Cold War Cultures

COLD WAR CULTURES
Perspectives on Eastern and Western European Societies

Edited by
Annette Vowinckel, Marcus M. Payk,
and Thomas Lindenberger

berghahn
NEW YORK · OXFORD
www.berghahnbooks.com

Published in 2012 by
Berghahn Books
www.berghahnbooks.com

©2012, 2014 Annette Vowinckel, Marcus M. Payk, and Thomas Lindenberger
First paperback edition published in 2014

All rights reserved. Except for the quotation of short passages
for the purposes of criticism and review, no part of this book
may be reproduced in any form or by any means, electronic or
mechanical, including photocopying, recording, or any information
storage and retrieval system now known or to be invented,
without written permission of the publisher.

Library of Congress Cataloging-in-Publication Data

Cold war cultures : perspectives on Eastern and Western European societies / edited by Annette Vowinckel, Marcus M. Payk, and Thomas Lindenberger.
   p. cm.
   Includes bibliographical references and index.
   ISBN 978-0-85745-243-6 (hardback) — ISBN 978-0-85745-244-3 (institutional ebook) — ISBN 978-1-78238-388-8 (paperback) — ISBN 978-1-78238-389-5 (retail ebook)
   1. Cold War—Social aspects—Europe. 2. Cold War—Social aspects—Europe, Western. 3. Cold War—Social aspects—Europe, Eastern. 4. Cold War in literature. 5. Cold War in motion pictures. 6. Cold War in mass media. 7. Cold War in popular culture. 8. Collective memory—Europe. 9. Collective memory—Europe, Western. 10. Collective memory—Europe, Eastern. I. Vowinckel, Annette. II. Payk, Marcus M. III. Lindenberger, Thomas, 1955–
   D1055.C53 2012
   940.55—dc23

2011029399

British Library Cataloguing in Publication Data

A catalogue record for this book is available from the British Library

Printed on acid-free paper

ISBN: 978-1-78238-388-8 paperback
ISBN: 978-1-78238-389-5 retail ebook

Contents

List of Illustrations ix

European Cold War Culture(s)? An Introduction 1
    Annette Vowinckel, Marcus M. Payk, Thomas Lindenberger

I. Mediating the Cold War: Radio, Film, Television, and Literature

Chapter 1. East European Cold War Culture(s): Alterities, Commonalities, and Film Industries 23
    Marsha Siefert

Chapter 2. "We Started the Cold War": A Hidden Message behind Stalin's Attack on Anna Akhmatova 55
    Olga Voronina

Chapter 3. Radio Reform in the 1980s: RIAS and DT-64 Respond to Private Radio 76
    Edward Larkey

Chapter 4. The Enemy Within: (De)Dramatizing the Cold War in U.S. and West German Spy TV from the 1960s 94
    Marcus M. Payk

Chapter 5. Cold War Television: Olga Korbut and the Munich Olympics of 1972 112
    Annette Vowinckel

II. Constructing Identities: Representations of the "Self"

Chapter 6. Catholic Piety in the Early Cold War Years; or, How the Virgin Mary Protected the West from Communism 129
    Monique Scheer

Chapter 7. The Road to Socialism Paved With Good Intentions: Automobile Culture in the Soviet Union, Romania, and the GDR During Détente 152
Luminita Gatejel

Chapter 8. Advertising, Emotions, and "Hidden Persuaders": The Making of Cold-War Consumer Culture in Britain from the 1940s to the 1960s 172
Stefan Schwarzkopf

Chapter 9. Survival in the Welfare Cocoon: The Culture of Civil Defense in Cold War Sweden 191
Marie Cronqvist

III. Crossing the Border: Interactions with the "Other"

Chapter 10. The Peace and the War Camps: The Dichotomous Cold War Culture in Czechoslovakia: 1948–1960 213
Roman Krakovsky

Chapter 11. Artistic Style, Canonization, and Identity Politics in Cold War Germany, 1947–1960 235
Joes Segal

Chapter 12. What Does Democracy Look Like? (And Why Would Anyone Want to Buy It?): Third World Demands and West German Responses at 1960s World Youth Festivals 254
Quinn Slobodian

Chapter 13. Drawing the East-West Border: Narratives of Modernity and Identity in the Northeastern Adriatic (1947–1954) 276
Sabina Mihelj

IV. The Legacies of the Cold War: Remembrance and Historiography

Chapter 14. A 1950s Revival: Cold War Culture in Reunified Germany 299
Andrew H. Beattie

Chapter 15. The Mikson Case: War Crimes Memory, Estonian Identity Reconstructions, and the Transnational Politics of Justice 321
Valur Ingimundarson

Chapter 16. The First Cold War Memorial in Berlin: A Short
    Inquiry into Europe, the Cold War, and Memory Cultures   347
        Petra Henzler

Notes on Contributors   370

Index   374

Illustrations

6.1. Image of Sister Lucia's 1925 visions of Mary asking for devotion to her Immaculate Heart — 136

6.2. *Der Spiegel* of 17 October 1949 — 141

6.3. Mary with a "crown of twelve stars" — 143

7.1. "Jedermann-Auto: Moskwich M 407" — 161

7.2. "Mercedes des Ostens, Volga Gaz-24" — 163

7.3. "Mercedes des Ostens, Volga Gaz-24" — 163

10.1. The poster for 6th Peace Race (Poland, Czechoslovakia, RDG, 1953) — 215

10.2. Poster of World Congress of Defenders of Peace (France, 1949) — 217

10.3. First Polish Peace Congress (Poland, 1950) — 217

10.4. Members of the Youth Union carrying the banner "Peace is for the People—War for Capitalists!" (May Day, Prague, 1949) — 218

10.5. Allegory of peace camp (May Day, Prague, 1949) — 219

10.6. The Hydra of the Reaction (May Day, Prague, 1951) — 220

10.7. Allegory of war camp (May Day, Ostrava, 1951) — 221

10.8. Allegory of peace camp (May Day, Ostrava, 1951) — 222

10.9. Allegory of war camp (May Day, Prague, 1950), with Wall Street skyscraper covered with inscriptions — 225

10.10. The first allegorical "burial" of the Western atomic bomb (May Day, Prague, 1950) — 227

10.11.	The burial of the war camp (May Day, Prague, 1957)	228
10.12.	The burial of the war camp (May Day, Prague, 1957)	228
12.1.	Helsinki World Youth Festival of 1962, promotional brochure	258
12.2.	Algiers World Youth Festival (planned for 1965, not realized), promotional brochure	260

EUROPEAN COLD WAR CULTURE(S)?
An Introduction

Annette Vowinckel, Marcus Payk, Thomas Lindenberger

Even though "Cold War" is a common term to describe the political conflict between Western liberal democracies and Eastern European Socialist states after World War II, it remained a Western expression until the "war" itself was over. In Eastern Europe and in the Soviet Union it was, as Muriel Blaive has pointed out, hardly used—except perhaps by intellectuals following Western discourse. Thus, even speaking of the "Cold War" already runs the risk of retrospectively applying common Western vocabulary and transforming it into an analytic term.[1] As a matter of fact, many North Americans and Western Europeans (admittedly the West Germans and the Swiss rather than the French or Austrians) would, to a certain extent, speak of "Cold War Culture" to summarize various aspects of the social and cultural history of their nations after 1945; in contrast, many Russians and Eastern Europeans would favor other terms to describe their experiences of the past.

In using the phrase "Cold War" as an analytical term in this volume, we do not want to level the diverse experiences, mentalities, and practices connected to the forty-year standoff between the Eastern and the Western camp. On the contrary, instead of applying a schematic model to the varying realities of the Cold War, we want to explore its different horizons and its multiple expressions—especially in their European forms. In fact, when considering the impact of the Cold War on Europe, we see a particularly broad range of different framings. While every European country had to adapt to the constraints imposed by the Cold War in a different way, there were also common conditions shared by almost all European states. These were, however, largely absent in the United States and the Soviet Union. Assessing the Cold War in Europe thus provides an excellent opportunity to understand how this global conflict altered, and was altered by, culture, media, mentalities, and everyday life in various national contexts.

By doing so, we acknowledge that the historiography of the Cold War has been deeply influenced by the unexpected end of the conflict in 1989–91. As Susan Buck-Morss and David Caute have pointed out,[2] the breakdown of the binary antagonism between East and West, capitalism and planned economy, liberal democracies and party dictatorships has paved the way for new historical perspectives on a familiar, yet unfamiliar era—familiar because its historians are contemporaries, unfamiliar because all of a sudden the era passed into history and historiography while the mental maps of its protagonists still seemed to be valid.

In the following, we will first provide a brief overview of the research on Cold War Culture after 1989–91, since the end of the global conflict was also accompanied by fresh methodological approaches, extending the historical research on the Cold War beyond the traditional focus on politics, diplomacy, and military developments.[3] In a second step, we will try to delineate recent research dealing with the cultural impact of the Cold War in Western and Eastern Europe, and then outline the various contributions to this volume and their diverse—yet not entirely diverging—answers to our key question: does it make sense to speak of a genuine *European* Cold War Culture?

American Cold War Culture

Already in the 1980s, some scholars had begun to study social and cultural aspects of the Cold War in U.S. history: George Lipsitz wrote a book on *Class and Culture in Cold War America*, Paul Boyer a history of the atomic age in *By the Bomb's Early Light,* and Lary May edited a classical volume of essays entitled *Recasting America: Culture and Politics in the Age of Cold War*.[4] Only months before the fall of the Berlin wall, May stated in the introduction to that collection that these contributions "represent a new departure in our understanding of postwar culture in the United States."[5]

Among the many excellent empirical studies on the 1950s and beyond, the pathbreaking book by Stephen Whitfield, *The Culture of the Cold War*, stands out.[6] It was not only an inspiring study, but also introduced the concept of a genuine *American Cold War Culture*—an idea in which the

Cold War is far more than just a term for the epoch that happened to end around the same time the book was published. For Whitfield, Cold War Culture is a key term to describe the 1950s as a decade in which American society was split in two: on the one side, there were (rather few) Communists, among them naïve do-gooders, reckless admirers of Stalin, and ordinary people who believed that freedom of opinion applied to everyone, including Communists. On the other side, there were those who believed that communism would subvert American society and that its supporters and "fellow travelers" had to be fought by all means—including the suppression of freedom of opinion, if necessary. On the one side, Western Communist cadres "flung down an unprecedented challenge, for they sought to enjoy the rights and benefits of a largely free society in order to demolish it. They habitually offered alibis for mass murder and denounced as 'slander' the effort to expose Soviet crimes. ... To call them Stalinists is ... a reminder to readers that American Communists were enemies of civil liberties, which they disdained as 'bourgeois' but which they invoked in their own behalf when opportune."[7] On the other hand, there was a "phobic overreaction"[8] on the part of American society and its political institutions. After all, the number of Communist Party members was negligible and had already reached its peak in 1950. Instead of sustaining democracy, the repressions "weakened the legacy of civil liberties, impugned standards of tolerance and fair play, and tarnished the very image of a democracy. This Red Scare was not a collective tragedy, but it was a disgrace."[9] According to Whitfield, the 1950s were thus dominated by a Cold War Culture that was not only anti-Communist, but also anti-liberal and anti-democratic. Only when it became clear that, after Stalin's death, Khrushchev would make an attempt to normalize international relations did the Red Scare in the United States slowly lose its sway over politics, society, and culture. Only then was the "subjugation of culture to politics" abolished.[10]

In the two decades following the publication of Whitfield's book, many aspects of this American Cold War Culture were investigated in greater detail. For example, Alan Nadel analyzed the impact of nuclear armament and of what he calls "containment culture." John Fousek contended that the culture of American nationalism (as supported by a white, male, Protestant, middle- and upper-class population) was one of the driving forces of the conflict between the two superpowers. Ron Robin drew attention to the cultural and political impact of the "military-intellectual complex" and its impact on social and behavioral studies, while Tom Engelhardt argued that the American defeat in Vietnam put an end to a culture of victory that had originally been established in early New England and in the days of the "Wild West."[11]

With the rise of media studies, the Cold War has also been scrutinized from various perspectives as a phenomenon of U.S. media. Over the last decade, many scholars have focused on different media (like newspapers, television, documentary, photography, novels, and music[12]), on genres like science fiction or documentary films,[13] and on different topics as presented by the media in general or in particular formats such as television series.[14] Finally, Ellen Schrecker wrote a book on Cold War memory politics entitled *Cold War Triumphalism*, in which she argues that history has turned into an armory after 1989–91, especially on the part of conservative politicians seeking to revise critical historiography in the United States.[15]

In 2005, Douglas Field published a selection of essays under the explicit title *American Cold War Culture*, covering the crucial fields of family, gender and sexuality, politics, mobility, and race as well as film, literature, television, and poetry.[16] In a way, the volume summarizes the state of the art of Cold War Culture research in U.S. history after the turn of the century, even if it does not come up with new concepts and interpretations that might enhance our understanding of the era.

However, the notion of a genuine culture of the Cold War, as proposed by Whitfield, Fields, and others, has not remained unchallenged. In 2001, Peter J. Kuznick and James Gilbert published an edited volume entitled *Rethinking Cold War Culture*.[17] While some of its contributors argue that the influence of the Cold War on American culture was not limited to the period from 1945 to 1960,[18] others maintain that the concept is too narrow to explain the postwar period as a whole, and that it is not appropriate to subsume all facets of American cultural production under only one term. Others claim that the term should not be reserved for the United States, but applied to other national cultures, including the Eastern European satellite states as well as Western European and non-European countries.

Consequently, in their introduction Kuznick and Gilbert argue that "Cold War culture is not synonymous with American culture, even at the height of its impact. It is the interaction between [the] unique elements of Cold War culture"—namely nuclear fear, anti-Sovietism, surrogate and covert wars, and the military-industrial complex[19]—and "the longstanding trends that existed independently and in large part antedated the Cold War that created American civilization in this age."[20] They conclude that apparently the principal effect of the conflict between East and West was a psychological one, as even those who had lined up to criticize McCarthyism made the mistake of centering their entire thinking around the Cold War: "Seeing the world through this dark, distorting lens and setting global and domestic policies to counter these fanciful as well as real threats was and is, then, the largest impact of the Cold War."[21]

European Cold War Culture(s)?

The aim to regain a sense of the complexity of the matter and to show that Cold War Culture was by no means homogenous, but rather a set of different, sometimes conflicting influences on culture in the twentieth century, is still highly topical. In the wake of this approach, the focus of research has shifted from earlier to later periods of Cold War history, and it has shifted from political and diplomatic to social, cultural, and media history, the history of ideas, utopias, and mentalities. Inevitably, the question arose whether the concept of Cold War Culture would also prove suitable for national (and international) contexts beyond the United States. Focusing on Europe, some scholars have warned against transferring a U.S. concept to the quite complex field of European postwar history, and pointed to the limits of its adaptability. However, the question of whether the concept would be useful to describe and analyze European Cold War Cultures so far remains unanswered.

In order to fill this gap, we have to reconsider briefly how we define the terms "culture" and "European." Obviously, we think of culture not in terms of "high" culture, or even in terms of "high" in contrast to "low" (or popular) culture, but as a very broad set of techniques, images, habits, mentalities, ways of producing and consuming, forms of communication, self-descriptions, and patterns of daily life. We thus agree with many scholars who have scrutinized the cultural Cold War in that "cultural" defines our methods and perspectives on Cold War history rather than the sources or subject matter itself.

Moreover, the notion of "Europe" as addressed in this volume requires further explanation. Geographically, Europe includes all countries between Iceland and Greece, Portugal and Estonia, Finland and Cyprus. However, there have been heated debates on whether the United States is "European" in that it was founded by Europeans, whether Turkey as a Muslim state and successor of the Ottoman Empire could be part of cultural Europe, whether the European colonies in Africa and Asia can be regarded as part of the continent (which, politically, they were), and on how to position Russia between "Europe" and "Asia." As Marsha Siefert suggests in her contribution to this volume, it seems useful to draw on those European self-descriptions of the 1980s and early 1990s that tried to relate to pre–World War II self-descriptions of Europe, including

Peter Sloterdijk's 1994 essay "Falls Europa erwacht" ("If Europe Awakes") or Milan Kundera's essay "Un occident kidnappé" ("A Kidnapped Occident," 1983). Sloterdijk defined Europe as the historical and mental unit that brought about modernity, and thus far more than just the sum of its various cultures. In his view, however, Europe (both East and West) was "squeezed" between the superpowers and thus "asleep" during the Cold War.[22] In contrast, Kundera argued that Czechoslovakia, Poland, and Hungary are not only geographically, but also historically and culturally at the center of the continent. In Kundera's view from the mid 1980s, Europe's main antagonist is Russia, for unlike Europe with its great variety of cultures sharing a limited space, the Soviet empire represents a minimum of variety on maximum territory. Like Sloterdijk, Kundera sees Europe embodied in its "culture and destiny,"[23] yet Central Europe was existentially confronted with Soviet imperialism and thus more deeply affected by the cultural Cold War than any Western European nation. Neither Sloterdijk nor Kundera provides an answer to the question of where Europe begins and where it ends in terms of geography.

This metageographical approach to Europe is a good starting point. We have thus decided not to limit our perspective to Central Europe or to define "Europe" in terms of maps and borders, but to leave room for different and differing approaches. In fact, the volume includes texts focusing on Iceland as well as Romania, on Great Britain as well as Sweden, on divided Germany, and even on the relationship between Russia and Britain as giving shape to the very early cultural Cold War. The result is an attempt to reconcile merely geographical definitions with cultural and historical notions of Europe, including the fringes of the continent that were in their own ways influenced by the conflict—Marie Cronqvist's chapter on Cold War Sweden is a case in point in this regard.

But even if we assume that virtually every European country was affected by the systemic conflict, the ways and the degrees to which they were influenced certainly differed. National, regional, and local traditions may have changed in different ways, and surely there were common trends in postwar Europe that hardly fit into the concept of the Cold War, for example urban reconstruction efforts after World War II, the expansion of the welfare state in the 1960s, the energy crisis of the 1970s, and the emergence of new media from the 1980s onwards (with the latter two not even being specifically European, but global phenomena). However, research is still dominated by national perspectives, in which common trends constitute a kind of background noise. Case studies centering on Western Europe refer to a wide variety of subjects, among them the process of decolonization, coming to terms with totalitarianism, collaboration, treason, civil war, and—most controversially—"Americanization."[24]

At the same time, studies often indicate that in all Western European countries, the Cold War was not only a political and cultural conflict imposed by the superpowers. In fact, conflicts between liberal or conservative democrats on the one hand and Socialist, Communist, or even anarchist groups on the other reflected deep-seated antagonisms that had been virulent long before the United States and the Soviet Union armed themselves with nuclear weapons, and long before the continent was divided by what was—in many ways—an impenetrable border. It would thus be appropriate to explore to what extent Western European societies suffered from inner ideological conflicts and how—if at all—they managed to overcome these conflicts after the end of the Cold War. Different case studies on the cultural Cold War in Western Europe have at least stressed national idiosyncrasies, for example Christopher Duggan and Christopher Wagstaff's book on Italy during the Cold War or Robert Hewison's early study of the cultural "anger" of British intellectuals and artists, which was at least partially connected to a loss of enthusiasm for Socialist and Communist ideas.[25] There are also quite a few comparative studies on Cold War Culture, like the conference volume on the cultural Cold War in Western Europe edited by Giles Scott-Smith and Hans Krabbendam. They come to the conclusion that in their feeling of obligation to fight totalitarianism, Western European countries were not only under the influence of the ideological antagonism, but also very much under the influence of their World War II experiences. American anti-communism was "thwarted by private initiatives, national elites, and local conditions" in Europe, where the politically active generation of the 1940s and 1950s was less skeptical toward the United States than the one dominating the 1960s.[26]

In contrast to this solely Western perspective, several authors try to compare Eastern and Western experiences of the Cold War, with comparisons between the two German states outnumbering all others by far. After all, here one nation was represented by both a Western liberal democracy and a Communist satellite state, dividing nation and society—even families—in two. From among the multifaceted literature on the topic, let us just briefly mention Uta Poiger's comparison of popular music in both East and West Germany under the influence of American musical culture and David Crew's selection of essays on consumer culture in the two German states.[27] In 2004, Patrick Major and Rana Mitter presented an edited volume on the social and cultural history of the Cold War that questioned traditional prejudices in both the Eastern and Western cultural traditions, addressed national as well as transnational developments, and focused on "home fronts" as well as international conflicts.[28] A year earlier, David Caute already provided a substantial study of cultural life in East and West in the context of the Cold War. He clearly cautioned against overlooking the many similarities between Eastern and Western attitudes toward the systemic conflict, which can only be fully understood if we dare to take multiple—sometimes contradictory but ideologically unbiased—perspectives on its history.[29] In her analysis of different delineations of modernity in the twentieth century, Susan Buck-Morss came to similar conclusions. With the end of the Cold War, she argued, the twentieth century ended and the modern dream of a better life—both the Socialist and the democratic or "Capitalist" utopia—was destroyed, for the "dream of mass sovereignty has led to world wars of nationalism and to revolutionary terror," while the "dream of industrial abundance has enabled the construction of global systems that exploit both human labor and natural environments."[30] Most recently, Jessica Gienow-Hecht has described the history of Cold War Culture as a conflict between the concept of "high culture," as favored by the Soviet Union and adopted by many Eastern European societies, on the one hand, and on the other the reality of American popular culture, which was both readily accepted and criticized on the grounds of traditional anti-Americanism while it served as a cultural paradigm for dissidents in Eastern Europe.[31]

Despite these remarkable accounts, we know relatively little about the cultural history of the Soviet Union and its Communist satellite states in Eastern Europe during the Cold War—to some extent because historians themselves were part of the system and under ideological supervision until 1989–91. The two volumes of essays, edited by David Crowley and Susan Reid, mark an important starting point for further research, however, as the authors focused on everyday life in Eastern Europe (including Russia) after 1945.[32] The essays in those volumes deal with consumerism and material culture, housing, city spaces, leisure areas, clothing, and aesthetics between 1947 and 1991, and try to identify analogies as well as differences between East and West. As Marsha Siefert points out in her contribution to the present volume, Eastern European societies are often conceived as the "other Europe" that came to redefine itself in the course of the 1980s and thus contributed to mitigating the conflict. While during the first decade after World War II Eastern European nations were regarded as mere "satellites" of the Soviet empire—and thus, in a way, "excommunicated" from what was sometimes labeled as "(good) old Europe"—they gradually succeeded in returning to the "center" of Europe. Even though the USSR remained the dominant power on various levels (politics, economy, military, ideology, culture), some Eastern European countries (such as Yugoslavia, Hungary, Czechoslovakia, and Poland) made more or less successful efforts to break ranks and reestablish pre-Soviet democratic or national traditions. In a way, these efforts seem to complement Western

European attempts to integrate Socialist and even Marxist elements into the framework of a liberal democracy (like the readmission of the Communist Party in the Federal Republic of Germany in the 1970s), but so far this question has not been systematically addressed.

* * *

The contributions to this volume try to increase and refine our knowledge about Cold War Culture in Europe and, in their specific ways, all address the following set of questions the authors were asked to consider: are there sufficient parallels between Eastern and Western European cultures to justify a specifically European perspective on the Cold War? Would it make more sense to stick to national perspectives on the one hand, and transnational perspectives independent of Cold War politics on the other? How strong was the influence of the United States and the Soviet Union, respectively, on the different European countries and cultures? Which peculiarities still at work in the present stem from the systemic conflict? What are the different ways in which societies remember the Cold War, and how do they deal with its material legacy (like bunkers and nuclear weapons)?

The volume's structure reflects four major areas of interest: (I) Mediating the Cold War: Radio, Film, Television, and Literature, (II) Constructing Identities: Representations of the "Self," (III) Crossing the Border: Interactions with the "Other," and (IV) The Legacies of the Cold War: Remembrance and Historiography. The first section discusses concepts and case studies in media history, which by its very nature comprises both national and transnational aspects. Taking as given the fact that different media attempted to disseminate political and ideological messages, the contributions to this section also try to point out in which ways media like radio or television pursued a common modern path of information dissemination and communication, sometimes drawing on cultural codes that had existed long before the beginning of the Cold War. Thus, daily media reception was not only an onslaught of "propaganda," but in some cases also a means of subversion.

In her account of Anna Akhmatova's 1946 meeting with British diplomat Isaiah Berlin, Olga Voronina draws parallels between the poet's statement that this very meeting marked the beginning of the Cold War, and Stalin's attempt to obtain a loan of several billion dollars from the U.S. government in order to rebuild his devastated country. What at first glance seems to be an expression of "self-aggrandizing tendencies" on Akhmatova's part turns out to coincide perfectly with Stalin's defeat. The dictator's attack on the journals *Zvezda* and *Leningrad*, as well as his attack on Akhmatova herself following her meeting with Berlin, may not have been the *cause* of the Soviet Union's turning against its World War II allies. However, by launching a campaign against the famous poet he could be sure to have his message delivered to the British government, and make sure that ideological and economic confrontation would not leave cultural production unaffected.

Edward Larkey compares the music program of West Berlin–based RIAS (Radio in the American Sector) with East Berlin–based DT 64—a music program aimed at young people, which was founded in 1964 and transformed into a new radio station in 1986—as a response to the growing demand for (Western) popular music in the GDR. Paying special attention to the process of commercialization on both sides of the Wall, Larkey comes to the conclusion that RIAS, especially the newly founded program RIAS 2, was subject to competition and driven by commercial interests—as was DT 64, which moreover also had to cater to East German youth's desire for "fun, excitement, innovation, and freedom." In the long run, Larkey concludes, the lack of popular music broadcasts by East German radio stations contributed to the failure of the Socialist experiment as much as the lack of consumer goods, freedom of speech, and political participation.

Marcus Payk focuses on "Spy Television" of the 1960s, comparing the West German series *John Klings Abenteuer* (The Adventures of John Kling) and the American *Mission: Impossible*. While intuitively one would think that in the midst of the Cold War, spy plots would feature "good" Western liberal defenders of law and order who protect their country against "bad," i.e., cold-blooded and ideologically fatuous Eastern spies, Payk's analysis yields rather different findings: both in the United States and in West Germany there is a strong tendency to maintain stability at all costs, to avoid open accusations of Eastern European governments or individuals. Payk concludes that during the 1960s the aggressive rhetoric of the very early Cold War gave way to a more subtle, ironic, even satirical approach, while political conflicts were transformed into internal and individual conflicts—the result being that the rhetoric of black-and-white lost its persuasive power, and simultaneously the audience lost interest in spy series.

Taking the gymnastic competition at the 1972 Munich Olympics as an example, Annette Vowinckel unfolds the argument that sports competitions in the Cold War were not necessarily ideological competitions—even if sports functionaries, commentators, and especially politicians were often glad to employ them for their purposes. Analyzing the 1972 competition at the uneven bars, which turned into a duel between Belarusian Olga Korbut and East German Karin Janz, Vowinckel shows that the live audience strongly favored Korbut despite the fact that Janz was a compatriot in West German eyes (only from beyond the Wall). It follows that the reception of sports performances was influenced by aesthetic aspects as well as political ideology, and that television audiences would only put up with political comments because avoiding them would have meant missing the sports event entirely. Vowinckel thus concludes that sport was one of many projection fields for different ideologies, but in the end it survived the Cold War and paved the way for postmodern habits of media reception.

Section II addresses matters of self-reflection and identity building as mirrored, for example, in religious practices, defense concepts, and consumer culture. The idea is that Cold War Culture became manifest in different cultural fields, including religious and metaphysical concepts and practices, national defense strategies, and self-depictions as reflected in material goods. Even if at first glance these fields appear quite disparate, there is a lot of evidence that in various ways the Cold War was integrated into different areas that were, for a long time, considered to be free of ideology.

As Monique Scheer shows in her investigation of Catholic piety, religion by no means remained untouched by politics during the Cold War. From the Western perspective, communism was a form of atheism and the Soviet Union was its bulwark; in the Socialist perspective, religion was "opiate for the masses" and needed to be overcome. Using the example of the cult of Fatima, which goes back to a supposed apparition of the Virgin Mary witnessed by three children in the village of Fatima, Portugal, in 1917 and later transformed into an anti-Soviet cult, Scheer argues that especially during the 1950s, aspects of Catholicism and anti-communism merged in Portugal as well as in Germany and France. While the alliance of lay Catholics and Cold Warriors lost some of its impact during the following decades, it was taken up again by Pope John Paul II, who believed that the Virgin of Fatima had saved him from being killed in 1981.

Taking a close look at automobile production in Romania and in the Soviet Union, Luminita Gatejel compares Eastern and Western ways of connecting mobility and consumerism with Communist and Capitalist ideology, respectively. She argues that not only did car production meet the needs of individuals on both sides of the Iron Curtain; Socialist— as well as Capitalist—societies rather used their cars as symbolic capital by which they attempted to promote an entire value system. While Western cars purported to be elegant, stylish, spacious, and economical, Eastern cars were promoted as being durable and inexpensive products of high-quality engineering. As we can easily imagine, it was difficult to sell Russian or Romanian cars in Western Europe or the U.S.—not only because they were regarded to be of lower quality, but also because they conveyed specific images. A car was not just a vehicle, it stood for an entire lifestyle—and the Socialist lifestyle was hard to sell beyond the Iron Curtain.

In his chapter on the British advertising industry in the early Cold War, Stefan Schwarzkopf points out that there were two approaches to advertising, reflecting by and large the binary structure of the Cold War. Those who favored advertising argued that the consumer's choice of products was an act of freedom in a free world. Those who opposed it—referring among other things to the experiment of subliminal advertisements in movie theaters—argued that this was a kind of manipulation, incapacitation, or even brainwashing. However, during the 1950s broad resistance to advertising campaigns lost ground in Britain. A conference hosting the International Advertising Convention in 1951 strongly supported the notion that without advertising, free consumers would not be able to make their choice. While during the 1960s leftist groups articulated a critique of consumerism, and of advertising as one of its main weapons, the topic of "free choice" was again taken up in the era of Ronald Reagan and Margaret Thatcher. However, Schwarzkopf argues, there is nothing particularly European about this debate and the respective positions. Especially in Britain, the influence of the United States was quite strong, whereas the establishment of a West European economic union rendered the Cold War obsolete long before the fall of the Berlin Wall. Still, it is clear that the debates of the 1950s reflect the mental map dominated by a "freely" consuming West and an "unfree" East suffering from lack of choice and—even worse—lack of a free advertising industry.

Marie Cronqvist asks why, during the Cold War, a small and neutral nation like Sweden would put more money and effort into civil defense than most other nations, including France, Great Britain, the United States, and the Soviet Union, making military preparedness a "home and family affair." She assumes that the *folkhem* (people's home) gave Swedish citizens a sense of stability in times of nuclear threat. Based on the analysis of a civil defense instruction manual entitled *If War Comes: Instructions for Sweden's Citizens*, she argues that the manual was not only about civil defense, but also about the construction and promotion of moral values, family ideals, work ethos, welfare, and cleanliness. While studies on the history of civil defense have so far often concentrated on the United States, Cronqvist offers a view of Sweden as one of those European countries that—like Switzerland—remained neutral, and thus developed a strong need for defense strategies. She concludes that Cold War Culture in Sweden was rather a sequel of than a break with World War II mentalities; one might even say that the World War continued in Sweden throughout the 1950s, causing a prolonged fear of the coming apocalypse and creating a grand vision of survival in the welfare cocoon.

Section III deals with different ways of "crossing borders": On the one hand, there are borders between nation-states, separating nations as well as societies, languages, and economic systems. On the other, there are borders between cultural and intellectual concepts. The articles in this section try to show that physical borders can be transcended, but that at the same time there are unbridgeable gaps splitting nations over questions of war and peace, artistic quality, or the distribution of power and wealth in an increasingly globalized world.

Roman Krakovsky takes a close look at symbolic representations of the peace camp (Socialist Eastern Europe) and the war camp (the Capitalist and imperialist West) designed to illustrate May Day celebrations in early postwar Czechoslovakia. He argues that the formation of Socialist self-images strongly depended on the construction of "the Other," namely the decadent capitalist warmonger, who was vividly depicted and sculpted for example by students of the Prague Academy of Arts, Architecture, and Design. While this strategy of demonizing "the Other" in order to reassert one's own commitment to peace and justice reached its peak during the 1950s, more complex images of Western society, politics, and everyday life came to dominate in the 1960s, after Khrushchev suggested that "peaceful coexistence" might rule out potential nuclear confrontation. Czech society, the author argues, became more liberal, viewing socialism no longer as a utopia, but reality, while at the same time audiovisual media helped to form a more differentiated picture of "the West."

Joes Segal investigates different concepts of art in postwar Germany, contrasting East and West (and at times also including the United States and the Soviet Union) between 1947 and 1960. While in general any artistic realism is regarded as (National) Socialist, and modern art (especially expressionist and abstract art) is mostly considered to be a product of individualism, decadence, or liberal democracy, Segal shows that the reality is more complex: followers of Joseph McCarthy in the United States and conservative art critics in the Federal Republic of Germany agreed with Soviet and East German art critics in their condemnation of modern art as decadent. In Germany the matter was even more complex, as both German states accused each other of continuing the National Socialist traditions. However, since there were realist as well as modernist tendencies in both East and West Germany, art in general became a kind of screen for ideological bickering. In the field of art politics, Segal concludes, reality became a matter of rhetoric.

Based on an analysis of the World Youth Festivals in Vienna (1959), Helsinki (1962), and Sofia (1968), Quinn Slobodian argues that "Third World" countries (both as actors and as objects of political analysis) played a major role in the competition between liberal and Socialist notions of democracy. Each bloc initially tried to convince participants from Africa or Southeast Asia that its respective model was superior and that it would also offer Third World countries better prospects for progress. However, in West Germany a significant change took place during the 1960s: whereas in 1959 visitors to the Youth Festival still tried to convince participants from Third World countries that German democracy was best, not least because it was economically highly successful, German attendees of the subsequent festivals in the 1960s addressed the topic by declaring solidarity with, for example, the Vietnamese people as victims of Western imperialism. At least in the microcosm of the Sofia Festival (and also within the German New Left), there was, as Slobodian concludes, a "third term" in German political culture beyond "socialism" and "capitalism."

Sabina Mihelj takes a close look at the Julian region, on the border between Italy, Slovenia, and Croatia. Until 1954, the city of Trieste was called Free Territory of Trieste (FTT) and divided into Zone A, controlled by the Allied military government, and Zone B, controlled by the Yugoslav army. It is striking that on the Italian side of the border, people thought of those living on the Slovenian side as uncivilized, atheist "Slavo-Communists." In contrast, in the Slovenian view it was not all Italians, but only the Italian Fascists, who were accused of being uncivilized, traditionalist Capitalists. Slovenians thought of themselves as being progressive, civilized, modern, and internationalist—and depicted their own eastern neighbors in many ways similar to how the Italians portrayed them. However, the cultural stereotypes underlying such constructions of one's own and others' identities date back much further than the Cold War; rather, the Cold War used and modified notions of a "civilized" Western and an "underdeveloped" Eastern Europe that can be traced back at least to the Enlightenment. Interestingly, in the Julian region all ethnic groups drew on a concept of modernity that expressed the antagonisms of progressive vs. backward and civilized vs. barbaric—the difference being that on one side progress was to be achieved through liberal democracy and a free market, while on the other it was to be achieved through Socialist egalitarianism in a worker-led society. Thus, as in many other case studies, the cultural differences between Eastern and Western perspectives on Europe, culture, and the Cold War turn out to differ less than one might have expected.

Section IV features different attempts to historicize and remember the Cold War. They refer both to material legacies (like Tempelhof Airport in Berlin) and to intellectual concepts dealing with Cold War history, as reflected in the public discourse of reunified Germany. While it is often assumed that Cold War Culture ceased to exist after the end of the Cold War, Andrew Beattie points out that there is a striking coincidence between anti-Communist narratives of the 1950s and historical accounts of the Cold War in the 1990s. Based on an analysis of two inquiries in the West German Bundestag, he argues that public memory was both highly contested and often instrumentalized in attacks on political opponents. There was, Beattie argues, a strong antagonism between post–Cold War triumphalism on the one hand and its critics on the other. While the latter argued that the triumphant West German conservatives lacked self-criticism regarding their own radical anti-communism and their lack of enthusiasm in prosecuting Nazi crimes during the Cold War, the former seemed to have "history itself" on their side—this resulted in massive attempts to resurrect the key features of Cold War Culture even if the Cold War itself was long over. There are, however, as Beattie points out, two major differences between the 1950s and the 1990s: Firstly, public memory of the 1990s was dominated not only by debates about eastern Germany's Communist past, but also by debates about the Nazi past that had already shaped the historical discourses of the previous decade. Secondly, anti-communism in the 1990s did not result in the legal prosecution of Communist individuals or the banning of the former East German state party, the SED/PDS. The author contends that the very presence of SED/PDS members in the German parliament disproves any attempt to equate the situation of the 1950s with the more recent past.

Valur Ingimundarsson tells the story of Evald Mikson, an Estonian war criminal, as framed by opposing Cold War and World War II narratives. Mikson joined the resistance against the Soviet occupation of Estonia in 1940 and collaborated with the Nazi occupation of 1941–1944, obviously because he thought of the Germans as better than the Soviet Communists. In 1944 he fled to Sweden, and moved on to Iceland in 1964, where he married, and eventually founded a massage parlor frequented by the Icelandic political elite. Several attempts to take him to court for imprisoning and murdering Jews and Communists failed because he was under the protection of the radically anti-Communist Icelandic government. Only in 1992 did Efraim Zuroff of the Simon Wiesenthal Center succeed in initiating a legal investigation against Mikson in Iceland. When Mikson died in 1993, the case was closed, and until today the charges against him have neither been proven on the basis of the strong evidence, nor have they been dismissed. However, as Ingimundarsson points out, the Mikson case vividly reflects how a certain Cold War narrative—in this case a joint Estonian-Icelandic anti-Communist narrative—could prevent a war criminal from being tried in court. It is one of history's ironies (or rather cynicisms) that Mikson died shortly before his case was brought to trial, and his former Nazi superior Martin Sandberger (also a staunch anti-Communist) died peacefully in his home in Stuttgart in

2010. Ingimundarsson's assumption that legal prosecution of war crimes is often subject to national and ideological interests proves to be more than true—a case in point that Cold War anti-communism had a stronger influence on the Mikson case than, for example, the need to convict him for collaborating with the Nazi occupiers or even killing Jews.

According to Petra Henzler, the Airlift Memorial at Berlin's Tempelhof Airport is the first memorial of the Cold War in Berlin. Yet it is not an exclusive and unchanging representation of the event itself, but subject to various interpretations, which in turn are subject to conflicting memories of the Cold War and its aftermath. Building on a discussion of different concepts of Europe, memory, and the Cold War, Henzler shows that before 1989 the Airlift was depicted as part of a transatlantic meta-narrative: it fostered Konrad Adenauer's politics of Westernization, democratization, and resistance to the Communist threat. In contrast, post–Cold War narratives are in general more ambivalent, accusing the United States of being imperialistic (here East German recollections as well as West German leftist opposition play a role). Thus, Henzler argues, Tempelhof and the Airlift not only generate memories; rather, they are "places of remembrance" (*Erinnerungsorte*) that have been transformed according to political circumstances and will most probably go on transforming in the future—even if (or perhaps because) the Cold War loses its impact on the present.

* * *

Naturally, different authors come to different conclusions when asked if there is any such thing as European Cold War Culture. However, there are some insights common to the essays presented in this volume: first of all, Susan Buck-Morss's argument that historiography needs a *critical* discourse on the Cold War and its ideological legacy appears more valid than ever. All authors would agree that from the perspective of a cultural historian, the respective political and economic systems of Eastern and Western Europe (and of the Soviet Union and the United States) present not only differences, but also analogies, similarities, and commonalities. They would moreover agree that although undeniably there are many important parallels between American and Western European culture on the one hand and Soviet and Eastern European culture on the other, these parallels are complemented by parallels between, for example, Austria and Hungary or Sweden and the GDR. However, what would make European Cold War Culture genuinely *European*?

The editors agree that European culture is in principle plural and multifaceted. Thus, we should rather speak of European Cold War *Cultures* than of one homogenous culture that is merely "represented" in different national variants. Secondly, we agree that the European perspective is shaped not only by Cold War experiences, but also by older traditions that were reshaped after World War II, but had never vanished completely (religious traditions, concepts of modernity, aesthetic ideals, etc.). Europe was the cradle of modernity, and the division of Europe by the Iron Curtain only reflects that modernity evolved along two different paths, even if one of them proved to be an impasse. The Socialist defeat, as Buck-Morss puts it, "cannot but place the whole Western narrative into question."[33] To focus on Europe as *one* theater of the Cold War means to reflect on Europe as the origin of enlightenment and democracy, as well as of science, industrialization, and totalitarian dictatorship. The Cold War shaped both Europe and other world regions for several decades, and Europe in turn shaped the Cold War in several ways. Research on European Cold War Culture(s) should thus take both of these aspects into account. It should emphasize the fact that notions of "Europe" are manifold, that Europeans brought forth socialism and communism as well as capitalism and democracy, and that any account of Europe between 1945 and 1991 should bear in mind that the continent was more than just a buffer area between the superpowers.

Notes

1. Muriel Blaive, "Utopian visions: The 'Cold War' and its political aesthetics," *Zeithistorische Forschungen/Studies in Contemporary History* 5 (2008): 313–322.
2. Susan Buck-Morss, *Dreamworld and Catastrophe* (Cambridge, Mass., 2000); David Caute, *The Dancer Defects* (Oxford, 2003).
3. For example Walter Lippmann, *The Cold War* (New York, 1947); James S. Allen and Doxey A. Wilkerson, eds., *The Economic Crisis and the Cold War* (New York, 1949); Wilfred G. Burchett, *The Cold War in Germany* (Melbourne, 1950); Salvador de Madariaga, *The Anatomy of the Cold War* (Belfast, 1955).
4. George Lipsitz, *Class and Culture in Cold War America* (New York, 1981); Paul Boyer, *By the Bomb's Early Light* (New York, 1985); Lary May, ed., *Recasting America* (Chicago, 1989).
5. May, "Introduction," in *Recasting America*, 1–16, 1.
6. Stephen J. Whitfield, *The Culture of the Cold War* (Baltimore, 1991), in the following cited from the second edition (1996).
7. Ibid., 3.
8. Ibid.
9. Ibid., 4.
10. Ibid., 240.
11. Alan Nadel, *Containment Culture* (Durham, 1996); John Fousek, *To Lead the Free World* (Chapel Hill, 2000); Ron Theodore Robin, *The Making of the Cold War Enemy* (Princeton, 2001); Tom Engelhardt, *The End of Victory Culture* (Amherst, 2007).

12. For example Thomas H. Schaub, *American Fiction in the Cold War* (Madison, Wisc., 1991); Lili Corbus Bezner, *Photography and Politics in America* (Baltimore, 1999); Thomas Patrick Doherty, *Cold War, Cool Medium* (New York, 2003); Bill Geerhart and Ken Sitz, *Atomic Platters* (Hambergen, 2005).
13. David Seed, *American Science Fiction and the Cold War* (Edinburgh, 1999); Michael Curtin, *Redeeming the Wasteland* (New Brunswick, 1995).
14. Michael Kackman, *Citizen Spy* (Minneapolis, 2005).
15. Ellen Schrecker, *Cold War Triumphalism* (New York, 2004).
16. Douglas Field, ed., *American Cold War Culture* (Edinburgh, 2005).
17. Peter J. Kuznick and James Gilbert, eds., *Rethinking Cold War Culture* (Washington, 2001).
18. Kuznick and Gilbert, "U.S. Culture and the Cold War," in idem, *Rethinking Cold War Culture*, 1–13, 1.
19. Ibid.
20. Ibid., 10.
21. Ibid., 11.
22. Peter Sloterdijk, *Falls Europa erwacht* (Frankfurt, 1994).
23. Milan Kundera, "Die Tragödie Mitteleuropas," in *Versunkene Welt*, ed. Joachim Riedl (Vienna, 1984), 132 (first published as "Un occident kidnappé ou la tragédie de l'Europe Centrale," in *Le Débat*, 27 November 1983).
24. Alexander Stephan, *The Americanization of Europe* (New York, 2006).
25. Christopher Duggan and Christopher Wagstaff, eds., *Italy in the Cold War* (Oxford, 1995); Robert Hewison, *In Anger* (London, 1981).
26. Giles Scott-Smith and Hans Krabbendam, "Introduction: Boundaries to Freedom," in *The Cultural Cold War in Western Europe 1945–1960*, ed. Giles Scott-Smith and Hans Krabbendam (London, 2003), 1–11, 10.
27. Uta Poiger, *Jazz, Rock, and Rebels* (Berkeley, 2000); David F. Crew, ed., *Consuming Germany in the Cold War* (Oxford, 2003).
28. Patrick Major and Rana Mitter, "East is East and West is West? Towards a Comparative Socio-Cultural History of the Cold War," in *Across the Blocs: Cold War Cultural and Social History*, ed. Patrick Major and Rana Mitter (London: Routledge, 2004), 1–22.
29. David Caute, *The Dancer Defects*.
30. Susan Buck-Morss, *Dreamworld and Catastrophe*, xi.
31. Jessica Gienow-Hecht, "Culture and the Cold War in Europe."
32. David Crowley and Susan Reid, eds., *Style and Socialism* (Oxford, 2000); idem, *Socialist Spaces* (Oxford, 2002).
33. Buck-Morss, *Dreamworld and Catastrophe*, xii.

Bibliography

Blaive, Muriel. "Utopian visions: The 'Cold War' and its political aesthetics." *Zeithistorische Forschungen/Studies in Contemporary History* 5 (2008), no. 2: 313–322.
Boyer, Paul. *By the Bomb's Early Light: American Thought and Culture at the Dawn of the Atomic Age*. New York: Random House, 1985.
Brooks, Jeffrey. *Thank you, comrade Stalin! Soviet Public Culture from Revolution to Cold War*. Princeton: Princeton University Press, 2000.

Buck-Morss, Susan. *Dreamworld and Catastrophe: The Passing of Mass Utopia in East and West*. Cambridge, Mass.: MIT Press, 2000.
Burchett, Wilfred G. *The Cold War in Germany*. Melbourne: World Unity Publications, 1950.
Caute, David. *The Dancer Defects: The Struggle for Cultural Supremacy During the Cold War*. Oxford: Oxford University Press, 2003.
Corbus Bezner, Lili. *Photography and Politics in America: From the New Deal into the Cold War*. Baltimore: Johns Hopkins University Press, 1999.
Crew, David F., ed. *Consuming Germany in the Cold War: Leisure Consumption and Culture*. Oxford: Berg, 2003.
Crowley, David, and Susan Reid, eds. *Style and Socialism: Modernity and Material Culture in Post-War Eastern Europe*. Oxford: Berg, 2000.
———. *Socialist Spaces: Sites of Everyday Life in the Eastern Bloc*. Oxford: Berg, 2002.
Curtin, Michael. *Redeeming the Wasteland: Television Documentary and Cold War Politics*. New Brunswick: Rutgers University Press, 1995.
Doherty, Thomas Patrick. *Cold War, Cool Medium: Television, McCarthyism, and American Culture*. New York: Columbia University Press, 2003.
Duggan, Christopher, and Christopher Wagstaff, eds. *Italy in the Cold War: Politics, Culture and Society 1948–58*. Oxford: Berg, 1995.
Engelhardt, Tom. *The End of Victory Culture: Cold War America and the Disillusioning of a Generation*. Amherst: University of Massachusetts Press, 2007.
Field, Douglas, ed. *American Cold War Culture*. Edinburgh: Edinburgh University Press, 2005.
Fousek, John. *To Lead the Free World: American Nationalism and the Cultural Roots of the Cold War*. Chapel Hill: University of North Carolina Press, 2000.
Geerhart, Bill, and Ken Sitz. *Atomic Platters: Cold War Music from the Golden Age of Homeland Security*. Hambergen, Germany: Bear Family Records, 2005.
Gienow-Hecht, Jessica. "Culture and the Cold War in Europe." In *The Cambridge History of the Cold War, Volume I: Origins*, ed. Melvyn P. Leffler and Odd Arne Westad. Cambridge: Cambridge University Press, 2010, 398–419.
Hewison, Robert. *In Anger: British Culture in the Cold War, 1945–60*. London: Weidenfeld and Nicolson, 1981.
Kackman, Michael. *Citizen Spy: Television, Espionage, and Cold War Culture*. Minneapolis: University of Minnesota Press, 2005.
Kundera, Milan. "Die Tragödie Mitteleuropas." In *Versunkene Welt*, ed. Joachim Riedl, 125–136.
Kuznick, Peter J., and James Gilbert, eds. *Rethinking Cold War Culture*. Washington: Smithsonian Institution Press, 2001.
Lippmann, Walter. *The Cold War: A Study in U.S. Foreign Policy*. New York: Harper, 1947.
Lipsitz, George. *Class and Culture in Cold War America: A Rainbow at Midnight*. New York: Praeger, 1981.
Madariaga, Salvador de. *The Anatomy of the Cold War*. Belfast: M. Boyd, 1955.
May, Lary, ed. *Recasting America: Culture and Politics in the Age of Cold War*. Chicago: The University of Chicago Press, 1989.
Nadel, Alan. *Containment Culture: American Narratives, Postmodernism and the Atomic Age*. Durham: Duke University Press, 1996.
Poiger, Uta. *Jazz, Rock, and Rebels: Cold War Politics and American Culture in a Divided Germany*. Berkeley and Los Angeles: The University of California Press, 2000.
Riedl, Joachim, ed. *Versunkene Welt*. Vienna: Jewish Welcome Service, 1984.

Robin, Ron Theodore. *The Making of the Cold War Enemy: Culture and Politics in the Military-Intellectual Complex*. Princeton: Princeton University Press, 2001.

Schaub, Thomas H. *American Fiction in the Cold War*. Madison: University of Wisconsin Press, 1991.

Schrecker, Ellen. *Cold War Triumphalism: The Misuse of History After the Fall of Communism*. New York: The New Press, 2004.

Scott-Smith, Giles, and Hans Krabbendam, eds. *The Cultural Cold War in Western Europe 1945–1960*. London: Cass, 2003.

Seed, David. *American Science Fiction and the Cold War: Literature and Film*. Edinburgh: Edinburgh University Press, 1999.

Sloterdijk, Peter. *Falls Europa erwacht: Gedanken zum Programm einer Weltmacht am Ende des Zeitalters ihrer politischen Absence*. Frankfurt am Main: Suhrkamp, 2002.

Stephan, Alexander. *The Americanization of Europe: Culture, Diplomacy, and Anti-Americanism after 1945*. New York: Berghahn, 2006.

Whitfield, Stephen J. *The Culture of the Cold War*. 2nd ed. Baltimore: Johns Hopkins University Press, 1996.

Part I

MEDIATING THE COLD WAR
Radio, Film, Television, and Literature

Chapter 1

EAST EUROPEAN COLD WAR CULTURE(S)
Alterities, Commonalities, and Film Industries

Marsha Siefert

At one end of Budapest's Freedom (Szabadság) Square stands a tall obelisk topped by a five-pointed star, with a dedication in Hungarian and Russian to the Soviet "heroes" who died "liberating" Budapest from Nazi occupation in 1945. It is surrounded by a person-high metal barricade, which was put up after the monument was defaced during the October 2006 demonstrations against the Hungarian government, on the fiftieth anniversary of the 1956 revolution. Across the walkway, for several months in 2008, stood a two-story tent, erected by a Hungarian nationalist organization and topped by a Hungarian flag. In front of the tent were three large wooden crosses, the taller middle one with two cross-pieces; on the highest cross-piece was nailed a map of pre-Trianon Hungary, with the lost territories colored in black. The sign in English and Hungarian proclaimed that the Hungarian flag had stood in that place and had been unlawfully torn down after 1945. Just a few paces from the monument and its constructed response, also on Freedom Square and enclosed by a person-high metal barricade, is the United States Embassy.

Symbol elision, juxtaposition, and overload are not unusual in "Eastern Europe," even after the twentieth anniversary of the fall of communism. Such abundant referents challenge any attempt to generalize about a cultural past in a part of the world so filled with boundary changes and so saturated in human tragedies. For this essay, which attempts to grapple with ways in which to approach the topic of Cold War Culture in this region as a whole, the assemblage on Szabadság Square links politics to culture, past to present, Europe to the Cold War, one superpower to another, while forging the longer-term historical trajectories so critical to differentiating the nations included in the Cold War geopolitical term "Eastern Europe." To speak of cultural commonalities, however, seems to go against the very heart of scholarship from this part of Europe since the fall of the Wall. Scholars from Hungary and Poland, Romania and Bulgaria, the emerged or reemerged countries of the Czech Republic and Slovakia, the former Yugoslav republics and the Baltic states, have reinvigorated national continuities in historicist terms. If Cold War Culture is mentioned, scholars from post-Socialist countries often see it as a limiting lens through which Western scholars interpreted everything, suppressing national specificities and reducing cultural products to the political. East European efforts to reclaim four decades of culture from ideological evaluation have revitalized the study of postwar music, art, film, and literature, with new themes of memory and everyday life and re-evaluated examples of aesthetic achievement.

Yet now, twenty years on, as most of these nations have become part of a new European aggregation, it may be possible to ask whether the new scholarship on the Cold War, and especially Cold War Culture, has anything to offer in thinking about the East European Cold War experience, without being either dominated or limited by that approach. This chapter will begin with some thoughts about how culture was linked to the Cold War in classic Anglo-American texts, and what happens when Europe is introduced into this equation. Particular attention will be paid to "Eastern Europe," which in Cold War symbolic geography includes countries today considered part of Central and Southeastern Europe. Next, the East European organizations and institutions created for cultural exchange and dissemination will be described in terms of their participation in bilateral and transnational relations of cultural import and export. Finally, the film industry is used to explore the implications of this approach, because during this period making films in Eastern Europe without state participation would have been technologically and practically prohibitive and because films were such an important component of Cold War cultural diplomacy. Overall, the goal is to give "the East" a place in the elaboration and critique of the concept of European Cold War Culture.

Cold War + Culture

The Cold War is no longer what it used to be. The years since the dissolution of the Soviet Union have seen increased scholarly attention to the Cold War's origin and ending. One result is that the time frame has broadened: looking specifically at U.S.-Soviet relations, some date the start of the Cold War as early as 1917, from the American intervention in the Russian Civil War.[1] Others have assessed Russian-American relations across the Revolutionary divide.[2] A central figure in this reexamination is Joseph Stalin, the Soviet ruler most identified with building the Soviet state during the 1930s and the postwar reconstruction of Eastern Europe. Obvious ideological continuities are evident in the persistence of Marxist-Leninist vocabulary, however any change in Stalin's policy and behavior following the dissolution of the wartime alliance might be construed.[3]

In the so-called cultural turn in scholarship on Cold War political and diplomatic relations,[4] especially as "soft power" has become an important explanatory factor in the rise of the United States after 1945,[5] the Cold War has been discursively related to culture in at least two ways. When "culture" is an adjective, the "cultural Cold War" hearkens back to Christopher Lasch's 1967 essay in *The Nation*, in which he used that term to discuss the CIA-backed Congress of Cultural Freedom (CCF).[6] After 1991, a new generation of scholars has revisited the history and the operation of institutions designed to "fight" the Cold War. The activities of the Ford Foundation and the Congress of Cultural Freedom, which published *Encounter*, *Preuves*, and *Der Monat*, along with the later cultural exchanges negotiated between governments, are identifiable manifestations of the cultural Cold War.[7] So too are the Western publications of dissident writings and the crises that arose in the process, from the Nobel prize awarded to Boris Pasternak to the well publicized defections and espionage scandals. The intertwining of high politics and high culture is a theme in contemporary accounts of its early decades.

In the context of the United States, using "Cold War" as an adjective to culture enlarges the frame to include cultural products—extending to attitudes and practices—specifically directed toward the domestic audience, sometimes called the Cold War "home front."[8] American Cold War Culture is often topically identified with books or movies that specifically address Cold War concerns, from the arms race to the space race, and include representations of "the Other," from spy films to science fiction, the Communist enemy within as well as in the East.[9] Everything from Hollywood to the evening television news, from serial music to abstract art, has been analyzed as Cold War Culture.[10] Thus in the U.S., the institutional structures that were created during the Cold War for exporting culture are related to, but not coterminous with Cold War Culture, much of which was produced for domestic consumption and within a commercial context. Two influential books written before the Cold War was "over" and "won" use a broader understanding of culture, with a small *c*. As exemplified by the table of contents of *The Culture of the Cold War*, Stephen

Whitfield lists not cultural categories, like film or music, but verbs of activity and agency. His chapter titles, like "Seeing Red," "Politicizing," "Assenting," "Informing," and "Dissenting,"[11] emphasize that Cold War Culture includes practices of cultural interpretation as well as cultural products. Lary May argues persuasively that American attitudes, as well as cultural products, created after 1945 were inflected by the Cold War and by a paradigm shift in America's perception of its own role as "leader of the free world."[12] Everyday life and its representation are part of the renewed interest in Cold War Culture.

However, the concept of Cold War Culture, even in the American case, has not been without its critics. Sometimes, for example, the Cold War seems to become a loose temporal marker for the 1950s, or for postwar America. In other cases it is used as an overdetermined metaphor that infuses cultural practice without adding to its understanding.[13] Reviews of the "Cold War Culture industry" remark on book titles using Cold War Culture as a marketing tool rather than an examined concept. Sometimes Cold War Culture is used to argue about something else entirely—for example the way the Hollywood Red Scare and the Vietnam War are used to critique the present,[14] or to express moral outrage over particular sets of values or assumptions now proven wrong.[15] Because culture, especially consumer culture and popular culture, has been credited with "winning" the Cold War, the nature of this culture's effects on "the Other" are often presumed or too baldly stated, with more attention to the message than to how it was received and interpreted.[16] Finally, focusing on the cultural product—the films or the blue jeans—can obscure the "big ideas" and political stakes of the Cold War enmity.[17] Cultural transfer, whether of American Cold War Culture or its conceptualization, can no longer be treated as self-evident.

Decentering America and Adding Europe

Adding Europe to the concept of Cold War Culture immediately invokes the bilateral West-East frame, as patently manifested by the symbolic geography of a Europe divided into West and East. In its simplest form, the term "European Cold War Culture" could apply to European domestic cultural products and practices similar to those identified by American scholars and commentators. But the attribution is complicated by Europe's role in the bilateral context, because in the matter of culture, Europe set the standard of achievement and value. Both the United States and the Soviet Union had traditions of cultural enlightenment and saw themselves as latecomers to the cultural contest in European high culture.[18] In this contest, the USSR pressed its advantage, reminding Europeans (both West and East) of its long and passionate commitment to and influence in theater, literature, dance, and music. The Soviet Union also shared with Europe the tradition of state sponsorship of the arts, and so the exposure of the American dependence on covert financing of their cultural projects abroad was more damaging in the lie than was government presence in the cultural sphere. Also, American efforts at exporting high culture in the early Cold War were demonstrably less successful than earlier Russian efforts in Western Europe. American CCF officials privately saw the 1952 Paris Festival "Masterpieces of the Twentieth Century" as a chance to counter "the traditional European misconception of the United States as a country lacking in culture, a misconception consistently exploited by Communist propaganda."[19]

Thus for Europe as a whole, and especially in Western Europe, it is sometimes difficult to separate what scholars label as "Americanization" from American Cold War cultural diplomacy.[20] Americanization is considered a longer-lived phenomenon. Victoria de Grazia, for example, addresses consumer culture as a twentieth-century phenomenon dating from 1914, bringing American products and techniques to Europe.[21] For the American film industry, the European market was intertwined with the rise of the Hollywood studio system, dominated by moguls of European origin, and exporting movies made for the domestic U.S. audiences was always part of the international marketing plan.[22] European reception of American Cold War Culture is part of a longer history of entangled cultural values.

European scholars have endeavored to introduce a more nuanced picture of the relationship between the United States and Western Europe by using the concept of "Westernization," which emphasizes the emergence of a transatlantic community of values. Here, cultural transfer is less about imposition and more about cooperation among the Western European countries, and importantly differentiates among the postwar histories of the many national and interest groups.[23] This European reinscription of "the West" into postwar culture, along with the national studies of the reception of U.S. culture in Europe,[24] affirms that generalizing about Europe or even Western Europe is fraught with qualifications and exceptions.

Europe is also a part of the enlarged spatial conception of the "global Cold War." The Cold War context certainly affected the way in which the postwar decolonization of European empires as well as the proxy and covert wars between Communists and anti-Communists that took place on "Third World" soil. But the Cold War did not determine the outcome.[25] One of the key words of Cold War theoretical discourse—"modernization"—also has a longer history, related to processes of technological development and urbanization that cut across the Cold War divide.[26] As Cox argues, especially beginning in the 1970s, Europe played a much more active role in the diplomatic and political as well as cultural life of the Cold War, especially through the European Community, than the America-centered narrative credits.[27] Overall, then, reinserting Europe into the cultural Cold War narrative also makes sense. Gienow-Hecht affirms: "In the case of … Europe, cultural relations and exchanges had been in place before, both on the level of high and popular culture. The Cold War highlighted, formalized and politicized these ties. It triggered programs to finance individual interactions that would otherwise not have been taking place. But it did not inspire new cultural affinities. … These had been in place before and they remained in place thereafter."[28] These European relations reached across the Iron Curtain as well.

East European Cold War Culture—An Alterity?

Adding "East" as an adjective to the concept of European Cold War invokes its long history as the "Other Europe," heightened perhaps but not invented in Cold War symbolic geography.[29] Germany is the perfect synecdoche, divided into East and West, with reunification offering closure for a Cold War case study,[30] but this model does not work for the rest of Eastern Europe. The term "Eastern Europe" is one of the constants of Cold War geopolitical vocabulary, but its definitional strength was resisted by intellectuals who redefined themselves as Central European, pushing the "dividing line" from the "Iron Curtain" to the edge of Latin Christianity.[31] The recitation of European Cold War political crises—highlighted most dramatically in Hungary 1956, Czechoslovakia 1968, Poland 1980–1981—also shapes external and internal perceptions of the core of Eastern Europe.[32] In the post–Cold War environment, the increasing frequency of the term "East-Central Europe," and the ways in which the adjectives of "old" and "new" Europe were applied after EU enlargement, demonstrate that "Eastern Europe" is no longer a consistent referent, but the term is used intentionally here in discussing Cold War Culture to include countries now referred to as Central and Southeastern Europe.

In Cold War discourse, "Eastern Europe" was a separate entity from the Soviet Union. In early Cold War rhetoric of the West, the states of Eastern Europe were referred to as "captive nations," "puppet states," and "Soviet satellites," among other phrases. However, Eastern Europe was often included with the Soviet Union in one of the most potent descriptors—"the bloc"—as the East was defined by the West. According to Kaldor, "bloc identity" was supposed to augment if not displace nationalism, and quarrels between and within nations were to be turned against "bloc enemies." "Bloc-ism" was based around abstract ideals like "freedom" or "socialism" rather than history, culture, or race, and therefore was supposed to be a more "progressive" civilizing agent. What held the bloc together, more than military integration through the Warsaw Pact, according to Kaldor, were interparty relations, dominated by the Soviet Communist Party and the *nomenklatura* system of party appointments, with linked networks of consultation, exchange, and negotiation between East European Communist parties. Interparty relations constituted ideological, physical, and economic forms of coercion.[33] "Bloc identity" expanded during the Cold War to include Communist countries outside Europe, like Cuba and Vietnam, while countries like Yugoslavia attempted to escape bloc identity by forming a nonaligned group. Still, it remains useful shorthand for describing a Cold War space that includes the USSR and Eastern Europe, whether the USSR or Russia is considered inside or outside of Europe.[34]

Specifically in the matter of cultural relations, East European nations were required to participate in the organizations for the circulation of cultural products within the bloc, and were subject to Soviet-style instruments of cultural diplomacy.[35] Soviet authorities were never able to monopolize the interactions of individual East European nations with the international system,[36] and many studies of Cold War Culture document the extent to which Western culture, from trophy films to jazz, was present even in the darkest days of Stalinism. But Bunce's observation that Soviet power was maintained through bilateral ties with each of the East European countries suggests that the Soviets attended to these relations in the cultural sphere as well.[37] Thus the term "bloc" is used here to describe the context of institutional relations between the Soviet Union and East European nations.

"Bloc" Builders in "Eastern Europe"

At least three types of cultural institution that relate to Cold War Culture were operative in Eastern Europe. Two of them represent those organizations or arrangements that typically are discussed within the concept of the cultural Cold War. The first includes those formal state agreements for the flow of culture between East and West, typified by the U.S.-USSR cultural exchange agreement of 1958, which supported the exchange of students, performers, media, and technology. In the West, organizations included the private, or in Lucas's term "private-state" foundations,[38] like the CCF or the Ford Foundation, as well as Radio Free Europe and Radio Liberty, that also sponsored the effort to project American identity abroad. The Soviet organizations for cultural relations with the West began already in the 1920s, when "Soviet Friendship Societies" were established in several countries, including the United States, Great Britain, and Germany, to foster sympathetic relations without formal ties to the Party. In 1927, the goal was described as creating "a whole solar system of organizations," and 1927 was also the year in which the International Association of the Friends of the Soviet Union was established.[39] The Soviet institution that arranged for cultural diplomacy, the All-Union Society for Cultural Relations with Foreign Countries, or VOKS (*Vsesoiuznoe obshchestvo kul'turnoi sviazi s zagranitsei*), lasted from 1924 to 1957. VOKS helped to foster exchange, tourism, and a PR bureau, and published newsletters and other bulletins in several languages. In the interwar period it was also responsible for arranging the visits of high-profile Americans and Europeans to witness the "Soviet experiment."[40]

While these organizations were gradually replaced by others after 1956,[41] their transformation over time, especially during the wartime alliance, and the lessons learned influenced the negotiation of subsequent agreements. For example, almost immediately after Stalin's death a new department for Ties with Foreign Communist Parties was created, which among other things was to oversee cultural affairs. While it created tension between Party control and the Ministry of Foreign Affairs, this change also concentrated Soviet efforts on consolidating relations with Eastern Europe as well as other countries. After various permutations, in 1967 a new Department of Cultural Relations was established within the Foreign Ministry that put these issues back under ministerial control,[42] and similar types of committees were established in the Soviet republics for cultural relations with their diaspora communities.[43] And of course, ideologically speaking, the Cominform, which on a smaller scale replaced the Comintern discontinued during the war and was itself disbanded as part of de-Stalinization after 1956, was a way of cultivating cultural ties.

A second type of state-sponsored organization supported intrabloc relations; some of these mirrored West European cooperative arrangements. For example, the Socialist trade organization Council for Mutual Economic Assistance or COMECON, established in 1947, was later revamped in part to rival Western Europe's Common Market.[44] In the important area of broadcasting, Intervision was created in 1960, as a counterpart to the West European institution Eurovision, for the exchange of broadcast news, sports, and other program materials within the Socialist bloc.[45] Bilateral treaties of "friendship, cooperation, and mutual assistance" governed intrabloc cooperation in a range of other fields, including science, education, tourism, and film. During the 1970s, Soviet sources on cultural links, primarily to Eastern Europe, cite more than seventy agreements and two hundred protocols in specific spheres of cultural relations. "Friendship Months" and "Days of Culture" celebrated Socialist achievements, and annual meetings of the Soviet and East European ministers of culture were supposed to aid bloc coordination.[46]

Competitions and festivals of various kinds allowed for the East-West cultural-achievement contest to be played out in real time by encouraging international participation.[47] The Soviet Tchaikovsky Competition in music became well known when an American pianist won first prize in 1958.[48] Other types of festival were held over time in different locations throughout the bloc. Biennial youth festivals, begun in 1947, were designed to bring together young people interested in socialism.[49] In sport, Socialist achievement was highlighted in the Olympics, but also encouraged through national competitions like the Spartakiads in Czechoslovakia and the Daciada in Romania.[50] Their discontinuation or transformation, documented in nation-based studies, is a part of the East European post–Cold War narrative.

A third set of cultural institutions represents those involved in the production, dissemination, interpretation, and consumption of domestic culture in the individual East European nations. Prominent among them are the "creative unions" that brought together musicians, writers, and artists. While ostensibly established to allow the artistic communities to oversee their professions, these unions soon saw the emergence of "cultural bosses" who managed the products, relations, and rewards of their membership.[51] As suggested by the history of the Soviet Filmmakers' Union, established in 1965 on the initiative of leading directors, the unions worked with the Party to maintain ideological purity, but also sometimes represented filmmakers in an attempt to work toward a minimum of creative freedom.[52] The "creative industries" included centralized state institutions for cultural production and dissemination, such as the state publishing houses, museums, and state broadcasting and recording bodies, as well as the Party- or state-financed publications that reviewed and critiqued cultural products from both East and West.

In the nations of Eastern Europe descriptions of postwar transformation of domestic cultural institutions during the late 1940s are usually connected to the debate about how Communist parties came to power in each East European country.[53] Recent scholarship stresses that the seemingly similar institutional structures and practices—including administrative hierarchies, Party oversight, and central planning—were much more diverse than previously described and emerged differently depending upon national contexts and historical experience.[54] This observation applies especially to East European culture. Just as Whitfield's formulation of American Cold War Culture uses active verbs or "practices," so too does the choice of verb become important in characterizing the various responses of local East European authorities to "Sovietization"[55]—hence the importance of national studies. To use Reid's eloquent formulation, one must remain "attentive to the specificity of the ways in which Soviet socialist ideology and organizational structures, and Soviet-style practices, were embedded, naturalized, appropriated, transformed, subverted or repulsed in different national contexts in the nations of Central and Eastern Europe."[56] New studies also argue that not only was the process varied, it was also incomplete. Archival evidence revealing disagreements among local Party elites, varying interpretations of the cultural formulae and aesthetics among intelligentsia and cultural creators, genuine interest in including socialism as part of postwar reconstruction, and significant achievements in what Reid and Crowley refer to as "Socialist style" has loosened the hold of the Sovietization paradigm in explaining East European Socialist culture.[57] The consistent use of the term "socialism" (sometimes but not always as "state socialism") in studies of East European countries serves as a distinction not only in Marxist-Leninist vocabulary but in describing a desired distance from the Soviet model.

Amid the greater latitude now attributed to local intelligentsia and members of the cultural sphere during the Socialist period, the question of local Party influence over the form, content, dissemination, and interpretation of culture in domestic and intrabloc contexts is still salient, though. As Zubkova has described Soviet-style decision-making, "the psychology of the regime was to design a model administrative unit endowed with a clearly stipulated element of initiative, easily defined and easily revised." The limited freedom of each administrative unit, with its hierarchical structure, gave bureaucrats at each level a "strange blend of plenary power and accountability" that allowed them to execute higher-level decisions in an optimal fashion without the necessity of heavy-handed supervision from above.[58] This description opens up possibilities at the local level for "creative" decision-making in the institutional hierarchies, rather than assuming only top-down instructions or formulaic products. It also explains how local decision-making can respond to the thaws and frosts in both local conditions and relations with the Soviet Union. As long as the cultural institutions remained intact, then, the potential for the reimposition of Party control—as happened after the Prague Spring in Czechoslovakia[59]—remained. In this way the Cold War could impinge upon and influence the domestic cultural products and practices of individual East European countries.

Writing about institutional considerations does not intend to reimpose a structural straitjacket on cultural products of the "bloc." Quite the contrary. The goal is to find a way to talk about Cold War Culture in Eastern Europe not only in terms of cultural artifacts, but also in a way that includes how intrabloc relations, institutional conditions, and local practices are affected directly and indirectly by Cold War considerations; and in the same way that the cultural industries in the "West" are also appraised as a part of a cultural economy.[60] Analyzing a given cultural product—a film, a piece of music, a novel, a painting—that is identifiably about a Cold War topic and then prospecting for the conditions of its production, reception, and interpretation allows the analyst to give it a Cold War reading. This happened frequently during the Cold War, when both West and East tried to read the political temperature from the "clues" in Socialist cultural products, as represented by the well-known Socialist expression "reading between the lines." The art works, music, stories, or films themselves often disappeared from view except in their role as indicator of or resistance to socialism, which is exactly what contemporary scholars in Eastern Europe dislike. As case studies have shown, while restrictive in many ways, the state structures also proved more flexible in practice, and many works of East European culture can be interpreted within broader aesthetic trends and also on their own terms, in addition to the Cold War reading.

The concept of East European Cold War Culture could also include the cultural products from the West that became available through the West-East programs and "illegal" forms of circulation. As I have described elsewhere, literature, art, music, and films from its Cold War enemy were present even in the Soviet Union throughout the period, and the *nomenklatura* always had privileged access.[61] East European Cold War Culture is also populated by any number of actors, from exiles and dissidents to nongovernmental organizations, who produced their own flow of people and cultural products across borders that explicitly operated outside of, or at least did not conform to, those of the state institutions.[62] These are celebrated aspects of Cold War Culture, and are especially valued in the East European narratives of this period. Still, investigating the transferability of a concept like Cold War Culture from the American use to Eastern Europe as a whole, one that includes the cultural Cold War as well as the representation of Cold War themes and products, would also require elaborating the institutional contexts and practices within the bloc. The film industries are used here to explore the potential for this type of analysis, with particular attention to intrabloc European relations.

East European Cold War Culture(s) and the "Film Factory"

The film industries of Eastern Europe, like other institutional formations in the bloc, were transformed in the late 1940s. Essentially this meant that local bureaucracies in charge of film production, education, labor, censorship, and distribution were reorganized according to local Party interpretations of socialist cultural production. The pattern had been set in the 1920s,[63] when the Soviet Union established regional film studios in the Soviet republics of Ukraine, Armenia, Georgia, Azerbaijan, and Central Asia, with the aim of producing films representing local nationalities. Their relative autonomy was soon brought under the umbrella of a more centralized Soviet film system, whose administrative units had a monopoly over distributing, importing, and exporting films. The USSR State Committee for Cinematography was responsible for overseeing film production as a whole, from concept to finished film. As in other Soviet industries, each year a proposed plan for film themes and genres, as well as individual proposals for each film, had to be submitted. During the approval process, film proposals moved up the hierarchical ladder to the local Party organs; screenwriters and directors were later chosen for approved proposals, and directors were paid according to the genre classification of the film. All stages of production and completed films were reviewed before release.[64] Film distribution was also regulated. In the Soviet Union, cinemas were supposed to show only a strictly defined number of films in particular thematic categories. Western films were not supposed to represent over 20 percent, or about thirty films per year, and no more than five or six were to be from the United States.[65]

During the postwar transformation, existing film industries in the Eastern bloc were brought into compliance with this system. East European countries like Bulgaria that had no viable film industry before the war built film studios in the 1950s, and the USSR supported the establishment of film studios in the Soviet republics of Estonia, Latvia, Lithuania, and Moldavia. Film schools were established in some of these countries to provide personnel. Iordanova compares the East European film studio system to the Hollywood studio system before 1948 in terms of the vertical integration of the industry from production to distribution, a "factory" model the USSR openly acknowledged in the 1930s.[66] In contrast to Hollywood, even though the authorities expected that films would make some money for reinvestment in the system, overall filmmakers were isolated from purely commercial concerns.

For countries like Poland, Hungary, Czechoslovakia, and East Germany that had relatively well developed cinema traditions and studios, the transformation of the film industries in the late 1940s was at the time sometimes called "nationalization,"⁶⁷ while developments over the whole Socialist period differed according to the inherited traditions of each cinema, material conditions after the war, and the thaws and frosts of relations with the USSR. Internal local politics were also an important factor in filmmaking, as many opportunists saw ways to gain favor within the national Communist Parties, and filmmakers in the Eastern bloc were likely to be subject to local demands and sanctions. Some practices, like the filmmaker ensembles begun in Poland in 1955, were adopted in other Socialist states like Hungary and Czechoslovakia, and later for some films in the USSR as well. Successful films, such as those produced in the "new wave" cinema or that had success on the festival circuit, also had an influence on the Soviet scene, for better and worse politically. On the other hand, "shelving" films that in the end did not fit the climate prevailing at the time the film was finished was also a common practice throughout the bloc.

During the Cold War, analyzing films from Eastern Europe inevitably invoked the political and aesthetic "doctrine" of "Socialist Realism." Introduced in the Soviet Writers Union in 1932 and elaborated in 1934, Socialist Realism has been a consistent category in discussing almost all Soviet cultural discourse and products, internally and externally. In fact, Dobrenko has recently suggested that "Socialist Realism," as represented in Stalinist art forms from novels and poems to songs and films, gave material form to "real Socialism" and was "Stalinism's most effective sociopolitical institution."⁶⁸ Even after Stalin's death, something like Socialist Realism was a touchstone from which to measure degrees of cultural freedom in the production of literary and other artistic products, both within and from outside the Soviet Union, even if there was no agreement about its definition.⁶⁹ East European cultural pronouncements through periods of thaw and frost often display a discursive irony and pay lip service to Socialist Realism. As Yurchak has argued, after the Stalinist period, "it was increasingly more important to reproduce precise ideological forms than to adhere to the precise meanings these forms were supposed to convey."⁷⁰ Thus, in these more recent interpretations of Soviet culture, the forms and institutions are crucial for understanding not only cultural products but socialism itself.

East European cinema, Iordanova argues, is not characterized by Socialist Realism, but by similar themes such as an emphasis on morality, or the relationship between the individual and social and historical processes.⁷¹ Often screenplays that were submitted for approval would be evaluated according to various ideological principles from the Socialist Realism vocabulary, like "the romanticism of revolutionary feats" or "Socialist humanism," as well as more negative characterizations such as "bourgeois morals" and "base individualism." Such phrases might also be used when the finished film was reviewed by the studio and local Party organs, and even in published reviews. But if audiences learned to read between the lines, so too did writers learn the lines to write.

East European filmmakers shared with their Soviet counterparts several strategies both to fulfill the objective demands and to evade the censors. Historical films, as an important thematic category, allowed filmmakers to locate a film in national history or biography, and dramatizing literary masterpieces spoke to the goal of exporting the best of high culture and emphasized the film as a work of art. National traditions also gave rise to complex symbols and metaphors, subtext and allusion, that allowed for ambiguity in interpretation. The use of documentary techniques gave films a type of film "positivism" that combined realism with social diagnosis. Iordanova cites elaborate camera movements, complexly staged long takes, meticulously choreographed scenes, and mastery of black-and-white photography as common to all national cinematic traditions of the region. These types of artistic and technical commonalities may also derive from the common education and the development of relations between the film personnel over the Socialist period, as well as their recognition as a "style" by the international film community.[72]

A Socialist Audiovisual Space?

Like the film industries of other nations, and notably with reference to Hollywood,[73] the Soviet film industry was interested in export and influence, and had a bureaucracy in place to pursue both those aims. Sovexportfilm was the unit of the State Cinema Committee (Goskino) in charge of all Soviet film sales and foreign film purchases. Other units handled promotion efforts, including the film festivals and the export magazine *Soviet Film*, which was published in six languages excluding Russian. In 1968, a unit called Sovinfilm was established to promote collaboration on films coproduced with foreign countries, as well as to earn foreign currency by providing services to foreign film producers.[74] Well publicized film exchanges between the USSR and the U.S. were launched as early as 1958, but in both the Soviet Union and Eastern Europe the preponderance of European imports as compared to American films speaks to the USSR's perceived ties with European culture more generally, and to the cost of Hollywood films.

East European countries were an important part of the Soviet efforts in film export, influence, and collaboration. One prime example is the numerous post-Stalinist Soviet films using what might be called "Cold

War genres"—espionage, military brinkmanship, Third World conflict, emigration, and cultural contacts—that were not commercially exported—except to the Socialist countries.[75] What Iordanova calls the geopolitically "forced togetherness"[76] of the Eastern bloc also led to numerous artistic interactions and mutual influences. A well developed system of cinematic barters between the bloc countries attempted to encourage mutual exchange or purchase of each other's films. Socialist cooperation was promoted through visiting delegations in the bloc countries, and by scheduled "Film Weeks" in which each country's films were screened with special events. For example, in 1980 *Soviet Film* listed film weeks and visiting delegations in a range of Soviet cities, from Minsk to Tashkent, with film weeks featuring all the East European countries, along with Spain, Italy, Denmark, Iceland, Turkey, Argentina, Mexico, Cuba, Niger, and Bangladesh.[77]

Film festivals also promoted Socialist film for the Eastern bloc as well as the rest of the world. By alternating the Moscow Film Festival with one in Karlovy Vary, Czechoslovakia, Eastern Europe was represented in a Socialist counterpart to famous film festivals in Cannes and Venice.[78] The international Tashkent Festival of Asian, African, and Latin American Cinema, founded in 1968, also was held in the "off years" to showcase films from the Central Asian republics—Uzbekistan, Kazakhstan, Kyrgyzstan, Tajikistan, and Turkmenistan.[79] The annual week-long "national" (All-Union) film festival rotated among the capital cities of the fifteen Soviet republics.[80] Included here also were arrangements with a range of "friendly" Third-World countries from Cuba to India,[81] along with other countries in Latin America, Africa, and Asia.

Film cooperation, trade, and exhibition within the Socialist bloc are underexplored areas. Anecdotal evidence suggests that East Europeans remember frequent showings of Soviet films in classrooms and local film theaters throughout the Socialist period. However, by the 1970s film exhibitors from those countries with larger film industries like Hungary, Czechoslovakia, Poland, and the GDR may have used the various forms of film barter and exchange in order to save their hard currency to purchase films from the West. National histories of East European countries stress the international and cosmopolitan nature of the East European capitals. So, for example, in Budapest in 1973, the "West" was represented by eleven films from the United States and twenty-three West European films, with French films the most numerous at eight. Meanwhile, Soviet films matched that number of eight, with the GDR supplying six, Czechoslovakia three, and one each from Poland, Romania, Bulgaria, and Yugoslavia.[82] *Soviet Film*, on the other hand, highlights the cooperation with the bloc countries. For example, one 1982 issue has a pair of articles on the named cinemas in each other's capital cities—"Prague" in Moscow and "Moscow" in Prague—with film weeks and events around each other's films and history.[83] The elaborate system of houses of culture, film clubs, and rural distribution in the USSR developed since the 1920s also reinforces the idea of support for as well as control of film circulation in the Socialist context.

Socialist film coproductions between the USSR and Eastern Europe suggest a very small but steady output of one or two a year, with some more complicated patterns exhibited during periods of perceived political uncertainty. One reason for this small output may be that some Socialist countries were much more interested in cultivating their own bilateral agreements with the West for exactly the same reasons that the Soviet Union was eager for coproduction—access to advanced filmmaking equipment and techniques, hard currency, and international stars. The success of their bilateral negotiations with each other and across the Curtain had actually been a spur to the Soviet effort.[84] Also, East European filmmakers' choices for coproductions within the bloc could be designed to satisfy or at least mollify Party oversight by selecting favored Soviet genres, and thereby opening open creative space in others. For example, of five Soviet coproductions with Hungary, two are biopics about Hungarian musicians, two are Revolutionary dramas, and the last is a World War II drama coproduced with several Socialist countries. Still, however, many of the most commercially successful of the fourteen "Easterns" or *Indianerfilme* made between 1965 and 1985 were coproductions that the East German studio DEFA made with various bloc countries—Yugoslavia, Bulgaria, Romania, the Soviet Union, and Cuba.[85]

In some cases, coproductions by East and West European countries revived long-standing cultural affinities, for example the Romanian historical epics directed by Sergiu Nicolescu that were coproduced with France.[86] In the 1980s, István Szabó from Hungary directed three well received films—*Mephisto* (1980/81), *Colonel Redl* (1984), and *Hanussen* (1987/88)—coproduced with West Germany. Some films were not officially coproductions, but offered foreign film companies the advantages of trained film personnel, lower costs, and historical settings, with Eastern Europe becoming a prime location for such "runaway" productions. For example, already in the 1960s Hollywood was filming in Eastern Europe for its "Russian" epics like *Taras Bulba* (J. Lee Thompson, 1962), which was coproduced with and in Yugoslavia, and *The Fixer* (John Frankenheimer, 1968), filmed in Hungary. Most famous is Czech émigré Miloš Forman's *Amadeus* (1984), filmed in Czechoslovakia.

East European countries also served another role in the intrabloc film industries: as an outlet for Soviet film criticism and opinions that could not be published in the USSR, a type of socialist *tamizdat*. One film magazine editor described how he "vacationed" in Warsaw, or entrusted film reviews to friendly officials in Moscow's Polish embassy, in order to have his more critical reviews published in the more liberal Poland.[87] In fact, East European countries were one of the main avenues for smuggling cultural products, including music and video cassettes, into the Soviet Union. Overall, efforts to create a "Socialist audiovisual space" are evident at the level of production and distribution and in various manifestations of sponsored intrabloc cooperation, however ineffective they may have been or were later interpreted. As with all communication during the Cold War, the boundaries were often permeable, and the system sometimes malleable. A few examples of intrabloc practices may be suggestive.

East European Cold War Film Practices: Intrabloc Examples

A first example suggests the ways in which "national" cinema, even within the Soviet Union, was perceived between the center and the republics. Although Lithuania was a Soviet republic during the Cold War, like other bloc countries it was independent in the interwar period, and returned to independence after 1991. After annexation in 1940, the Soviet authority supported the development of a "national" cinema, first through a newsreel studio during and after the war, and culminating in the establishment of the Lithuanian Film Studio in Vilnius in 1956. The Lithuanian Film Studio operated like all republic studios, by fulfilling a thematic and genre plan and submitting film scenarios to the Studio's Scenario Editorial Board, and then to Lithuania's State Cinematographic Committee, which served as a censor and a surrogate for Goskino; a representative from Moscow was often present at regular debates over individual films.

As with many films throughout the bloc in the decades after the war, the portrayal of the past, especially the past related to the war years, was a prime topic. The 1965 film *Niekas nenorėjo mirti* (Nobody Wanted to Die) and its director Vytautas Žalakevičius came to represent Lithuanian filmmaking in discussions of East European and Soviet cinema both within and outside the Soviet Union.[88] Like many films about a national past, the scenario met the generic and ideological expectations of the Soviet film industry, while providing the possibility of visualizing national Lithuanian symbols and events to carry the ambiguities of allegory and metaphor on film. In *Soviet Film*'s summary, the action "takes place a year after the war, when bands roamed the forests of Lithuania, terrorizing the population. That was their way of fighting against the Soviet system in Lithuania. The bandits shot down women and children and slaughtered entire families. 'Nobody Wanted to Die' tells of the four sons of Lokis who led the struggle against the bandits in their village."[89] The "bandits" are Lithuanian partisans; the summary neglects to say that Lithuanian partisans were fighting the Soviet "occupation" as late as 1955. The mise-en-scène includes several Lithuanian national symbols that become the basis of later "resistant" readings, particularly as the film became a founding film of Lithuanian cinema.

In 1966, the film was dubbed into Russian and exported to other Soviet republics. It won the "Big Amber" film festival of the Soviet western republics—Lithuanian, Latvia, Estonia, Moldavia, and Belarus. The review of the film by Ina Solovieva in the magazine *Iskusstvo Kino* (Film Art) was translated, excerpted, and illustrated by six stills in the Soviet export film magazine *Soviet Film*,[90] and the film was exported to eighty-five countries outside the Soviet Union. All these signs of success rebounded upon its director and star in the Soviet system. Žalakevičius moved to Moscow in the 1970s, where he made "political films" about Chile and Cuba,[91] and Donatas Banionis, the film's lead actor, also became a Soviet star in several prestige films. The story of this film's production as told by the Lithuanian archives gives no indication that these resistant readings were perceived by the state's reviewers or censors, although numerous other Lithuanian films of that period showed a heavier hand. A tantalizing rumor, which surfaced in June 2005 from a retrospective on its director shown on Russian television (RTR Planeta), also available in Lithuania, claimed that the local Lithuanian censors did not initially approve the film. So the director "stole it" from the Lithuanian Cinema Studio and took it to Moscow, where its quality was recognized. While this rumor could not be verified in the Lithuanian Archives of Literature and Art,[92] it suggests that the cinematic relations between the center and the republics deserve exploration. As the Soviet critic ends her review, "each person will see this film in his own way."

A second example involves the expensive and ambitious practice of film coproduction between bloc countries. One significant coproduction portraying the life of Goya was initiated by the East German DEFA Studio, with its most prestigious director, Konrad Wolf. The story is based on the 1951 novelized biography written in Hollywood by Leon Feuchtwanger. Feuchtwanger's work, also translated into Russian, had a checkered but noticeable career in the USSR following his 1937 visit. Goya's transformation from a court portrait painter to an artist of revolution seemed the perfect Socialist biographical vehicle. The film coincided with the interest in appropriating the traditional literary canon that emerged in the GDR in the early 1970s.[93] "Künstler-Filme" could also be considered "safer places" than contemporary settings, even though the launch of Willy Brandt's *Ostpolitik* in 1969 seemed to herald a more liberal artistic environment in which a biopic could use the artist's role in society to provide oblique social commentary.[94] According to Liehm and Liehm, *Goya* aimed to synthesize three values that DEFA films had until then been trying in vain to achieve: artistic quality, recognition abroad, and box-office success.[95] These last two qualities correspond to the Soviet reasons for pursuing coproductions. The film also represents an attempt at a larger Socialist collaboration, for in addition to DEFA and Lenfilm, the second Soviet studio, both Sofia Feature Film Studio of Bulgaria and Bosna Film of Yugoslavia participated. The film starred Donatas Banionis, the Lithuanian actor mentioned above, in the title role. The lavish sets, the two-part story, the re-creation of Inquisition Spain, the large amount of film stock used, the detailed 150-page book accompanying the production—all evidenced the economic investment and cultural hopes behind the project. The appearance of many such prestige biopics of "creators" coproduced throughout the bloc during this period, like the Soviet-Hungarian *Loves of Liszt* (Márton Keleti, 1971), and the GDR-Polish *Kopernik* (Ewa Petelska, Czeslaw Petelski, 1973), along with Mosfilm's *Tchaikovsky* (Igor Talankin, 1969),[96] could represent a fashion, a genre perceived to offer space for both critical commentary and a "positive hero," or a nod to perceived preferences in the chilled climate at the end of the 1960s.[97] Whatever the complex calculations in the film plans and practice, the patterns of film genres represent a potential category for comparison across the bloc.

A third example derives from the Soviet practice of hosting visiting filmmakers from the bloc as a part of the selection and purchasing of films. One account from 1980[98] demonstrates the relative independence of film practice in the bloc by that time. On a particular evening, about forty Soviet film people, including *Iskusstvo Kino* editors and contributors, attended a preview of three Hungarian films. Overheard among the professionals were adjectives like "courageous," "artistic," and "unusual," but already it was known that these films would not be "officially distributed" in the USSR because they were critical of the contemporary Socialist system in Hungary. Meanwhile, a Hungarian delegation of film directors and writers screened new Soviet films at the Union of Film Workers building, including *Moscow Does Not Believe in Tears*, which had generated long lines at the Soviet box office and represented what was debated as "the new commercialism" in Soviet cinema. A rumor had already circulated that the Hungarian delegation walked out in the middle of the film, presumably because of its apolitical and sentimental view of Soviet social life.[99]

The next morning, both delegations attended a meeting at the Union of Film Workers, with a Central Committee representative from the department on East European Socialist countries also present. At two parallel tables, Hungarians on one side and Soviet filmmakers on the other, official welcoming speeches were followed by the Hungarians' explanations of their films. The Soviet participants then spoke about the Hungarian films, mildly rebuking their pessimism. "Why were so many Soviet songs included in the Hungarian film?" one Moscow critic asked. But he knew the answer: the presence of Soviet songs acted as an indirect accusation of Soviet "complicity in the problems of Hungarian life."[100]

These rituals of meeting, critique, rebuke, and praise among the filmmakers and at the Union of Film Workers, with the hovering presence of the Party, are familiar from other analyses of intrabloc encounters as well as the more famous incidents of "peer" criticism during the Cold War, for example, of Pasternak and Solzhenitsyn. But they also provide glimpses into the everyday practices that give texture and explanatory power to the films produced in the bloc during these decades.

These three brief examples illustrate how films not on identifiable Cold War topics can represent practices that illustrate Soviet-East European cultural relations. The circumstances surrounding their production, interpretation, or reception also represent patterns of relations between bloc members and their attempts to support, reward, or resist bloc solidarity. The examples all represent some type of relation across borders, whether internal to the USSR or across the bloc. All three films—*Nobody Wanted to Die*, *Goya*, and *Moscow Does Not Believe in Tears*—were exported and represented in film festivals, and in the U.S. the last won an Academy Award for Best Foreign Film. Thus, they are not unimportant films, and unlikely to be unique incidents. According to the argument presented in this chapter, these intrabloc relations regarding particular films represent a manifestation of East European Cold War Culture. Asking the question about whether there was such a thing as East European Cold War Culture prompted an examination of practice as well as product, relations as well as interpretations. The answer required an assessment of the particular Cold War symbolic geography of the Eastern bloc, and suggested that the cultural flows and relations across borders within the bloc exemplified a type of East European culture that existed only within that period in that particular way.

East European Cold War Culture(s)? By Way of Conclusion

On 29 June 2011 a new statue was unveiled on Budapest's Freedom Square—a 7-foot bronze likeness of Ronald Reagan. He is caught in midstride as if intending to walk past the Soviet War Memorial toward the

U.S. Embassy. Press photos show the statue against the backdrop of the Hungarian Parliament building. The Hungarian government stated that Reagan was being honored for his role in "bringing the Cold War to a conclusion, and for the fact that Hungary regained its sovereignty in the process."[101]

Yet, even as new generations of scholars from and of Eastern Europe study or teach in the "West," and thereby become familiar with the Cold War decades as time period, history, and metaphor of power, their scholarship may decenter the American Cold War narrative in the European direction. Even as the legacy of socialism plays out in the headlines of newly discovered police informers or debates over the merits and meanings of films made under socialism,[102] new scholarship can afford to use new approaches that are not limited to the politics of Cold War Culture, especially as the global Cold War has given license to connecting cultures beyond Europe to European trends. Even as scholars criticize the limiting aspects of linking the terms "Eastern Europe" and "Cold War," they recognize that in some form the term undercuts more essentialist narratives of national cultures, and recalls the shared regional histories.[103] Even as state support for the arts collapsed with the coming of global capitalism, gradually new coalitions of filmmakers are forming that replace the East European "bloc-builders" with pan-European institutions.[104] Even as the perceived heroism of the political oppositional art of the Socialist era is deemed no longer necessary or relevant in the post–Cold War era, and Eastern Europe seeks ways to reinsert itself into global culture, nostalgic representation of the past—specifically the Socialist past—represents a new layer of analysis.[105] It may well be that the Cold War "did not absorb the internal dialectic of European modernity," even though it affected and was affected by its processes.[106] But new generations still applaud the heroic representation of the Cold War's failure to engineer the human soul, as the West represents the redemption of Eastern Europe in the "lives of others."[107]

And what of the concept, "East European Cold War Culture(s)"? Snyder argues that the term Eastern Europe has a deeper significance, which transcends the Cold War experience due to differences in historical memory and experience.[108] He links the points of divergence and overlap between the West European, East European, and Soviet narratives to World War II and postwar experiences, although East European national narratives stretch much farther back, as a look at other statues on Hungarian's Freedom Square would reveal. Perhaps a place to begin is to credit that the concept of Cold War Culture as originating in America is an uneasy transplant into the rich and fertile histories of East European nations, not only because of that history but also because of the multiple relations with Europe, whether further west or further east. The superpower, bilateral rhetorical images still potent in characterizing American-Russian relations are often tautological, and limit an appreciation of the active role of Europeans from both sides of the "Curtain." For Eastern Europe in particular, going beyond symbolic geography to recognize the elaborated, negotiated stances and roles available to the individuals and nations of Eastern Europe between 1945 and 1989 helps to deconstruct the bloc, undermine the presumed linearities of cultural influence, and at the same time offer new insights into the dominating constraints of a superpower construct of the Cold War.

Notes

1. J. D. Parks, *Culture, Conflict and Coexistence* (Jefferson, 1983).
2. David S. Foglesong, *The American Mission and the "Evil Empire"* (Cambridge, Mass., 2007).
3. Recent books that stress this continuity include Geoffrey Roberts, *Stalin's Wars, 1939–1953* (New Haven, 2007) and Gerhard Wettig, *Stalin and the Cold War in Europe* (Lanham, Md., 2008).
4. Robert Griffith, "The Cultural Turn in Cold War Studies," *Reviews in American History* 29, no. 1 (March 2001): 150–157.
5. See, e.g., Walter L. Hixson, *Parting the Curtain* (New York, 1996).
6. Christopher Lasch, "The Cultural Cold War," *The Nation* (11 September 1967).
7. Peter Coleman, *The Liberal Conspiracy* (New York, 1989); Frances Stonor Saunders, *The Cultural Cold War* (New York, 1999); Giles Scott-Smith, *The Politics of Apolitical Culture* (London, 2002); and more generally Hugh Wilford, *The Mighty Wurlitzer* (Cambridge, Mass., 2008).
8. Rana Mitter and Patrick Major, "East is East and West is West? Towards a Comparative Socio-Cultural History of the Cold War," in *Across the Blocs*, ed. Patrick Major and Rana Mitter (London, 2004), 1–22, here 6.
9. Tony Shaw, *Hollywood's Cold War* (Amherst, 2007); Patrick Major, "Future Perfect? Communist Science Fiction during the Cold War," in Major and Mitter, *Across the Blocs*, 56–74.
10. Jane de Hart Mathews, "Art and Politics in Cold War America," *American Historical Review* 81, no. 4 (October 1976): 767–87; Nancy E. Bernhard, *U.S. Television News and Cold War Propaganda, 1947–1960* (New York, 1999); Martin Brody, "'Music for the Masses,'" *Musical Quarterly* 77, no. 2 (Summer 1993): 161–192.
11. Stephen Whitfield, *The Culture of the Cold War* (Baltimore, 1991).
12. Lary May, "Introduction," in *Recasting America: Culture and Politics in the Age of Cold War*, ed. Lary May (Minneapolis, 1989).
13. Susan L. Carruthers, review of Douglas Field (ed.), *American Cold War Culture* (Edinburgh, 2005), *Modernism/Modernity* 13 (2006), no. 1: 956–958.
14. For example, the cultural history of the impact of the Vietnam War on America: Tom Engelhardt, *The End of Victory Culture* (New York, 1995) was reissued in 2007.

15. Michael David-Fox recalls postwar books written about fellow travelers that emphasize how their utopian hopes for the USSR project their agendas for their own societies. "The Fellow Travelers Revisited" *Journal of Modern History* 75 (June 2003): 300–335, here 300–304.
16. See, for example, Frank Ellis, "The Media as Social Engineer," in *Russian Cultural Studies*, ed. Catriona Kelly and David Shepherd (Oxford, 1998); Peter G. Boyle, "The Cold War Revisited: Review Article," *Journal of Contemporary History* 35, no. 3 (July 2000): 479–489, here 488.
17. David Caute, "Foreword," in *The Cultural Cold War in Western Europe, 1945–1960*, ed. Giles Scott-Smith and Hans Krabbendam (London, 2004), vii–ix.
18. David Caute, *The Dancer Defects* (Oxford, 2003), 2–8.
19. Cited in Ian Wellens, *Music on the Frontline* (London, 2002), 50.
20. See Jessica C.E. Gienow-Hecht, "Academics, Cultural Transfer, and the Cold War—A Critical Review," *Diplomatic History* 24, no. 3 (Summer 2000): 465–494, and the responses to this review. In the 1980s, critics on the Left labeled this process as "cultural imperialism."
21. Victoria de Grazia, *Irresistible Empire* (Cambridge, Mass., 2005).
22. Marsha Siefert, "Twentieth-Century Culture, 'Americanization,' and European Audiovisual Space," in *Conflicted Visions: Europeanizing Contemporary Histories*, ed. Konrad Jarausch and Thomas Lindenberger (New York, 2007): 164–193.
23. See, e.g., Holger Nehring, "'Westernization,'" *Cold War History* 4 (2004), no. 2: 175–191.
24. See the country studies in Alexander Stephan (ed.), *The Americanization of Europe* (New York, 2006).
25. Odd Arne Westad, *The Global Cold War* (Cambridge, 2005).
26. David C. Engerman, et al., eds., *Staging Growth* (Amherst, 2003).
27. Michael Cox, "Another Transatlantic Split?" *Cold War History* 7, no. 1 (February 2007): 121–146.
28. Jessica C.E. Gienow-Hecht, "'How Good Are We?' Culture and the Cold War," in Scott-Smith and Krabbendam, *Cultural Cold War*, 269–282, quotation 279.
29. Larry Wolff, *Inventing Eastern Europe* (Stanford, 1994); W. Brian Newsome, "'Dead Lands' or 'New Europe'?" *East European Quarterly* 36, no. 1 (March 2002): 39–62.
30. See, for example, the comparative possibilities in Uta G. Poiger, *Jazz, Rock, and Rebels* (Berkeley, 2000).
31. This concept became more visible with the publication of Milan Kundera's "The Tragedy of Central Europe" in the *New York Review of Books* (26 April 1984): 33–38. See also Maciej Janowski et al., "Why Bother about Regions," *East-Central Europe: L'Europe du Centre Est. Eine wissenschaftliche Zeitschrift* 1 (2005), no. 1–2: 5–58.
32. Every country, with the possible exception of Bulgaria, experienced serious crisis with the Soviet Union during the Cold War. For its relation to film history, see Diana Iordanova's discussion of this problem in "The Cinema of Eastern Europe: Strained Loyalties, Elusive Clusters," in *East European Cinemas*, ed. Anikó Imre (New York, 2005).
33. Mary Kaldor, *The Imaginary War* (Oxford, 1990), 25, 68.
34. The role of Europe in debates about Russian identity has a long history. See, for example, Iver B. Neumann, *Russia and the Idea of Europe* (London, 1996).
35. Frederick G. Barghoorn, *The Soviet Cultural Offensive* (Westport, 1976 [1960]).
36. The relations between the Soviet Union and Eastern Europe generated scores of analyses during and after the Cold War, including H. Gordon Skilling, *Communism National and International* (Toronto, 1964); Jonathan C. Valdez, *Internationalism and*

the Ideology of Soviet Influence in Eastern Europe (Cambridge, 1993). I found particularly useful Robert Service's discussion of routine difficulties and structural problems in the relationship: Robert Service, "The Communisation of Eastern Europe: Soviet Model or National Variants?" Lecture, 23 April 2007, St. Antony's College, Oxford University.

37. Valerie Bunce, *Subversive Institutions* (Cambridge, 1999), 38–41.
38. Scott Lucas, *Freedom's War* (Manchester, 1999).
39. Louis Nemzer, "The Soviet Friendship Societies," *Public Opinion Quarterly* 13, no. 2 (Summer 1949): 265–284; Jan C. Behrends, "Agitation, Organization, Mobilization: The League for Polish-Soviet Friendship in Stalinist Poland," in *The Sovietization of Eastern Europe*, ed. Balázs Apor, Péter Apor, and E.A. Rees (Washington, 2008), 181–200.
40. Michael David-Fox, "From Illusory 'Society' to Intellectual 'Public,'" *Contemporary European History* 11 (2002), no. 1: 7–32.
41. The organization that replaced VOKS—the Union of Soviet Societies for Friendship and Cultural Relations with Foreign Countries, constituted in February 1958—was called by its critics "VOKS under another name" because of the continuity in personnel. Open Society Archive (hereafter OSA) 300-8-3, Records of the Research Institute of Radio Free Europe/Radio Liberty, Radio Free Europe Background Report, "New Organization to Control 'Friendship,'" 25 April 1958.
42. Nigel Gould-Davies, "The Logic of Soviet Cultural Diplomacy," *Diplomatic History* 27, no. 1 (April 2003): 193–214.
43. See, for example, Ieva Zake, "Controversies of US-USSR Cultural Contacts During the Cold War," *Journal of Historical Sociology* 21, no. 1 (March 2008): 55–81.
44. From the extensive literature on this topic, see for example Randall W. Stone, *Satellites and Commissars* (Princeton, 1996).
45. Tapio Varis, "Global Traffic in Television Programming," in *World Communication: A Handbook*, ed. George Gerbner and Marsha Siefert (New York, 1984), 143–152.
46. Robert L. Hutchings, *Soviet-Eastern European Relations* (Madison, 1983), 223–226.
47. The idea of cultural contests is well developed in Caute, *The Dancer Defects*.
48. Marsha Siefert, "From Cold War to Wary Peace: American Culture in the USSR and Russia," in *The Americanization of Europe*, ed. Alexander Stephan (New York, 2006), 185–217.
49. Allen Kassof, *The Soviet Youth Program* (Cambridge, Mass., 1965).
50. Petr Roubal, "Mass Gymnastic Performances under Communism: The Case of Czechoslovak Spartakiads," in Apor et al., *Sovietization of Eastern Europe*, 171–180.
51. Vera Tolz, "'Cultural Bosses' as Patrons and Clients," *Contemporary European History* 11 (2002), no. 1: 87–105.
52. George Faraday, *Revolt of the Filmmakers* (University Park, 2000); Daniil Dondurei and Natalie Venger, "The Film Sector in the Russian Federation," Report for European Audiovisual Observatory (Moscow, 2001), 6, accessed 29 July 2009 at www.obs.coe.int/oea_publ/eurocine/doubled_film.pdf.
53. See, e.g., Apor et al., *Sovietization of Eastern Europe*; Norman M. Naimark, "The Sovietization of Eastern Europe, 1944–1953," in *The Cambridge History of the Cold War*, vol. 1, ed. Melvyn P. Leffler and Odd Arne Westad (Cambridge 2010), 175–197.
54. The classic comparative analysis that elaborates these differences is John Connelly, *Captive University* (Chapel Hill, 2000). See also Michael David-Fox and György Péteri, eds., *Academia in Upheaval* (Westport, 2000).
55. Norman M. Naimark, "Post-Soviet Russian Historiography on the Emergence of the Soviet Bloc," *Kritika* 5, no. 3 (Summer 2004): 561–580.

56. E.A. Rees, "Introduction," in Apor et al., *Sovietization of Eastern Europe*, 1–28; quotation by Susan E. Reid, back cover.
57. Susan E. Reid and David Crowley, eds., *Style and Socialism* (Oxford, 2000); David Crowley and Susan E. Reid, eds., *Socialist Spaces* (Oxford, 2002), idem, *Pleasures in Socialism* (Chicago, 2010).
58. Elena Zubkova, *Russia After the War*, trans. and ed. Hugh Ragsdale (Armonk, 1998), 14, also citing Mikhail Gefter, "V predchuvstvii proshlogo," *Vek XX i mir* no. 9 (1990): 34.
59. See, for example, Libora Oates-Indruchová, "The Limits of Thought?" *Europe-Asia Studies* 60, no. 10 (December 2008): 1767–1782.
60. For a cultural economy approach, see for example Toby Miller et al., *Global Hollywood: No. 2* (London, 2008).
61. Siefert, "From Cold War to Wary Peace."
62. Friederike Kind-Kovács, "'Out of the Drawer and into the West,'" Doctoral dissertation, University of Potsdam, 2008.
63. Natalia Nussinova, "The Soviet Union and the Russian Émigrés," in *Oxford History of World Cinema*, ed. Geoffrey Nowell-Smith (Oxford, 1997), 162–174, here 163.
64. Yuri Bogomolov, "The Revitalization of the Soviet Film Industry," in *Mass Culture and Perestroika in the Soviet Union*, ed. Marsha Siefert (New York, 1991), 39–40; Dondurei and Venger, "Film Sector," 6.
65. Miron Chernenko, "Film Production in Russia," in *Central and Eastern Europe: Audiovisual Landscape and Copyright Legislation*, ed. Karol Jakubowicz, EUREKA Audiovisuel, and Pierre Jeanray (Antwerp, 1995), 62–74, here 74.
66. Diana Iordanova, *Cinema of the Other Europe* (London, 2003), 27; Richard Taylor and Ian Christie, eds., *The Film Factory* (Cambridge, Mass., 1988).
67. See, for example, István Nemeskürty, *Word and Image* (Budapest, 1968), 149.
68. Evgeny Dobrenko, *Political Economy of Socialist Realism* (New Haven, 2007).
69. Leonid Heller, "A World of Prettiness: Socialist Realism and Its Aesthetic Categories," in *Socialist Realism without Shores*, by Thomas Lahusen and Evgeny Dobrenko (Durham, 1997), 51–75.
70. Alexei Yurchak, "Soviet Hegemony of Form," *Comparative Studies in History and Society* (2003): 480–510, here 504.
71. Iordanova, *Cinema of the Other Europe*, 13.
72. This description derives from several sources, including Iordanova, ibid.; Marek Hendrykowski, "Changing States in East Central Europe," in Nowell-Smith, *Oxford History of World Cinema*, 632–640; Károly Nemes, *Films of Commitment*, trans. András Boros-Kazai (Budapest, 1985); Jerzy Toeplitz, "Cinema in Eastern Europe," *Cinema Journal* 8, no. 1 (Autumn 1968): 2–11.
73. Marsha Siefert, "Twentieth-Century Culture."
74. Marsha Siefert, "Co-Producing Cold War Culture," in *Divided Dreamworlds: The Cultural Cold War in East and West*, ed. Giles Scott-Smith and Joes Segal (Amsterdam, forthcoming).
75. Sergei Dobrynin, "The Silver Curtain," *History Compass* 7 (2009), no. 3: 862–878, here 863, 874.
76. Iordanova, *Cinema of the Other Europe*, 13.
77. Anna Kagarlitskaya, "Broad Panorama," *Soviet Film* (October 1980): 25–27.
78. Lars Karl, "Zwischen politischem Ritual und kulturellem Dialog: Die Moskauer Internationalen Filmfestspiele im Kalten Krieg 1959–1971," in *Leinwand zwischen Tauwetter und Frost*, ed. Lars Karl (Berlin, 2007), 279–298.

79. Ron Holloway, "Festival Wars: Goskino versus Union of Soviet Filmmakers," *Moving Pictures Magazine*, accessed 3 June 2008 at http://www.movingpicturesmagazine.com/festivities/articles/festivalwarsgoskinoversusunionofsovietfilmmakers.
80. Val S. Golovskoy, with John Rimberg, *Behind the Soviet Screen*, trans. Steven Hill (Ann Arbor, 1986), 69.
81. See, for example, Sudha Rajagopalan, *Indian Film in Soviet Cinemas* (Bloomington, 2009).
82. Figures from Peter A. Toma and Ivan Volgyes, *Politics in Hungary* (San Francisco, 1977), 113–114. Other years give a different picture. For example, in 1968 thirty-four Soviet films were released in Hungary, as compared to twenty-two Hungarian films, forty-eight films from bloc countries, and thirty from Western Europe. Thirteen American films were released that year. (OSA 300-8-3 Records of the Research Institute of Radio Free Europe/Radio Liberty, Radio Free Europe Research Report, "Hungary's Windows to the West," 28 October 1970, 18.)
83. Alexander Abdrashitov, "Prague in Moscow," and Alexei Galkin, "Moscow in Prague," *Soviet Film* (October 1982), 23.
84. Siefert, "Co-Producing Cold War Culture."
85. Ute Lischke and David T. McNab, "Indian Films of the Deutsche Film Aktiengesellschaft," in *Germany and the Americas*, ed. Thomas Adam (Santa Barbara, 2005), 546–550, here 546; Gerd Gemünden "Between Karl Marx and Karl May," *New German Critique* 82 (Winter 2001): 25–38.
86. Anne Jäckel, "France and Romanian Cinema 1896–1999," *French Cultural Studies* 11, no. 2 (October 2000): 409–425.
87. Golovskoy, *Soviet Screen*, 76, 81.
88. See, for example, Mira Liehm and Anton J. Liehm, *The Most Important Art* (Berkeley, 1980), 329.
89. "Nobody Wanted To Die," *Soviet Film* (May 1966): 6.
90. Ina Solovieva, "People, Memory and History," *Iskusstvo kino* no. 3 (1966), 30; translated and excerpted in "Nobody Wanted To Die," 6–7.
91. Golovskoy, *Soviet Screen*, 142.
92. The archival investigation was done in the Lithuanian Archives of Literature and Art, but the author was not able to check the Soviet archives. See Gintare Kurtinaityte, "Constructing 'Unofficial' History" (unpublished master's thesis, Central European University, Budapest 2005), 45, note 110.
93. Daniela Berghahn, "The Re-Evaluation of Goethe and the Classical Tradition in the Films of Egon Günther and Siegfried Kühn," in *DEFA: East German Cinema, 1946–1992*, ed. Seán Allan and John Sandford (New York, 1999), 222–223.
94. Seán Allan, "DEFA: An Historical Overview," in Allan and Sandford, *DEFA: East German Cinema*, 15–16.
95. Liehm and Liehm, *The Most Important Art*, 363.
96. Marsha Siefert, "Russische Leben, sowjetische Filme: Die Filmbiographie, Cajkovskij und der Kalte Krieg," in Karl, *Leinwand zwischen Tauwetter und Frost*, 133–170.
97. Steven P. Hill, "The Soviet Film Today," *Film Quarterly* 20, no. 4 (Spring 1967): 33–52.
98. "A Typical Week in the Life of a Film Magazine Editor," in Golovskoy, *Behind the Soviet Screen*, 71–85.
99. For more on the Soviet and international debate on this film, see David MacFadyen, "Moscow Does Not Believe in Tears," *Studies in Russian and Soviet Cinema* 1, no. 1 (November 2006): 45–67.
100. Golovskoy, *Soviet Screen*, 80.

101. "Ronald Reagan Statue Unveiled in Budapest," *Wall Street Journal* (29 June 2011). Accessed at WSJ.com.
102. For example, the 2004 revelation that Hungarian film director István Szabó had been a police informant led to reinterpretations of his films. See István Rév, "The Man in the White Raincoat," in *Past for the Eyes*, ed. Péter Apor and Oksana Sarkisova (Budapest, 2008), 3–57.
103. Anikó Imre, "East European Cinemas in New Perspectives," in *East European Cinemas*, ed. Anikó Imre, xi–xxvi, here xvii.
104. Anne Jäckel, "Cultural Cooperation in Europe," *Media, Culture & Society* 9 (1997), no. 1: 111–120.
105. Péter Apor and Oksana Sarkisova, eds., *Past for the Eyes* (Budapest, 2008).
106. Goran Therborn, *European Modernity and Beyond* (Thousand Oaks, 1995), 30.
107. *The Lives of Others* is an Academy Award–winning German film from 2007 that portrays a Stasi officer who protects the object of his surveillance. For analysis, see Thomas Lindenberger, "Stasiploitation—Why Not?" *German Studies Review* 31 (2008), no. 3: 558–566.
108. Timothy Snyder, "The Historical Reality of Eastern Europe," *East European Politics and Societies* 23, no. 1 (February 2009): 7–12.

Bibliography

Abdrashitov, Alexander. "Prague in Moscow," and Alexei Galkin, "Moscow in Prague," *Soviet Film* (October 1982).
Allan, Seán, and John Sandford, eds. *DEFA: East German Cinema, 1946–1992*. New York: Berghahn, 1999.
Apor, Balázs, Péter Apor, and E.A. Rees, eds. *The Sovietization of Eastern Europe: New Perspectives on the Postwar Period*. Washington, DC: New Academia, 2008.
Apor, Péter, and Oksana Sarkisova, eds. *Past for the Eyes: East European Representations of Communism in Cinema and Museums after 1989*. Budapest: Central European University Press, 2008.
Barghoorn, Frederick G. *The Soviet Cultural Offensive: The Role of Cultural Diplomacy in Soviet Foreign Policy*. Westport, Conn., 1976 (1960).
Bernhard, Nancy E. *U.S. Television News and Cold War Propaganda, 1947–1960*. New York: Cambridge University Press, 1999.
Bogomolov, Yuri. "The Revitalization of the Soviet Film Industry." In *Mass Culture and Perestroika in the Soviet Union*, ed. Marsha Siefert (New York, 1991), 39–40.
Boyle, Peter G. "The Cold War Revisited: Review Article." *Journal of Contemporary History* 35, no. 3 (July 2000): 479–489.
Brody, Martin. "'Music for the Masses': Milton Babbitt's Cold War Music Theory." *Musical Quarterly* 77, no. 2 (Summer 1993): 161–192.
Bunce, Valerie. *Subversive Institutions: The Design and the Destruction of Socialism and the State*. Cambridge: Cambridge University Press, 1999.
Carruthers, Susan L. "Review of Douglas Field (ed.), *American Cold War Culture* (Edinburgh, 2005)." *Modernism/Modernity* 13 (2006), no. 1: 956–958.
Caute, David. *The Dancer Defects: The Struggle for Cultural Supremacy during the Cold War*. Oxford: Oxford University Press, 2003.

Chernenko, Miron. "Film Production in Russia: A Riddle Wrapped in an Enigma." In *Central and Eastern Europe: Audiovisual Landscape and Copyright Legislation*, ed. Karol Jakubowicz, EUREKA Audiovisuel, and Pierre Jeanray (Antwerp, 1995), 62–74.

Coleman, Peter. *The Liberal Conspiracy: The Congress for Cultural Freedom and the Struggle for the Mind of Postwar Europe*. New York: Free Press, 1989.

Connelly, John. *Captive University: The Sovietization of East German, Czech and Polish Higher Education, 1945–1956*. Chapel Hill: University of North Carolina Press, 2000.

Crowley, David, and Susan E. Reid, eds. *Socialist Spaces: Sites of Everyday Life in the Eastern Bloc*. Oxford: Berg, 2002.

———. *Pleasures in Socialism: Leisure and Luxury in the Eastern Bloc*. Evanston, Ill.: Northwestern University Press, 2010.

Cox, Michael. "Another Transatlantic Split? American and European Narratives and the End of the Cold War." *Cold War History* 7, no. 1 (February 2007): 121–146.

David-Fox, Michael. "From Illusory 'Society' to Intellectual 'Public': VOKS, International Travel, and Party-Intelligentsia Relations in the Interwar Period." *Contemporary European History* 11 (2002), no. 1: 7–32.

———. "The Fellow Travelers Revisited: The 'Cultured West' through Soviet Eyes." *Journal of Modern History* 75 (June 2003): 300–335.

David-Fox, Michael, and György Péteri, eds. *Academia in Upheaval: Origins, Transfers, and Transformations of the Communist Academic Regime in Russia and East Central Europe*. Westport, Conn.: Bergin & Garvey, 2000.

de Hart Mathews, Jane. "Art and Politics in Cold War America." *American Historical Review* 81, no. 4 (October 1976): 767–787.

Dobrenko, Evgeny. *Political Economy of Socialist Realism*. New Haven: Yale University Press, 2007.

Dobrynin, Sergei. "The Silver Curtain: Representations of the West in Soviet Cold War Films." *History Compass* 7 (2009), no. 3: 862–878.

Dondurei, Daniil, and Natalie Venger. "The Film Sector in the Russian Federation." Report for European Audiovisual Observatory (Moscow, 2001), 6. www.obs.coe.int/oea_publ/eurocine/doubled_film.pdf (accessed 29 July 2009).

Ellis, Frank. "The Media as Social Engineer." In *Russian Cultural Studies*, ed. Catriona Kelly and David Shepherd (Oxford: Oxford University Press, 1998).

Engerman, David C., Michael E. Latham, Mark H. Haefele, and Nils Gilman, eds. *Staging Growth: Modernization, Development, and the Global Cold War*. Amherst, Mass.: University of Massachusetts Press, 2003.

Engelhardt, Tom. *The End of Victory Culture: Cold War America and the Disillusioning of a Generation*. New York: Basic Books, 1995, reissued in 2007.

Faraday, George. *Revolt of the Filmmakers: The Struggle for Artistic Autonomy and the Fall of the Soviet Film Industry*. University Park, Penna.: Pennsylvania State University Press, 2000.

Foglesong, David S. *The American Mission and the "Evil Empire": The Crusade for a "Free Russia" since 1881*. Cambridge, Mass.: Cambridge University Press, 2007.

Gefter, Mikhail. "V predchuvstvii proshlogo." *Vek XX i mir* no. 9 (1990): 34.

Gemünden, Gerd. "Between Karl Marx and Karl May: The DEFA Indianerfilme (1965–1983)." *New German Critique* 82 (Winter 2001): 25–38.

Gienow-Hecht, Jessica C.E. "Academics, Cultural Transfer, and the Cold War—A Critical Review." *Diplomatic History* 24, no. 3 (Summer 2000): 465–494.

Golovskoy, Val S., with John Rimberg. *Behind the Soviet Screen: The Motion-Picture Industry in the USSR 1972–1982*, trans. Steven Hill. Ann Arbor: Ardis, 1986.

Gould-Davies, Nigel. "The Logic of Soviet Cultural Diplomacy." *Diplomatic History* 27, no. 1 (April 2003): 193–214.
Grazia, Victoria de. *Irresistible Empire: America's Advance through Twentieth-Century Europe*. Cambridge, Mass.: Harvard University Press, 2005.
Griffith, Robert. "The Cultural Turn in Cold War Studies." *Reviews in American History* 29, no. 1 (March 2001): 150–157.
Hill, Steven P. "The Soviet Film Today." *Film Quarterly* 20, no. 4 (Spring 1967): 33–52.
Hixson, Walter L. *Parting the Curtain: Propaganda, Culture, and the Cold War*. New York: St. Martin's Griffin, 1996.
Holloway, Ron. "Festival Wars: Goskino versus Union of Soviet Filmmakers." *Moving Pictures Magazine*. http://www.movingpicturesmagazine.com/festivities/articles/festivalwarsgoskinoversusunionofsovietfilmmakers.
Hutchings, Robert L. *Soviet-Eastern European Relations: Consolidation and Conflict, 1968–1980*. Madison, Wisc.: Univ of Wisconsin Press 1983.
Imre, Anikó. "East European Cinemas in New Perspectives." In *East European Cinemas*, ed. Anikó Imre (New York: Routledge, Taylor & Francis, 2005), xi–xxvi.
Iordanova, Diana. *Cinema of the Other Europe*. London: Wallflower, 2003.
Jäckel, Anne. "Cultural Cooperation in Europe: The Case of British & French Co-productions with Central and Eastern Europe." *Media, Culture & Society* 9 (1997), no. 1: 111–120.
———. "France and Romanian Cinema 1896–1999," *French Cultural Studies* 11, no. 2 (October 2000): 409–425.
Janowski, Maciej, Constantin Iordachi, and Balázs Trencsényi. "Why Bother about Regions: Debates over Symbolic Geography in Poland, Hungary and Romania." *East-Central Europe: L'Europe du Centre Est, eine wissenschaftliche Zeitschrift* 1 (2005), no. 1–2: 5–58.
Kagarlitskaya, Anna. "Broad Panorama: Foreign Films in the USSR." *Soviet Film* (October 1980): 25–27.
Kaldor, Mary. *The Imaginary War: Understanding the East-West Conflict*. Oxford: Blackwell, 1990.
Karl, Lars, ed. *Leinwand zwischen Tauwetter und Frost: der osteuropäische Spiel- und Dokumentarfilm im kalten Krieg*. Berlin: Metropol, 2007.
Kassof, Allen. *The Soviet Youth Program: Regimentation and Rebellion*. Cambridge, Mass.: Harvard University Press, 1965.
Kind-Kovács, Friederike. "'Out of the drawer and into the West': Tamizdat from the Other Europe and its Vision and Practice of a Transnational Literary Community (1956–1989)." Doctoral dissertation, University of Potsdam, 2008.
Kundera, Milan. "The Tragedy of Central Europe." In *The New York Review of Books* (26 April 1984): 33–38.
Kurtinaityte, Gintare, "Constructing 'Unofficial' History: Lithuanian Filmmakers and Soviet Censorship, 1956–1970." Unpublished master's thesis, Central European University, Budapest, 2005.
Lahusen, Thomas, and Evgeny Dobrenko. *Socialist Realism without Shores*. Durham, N.C.: Duke University Press, 1997.
Lasch, Christopher. "The Cultural Cold War." *The Nation*, 11 September 1967.
Liehm, Mira, and Anton J. Liehm. *The Most Important Art: Eastern European Film after 1945*. Berkeley and Los Angeles: University of California Press, 1980.
Lindenberger, Thomas. "Stasiploitation—Why Not? Reconciliation and Misogyny in Florian von Donnersmarck's *The Lives of Others*." *German Studies Review* 31 (2008), no. 3: 558–566.

Lischke, Ute, and David T. McNab. "Indian Films of the Deutsche Film Aktiengesellschaft." In *Germany and the Americas: Culture, Politics, and History: A Multidisciplinary Encyclopedia*, ed. Thomas Adam (Santa Barbara: ABC-Clio, 2005), 546–550.

Lucas, Scott. *Freedom's War: The US Crusade against the Soviet Union, 1945–1956*. Manchester: Manchester University Press, 1999.

MacFadyen, David. "*Moscow Does Not Believe in Tears*: From Oscar to Consolation Prize." *Studies in Russian and Soviet Cinema* 1, no. 1 (November 2006): 45–67.

Major, Patrick, and Rana Mitter, eds. *Across the Blocs: Exploring Comparative Cold War Cultural and Social History*. London: Cass, 2004.

May, Lary, ed. *Recasting America: Culture and Politics in the Age of Cold War*. Chicago: University of Chicago Press, 1989.

Miller, Toby, Nitin Govil, John McMurria, Ting Wang, and Richard Maxwell. *Global Hollywood: No. 2*. London: British Film Institute, 2008.

Naimark, Norman M. "Post-Soviet Russian Historiography on the Emergence of the Soviet Bloc." *Kritika* 5, no. 3 (Summer 2004): 561–580.

———. "The Sovietization of Eastern Europe, 1944–1953." In *The Cambridge History of the Cold War*, vol. 1, ed. Melvyn P. Leffler and Odd Arne Westad (Cambridge: Cambridge University Press, 2010), 175–197.

Nehring, Holger. "'Westernization': A New Paradigm for Interpreting European History in a Cold War Context." *Cold War History* 4 (2004), no. 2: 175–191.

Nemes, Károly. *Films of Commitment: Socialist Cinema in Eastern Europe*. Trans. András Boros-Kazai. Budapest: Corvina, 1985.

Nemeskürty, István. *Word and Image: History of the Hungarian Cinema*. Budapest: Corvina, 1968.

Nemzer, Louis. "The Soviet Friendship Societies." *Public Opinion Quarterly* 13, no. 2 (Summer 1949): 265–284.

Neumann, Iver B. *Russia and the Idea of Europe: A Study in Identity and International Relations*. London: Routledge, 1996.

Newsome, W. Brian. "'Dead Lands' or 'New Europe'? Reconstructing Europe, Reconfiguring Eastern Europe: 'Westerners' and the Aftermath of the World War." *East European Quarterly* 36, no. 1 (March 2002): 39–62.

Nowell-Smith, Geoffrey, ed. *Oxford History of World Cinema*. Oxford: Oxford University Press, 1997.

Oates-Indruchová, Libora. "The Limits of Thought? The Regulatory Framework of Social Sciences and Humanities in Czechoslovakia (1968–1989)." *Europe-Asia Studies* 60, no. 10 (December 2008): 1767–1782.

Parks, J.D. *Culture, Conflict and Coexistence: American-Soviet Cultural Relations, 1917–1958*. Jefferson, N.C.: McFarland, 1983.

Poiger, Uta G. *Jazz, Rock, and Rebels: Cold War Politics and American Culture in a Divided Germany*. Berkeley and Los Angeles: University of California Press, 2000.

Rajagopalan, Sudha. *Indian Film in Soviet Cinemas: The Culture of Movie-Going after Stalin*. Bloomington, Ind.: Indiana University Press, 2009.

Reid, Susan E., and David Crowley, eds. *Style and Socialism*. Oxford: Berg, 2000.

Rév, István. "The Man in the White Raincoat." In *Past for the Eyes: East European Representations of Communism in Cinema and Museums after 1989*, ed. Péter Apor and Oksana Sarkisova (Budapest: Central European University Press, 2008), 3–57.

Roberts, Geoffrey. *Stalin's Wars, 1939–1953*. New Haven: Yale University Press, 2007.

Scott-Smith, Giles. *The Politics of Apolitical Culture: The Congress for Cultural Freedom, the CIA and Post-War American Hegemony*. London: Routledge, 2002.

Scott-Smith, Giles, and Hans Krabbendam, eds. *The Cultural Cold War in Western Europe, 1945–1960*. London: Cass, 2004.
Scott-Smith, Giles, and Joes Segal, eds. *Divided Dreamworlds: The Cultural Cold War in East and West*. Amsterdam: Amsterdam University Press, forthcoming.
Shaw, Tony. *Hollywood's Cold War*. Amherst, Mass.: University of Massachusetts Press, 2007.
Siefert, Marsha. "Twentieth-Century Culture, 'Americanization,' and European Audiovisual Space." In *Conflicted Visions: Europeanizing Contemporary Histories*, ed. Konrad Jarausch and Thomas Lindenberger (New York: Berghahn, 2007), 164–193.
———. "Co-Producing Cold War Culture: East-West Filmmaking and Cultural Diplomacy." In *Divided Dreamworlds: The Cultural Cold War East and West*, ed. Giles Scott-Smith and Joes Segal (forthcoming).
Skilling, H. Gordon. *Communism National and International: Eastern Europe after Stalin*. Toronto: Canadian Institute of International Affairs, 1964.
Snyder, Timothy. "The Historical Reality of Eastern Europe." *East European Politics and Societies* 23, no. 1 (February 2009): 7–12.
Solovieva, Ina. "People, Memory and History," *Iskusstvo kino* no. 3 (1966): 30.
Stephan, Alexander, ed. *The Americanization of Europe: Culture, Diplomacy and Anti-Americanism After 1945*. New York: Berghahn, 2006.
Stone, Randall W. *Satellites and Commissars: Strategy and Conflict in the Politics of Soviet-Bloc Trade*. Princeton: Princeton University Press, 1996.
Stonor Saunders, Frances. *The Cultural Cold War: The CIA and the World of Arts and Letters*. New York: New Press, 1999.
Taylor, Richard, and Ian Christie, eds. *The Film Factory: Russian and Soviet Cinema in Documents, 1896–1939*. Cambridge, Mass.: Harvard University Press, 1988.
Therborn, Gorän. *European Modernity and Beyond: The Trajectories of European Societies, 1945–2000*. Thousand Oaks, Calif.: Sage, 1995.
Toeplitz, Jerzy. "Cinema in Eastern Europe." *Cinema Journal* 8, no. 1 (Autumn 1968): 2–11.
Tolz, Vera. "'Cultural Bosses' as Patrons and Clients: The Functioning of the Soviet Creative Unions in the Postwar Period." *Contemporary European History* 11 (2002), no. 1: 87–105.
Toma, Peter A., and Ivan Volgyes. *Politics in Hungary*. San Francisco: W. H. Freeman, 1977.
Valdez, Jonathan C. *Internationalism and the Ideology of Soviet Influence in Eastern Europe*. Cambridge: Cambridge University Press, 1993.
Varis, Tapio. "Global Traffic in Television Programming." In *World Communication: A Handbook*, ed. George Gerbner and Marsha Siefert (New York: Longman, 1984), 143–152.
Wellens, Ian. *Music on the Frontline: Nicholas Nabokov's Struggle against Communism and Middlebrow Culture*. London: Ashgate, 2002.
Westad, Odd Arne. *The Global Cold War: Third World Interventions and the Making of our Times*. Cambridge: Cambridge University Press, 2005.
Wettig, Gerhard. *Stalin and the Cold War in Europe: The Emergence of East-West Conflict, 1939–1953*. Lanham, Md.: Rowman & Littlefield, 2008.
Whitfield, Stephen. *The Culture of the Cold War*. Baltimore: Johns Hopkins University Press, 1991.
Wilford, Hugh. *The Mighty Wurlitzer: How the CIA Played America*. Cambridge, Mass.: Harvard University Presss, 2008.

Wolff, Larry. *Inventing Eastern Europe: The Map of Civilization on the Mind of the Enlightenment*. Stanford: Stanford University Press, 1994.

Yurchak, Alexei. "Soviet Hegemony of Form: Everything Was Forever Until It was No More." *Comparative Studies in History and Society* 45 (2003), no. 3: 480–510.

Zake, Ieva. "Controversies of US-USSR Cultural Contacts During the Cold War: The Perspective of Latvian Refugees." *Journal of Historical Sociology* 21, no. 1 (March 2008): 55–81.

Zubkova, Elena. *Russia After the War: Hopes, Illusions, and Disappointments, 1945–1957*. Trans. and ed. Hugh Ragsdale. Armonk, N.Y.: M. E. Sharpe, 1998.

Chapter 2

"WE STARTED THE COLD WAR"
A Hidden Message behind Stalin's Attack on Anna Akhmatova

Olga Voronina

An ideological—as well as political and economic—confrontation between Soviet-dominated Eastern Europe and the United States and its allies, the Cold War manifested itself in cultural actions as much as it did in military and diplomatic crises. The onset of the "political" Cold War is generally tied to President Truman's introduction of the Containment Policy Doctrine in March 1947.[1] The beginning of the Cold War as an opposition of cultures is not as easy to pin down. I suggest that the Soviet government launched it nine months earlier, and that the resolution "About the journals *Zvezda* and *Leningrad*," adopted on 14 August 1946, was a significant step toward the new confrontation. Generally regarded as the beginning of a new stage in the persecution of the intelligentsia, this decree of the Organizational Bureau of the Central Committee of the Communist Party (CCCP) in fact targeted two audiences: while attempting to curb postwar free thinking within the country, it also signaled to foreign nations the complete ideological break with the former Allies in the anti-Hitler coalition. In the following, I will attempt to reveal the content of the message by chronologically analyzing the resolution's preparation as well as exploring the relationship between the people who were united by it: Anna Akhmatova, Isaiah Berlin, and Joseph Stalin.

Although even the listing of their names together creates a dissonance, each of the three people in this group, the poet, the scholar-diplomat, and the dictator, played a role in delivering the Soviet message to the West. Akhmatova, who had earlier been silenced several times as a voice of dissident prerevolutionary culture, in 1946 turned out to be one of the two main targets of the Party's ideological attack. This time, however, she was blamed not for her backwardness or indifference towards politics, but for "cultivating the ... spirit of servility towards contemporary bourgeois Western culture."[2] The seriousness of this accusation lay in Stalin's personal campaign against "servility towards the West," which he launched shortly after the end of the war. Citing the need to promote "Soviet patriotism" as the chief slogan of the day, Stalin initiated the crusade, according to Konstantin Simonov's shrewd observation, with the bitterness of a leader of a "winner country which had been completely ruined."[3]

The three visits that the Oxford scholar and British Foreign Office employee Isaiah Berlin paid Akhmatova during the winter of 1945–46 provided her, at least until Pasternak won the Nobel Prize for literature in 1958, with the status of a Soviet poet of the greatest interest to foreign readers.[4] After the resolution, which she believed Berlin "earned" for her,[5] Akhmatova became the main symbol for the potential postwar liberalism nipped in the bud by Stalin's preventive measures against the "corrupting influence" of European and American culture. Meanwhile, Berlin became the main target of Stalin's anti-Western agenda. He played his part perfectly by writing, as early as December 1946, a memoir about his postwar meetings with Soviet writers in which the notion of silenced voices and tortured consciousnesses came to the fore, instead of the memorandum about international Soviet politics as commissioned by the Foreign Office.[6] Burdened by the accusation of having endangered Akhmatova by visiting her in her apartment and therefore exposing her to Stalin's wrath, Berlin carried his mission even further: all his life he analyzed the relationship between an individual as an agent of history and a historian as its author. In "The Sense of Reality," one of his central essays, he defined the main task of the "historian of ideas" (which he considered himself to be) as that of grounding history in real-life experiences: "A mere recital of facts is not history, not even if scientifically testable hypotheses are added to them; only the setting of them in the concrete, at times opaque, but continuous, rich, full texture of 'real life'—the intersubjective, directly recognizable continuum of experience—will do."[7] His meetings with Akhmatova did just that: they completely overturned the lives of their participants while providing a solid base for an important historical event.

Akhmatova herself made the connection between her status as one of the main victims of Stalin's postwar ideological campaign and the beginning of the confrontation between the East and the West by stating, on various occasions and to a number of her confidants, that she and Berlin had started the Cold War.[8] Her statement, however, remained both unproven and a subject of commentary on Akhmatova's self-aggrandizing tendencies by several scholars—including Berlin. In "Meetings with Russian Writers in 1945 and 1956," Berlin replied to Akhmatova's words about their role in world history with a deprecating comment that befitted his status as one of Europe's most skeptical minds:

> She attributed her misfortunes to Stalin's personal paranoia. When she told me this in Oxford, she added that in her view we—that is, she and I—inadvertently, by the mere fact of our meeting, had started the cold war and therefore changed the history of mankind. She meant this quite literally; and ... was totally convinced of it, and saw herself and me as world-historical personages chosen by destiny to begin a cosmic conflict.... I could not protest that she had perhaps, even if the reality of Stalin's violent fit of anger and of its possible consequences were allowed for, somewhat overestimated the effect of our meeting on the destinies of the world, since she would have felt this as an insult to her tragic image of herself as Cassandra—indeed, to the historico-metaphysical vision which informed so much of her poetry. I remained silent.[9]

Sir Isaiah's observation about Akhmatova's penchant for seeing history through thick metaphysical lenses was certainly true. However, although it would be impossible—and inexpedient—to attempt to defend the poet's assertion on purely political terms, evidence supporting her conviction does exist. It is hidden behind the "continuous, rich, full texture of 'real life'"—Akhmatova's as well as that of the country with which she shared her destiny.

"It Is Death That He Bears":
Berlin/Akhmatova, Stalin/Churchill

Berlin claimed that when he arrived in the Soviet Union in the fall of 1945, he did not know that Akhmatova had survived the war.[10] Appointed British press attaché in Moscow, he had come to Leningrad in order to escort Randolph Churchill, the son of the former Prime Minister, on his tour of the city. Unofficially, Berlin was there to buy rare books for his collection. His familiarity with Russian literature was a result of his semi-Russian upbringing, which had prompted him to study philosophy and Russian literature at Oxford before embarking on his diplomatic career.

Among the Gogolian and Dostoevskian characters Berlin encountered on his visit was Gennady Rakhlin, a bookseller in Writers' Bookshop on Nevsky Prospekt, who knew lots of people, read everything, and could, through a vast network of clients, introduce Berlin to almost anyone in the city.[11] In the "inner sanctum" of Rakhlin's store, Berlin learned from another book buyer that Akhmatova was not only alive, but that she fortuitously lived around the corner, in Sheremetiev Palace on Fontanka. It took one phone call to arrange the meeting. For Akhmatova, apart from a Polish translator whom she had met during the war, Berlin was the first foreign visitor since 1917.[12] In 1945, she was fifty-six and living with her former husband and his family in a cramped communal apartment. Berlin was twenty years younger, and fascinated with Akhmatova's life (at least with what he had heard about it) and poetry—which, as it turned out during their meeting, he was not all that acquainted with.

The nightlong meeting of 15–16 November 1945, which György Dalos has termed a three-act drama, is well documented.[13] Berlin came early in the evening but the conversation did not take off right away, partly because Akhmatova had another visitor, and partly because they were interrupted: Randolph Churchill, drunk and in search of a companion, appeared around nine o'clock under Akhmatova's window and, to Berlin's horror, began to shout his name. Only after Berlin escorted Churchill back to the hotel and returned to Akhmatova could they talk without interruption.[14] She inquired about her former lovers, friends, and acquaintances who had emigrated to Europe, told him about her life, and recited her poetry. Among the lines she spoke were stanzas from her then unfinished *Poem Without a Hero*, the then unpublishable *Requiem*, poems from *Anno Domini*, *The White Flock*, and *From Six Books*—the collections that had been published. Twice she broke down, remembering Nikolai Gumilev, her first husband, who was executed in 1921, and Osip Mandelstam, who had been arrested in front of her in 1934 and who, after his second arrest, perished in a Kolyma camp in 1938. However, in spite of these tears (or perhaps because of them), Berlin compared Akhmatova's speech to that "of a princess in exile, proud, unhappy, unapproachable."[15]

The meeting ended with his asking her to write down the *Poem Without a Hero*, which she declined to do. Several days later, Berlin left for Moscow. He returned to Leningrad and Akhmatova on 5 January 1946, the Russian Epiphany Eve, and she then presented him with her new collection that bore the inscription of a poem from *Cinque*, dedicated to him. Ten years later, Akhmatova added the third and last dedication to *Poem Without a Hero*—the one to Berlin—and included him in the poem as the "Guest from the Future," an enigmatic figure whose twentieth-century provenance stands in stark opposition to the nostalgic prerevolutionary appearances of other characters.[16] She dated the dedication 5 January 1956, thus celebrating the anniversary of Berlin's second visit.

The much-quoted dedication stands out both as a confession of Akhmatova's love for Berlin and as a statement of their joint mission:

> Long enough I have frozen in fear,
> > Better to summon a Bach Chaconne,
> > > And behind it will enter a man,
> He will not be a beloved husband to me
> > But what we accomplish, he and I,
> > > Will disturb the Twentieth Century.
> I took him by mistake
> > For someone mysteriously bestowed,
> > > The most bitter of fates.
> ...
> But it's not the first branch of lilac,
> > Not a ring, not the sweetness of prayers—
> > > It is death that he bears.[17]

In critical discourse, much has been theorized on Akhmatova's falling for Berlin.[18] After all, he appeared in her life at a time when she, once a famous beauty, was getting over a bitter breakup with Vladimir Garshin, a man she had hoped to marry.[19] However, her love affairs were as often imaginary as real, and her obvious infatuation with her guest may have been as much a result of his personal charm as of his being a messenger from England, the country of Akhmatova's favorite foreign writers (Shakespeare, Byron, and Keats) and the land to which her lovers Boris Anrep and Arthur Lourie escaped in the 1920s.[20]

It is the second key motif of the stanza, Akhmatova's prophetic writing about her own downfall brought on by the "guest from the future," that appears to be more enigmatic—and more relevant with regard to her statement about their role in provoking the Cold War. To understand it, one must keep in mind the Russian literary tradition of poetic prophesying. In "Prophet," a poem from 1826, Pushkin proclaimed that the poet, God-chosen to deliver the word of truth to the people, becomes a seer and an oracle by shedding his mortal appearance, suffering torture, and gaining a new, superhuman power of vision and speech. Although there is no direct reference to "Prophet" in *Poem Without a Hero,* it seems curious that the Biblical text Pushkin reworked, and in places almost directly quoted, is the *Book of Isaiah*.[21] Akhmatova took special pride in her Pushkin scholarship and therefore could have hardly missed the allusion.

After the adoption, publication, and enforcement of the resolution "About the journals *Zvezda* and *Leningrad,*" Akhmatova's fatalism became sustained not only by the poet's awareness of her literary heritage, but also by the historical circumstances. The public denunciation of the poet and some of her colleagues, most notably the writer Mikhail Zoshchenko, began with an excoriating speech by the Party's chief ideologue Andrei Zhdanov, then the chairman of the Supreme Soviets Council of the USSR, the official head of the Propaganda and Agitation Department of the politburo of the Central Committee of the Communist Party (CCCP), and the secretary of the Leningrad Party Committee. On 4 September, he spoke at the specially—and hastily—gathered meeting of Leningrad writers and Party executives in Smolny Palace. In his address, Zhdanov attacked *Zvezda* and *Leningrad* as periodicals with ideological positions that the Party found "unsatisfactory." The journals' foremost crime was their decision to publish Akhmatova and Zoshchenko, who "brought elements of ideological instability and disorganization into Leningrad's writing circles."[22] The Writer's Union and the Literature Union expelled the two writers, thus depriving them of the right to get their work printed, and consequently of their income and bread rations.[23]

Although Akhmatova was not invited to Smolny and, according to her own account, discovered that she had been ostracized from the *Leningradskaia Pravda*, in which the resolution appeared, she immediately felt a social vacuum forming around her.[24] People shunned her as they would victims of the prewar purges: for those who had witnessed the trials of the late 1930s, the resolution's most notorious paragraph about Akhmatova sounded like an epitaph:

> Akhmatova's work is typically representative of a kind of ideologically empty poetry alien to our people. Her poetry, steeped in pessimism and a spirit of decline, expressing tastes like those of the former drawing-room poetry, has become ossified in a stance of bourgeois aristocratic aestheticism—of "art for art's sake"—which refuses to follow in the footsteps of the people, is harmful to our youth and cannot be tolerated in Soviet literature.[25]

It is noteworthy that in private conversations Akhmatova did speculate that the Party's decision to subject her to public flogging could have more than one reason behind it. For example, she told Natalia Roskina and Nadezhda Mandelstam that Stalin could have been jealous of the ovations she received at one of the public readings in the spring of 1946.[26] However, the poet mostly preferred to interpret her falling into disgrace as a punishment for transgressive behavior. Reinforced by the earlier prophetic visions of her doomed fate and aware of the treatment that foreigners and those who communicated with them received in her country, she was certain that the resolution was Stalin's personal revenge for the act of civil disobedience she had committed by hosting a British diplomat in her apartment.²⁷ In "Meetings with Russian Writers in 1946 and 1956," Berlin records:

> When we met in Oxford in 1965 ... Akhmatova told me that Stalin had been personally enraged by the fact that she ... had committed the sin of seeing a foreigner without formal authorization, and not just a foreigner, but an employee of a capitalist government. "So our nun now receives visits from foreign spies," he remarked (so it is alleged), and followed this with obscenities which she could not at first bring herself to repeat to me.²⁸

The circuit made by this bit of information, passed down from the Kremlin to Akhmatova, and from Akhmatova to Berlin, signifies how strangely intimate all the participants of this event were. Akhmatova was convinced of Stalin's constant awareness of all her doings. In the past, she had overcome the distance between herself and the dictator many times. After Osip Mandelstam's arrest in 1934, she found a way to see Abel Yanukidze, Stalin's close aide and one of the top officials in the Council of People's Commissars, in order to plead for her friend's release.²⁹ In 1935, her son Lev Gumilev and former husband Nikolai Punin were released from prison after she had appealed to Stalin through her friends.³⁰ Her intervention in 1938, when Lev was rearrested, proved ineffective, but it was still an attempt to reach Stalin himself, and yet another confirmation of Akhmatova's certainty that every political decision concerning her life came from the very top.³¹ In the 1960s, describing to her secretary Anatoly Nayman the release of Gumilev and Punin from prison after her interference in 1935, Akhmatova concluded: "That, Tolya, ... is the prehistory of my relationship with Stalin. The old cockroach didn't always ask: 'What's the nun doing?'"³²

For Stalin, with his octopus-like apparatus of secret-service agents, keeping an eye on Akhmatova was easy. The ever so helpful bookseller Rakhlin was most likely an agent of the Ministry of State Security (MGB, a successor of NKVD), and the lady who had been visiting Akhmatova at the time of Berlin's arrival was certainly one as well.³³ Soon after Berlin's second visit, when Akhmatova was out, someone came to install listening devices in her apartment. The agents did not even bother to clean up the rubbish left from drilling the walls.³⁴

Akhmatova's understanding of her role in the politics of 1946 was based not only on her belief in Stalin's omnipresence (and his interest in her person), but also on the supposition that the Soviet leadership saw in Berlin an agent of foreign intelligence rather than a lover of literature, the guise under which "the guest from the future" had approached her. Although Berlin denied all his life the assumption that his work in the Soviet Union had anything to do with spying, he was a likely candidate for Stalin's rage.³⁵ Not only did he work at the British Embassy, where all conversations were secretly taped and then sent, in transcript, to Stalin in Sochi,³⁶ but he was also a friend of Winston Churchill's son, and therefore a person dangerously close to the former Prime Minister. Stalin may not have known that Berlin's assignment in Moscow was to write a long dispatch about postwar American-British-Soviet relations and that Berlin gave it up in order to record his meetings with Akhmatova and other Russian writers.³⁷ Nevertheless, he certainly had a negative opinion of Randolph Churchill, who came to the Soviet Union shortly after the war as a correspondent of the *Daily Telegraph* and *Morning Post* and who, in a December article about the Soviet government, speculated about the possible heir of the Soviet leader, who was then recovering from a stroke in Crimea. (On 4 December 1945, TASS issued a short summary of the article).³⁸ Curiously, his dislike of the Prime Minister's son had been formed even before the ill-fated article appeared in print.

During Stalin's absence from Moscow, principal members of the CCCP's Political Bureau Molotov, Malenkov, Beria, and Mikoian acted in his place. When on 7 November 1945 they held a traditional banquet at the Kremlin for members of the diplomatic corps to celebrate an anniversary of the Revolution, Randolph Churchill approached Molotov with a request for a private interview. Molotov, whom Churchill and others saw as Stalin's successor, and who was then behaving more recklessly than usual, agreed to grant the interview without consulting his boss or his colleagues. Shortly afterwards, Malenkov, Beria, and Mikoian expressed their displeasure with this decision and the interview was cancelled. However, on 7 December 1945, when the threesome launched a campaign against Molotov, they decided to present this accident to Stalin as an example of their colleague's gross misdemeanor—and as an illustration of his flawed judgment.³⁹ If an unsanctioned meeting that never took place is sufficient reason for such an assertion, then Randolph Churchill was indeed a persona non grata in Stalin's eyes. Metonymically, Berlin would belong to the same category.

Akhmatova's interpretation of Berlin's interference in her life as that of a "death-bearing" messenger had little to do with knowing about the actual alignment of political forces in the early postwar era. However, her intuition did not betray her. In a note dictated to Amanda Haight, her first biographer, she remarked: "I think it is a lucky discovery to juxtapose what they were saying about Zoshchenko and Akhmatova (in 1946) and what they were saying about Churchill."⁴⁰

Akhmatova associated the name of the former British Prime Minister with Berlin because the latter had come to Leningrad and happened to be seen beneath the windows of her apartment together with Churchill's son. But other facts in Berlin's biography—for example that while working in Washington during the war he had made friends with George Kennan, or that he had been part of the British delegation at the United Nations' founding conference in the summer of 1945—that were not available to the poet, could easily have reached the Kremlin.[41] It is tempting to suggest that for Stalin, who considered politics as much a personal affair as an interplay of objective factors, Berlin represented the closely knit inner circle of the Western political elite. Never really accessible to the Soviets, except for the cautiously orchestrated cordiality of Teheran, Yalta, and Potsdam, this world shut itself off completely in March 1946, when Winston Churchill proclaimed that Communists were "a growing challenge and peril to Christian civilization."[42] Naturally, after the Fulton speech Churchill's name became an anathema among Moscow civil servants, military officials, and diplomats almost overnight.[43]

To the Soviet leader, Churchill's quick and harsh renunciation of the ties between the countries of the Grand Alliance was an act of personal betrayal. Not only had Stalin considered the British Prime Minister the cleverest of his counterparts, he also saw American democracy as a regime without a leader, and therefore lifeless and prone to such potential failures as a major financial crisis.[44] Having underestimated the U.S.A.'s strength before the announcement about the bomb was made, for a while he envisaged the possibility of a British, and not American-dominated Western bloc in Europe.[45] By shattering these hopes in Fulton, Churchill both deprived Stalin of certain political illusions and helped to reinforce the dictator's hatred of foreigners.[46]

In November 1945 and even in January 1946, however, Great Britain was officially still an ally, and Berlin's visit to Akhmatova, albeit conspicuous because of the visitor's connection to Randolph Churchill, could not count as a gross infringement of political etiquette or even a violation of a security taboo. Akhmatova's tragic prognostications were still unconfirmed. Things began to get nasty much later, namely in the summer of 1946. It is the mysterious gaps between Berlin's visits to Akhmatova in November and January, Churchill's Fulton speech in March, and the adoption of the resolution "About the journals *Zvezda* and *Leningrad*" in August that reveal how the meetings of a poet and a scholar-diplomat became reinterpreted as a political crime, followed by a severe and momentous punishment.

Investigating the Improbable: A Delayed Punishment and a Hushed-up Propaganda Campaign

Akhmatova's interpretation of the Party's resolution "About the journals *Zvezda* and *Leningrad*" as the first Cold War move contains several contradictions. For example, her statement can be refuted by the mildness of Stalin's reaction to their meeting. If Akhmatova was indeed being disciplined for seeing Berlin, was not the campaign against her unusually lenient? In 1937, simply for being his father's son, Lev Gumilev had been convicted to ten years of forced labor.[47] Osip Mandelstam had to go through the ordeal in Lubyanka (the infamous prison in the basement of the NKVD headquarters) and then perished because he failed to satisfy the dictator as a poet. Accused of "anti-Soviet activities," he certainly never committed a crime comparable to meeting "British spies."[48] Aware of these and other cases, and keeping in mind Stalin's methods of prosecution, conviction, and elimination, Akhmatova herself expected a much harsher retribution—but did not receive it. The attack of 1946 seems to have been aimed at putting her in the negative spotlight, but not at physically destroying her.[49]

The postponement of punishment also undermines Akhmatova's conviction that Stalin's "enragement" was provoked by her meeting with Berlin as a "British spy." Why was the resolution adopted in August? Rancorous and prone to quick, vengeful attacks, this time Stalin waited nine months to launch his campaign against the poet. An earlier case of Akhmatova's falling into disgrace shows how unusual this was. In 1924, after she gave a public reading of her "New Year's Ballad" at a literary soiree in Moscow, the CCCP had almost immediately accepted a resolution banning her work.[50] In the spring and early summer of 1946, however, she was able to enjoy relative success and prosperity. In July 1946, she went to Moscow to give a reading with Boris Pasternak. On 7 August, she read at the Bolshoi Drama Theater in Leningrad. She was also preparing two new books for publication—with flattering print runs of 100,000 copies each.[51]

And yet, as difficult as it is to prove Akhmatova's statement about her and Berlin's role at the beginning of the Cold War, there is no evidence to the contrary. Several theories put forward in explanation of Akhmatova's "martyrdom" are also hard to agree with, such as Akhmatova's own theory that the resolution was a result of Stalin's jealous reaction to the ovations she received after the Bolshoi Drama Theater reading. However, the memorandum "About the unsatisfactory condition of the journals *Zvezda* and *Leningrad*," signed by Egolin and Alexandrov, two leading apparatchiks of the Propaganda and Agitation Department, was submitted to Zhdanov along with the first draft of the resolution on the same day the reading took place.[52] This means that it was prepared before the reading and therefore could not have been provoked by it. Then again, the timing of Stalin's selection of Akhmatova as an object of his wrath could be one of the key arguments supporting her Cold War statement. Unlike

Zoshchenko, she appeared in the resolution almost overnight. Moreover, as has recently become clear from transcripts of several Kremlin meetings during which the resolution was being prepared, her name had been added to the list of writers picked out for ostracism no earlier than July 1946.[53]

The most telling of these sources is a transcript of the 9 August 1946 meeting of the Organizational Bureau of the CCCP. Hastily summoned, the gathering included several writers and editors, which was in itself a rare incident. According to the transcript, Stalin asked the poet Alexander Prokofiev to give him a sufficient reason to persecute Akhmatova: "Anna Akhmatova, in addition to having an old name, what else can we find on her?" Although Prokofiev tried to resist the pressure by praising a few of Akhmatova's works written after the war, Stalin persevered: "One, two, three poems and that's it, no more." After Prokofiev had told the generalissimo that some of Akhmatova's poems, rejected by *Zvezda*, had appeared in another periodical, *Znamya*, Stalin grunted: "We will get to *Znamya*, too, we will get to everyone."[54] This search for reasons to discredit Akhmatova, as well as Stalin's general indisposition towards her, indicate that, desperate to condemn the poet but unable to outline her real "crime" to his audience, he was trying to make others provide an indictment. When it became clear that none was to be found, Zhdanov came up with a set of ideological accusations, some of which were based on the old, and none so vicious, criticism by historian and literary scholar Boris Eikhenbaum.[55]

The timing of Stalin's decision to publicly crush Akhmatova also helps to challenge the widespread notion that Akhmatova was made a victim of the Party's attack on the intelligentsia liberated by the war because she was the most talented of contemporary poets. This notion implies that by injuring an outstanding figure such as Akhmatova, Stalin was carrying out a symbolic act of reining in culture.[56] Chronologically, however, the resolution "About the journals *Zvezda* and *Leningrad*" was not the Party's first postwar move against nonconformist intellectuals and the institutions that harbored them. The ideological crackdown began in the fall of 1945 with the revision of government agencies in charge of information distribution, propaganda, and foreign relations. On 14 November 1945, a committee of top-ranking party officials was ordered "to conduct a checkup of the Telegraph Agency of the Soviet Union" (TASS) and "present to the politburo its suggestions about the serious strengthening of the leadership" of the agency.[57] On 28 November 1945, the Press Department of the People's Commissariat of Foreign Affairs was charged with censoring articles prepared by foreign correspondents, who no longer were allowed to transmit abroad any "materials that could cause damage to the state interests of the USSR."⁵⁸ In the spring, this campaign intensified. On 13 April 1946, the CCCP met to discuss drawbacks in the Party's ideological work.⁵⁹ Stalin, who presided over the meeting, gave a speech in which he suggested that "current ideological work is to be considered seriously flawed." Among others, he condemned Alexander Tairov, head of the Moscow Chamber Theater, and criticized several literary works published in "thick journals," including *Zvezda*. Thus the later attack on *Zvezda* and *Leningrad*—Akhmatova and Zoshchenko—was only a continuation of this combing out of the intelligentsia, which by August had become almost routine.⁶⁰

Stalin's decision to ostracize Akhmatova, made in the middle of the summer and not earlier, suggests that her meeting with Berlin, seemingly "forgotten" in the winter of 1946, was "remembered" much later. In which connection could it be brought up again? The chronology of the 1946 anti-British propaganda campaign provides an answer to this question. According to Vladimir O. Pechatnov, it began in the fall of 1945 as a counterintelligence operation, a response to British propaganda that was conducted, in part, through the magazine *British Ally* (*Britanskii Soyuznik*).⁶¹ However, before the summer of 1946 the intensity of the anti-British and, somewhat later, the anti-American crusade was low. Even though Stalin was infuriated by Churchill's "betrayal" in Fulton, up until August the official rhetoric was contained within the frame of "cautious optimism," to use an idiomatic expression characteristic of the relations between the Allies. It was only in the late summer and fall that the institutions in charge of exchange of information and literature with other countries, such as the Soviet Information Bureau and International Book, were scrutinized for their failure to fight the West as a treacherous ideological enemy. The official status of *British Ally* and its twin American publication, *America*, was not changed until August, when the circulation of these magazines was reduced by half. Access to other foreign periodicals, through subscriptions to libraries and academic institutions, was also limited around that time.⁶²

Even if negative pronouncements about Great Britain and the U.S. were made in the spring of 1946, they seemed tame in comparison to the accusations leveled during late summer of that year and the decades that followed. For example, Stalin's speech in the Supreme Soviet on the eve of the general election on 10 February 1946, in which he stated the inevitability of the crisis inherent in international capitalism and called for a "new mighty upsurge in the national economy," illustrates how muted his desire to aggressively attack the Allies was. Although Stalin's words are believed to have provoked both Kennan's *Long Telegram* and Churchill's

Fulton diatribe, they were really a domestic propaganda product not intended for export. Stalin's main goal was to assert himself as the national leader who would resurrect his country after the destruction of World War II—the stance he believed essential for maintaining the overwhelming support of the impoverished, exhausted nation. As Vladimir Zubok and Constantine Pleshakov emphasize in *Inside the Kremlin's Cold War*, the former Allies overreacted, hearing a war cry behind his declarations. At the time of the elections, Stalin simply could not afford a "premature confrontation with the British and the Americans."[63]

Zubkov and Pleshakov's explanation of Stalin's nonaggressive attitude towards the former Allies in the spring of 1946 is based on the presumption that the Soviet leader, concerned by the United State's possession of the nuclear bomb, "wanted a breathing spell in order to rearm."[64] Although convincing, this statement does not address another important factor that bridled Stalin's rage against the former Allies: the postwar devastation of the Soviet Union and the hope of improving his country's economic stability with the help of a major loan from the West. It is well known that in the first eight months of 1945, even before the Lend-Lease aid was terminated, the Soviet government made two formal applications to the United States government for large-scale credits for postwar reconstruction.[65] What is less known—or rather completely overlooked—in the scholarly analysis of the anti-West and especially anti-British ideological campaigns of 1946 is that the disappointment of Stalin's expectations of American financial aid coincided with the beginning of his attack on Akhmatova.

The British Loan and the End of Restraint in the Soviet Ideological Campaign Against the West

The failure of Soviet expectations of receiving significant financial aid from the U.S. was especially painful because the Soviet Union had to compete for the grants with Great Britain, its former ally. The Soviet request for $6 billion got stuck between the State Department and the Treasury, while the British application for the same amount was not only heatedly discussed in the House of Representatives and the Senate, but also, by the end of 1945, began to be considered a matter of precedent.[66] According to some in the American press, if the British were to receive their credit, other countries, including the Soviet Union, could apply for—and expect to receive—money as well. For example an editorial in the Washington *Daily News* said:

> A loan to the British Government is only the first on our loan list. What we do about this we must be ready to do for many other nations.
>
> France came in for a $550,000,000 loan last week. Russia, China, Italy, Belgium, Poland, and a dozen of other nations also are waiting to see what ruler book we write for the billions for Britain.
>
> Each nation expects equal treatment. We are setting a foreign-loan pattern, many times larger than after the last war.[67]

For Stalin, who pushed for the loan relentlessly, the competition with Great Britain marked a new alignment of forces in international politics. With the death of President Roosevelt on 11 April 1945, the USSR lost its biggest sympathizer in the Grand Alliance. According to Sir Frank Roberts, British Head of Central Department from 1943 to 1945 and Minister at the British Embassy in Moscow from 1945 to 1948, it was then that the "Anglo-Saxon preference for wide international co-operation instead of the Big Three procedure favored by the Russians" became apparent.[68] For Stalin, this meant having to face the incompatibility between his domestic political role—that of a dictator in total control of everything from nuclear-bomb research to poetry—and the role he was playing in the international arena, where he had to exhibit an attitude of flexibility and even compliance.

As the Congressional discussions of foreign loans demonstrate, America's postwar prosperity allowed it not only to launch an extensive program of rehabilitation of the former Allies,[69] but also to measure the countries applying for financial aid against each other for ideological malleability, usefulness to the U.S. as trade partners, and reliability as guarantors of world peace. In the beginning of the discussions, lawmakers and the press tended to equate rather than separate the USSR and Great Britain, pairing them up against weaker and less reliable applicants such as Poland or France. Thus, on 6 December 1945, Congressman Daniel A. Reed of New York quoted an article from the *Washington Star,* in which the Soviet Union and Great Britain were both considered worthy of financial aid because of their solvency.[70] Even the facts concerning the Soviet Union's unlawful behavior in Europe—looting and the use of slave labor were the two examples that Congressman Reed gave in his speech—did not curb the overwhelming sympathy towards the Soviet Union, which meant that in the winter of 1945 it stood a good chance of getting its loan.

Stalin's willingness to compromise and yield to the pressure the U.S. government was trying to put on the aid applicants had also made a good impression. Even after Congress minimized the figure of the Soviet loan to $1 billion, the Soviets still stayed in the game. In April, the USSR accepted with almost no changes the American conditions under which the minimized loan could be made.[71] This tactic of nonconfrontation can help explain why Stalin was reluctant to start a major propaganda campaign against the former Allies until the decision on the loan was made. It seems that as long as there was a possibility of getting the money, he was willing to continue placating the West.

In the summer of 1946, however, the tone of discussions in Congress changed. On 8 July, President Truman sent a letter to the House of Representatives endorsing the British loan. The main reasons for favoring Great Britain over the Soviet Union, as stated in this message as well as in Congressmen's remarks, were economic. They referred to the fact of British trade dominance in the prewar world. If the British economy collapsed, the reasoning went, so would world trade. However, the ideological arguments against the Soviet Union lay too close to the surface to remain unnoticed. American-British cooperation was presented as a guarantor of the economic supremacy of non-Socialist countries on the world market. Although several voices were raised against helping the new British government, with its strong National Socialist tendencies, Stalin's ideological unreliability was considered a much weightier counterbalance. Loaning money to the British partner would enable it to maintain a strong influence in its current and former colonies, which would then be harder for the Communist bloc to control.[72]

Stalin did not need to eavesdrop on the debates in Congress to understand how precarious his position as an applicant for financial aid was. The American press was full of commentaries on the discussion. The *New York Times* editorial of 2 July 1946, for example, was already pairing Great Britain and France, as U.S. allies, against the Soviet Union as its main ideological, political, and strategic opponent:

> Great Britain and France are eastern bastions of human liberty. We have recognized almost instinctively that there are impelling reasons why we should strive to make these bastions secure. We have granted a loan to the French Republic. It is a matter of immediate national concern that we follow this by granting a loan to Great Britain. If we allow anything to prevent us from doing so, only the Soviet Union will rejoice. For the Kremlin would inevitably see in this a blow to those fraternal ties which today offer the only effective resistance to its further encroachments.[73]

The anti-Soviet tone of the debate and the number of voices raised in favor of Great Britain reached its peak in early summer. On 14 June 1946, the House Banking and Currency Committee adopted a resolution approving the British loan of $3.75 billion. On 13 July the loan passed. Five days later, at a press conference, President Truman announced that he had no intention of requesting from Congress additional authorization for foreign loans.[74] This was the end of the Soviet Union's hope of getting a grant from the U.S.—its loan went to Great Britain. Several days later, Egolin and Alexandrov got the assignment to prepare a memorandum about the deficiencies in the work of *Zvezda* and *Leningrad*. And on 9 August, at the meeting of the Organizational Bureau of the CCCP, Stalin grilled Prokofiev about Akhmatova's faults. If he ever "remembered" Akhmatova and her meeting with "British spies," it was then, when the former ally had become not only an ideological opponent, but a rival in the battle for economic survival.

The fact that the end of the British loan debate in the U.S. Congress marked the beginning of the rabid anti-British and anti-American propaganda campaign in the Soviet Union can be accepted on pragmatic terms. The postwar campaign against "servility towards the West," initially directed at the domestic audience, changed its course in the summer of 1946, after Stalin, no longer entertaining any hopes of being supported by the West, began to feel free to charge at it as the Soviet Union's enemy. The concurrence between the loan fiasco and the preparation of the resolution "About the journals *Zvezda* and *Leningrad*," however, is based on a more convoluted logic. Can we really say that Stalin initiated the anti-Akhmatova campaign after he had received the news about the USSR's failure to get the loan and Britain's success in securing it? Although there is no direct evidence that the attack on Akhmatova was Stalin's attempt to inform the West about the complete break, three factors allow me to back up the poet's statement about the role she and Berlin played in the Cold War: Berlin's professional connections with Winston Churchill, his acquaintance with George Kennan, and his personal closeness to Randolph Churchill.[75] Had Stalin known how almost accidental Berlin's first visit to Akhmatova was, he might have looked for another victim. But dictators, as well as poets, see no accidents in history.

The resolution targeted culture as the dawning war's new weapon. Just as Soviet readers had to be made aware that their access to "contemporary bourgeois Western culture" was from then on going to be extremely limited,[76] the former Allies had to understand that for them too, Soviet culture was now placed under a ban. The artists and writers they liked were to be terribly punished; the art they admired or inspired was to be labeled "cosmopolitan" and either destroyed or hidden from public view. Berlin realized this predicament in writing about his visit to Akhmatova in the memorandum for the British Foreign Office, which his biographer calls "probably the first Western account of Stalin's war against Russian culture."[77] As a courier, Berlin was well chosen. By directing his rage against Akhmatova, Stalin could be certain that his message would be delivered quickly and to the right address.

Notes

1. William Taubman, *Stalin's American Policy* (New York, 1982), 99–165.
2. A. Zhdanov, *The Central Committee Resolution and Zhdanov's Speech on the Journals "Zvezda" and "Leningrad,"* transl. Felicity Ashbee and Irina Tidmarsh (Royal Oak, Mich., 1978), 50.
3. Konstantin Simonov, *Glazami cheloveka moego pokoleniya* (Moscow, 1989), 96.
4. In his memoirs, Berlin repeats the rumors that circulated in Leningrad after his visit. One of them was that a delegation from England had come to convince Akhmatova to leave Russia. Another even more blatant rumor stated that Winston Churchill had been Akhmatova's admirer all his life and therefore was sending an airplane to take her to England. See Roberta Reeder, *Anna Akhmatova* (New York, 1994), 287.
5. Lidiya Chukovskaya, *Zapiski ob Anne Akhmatovoi*, vol. 2 (Saint Petersburg, 1996), 415.
6. Michael Ignatieff, *Isaiah Berlin: A Life* (New York, 1998), 161. Berlin submitted the first version of the essay to the Foreign Office under the title "A Note on Literature and the Arts in the RSFSR in the Closing Months of 1945." He reworked the text several times throughout his life and published it extensively.
7. Isaiah Berlin, *The Sense of Reality* (New York, 1996), 26.
8. Joseph Brodsky, *Vspominaia Akhmatovu: Iosif Brodskii—Solomon Volkov. Dialogi* (Moscow, 1992), 38.
9. Isaiah Berlin, "Meetings with Russian Writers in 1946 and 1956," in *Personal Impressions* (London, 1980), 156–210, 202.
10. This claim has now been refuted. L. Kopylov et al., *"I eto bylo tak": Anna Akhmatova i Isaiia Berlin* (Saint Petersburg, 2009), 9–16, 25–36.
11. Isaiah Berlin, *Flourishing: Letters 1928–1946*, ed. Henry Hardy (London, 2004), 604.
12. György Dalos, *The Guest From the Future: Anna Akhmatova and Isaiah Berlin* (New York, 1996), 25.
13. Ibid., 33.
14. Ignatieff, *Isaiah Berlin*, 155.
15. Berlin, "Meetings with Russian Writers," 193.
16. Nancy Anderson, "War and Late Stalinism," in *Anna Akhmatova, The Word That Causes Death's Defeat: Poems of Memory*, ed. and trans. Nancy Anderson (New Haven, 2004), 105f.; Reeder, *Anna Akhmatova*, 287f.
17. Anna Akhmatova, *The Complete Poems of Anna Akhmatova*, trans. Judith Hemschemeyer, ed. Roberta Reeder (Somerville, Mass., 1990), 407.
18. Dalos, *The Guest From the Future*, 40f.
19. Reeder, *Anna Akhmatova*, 278–281.
20. Anatoly Nayman, *Remembering Anna Akhmatova*, trans. Wendy Rosslyn (New York, 1989), 99.
21. Boris Gasparov, *Poeticheskii iazyk Pushkina kak fakt istorii russkogo literaturnogo iazyka* (Saint Petersburg, 1999), 242f.
22. Zhdanov, *Central Committee Resolution*, 42.
23. Reeder, *Anna Akhmatova*, 291ff.
24. Chukovskaya, *Zapiski ob Anne Akhmatovoi*, vol. 2, 53; Dalos, *The Guest From the Future*, 76.
25. Zhdanov, *Central Committee Resolution*, 42.
26. Konstantin Polivanov, ed., *Anna Akhmatova and Her Circle*, trans. Patricia Beriozkina (Fayetteville, 1994), 165; Nadezhda Mandelstam, *Hope Against Hope* (New York, 1970), 375.

27. The poet began her catastrophic self-prophesying in an earlier work, the drama *Enuma Elish*, written at the beginning of the 1940s in Tashkent and later burnt (only short reconstructed abstracts have survived). In *Enuma Elish*, Akhmatova told the story of a poet and actress upon whom a "guest from the future" descended in a dream, bringing with him the failure of the production of the play, the heroine's trial, and her tragic death. Akhmatova, *Complete Poems*, 768f.
28. Berlin, "Meetings with Russian Writers," 201f..
29. Vitaly Shentalinsky, *Arrested Voices* (New York, 1993), 175.
30. Nayman, *Remembering Anna Akhmatova*, 71.
31. Dalos, *The Guest From the Future*, 88.
32. Nayman, *Remembering Anna Akhmatova*, 71.
33. Berlin, *Flourishing*, 604f.; Oleg Kalugin, "Delo KGB na Annu Akhmatovu," in *Gosbezopasnost' i literatura* (Moscow, 1994), 72–79. Quoting Rakhlin's daughter and the protocols of Rakhlin's secret police interrogations, Kopylov et al. prove that the bookseller was closely connected to the MGB (*"I eto bylo tak,"* 44, 48). They reveal that during Berlin's visit to Leningrad, Rakhlin invited him and Randolph Churchill to visit his apartment, and that MGB provided groceries for their dinner that night. Rakhlin was arrested and tried in 1949 for his meeting with Berlin. For information about Sofia Ostrovskaya and Antonina Oranzhereeva, two of Akhmatova's friends who kept a close eye on the poet for the MGB, see ibid., 29–36. See also Mikhail Kralin, "Sof'ia Kazimirovna Ostrovskaia—drug ili oboroten'?" in *Pobedivshee smert' slovo*, ed. M. Kralin (Tomsk, 2000), 222–241.
34. Ignatieff, *Isaiah Berlin*, 164.
35. Mikhail Kralin, *Pobedivsheye smert' slovo*, 202; Brodsky, *Vspominaya Akhmatovu*, 37.
36. Information about the materials Stalin received from his aides during his fall vacations in Crimea in 1945 and 1946 includes "records of conversations in the British Embassy" (RGASPI *Perepiska s I.V. Stalinym vo vremya otpuskov*).
37. Ignatieff, *Isaiah Berlin*, 134, 161.
38. Boris Sokolov, *Stalin: vlast' i krov'* (Moscow, 2004), 301.
39. Ibid., 304.
40. Amanda Haight, *Anna Akhmatova* (Moscow, 1991), 243.
41. Ignatieff, *Isaiah Berlin*, 110, 133. Berlin was introduced to Kennan in the early 1940s in the house of Charles Bohlen, the founder of scholarship known as Kremlinology. Berlin, Kennan, and Bohlen formed the center of the Dumbarton Avenue intellectual circle. Before the war, they represented a minority who knew, in Kennan's words, that "Stalinism is irreversible." Frances Stonor Saunders, *The Cultural Cold War* (London, 1999), 36.
42. Martin Gilbert, *Winston Churchill*, vol. 8 (London, 1988), 202.
43. Vladimir O. Pechatnov, "'Strelba kholostymi,'" 113.
44. Jonathan Haslam, "Russian archival revelations and our understanding of the Cold War," *Diplomatic History* 21, no. 2 (Spring 1997): 217–229, 224.
45. Sean Greenwood, *Britain and the Cold War 1945–91* (London and New York, 2000), 12.
46. Konstantin Simonov testifies to Stalin's hatred of foreigners in his record of their private conversation on 13 May 1947. Konstantin Simonov, *Glazami cheloveka moego pokoleniya*, 129.
47. Nancy Anderson, "Terror and the Muse," in Akhmatova, *The Word That Causes Death's Defeat*, 76f.
48. Shentalinsky, *Arrested Voices*, 189f.
49. Chukovskaya, *Zapiski ob Anne Akhmatovoi*, vol. 2, 13.

50. This ban was lifted in 1929. See Haight, *Anna Akhmatova*, 239.
51. Dalos, *Guest From the Future*, 75; Reeder, *Anna Akhmatova*, 288.
52. D.L. Babichenko, ed., *"Literaturnyi front"* (Moscow, 1994), 191.
53. Even in the memorandum handed in by Egolin and Alexandrov on 7 August, Akhmatova still does not stand out as a key figure. See "G.F. Alexandrov, A.M. Egolin—A.A. Zhdanovu: O neudovletvoritel'nom sostoianii zhurnalov 'Zvezda' i 'Leningrad,'" in Babichenko, *"Literaturnyi front,"* 191–197.
54. "Stenogramma zasedaniia Orgburo TsK VKP(b) po voprosu 'O zhurnalakh 'Zvezda' i 'Leningrad,'" in Babichenko, *"Literaturnyi front,"* 204.
55. Reeder, *Anna Akhmatova*, 292.
56. Ibid., 290; Haight, *Anna Akhmatova*, 145.
57. Yurii Zhukov, *Stalin: tainy vlasti* (Moscow, 2005), 322.
58. Ibid.
59. Ibid., 351.
60. Ibid., 323, 355f.
61. Vladimir O. Pechatnov, "The Rise and Fall of *Britansky Soyuznik*," *The Historical Journal* 41 (1998), no. 1: 293–301, 295. Coincidentally, while working at the British Embassy in Moscow, Berlin served as the curator of the magazine. Roman Timenchik, *Anna Akhmatova v 1960-e gody* (Moscow, 2005), 35.
62. Pechatnov, "Strelba kholostymi," 114–129.
63. Vladislav Zubok and Constantine Pleshakov, *Inside the Kremlin's Cold War* (Cambridge, Mass., 1996), 117.
64. Ibid., 119.
65. Leon Martel, *Lend-Lease, Loans, and the Coming of the Cold War* (Boulder, 1979), 169.
66. Although Britain applied for $6 billion, $4.4 billion is the biggest amount for the British loan that came up in discussions in the U.S. Congress. The final figure was reduced almost by half to $3.75 billion. U.S., Congress, Senate, *Congressional Record*, 79th Cong., 2nd sess., 1946, 92, pt. 7, 8416–8417.
67. Quoted in Senate, *Congressional Record*, 79th Cong., 2nd sess., 1946, 92, pt. 7, 3922.
68. Sir Frank Roberts, "On Soviet Policy, 26 and 31 October 1945," in *The Foreign Office and the Kremlin*, ed. Graham Ross (Cambridge, Mass., 1984), 264.
69. Senate, *Congressional Record*, 79th Cong., 1st sess., 1946, 91, pt. 13, 8346.
70. Ibid., 5330.
71. Martel, *Lend-Lease*, 191, 197ff., 218.
72. Senate, *Congressional Record* 92, pt. 7, 8393–8409.
73. Quoted Senate, *Congressional Record* 92, pt. 12, A3964.
74. Martel, *Lend-Lease*, 219.
75. Joseph Brodsky, who knew both Akhmatova and Berlin, seemed to believe that the latter factor indeed triggered Stalin's jealous rage. Brodsky, *Vspominaya Akhmatovu*, 37.
76. Zhdanov, *Central Committee Resolution*, 50.
77. Ignatieff, *Isaiah Berlin*, 161.

Bibliography

Akhmatova, Anna. *The Complete Poems of Anna Akhmatova*. Trans. Judith Hemschemeyer, ed. Roberta Reeder. Somerville, Mass.: Zephyr Press, 1990.

———. *The Word That Causes Death's Defeat: Poems of Memory*. Ed. and trans. Nancy Anderson. New Haven: Yale University Press, 2004.
Babichenko, D.L., ed. *"Literaturnyi front": istoriia politicheskoi tsenzury 1932–1946*. Moscow: Entsiklopediia rossiiskikh dereven', 1994.
Berlin, Isaiah. "Meetings with Russian Writers in 1946 and 1956." In *Personal Impressions*, by Isaiah Berlin (London: The Hogarth Press, 1980), 156–210.
———. *The Sense of Reality*. New York: Farrar, Straus, and Giroux, 1996.
———. *Flourishing: Letters 1928–1946*, ed. Henry Hardy. London: Chatto & Windus, 2004.
Brodsky, Joseph. *Vspominaya Akhmatovu: Iosif Brodskii—Solomon Volkov. Dialogi*. Moscow: Nezavisimaia gazeta, 1992.
Chukovskaya, Lidiya, *Zapiski ob Anne Akhmatovoi*, vol. 2. Saint Petersburg: Neva, 1996.
Dalos, György. *The Guest From the Future: Anna Akhmatova and Isaiah Berlin*. New York: Farrar, Straus, and Giroux, 1996.
Gasparov, Boris. *Poeticheskii iazyk Pushkina kak fakt istorii russkogo literaturnogo iazyka*. Saint Petersburg: Akademicheskii proekt, 1999.
Gilbert, Martin. *Winston Churchill*. Vol. 8. London: Heinemann, 1988.
Greenwood, Sean. *Britain and the Cold War 1945–91*. London: MacMillan Press, New York: St. Martin's Press, 2000.
Haight, Amanda. *Anna Akhmatova: poeticheskoe stranstvie. Dnevniki, vospominaniia, pis'ma*. Moscow: Raduga, 1991.
Haslam, Jonathan. "Russian archival revelations and our understanding of the Cold War." *Diplomatic History* 21, no. 2 (Spring 1997): 217–229.
Ignatieff, Michael. *Isaiah Berlin. A Life*. New York: Henry Holt and Co., 1998.
Kalugin, Oleg. "Delo KGB na Annu Akhmatovu." In *Gosbezopasnost' i literatura: na opyte Rossii i Germanii (SSSR i GDR)*, ed. E.V. Shukshina and T.V. Gromova (Moscow: Rudomino, 1994), 72–79.
Kopylov, L., T. Pozdniakova, and N. Popova. *"I eto bylo tak": Anna Akhmatova i Isaiia Berlin*. Saint Petersburg: Muzei Anny Akhmatovoi v Fontannom Dome, 2009.
Kralin, Mikhail. *Pobedivshee smert' slovo*. Tomsk: Vodolei, 2000.
Mandelstam, Nadezhda. *Hope Against Hope*. New York: Atheneum, 1970.
Martel, Leon. *Lend-Lease, Loans, and the Coming of the Cold War: A Study of the Implementation of Foreign Policy*. Boulder, Colo.: Westview Press, 1979.
Nayman, Anatoly, *Remembering Anna Akhmatova*, trans. Wendy Rosslyn. New York: Henry Holt and Co., 1989.
Pechatnov, Vladimir O. "The Rise and Fall of *Britansky Soyuznik:* A Case Study in Soviet Response to British Propaganda of the Mid-1940s." *The Historical Journal* 41 (1998), no. 1: 293–301.
———. "'Strel'ba kholostymi': sovetskaia propaganda na zapad v nachale kholodnoi voiny (1945–1947)." In *Stalinskoe desiatiletie kholodnoi voiny: fakty i gipotezy*, ed. A.O. Chubarian (Moscow: Nauka, 1999), 108–133.
Polivanov, Konstantin, ed. *Anna Akhmatova and Her Circle*. Trans. Patricia Beriozkina. Fayetteville, Ark.: University of Arkansas Press, 1994.
Reeder, Roberta. *Anna Akhmatova: Poet and Prophet*. New York: St. Martin's Press, 1994.
Roberts, Sir Frank. "On Soviet Policy, 26 and 31 October 1945." In *The Foreign Office and the Kremlin: British Documents on Anglo-Soviet Relations, 1941–1945*, ed. Graham Ross (Cambridge, Mass.: Cambridge University Press, 1984).
Shentalinsky, Vitaly. *Arrested Voices: Resurrecting the Disappeared Writers of the Soviet Regime*. New York: The Free Press, 1993.

Simonov, Konstantin. *Glazami cheloveka moego pokoleniia: razmyshleniia o I.V. Staline.* Moscow: Novosti, 1989.
Sokolov, Boris. *Stalin: vlast' i krov'*. Moscow: AST Press, 2004.
Stonor Saunders, Frances. *The Cultural Cold War: The CIA and the World of Arts and Letters.* London: Granta Books, 1999.
Taubman, William. *Stalin's American Policy: From Entente to Détente to Cold War.* New York, London: W.W. Norton & Co., 1982.
Timenchik, Roman. *Anna Akhmatova v 1960-e gody.* Moscow: Vodolei Publishers, Toronto: the University of Toronto Press, 2005.
Zhdanov, A. *The Central Committee Resolution and Zhdanov's Speech on the Journals "Zvezda" and "Leningrad."* Bilingual ed.; transl. Felicity Ashbee and Irina Tidmarsh. Royal Oak, Mich.: Strathcona Publishing Co., 1978.
Zhukov, Yurii. *Stalin: tainy vlasti.* Moscow: Vagrius, 2005.
Zubok, Vladislav, and Constantine Pleshakov. *Inside the Kremlin's Cold War.* Cambridge, Mass.: Harvard University Press, 1996.

Further documents

U.S., Congress, Senate. *Congressional Record.* 79th Cong., 1st sess., 1945, 91, pt. 13.
———. *Congressional Record.* 79th Cong., 2nd sess., 1946, 92, pt. 7.
———. *Congressional Record.* 79th Cong., 2nd sess., 1946, 92, pt. 12.
RGASPI (Rossiiskii gosudarstvennyi arkhiv sotsialno politicheskoi istorii). *Perepiska s I.V. Stalinym vo vremia otpuskov.* Fund 558, inventory 11, case 100 (June 25, 2005).

Chapter 3

RADIO REFORM IN THE 1980s
RIAS and DT-64 Respond to Private Radio

Edward Larkey

In the introduction to the volume *Pop und Propaganda*, editors Klaus Arnold and Christoph Classen[1] point to the curious situation of the electronic media of both German states before unification: although they arose out of competing and antagonistic social, economic, and political systems, and even developed according to different concepts,[2] programming of the broadcasting networks in both states gradually achieved a similarity, with increased orientation to specific target audiences and audience distinctions.[3] Moreover, while the political or propaganda programs were neither credible nor popular among most people in the GDR, Arnold and Classen surmise that the entertainment shows popular among GDR citizens could have promoted identification with the state, and thus may have indirectly reinforced the legitimacy of the governing elite.[4] The similarities in program structure in spite of the antagonistic political systems is usually traced back to the needs and preferences of the audience, for whom music on the radio forms the "background noise" for primary activities during the day.[5] This essay will argue that the evolution toward similar programming of the East and West German media goes deeper than just the "needs of the audience." Instead, these changes are rooted in socioeconomic and sociocultural transformations that may be analyzed within the framework of more recent theories on cultural industries, in which cultural production and circulation—such as that in the mass media—achieves a more prominent role in reproducing the capitalist system in competition with the Eastern bloc's "real existing socialism." The changes are rooted in a process that we shall call *commercialization*. For the purposes of this chapter, *commercialization* will refer to the penetration of capitalist logic and rationality into the popular music and media sphere of the GDR, and its expansion into RIAS programming. Commercialization can be considered an instrument of European cultural modernity that expanded into Eastern Europe, and in particular the GDR. This essay will also suggest that any legitimacy or loyalty gained by the state was at best tentative and temporary, and tempered by people's daily experience of their political and economic subordination in the media and in life.

A Cultural Industries Approach to GDR Media Culture

At the heart of East-West media confrontations were the manifestations of increased competition between a new, flexibly networked, globally functioning elite in the West and the more traditional, command-style management of industrial capitalism. Within these newer groupings among the elite, greater autonomy in cultural creativity was combined with strict regulation of circulation and management of symbolic goods. While the newer sectors were successfully competing in the West at the expense of the political domination of the older elite based in the traditional industries with a top-down, command style of management, this competition also played into the SED party bureaucracy's management of cultural and social processes, which tolerated no open competition. In the West, members of a newer elite were recruited from the ranks of the new electronic and computer industries, advertising, and other sectors involved in the production, circulation, and management of symbolic goods. These same industries were also growing in the GDR, but their political activity was severely constrained by Party dogma.

This paper assumes with Louw and with Hesmondhalgh that the new cultural industries were not only crucial for the reproduction of modern capitalist society, but were also important for the reproduction and ultimate demise of the GDR's "real existing" socialist society.[6] Reform plans in radio broadcasting in both East and West reflected this competition between old and new elites. The increased importance of this sector for maintaining the system gave heightened prominence to the control of political, cultural, and social discourse, and to the ultimately futile attempts by the East German political leadership to achieve discursive closure within the country. Western media, however, which prevented discursive closure in the GDR, practiced a more pluralist form than the command style of GDR political and ideological discourse. Despite this, through various measures designed to counteract Western influence, the GDR authorities maintained a highly contested discursive hegemony that included popular music programming. One of the elements of government legitimacy was its ability to manage an internationally networked and culturally credible popular music sector.

On the basis of the cultural-industries approach outlined above, this essay will explain how these issues played out in the competition between RIAS, the U.S.-owned and German-operated network in West Berlin, on the one hand, and DT 64, the primary East German program, which became its own youth network in the mid 1980s, on the other. The following aspects will be discussed: first, the consolidation of GDR radio programming into one youth network, Jugendradio DT 64, prompting greater output from largely private GDR producers; second, the two reform strategies for the Radio in the American Sector (RIAS) network in the 1980s, which forced the GDR networks to adopt a similar commercially oriented program model; third, the creation of a new radio pop music studio rooted in commercial pop concepts; and fourth, dubbing programs like *Duett—Musik für den Rekorder*, to compensate for the lack of Western LP recordings on the GDR domestic market.

GDR Media and Cultural Policies: A Short Overview

A cursory overview of GDR cultural policies toward popular music will contextualize these developments. In the mid 1950s and the 1960s, Western influences were to be counteracted by creating a Socialist alternative. The failure of these early strategies was symptomatic of a lack of insight into the necessity of creating a networked cultural industry in the GDR. In the 1970s, these efforts were modified to accommodate more commercial popular music influences from the West, while still pursuing the creation of distinctly Socialist popular music. This led to a significant increase in the amount of Western music broadcast by GDR networks.

Popular music policies were intimately linked to how the GDR command-oriented political elite positioned itself on the question of managing the creation and development of multifaceted and cooperatively networked cultural industries. The GDR asserted that Marxist cultural theory allowed for the political management and planning of society's cultural development.[7] In actuality, GDR policies toward mediated culture were piecemeal, fraught with intermedia rivalries, and based on an artisanal understanding of cultural production and distribution. These approaches hindered the development of viable alternatives to the cultural industries of the West, especially when the institutions possessed little autonomy to decide their own policies. The existence of a censorship board (*Lektorat*) for each medium—record company, radio network, and television broadcasting service—typifies the potential for institutional rivalries that were brought into the open in the latter half of the 1980s, when each of them released songs that were prohibited in another medium for either political or aesthetic reasons. Historically, GDR cultural and political bureaucracies could not cope with the continuous innovations flowing across the border from the West, which led to a state security discourse of threat and defensiveness that clashed with the discourse of the global popular music with its values of fun, hedonism, enjoyment, consumption, and popularity.[8] Bands as well as radio broadcasts were obligated to mediate these competing discourses by attempting to accommodate the ritualized official language of the political institutions with the daily vernacular speech of youth culture. Youth cultural and popular music phenomena, behaviors, and values that did not conform to narrow Party dictates were considered threats to socialism, the GDR, and the working class—instigated at the behest of Western imperialists.[9] With increasing commercialization, more spaces opened up for competing narratives about GDR reality, not only in the so-called independent scene, but also among established bands.[10]

In the absence of a comprehensive approach to creating mass-mediated cultural industries, GDR authorities made concessions to spontaneously generated cultural influences from the West that had taken root in GDR society, but were perceived as a threat to its political and cultural monopoly; not only relatively innocuous influences like disco music, but culturally more challenging ones like punk. Programming, styles of moderating, musical sounds, and discursive conventions and concepts, as well as Capitalist laws of market rationality, found their way into the GDR media sector for the purpose of generating loyalty within the population.[11] Reliance on market structures and thinking, an unintended side effect of concessions to these influences, helped undermine the SED/GDR leadership's determination to lead and plan society's cultural development, further undercutting its legitimacy.

Political functionaries, in an effort to mitigate the influences of Western music and youth culture, employed a variety of distancing strategies: requiring German lyrics; implementing the 60:40 rule for radio and performance repertoire in 1958, which stipulated that sixty percent had to come from Socialist countries and forty percent from the West; refusing to play song titles that seemed incompatible with narrowly defined Party ideological and aesthetic precepts; compelling bands to obtain and renew annual performance licenses; prohibiting the sale of Western recordings and popular music periodicals; submitting all songs to a censorship board, the *Lektorat*, before production; restricting the import of musical instruments; maintaining a state monopoly on the production of recordings in studios of the radio stations, TV stations, and the pop music label Amiga; preventing most GDR rock bands from performance tours and recordings in the West; and severely restricting the performances and distribution of recordings of Western bands in the GDR. Western radio stations were not bound by such prohibitions and played much of the music sought after by GDR youth audiences. On that basis, the band Klaus Renft was outlawed in 1975,[12] while Party bureaucrats refused to allow West German rock acts like Udo Lindenberg or BAP to go on performance tours through the GDR.[13] Also, the Politbüro intervened in the programming of songs or bands whose lyrics seemingly went against Party economic, cultural, or social policies.[14]

In the course of the 1980s, commercialization pressures diluted these strategies. Private recording studios emerged to produce music commissioned by the state radio broadcasting network.[15] Also, more GDR bands were producing original songs using English lyrics, and the government allowed an increase in the number of GDR bands authorized to perform and release recordings in the West. By far some of the most far-reaching commercialization tendencies were to be found, paradoxically, in the state broadcasting network, with the creation of the youth broadcasting network Jugendradio DT 64. The ultimate aim of popular music broadcasting in the GDR was to help construct a national popular music community, if possible with a stylistically recognizable (Socialist and German) identity, able to compete with Western productions on both the domestic and international markets. This goal proved to be elusive.

Instead of addressing the underlying causes of insufficient political and cultural legitimacy, i.e., the restrictions on free speech, travel, democratic participation, and legal recourse through the courts and the ability to address these issues in the media, GDR media policies were designed to attract the majority of its youth who listened to Western media outlets. These policies sought to emulate the successful formats and programming in the West, in the hope of binding GDR youth to East German broadcasts and promoting identification with GDR media outlets and programming. Innovations in broadcasting initiated by these objectives were far-reaching, and included first, the introduction of Western moderation styles; second, catering to segmented music audiences while slightly reducing the predominance of political propaganda in some youth broadcasts; third, creating informative music magazine shows with background information on the capitalist pop world; fourth, assessments of GDR popular music based on commercial criteria; fifth, creating chart radio shows for generating popularity, innovation, and obsolescence.

These innovations were introduced in competition with radio stations in the West, most notably with RIAS. For instance, the all-night call-in show *Lange Nacht des RIAS* or *Rock over RIAS* was duplicated on GDR broadcasting networks. RIAS was particularly instrumental in inducing changes to programming at DT 64 and other networks in the 1980s in response to the challenge of the dual broadcasting system in West Germany and its competition with SFB.[16] Finally, several new radio programs were created or adapted to appeal to segmented audience communities, for instance *Parocktikum*[17] to cater to audiences interested in the independent scene, or the *Hard and Heavy* segment in *Beatkiste*, a program continued from Stimme der DDR.

The next section looks at developments at RIAS and DT 64 that led to a greater degree of commercialization. These include: first, the creation of Jugendradio DT 64; second, the construction of a new high-tech pop music recording studio for producing commercially oriented pop to fill up broadcasting time on the new youth radio network, which expanded its operations to twenty hours within the next two years; and third, the use of music dubbing programs to distribute Western music to GDR audiences for their tape collections. These changes will be framed by the reform steps undertaken at RIAS in the 1980s, which made RIAS 2 the most highly developed model for a commercial-format radio station in the entire German-speaking realm. This had serious repercussions for the programming of DT 64 because of the competition between the two networks.

The Creation of Jugendradio DT 64

The West German Constitutional Court's decision in 1984 to permit private radio and television induced changes in both RIAS and East German programming. Two of the most prominent East German radio programs, *Hallo—das Jugendjournal* (on Stimme der DDR) and DT 64 (on the Berliner Rundfunk network) extended their programming to weekend broadcasts (in 1981) and expanded broadcasting into the previously unused 101–108 MHz frequencies in 1984 and 1985.[18] In 1986, all youth broadcasts (on Radio DDR I and II, Stimme der DDR, and Berliner Rundfunk) were consolidated into one network, called Jugendradio DT 64, on the FM frequencies of Berliner Rundfunk. Its main intention, to compete for GDR youth listeners, did not succeed as planned. Other unintended consequences made a severe impact on they way music was produced and distributed in the GDR. For one thing, after its initial eleven-hour daily broadcasting schedule was established, the broadcast day was extended to twenty hours[19] with an early morning magazine show (*Morgenrock*), and programming until 11:30 PM. This meant filling up a comparatively large amount of airtime with new programming where no need had existed before. This put further pressure on the state's popular music production facilities, which had been unable to keep up with demand even before the creation of Jugendradio DT 64. These developments led to greater use of commissioned productions from private recording studios owned by prominent GDR bands. By the mid 1980s, at least twelve of these were operating as suppliers to GDR broadcasting networks, ostensibly supplying "demo tapes," but in reality providing almost-completed productions. The number of song titles produced in private studios rose from eleven in only one studio in 1982 to 130 in twelve studios in 1988.[20]

While these private studios were initially only paid after their recordings passed the scrutiny of the *Lektorate*, they also allowed the bands to experiment with both sounds and lyrics without the direct control and supervision of station bureaucrats and functionaries. Even though equipment investment was left to the studio owners, the bands were willing to operate the studios for their own and others' productions. With the earnings from the commissioned recordings, many of the bands placed their studios at the disposal of younger, more experimental bands, thus allowing a small market for recordings outside the state structures to grow into an "independent scene" with some hallmarks similar to that in the West. Songs produced in this manner were not subject to direct *Lektorat* control, but could instead be broadcast in a program like *Parocktikum* without being officially "archived" for broadcast in other programs.[21] The Stasi was concerned with the uncontrolled production of music outside of government-controlled media because of its potential for release outside of the country, fearing publicity for dissident and nonconformist sentiment and behavior of GDR citizens in the foreign media.

The Construction of a New Pop Studio

Another step in the further commercialization of the GDR media and popular music was taken with the construction of a new pop music studio, designed to promote new productions of a particular kind of pop music catering to mainstream GDR audiences. The reasoning behind this was that innovation and experiment would be left to the private studios, whereas the radio pop studio would focus on the GDR musical mainstream disadvantaged by competitive recordings from the West. To that end, the studio strove to replicate the sophisticated sounds of Western popular music and enable bands (and especially single vocalists with the need to hire a backup band) to compete on the airwaves with Western productions. This strategy was based on the assumption that producing pleasing yet banal international-style pop such as that of IC Falkenberg and Arnulf Wenning would fill up airtime, be accepted as a legitimate cultural expression by GDR audiences, and attract more listeners to GDR radio programs, and thus help them compete with broadcasters like RIAS and SFB, which were expanding their broadcasting to compete with both the private stations in the West and GDR programming. However, to fill up airtime, many of the *Lektorat*'s once seemingly indispensable political and aesthetic criteria for determining the "quality" of a song had to be disregarded or reduced to secondary importance. *Lektorat* officials authorized recordings that they earlier would have rejected for quality reasons. This reliance on quantity rather than pursuing political, ideological, or other criteria derived from an institutional aesthetic traditionally based on the *Schlager* tradition and its audiences in the 1960s and 1970s marks an important step in the commercialization process, which relies on market forces and the overproduction of mediocre recordings in order to generate the occasional hit. In 1987, sixty-three song titles in the rock/pop category were produced in the studio. One year later, the studio produced seventy, and the plan for 1989 projected a total of 100 songs, a goal that was not reached.[22]

GDR radio officials underestimated both the cost and the effort associated with continuously upgrading recording equipment, as well as the ability to acquire the know-how to produce a competitive sound that would not be immediately identifiable as a lower-quality GDR-engineered recording. This was especially evident when GDR bands with the privilege of performing in the West in the 1980s, like the Puhdys, Karat, Silly, Pankow, and others, convinced either Amiga or the radio broadcasting functionaries to employ Western sound engineers and producers. The one or two GDR producers with enough expertise to make a competitive recording were completely overworked by the quantity of production demanded of them to maintain a continuous presence of GDR songs in the programs.[23] Even if the pop studio producers did achieve intermittent success with a few songs, continuous production of successful and popular hit recordings proved to be unattainable, particularly the more exacerbated the crisis of political legitimacy became with the approach of 1989.

Dubbing Programs

One specific form of radio program for GDR stations was the *Mitschneidesendung*, or dubbing program, in which popular songs of the West were broadcast in half-hour segments without interruption in alternation with GDR productions, so that GDR listeners could record them on tape for their own collections. This was due to the unavailability of the Western commercial recordings themselves in the GDR. In order to compensate for this lack, the GDR created a specific one-hour program, *Duett—Musik für den Rekorder* [Duet—music for the recorder].[24] This program was broadcast daily from 3:00 to 4:00 PM on the Berliner Rundfunk network, before the creation of Jugendradio DT 64. The program was aired in two parts, one before the news at 3:30, and one part after the news from 3:35 to 4:00 PM. It was preproduced weeks before the broadcast date and featured an announcer of the titles, who gave a short introduction about each band or vocalist before all the music was played.

This kind of program required that GDR youth already be familiar with recordings that were available to them not through GDR record stores or radio shows but by listening to Western radio stations. The compensatory character was evident in that music on tape was not as readily accessible as were LP records. Also, substantial symbolic and monetary value was attached to the possession of the vinyl recording, even if its importation was not prohibited, which it often was. Furthermore, many GDR youths assigned great symbolic value to collections of these tape recordings, and spent hours at a time waiting to record songs that they needed for their collections.[25] Another factor was the necessity of producing newer radio cassette recorders that could record directly to an audiocassette. GDR radiocassette recorders were notoriously unreliable and prone to failure. In addition, audiocassettes themselves were fairly expensive and sometimes difficult to obtain in retail outlets, although they were readily available in *Intershop* stores for Western currency. The cassette-based independent scene solved this supply problem by requiring empty cassettes to be traded for fully recorded ones of the favorite bands. The hurdles in obtaining the commercial vinyl LPs represent a continuous reminder of the subordinate, discriminatory, and humiliating position of GDR youth on the international pop-music market. The dependence of tape collections on the whims of program producers further exacerbated feelings of resentment and frustration.

Changes to RIAS 2

Two developments at RIAS contributed to a further commercialization of the media landscape in both German states. The first was the program reform from 1980 to 1982, an attempt at a consensual, inclusive programming reform that was ultimately rejected by the RIAS management for both political and financial reasons. The second attempt at reform was more successful. While it seemed to accommodate the reform wishes of the newer programmers at RIAS who pushed for the supremacy of popular music as the primary path to political and ideological influence among East German audiences, their triumph over the historically dominant faction promoting the preeminence of ideological and political broadcasts at the expense of popular music was short-lived. The rigor with which a new commercially modeled station identity and music programming regime were installed by a series of politically connected station managers and department heads led to a large exodus of broadcast personalities involved in popular music who had originally supported the reform, but who were appalled by the transformation of RIAS 2[26] into a commercial radio format that severely restricted their autonomy and choice of music styles.

The First "Democratic" RIAS Reform, 1980–1982

The first effort[27] to revamp the programming of RIAS in the 1980s centered around the issue of creating a separate musical image for the second of two RIAS channels, RIAS II, with its highly successful afternoon magazine program called *Treffpunkt*, broadcast Monday to Saturday between 4:00 and 6:00 PM. On the basis of survey data and letters sent to the radio station, the advocates of creating a separate identity for RIAS II[28] thought that this identity should be rooted in the distinction of two separate audiences: the first audience comprised youths whose musical experiences started with the Beatles in the mid 1960s and was based in international, English-language pop. In the eyes of supporters, this group would best be served by a predominance of this kind of music in all of the RIAS II programming, whereas RIAS I would retain the more traditionally oriented, older audiences whose music tastes would be based in the German *Schlager*. The younger group of advocates for a separate identity for RIAS II also believed that it should have its own separate morning magazine show, catering to the same musical tastes and information needs as the rest of RIAS II programming. The older generation, based in the politics, history, and foreign affairs departments, wanted to retain the traditional model, whereby these departments were responsible not only for the news and information content on both channels, but for the music as well. According to their thinking, the music choice was less important than the political content in broadcasts to the East.[29] Unlike the other faction, they did not distinguish music audiences according to tastes and experiences, and disregarded the suggestions of the *L-Musik* (*leichte*

Musik, or "easy-listening music") division to choose music according to its popularity on the pop charts. The youth music faction countered that the musical identity of a particular channel was crucial for forming political viewpoints. The impasse generated in this conflict prevented sweeping structural reforms from being implemented in RIAS programming, and in 1982 the fifteen-member committee resigned in protest when only slight changes were introduced to the program, after the political, foreign, and information departments refused to go along with it and the changes proved to be over budget.[30]

This first reform effort represented a setback for the faction supporting the broadcasting of more commercially oriented youth music, and their attempts to anchor the concept of music identity as a primary factor in station identity at the expense of political ideology. However, it paved the way for more rigorous and drastic changes. In the second attempt, this faction would see many of its ideas implemented, but it would be disappointed with the extent to which the commercial model became a dictatorial imperative that abolished this faction's autonomy and prevented it from broadcasting more diverse, avant-garde, and innovative music.

The Second "Commercial" Reform

On 31 July 1984, newly named RIAS superintendent Peter Schiwy commissioned Munich Media consultant Dr. Klaus Schönbach to evaluate the media market and media usage by listeners and complete a position paper with suggestions for changing the program structure and content of RIAS. Schönbach's report was based on thinking from the first media reform campaign, giving primacy to music in delineating the attraction and identity of the RIAS programs, and thus was in step with the faction of the *L-Musik* division. The final version of the report, submitted on 30 November 1984,[31] was approved by the RIAS management on 29 April 1985 and became the foundation for a new program structure, with a new reformed RIAS II at its core, and a strict distinction between the programs of RIAS 1 and 2, which became the new designations for each program. In the course of these transformations, new program directors sympathetic to these changes were brought in to ensure that *Treffpunkt* as well as other programs on RIAS 2, like the innovative *Music Special*, adhered to the strict programming requirements regarding music choice, verbal content, and style.

The new station identity of RIAS 2 was rooted in a unified concept of music based on the perceived needs of listeners between 19 and 35 years old. In addition to restricting spoken contributions in all programs to 3.5

minutes in length,[32] the concept required the carefully prescribed use of several dozen stylistically different new station jingles for each particular program, according to management guidelines regarding their frequency and placement.[33] Not only was the usage of previous jingles or even self-made jingles prohibited, no divergence from these guidelines was allowed for any moderator or disc jockey. After the start of Jugendradio DT 64, RIAS Program Director Gerhard Besserer decreed a change in the music choices broadcast in *Treffpunkt* and other RIAS 2 programs to reflect a more unified and moderate "color" based on the systematic use of four different types of music, designated by "baskets" (*Körbe*) of types: A (RIAS 2-Top-60), B (oldies, older than 1980, super-oldies, and popular super-oldies), C (top hits from Germany, Great Britain, and the U.S., as well as Italy and France), and D (new releases and LP tracks). Inside of an hour, five A-titles should be played and in the course of the 24 hours these should be played a second time.[34] All spoken reports were also to be banned from music programs.

After the implementation of the new RIAS 2 plans, the *Treffpunkt* team lost its autonomy and was placed under the direct supervision of the RIAS 2 program director, leading to the transfer of the head of the youth department, Richard Kitchigin, to the sports department. Other *Treffpunkt* employees transferred to RIAS 1, which focused on political and information programs with musical framing.[35] Also, the rock music department was removed from the *L-Musik* division, prompting the resignation of most of the nine members of the rock department. The most bitter confrontation was between Siegfried Schmidt-Joos and both the new program director Gerhard Besserer and his program manager Jörg Brüggemann. Schmidt-Joos sought to defend innovative programming and the autonomy of his show *Music Special*. His bid ended unsuccessfully when his special relationship to the upper-echelon RIAS-management was terminated upon the installation of the new superintendent Bernhard Rohe in 1987. Schmidt-Joos left RIAS in November 1987.

Discursive Closure and Global Capitalist Cultural Management

The DT 64 changes and the RIAS reforms represent two different kinds of state response to the commercialization process in the cultural industries. They entail two different kinds of policy strategies directly affecting the distribution of popular music, while enabling small collectives of creators in the recording industry to produce music for distribution through the media. While these bands, sound engineers, producers, and studio technicians could, within their financial means, create music in their own studios and thus have relatively autonomous control over their creations, the media policies of both RIAS and DT 64 were directed more toward managing and controlling the circulation of these products on the domestic, and even international, markets. In the GDR, the control of these products was overpoliticized and ideologized, while the control exerted by the newly reformed RIAS 2 was by the highly monopolized popular music industry's political and ideological advocates of a market economy, who were brought in to manage the station's identity in the newly privatized media landscape of West Berlin. In both cases, managing the station's image and identity through music programming was crucial, coinciding with Louw's and Hesmondhalgh's views about the increasing prominence of the cultural industries in the reproduction of the capitalist system. Both broadcasters were positioning themselves on the highly competitive Berlin market of dual broadcasting, in which private broadcasting outlets were now participating as well.

The DT 64 programming changes were precipitated by the influence of the Western media inside the GDR. Audiences were empowered to establish their own relationship to Western popular music in spite of hegemonic discourse against many forms of the music. The capitalist industry's ability to insert itself into the circulation of cultural and symbolic goods in the GDR meant the incorporation of the country into the global circulation of popular music products, albeit as a subordinate and peripheral outpost. GDR youth were drawn to Western radio stations because they offered alternative and supplemental political viewpoints and musical experiences to those of the GDR state radio. In addition, the music shows seemed less politicized than those in the GDR, and offered critical insights into Western society and the music scene. The radio stations of the West also helped construct a mediated network of like-minded, culturally and musically conscious fans that reached beyond the narrow confines of the GDR. Finally, West German media symbolized the spectacular and extraordinary, embodying the fun, excitement, innovation, and freedom that was missing from the experience of daily life in the GDR.

While commercializing changes to DT 64 opened up new spaces for social and cultural narratives within a system that prohibited alternative views of social and political development, the commercialization of RIAS programming instituted by the second reform wave in the late 1980s represented a restriction of previously open spaces and autonomy afforded to radio producers for alternative narratives. Reform-oriented producers and editors like Siegfried Schmidt-Joos, Olaf Leitner, and others originally supported the reforms. In the beginning, they saw no incompatibility between steps to increase the broadcasting of more songs popularized by the commercial recording industry on the one hand, and their efforts to distribute more innovative and culturally challenging, but also less popular music narratives on the other.

Cross-border media influences involved making certain kinds of music accessible for GDR audiences and establishing aesthetic criteria in popular music for GDR artists and audiences. They also introduced a completely new way of thinking on how to produce, distribute, and consume music, and how to create and manage cultural industries. They contributed to changing social discourse in the GDR by inserting other narratives and cultural and musical experiences into the creation, management, and circulation of symbolic goods on the domestic GDR market. This happened in the face of an explicit counterstrategy, vigorously pursued by the GDR from the 1950s and 1960s into the 1970s, that cast GDR popular music as an alternative to the capitalist entertainment industry. The evolution in the GDR of a new popular music industry that was integrated as a subaltern sector of the global capitalist entertainment market helped to undermine the GDR strategy of economic and industrial autarchy, and aided efforts at cultural self-sufficiency and autonomy that persisted until the mid and even late 1970s.

Any attempt by GDR authorities to attain discursive closure or maintain a hegemonic stance with regard to popular music, its social and political role in society, and its use by audiences, was always a tentative accomplishment which depended on the degree of legitimacy provided to the government and the Party by the people in general and audience communities in particular. The continuing legitimacy deficit prompted by consumer shortages, lack of democracy and openness, and the loss of the utopian ideals embodied in the notion of "real existing socialism" in the 1980s were the basis for shifting loyalties that eventually led to the fall of the Berlin Wall and the dissolution of the GDR.

Notes

1. See Klaus Arnold and Christoph Classen, "Radio in der DDR," in *Pop und Propaganda*, ed. Klaus Arnold and Christoph Classen (Berlin, 2004), 13–25.
2. Ibid., 18.
3. Ibid., 16
4. Ibid., 20.
5. Ibid., 19.
6. Eric Louw, *The Media and Cultural Production* (London, 2001), 62; David Hesmondhalgh, *The Cultural Industries* (London, 2002), 3.
7. See especially Jürgen Marten and Holger Martin, *Wie ist Kultur planbar?* (Berlin, 1981).

8. Police and the state security service applied this discourse to social and political phenomena manifested in popular music culture, such as youths hitchhiking around the country to various concerts, getting drunk, and behaving in what the police considered "disorderly" fashion. To prevent these "special incidents" (*besondere Vorkommnisse*) which revealed non-Socialist or anti-Socialist behavior, bands were banned or their concerts restricted. Also, song lyrics were considered political ideology and proscribed for being "nihilist," "pessimist," "unfriendly to the working class," or "ideologically deviant."
9. For the story of how this was manifested in various subcultural scenes in the GDR, see *Wir wollen immer artig sein*, ed. Ronald Galenza and Heinz Havemeister (Berlin, 1999). See also Michael Rauhut and Thomas Kochan, eds., *Bye Bye, Lübben City* (Berlin, 2004) for oral histories and other stories.
10. See for instance City. *Am Fenster*, recorded by Thomas Otto (Berlin, 1997), particularly the interview with Alfred Roesler on producing the album "Casablanca," 296–317.
11. I will be using Sigrid Meuschel's distinction between loyalty and legitimacy: cf. *Legitimation und Parteiherrschaft in der DDR* (Frankfurt, 1992). She explains that with loyalty, "individuals orient themselves according to subjective interests or values that can be pursued independent of a nonshared offical purposiveness and valorization," while legitimacy is a more comprehensive coincidence of socially dominant values and norms of the political system (p. 23, author's translation).
12. Two books contain oral histories and reminiscences from band members about this: Klaus Renft, *Zwischen Liebe und Zorn*, ed. Hans-Dieter Schütt (Berlin: Schwarzkopf & Schwarzkopf, 1997), and Delle Kriese, ed., *Nach der Schlacht* (Berlin, 1998).
13. Michael Rauhut, *Schalmei und Lederjacke* (Berlin, 1996), 67–127.
14. For the story of Freygang's treatment by the cultural authorities from the viewpoint of the leader of the band, André Greiner-Pol, see the autobiographical narrative *Peitsche Osten Liebe* (Berlin, 2000). If a band was not licensed by the district cultural authorities to perform, or had its performance license rescinded, like Freygang, the band was excluded from GDR radio networks.
15. For details on these studios, consult Larkey, *Rotes Rockradio*, especially chapter 2 on the *Lektorate* and chapter 3 on the modernization steps undertaken by the official radio networks.
16. For details on how RIAS shows were emulated, see Larkey, *Rotes Rockradio*, chapter 6.
17. For more information on *Parocktikum*, see Larkey, *Rotes Rockradio*, 171–175.
18. See *Vorschlag über die weitere Entwicklung des Rundfunks der DDR in den Jahren 1985 bis 1990*, 22 Oct. 1984, Barch, DR 6/942, 1.
19. The eleven hours of broadcast time on Jugendradio DT 64 were maintained for about a year, until around the end of 1987, when the broadcasting day was extended to twenty hours.
20. See "Zuarbeit zum Bilanzmaterial Rundfunk in Vorbereitung des Kongresses der Unterhaltungskunst am 1. und 2. März 1989," 7 January 1989 (DRA repository Potsdam-Babelsberg, HA Musik/Abt. JM 1989, 1).
21. For an explanation on the concept of "archiving" for supplying music to all of the radio network's programs, see Larkey, *Rotes Rockradio*, 100f.
22. See Walter Cikan, "Entwurf zum Bilanzmaterial Rundfunk in Vorbereitung des Kongresses der Unterhaltungskunst am 1. und 2. März 1989" (DRA repository Potsdam-Babelsberg, Historisches Archiv, HA Musik, Abt. JM 1989, 1).
23. See the critique of the *Lektorat* work by Walter Cikan, "Die Qualität der DDR-Musik

unter dem Einfluss zunehmender Internationalisierung" (DRA repository Potsdam-Babelsberg, Historisches Archiv, HA Musik, Abt. TM 1985, 1ff.).
24. For an extensive analysis of the moderation and music in the program *Duett—Musik für den Rekorder*, please see Larkey, *Rotes Rockradio*, 150–158.
25. Some of these complaints were lodged in letters to the networks and the program producers, who were quick to assure their irate listeners that there were special programs for recording their songs. Some of these letters and the complaints are analyzed in Larkey, *Rotes Rockradio*, 311–328. GDR listeners tried to dub all songs broadcast in the programs, but ran into difficulties when the disc jockeys or announcers interrupted them with information or other kinds of verbiage that were a part of the program, but detracted from the dubbing of the complete song or instrumental.
26. In this chapter, the use of Roman numerals to designate the first and second channels of RIAS (RIAS I, RIAS II) will be restricted to the period before the second program reform in 1986, while Arabic numbers (RIAS 1, RIAS 2) will designate the two channels after the second reform.
27. Most information on this first reform effort was contained in position papers completed during the consultations the fifteen-member committee comprising representatives from most of the departments. See "Abschließendes Positionspapier zum Entwurf der Arbeitsgruppe Programm-Reform—nach kritischer Durchsicht des Programm-Vorschlags von Kundler," 15 February 1982 (DRA repository Potsdam-Babelsberg, Historisches Archiv, RIAS 6/91/1).
28. Siegfried Schmidt-Joos, Olaf Leitner, and Walter Bachauer wrote position papers explaining the need to distinguish both channels in terms of the music listening experiences and tastes of different audiences. See Walter Bachauer, "Vorschläge zu einer generellen Reform der RIAS-Musikprogramme innerhalb des existierenden Programmrahmens," n.d. (DRA repository Potsdam-Babelsberg, Historisches Archiv, RIAS 10/92/2). See also Olaf Leitner, "Blick über die Mauer, oder: Der Versuch, eine für beendet erklärte Diskussion noch einmal in Schwung zu bringen," in *Beiträge zur Programm-Debatte*, ed. RIAS-Berlin, April 1981, DRA repository Potsdam-Babelsberg, Historisches Archiv, RIAS 6/92/1. See also Siegfried Schmidt-Joos, "Konzept eines zweiten Morgenprogramms" (DRA repository Potsdam-Babelsberg, Historisches Archiv, RIAS 10/92/2).
29. See "Vorlage der Abt. Aktuelles zur geplanten Programmstruktur-Reform vom 23. April 1981" (DRA repository Potsdam-Babelsberg, Historisches Archiv, RIAS 6/92/1, 1).
30. This was the reaction to Program Director Herbert Kundler, who although generally supportive of the idea of separating RIAS I and II on the basis of different music tastes and experiences, nonetheless was skeptical about the whole reform project. When the technical and financial barriers proved to be prohibitive under current conditions, he called off the reform attempt and implemented only slight changes to the programming. See Herbert Kundler, "Programm-Innovation," 24 April 1981, in *Beiträge zur Programm-Debatte*, ed. RIAS-Berlin, Part IV, April 1981 (DRA repository Potsdam-Babelsberg, Historisches Archiv, RIAS 6/94/1). On the resignation of the reform committee, see "Protokoll über die außerordentliche Sitzung der Arbeitsgruppe," 27 April 1982, ed. Arbeitsgruppe Strukturreform (DRA repository Potsdam-Babelsberg, Historisches Archiv, RIAS 6/92/1, 1).
31. See "Radiohören heute: Umrisse einer neuen Programmkonzeption für den RIAS," 12 November 1984. This draft was slightly reworked and implemented along with a new program concept for RIAS 2, which was adopted on 10 September 1985. See "Anlage zum Schreiben von Gerhard Besserer an Chairmen, Intendant, Direktoren,

Hauptabteilungsleiter und Abteilungsleiter," 10 September 1985 (DRA repository Potsdam-Babelsberg, Historisches Archiv, RIAS 29/95/20).
32. These changes were contained in a new design concept for RIAS 2 by Thomas Dittrich from the *L-Musik* division and based on Schönbach. See "Zur Programmreform RIAS-Berlin (Dittrich), Anlage zum Schreiben an Schiwy," 4 March 1985 (DRA repository Potsdam-Babelsberg, Historisches Archiv, RIAS 5/98/93).
33. These requirements were laid out in a series of memoranda sent to those in the *L-Musik* division by Program Director Besserer, who compiled a detailed list of different jingles that would be required. See the letter from Besserer to the *L-Musik*, Youth, and News divisions from 29 September 1985 (DRA repository Potsdam-Babelsberg, Historisches Archiv, RIAS 9/92/308), explaining that because no other suggestions had been made, he would commission a series of new jingles for RIAS 2 programs. See also the letter of 9 October 1985 from Besserer to the *L-Musik*, Youth, Sports, News, and Magazines divisions (DRA repository Potsdam-Babelsberg, Historisches Archiv, RIAS 5/98/11).
34. See "Anlage RIAS 2, *Musikschema zu vorgesehenen Musik- und Layout-Korrekturen*," n.d. (DRA repository Potsdam-Babelsberg, Historisches Archiv RIAS 5/98/11).
35. Details of this development can be found in Larkey, *Rotes Rockradio*, 266–70.

Bibliography

Arnold, Klaus, and Christoph Classen. "Radio in der DDR: Einleitung." In *Pop und Propaganda: Radio in der DDR*, ed. Klaus Arnold and Christoph Classen (Berlin: Christoph Links Verlag, 2004), 13–25.

Bachauer, Walter. "Vorschläge zu einer generellen Reform der RIAS-Musikprogramme innerhalb des existierenden Programmrahmens." DRA repository Potsdam-Babelsberg, Historisches Archiv, RIAS 10/92/2.

Besserer, Gerhard. Letter to the *L-Musik*, Youth, and News divisions, 29 September 1985. DRA repository Potsdam-Babelsberg, Historisches Archiv, RIAS 9/92/308.

———. Letter to the *L-Musik*, Youth, Sports, News, and Magazines divisions, 9 October 1985. DRA repository Potsdam-Babelsberg, Historisches Archiv, RIAS 5/98/11.

Cikan, Walter. "Die Qualität der DDR-Musik unter dem Einfluss zunehmender Internationalisierung." DRA repository Potsdam-Babelsberg, Historisches Archiv, HA Musik, Abt. TM 1985.

———. "Entwurf zum Bilanzmaterial Rundfunk in Vorbereitung des Kongresses der Unterhaltungskunst am 1. und 2. März 1989." DRA repository Potsdam-Babelsberg, Historisches Archiv, HA Musik, Abt. JM. 1989.

Dittrich, Thomas. "Zur Programmreform RIAS-Berlin (Dittrich), Anlage zum Schreiben an Schiwy," 4 March 1985. DRA Standort Potsdam-Babelsberg, Historisches Archiv, RIAS 5/98/93.

Galenza, Ronald, and Heinz Havemeister, eds. *Wir wollen immer artig sein…: Punk, New Wave, HipHop, Independent-Szene in der DDR 1980–1990*. Berlin: Schwarzkopf & Schwarzkopf, 1999.

Greiner-Pol, André. *Peitsche Osten Liebe. Das Freygang-Buch*. Berlin: Schwarzkopf & Schwarzkopf, 2000.

Hesmondhalgh, David. *The Cultural Industries*. London: Sage Publications, 2002.

Kriese, Delle, ed. *Nach der Schlacht: Die Renft-Story—von der Band selbst erzählt.* Berlin: Schwarzkopf & Schwarzkopf, 1998.
Kundler, Herbert. "Programm-Innovation." 24 April 1981. In *Beiträge zur Programm-Debatte*, ed. RIAS-Berlin, Part IV, April 1981, DRA repository Potsdam-Babelsberg, Historisches Archiv, RIAS 6/94/1.
Larkey, Edward. *Rotes Rockradio: Populäre Musik und die Kommerzialisierung des DDR-Rundfunks.* Berlin: LIT-Verlag, 2007.
Leitner, Olaf. "Blick über die Mauer, oder: Der Versuch, eine für beendet erklärte Diskussion noch einmal in Schwung zu bringen." In *Beiträge zur Programm-Debatte*, ed. RIAS-Berlin, April 1981, DRA repository Potsdam-Babelsberg, Historisches Archiv, RIAS 6/92/1.
Louw, Eric. *The Media and Cultural Production.* London: Sage Publications, 2001.
Marten, Jürgen, and Holger Martin. *Wie ist Kultur planbar?* Berlin: Dietz Verlag, 1981.
Meuschel, Sigrid. *Legitimation und Parteiherrschaft in der DDR.* Frankfurt am Main: Suhrkamp Taschenbuchverlag, 1992.
Otto, Thomas, ed. *City. Am Fenster: Die Band, die Songs, die Story.* Berlin: Schwarzkopf & Schwarzkopf, 1997.
Rauhut, Michael. *Schalmei und Lederjacke. Udo Lindenberg, BAP, Underground: Rock und Politik in den achtziger Jahren.* Berlin: Schwarzkopf & Schwarzkopf, 1996.
Rauhut, Michael, and Thomas Kochan, eds. *Bye Bye, Lübben City. Bluesfreaks, Tramps und Hippies in der DDR.* Berlin: Schwarzkopf & Schwarzkopf, 2004.
Renft, Klaus. *Zwischen Liebe und Zorn. Die Autobiographie.* Ed. Hans-Dieter Schütt. Berlin: Schwarzkopf & Schwarzkopf, 1997.
Schmidt-Joos, Siegfried. "Konzept eines zweiten Morgenprogramms." DRA repository Potsdam-Babelsberg, Historisches Archiv, RIAS 10/92/2.

Further documents

From the Federal Archives:
"Vorschlag über die weitere Entwicklung des Rundfunks der DDR in den Jahren 1985 bis 1990." 22 Oct. 1984, Barch, DR 6/942.

From the *Deutsches Rundfunkarchiv:*
"Zuarbeit zum Bilanzmaterial Rundfunk in Vorbereitung des Kongresses der Unterhaltungskunst am 1. und 2. März 1989." 7 January 1989. DRA repository Potsdam-Babelsberg, HA Musik/Abt. JM 1989
"Abschließendes Positionspapier zum Entwurf der Arbeitsgruppe Programm-Reform—nach kritischer Durchsicht des Programm-Vorschlags von Kundler." 15 February 1982, DRA repository Potsdam-Babelsberg, Historisches Archiv, RIAS 6/91/1.
"Vorlage der Abt. Aktuelles zur geplanten Programmstruktur-Reform vom 23. April 1981." DRA repository Potsdam-Babelsberg, Historisches Archiv, RIAS 6/92/1.
"Anlage zum Schreiben von Gerhard Besserer an Chairmen, Intendant, Direktoren, Hauptabteilungsleiter und Abteilungsleiter," 10 September 1985. DRA Standort Potsdam-Babelsberg, Historisches Archiv, RIAS 29/95/20.
"Anlage RIAS 2, *Musikschema zu vorgesehenen Musik- und Layout-Korrekturen*," n.d. DRA repository Potsdam-Babelsberg, Historisches Archiv RIAS 5/98/11.
"Radiohören heute: Umrisse einer neuen Programmkonzeption für den RIAS," 12 November 1984. DRA repository Potsdam-Babelsberg, Historisches Archiv RIAS 5/98/92.

Chapter 4

THE ENEMY WITHIN
(De)Dramatizing the Cold War in U.S. and West German Spy TV from the 1960s

Marcus M. Payk

The preeminent symbol of the Cold War was the atomic bomb, and the threat of a nuclear Armageddon hovered relentlessly over humankind between the late 1940s and the early 1990s. While the complex political, social, and cultural effects of this prime Cold War angst have been the subject of many books and papers,[1] my approach is slightly different. I am interested in the "minor" fears of this conflict: those we are generally familiar with as the classic themes of espionage and counterintelligence—Communist infiltration, subversion, the theft of military arcana, the abduction of scientists, etc. But instead of concentrating on "real" covert missions during the Cold War, I am concerned with the depiction and dramatization of these topics in U.S. and West German TV series from the 1960s, reading those entertainment narratives as a characteristic expression of widespread fears in society. The new cultural history has repeatedly pointed out that media narratives express the mentalities dominant in a society, and that they "reveal the work of ideology and discourse in both plot and presentation."[2] Even though their impact on social structures or individual mindsets may be vague, one can read media products as both the expression and the representation of cultural constellations in shifting historical contexts.

The influence of the Cold War and its competing ideologies on the culture of the societies involved has attracted increasing attention in recent years. Summed up under the heading of a unique "Cold War Culture," many studies have introduced new issues and methodologies or raised new questions in Cold War research, often tackling the construction of identities or the roles of race, class, and gender.[3] In this context, much research has been devoted to Cold War Culture in film. While taking the findings of these studies into consideration, I want to draw attention away from the silver screen and to the TV screen, arguing that during the 1960s the film industry faltered while television was well on its way to becoming the dominant medium. Admittedly, the development of television and its impact varied widely across countries during this phase of the Cold War. While the United States was the uncontested pacemaker, other countries like West Germany followed with a delay of several years. In both countries, however, TV entertainment grew to be a major factor in the lives of many people during the 1960s, epitomizing moral standards and societal values.[4]

In order to explore the complex interplay between these societal principles, the internal logic of entertainment media, and the variable influence of the Cold War, I will concentrate on two TV series from this decade: *Mission: Impossible* from the United States and *John Klings Abenteuer* from West Germany. Comparing a North American and a European example of TV entertainment offers insights into the similarities and differences between the two nations as well as the modes of cultural transfer between the continents.[5] After a general overview of espionage fiction as part of the entertainment industry, I will analyze the plot structures and their highly standardized narratives of two episodes from these TV series within the framework of the Cold War. Aside from the national differences that can be found in these two series, I am especially interested in the transformation and dedramatization of Cold War ideology and dichotomy during a decade of rapid cultural and social change.

Espionage Fiction as Media Genre

The fear and fascination of espionage as a widespread phenomenon in both society and the media arose at the time of World War I, expressing anxieties about an invisible menace under the surface of a society in crisis. In contrast to more easily recognizable threats, spies could be suspected almost anywhere, fostering the popular imagination of subversive powers and occasionally sparking attacks against particular individuals or groups.[6] On the other hand, myth-building "master spies" like the notorious Mata

Hari brought the conventions and fascinations of espionage to the attention of a large public. As a result, espionage fiction was established as a subgenre of pulp criminal literature in the first half of the twentieth century, quickly spreading across all media formats of the entertainment industry. The popular depiction of spies and counterintelligence intensified during World War II and the hysterical Red Scare of the early Cold War.[7] In the 1950s, Hollywood developed not only dozens of spy movies with a strong anti-Communist, patriotic sentiment, but also genuine TV espionage series like *I Led Three Lives* (1953–1956), which was based on actual cases and employed a strongly documentary approach.[8] Other media products fictionalized the intrusion of a foreign power in the shape of Native Americans, monsters, or space aliens.[9] In contrast to the numerous productions from the U.S., West German film and TV makers were more reluctant and reserved in picking up espionage motifs. One of the notable exceptions is *Menschen im Netz* (Men in the Net) (1959), admittedly a movie, or the semirealistic TV series *Die fünfte Kolonne* (The Fifth Column) (1963–1968).[10]

Although the spy genre has seldom met with critical acclaim, its popularity among the audience began to rise steeply by the early 1960s. The highly profitable James Bond movies like *Dr. No* (1962), *From Russia with Love* (1963), or *Goldfinger* (1964) initiated and pioneered a downright "spy craze" in the entertainment industry.[11] The huge success of these films inspired countless other productions with espionage-themed content, often displaying fantastic technological possibilities that underscored the industrial progress of the West and at the same time transferred it into a utopian realm. Basically, there were two types of narrative: action-oriented stories with heavy use of technical gadgets and simple good-versus-evil storylines on the one hand, and melancholy, sometimes cynical stories like *The Spy Who Came in from the Cold* (1965) or *Funeral in Berlin* (1966) on the other, to name only two of the more prominent examples.

In contrast to these movies, popular television series dealing with espionage pursued a slightly different approach. Low budgets and the demands of TV broadcast programming enforced not only a restricted use of sensational and expensive special effects, but also a certain internal structure, like resorting to standard plots or an easily recognizable group of central characters. These patterns were already quite common in radio serials at the time, and they were transferred to TV family dramas and crime series with the advent of the new medium in the 1950s. This often leads to the misinterpretation that TV espionage series were mere crime stories. Viewed from the perspective of Cold War history, however, one cannot help but notice dozens of traits that were associated with the antagonism of the two rival superpowers and its impact on society, for example the clear-cut dichotomy of two opponents, the necessity of taking sides, and the unstable relationship between governmental institutions and private citizens. Within the general and stable framework of the series, societal and cultural value settings inseparably linked with the Cold War were thus replayed, condensed, and dramatized, making the spy genre one of the most popular fiction themes of the mid 1960s.[12]

"The Short Tail Spy": *Mission: Impossible*

My first example is a 45-minute episode taken from the television show *Mission: Impossible*, broadcast on CBS between September 1966 and March 1973 in about 168 episodes. This series dealt with the adventures and operations of a team of secret agents (the Impossible Missions Force, IMF), employed, but not officially acknowledged, by the United States government (or, to be more precise, by an anonymous agency called "the secretary"). The team is sent on covert missions to combat dictators, reveal spies and traitors, or recover stolen military and technological secrets, thus silently protecting U.S. security interests at home and abroad. Its leader is Dan Briggs (Steven Hill), later replaced by Jim Phelps (Peter Graves), who is usually charged with forming a mission team composed of various agents who come from a multitude of professions and walks of life. The core group in the early seasons typically includes Cinnamon Carter (Barbara Bain), a fashion model and actress, Barney (Greg Morris), an electronics genius, and Rollin Hand (Martin Landau), a noted actor, escape artist, and magician.[13]

To analyze some of the Cold War anxieties comprised in this series, I will mainly concentrate on the episode "The Short Tail Spy," broadcast on 17 December 1966. The plot line is easily summarized: The Impossible Missions Force team learns that two rival spy groups from a foreign—supposedly Eastern/Russian—power are active in the United States, both intending to assassinate a highly acclaimed professor who has defected to the West. The IMF must prevent this assassination at all costs; and to neutralize the younger, more dangerous of these two groups, attractive agent Cinnamon Carter tries to seduce its chief assassin Andrei Fetyukov. The two play a dangerous romantic game while Briggs convinces Shtemenko from the older group that Fetyukov has betrayed him to the Americans. This intrigue works out, and while Shtemenko is forced to leave the country without doing any harm, Fetyukov is arrested in a dramatic showdown.

Even though this episode is neither an example of exceptional TV entertainment nor an aesthetic pleasure, it provides insights into the depiction and dramatization of the Cold War in the mid 1960s. On the surface, the threat posed by the spies operating within U.S. borders is relatively clear. The arcane knowledge embodied in a highly proficient (albeit unworldly) scientist has to be "secured," as it could give one of the two rival sides a decisive advantage. The professor's field of specialization remains unclear in this episode, but standard topics would be rocket science, nuclear science, computers, or electronics—genuine technologies of Cold War rivalry as well as of a mid-century faith in progress and modernity. The empirical and nonideological nature of these fields is usually accompanied by a binary code of its "good," "white," and "civilian" versus its "bad," "black," and "military" utilization. Also, the defection of scientists from East to West (and occasionally from West to East) is a classic subject of the espionage genre during the Cold War, often including the scientist's families (especially their attractive daughters) and/or blackmail as dramaturgical amplifiers.

However, a closer look at the episode "The Short Tail Spy" reveals certain subtextual complexities and ambivalences. First, both the assailants and the defenders of U.S. national security share a tacit form of agreement: in the dense vicinity of the hotel where most of the story takes place, the secret teams get to know each other fairly well, and there is a strange and implicit correspondence between the IMF and the enemy group under the command of Colonel Shtemenko throughout the episode. Both sides share a common interest and form an unspoken alliance by opposing the younger spy group of Colonel Fetyukov, whose aggressions threaten the fragile balance between two established opponents. To get this less hostile "enemy partner" out of the way in the most harmless manner, the IMF sets a trap and photographs Shtemenko in a compromising situation. Shtemenko is hence forced to leave the country, but he does so as a free man, provided with an airline ticket and a mere word of warning never to return to the United States as his only punishment.

The attention then shifts to the sinister business of Fetyukov, who is identified as the real danger. It is interesting that the Eastern master spy reveals ever stronger traits of a mercenary in the course of events. At one point Fetyukov stresses his autonomy from ideals and loyalties and openly admits that he has "never done anything for anybody," working only for himself. This portrayal as not only an immoral killer but an incalculable menace to the equilibrium of spies and counterspies darkens his character even further. However, balance of power, stability, and predictability were central themes of the Cold War, especially during the détente of the 1960s. In contrast to Fetyukov, the group of older spies mirrored and personified these qualities. Even though they were undoubtedly enemies of the "good" side, they had a similar code of honor, identifiable objectives, and no interest in violating the informal rules of the "spy game."

Fetyukov, in turn, is presented not only as a ruthless villain, but also as a womanizer who is known to have killed his former girlfriends—mostly female agents—in cold blood. Even though Cinnamon is warned by Briggs at the very beginning of the episode, she starts to play a dangerous game of seduction and affection with Fetyukov. The true nature of the relationship between the American agent and the Eastern spy remains ambivalent throughout most of the plot, with both Cinnamon and Fetyukov appearing both as passionate lovers and as coolly calculating manipulators. Cinnamon gives a slight hint that her affection for the Eastern master spy might be more than just play-acting for a greater cause only in the very last scene of the episode. In this light, one of Cinnamon's final actions in the story—taking the bullets out of Fetyukov's gun—can be interpreted in two ways: as sabotage of his intentions or as protecting him from a firefight, which would most certainly have resulted in his death.

But with the line between irrational passion and rational restraint blurred, the importance of emotions in the episode's storyline becomes even clearer. There is an intense interplay between the narrative about the shallows and depths of love (and lust) and the narrative about Cold War espionage, both equally charged with fear and insecurity. On the one hand, we can read the complicated love story between Cinnamon and Fetyukov as an expression of the fear that Western women could be seduced and exploited for espionage purposes. Obviously, this has a strong sexual component, associated with devotion, dependence, and eventually the penetration of moral and bodily integrity and national security likewise.[14] A further exploration could link this dimension to widespread fears of new mind-controlling or manipulative psychological techniques developed during the 1950s and 1960s. To give just one example: the contemporary discussion on modern advertising's evoking hidden sexual desires was deeply rooted in the Cold War context as well.[15]

On the other hand, Cinnamon is portrayed as a strong and self-determined woman—a far cry from the hesitant and fearful female stereotypes occasionally used as plot elements in the 1950s. The agent claims to be fully aware of the situation, trying to deceive and mislead the Eastern master spy herself. However, while this might hint at gradual changes in the picture of women in American culture, it also conveys a rather ambivalent message, as the demands of self-control and self-integrity transform the Cold War conflict into an inner crisis and an individual problem. Not the outer enemy is the real fiend; it is one's own self in an entangled contest between loyalty, rationality, and sentiment.

"Der Fall Pünköschky": *John Klings Abenteuer*

For the German case, I will explore some peculiarities of Cold War Culture in the Federal Republic of Germany by taking a closer look at the TV series *John Klings Abenteuer* (The adventures of John Kling). The protagonist's name may be familiar from other contexts, as John Kling is a classic of twentieth-century German pulp fiction.[16] A main character already in dozens of pulp novels in the Weimar Republic and even in the first years of the "Third Reich," he and his humorous sidekick Jones Burte were revived in the 1950s and eventually adapted to a television series by the mid 1960s. Starring Hellmut Lange and Uwe Friedrichsen, twenty-six episodes were produced by TV-Union Berlin on behalf of ZDF (one of the two main public networks in Germany) and broadcast in the early evening program at 6:55 PM (later at 7:10 PM), a prime time in the 1960s.

In the two seasons it ran (1965/66 and 1969/70), audience reception of *John Klings Abenteuer* was quite good, even though it lost slightly to *Percy Stuart*, a comparable TV series also based on a pulp-fiction story and running opposite *John Klings Abenteuer*. As indicated by their names, the protagonists of both series had an aura of Anglo-Saxon descent. Just like James Bond on the movie screen or the characters of *Mission: Impossible* on TV, they symbolized modernity, manliness, and a cosmopolitan flair. These German TV shows also shared a particular fondness for remote countries and exotic locations, fitting perfectly into a time of dramatic international changes like decolonization or the rise of nonaligned movements in some parts of the "Third World."

In contrast to the majority of German TV series, the Cold War served as a narrative background for most (but not all) episodes of *John Klings Abenteuer*. Nearly every episode began with some high-ranking official calling in private investigators John Kling and Jones Burte for a secret assignment that, for some reason or another, could not be executed by the official institutions or regular counterintelligence of the nations in question. As in *Mission: Impossible*, these assignments were rather intricate: finding an abducted rocket scientist, protecting an Arab potentate, securing a chemical formula for oil production, etc.

I want to detail some aspects by closely reading the episode "Der Fall Pünköschky" (The Pünköschky case), telecast on ZDF on 27 October 1965. Just like the example of "The Short Tail Spy" discussed above, this episode adds emotional tribulations and gender issues to the espionage theme. Again, the plot structure is rather simple and predictable: Kling and Burte are called in to investigate the death of a high-ranking Hungarian official called Pünköschky, who had worked at the Ministry of Economic Affairs in Budapest. He was well known as a supporter of economic cooperation with the West, and it soon becomes clear that he did not commit suicide, as was publicly announced. Put in charge by an undisclosed Western agency, Kling and Burte travel behind the "Iron Curtain," where they are assisted by the attractive Communist Party functionary Ilonka. While John Kling is lured into a trap and arrested, Burte and Ilonka find out that a friend of the Pünköschky family, Imre Istevan, is the culprit. Istevan had fallen in love with Marika, Pünköschky's wife, and killed her husband out of jealousy. He also murders Marika when she rejects his advances. In a final confrontation, he confesses his guilt to Ilonka and is arrested before he succeeds in killing her as well.

Several aspects of this narrative are rather striking. The Cold War is very much toned down and reduced to a worry about a possible breakdown of economic negotiations and cooperation between East and West. No direct or indirect links to military or even nuclear threats are provided, and even the harmless shadowing of Kling and Burte by the Hungarian secret police is only employed as a moment of comic relief. Instead, the story soon breaks down Cold War fronts, as Western secret agents and Eastern officials begin to work together on the murder case. Even though there are slight hints at dissonance within the Party bureaucracy, the smart and charismatic Ilonka is used to portray a Communist "reformist faction" that wants to cooperate with the West—in this particular murder case at any rate. Evidently, this motif hints at the new economic course of Hungary initiated in the mid 1960s by Prime Minister János Kádár, who tried to improve foreign trade with West European Countries and especially with the Federal Republic.[17] These political aspects are not elaborated, however, but rather constitute the background of a general will to collaborate on both sides. Embodied by the main characters, East and West share the mutual intention to maintain stability between the blocs and to continue efforts at (economic) cooperation. This balance even extends to analogies between Eastern and Western rule of law toward the end of the episode, especially when it comes to the persecution of nonpolitical crimes.

This affiliation between East and West is moreover emphasized by the relationship between Burte and Ilonka, which develops in the course of events. No explicit references are made to love or even sexuality, but Burte's behavior evolves from reservation to fondness and affection in a most obvious way. As the humorous, witty, and sometimes frivolous assistant to the cool, gentleman-like character of John Kling, he gently teases Ilonka about the bureaucratic customs of communist Hungary, mixing courtship and critique. In the final showdown, however, Burte fails to protect Ilonka and is easily overwhelmed by main villain Imre Istevan. Unsurprisingly, John Kling suddenly appears on the scene as a superior, nonpartisan sovereign. Assisted by Hungarian police officials, he quickly resolves the situation through the virtues of self-control and emotional distance.

This plot line points at yet another East-West analogy: the emotional and immature tempers of both Burte and Imre Istevan have made them blind, temperamental, and vulnerable, thus endangering stability and balance. In contrast, the sovereignty, discipline, and coolness embodied by John Kling are displayed as the main preconditions for the peaceful coexistence of the blocs. Understanding and cooperation between East and West, as negotiated within the fictional framework of this TV show, can only prosper on a moderate, unbiased, and restrained basis, with ideologies and emotions left aside on both sides. This obviously relates to the actual developments of the 1960s, with the atmosphere between the Western and the Eastern states, between the Federal Republic and the GDR slowly moving toward a détente. As is well known, a new *Ostpolitik* was taking shape, guided by the motto "change through rapprochement," which had been coined by the West German politician Egon Bahr just two years earlier.

To take this point one step further: in the narrative of "Der Fall Pünköschky," the negative and positive impacts of emotions are the same on both sides of the "Iron Curtain." But while affection and jealousy, trust and suspicion are described as universal human feelings, only their control allows for mutual understanding. As in *Mission: Impossible*, Cold War stability depends on emotional control and self-restraint. Politics have to be disentangled from irrational motifs and anxieties. This not only conforms to the technocratic spirit that prevailed in most Eastern and Western societies during the 1960s, but also refers to a major characteristic of the Cold War: every misunderstanding, resentment, or irrational passion harbors the risk of a destructive nuclear chain reaction, as depicted in the satire *Dr. Strangelove; or, How I Learned to Stop Worrying and Love the Bomb* (1964).[18] In a German TV series like *John Klings Abenteuer* there was, of course, little room for such paranoia-ridden burlesque. As in most other media products, order is restored in an essentially happy ending. However, the main message is that the virtues of objectivity and coolness are necessary to preserve—and to restore—the fragile stability of the Cold War.

From Externalization to Introspection

In reassessing these two examples of a West German and a U.S. TV production, one cannot help but notice apparent national differences on the one hand, and striking similarities in the alteration and dedramatization of the Cold War on the other. In the following section, I will discuss these two aspects, concentrating on the varying depictions of the enemy as well as on the role of emotions in these two narratives. Both facets, I would argue, allow us to study in detail how the Cold War was refashioned and modified in the course of the 1960s.

At first glance, the narratives of both episodes seem to replicate the sharp confrontation between East and West. But unlike the vast majority of media products from the 1950s, the U.S. show deliberately tried to avoid any explicit references to the Soviet Union or any other real Eastern bloc country, using implicit references instead. Rather than being marked as Soviet or Russian, almost all of the hideous villains in *Mission: Impossible* appear to be of anonymous Slavic or Baltic origin. Also, enemy countries in this TV series were named "European People's Republic" or "Eastern European Republic" or similar fictitious names. In contrast, the clear reference to communist Hungary in the above-mentioned episode of *John Klings Abenteuer* is a telling exception. Although not repeated in other episodes, this explicit reference hints at the strong semirealistic and "objective" approach of the German TV show. Also, Western countries like France, Great Britain, Italy, or Turkey were often central to the plot structure and added to the special flair of "internationalism." There was only one notable exception: the GDR was never even mentioned in *John Klings Abenteuer*.

While the reservation (or caution) of U.S. TV-makers about clearly marking the villains as Soviets continually increased during the 1960s and into the 1970s, the clumsy "realism" of the West German series avoided the demonization of the enemy from the outset, employing narratives of mutual understanding instead. But both TV shows indicate the beginnings of a fundamental shift. Later episodes of *Mission: Impossible* as well as other series from the U.S.—or Great Britain—were even more advanced, anticipating the latest changes in foreign policy as well as popular opinion. In a time of international détente and the prevalence of a more introspective, self-centered atmosphere in most Western societies,[19] the Eastern bloc was neglected or even abandoned as the prime enemy. Instead, more fantastic opponents came into play, especially large crime cartels that threatened the entire world and often got hold of nuclear weapons or equally destructive devices. A forerunner in this context is the transformation of SMERSH in the James Bond novels, a Soviet counterintelligence agency with the mission to subvert and weaken the West. In the 1960s film version it was changed to SPECTRE, a fictional terrorist organization without any ideology or political agenda but still with a relentless lust for power.[20] A more elaborate variant was introduced in the

TV series *The Man from U.N.C.L.E.*, where ideologically opposed secret agents from the United States and the Soviet Union actually worked together in a constant struggle against a vast criminal organization known as THRUSH.[21] In the series *Get Smart*, this was satirized by the two opposing groups CONTROL versus KAOS.[22] Also, Nazis were revived here and there, as in the *Mission: Impossible* episode "The Legend." In this episode, telecast on 11 February 1967, a clandestine group of top-ranking Nazis intended to reestablish the "Third Reich" in the fictitious South American country "Puerto Ubera." Leaving the imaginary content of a Nazi revival aside, this episode is also a good example of how the growing attention for the concerns of the "Third World" in the late 1950s and 1960s was reproduced in these TV series (as well as in contemporary movies). Many narratives were transferred from the stages of the main Cold War nations—Europe, the United States, and the Soviet Union—to peripheral countries, "banana republics," or desert islands. Again, espionage fiction in literature paved the way for this shift, as some of Graham Green's novels indicate: *Our Man in Havana* (1959) is set in pre-Castro Cuba, *A Burnt-out Case* (1961) in the Belgian Congo, and *The Comedians* (1966) in Haiti. Another good example would once again be the James Bond stories, in both books and films.[23]

While the reluctance to identify TV enemies with "real" enemies as well as the shift toward a more remote and exotic scenery may have facilitated the acceptance of U.S. espionage fiction among European audiences, it also hints at the increasing fictionalization of the Cold War. This tendency is mirrored by the way in which emotions and emotionality were integrated into the plot of espionage narratives. Needless to say, emotions ranging from love to distrust and hate are common ingredients of all kinds of media entertainment, from folk tales to TV series, and at almost all times. Usually they intensify plot structures and function as dramatic amplifiers. Looking at the ways emotions were employed in the dramatization—and dedramatization—of the Cold War, however, we can detect some notable changes in the entertainment media of the 1960s. Especially the binary moral logic of the early Cold War, which was centered on good family virtues as the foundation of national security, versus negative associations of insubordinate behavior, female independence, or permissive sexuality (and, in particular, homosexuality), was slowly broken up. Moral standards, attitudes toward authority, and codes of conduct were increasingly transformed and emotionally refashioned in the course of the 1960s, undermining what has been called "containment culture."[24]

Both *Mission: Impossible* and *John Klings Abenteuer* reflect this cultural liberalization in their own ways. We have seen that the underlying conflict in the narratives is not so much the Cold War, but rather an emotional struggle. Both series suggest that the most dangerous threat to one's own "good order" would result from matters involving morality, emotions, and interpersonal relationships. Consequently, the possible nuclear confrontation of the two superpowers, which might unleash angst on an epic scale, remained abstract and isolated in narratives that drew attention away from big politics to everyday life. There are dozens of TV episodes, movies, books, and comics from the 1960s that can be read as Cold War stories considering the threat posed to national security by some foreign mastermind.[25] In the majority of cases, however, the pivotal point was not so much the aggression of a cunning spy, but rather the ambiguity of the protagonists' emotions, dramatized in patterns of betrayal versus integrity or moral weakness versus human sincerity.

Emotional turmoil of this kind fundamentally challenged the rigid and unambiguous logic of the early Cold War, and allowed for a cynical or ironic distancing of any good-versus-evil dichotomy. New heroes and villains had to be introduced, often followed by the construction of a new masculine rationality for which the wit, self-irony, sex appeal, and coolness of James Bond became the uncontested paradigm. But these innovations also reflect substantial differences between the developments in U.S. and European espionage fiction. Altogether, the American culture industry was much more responsive to new trends, moods, and popular demands, quickly adapting narrative conventions to atmospheric changes in society at large. While the already scant production of spy movies and television programs in West Germany remained entranced by a different reality of the Cold War—a divided country trying to ease tensions across an interior dividing line—U.S. and British productions were free to transform the entire spy genre into an almost apolitical entertainment theme with hilarious, cynical, or melancholy self-references. Whether considering *James Bond*, fast-paced action series like *Mission: Impossible*, *The Man from U.N.C.L.E.*, or satirical shows like *Get Smart*, we can discern a new pop aesthetic superseding traditional styles, as well as new forms of emotionality transcending the moral inhibitions of the 1950s.

These new shows from the United States and Great Britain were quite successful on the European continent as well, soon outrunning any domestic serial and triumphantly dominating at least West German TV screens from the 1970s onward.[26] Even though *John Klings Abenteuer* tried to adapt to the new demands of TV entertainment, its characters still acted within the stale logic of seriousness, sobriety, and objectivity. Interestingly enough, while these narrative customs missed audience expectations of a more relaxed and imaginative form of TV entertainment, their reservation toward any combination of politics and emotions might reflect a nationally encoded restraint, as it can be observed for espionage fiction made in the GDR as well. Here, the alteration of the Manichean setting of the Cold War was even more limited than in West Germany. The DEFA-produced movie *For eyes only—Streng Geheim* (1963) was a box-office hit in the GDR, employing precisely the same narrative pattern found in Western films as well: smart agents who prevent the warmongering efforts of hideous villains. But the film nonetheless maintained strict documentary claims, purporting to be based on a real-life case. In addition, the Eastern reception of Western spy fiction like the James Bond films remained much more charged with an aggressive Cold War rhetoric. For instance, reviews of *Thunderball* (1965) in East German newspapers decried James Bond as a murderer, sexist, and super-agent of anti-humanism who would popularize fascism among Western youth.[27]

Conclusion

Against this backdrop, I would argue that the dedramatization of the Cold War by satirizing it in espionage fiction was a genuinely American form of coping with the cultural demands of the international conflict. It was picked up only hesitantly by German TV makers, but nevertheless strongly welcomed by the audience in the Federal Republic, perhaps reflecting the latter's growing cultural orientation toward the West. Of course, the overtly aggressive rhetoric of the early Cold War was losing ground in almost all societies during the 1960s. After the Cuban Missile Crisis of 1962, international relations slowly moved toward a détente, resulting in the SALT I and II treaties. But—paradoxically enough—it was primarily the U.S. culture industry that fostered a growing dedramatization of the conflict in the public perception through the increasing fictionalization and spectacular exaggeration of the Cold War for the sole purpose of entertainment. In contrast, European approaches to alleviating and mitigating Cold War tensions in the course of the 1960s followed different national traditions, with German narratives, as we have seen, centering mostly on concepts of reconciliation, bloc parity, and stability.

Although the two TV series under scrutiny here only represent a fragment of a broader picture, both hint at the changing significance of the Cold War in Western societies during the 1960s. Instead of perpetuating the binary logic with its aggressive constructions of a "good" versus a "bad" side, these TV series—as well as other media narratives—renegotiated the basic conditions and assumptions of the 1950s. While the abstract threat of a nuclear apocalypse was even further externalized from and repressed in public awareness, a more flexible treatment of the Cold War in entertainment narratives began to take shape, incorporating ideas of cooperation between the superpowers as well as elements of humor, irony, and sarcasm.[28]

More importantly, fears of subversion and hidden danger were internalized and recast as internal conflicts on the levels of both society and the individual. New societal anxieties began to interfere with the Cold War logic, slowly shifting the focus from external intruders to the problems and inner contradictions of one's own side. Spies no longer embodied the absolute evil, and secret agents no longer personified the flawless good. Just as representations of police officers or criminals drastically changed in the late 1960s and early 1970s—first in the U.S., somewhat later in West Germany—it became unclear what the "right side" was all about.[29] In this crisis of confidence, the feared subversion and infiltration of society's emotional integrity shifted from alien intruders to indigenous institutions. The murky business of counterintelligence became a prime object for popular suspicion and distrust among large parts of the population. Espionage fiction rapidly lost its attraction and resonance during the 1970s, whereas government agencies soon displayed a previously unknown dubiousness in real life, reflected most spectacularly by the Watergate affair. In conclusion, one might say that the outer enemy was transformed into—or at least merged with—the enemy within.

Notes

1. See for example Paul Boyer, *By the Bomb's Early Light* (Chapel Hill, 1994). For Germany, cf. Ilona Stölken-Fitschen, *Atombombe und Geistesgeschichte* (Baden-Baden, 1995).
2. John Hartley, *Communication, Cultural and Media Studies* (London, 2006), 154.
3. E.g., Elaine Tyler May, *Homeward Bound* (New York, 1999); Stephen J. Whitfield, *The Culture of the Cold War* (Baltimore, 1991); Peter J. Kuznick and James Gilbert, eds., *Rethinking Cold War Culture* (Washington, 2001); John Fousek, *To Lead the Free World* (Chapel Hill, 2000).
4. Barbara Moore, Marvin R. Bensman, and Jim Van Dyke, *Prime-time Television* (Westport, 2006), 121–170. For Germany, cf. Helmut Kreuzer and Christian W. Thomsen, eds., *Geschichte des Fernsehens in der Bundesrepublik Deutschland* (Munich, 1993–1994).
5. This relationship is often (and imprecisely) called "Americanization"; see, for instance, Alexander Stephan, ed., *The Americanization of Europe* (New York, 2006). However, I will not pick up the discussion about the validity of "Americanization" as a useful category of historical research. See also Victoria de Grazia, *Irresistible Empire* (Cambridge, Mass., 2005), 554–556.
6. John G. Cawelti and Bruce Rosenberg, *The Spy Story* (Chicago, 1987), 34ff.; Florian Altenhöhner, "Spionitis," in *Kollektive Identitäten und kulturelle Innovationen*, ed.

Werner Rammert et al. (Leipzig, 2002), 77–91. For an epistemology of the spy, see also Eva Horn, "Der Spion," in *Grenzverletzer*, ed. Eva Horn, Stefan Kaufmann, and Ulrich Bröckling (Berlin, 2002), 136–155.
7. Timothy Melley, *Empire of Conspiracy* (Ithaca, 2000), 133ff.
8. Nora Sayre, *Running Time* (New York, 1982); Michael Kackman, "Citizen, Communist, Counterspy," *Cinema Journal* 38 (1998): 98–114.
9. Stanley Corkin, *Cowboys as Cold Warriors* (Philadelphia, 2004); Cyndy Hendershot, "The Cold War Horror Film," *Journal of Popular Film and Television* 29 (2001), no. 1: 20–31; David Seed, *American Science Fiction and the Cold War* (Edinburgh, 1999).
10. Ingrid Brück, et al., *Der deutsche Fernsehkrimi* (Stuttgart, 2003), 141–147.
11. Tony Bennett and Janet Woollacott, *Bond and Beyond* (London, 1987); James Chapman, *Licence to Thrill* (London, 1999), 111–114; Jason Mulvihill, "The Golden Age of Bond," parts 1 and 2, *International Journal of Instructional Media* 28 (2001): 225–237 (part 1), 337–353 (part 2).
12. Michael Kackman, *Citizen Spy* (Minneapolis, 2005); Toby Miller, *Spyscreen* (Oxford, 2003), 88–153; Wesley Britton, *Spy Television* (Westport, 2004), 35ff. For an additional overview of the genre of the political thriller and its connection to spy fiction see Brett F. Woods, *Neutral Ground* (New York, 2008).
13. The following is a useful episode guide: Patrick J. White, *The Complete Mission Impossible Dossier* (New York, 1991).
14. See also Melley, *Empire of Conspiracy*, 81ff., 107ff.
15. For Britain, cf. Stefan Schwarzkopf, "'They do it with mirrors,'" *Contemporary British History* 19 (2005), no. 2: 133–150. Cf. also Schwarzkopf's contribution in this volume.
16. Inge Marßolek, "Internationalität und kulturelle Klischees am Beispiel der John-Kling-Heftromane der 1920er und 1930er Jahre," in *Amerikanisierung: Traum und Alptraum im Deutschland des 20. Jahrhunderts*, ed. Alf Lüdtke, Inge Marßolek, and Adelheid von Saldern (Stuttgart: Steiner, 1996), 144–160.
17. Rudolf L. Tökés, *Hungary's Negotiated Revolution* (Cambridge, 1996), 47f.
18. See Charles Maland, "Dr. Strangelove (1964)," in *Hollywood as Historian*, ed. Peter C. Rollins (Louisville, 1998), 190–210.
19. The relationship between foreign affairs and internal protest during the 1960s is discussed in Jeremi Suri, *Power and Protest* (Cambridge, Mass., 2005).
20. Thomas J. Price, "The Changing Image of the Soviets in the Bond Saga," *Journal of Popular Culture* 26 (1992), no. 1: 17–37; Christoph Lindner, "Criminal Vision and the Ideology of Detection," in *The James Bond Phenomenon*, ed. Christoph Lindner (Manchester, 2003), 76–90 (81ff.).
21. Rick Worland, "The Cold War Mannerists," *Journal of Popular Film and Television* 21 (1994): 150–162; Kackman, *Citizen Spy*, 79–98.
22. Kackman, *Citizen Spy*, 99–105.
23. Vivian Halloran, "Tropical Bond," in *Ian Fleming and James Bond*, ed. Edward P. Commentale et al. (Bloomington, 2005), 158–177.
24. Alan Nadel, *Containment Culture* (Durham, 1996). For this transformational period, cf. Arthur Marwick, *The Sixties* (Oxford, 1998).
25. A similar point is made in Worland, "Cold War Mannerists," 151f. The author stresses the increased use of comic and ironic elements in a TV series like "The Man from U.N.C.L.E." in the 1960s.
26. See for instance "Solo nach Emma," *Der Spiegel*, issue 20 (1967), 186.
27. See for example Helga Radmann, "Feuerball als NATO-Reklame-Show," *Thüringische Landeszeitung* (Weimar), 14 January 1966; "James Bond—und kein Ende," *Der*

Neue Weg (Halle), 30 December 1966. See also Peter Ulrich Weiß, "Wo das Wolfsgesetz regiert," in *Umworbener Klassenfeind*, ed. Uta Balbier and Christiane Rösch (Berlin: Christoph Links Verlag, 2006), 160–179. An apolitical article in the West German press would be "So kämpft James Bond!" *Bravo*, 6 December 1965.

28. This development had some forerunners in 1950s movies: cf. John H. Lenihan, "Hollywood Laughs at the Cold War, 1947–1961," in *Hollywood as Mirror*, ed. Robert Brent Toplin (Westport, Conn., 1993), 139–155.
29. On these conflicted heroes see Douglas Snauffer, *Crime Television* (Westport, Conn., 2006), 65–112; Brück, *Der deutsche Fernsehkrimi*, 147, 188ff.

Bibliography

Altenhöhner, Florian. "Spionitis: Reale Korrelate und Deutungsmuster der Angst vor Spionen, 1900–1914." In *Kollektive Identitäten und kulturelle Innovationen: Ethnologische, soziologische und historische Studien*, ed. Werner Rammert et al. (Leipzig: Leipziger Universitätsverlag, 2002), 77–91.

Bennett, Tony, and Janet Woollacott. *Bond and Beyond: The Political Career of a Popular Hero*. London: Routledge, 1987.

Boyer, Paul. *By the Bomb's Early Light: American Thought and Culture at the Dawn of the Atomic Age*. Chapel Hill: University of North Carolina Press, 1994.

Britton, Wesley. *Spy Television*. Westport, Conn.: Praeger, 2004.

Brück, Ingrid, Andrea Guder, Reinhold Viehoff, and Karin Wehn. *Der deutsche Fernsehkrimi: Eine Programm- und Produktionsgeschichte von den Anfängen bis heute*. Stuttgart: Metzler, 2003.

Cawelti, John G., and Bruce Rosenberg. *The Spy Story*. Chicago: University of Chicago Press, 1987.

Chapman, James. *License to Thrill: A Cultural History of the James Bond Films*. London: Tauris, 1999.

Corkin, Stanley. *Cowboys as Cold Warriors: The Western and U.S. History*. Philadelphia: Temple University Press, 2004.

De Grazia, Victoria. *Irresistible Empire: America's Advance through Twentieth-Century Europe*. Cambridge: Harvard University Press, 2005.

Fousek, John. *To Lead the Free World: American Nationalism and the Cultural Roots of the Cold War*. Chapel Hill: University of North Carolina Press, 2000.

Halloran, Vivian. "Tropical Bond." In *Ian Fleming and James Bond: The Cultural Politics of 007*, ed. Edward P. Commentale, Skip Willman, and Steven Watt (Bloomington: Indiana University Press, 2005).

Hartley, John. *Communication, Cultural and Media Studies: The Key Concepts*. 3rd edition. London: Routledge, 2006.

Hendershot, Cyndy. "The Cold War Horror Film: Taboo and Transgression in The Bad Seed, The Fly, and Psycho." *Journal of Popular Film and Television* 29, no. 1 (2001): 20–31.

Horn, Eva. "Der Spion." In *Grenzverletzer: Zur politischen Subversion territorialer Ordnung*, ed. Eva Horn, Stefan Kaufmann, and Ulrich Bröckling (Berlin: Kadmos, 2002), 136–155.

Kackman, Michael. "Citizen, Communist, Counterspy: I Led 3 Lives and Television's Masculine Agent of History." *Cinema Journal* 38 (1998): 98–114.

———. *Citizen Spy: Television, Espionage, and Cold War Culture*. Minneapolis: University of Minnesota Press, 2005.

Kreuzer, Helmut, and Christian W. Thomsen, eds. *Geschichte des Fernsehens in der Bundesrepublik Deutschland*. Munich: W. Fink, 1993–94.

Kuznick, Peter J., and James Gilbert, eds. *Rethinking Cold War Culture*. Washington: Smithsonian Institution Press, 2001.

Lenihan, John H. "Hollywood Laughs at the Cold War, 1947–1961." In *Hollywood as Mirror: Changing Views of "Outsiders" and "Enemies" in American Movies*, ed. Robert Brent Toplin (Westport, Conn.: Greenwood, 1993), 139–155.

Lindner, Christoph. "Criminal Vision and the Ideology of Detection." In *The James Bond Phenomenon: A Critical Reader*, ed. Christoph Lindner (Manchester: Manchester University Press, 2003), 76–90.

Maland, Charles. "Dr. Strangelove (1964): Nightmare Comedy and the Ideology of Liberal Consensus." In *Hollywood as Historian: American Film in a Cultural Context*, ed. Peter C. Rollins (Louisville: University Press of Kentucky, 1998), 190–210.

Marßolek, Inge. "Internationalität und kulturelle Klischees am Beispiel der John-Kling-Heftromane der 1920er und 1930er Jahre." In *Amerikanisierung: Traum und Alptraum im Deutschland des 20. Jahrhunderts*, ed. Alf Lüdtke, Inge Marßolek, and Adelheid von Saldern (Stuttgart: Steiner, 1996), 144–160.

Marwick, Arthur. *The Sixties: Cultural Revolution in Britain, France, Italy, and the United States, c. 1958–1974*. Oxford: Oxford University Press, 1998.

May, Elaine Tyler. *Homeward Bound: American Families in the Cold War Era*. New York: Basic Books, 1999.

Melley, Timothy. *Empire of Conspiracy: The Culture of Paranoia in Postwar America*. Ithaca, N.Y.: Cornell University Press, 2000.

Miller, Toby. *Spyscreen: Espionage on Film and TV from the 1930s to the 1960s*. Oxford: Oxford University Press, 2003.

Moore, Barbara, Marvin R. Bensman, and Jim Van Dyke. *Prime-time Television: A Concise History*. Westport, Conn.: Greenwood Publishing Group, 2006.

Mulvihill, Jason. "The Golden Age of Bond: Creation of a Cold War Popular Hero," parts I and II. *International Journal of Instructional Media* 28 (2001): 225–237 (part I), 337–353 (part II).

Nadel, Alan. *Containment Culture: American Narrative, Postmodernism, and the Atomic Age*. Durham: Duke University Press, 1996.

Price, Thomas J. "The Changing Image of the Soviets in the Bond Saga: From Bond-Villains to 'Acceptable Role Partners,'" *Journal of Popular Culture* 26 (1992), no. 1: 17–37.

Sayre, Nora. *Running Time: Films of the Cold War*. New York: Dial Press, 1982.

Schwarzkopf, Stefan. "'They do it with mirrors': Advertising and British Cold War Consumer Politics." *Contemporary British History* 19 (2005), no. 2: 133–150.

Seed, David. *American Science Fiction and the Cold War: Literature and Film*. Edinburgh: Edinburgh University Press, 1999.

Snauffer, Douglas. *Crime Television*. Westport, Conn.: Greenwood, 2006.

Stephan, Alexander, ed. *The Americanization of Europe: Culture, Diplomacy, and Anti-Americanism after 1945*. New York: Berghahn, 2006.

Stölken-Fitschen, Ilona. *Atombombe und Geistesgeschichte: Eine Studie der fünfziger Jahre aus deutscher Sicht*. Baden-Baden: Nomos, 1995.

Suri, Jeremi. *Power and Protest: Global Revolution and the Rise of Détente*. Cambridge: Harvard University Press, 2005.
Tökés, Rudolf L. *Hungary's Negotiated Revolution: Economic Reform, Social Change, and Political Succession, 1957–1990*. Cambridge: Cambridge University Press, 1996.
Weiß, Peter Ulrich. "Wo das Wolfsgesetz regiert: Agent Hansen ermittelt. Amerikabilder in DEFA-Produktionen zu Beginn der 1960er Jahre." In *Umworbener Klassenfeind: Das Verhältnis der DDR zu den USA*, ed. Uta Balbier and Christiane Rösch (Berlin: Christoph Links Verlag, 2006), 160–179.
White, Patrick J., *The Complete Mission Impossible Dossier* (New York: Avon Books, 1991).
Whitfield, Stephen J. *The Culture of the Cold War*. Baltimore: Johns Hopkins University Press, 1991.
Woods, Brett F. *Neutral Ground: A Political History of Espionage Fiction*. New York: Algora, 2008.
Worland, Rick. "The Cold War Mannerists: The Men From U.N.C.L.E. and TV Espionage in the 1960s." *Journal of Popular Film and Television* 21 (1994): 150–162.

Further documents

"Solo nach Emma." *Der Spiegel* 20 (1967), 186.
Radmann, Helga. "Feuerball als NATO-Reklame-Show." *Thüringische Landeszeitung* (Weimar), 14 January 1966.
"James Bond—und kein Ende." *Der neue Weg* (Halle), 30 December 1966.
"So kämpft James Bond!" *Bravo*, 6 December 1965.

Chapter 5

COLD WAR TELEVISION
Olga Korbut and the Munich Olympics of 1972

Annette Vowinckel

Sport is an integral part of postmodern everyday life—in the form of daily exercise and even more as a media phenomenon. However, sport is usually not reflected upon as a mere phenomenon; rather, it is perceived as indirectly informing us about politics, societies, and economic and media developments. In both the sociology and the history of sports, it has been common to speak of sports as an image or mirror of social reality, to charge sports with ideological meaning and to assume that they are influenced by various—and sometimes opposing—interests. The reality of sports in the twentieth century has in many ways abetted such projections, and few sports events are more apt to support this approach than the Olympics. In their context, sport has become a "universal metaphor"[1] for anything but sport itself.[2] It seems to be self-evident that teams represent nations, that athletes strive for medals in order to elate their compatriots and to serve their country and upgrade its standing in the world. In a concept of "Cold War sports," there seems to be no place for athletes who refuse to represent their countries—as, for example, Jürgen Sparwasser, a famous East German soccer player who relocated to the Federal Republic of Germany in 1988.

In this essay, I will argue that the Cold War did provide a framework for the reception of sports and sports events, but that there are also limits regarding the applicability of this framework. By analyzing the Olympics as a media event, which has been broadcast in real time since the early days, I will show that the games are not only a political and/or economic enterprise, but that, as Hans Ulrich Gumbrecht has described it, they make a case for the "production of presence" as opposed to the "production of meaning."[3]

Taking Russian gymnast Olga Korbut's 1972 performance in Munich as an example, I will argue that she was the declared darling of the public because she succeeded in being "most present"—despite the fact that she competed directly with (East) German Karin Janz, who won the gold medal in this competition. I will describe the very special atmosphere that was generated by the Munich audience and commented upon by sports journalists of different nationalities in order to show that sports events—within certain limits—managed to establish an autonomous sphere that transcended political borders between blocs and nations instead of confirming and reproducing them. I will thus explore which elements, aside from economy and political representation, make postmodern sports attractive for mass audiences. Moreover, I will examine whether there is a shift from political to aesthetic reception, and whether this shift teaches us anything about (European) Cold War Culture.

The Modern Olympics

The modern Olympics were founded by the French aristocrat Pierre de Coubertin in the late nineteenth century—or, more accurately, they were revived in the style of the ancient Olympic games. Since in antiquity the athletes were professionals and the games were anything but a feast of peace and friendship, the establishment of the modern Olympics is truly a case of *invention of tradition*.[4] Only in the twentieth century was the amateur status of the sportsmen stressed, and the attitude that participation matters more than victory is also genuinely modern. Such an attitude would have been utterly strange to the ancient Greeks, who went for victory or defeat as they went for life or death.

When Coubertin founded the modern Olympics, he replaced the competitive principles of the ancient games with an ideology of "fair play," which was emphatically opposed to any kind of military training. For him, the games' primary aim was not to win but to bring about peace—and to reaffirm social distinctions within European societies. While soccer was held to be a "school for the body" that allowed for some individuals to join the upper classes, the Olympic movement was, in Coubertin's view, a "school for the character" of the aristocratic elite. Thus, according to

Pierre Bourdieu, "fair play" was for Coubertin "the kind of game of those who as future leaders knew to keep distance according to their social role."[5] In this perspective, sport would never be an end in itself but a school for managers who had to persist in social competition.

Consequently, the Olympic movement gained the reputation of stabilizing class society, and likewise it is not surprising that the Olympic ideal was damaged in many ways in the course of the twentieth century. In their early years, the games were overshadowed by long-distance traveling and poor organization—the games of 1900, for example, lasted five months. Also, it did not take long for politicians of all parties to discover that the games were a perfect stage for political propaganda of all sorts: the 1936 Berlin Olympics were misused for a campaign to support Hitler and National Socialism, the 1972 Munich games turned into a stage for Palestinian terrorists, and the 1980 Moscow games are remembered as "Boycott games," since several Western teams stayed home because of the Soviet invasion of Afghanistan. Especially in the context of the Cold War, both Socialist and democratic governments tried to ideologically exploit the Olympics. Hence the sports competition was always also a competition of political systems.

On the part of the Soviet Union, whose team first attended the competition in 1952, the games were staged as an exhibition of Socialist virtues and rhetorically marketed as a service for peace in the Coubertinian spirit. In the Western world, the games were perceived as a free competition of free individuals whose successes were, however, in the end also conceived as a victory of democracy and free-market economy. Thus, the games became a showcase for ideological arguments of all sorts and respective accusations against the antagonist. In 1980, the Soviets were accused of abusing the games in order to distract public attention from the war in Afghanistan, while the American boycott campaign was allegedly run by Jimmy Carter in order to divert attention from domestic problems in the United States.[6]

In contrast, Uta Balbier has argued that at least the Munich games of 1972, which were destined to stage the Cold War in a divided Germany, conspicuously abstained from using Western symbols and representations in favor of pop cultural and transnational symbols. For example, the double performance of the West German anthem during the opening ceremony of 1972—once for the country's status as a participating nation, once as the host—was reduced to a single performance, and the arrival of the athletes in the stadium was accompanied by pieces like *Hoch auf dem gelben Wagen* (a German folk song) for the West German team and *When the Saints Go Marching In* for the U.S. athletes.[7] This shows that—aside from common Cold War programmatic elements—there are also traditions and developments that oppose the common cliché of sports events as a playground for Cold War protagonists.

Still, there is no doubt that Balbier, too, would locate the general cultural and historical meaning of the games in the political realm, even though the equation of sports and politics is a one-way street: even if we can speak of sports as reproducing politics, we would hardly speak of politics as reproducing or reflecting sports. I would thus encourage a heuristic separation of sports and politics, and will focus on the media coverage of sports events during the Cold War, assuming that audiences in both East and West watched the Olympics (soccer championships etc.) not *because of* but *despite* the propaganda that accompanied it. I will argue, in other words, that we can only fully understand the meaning of sports events if we also analyze their aesthetic, performative, and playful qualities, and that sometimes politics and aesthetics radically oppose each other.

Media Coverage of Sports

During the Cold War, the Olympics became an integral part of entertainment culture on both sides of the Iron Curtain. During the first decades of the twentieth century, sports audiences had to visit the athletes' arena, listen to the radio, or read about sports events in the paper the following day. Starting in the second half of the century, television became increasingly important. Live coverage began to shape the face of sports, naturally focusing on visual and performative aspects rather than on mere results. Consequently, a new mode of following sports developed, and simultaneously a gradual change in television's time management.

During the Melbourne games in November 1956, both Hessischer Rundfunk in West Germany and Deutscher Fernsehfunk in East Germany broadcast only one daily report, summarizing the results of all competitions. During the Rome Olympics of 1960, West German television already broadcast three programs per day, and some competitions were covered live for the first time after the war. Reports started at 2:55 PM, followed by a five-minute summary at 8:20 PM and a flexible late program.

During the Tokyo games of 1964, the number of broadcasts rose to a maximum of six per day on West German TV. Due to the seven-hour time shift and an insufficient number of satellites, most of them were summary reports. ARD (the "first" public TV station) covered the broadcasts before 8:00 PM, the ZDF (the "second" public station) covered the later broadcasts, or vice versa, alternating daily. East German television broadcast five reports per day, the first one already at 10:00 AM.

During the Mexico games of 1968 (again with a seven-hour time shift for European audiences), there was still a maximum of six reports on West German television and three in the GDR. However, these three programs were significantly longer than before. In fact, there was no less TV coverage but fewer interruptions between the various reports. Basically, there was nonstop reporting on the Mexico games in both East and West Germany, as well as significantly more live coverage. While in 1968 color programs (including all reports from Mexico) were labeled as such in TV program guides, in 1972 black and white programs (now a minority) had to be labeled instead.

In the course of the 1960s, live coverage of sports competitions became more and more important, and in the wake of substantial time differences they led to an inversion of daily schedules for many Europeans. For many people, participation in a televised sports event became more important than a good night's sleep—at least in West Germany, where in 1968 reports often lasted until 2:00 AM, while in East Germany people were "sent to bed" already at 11 PM (possibly against their will). Likewise, the Olympics became more and more of a spectacle,[8] and its entertainment value was only exceeded by the soccer World Championships, which unlike the Olympics have continued to gain in importance since the end of the Cold War. This indicates that the fascination of televised sports is neither based on information, nor is it necessarily connected to national exaltation. Rather, the fascination is rooted in a shared aesthetic experience in real time—an experience which in the context of sports lives not on language and information but on moving images and the pleasure they bring about. Anne Fleig has argued that the visualization of the moving body is an important step on the path to a modernity shaped by mass observation—even if she speaks of athletes in the sports stadium rather than bodies on television.[9] Hence, it is not the ideological conflict of communism versus capitalism or democracy that draws people to the stadium or to the television set, but the visual presence of the athletes.

If this argument is valid both for Socialist and for democratic countries—and regarding the history of sports television there is no significant difference between East and West—we should assume that the most important change in the perception of sports was caused not by the Cold War, but by the establishment of television as the key medium in the second half of the twentieth century. We should therefore first analyze some changes in the reception of sports that are not so much influenced by politics, but rather by the evolution of media coverage.

After the establishment of television, it was no longer necessary to go to the stadium in order to watch a game. The perspective of the individual in the stadium, who was able to survey the entire field, was replaced by partial perspectives and complemented by close-up views of single players and faces. However, the increasing presence of moving bodies on television has paradoxically prompted their disappearance. As anthropologist Dietmar Kamper put it, the body has been "staged as an image and assigned to consumption. Thus, it comes close to garbage and litter. Insofar as postmodernism is seen as the defeat of modernism, sport is apt to show modernism's 'real' face."[10] It is a paradox that media images depend on the presence of athletes, while at the same time they make the audience watch these images instead of the athletes' bodies. However, sometimes the reactions of "real" audiences get closely entangled with the reactions of television audiences and commentators—as was the case during Olga Korbut's performance at the uneven bars during the Munich Olympics of 1972.

Duel on the Uneven Bars: Olga Korbut versus Karin Janz

On 31 August 1972, the Olympic finals in women's gymnastics took place in Munich. The uneven bars competition, which was in fact a competition between the Soviet Union and the German Democratic Republic, attracted a great deal of attention.[11] The East German gymnast Karin Janz won the gold medal, while her compatriot Erika Zuchold and Belarusian gymnast Olga Korbut got identical scores and thus shared the silver medal. Seventeen-year-old Olga Korbut, also named "the sparrow from Minsk," was the darling of the Munich public despite (or because of) the fact that she failed at the all-around competition. When the individual competition at the uneven bars started, the audience hoped for her to win the gold medal, which with respect to the difficulty of her performance and her very special aura—a mixture of elegance and adolescent charm—she would surely have deserved. She was the first athlete to perform a flic-flac on the upper bar and a very elaborate stretched back salto, but scored only 9.8 points, while Karin Janz, who had presented a somewhat less difficult and rather stiff performance, scored 9.9 points.[12]

When the scores were displayed the audience became furious. People started to whistle and stamp in order to articulate their protest; they unmistakably disapproved of the jury, and it took almost ten minutes for the audience to calm down—which was, not only by television standards, a very long time.

The comments of different journalists in East and West are very revealing. On the occasion of Karin Janz's victory in the leapfrog competition, an East German commentator had asserted that there was "no envy between these girls."¹³ They had practiced together with the Soviet girls, and whenever one of them won a medal, all the others would congratulate her. But now the commentator had to admit that there was a keen competition between the gymnasts of the two countries after all—both for medals and for the affection of the audience—and that there appeared to be clear limits to *Völkerfreundschaft* ("friendship of the nations") when it came to the distribution of precious metals.¹⁴

During the upheaval caused by the bad scores for Olga Korbut, the East German commentator kept repeating that the jury was international and that its judgments had to be respected—even if Olga Korbut was the audience's declared favorite. He got rather angry when the hail of catcalls continued during the performance of East German gymnast Angelika Hellmann, who was next in line after Korbut and would finish sixth. According to the commentator, "the audience's protest did not address the jury any more but Angelika Hellmann—this needs to be said loud and clear." He continued attacking the West German spectators in a way previously unknown in sports journalism:

> "Maybe there are people in this hall who have read too many sport articles in the *Bild-Zeitung* [West Germany's largest tabloid]. We're not on a soccer field here, where it is common to appeal against the audience's, err, jury's decision and to whistle in order to show disapproval and disdain for the athletes. We are in an Olympic stadium; the athletes deserve our attention and they deserve to be supported; one should not put a spoke in someone's wheel, as was done with Angelika Hellmann."¹⁵

Obviously, the situation was unprecedented and the commentator's attack on the audience was rather inconsiderate. He was caught in a double bind, since he himself had just previously maintained that friendship between the GDR and the Soviet Union did not allow for envy and competition. Then he suddenly saw himself forced to defend his own candidate against a Western audience, which—contrary to the ideological "requirements" of the Cold War—favored a Soviet athlete and not the German compatriot from the "other side of the Wall." Had Korbut's rival been a West German athlete, he might have gone along with the audience and supported the Belarusian gymnast.

What is most striking in this context is not the East German commentator's furious attack on the audience, but the fact that both the Munich audience and Western reporters enthusiastically favored an athlete representing the Soviet Union. This becomes particularly clear in the comments of two U.S. journalists who had the following conversation during Korbut's performance:

Commentator 1: "Watch this, watch this: back salto right to the other bar."
Commentator 2: "Has that been done before by a girl?"
Commentator 1: "Never, never. Not by any human that I know of ... look at that! And she's second best? I don't believe it!"
Commentator 2: "This is a historical format we're watching right now in gymnastics."
Commentator 1: "She's a Cathy Rigby size ... oh my God! Olga Korbut!"[16]

In fact, the remark "she's second best? I don't believe it!" refers not to her being second after Karin Janz (which at that point the commentators did not know yet) but to Olga Korbut's being rated second best on her own team. Still, the commentators' voices cracked and they radiated enormous enthusiasm for the Belarusian girl—an enthusiasm which we intuitively still understand when watching the performance on YouTube today. After all, the video was clicked more than 450,000 times between February 2006 and May 2009.[17]

It seems quite likely that Korbut's personality caused this enthusiasm: a combination of aura and vocation made her appear outstanding; anybody watching her performances, be it in rhythmic gymnastics, on the bars, or on the balance beam, intuitively understands why it was she of all athletes who became the audience's darling in Munich. She radiated childish optimism as well as courage, creativity, charm, and lightness—a combination of qualities that also made it easy to recognize her quickly among dozens of gymnasts. Her mishap at the bars made her even more likable, for it moved her closer to "ordinary people" in the audience—who were all the more upset when she missed the gold medal despite having performed outstandingly in the individual competition.

During the competition, the focus was clearly not on politics, ideology, or nationality. Rather, Korbut provided a screen onto which ordinary people could project their desires and disappointments. Consequently, the fact that she represented the Soviet Union hardly mattered to the audience. In fact, the Munich episode teaches us that sports audiences, even at the peak of the Cold War, did not blindly support their own compatriots. On the contrary: Korbut's home page today still claims that she "did more to ease the tensions of the Cold War than all the politicians and diplomats of the day put together"—and this may very well be true.[18]

Of course, we could first argue that Olga Korbut attracted Western audiences because she did *not* match the stereotypes of Russian athletes at that time, who were by large characterized as viragos.[19] In contrast, Korbut was a "chick," appealing to the (male) audience's protective instincts. We could argue secondly that support for athletes of other nations was more common in "aesthetic"—and therefore "female"—disciplines like gymnastics, ice skating, high diving, water ballet, horseback riding, etc. than in competitive team sports like soccer, hockey, or basketball. It mattered, thirdly, that no athlete from either the United States or West Germany was in the competition any more, making it easier for a West German audience to support the Belarusian teenager. However, we might also think of Korbut's performance on the uneven bars as paradigmatic for a general switch from national identification to aesthetic pleasure in the reception of sports in postmodern media societies.

On the one hand, this shift mirrors the fact that the television broadcasting of sports events has exploded and that television has provided a variety of aesthetic gadgets like repetition, slow motion, close-up, and split screen. Sports have become part of entertainment (or, for that matter, infotainment) and of a popular culture that is by nature transnational. Identity and identification seem to become gradually "denationalized," and even in national teams matters of nationality have lost significance, especially in societies that have a high percentage of immigrants like England and France or, more recently, Germany.

(European) Cold War Cultures?

I initially raised the question whether Cold War sports are in fact *Cold War* sports or whether they just happen to be sports in the Cold War era. If we look at the Olympic Games from a political or sociological perspective, it becomes clear that they were strongly shaped by ideologies of different sorts. Lincoln Allison even assumes that the collapse of the Soviet Union and the subsequent collapse of amateurism will marginalize the Olympics in the near future. He is convinced that the Olympic movement nowadays "lacks the drama and impetus it had in the Cold War. Its mythology has been thoroughly deconstructed; it is threatened by drug scandals. It cannot reconstitute itself as a kind of World professional Games ... because the international federations of the major sports cannot fit it into their schedules and are jealous of their own power. Logically, the Olympics should be on the skids."[20] Without the competition between socialism and liberal democracy, between the Soviet and the Western blocs, there seems to be no reason to keep the Olympic movement alive. However, Allison concedes that the Olympic movement is

> as important to the Chinese and certain Third World governments now as it used to be to the Russians. It is one of the few events, in some respects

> the only one, that seems to capture the spirit of a global village: Barcelona '92 was the place to be.... The income from U.S. television for the summer games has soared: $2 million in 1964, $25 million in 1976, $225 million in 1984, though it has leveled off at around $400 million. Myths are deconstructed intellectually; the deconstructed myth may leave you muttering, "this is all nonsense, you know," but with a tear in your eye. Olympic myth, with its universalism, historical dubiety, and claim to be on a higher plane, is in some respects parallel to that of the Roman Catholic Church. I would not bet on its decline.[21]

Allison argues that the longevity of the Olympics is due to its financial success. However, this success is itself due to the popularity of the Games. If the popularity of the Olympic games after World War II had been a byproduct of the Cold War, they would have declined after its end. Since they did not decline, they cannot have been a Cold War phenomenon in an intrinsic sense, but only in terms of temporal coincidence. I would add that, just like the Olympics, television also happened to reach its peak simultaneously with the Cold War, and that thus the three are closely related in the sense that they all happen to be significant for the emergence of a globalized, yet fragmented postmodern culture in the second half of the twentieth century—a culture which tends both to aestheticize politics and to politicize aesthetics.

Finally, we should again raise the question whether there is any difference between *European* Cold War Olympics and Cold War Olympics elsewhere. Again, I would like to take media coverage as a starting point. It is obvious that in times of globalization, media formats and aesthetics tend to be leveled and homogenized. Olympic images are the same worldwide, and even verbal comments may not significantly differ unless there is a compatriot of the commentator taking part in the competition—which used to be likely for the Soviet Union or the United States and rather unlikely for countries like Benin or Peru. However, it does make a difference that in Europe, a variety of neighboring nations took pride in scoring medals against *both* superpowers. For example, in the Melbourne Olympics of 1956 the Hungarian team scored twenty-six medals and ranked fourth on the list of medal winners behind the USSR, the United States, and Australia (making a home match). This was a real success in terms of sports, and it strengthened the small nation's self-esteem, which had been undermined by the Soviet invasion of the same year. Furthermore, in 1972 the German Democratic Republic and the Federal Republic of Germany ranked third and fourth immediately behind the respective superpowers, thus indicating that the competition took place in the heart of Europe and even inside the German nation.

Conclusion

In general, Olympic audiences were less interested in politics than were sports officials, Cold Warriors, or governments. It is quite likely that they put up with politics simply because they could not escape it. For example, during the Moscow Games of 1980, the marginalized West German *Zonenrandgebiet* ("border area") suddenly turned into an attractive region for tourists who wanted to watch the Olympics on East German television, since West German television did not cover the event. The West German Communist Party (DKP) set up television sets in marketplaces to display East Germany's live coverage of the Olympics, and this service was even accepted by anti-Communist members of established political parties.[22] Quite obviously, West Germans preferred watching the Olympics commented by East German reporters to not watching them at all.

Interestingly, the shift from a political and nationalistic reception of sports to a rather aesthetic approach—in which sport is closer to theater than it is to ideology—occurred simultaneously in East and West. Thus, citizens of the Socialist states in Central and Eastern Europe were able to smoothly adapt to the norms and practices of Western media societies after the demise of state socialism. One could even argue that large sports events—especially soccer championships and the Olympics—are the real winners of the Cold War, and, paradoxically, contribute substantially to saving television from doom in the age of digital media.[23] While television ceased to be a mass medium—in the sense that many people watch the same public program at the same time—and gradually turned into a rather individual medium during the 1980s and 90s, sports events as the last remaining blockbusters remind us of the good old times of television, which happened to coincide with the Cold War—and not only in Europe.[24]

Notes

1. Bernd Wirkus, "Präsenz und Transzendenz im Sportsieg," in *Dimensionen der Ästhetik*, ed. M. Lämmer (Sankt Augustin, 2005), 62–75.
2. For example: Lincoln Allison, ed., *The Politics of Sport* (Manchester, 1986); Uta A. Balbier, *Leistungskonkurrenz* (Paderborn, 2006); Wolfgang Berens and Gerhard Schewe, eds., *Profifußball und Ökonomie* (Hamburg, 2003); Tobias Blasius, *Olympische Bewegung, Kalter Krieg und Deutschlandpolitik 1949–1972* (Frankfurt, 2001); Gunter Holzweißig, ed., *Diplomatie im Trainingsanzug* (Munich, 1981); Matthias Marschik and Doris Sottopietra, eds., *Erbfeinde und Haßlieben* (Münster, 2000).
3. Cf. Hans Ulrich Gumbrecht, *Production of Presence* (Stanford, 2004).

4. Cf. Lincoln Allison, "The Olympic Movement and the End of the Cold War," *World Affairs* 157 (1994), no. 2: 92–97; Eric Hobsbawm, ed., *The Invention of Tradition* (Cambridge, 1996).
5. Pierre Bourdieu, "Historische und soziale Voraussetzungen des modernen Sports," *Merkur* 39 (1985), no. 437: 575–590, here 587: "die Spielweise derer, die den späteren Rollen der künftigen Führungskräfte inhärente 'Rollendistanz' zu wahren wissen."
6. See Evelyn Mertin, "Der Boykott der Olympischen Spiele 1980 in Moskau in der sowjetischen Presse," *Stadion: Internationale Zeitschrift für Geschichte des Sports* 29 (2003): 251–262.
7. Uta A. Balbier, "'Der Welt das moderne Deutschland vorstellen,'" in *Auswärtige Repräsentationen*, ed. Johannes Paulmann (Cologne, 2005), 105–119. Quote on p. 116.
8. Guy Debord, *Die Gesellschaft des Spektakels* (Hamburg, 1978).
9. Anne Fleig, "'Siegesplätze über die Natur,'" in *Leibhaftige Moderne*, ed. Michael Cowan and Kai Marcel Sicks (Bielefeld, 2005), 81–96, here 84.
10. "[Der Körper wird] als Bild inszeniert und dem Konsum überlassen. Damit gerät er definitiv in die Nähe des Abfalls und des Mülls. Insofern die Postmoderne als Niederlage der Moderne bezeichnet werden kann, zeigt der Sport immer deutlicher das 'wahre' Gesicht der Moderne." Dietmar Kamper, "Keine Chance für die Geistesgegenwart," in *Olympische Spiele, die andere Utopie der Moderne: Olympia zwischen Kult und Droge*, ed. Gunter Gebauer (Frankfurt am Main, 1996), 256–263, here 261 (author's translation).
11. See Harald Lechenperg, *Olympische Spiele 1972* (Munich, 1972), 263.
12. There is no evidence as to why the jury did not give higher scores. Possibly its members did not find it appropriate to award the gold medal to an athlete who had failed in the team competition. In fact there was no tendency to rate East German gymnasts higher than others, and aside from this incident there were no complaints about the jury or the rating system.
13. "Olympia aktuell," DDR-2, 31 August 1972, 10:00 AM–2:00 PM, Deutsches Rundfunkarchiv Babelsberg (DRAB) AC4432/DRAB/1/1, identification no. 77614, 10'45".
14. Ever after 1972, Korbut's contribution to the friendship of the nations during the Cold War has been stressed. Cf. www.olgakorbut.com.
15. "Vielleicht gibt's tatsächlich hier in der Halle einige Leute, die zu oft die Sportberichte in der Bildzeitung lesen. Wir sind hier nicht auf einem Fußballbundesligaplatz, wo es üblich ist, Zuschauer-, äh, Schiedsrichterentscheidungen zu kritisieren und mit solchen Pfiffen zu belegen, sie nicht anzuerkennen. Wir sind hier in einer olympischen Arena, die Sportlerinnen haben verdient, dass man ihnen Aufmerksamkeit schenkt und dass man sie in ihrem Kampf unterstützt und ihnen nicht noch Knüppel zwischen die Beine wirft, wie das bei Angelika Hellman eindeutig geschehen ist" (author's translation). "Olympia aktuell," 31 August 1972, 11'07".
16. "ABC-Interview München '72," ABC television, February 1987, archive of the Deutscher Olympischer Sportbund (DOSB, German Olympic Committee) Frankfurt, no. 72, 2'50". Cathy Rigby was a U.S. gymnast who won a silver medal on the balance beam in the 1970 world championship in gymnastics, but did not participate in the Munich Olympics because of an injury.
17. See http://de.youtube.com/watch?v=yOOmFgBAdIA (Korbut at the uneven bars) and http://de.youtube.com/watch?v=wF40nzErqC0 (the performance of the team competition, in which Korbut failed rather badly).
18. See http://www.olgakorbut.com.

19. See Stefan Wiederkehr, "Wer ist 'olympisch gesehen eine Frau'?" *New Aspects of Sport History*, Proceedings of the 9th ISHPES-Congress, ed. Karl Lennartz, Stephan Wassong, and Thomas Zawadzki (Sankt Augustin, 2007), 185–192; idem, "'Unsere Mädchen sind alle einwandfrei,'" in *Sport zwischen Ost und West*, ed. Arie Malz, Stefan Rohdewald, and Stefan Wiederkehr (Osnabrück, 2007), 269–286.
20. Allison, "The Olympic Movement," 96f.
21. Ibid., 97.
22. See "Hintergrundbericht zur Olympiade," DDR-1, 26 July 1980, 3:25 PM; DRAB AS8005721/DRAB/1/1, identification no. 98841.
23. Cf. Stefan Münker, "Epilog zum Fernsehen," in *Televisionen*, ed. Stefan Münker (Frankfurt, 1999), 220–236, here 221.
24. Ibid.

Bibliography

Allison, Lincoln. "The Olympic Movement and the End of the Cold War." *World Affairs* 157 (1994), no. 2: 92–97.

———, ed. *The Politics of Sport*. Manchester, 1986.

Balbier, Uta A. "'Der Welt das moderne Deutschland vorstellen': Die Eröffnungsfeier der Spiele der XX. Olympiade in München 1972." In *Auswärtige Repräsentationen: Deutsche Kulturdiplomatie nach 1945*, ed. Johannes Paulmann (Cologne, 2005), 105–119.

———. *Leistungskonkurrenz: Der deutsch-deutsche Sport 1950–1972: Eine Ost-West-Beziehungsgeschichte im Kalten Krieg*. Paderborn, 2006.

Berens, Wolfgang, and Gerhard Schewe, eds. *Profifußball und Ökonomie*. Hamburg, 2003.

Blasius, Tobias. *Olympische Bewegung, Kalter Krieg und Deutschlandpolitik 1949–1972*. Frankfurt am Main, 2001.

Bourdieu, Pierre. "Historische und soziale Voraussetzungen des modernen Sports." *Merkur* 39 (1985), no. 437: 575–590.

Debord, Guy. *Die Gesellschaft des Spektakels*. Hamburg, 1978.

Fleig, Anne. "'Siegesplätze über die Natur': Musils Kritik am Geist des modernen Wettkampfsports." In *Leibhaftige Moderne: Körper in Kunst und Massenmedien 1918 bis 1933*, ed. Michael Cowan and Kai Marcel Sicks (Bielefeld, 2005), 81–96.

Gumbrecht, Hans Ulrich. *Production of Presence: What Meaning Cannot Convey*. Stanford, 2004.

Hobsbawm, Eric, ed. *The Invention of Tradition*. Cambridge, 1996.

Holzweißig, Gunter, ed. *Diplomatie im Trainingsanzug: Sport als politisches Instrument der DDR in den innerdeutschen und internationalen Beziehungen*. Munich, 1981.

Kamper, Dietmar. "Keine Chance für die Geistesgegenwart: Wie der Körper als Bild im Sport sein Dasein fristet." In *Olympische Spiele, die andere Utopie der Moderne: Olympia zwischen Kult und Droge*, ed. Gunter Gebauer (Frankfurt am Main, 1996), 256–263.

Lechenperg, Harald. *Olympische Spiele 1972: Sapporo—München*. Munich, 1972.

Marschik, Matthias, and Doris Sottopietra, eds. *Erbfeinde und Haßlieben: Konzept und Realität Mitteleuropas im Sport*. Münster, 2000.

Mertin, Evelyn. "Der Boykott der Olympischen Spiele 1980 in Moskau in der sowjetischen Presse." *Stadion: Internationale Zeitschrift für Geschichte des Sports* 29 (2003): 251–262.

Münker, Stefan. "Epilog zum Fernsehen." In *Televisionen*, ed. Stefan Münker (Frankfurt am Main, 1999), 220–236.

Wiederkehr, Stefan, "Wer ist 'olympisch gesehen eine Frau'? Die Schweizer Presse im Jahre 1968 über Spitzensportlerinnen aus dem Ostblock und die Einführung von Geschlechtertests." *New Aspects of Sport History: The Olympic Lectures*. Proceedings of the 9th ISHPES-Congress, ed. Karl Lennartz, Stephan Wassong, and Thomas Zawadzki (Sankt Augustin, 2007), 185–192.

———. "'Unsere Mädchen sind alle einwandfrei.' Die Kobukowska-Affäre von 1967 in der zeitgenössischen Presse (Polen, BRD, Schweiz)." In *Sport zwischen Ost und West: Beiträge zur Sportgeschichte Osteuropas im 19. und 20. Jahrhundert*, ed. Arie Malz, Stefan Rohdewald, and Stefan Wiederkehr (Osnabrück, 2007), 269–286.

Wirkus, Bernd. "Präsenz und Transzendenz im Sportsieg." in *Dimensionen der Ästhetik: Festschrift für Barbara Ränsch-Trill*, ed. M. Lämmer (Sankt Augustin, 2005), 62–75.

Audiovisual material

"Olympia aktuell." DDR-2, 31 August 1972, 10:00 AM–2:00 PM, Deutsches Rundfunkarchiv Babelsberg (DRAB) AC4432/DRAB/1/1, identification no. 77614.

"ABC-Interview München '72." ABC television, February 1987, archive of the Deutscher Olympischer Sportbund ("German Olympic Committee," DOSB), Frankfurt am Main, no. 72.

"Hintergrundbericht zur Olympiade." DDR-1, 26 July 1980, 3:25 PM; DRAB AS8005721/DRAB/1/1, identification no. 98841.

Web sites

http://de.youtube.com/watch?v=yOOmFgBAdIA (Korbut at the uneven bars)
http://de.youtube.com/watch?v=wF40nzErqC0 (Korbut failing on the uneven bars)
http://www.olgakorbut.com (Korbut's official website)

Part II

Constructing Identities
Representations of the "Self"

Chapter 6

CATHOLIC PIETY IN THE EARLY COLD WAR YEARS, OR
How the Virgin Mary Protected the West from Communism

Monique Scheer

An important dimension of everyday culture in the United States during the Cold War was the foregrounding of the notion that American national identity was tightly bound up with religious commitment. One of communism's most salient features was its self-proclaimed atheism; by inverse conclusion, to be anti-Communist (and therefore a "good American") was to be God-fearing. Regular attendance at religious services, and perhaps even more importantly "a highly favorable attitude toward religion became forms of affirming 'the American way of life' during the Cold War," and at the same time "the most effective shield against the suspicion of subversiveness."[1] Among politicians, the idea took hold that American government was somehow fundamentally grounded in religion, in spite of the meager references to God in the founding documents of the country. Congress passed a law in 1954 adding the phrase "under God" to the "Pledge of Allegiance" to the flag, because, as one Congressman put it, "it highlights one of the real fundamental differences between the free world and the Communist world."[2] The public was to understand that the political and military threat communism represented to the country was intimately connected to the dangers it posed to the souls of the American people. Promoting pious behavior was considered tantamount to constructing a bulwark against Communist ideology. Though he had a large nuclear arsenal at his disposal, President Eisenhower nevertheless maintained that "spiritual weapons [are] our country's most powerful resource."[3] Religious leaders—particularly of the Christian churches—took advantage of this opportunity to have a stronger public voice. The issue of personal salvation, traditionally their domain, had now become politically relevant, as the Cold War was perceived as not only a military struggle, but also one for the hearts and minds of the population.

To what extent such observations on the religious culture of the Cold War in the United States apply to the European case has yet to be systematically investigated. Certainly there appear to be some parallels: politics was religiously charged in Europe after 1945, and religion was politically charged. The Catholic Church in particular set aside the defensive attitude it had maintained through decades of secularization and went on the offensive, not only against the Communist threat from an expanding sphere of Soviet control, but against the appeal of Communist parties in European countries, particularly France and Italy. The national elections in Italy in April of 1948, for example, were highly charged with religious implications. The Vatican put out the slogan: "essere con Cristo o contro Cristo: e tutta la questione"—Italian voters, it said, were either for Christ or against him, making clear to them the spiritual dimensions of their political decisions.[4] In West Germany, the traditional confessional geography was in flux: Catholics were no longer a minority and enjoyed social recognition as a community that had ostensibly not succumbed as fully as others to Nazi indoctrination.[5] German Catholics were emerging from their enclave, and they brought their perceived moral integrity and newfound confidence to bear in postwar politics, embodied in the first postwar chancellor, the Catholic Konrad Adenauer. The sense that Western European identity was closely bound up with Christian faith[6] in opposition to a "godless communism" was also part of the dominant Cold War discourse in Europe. It is in this context that we find Konrad Adenauer echoing Eisenhower's words that it is necessary "to fight communism with spiritual weapons. … Without the help of prayer, we cannot defeat evil."[7] As in the United States, German Catholicism's traditional anti-Communist stance now dovetailed with the concerns of a broader sector of society, facilitating the integration of Catholic discourse into the mainstream as well as providing the religious activities of particularly eager believers a sort of political legitimacy.

Historians have long recognized that the Cold War had a strong religious dimension and that it gave everyday piety a political overlay, but they have not yet spent much time exploring these issues. The historian Dianne Kirby finds, in fact, that the subject has been "systematically neglected" in political histories of the conflict, and almost the same could be said of cultural histories as well.[8] However, the few studies that have been presented are beginning to show that in the everyday culture of the Cold War religion "mattered."[9] Indeed, "for many who lived through the period, the Cold War was one of history's great religious wars."[10] Believers saw their faith no longer just as a source of solace and support in the face of a military conflict, but rather as something to be militantly defended. Furthermore, they understood their nation to be the target of Soviet aggression precisely *because* it was a "Christian nation." Everyday religious activities thus acquired a stratum of anti-Communist discourse.

Billy Graham's apocalyptic message and fervent anti-communism went hand in hand with an urgent sense that the Christian message must be spread[11]—a sentiment he certainly shared with most European Christians, Catholic and Protestant alike. When he visited Germany after 1945, some Protestant groups in Germany, especially Pietists and the emerging German evangelical movement, found his large-scale missionary work to be an inspiring model for the "re-Christianization" of the European continent.[12] Mainstream Lutherans in Germany, however, distanced themselves from the evangelicals' emotional preaching style. Furthermore, mainline Protestantism seemed more concerned with working through its compromised past than fighting Soviet aggression. Important Lutheran figures like Martin Niemöller placed a higher value on national unity between East and West Germany than on freedom from Communist rule, and maintained that recognizing the guilt of the German people was the appropriate starting point for reestablishing a Christian foundation for German society.[13] Pietists, on the other hand, shared the Catholic view that this was not necessary,[14] though they still struggled with the question of how much to become involved in politics and were institutionally at a disadvantage.[15] The smaller, more conservative Pietist or evangelical groups had to either exist in a niche within the larger, predominantly Lutheran state church, or else organize as "free churches" without state support. Thus, staunchly anti-Communist Protestant groups, unlike in the U.S., where all denominations "competed" equally on an open religious "market," were hindered from gaining a foothold in European Cold War society.[16] This contributed to well organized and institutionally supported Catholicism's more prominent position in Europe as *the* Christian denomination with the most stalwart and reliable anti-Communist stance.

For all its centralist and hierarchical structure, however, the Catholic community was by no means monolithic, and there were in fact some small groups which favored friendlier relations between Catholics and

Communists, even during the Cold War. In spite of strong anti-modernist pressure coming from the Vatican since the mid nineteenth century (which made its presence concretely felt in the "Oath against Modernism" required at the ordination of every Catholic priest from 1910 to 1967), there were nevertheless theologians who were interested in integrating some Socialist principles into their work. A prime example is the "nouvelle théologie" embodied in the work of Yves-Marie-Joseph Congar (1904–1995) and Marie-Dominique Chenu (1894–1989), who advised and supported the worker-priest movement in France.[17] In postwar Germany, left-wing Catholic sentiment was represented in the *Frankfurter Hefte*, edited by Walter Dirks and Eugen Kogon. However, its following remained more or less limited to an intellectual elite without the capacity to wield political power, particularly in the dominantly conservative atmosphere of the time.[18] Furthermore, the Vatican consistently and unequivocally condemned any activities that sought to reconcile Catholicism with Marxist thought, and had undisputedly enormous influence. Therefore, despite some small pockets of nonconformity, it can be safely said that the dominant strands of European and American Catholicism in this period were overwhelmingly anti-Communist.

If Catholicism felt particularly called to the engagement against communism, then it also had a particularly well-suited vehicle for bringing it down to the level of the common believer: the cult of Mary. The melding of Cold War politics with personal piety will therefore be explored in the following using the example of Catholic devotion to Mary, which experienced a remarkable surge in popularity and publicity during the late 1940s and 1950s all over the world. Catholicism, besides being a theology and an institution, is understood in this essay from an anthropological perspective as a worldview expressed in and supported by an elaborate symbolic system.[19] That is to say, it is not the theology per se that is the focus here, but the symbols and narratives that the cult of Mary provides its believers to make sense of their experiences. These are provided within the institutionalized Church and flourish in popular piety. The way each impinges upon the other will also be shown as this essay seeks to demonstrate the extent to which the Cold War shaped devotion to Mary, and conversely how believers' perceptions of a looming threat were shaped by their devotion to this saint.

War and the "Marian Century"

The "Marian Century" was a period of increasing attention to the Virgin Mary in Catholicism, ushered in by the declaration of the dogma of the Immaculate Conception in 1854 and culminating in the announcement of the Assumption dogma in 1950.[20] It was also a century of great bloodshed in Europe. The wounds of wartime were still quite fresh when tensions with the Soviet Union began to rise, and in the fall of 1949 the first Soviet nuclear bomb was tested. Fear of a renewed conflict much like the past one—or even worse—ran high, and some individuals funneled this emotional energy into their religious beliefs and practices. In his declaration of the dogma in 1950, Pope Pius XII noted that "piety toward the Virgin Mother of God is flourishing and daily growing more fervent." The hardship associated with wartime had caused the faithful to be more "vigorously aroused to a more assiduous consideration of [Mary's] prerogatives," and so the truth of her glorification had "shone forth more clearly."[21] The wording of the encyclical confirms the observation of a connection between Marian piety and wartime, indicating that the cult of Mary provided cultural resources for coping with war experience by providing interpretive schemes with which to make sense of political events that ultimately caused people to suffer greatly.

One of these schemes was the interpretation of war as divine punishment. Far from being a medieval relic no longer understood by modern Europeans, this teaching was recalled, for example, by the Bishop of Münster in 1945 as he spoke to his flock from the steps of what had once been the city hall, now a pile of rubble after the Allied bombing attacks. The Germans had brought this punishment upon themselves, he said, because "wide sections of the German people have increasingly renounced the belief in God and in Christ, and have left the Church," getting caught up in "truly satanic entanglements" with the regime.[22] From the Catholic point of view in Germany after 1945, Nazism had been the logical extreme of a generally anthropocentric trend that had begun with the Renaissance—or, at the latest, with the French Revolution.[23] The consequence (phrased in religious terms as "punishment") had been war. As soon as the threat of the next World War became tangible, this interpretive scheme could be reapplied: God would lower his rod again to punish the West for its secularism by unleashing another war through an atheist regime—this time the Soviet Union.

For Catholics, one of the most fundamental functions of the saints' cults is to provide a divine personage to turn to in times of crisis, who can intervene with God on behalf of the petitioner, that he might remove his punishment. During the "Marian century," this function was focused increasingly on Mary, who was believed to have the greatest power of intervention with her son. The Marian pilgrimage shrines and her churches, chapels, and side altars are locations at which the presence of the Virgin was symbolized and the faithful communicated their petitions to her through prayer, hymn, and the lighting of candles. And increasingly, Mary began to answer: people gathered in large numbers at sites where it was believed that she herself had appeared on earth to speak to certain visionary individuals. Most of the time, Mary's message informed her followers that the community as a whole had sinned, and gave them instructions on how to avert further punishment by her son, usually through prayer and penance, often also the building of a shrine at the apparition site.[24] The basic pattern of the Marian apparition evolved in France during the nineteenth century, the apparitions at Lourdes in 1858 attaining the greatest prominence. Several apparitions were approved by the local bishops according to rules and procedures set out by the Church centuries before, meaning that while Catholics were not required to believe they had actually happened, the Church recognized the possibility that they were real and supported them with pilgrimages. The French tradition of annual "national pilgrimages" to Lourdes began in 1872 after the country's defeat at the hands of Prussia, interpreted within Catholicism as divine punishment for the sins of the Republic and the Paris Commune.[25] Throughout the "Marian Century," the modern apparition cult was given impetus and charge through war experiences.

This reading of the function of apparition cults is supported by the fact that, as Europe was just recovering from the aftermath of World War II and confronting the possibility of yet another war of probably even greater destructive dimensions, a wave of Marian apparitions swept across the continent greater than any that had come before. Between 1947 and 1954 there were an average of thirteen to fourteen apparitions reported to the diocesan authorities each year, more than three times the average of the preceding and following decades.[26] The majority were reported in Italian parishes, but in Germany, Spain, and France as well, there was more than one sighting of the Virgin on average in each country each year, sometimes drawing crowds that numbered in the tens of thousands for weeks and months on end. Catholics on the other side of the "Iron Curtain" also felt Mary's special attention to their plight: in the cathedral of Lublin, Poland, for example, a statue of Mary reportedly began to weep, drawing crowds of up to 100,000 a day. These gatherings were interpreted by the authorities as anti-Communist demonstrations, and the police were instructed to intervene.[27] In Western Europe, however, the secular authorities did not see the outbreak of an apparition cult in the countryside as a threat and left the regulation of the affair to the Church authorities, who seemed increasingly taken aback by this development, and in contrast to their practice up to the 1930s gave none of these apparitions official approval. The "piety toward the Virgin Mother of God" which Pius XII had praised in November 1950 as "flourishing and daily growing more fervent" needed to be reined in, as Cardinal Ottaviani noted in *L'Osservatore romano* only months later (4 February 1951). What the clergy perceived as "excess," however, was of their own making, as William Christian, Jr., has argued, particularly because missionary activity in the postwar period drew strongly on the symbolic capital that Mary provided, including the belief in her appearances on earth.[28]

Fatima and the "Marianization of the Masses"

The canon of approved French apparitions, most especially Lourdes, remained important points of reference for the dramaturgy and "look" of the new apparitions, but even more relevant for the Cold War period were the apparitions in Fatima, Portugal, which had been reported by three young children between May and October of 1917. The immense popularity of Fatima beginning in the 1940s is closely connected to war experience and the fear of Soviet aggression. Initially a response to Portugal's entry into World War I in March of 1917, when unprecedented numbers of young men were recruited and sent to the western front, Mary's appearances took on new meaning as time went by. After some initial difficulties, including resistance from the secular authorities as well as a temporarily vacant Episcopal seat, a diocesan commission finally confirmed the authenticity of the Fatima apparitions in 1930. From then on, the pilgrimage site was firmly supported by the Church and the Salazar regime as a symbol of the triumph, achieved through Mary's intervention, over the anticlerical, secular government.[29] From 1937 to 1941, one of the visionary children, now a nun, submitted to her bishop a written record of her memories of all these events, now clearly colored by her experience of the Spanish Civil War in the intervening years.[30] Perhaps the most significant new piece of information for the general public was her recollection in 1941 that Mary had told her three "secrets" in 1917, two of which she could now reveal.[31] She claimed that Mary had prophesied the coming of World War II, identifying not Nazi Germany but the Soviet Union as the aggressor. To avoid further war, Mary had recommended making the "Five First Saturdays" a special devotion to her Immaculate Heart, in order to "convert Russia." Finally, Mary asked that Russia be consecrated to her Immaculate Heart, also to ensure peace through the conversion of its people to Christian belief (see Illustration 6.1). This much later version of the story of Fatima was published in 1943 and distributed internationally, becoming the new dominant narrative of the apparition events.[32]

Illustration 6.1. Image of Sister Lucia's 1925 visions of Mary asking for devotion to her Immaculate Heart. Statue in the Carmelite convent in Coimbra, Portugal.
From Bote von Fatima, August 1951, 503. (All illustrations from the author's archive.)

The years 1942–43 were to become a turning point for the Fatima apparition cult also because of the attention paid to it by Pope Pius XII. In Fatima, the twenty-fifth anniversary of the apparitions was celebrated in

1942, with the high point of the closing ceremonies on the evening of 31 October being an address delivered by the pope via Vatican radio.[33] His speech began by recognizing the role of "divine intervention," as he phrased it, in the restoration of Catholic rule to Portugal and the successful aversion of the "red menace" in nearby Spain during the mid 1930s, due to the tide of devotion stimulated by Mary's appearances in Fatima. The protection that she had provided Portugal was now needed elsewhere, moving the pope to close his speech with a prayer to Mary, consecrating not only the Church, but "the entire world torn by violent discord, scorched in a fire of hate, victim of its own iniquities" to her "Immaculate Heart" and asking for her aid and intercession to end World War II.[34] During the following year, Catholic bishops were requested by the curia to reiterate the ritual at the local level by consecrating their dioceses to Mary, triggering a wave of commemorative activities in 1943 that were often accompanied by sermons on the significance of Marian apparitions in times of war. After the war's end, on 13 May 1946, a papal emissary crowned the Fatima statue before a crowd of 600,000.[35] The Church's uses of the Fatima message throughout Europe in the following years throughout Europe were met with great enthusiasm. Traveling madonnas, special missionary events, and Fatima masses all contributed to making Fatima a household word by 1950.[36]

The Fatima-led Marian revival of the early Cold War period was as much a result of Church-guided efforts as it was a movement from below. It began as a result of activities begun during World War II, and in a seamless transition after the war, Mary's special protection was specifically, explicitly, and almost exclusively aimed at the Communist/Soviet/Russian threat, a development that may also have reflected an increasing influence of American Catholicism in the Church as a whole,[37] and in the organization of the Fatima cult itself. In 1952, the tenth anniversary of his consecration of the world to the Immaculate Heart of Mary, Pope Pius XII issued an apostolic letter stating that he would now consecrate the peoples of the Soviet Union to Mary's Immaculate Heart, thereby granting a request made in countless letters he had received in the last two years.[38] Such letter-writing campaigns were among the instruments that the many Fatima-inspired organizations used to further their cause of "fulfilling the demands Mary made at Fatima." Perhaps the most high-profile of these organizations was the Blue Army of Fatima, founded in the United States in 1947 and boasting millions of members worldwide within a few years.[39] The organization spread quickly throughout Europe, reaching West Germany in 1951. Membership in the Blue Army entailed a pledge to pray the rosary daily, to make the First Five Saturdays, to consecrate oneself to Mary's Immaculate Heart, and to wear a medal or scapular as a sign of this pledge.[40] Thus, it did not preclude or hinder membership in the many other Marian organizations that already existed, some of which now also raised the banner of Fatima, perhaps also in an effort to boost their membership. "Rosary Crusades," prayer groups led by the Franciscan order in Vienna, were soon started up in other countries. The centuries-old Catholic practice of praying the rosary was given a Fatima-inspired, anti-Communist thrust, becoming almost as much a political act as a pious one. The "message of Fatima" was integrated into the enormous infrastructure of Marian piety that had been built up in Europe since the mid nineteenth century—Marian congregations, sodalities, brotherhoods, the Legion of Mary, the Militiae Immaculatae, Schönstatt—none of these organizations could ignore Fatima, nor did they necessarily want to.[41] Protest or criticism of Church-approved apparitions was, at this time, quite rare and only occurred with a strong sense of breaking a taboo.[42]

In the U.S., the electronic media were enlisted in the "Marianization of the masses."[43] The radio waves were replete with religious orders and other organizations offering "Rosary Prayer Hours" and other religious programming. Archbishop Fulton Sheen's popular television show, *Life is Worth Living*, awarded an Emmy in 1952, was known for its staunchly Christian and anti-Communist message. It was broadcast in prime time (Tuesday evenings from 8:00 to 8:30 PM) and enjoyed a viewing audience of some twenty-five million, Catholic and non-Catholic alike.[44] The use of this medium seems to have been less pronounced in Europe: the charismatic Jesuit Johannes Leppich relied on public speaking and best-selling books to get across his anti-Communist and revivalist message. What did cross over, however, were American films, among them the Oscar-winning *Song of Bernadette*, based on Franz Werfel's novelization of the Lourdes story.[45] This film, released in West German cinemas between the fall of 1948 and the spring of 1949, struck a chord with audiences; in some areas of Germany it was the film with the largest audience of the year 1949.[46] When in the very same year young girls at two different sites in West Germany claimed to have visions of the Virgin Mary similar to those of Bernadette, the young seer of Lourdes, many commentators attributed this directly to the influence of the film, which the girls had admittedly seen.[47] Both the popularity of the film and the attractiveness of the apparition cults for tens of thousands of pilgrims are evidence of the Marian fervor of the early Cold War years, feeding off deep-seated fears of another war, amplified by Church efforts to profit from the energies created by popular devotion to Mary, especially in apparition cults, and given free reign by a political culture committed to supporting piety as a "weapon" in the Cold War. By offering the key to understanding the "deeper causes" of the Cold War as a spiritual struggle, this formerly local

Portuguese pilgrimage site entered the consciousness of the entire Catholic world, with consequences for popular religious culture in Europe.

Visions of Conversion

As the example of the Fatima cult demonstrates, the Church set great store by the missionizing effects of "popular piety," but by 1951 saw it spinning out of its control. While the Church managed and legitimized the symbolic language that constituted the cult of Mary, believers used this language to articulate their hopes and fears in ways that the many clerics and Church leaders did not accept. Fatima offered Catholics a narrative that resonated so strongly with them that it caused an unprecedented number of reported visions of Mary to attract droves of believers. These new apparitions followed more or less faithfully the dramaturgy of the canonized apparitions of Lourdes and Fatima, most often with young girls as seers and an apparition prophesying war with the Soviet Union, one that could only be averted if the faithful prayed hard enough and did penance for the sins of mankind against God. These sins were identified primarily as a "turning away from God" in the drive toward secularism and modernization, thus the recurring theme of "conversion" in many of the apparitions.[48] "Conversion" usually meant a return to active religious belief and conformity with Catholic rules of conduct. The story of the apparitions at the Trappist monastery of Tre Fontane just outside Rome illustrate this theme perhaps most clearly: The seer was a 33-year-old veteran of the Spanish Civil War, where he had volunteered on the Republican side and learned to despise the pope and the Catholicism of his childhood. On 12 April 1947, while strolling with his children on the grounds of the abbey, first his children and then he himself reportedly had a vision of Mary, in which she called him back to the fold. The seer had several more visions in the following months, and within the year the site was transformed into a pilgrimage shrine to accommodate the thousands of believers.[49] Two years later, in Fehrbach, a village near the German–French border, a twelve-year-old girl claimed to see and converse with Mary, who demanded prayer and penance from the community and called herself the "Mother of the Conversion of Sinners," drawing a crowd of as many as 15,000 from the spring of 1949 to the fall of 1952.[50]

The specific message of Fatima, however, that war could be averted through the "conversion of Russia," was perhaps nowhere more dramatically rendered than in the "Russian Visions" (*Russenvisionen*) of 1950 that were part of the apparition cult in Heroldsbach-Thurn, a village in southeastern Germany. It had begun in October 1949, as reports of daily appearances of the Virgin Mary to a group of young girls became the focus of regular devotional gatherings, drawing crowds of up to 50,000.[51] Questions about the whereabouts of relatives still being held as prisoners of war in the Soviet Union were often asked, as was the simple question: "Will there be another war?" Mary's answer was always: "Not if you pray." The West German press, only recently reinstituted, pounced upon these events, sending in photographers and reporters to document what might be the beginning of a "German Lourdes." The reports presented the apparition cults as symptomatic of the times. While southern German newspapers tended to emphasize the theme of religious revival nourished by the deep piety typical of rural folk, especially women, the northern German, big-city gazettes such as *Der Spiegel* were more skeptical, but nevertheless impressed by the hope these "miraculous" happenings had awakened in the local population.[52] It placed a photo of the visionary girls on its cover during the first weeks of the Heroldsbach events, with a suggestive caption taken from a popular nursery rhyme: "Your father's in the war" (see Illustration 6.2). The choice of the *Spiegel* cover illustration indicates that the image of children leading the community in prayer, even for outsiders, somehow captured the spirit of that historical moment, somewhere between a war that was not yet over and one that had not yet begun, and the resulting hunger for some sort of divine intervention.

The diocesan authorities in Bamberg denied the authenticity of the apparitions at Heroldsbach, and in March 1950 prohibited all members of the clergy from attending the devotions there. From this point onward, the cult activities were left entirely to a rather zealous laity, who took on the roles formerly occupied by clergy, such as leading the prayers, hymns, and processions, giving sermons, and most importantly acting as liaison between the visionaries and the audience. They also interviewed the seers about all they had seen and heard and meticulously recorded this information for the Church investigators they still hoped would one day take up their cause. These records relate the following series of visions as reported by the young seers.[53]

On 15 May 1950, one of the visionary girls said Mary was telling her that the "Russians were coming" and the people should bring her candles and matches to bless. For several days, the girls repeatedly had a vision of soldiers in close combat, the one side dressed in brown, the other in black. The men in brown went into the houses of the village and brought out the old people, women, and children, and shot them point blank. One of the girls said: "The soldiers are standing in blood up to their ankles."[54] The girls claimed to hear Mary's voice saying: "It won't be long now. ... The Russians will come."[55] At the same time, the girls repeatedly claimed to see their village, and above it Mary spreading out her mantle

Illustration 6.2. *Der Spiegel* of 17 October 1949.

to cover it in a gesture of heavenly protection. One day, the girls claimed they had seen a Russian soldier standing directly before them and showed him their rosaries, explaining that they prayed to Mary with them. They then claimed to see the soldier kneel before a statue of Mary and pray as well. The girls reported that more and more Russian soldiers were arriving at the scene and, like their comrade before them, were so moved by the pure, innocent piety of these young girls that they also fell to their knees and prayed. The children repeated over and over "We have seen the Madonna" until they had converted each and every one. Then they said the soldiers gave them bread, chocolate, and candy.[56]

The group conversion of the Soviet soldiers was a reference to and confirmation of the "secret" of Fatima, that future wars would be started by the Soviet Union's attempting to spread its atheist ideology, and thus could only be stopped by a "conversion" of the country. The fighting ends, the vision told its listeners, when the foe kneels and prays to Mary together with us. In the diocesan archives, letters from individuals who had witnessed these events reflect their belief that the children could not possibly have invented these visions, as due to their youth they could have no understanding of their political meaning.[57] Whether or not this is the case, it is clear that the girls acted as antennas for the fears of this community, located less than a hundred miles from the border with the Soviet bloc, and that they bore the burden of ritually driving out those fears for the sake of the collective.

Marian Piety in European Cold War Culture

Catholic clergy in Europe launched many commemorative events in the early postwar years—the annual reiteration of the papal consecration of the world to Mary's Immaculate Heart of 1942, the "wandering virgin" recalling the events in Fatima, the declaration of the Assumption dogma in 1950, the Marian Year of 1954—which kept Mary in the public eye and at the forefront of Catholic consciousness. There are many reasons why the Church placed so much emphasis on the cult of Mary during these years, including the fact that the Marian revival had been under way for a century already and proven itself effective in rekindling religious participation in the past. Adapting the cult of Mary to the concerns of the Cold War, then, involved reactivating strata of symbolic meaning that had lain more or less dormant since the wars of religion in the sixteenth and seventeenth centuries. This reactivation was quite conscious: Catholic commentators frequently referred to similarities between earlier wars against heretics and nonbelievers in order to legitimate a reliance on Mary as a special patroness in this new "religious war."[58] They did this for good pastoral reasons: legends of Mary's intervention in wars against Christendom, as well as the image of *Maria della Victoria*, demonstrated that it was worthwhile to place one's faith in her aid, as it had proven successful time and time again, thus offering solace to those fearing another world war.

Participation in this religious activity meant participating in a cognitive frame that interpreted the war in two ways that appear on the surface contradictory, but which ultimately made sense within the Catholic worldview of the time: On the one hand, war was seen as God's punishment of an unfaithful human collective, an interpretation which had its roots in the Hebrew Bible.[59] The pain of recognizing one's own responsibility for the war in sin and guilt could be ameliorated by praying for forgiveness and performing acts of penance, precisely the prescription handed out at Fatima and the other apparition sites. On the other hand, war against a Christian collective by non-Christians was seen as a religiously motivated attack that God would certainly not tolerate, particularly if the community proved itself worthy through its moral example. Thus, guilt and fear give way to hope, even confidence, and the appearances of Mary underline the supernatural truth of these beliefs. It was on the power of this cognitive structure that politicians and church leaders drew when they claimed that communism must be fought with "spiritual weapons."

Illustration 6.3. Mary with a "crown of twelve stars." Altar with Fatima madonna in the Carmelite church of Bamberg, West Germany, in December 1949.

From *Bote von Fatima*, January 1950, 343.

But not only did the discourses of the Cold War era find their way into the religious beliefs and practices of ordinary Catholics, but the cult of Mary also seemed to have something important to say to the culture at large about the truth of Cold War values. The Virgin of the apparition cults was often depicted with the attributes of the "woman of the apocalypse," a female figure described in the Book of Revelations as "clothed with the sun, with the moon under her feet, and on her head a crown of twelve stars"[60] (see Illustration 6.3), suggesting that the struggle through which Mary had come to guide her followers was somehow the Final Battle between Good and Evil.[61]

This particular iconography—as opposed to, say, the image of the Pièta—resonated with apocalyptic Cold War narratives, characterizations of the Soviet Union as an "evil empire," and polarized views of politics and morality ("essere con Cristo o contro Cristo"). At the same time, the Church continued to propagate images of Mary as Mother, the ultimate in womanhood, more a maternal ideal to be emulated than a victorious virgin goddess to be worshiped. This aspect, too, harmonized with Cold War Culture by supporting the "family values" that placed a premium on motherhood.[62] The image of Mary oscillates in this period between these two poles, serving the needs of those wanting to provide a moral orientation seen as necessary to shore up national unity in the face of the Communist threat, as well as more basic needs for divine intervention in the face of a coming war.

Perhaps partly as a result of the experiences of the "fervent fifties," the Second Vatican Council of the mid 1960s, with its far-reaching liturgical reforms, consciously limited the importance of the cult of Mary. Throughout the 1960s and 1970s, the Marian cult was seen as incompatible with progressive Catholicism, a legacy of the Cold War imprint on the cult that is still difficult to shake off. Not until the pontificate of John Paul II did the cult of Mary begin to regain some importance. Viewed against the backdrop of the material presented here, it seems rather significant that this renaissance took place during the Reagan years, which were widely perceived as a sort of revival of 1950s Cold War Culture. The Polish pope was known for his preference for Mary's protection and believed the Virgin of Fatima had saved him from the attempt on his life in 1981. For Fatima believers it was this kind of devotion that was the deeper and truer cause of the eventual fall of communism.

Notes

1. Stephen J. Whitfield, *The Culture of the Cold War* (Baltimore, 1991), 83.
2. Ibid., 89.
3. Ibid., 90.
4. Robert A. Ventresca, "The Virgin and the Bear," *Journal of Social History* 37 (2003): 439.
5. See Damian van Melis, "'Strengthened and Purified Through Ordeal by Fire,'" in *Life After Death*, eds. Richard Bessel and Dirk Schumann (Washington, 2003), 231–242.
6. See, for example, Anselm Doering-Manteuffel, "Kirche und Katholizismus in der Bundesrepublik der Fünfziger Jahre," *Historisches Jahrbuch* 102 (1982): 113–134.
7. Konrad Adenauer, in a speech given in Schaumburg Palace in Bonn on 30 May 1954, upon receiving the first Peace Prize instituted by the "Blue Army," an international organization dedicated to promoting devotion to Mary Fatima. He was awarded the prize for "excellent service in the battle against godless communism and for world

peace," according to the report in the German devotional periodical *Maria siegt*, no. 4 (May 1955). See also Andreas Johannes Fuhs, *Fatima und der Friede*, 2nd ed. (Steyl, 1961), 168, 238 (n. 2).

8. Dianne Kirby, "Religion and the Cold War—An Introduction," in *Religion and the Cold War*, ed. D. Kirby (Houndmills and New York, 2003), 1. Whitfield's inclusion of a chapter on the religious revival in America in connection with anti-communism in his study *The Culture of the Cold War* seems, in fact, to be an exception, as the many cultural histories of the Cold War that emerged in the 1990s either do not include studies of religion or only treat them in passing. For an overview of the literature, see Robert Griffith, "The Cultural Turn in Cold War Studies," *Reviews in American History* 29 (2001): 150–157.

9. In addition to Kirby's collection, see Robert S. Ellwood, *The Fifties Spiritual Marketplace* (New Brunswick, N.J., 1997). On devotion to the Virgin Mary during the Cold War, see William Christian, Jr., "Religious Apparitions and the Cold War in Southern Europe," in *Religion, Power, and Protest in Local Communities*, ed. Eric R. Wolf (Berlin, 1984), 239–265; Thomas Kselman and Steven Avella, "Marian Piety and the Cold War in the United States," *Catholic Historical Review* 72 (1986): 403–424; Nicholas Perry and Loreto Echeverría, *Under the Heel of Mary* (London and New York, 1988); Paula M. Kane, "Marian Devotion since 1940: Continuity or Casualty?" in *Habits of Devotion*, ed. James M. O'Toole (Ithaca, N.Y., 2004), 89–129; Monique Scheer, *Rosenkranz und Kriegsvisionen* (Tübingen, 2006).

10. Kirby, "Introduction," 1.

11. On Graham's early Cold War activities and message, see Whitfield, *Culture of the Cold War*, 77–82.

12. See Eberhard Busch, "Der Pietismus in Deutschland seit 1945," in *Der Pietismus im 19. und 20. Jahrhundert*, ed. Ulrich Gäbler, vol. 3 of *Geschichte des Pietismus*, eds. Martin Brecht et al. (Göttingen, 2000), 535; see also Friedhelm Jung, *Die deutsche Evangelikale Bewegung* (Bonn, 1994), 35.

13. Niemöller was widely cited as having stated in an interview with the *New York Herald Tribune*: "Most Germans would prefer the reunification of their country under communism to the continuation of its current divide into East and West." Cited in Martin Greschat, *Die evangelische Christenheit und die deutsche Geschichte nach 1945* (Stuttgart, 2002), 397 (my translation). On the question of the Protestant treatment of German guilt, see ibid., 139–147.

14. Cf. Busch, "Der Pietismus in Deutschland," 534. Pietists distanced themselves from the Lutherans' "Stuttgart Declaration of Guilt" made in October 1945, claiming that Christians "cannot do penance for anti-Christendom." Catholics were by and large also free of a sense of obligation to feel a collective German guilt, particularly since Pope Pius XII had made clear as early as his Christmas address of 1944 and again in an address to the College of Cardinals on 2 June 1945 that there was no collective guilt for Germans. See Ludwig Volk, ed., *Akten deutscher Bischöfe über die Lage der Kirche 1933–1945*, vol. 6, Veröffentlichungen der Kommission für Zeitgeschichte A 38 (Mainz, 1985), 886–890.

15. Cf. Busch, "Der Pietismus in Deutschland."

16. Scholars of the "economics of religion" have explored these differences between the European and American "religious markets." See, for example, Rodney Stark and Laurence R. Iannaccone, "A Supply-Side Reinterpretation of the 'Secularization' of Europe," *Journal for the Scientific Study of Religion* 33 (1994): 230–252.

17. Chenu's book outlining his main ideas, *Une école de théologie: le Saulchoir*, published in 1937, was forbidden by the Vatican in 1942. The pope put a stop to the worker-

priest movement in France in 1953. See also Paul Hainsworth, "Cold War on High and Unity from Below: The French Communist Party and the Catholic Church in the Early Years of the Gaullist Fifth Republic," in Kirby, *Religion and the Cold War*, 145–162.
18. Dirks expresses his resignation to this situation in "Der restaurative Charakter der Epoche," *Frankfurter Hefte* 5 (1950): 942–954. On German left-wing Catholicism, see Heiner Ludwig and Wolfgang Schroeder, eds., *Sozial- und Linkskatholizismus* (Frankfurt am Main, 1990).
19. Clifford Geertz, "Religion as a Cultural System," in *The Interpretation of Cultures* (New York, 1973), 87–125 (first published in *Anthropological Approaches to the Study of Religion*, ed. M. Banton, [London, 1966]).
20. Cf. the apostolic constitutions *Ineffabilis Deus* and *Munificentissimus Deus*, in William J. Doheny and Joseph P. Kelly, eds., *Papal Documents on Mary* (Milwaukee, 1954).
21. *Munificentissimus Deus*, in Doheny and Kelly, *Papal Documents*, 221.
22. Cited in Wilhelm Damberg, *Abschied vom Milieu?* (Paderborn, 1997), 107–108.
23. This interpretation was included in the party program of the CDU (the "Kölner Leitsätze") in 1946; see Eike Wolgast, *Die Wahrnehmung des Dritten Reichs in der unmittelbaren Nachkriegszeit (1945/46)*, Schriften der Philosophisch-historischen Klasse der Heidelberger Akademie der Wissenschaften 22 (Heidelberg, 2001), 129.
24. See Sandra Zimdars-Swartz, *Encountering Mary* (Princeton, 1991), 3–12.
25. Ruth Harris, *Lourdes* (London, 2000), 249–255.
26. In the decades before this period, from 1931 to 1946, the average number of apparitions reported in Europe was four per year; in the decades following, i.e., from 1955 to 1975, an average of three per year were reported. See the table in Christian, "Religious Apparitions and the Cold War," 242, which builds on the statistics presented in 1971 to the Société française d'études mariales in Pontmain, published in Bernard Billet et al., eds., *Vraies et fausses apparitions dans l'Eglise*, 2nd ed. (Paris, 1976), 11–24.
27. On Lublin, see Izabella Main, "Weeping Virgin Mary and the Smiling Comrade Stalin," in *Sphären von Öffentlichkeit in Gesellschaften sowjetischen Typs*, eds. Gábor T. Rittersporn, Malte Rolf, and Jan C. Behrends (Frankfurt am Main and New York, 2003), 255–278.
28. Christian, "Religious Apparitions and the Cold War," 249.
29. For a highly critical account of the relationship between Fatima and the Salazar regime, see Perry and Echeverría, *Under the Heel of Mary*, 181–193.
30. These documents have been published in edited form in Antonio Maria Martins and Robert J. Fox, eds., *Documents on Fatima and Memoirs of Sister Lucia* (Alexandria, S. Dak., 1992). See also Scheer, *Rosenkranz und Kriegsvisionen*, 58–71.
31. The mysterious "third secret of Fatima" was the source of much speculation during the Cold War period, and plays into a broader theme of "secrecy" in Cold War culture. The most commonly held belief was that it was a prophecy of nuclear apocalypse. The story circulated widely that the real reason for the resolution of the Cuban missile crisis was the revelation of the third secret to Kennedy and Khrushchev. For more on the Cold War anxieties, apocalypticism and the third secret, see Zimdars-Swartz, *Encountering Mary*, 201–219.
32. The Italian original from Luigi Gonzaga da Fonseca, *La Meraviglie de Fátima*, first published in Casale Monferrato in 1931, was revised and approved by the visionary and published in Rome in 1942. Casimir Barthas presented Fonseca's material in the French translation in the same year, and an English translation was prepared based on his book with the title *Our Lady of Light* (published in Dublin and Milwaukee in

1947). The book was published in a German translation in 1944 in Fribourg, Switzerland, under Fonseca's name with the title: *Maria spricht zur Welt! Geheimnis und weltgeschichtliche Sendung Fátimas*.
33. The salutation "Benedicite Deum" was printed in full on the front page of the Vatican newspaper the next day with the headline: "Il Radiomessagio del Sommo Pontefice al Portogallo: Il Supremo Pastore nella grave ora presente consacra il genere umano al Cuore Immacolato di Maria," *L'Osservatore Romano*, 2/3 November 1942, 1.
34. See the text of the "Consecration of the World to the Immaculate Heart of Mary" in Doheny and Kelly, *Papal Documents on Mary*, 202–204. The pope solemnly renewed the consecration on the Feast of the Immaculate Conception, 8 December 1942, in St. Peter's Basilica, see "Il Sacro Rito Espiatorio e Impetratorio nella Basilica Vaticana: Il Sommo Pontefice in unione al Suo popolo rinnova la Consacrazione dell' umanità al Cuore Immacolato di Maria," *L'Osservatore Romano*, 9/10 December 1942, 1.
35. See link to Bote von Fatima home page:
36. Cf. Christian, "Religious Apparitions and the Cold War," 247ff.; Scheer, *Rosenkranz und Kriegsvisionen*, 127–160.
37. Perry and Echeverría argue that the loss of access to Eastern Europe shifted the focus of the Vatican westward, particularly to the U.S., where Catholics were now becoming the largest Christian denomination. Perry and Echeverría, *Under the Heel of Mary*, 232.
38. Cf. *Carissimis Russiae Populis*, 7 July 1952, in Doheny and Kelly, *Papal Documents on Mary*, 249–251. See also the Latin version (*Epistula Apostolica ad Universos Russiae Populos*) published on 4 August 1952 in Acta Apostolicae Sedis, vol. 44 (1952), 505–511.
39. Cf. Kselman and Avella, "Marian Piety and the Cold War," 409f.
40. "Kleiner Katechismus der Blauen Armee Mariens," in Andreas Johannes Fuhs, *Fatima und der Friede*, 3rd ed. (Steyl, 1983), 246.
41. For an overview of Marian organizations in Germany during this period and their attitude toward Fatima, see Scheer, *Rosenkranz und Kriegsvisionen*, 96–108.
42. See, for example, Pater Bernardus, "Fatima—Wahrheit oder Täuschung?" *Ökumenische Einheit* 2 (1951): 255–271. Even in this openly reformist journal, the author prefers to use a pseudonym, a fact discussed in a letter in the archive of the Ordinariate of the Archdiocese of Munich (letter from a pastor dated 8 May 1954, in EOM, Registratur des Generalvikariats, Signatur Fatima, box no. 1313). For an overview of Fatima critiques in Germany, see Scheer, *Rosenkranz und Kriegsvisionen*, 109–119 and 254–260.
43. Perry and Echeverría, *Under the Heel of Mary*, 238.
44. Whitfield, *Culture of the Cold War*, 170ff.
45. Werfel fled Europe in 1940 via Lourdes, where he vowed to write the novel in return for his safe passage to the U.S. The book was completed the following year, appearing first in German (*Das Lied von Bernadette* [Stockholm, 1941]), then in an English translation (*The Song of Bernadette*, trans. Lewis Lewisohn [Garden City, N.Y., 1942]), and became the surprise top seller of the Book-of-the-Month-Club. The movie rights were immediately bought by 20th Century-Fox, and the film was released in December 1943. It was nominated for an Academy Award in the categories Best Film and Best Screenplay; Jennifer Jones, who played the role of Bernadette Soubirous, the young visionary of Lourdes, received the Oscar for Best Actress. See Peter Stephan Jungk, *Franz Werfel: Eine Lebensgeschichte* (Frankfurt am Main, 1987), 290–297. Kselman and Avella also note that the release of the film gave "major impetus" to the Lourdes cult in the U.S. ("Marian Piety and the Cold War," 408).

46. Statistics are hard to come by, but this result is documented for the city of Ludwigshafen in the French occupation zone. See Peter Gleber, "Kino als Überlebensmittel," *Zeitschrift für die Geschichte des Oberrheins* 145 (1997): 422. See also Scheer, *Rosenkranz und Kriegsvisionen*, 143.
47. This was noted in the case of the apparitions in Fehrbach and Heroldsbach in West Germany; see Scheer, *Rosenkranz und Kriegsvisionen*, 197, 213.
48. Christian notes the prominence of this theme in the Cold War apparitions in Southern Europe ("Religious Apparitions and the Cold War," 252f.); the same can be said of those in Germany.
49. Gottfried Hierzenberger and Otto Nedomansky, *Erscheinungen und Botschaften der Gottesmutter Maria* (Augsburg, 1993), 350–354.
50. Cf. Scheer, *Rosenkranz und Kriegsvisionen*, 193–207.
51. Cf. ibid., 207–245. See also Cornelia Göksu, *Heroldsbach* (Würzburg, 1991).
52. "Heller Schein im gelben Laub: Auges eines verschreckten Rehes," *Der Spiegel*, 27 October 1949, 31f. See also the series of local reports in the *Nürnberger Zeitung*, *Nürnberger Nachrichten*, and *Fränkischer Tag*.
53. Johann Baptist Walz, *Die Protokolle von Augenzeugen zu den "Muttergottes-Erscheinungen" von Heroldsbach-Thurn*, vols. 1–3 (Mönchengladbach, 1958).
54. Walz, *Protokolle*, vol. 1, 242.
55. Ibid.
56. Ibid., 244.
57. See, for example, letters filed under "Heroldsbach" (5954) in the Faulhaber Papers, Archives of the Archdiocese of Munich (Erzbischöfliches Archiv München, EAM).
58. Examples of the comparison of the Cold War to the wars of religion in the episcopal letters from Rottenburg (*Kirchliches Amtsblatt für die Diözese Rottenburg* 53 [7 June 1948], 93) and Augsburg (*Amtsblatt für die Diözese Augsburg* 53 [21 April 1943], 77) could stand in for countless such references from bishops all over Europe during this period. See also Christian, "Religious Apparitions and the Cold War," 249f.
59. On the religious interpretations of war in the context of popular piety in the early modern period, cf. Klaus Schreiner, *Märtyrer, Schlachtenhelfer, Friedenstifter* (Opladen, 2000).
60. Revelations 12:1, quoted from *The New American Bible*, Catholic version (Nashville, 1970).
61. For a detailed analysis of the iconography of Marian apparitions and its connection with war experience, see Scheer, *Rosenkranz und Kriegsvisionen*, 263–298.
62. On American Cold War "family values," see Elaine Tyler May, *Homeward Bound* (New York, 1988).

Bibliography

Billet, Bernard, Joaquim-Maria Alonso, Boris Bobrinskoy, Marc Oraison, and René Laurentin, eds. *Vraies et fausses apparitions dans l'Eglise*. 2nd ed. Paris: Lethielleux, 1976.
Busch, Eberhard. "Der Pietismus in Deutschland seit 1945." In *Der Pietismus im 19. und 20. Jahrhundert*, ed. Ulrich Gäbler. Vol. 3 of *Geschichte des Pietismus*, ed. Martin Brecht, Klaus Deppermann, Ulrich Gäbler, and Hartmut Lehmann (Göttingen: Vandenhoeck & Ruprecht, 2000).

Christian, William, Jr. "Religious Apparitions and the Cold War in Southern Europe." In *Religion, Power, and Protest in Local Communities: The Northern Shore of the Mediterranean*, ed. Eric R. Wolf (Berlin: Mouton, 1984).
Damberg, Wilhelm. *Abschied vom Milieu? Katholizismus im Bistum Münster und in den Niederlanden 1945–1980*. Paderborn: Schöningh Verlag, 1997.
Dirks, Walter. "Der restaurative Charakter der Epoche." *Frankfurter Hefte* 5 (1950): 942–954.
Doering-Manteuffel, Anselm. "Kirche und Katholizismus in der Bundesrepublik der Fünfziger Jahre." *Historisches Jahrbuch* 102 (1982): 113–134.
Doheny, William J., and Joseph P. Kelly, eds. *Papal Documents on Mary*. Milwaukee: Bruce Publishers, 1954.
Ellwood, Robert S. *The Fifties Spiritual Marketplace: American Religion in a Decade of Conflict*. New Brunswick, N.J.: Rutgers University Press, 1997.
Fuhs, Andreas Johannes. *Fatima und der Friede*. 2nd ed. Steyl: Steyler Verlag, 1961.
Geertz, Clifford. "Religion as a Cultural System." In *The Interpretation of Cultures: Selected Essays by Clifford Geertz* (New York: Basic Books, 1973).
Gleber, Peter. "Kino als Überlebensmittel: Anfänge und Bedeutung dieses Mediums in der französischen Zone unter besonderer Berücksichtigung der Großstadt Ludwigshafen am Rhein 1945–1949." *Zeitschrift für die Geschichte des Oberrheins* 145 (1997): 403–429.
Göksu, Cornelia. *Heroldsbach: Eine verbotene Wallfahrt*. Würzburg: Echter Verlag, 1991.
Gotto, Klaus. "Zum Selbstverständnis der katholischen Kirche im Jahre 1945." In *Politik und Konfession: Festschrift für Konrad Repgen zum 60. Geburtstag*, eds. Dieter Albrecht et al. (Berlin: Duncker & Humblot, 1983).
Greschat, Martin. *Die evangelische Christenheit und die deutsche Geschichte nach 1945: Weichenstellungen in der Nachkriegszeit* (Stuttgart: Verlag W. Kohlhammer, 2002).
Griffith, Robert. "The Cultural Turn in Cold War Studies." *Reviews in American History* 29 (2001): 150–157.
Harris, Ruth. *Lourdes: Body and Spirit in the Secular Age*. London: Penguin Books, 2000.
Hierzenberger, Gottfried, and Otto Nedomansky. *Erscheinungen und Botschaften der Gottesmutter Maria: Vollständige Dokumentation durch zwei Jahrtausende*. Augsburg: Pattloch Verlag, 1993.
Jung, Friedhelm. *Die deutsche Evangelikale Bewegung: Grundlinien ihrer Geschichte und Theologie*. Bonn: Verlag für Kultur und Wissenschaft, 1994.
Jungk, Peter Stephan. *Franz Werfel: Eine Lebensgeschichte*. Frankfurt am Main: Fischer Verlag, 1987.
Kane, Paula M. "Marian Devotion since 1940: Continuity or Casualty?" In *Habits of Devotion: Catholic Religious Practice in Twentieth-Century America*, ed. James M. O'Toole (Ithaca, N.Y.: Cornell University Press, 2004).
Kirby, Dianne, ed. *Religion and the Cold War*. Houndmills and New York: Palgrave Macmillan, 2003.
Kselman, Thomas, and Steven Avella. "Marian Piety and the Cold War in the United States." *Catholic Historical Review* 72 (1986): 403–424.
Ludwig, Heiner, and Wolfgang Schroeder, eds. *Sozial- und Linkskatholizismus: Erinnerung—Orientierung—Befreiung*. Frankfurt am Main: Knecht Verlag, 1990.
Main, Izabella. "Weeping Virgin Mary and the Smiling Comrade Stalin: Polish Catholics and Communists in 1949." In *Sphären von Öffentlichkeit in Gesellschaften sowjetischen Typs: Zwischen parteistaatlicher Selbstinszenierung und kirchlichen Gegenwelten*, eds. Gábor T. Rittersporn, Malte Rolf, and Jan C. Behrends (Frankfurt am Main and New York: Peter Lang, 2003).

Martins, Antonio Maria, and Robert J. Fox, eds. *Documents on Fatima and Memoirs of Sister Lucia*. Alexandria, S.Dak.: Fatima Family Apostolate, 1992.
May, Elaine Tyler. *Homeward Bound: American Families in the Cold War Era*. New York: Basic Books, 1988.
Pater Bernardus, "Fatima—Wahrheit oder Täuschung?" *Ökumenische Einheit* 2 (1951): 255–271.
Perry, Nicholas, and Loreto Echeverría. *Under the Heel of Mary*. London and New York: Routledge, 1988.
Repgen, Konrad. "Die Erfahrungen des Dritten Reichs und das Selbstverständnis der deutschen Katholiken nach 1945." In *Die Zeit nach 1945 als Thema kirchlicher Zeitgeschichte*, ed. Victor Conzemius, Martin Greschat, and Herman Kocher (Göttingen: Vandenhoeck & Ruprecht, 1988).
Scheer, Monique. *Rosenkranz und Kriegsvisionen: Marienerscheinungskulte im 20. Jahrhundert*. Tübingen: Tübinger Vereinigung für Volkskunde, 2006.
Schreiner, Klaus. *Märtyrer, Schlachtenhelfer, Friedenstifter: Krieg und Frieden im Spiegel mittelalterlicher und frühneuzeitlicher Heiligenverehrung*. Otto-von-Freising-Vorlesungen der Katholischen Universität Eichstätt. Opladen: Leske + Budrich, 2000.
Stark, Rodney, and Laurence R. Iannaccone. "A Supply-Side Reinterpretation of the 'Secularization' of Europe." *Journal for the Scientific Study of Religion* 33 (1994): 230–252.
Van Melis, Damian. "'Strengthened and Purified Through Ordeal by Fire': Ecclesiastical Triumphalism in the Ruins of Europe." In *Life After Death: Approaches to a Cultural and Social History of Europe During the 1940s and 1950s*, ed. Richard Bessel and Dirk Schumann (Washington: German Historical Institute and Cambridge: Cambridge University Press, 2003).
Ventresca, Robert A. "The Virgin and the Bear: Religion, Society and the Cold War in Italy." *Journal of Social History* 37 (2003): 439–456.
Volk, Ludwig, ed. *Akten deutscher Bischöfe über die Lage der Kirche 1933–1945*, vol. 6. Veröffentlichungen der Kommission für Zeitgeschichte A 38. Mainz : Matthias-Grünewald-Verlag, 1985.
Walz, Johann Baptist. *Die Protokolle von Augenzeugen zu den "Muttergottes-Erscheinungen" von Heroldsbach-Thurn: Von Anfang an bis zum 2. Römischen Dekret (9. Okt. 1949 bis 25. Juli 1951)*. 3 vols. Mönchengladbach: Altgott, 1958.
Whitfield, Stephen J. *The Culture of the Cold War*. Baltimore: Johns Hopkins University Press, 1991.
Wolgast, Eike. *Die Wahrnehmung des Dritten Reichs in der unmittelbaren Nachkriegszeit (1945/46)*. Schriften der Philosophisch-historischen Klasse der Heidelberger Akademie der Wissenschaften 22. Heidelberg: Universitätsverlag Winter, 2001.
Zimdars-Swartz, Sandra. *Encountering Mary: Visions of Mary from La Salette to Medjugorje*. Princeton, N.J.: Princeton University Press, 1991.

Further documents

Amtsblatt für die Diözese Augsburg 53 [21 April 1943].
Epistula Apostolica ad Universos Russiae Populos, published on 4 August 1952 in *Acta Apostolicae Sedis*, vol. 44 (1952): 505–511.
"Il Radiomessagio del Sommo Pontefice al Portogallo: Il Supremo Pastore nella grave ora presente consacra il genere umano al Cuore Immacolato di Maria." *L'Osservatore Romano* No. 256, 2/3 November 1942.

"Il Sacro Rito Espiatorio e Impetratorio nella Basilica Vaticana: Il Sommo Pontefice in unione al Suo popolo rinnova la Consacrazione dell' umanità al Cuore Immacolato di Maria." *L'Osservatore Romano*, 9/10 December 1942.

"Heller Schein im gelben Laub: Auge eines verschreckten Rehes." *Der Spiegel*, 27 October 1949, 31f.

Kirchliches Amtsblatt für die Diözese Rottenburg 53 [7 June 1948].

Letters filed under "Heroldsbach" (5954) in the Faulhaber Papers, Archives of the Archdiocese of Munich (Erzbischöfliches Archiv München, EAM).

Ordinariate of the Archdiocese of Munich. (Letter from a pastor dated 8 May 1954, in EOM, Registratur des Generalvikariats, Signatur Fatima, box no. 1313).

The New American Bible, Catholic version. Nashville: Thomas Nelson Publishers, 1970.

Chapter 7

THE ROAD TO SOCIALISM PAVED WITH GOOD INTENTIONS
Automobile Culture in the Soviet Union, Romania, and the GDR During Détente

Luminita Gatejel

In 1960, the West German Journalist Helmut Müller traveled to the Soviet Union by car. In Moscow, he noted the following event in his diary:

> Stoi! The policeman on Gorky Street waves a red flag. We should stop the car! Around us, all the other drivers stop, too.... After five more minutes, the whole street is full of cars. Either Khrushchev is passing by, or in front of us a portion of the street was missing.... The policemen start to wave their flags again. We get it: davai, davai, go, go. The whole jam is set in motion again. On a balcony, we see a camera with a telephoto lens pointing down at the traffic on Gorky Street. We are astonished. After a few meters, we understand. A TV cameraman is filming the "giant" traffic in Moscow for some broadcast or television.... And the comrades in Komi and Kazakhstan will hold their breath while watching the coverage. With genuine conviction, they will tap foreign visitors on the back and say, "I recently saw a film about Moscow—well, you should have seen it, too. Then you would have a clear picture of how our traffic is about to overtake the West." Yes yes, comrades...ever heard of Potemkin?[1]

I chose this passage as an introduction for several reasons. Firstly, I would like to stress the importance of automobility in the self-presentation of the Soviet Union during the 1960s. Secondly, the quotation is a typical example of a Western glimpse into the Eastern camp intended to uncover the "hidden truth" behind the Iron Curtain for the audience back home. And thirdly, it refers to Khrushchev's dogma of peaceful Cold War competition—to "overtake the West without catching up." In this context, I argue that the history of the Socialist automobile cannot be understood without taking the Cold War paradigm into consideration. In addressing the meaning of the label "Socialist" with reference to cars in the 1960s and 1970s, my purpose is twofold: first, to discuss the impact of Western technology imports on the discourse surrounding the Socialist automobile, and then, in a second step, to assess the way Socialist cars were sold abroad on Western markets. The GDR will not be addressed in the first part of the essay, because East German cars were for the most part developed and produced domestically.

How important were cars to Socialist countries? The history of post-Stalinist socialism as seen through the windscreen of a car is a complex issue that encompasses various discursive patterns. In this paper, I adopt a view in which cars function as a kind of crossroads of the political economy, sociopolitical legitimacy, and personal lifestyle in Socialist societies. Brezhnev's and Ceaușescu's seizing power in 1964 and 1965, respectively, entailed a change in policy that did not, of course, endanger the system as a whole.[2] There are, however, some obvious differences. While Brezhnev attempted to contain his predecessor's reforms in the Soviet Union, the first years of Ceaușescu's rule brought about a political thaw. Nevertheless, both new leaders launched similar legitimizing campaigns. One of the key elements in these campaigns was the shift from a production-centered economic policy to an interest in consumption. The production of goods now began to aim at satisfying the populations' needs and demands. Even if the so-called consumerist turn in the Eastern block is attributed to Khrushchev,[3] it was his successor Brezhnev who converted the former general secretary's hasty decisions into a stable rule of power. Brezhnev succeeded in turning Khrushchev's initial reforms into a comprehensive, state-run service and welfare package that was then sold to the population as Socialist.[4] In this respect, the GDR was rather an exception, since its consumption rhetoric and practice was more influenced by its proximity to the Federal Republic of Germany. The gaze toward the West molded people's perception of consumption. Soon after the end of World War II, we can observe a strong preoccupation with consumption on the part of the East German population as well as the political elite.[5]

Broad political acceptance of the mass-produced personal car was anything but the predicted outcome of the debate regarding the role of the car in Socialist societies. Khrushchev envisioned a system of retail centers in order to avoid private car ownership and stressed his commitment to collective values.[6] A major shift in attitude toward automobility occurred in the 1960s, coinciding with the appearance of the new leaders on the political scene in Moscow and Bucharest. Improving the automobile sector turned into a priority for both Brezhnev and Ceaușescu. The new investment programs for automobile production were partly justified by increased consumption rates.[7] In the face of rising living standards, the new needs and desires of the population had to be satisfied. Political decision-makers in both countries were aware that a personal car belonged to a modern way of life. However, not only the disastrous material basis of the retail parks, but also the influence of Western car imagery contributed to this ideological shift. Placing the flexibility, comfort, and even "freedom" of the passenger at the center of the car-consumption ideology proved decisive in this respect.[8] In the so-called Informal Pact, a minimum of material satisfaction among the population was traded for political obedience. The car was an important item that Socialist governments used to lure their citizens into tolerating the system. To put it bluntly: the people in Socialist countries were bribed by their governments with consumer goods—the most prominent among them the car—to keep quiet. And in this sense, the car as private property became also a broad consensus among the various political and societal groups.[9] Another reason for this change of attitude was the ambition of both governments to establish themselves as modern industrial nations. And what better proof could they bring than modern assembly lines for automobiles? However, in order to achieve this, technological help from Western countries was needed.

Cooperation contracts with Renault in Romania and Fiat in the Soviet Union invited Western corporations to work behind the Iron Curtain. In Tol'yatti (Soviet Union) and in Pitești (Romania), new automobile plants were constructed under their supervision. The industrial cooperation with Western automobile firms is just one example of a wider transfer of knowledge and technology between East and West during détente.[10] Why were these Western automobile makers interested in investing in Socialist countries? Several factors contributed to their desire to expand their production into the Eastern camp. First and foremost, the automobile companies were looking for new markets to expand their business because they had to deal with a saturated internal car market and aggressive American competition at home. The doctrine of peaceful coexistence, which dates back to the beginning of the 1960s, offered them ideological support for making a profit on the enemy. Not only managers, but also politicians believed that through direct economic exchange, the West could prove its material superiority to the Soviet Union and its satellites.[11] Yet another material incentive, this time for the governments in Western Europe, was at stake here: cheap oil and gas. Before even beginning the negotiation process with Fiat, the Soviet government offered the Italian Energy Company (ENI) a significant amount of oil and gas under the market price via the Italian government. Thus the last ideological doubts on the Italian side were dispelled.[12]

In the East, the ideological dilemmas could not be so simply bought off. A much more intense public campaign was initiated to explain and justify these unorthodox exchanges. In the following, I will focus on how the production of Western cars was perceived and discussed in the East. Which discursive mechanisms were used to justify the importation of automobile technology—the symbol of mobility, freedom, and the "capitalist way of life"—while preventing Western ideas from trickling through to the population? In this context, we have to come to terms with an internal contradiction: while decision-makers in Socialist countries had a sense of their political systems' backwardness, they simultaneously believed in the one right path to Socialist modernity.[13]

We must, however, differentiate between the local contexts in Romania and the Soviet Union. Romania was a newcomer to the world of automobile production. Developing a new car entirely by local means proved to be an unrealistic undertaking. Thus, political decision-makers and administrative personnel decided in favor of a license contract with a Western automobile firm. Economic cooperation with the West did not pose a moral dilemma for the members of the Romanian politburo. Ceaușescu even voiced his disdain for those who warned against the influence of capitalism while at the same time closely cooperating with the West (probably hinting at the Soviet Union). Furthermore, he harshly criticized what he called the "unproductive Romanian reservations toward an exchange with the capitalist world." According to him, such an exchange could only improve the country's technological development.[14] It was never openly addressed that the official discourse in Romania also attempted to mediate between two irreconcilable positions: On the one hand, Romania situated itself on the Socialist side in the psychological Cold War. On the other hand, it pursued an independent economic policy. Without formally leaving the Socialist military and economic alliances, Romania came to occupy a special position in the Eastern camp that more resembled that of an unaligned state.[15]

In Romania, economic as well as political considerations played a role in the contest for the license. The discussions in the Central Committee and the Council of Ministers primarily addressed economic considerations. Peugeot, Fiat, and Renault were in close competition for the license contract. Peugeot's offer was quickly rejected, as it was too expensive. Central Committee member Alexandru Bîrlădeanu justified the decision as follows: "We need a modest car with low gas consumption that will be accepted by the greater public."[16] With Fiat and Renault, other problems arose. Although the Italians' international experience was highly praised, the technology of the 124 model was considered outdated after a mere five years of mass production. The French firm impressed Romanian engineers with a brand-new prototype. Thus, a provisional solution was agreed upon. After building the plant in Pitești in the record time of twelve months, the Renault 8 was produced there for two years until September 1970, when the new model 12 was issued simultaneously in Romania and at the parent plant in France.

However, these economic reasons were closely intertwined with political considerations. Since Ceaușescu's political takeover in 1965, a privileged Romanian-French relationship had begun to take shape. The seemingly obvious assumption that the French Communist Party had played an important part during the negotiations could not be confirmed by the sources in the Romanian National Archives. Instead, the French state was regarded as an important negotiating partner, especially due to the shares it held at Renault. A symbolic element completed the picture: Ceaușescu staged himself as de Gaulle's political spitting image on the Socialist side. The two statesmen shared a strategy that involved distancing themselves from the two superpowers and their military strategies, and was expressed in a "national" policy (in the broad meaning of the term).[17] However, Romania lacked the economic resources to sustain its course toward independence in a convincing way. Therefore, help from the French was gratefully accepted.[18] The outstanding position France inhabited in Romania's political discourse was expressed in the metaphor of a Latin brotherhood, which at the same time functioned as a dissociation from the Socialist family rhetoric.[19]

In the Soviet Union, the conditions for the transfer of Fiat technology were completely different. The VAZ plant in Tol'yatti was just one among many locations where cars were produced with the help of Western technology. This tradition went back to the early Soviet era, when the first Ford automobiles were built in the town of Gorky on the Volga. By the end of the 1960s, a vast program to modernize Soviet automobile production was launched. Kosygin's speech before GOSPLAN, the State Planning Commission, is considered the starting point for this immense investment program. He harshly criticized his predecessor Khrushchev for ignoring this vital segment of domestic industry and admitted that the

Soviet Union was still producing old-fashioned cars that were rejected by Western consumers.[20] In consequence, the Moskvich plant near Moscow was to benefit from Renault's technological know-how in the development of the new Kamaz truck.

The Soviets collaborated with several automobile firms, among them Liebherr and Renault. But the case of Fiat in Tol'yatti was unique, inasmuch as both the construction of the new plant and the development of a new model were entirely supervised by a single Western company.[21] According to Lewis Siegelbaum, citing the correspondence of a former KGB agent in Rome, the contract with Fiat (worth around $800 million) was the biggest contract ever to be signed by the Soviet Union and a Western company.[22] Thus it is not surprising that the CIA closely monitored the negotiation process. From the U.S.A.'s point of view, as dictated by the logic of the Cold War, the technological improvement of the Soviet civilian automobile sector was a matter of concern because new technology could easily be applied in the military sector as well. This also explains why American companies were so reluctant to invest in the Soviet Union at that time, which had not been the case during the interwar period, for example.[23]

However, my aim is not to assess the success or failure of these technological exchanges. Rather, I am concerned with the way the interactions between the two ideological spheres were mirrored in the official discourse of the time. How was the cooperation with the West discussed during these times of harsh systemic competition? Seen from the vantage point of automobility, how was it possible to create Socialist symbols out of these foreign products? Taking into consideration that the twin cars were identical—at least with regard to their exterior design—by what means was it possible to construct "national" Socialist patterns of identification? The naming of the cars significantly contributed to erasing the traces of these newborn products' origins. In the Soviet Union, the Fiat 124 was dearly named Zhiguli, after the Zhiguli hills surrounding the town of Tol'yatti. The geographical origin of the car was thus clearly placed in the foreground. The model issued in Romania was called Dacia, which stands for an ancient region located north of the river Danube, once the land of the Dacian people, which roughly corresponds to the southern part of today's Romania. Although I do not wish to overinterpret an ordinary car name, the selected name seems to correspond perfectly to the pseudonationalist tone of official Romanian discourse. Moreover, the Romanian national symbol—the eagle—was chosen to represent the car.

As it was talked about in Romania, the new car was closely linked to a consensus among the local industry, political decision-makers, and plan commissioners, namely that without Western technological imports, no qualitative or quantitative improvements could be achieved in the domestic automobile industry. Under these circumstances, they wanted to learn from the best. The Soviet Union and Romania were proud to cooperate with two renowned automobile companies, as was often stressed in the local and national press. However, the divide between domestic and foreign so characteristic of Cold War propaganda remained omnipresent in both countries. A typical differentiation referred to Western knowledge on the one hand and Socialist quality work on the other. The quick implementation of the newly acquired knowledge was admired in the press. For the record, the foreign helpers were showered with lavish gratitude, but at the same time it was stressed that the local workers had the most difficult job to do. And of course, the workers in Tol'yatti supposedly worked under improved conditions as compared to their Italian colleagues: "A representative of the Soviet [Automobile Builders'] trade union was sent to Turin to make sure that the project of the new plant in Tol'yatti respected the regulations of Soviet labor legislation.… The workrooms are higher and larger than in Turin, the warm wall colors ought to have a pleasant effect on the workers even when the weather is gloomy, and the power of the ventilation and the air conditioning system was increased by three to five times."[24] Another preferred strategy to set the two cars apart was to overemphasize the changes that Socialist engineers had applied to the Western model: "The Zhiguli model Vaz 2101 is not the same car as the Fiat 124. The Soviet and Italian designers went to a lot of trouble to adapt the new car to the harsh weather conditions in the Soviet Union. In the end, they developed a new model that resembles its predecessor as much as the Russian winter resembles the Italian winter."[25] Both Socialist governments pursued the same goal, namely to free themselves as quickly as possible of the contract obligations. After an initially enthusiastic phase of East-West exchange during which the qualities of the foreign partners were often stressed, one can observe how Fiat and Renault were gradually erased from the "biographies" of the two Socialist cars.

These technological exchanges across the Iron Curtain would not have been possible without the doctrine of peaceful coexistence, which allowed for economic cooperation between the two blocks. Nevertheless, these isolated "friendly" exchanges were overlain with a fierce ideological battle. With military conflicts banished to the Third World, direct confrontation between the two systems was replaced by the so-called psychological warfare.[26] In this new phase of the East-West confrontation, both sides competed for the one "right" interpretation of the world. Vast resources were invested in presenting their part of the story as the only viable one. In this "quest for civilization," the ultimate truth could only be either Capitalist or Socialist.[27] Military engagement gave way to a contest of images surrounding modernity and success. In the second part of this analysis, I will focus on a certain type of image produced to convince the Western public of the superiority of the Socialist production system and way of life. In this context, I analyze several advertising brochures designed to sell Socialist cars on capitalist markets. It is striking that among the automobiles selected to demonstrate Socialist efficiency and technological might, we also find those manufactured under Western licenses.

Before embarking on this analysis, I would like to elucidate the general framework of discourse on the superiority of socialism. Many scholars have come to consider the so-called kitchen debate between Khrushchev and Nixon, during a visit to the American exhibition in Moscow in 1959, a turning point in the domestic policies of the Eastern states. In an ultramodern kitchen displayed at this exhibition, Nixon affirmed the superiority of the American way of life because it provided the best material well-being for its citizens. This claim had quite an impact on Khrushchev and his future social policy. What followed was an increased concern with providing for the material needs of the population. After this, every Soviet citizen was turned into a consumer whose lifestyle and living conditions became relevant categories in the context of the East-West competition.[28] Although the GDR was a front runner in the realm of Socialist consumption, the shift in Soviet policy was welcomed as a beacon for further political relaxation.[29] Romania lagged behind in this respect until consumption discourse and practice came into full flower during the first years of Ceaușescu's rule.[30] A utopian vision for the future and the conquest of the universe would have been the topics of choice for systemic comparisons in the Soviet Union until the West imposed the issue of consumption. Thus Soviet politicians had to abandon the promise of happiness that lay beyond the horizon, toward which the Soviet people were marching in discipline, and turn instead to more earthly problems such as the organization of everyday life.

Although the rules of the game were imposed on them by their adversary, the Socialist states were willing to learn. What appeared to be a lost cause at the beginning gradually turned into a successful endeavor. By learning the rules of the consumption game, Socialist countries were able to withstand the one-directional penetration of Western ideas and images from behind the Iron Curtain. A number of sources will illustrate this learning process, and show how the persuasive methods of advertising became more refined over the years. I will start with a quite simple leaflet designed to sell the Soviet car Moskvich in the Federal Republic of Germany from 1960, continue with a brochure from 1970 that presents the Soviet Volga Gaz-24 to the same West German public, and close with what seems like an endless series of scenes presenting the East German Wartburg in various settings across Europe.

The specificity of this type of source lies in the fact that ideological components are closely intertwined with economic considerations. Socialist cars, especially in the private car sector, were exported in order to obtain valuable foreign currency. However, economic figures are not of primary importance in this context. Rather, I intend to depict the image (or images) of Socialist cars on capitalist markets, including their product identities and sales management. The Socialist exporters had to deal with a completely different situation in capitalist markets—they had to envision a distinct personality for their products, with easily recognizable features. I should add that regarding consumers at home, no sales campaign was necessary, owing to high consumer demand and the low availability of cars. This does not mean that consumption motives in the West and the images and texts designed for the Western public were utterly different from those in Socialist countries. The strategies behind the campaigns varied, however. The very same images that functioned as clever sales strategies in the West portrayed the ideal world of an advanced Socialist society in the East. What was missing in the West, as compared to the advertising at home, was the anti-bourgeois (or anti-capitalist) stance. Sales brochures for Socialist cars were intended to advocate the Socialist way of life without openly "exposing" the flaws of capitalism. The primary goal of the marketing campaign was to sell as many cars as possible, but equally important was the aim of getting the right message across to the capitalist Other. First and foremost, Socialist cars were not only competitive automobiles, but also products of a different political and social system. Thus, Socialist cars were supposed to convey the viability of the Socialist production process in the West. I begin my analysis with a leaflet that introduces the Moskvich (see Illustration 7.1) to its potential buyers:

> Moskvich 407—A car for everyone
> It is a real four-seater in which four adults can fit comfortably; it has a big trunk for lots of luggage, and the 4 doors allow for easy getting in and out…. On long journeys, driving is pleasant and not tiresome. The M-407 is resistant to wind and rain, its interior remains comfortable under extreme weather conditions, through snow and bitter cold. It gets through in all road conditions. It can easily pull a trailer or a caravan. For all these benefits, it needs no special servicing; it remains modest and economical throughout its life. However, its designers did not think highly of technical trifles or fashionable details. They built the M-407 for sensible buyers.[31]

If we closely scrutinize the above quote, we are immediately struck by what one would consider the typical virtues of Socialist products: their

Illustration 7.1. "Jedermann-Auto: Moskwich M 407," commercial, 1959/1960. (Guido Esling collection. Every effort has been made to trace the copyright holder and to obtain permission for this image.)

durability, high quality-engineering, and last but not least their low price. Compared to Western automobile advertisements, certain key topics such as unique features, design, and interior accommodations are not addressed. In the case of the Moskvich, these details are explicitly disregarded. To put it simply: if Socialist products are supposed to renounce commodity fetishism, why should they follow the ideals of the throwaway society, where details are more appealing than fundamental components? Ironically enough, the car is presented as if the advertisement were still addressing a Soviet audience. Mentioning extreme weather conditions and bad roads seems somewhat out of place for the Federal Republic of Germany. The included pictures are just as simple and straightforward as the text below them. Without any unnecessary details, they leave the car to speak for itself.

A similar example from a Dacia advertisement in Canada shows that these simple and quite poor ads were to remain characteristic of Socialist advertising irrespective of the year (this advertisement being from 1978):

> Dacia, a name recognized by more and more people. A Dacia is built to last. Its body construction made of extra heavy gauge steel and its factory

applied anticorrosion treatment makes it a very durable car, capable of withstanding all the rigors of our climate. It is a 4-door car at a 2-door price.... In simple terms, a Dacia is built to be driven safely on the most difficult roads, in even the toughest weather conditions.[32]

In my view, these texts are timid approaches to selling Socialist values to capitalist buyers. The cars were in fact popular among a certain type of Western buyer: employees from the low-wage sector who wanted a new car but could not afford a Western brand and quite often lived in remote areas.[33] However, not only economic reasons prompted Western buyers to choose a Socialist car. A certain strange fascination with the material culture of the Other, the possibility of crossing a strict demarcation line, or silent protest against the establishment were also important determinants. However, this group that made an overt political statement by choosing a car manufactured in a Socialist country most likely constituted only a small minority among the quite large number of buyers. Nevertheless, several drawbacks spoke against the purchase of a Socialist vehicle: a thin service net, high gas consumption, and in certain cases construction flaws. On the other hand, political factors—in rare cases outspoken—played an important part in shaping consumers' wishes. Although it was not forbidden to own Socialist products, commitment to the political system was expected of a loyal citizen, and deviant personal choices were frowned upon; not to mention that very aggressive anti-Socialist propaganda kept Western consumers away from Socialist products.

In spite of their bad reputation, cars produced in Socialist countries were similar to their Western counterparts as far as technical characteristics and engineering were concerned. This is further evidence toward the obvious conclusion that the act of buying a car has more to do with the fulfillment of desires and less with the car's technical data. A convincing commercial delivers a fusion of reality and fantasy.[34] If we take a closer look at a second brochure, for the Volga Gaz-24 designed for West Germany, we can note some striking changes (see Illustrations 7.2 and 7.3). While the expected features of a Socialist car mentioned above (like the solid engine, stability, and reliability) can also be found, references to fashionable details are placed in the foreground here:

> The beautiful, soft seats with comfortable backs are quite cozy for the passengers. Each of the front seats can be easily adjusted.... If needed, the seats can be turned into a sleeping accommodation. The car is equipped with a transistor radio with long, medium, and shortwave bands and an automatic antenna.[35]

As compared to the previous Soviet advertisement, the pictures accompanying the text are more colorful and more carefully staged. Before analyz-

Illustration 7.2. "Mercedes des Ostens, Volga Gaz-24," commercial, 1970.
(Guido Esling collection. Every effort has been made to trace the copyright holder and to obtain permission for this image.)

Illustration 7.3. "Mercedes des Ostens, Volga Gaz-24," commercial, 1970.
(Guido Esling collection. Every effort has been made to trace the copyright holder and to obtain permission for this image.)

ing the images in depth, a few words should be said about the specificity of the Volga on Socialist roads. If we compare this brand to the Moskvich, it is striking that in Socialist societies distinction mechanisms worked similarly to those in the capitalist system. Whereas in the latter, boundaries between social groups were fluid and constantly changing, the existence of a rigid bureaucratic elite, as represented by the *nomenklatura*, was characteristic of Socialist societies. The Volga was created to cater to their specific needs. Among the Soviet population, the Volga was known as the "wheels of the big bosses." Moreover, the black Volga stood for the permanent surveillance of the secret police. When such a car passed by, people often wondered who was being picked up for interrogation or what kinds of other secret things were taking place behind the tinted windows.

This image was not suitable for export to the West. Thus, a completely new product identity was created for the sales brochure. Dominated by the visual element, the included text appears as a welcome interjection. However, the message is primarily delivered through the images. Taken together, the pictures compose a little story. Three elegant young people (one man and two women) stand by the car. A holiday setting has been carefully staged for them. A majestic luxury yacht gliding over the waters of the river Volga (almost certainly) completes the background of the picture. The three people are obviously tourists and convey a relaxed impression. The smart young man is of course a perfect gentleman, carrying the luggage into the hotel himself. Instead of the Socialist ideal of equal rights and shared obligations for men and women alike, we find old-fashioned courtesy. All this play with gender connotations and holiday scenery is, however, only a pretext to cast a positive light on the oversized automobile. It dominates the scenery, saying to the viewer that bigger is better. From the angle from which the picture was taken, the car clearly outstrips the boat in the background. Thus, the Volga is the embodiment of style and grace on land. In spite of the car's huge dimensions, the warm pastel colors of the scenery give the scene a dreamy note. A snapshot taken through the Volga's windshield enables the viewer to take a closer look at the interior of the car while at the same time looking out onto the road, conveying the feeling of driving. Every detail was carefully selected here, the interactions between the elements scrupulously planned, and the viewer subtly drawn into the picture.

Although Volga was a well-known brand name among automobile fans, it could only rarely be encountered on West German roads. Its nickname—"Mercedes of the East"—says everything about the position it occupied in the automobile scene: a (cheap) copy of the original Mercedes. The Volga could not establish a market position for itself in the West, or even find a niche. In this respect, it is striking that in spite of its low sales numbers, the Volga came to inhabit a permanent place in the iconography of the Cold War. To put it boldly: if the Volga had not been developed before the war, it would have had to be invented afterwards, as the Socialist counterpart to the epitome of automobile excellence.

The East German Wartburg also played an important role in the imagery of the Cold War. The Wartburg was less associated with a repressive system, although it shared with its Soviet counterpart the same exclusiveness and pretty much the same elite clientele. The unique position that the GDR automobile industry occupied in the Eastern camp explains some of the distinctive features that shaped its product identity. Among my case studies, the GDR is the only country with a highly developed automobile sector during the interwar period—referring not only to the manufacturing process, but also to a functioning and efficient retail system and a widespread service net, as well as extensive advertising and sales strategies. The GDR was among the first European countries to develop new cars immediately after the end of World War II.[36] My last example presents the Wartburg in all its glory:

> 70 Years of Automobile Building in Eisenach. 70 Years of International Reputation.
>
> With the new Wartburg 1000, the automobile producers of Eisenach accomplished a work of superior mastership. Both at home and abroad, this series-built car has won many friends. This illustrated folder is intended to convey to all prospective "Wartburg" owners an idea of some countries to which exports of this approved and reliable car automobile type go.[37]

The key element in this text is tradition. The Wartburg is not a new car that is yet to be introduced to potential buyers. Rather, the message alludes to an easily recognizable product. The reference to its pre-Socialist past was not only a convenient side effect, but the main focus and a persistent leitmotif of all Wartburg advertising campaigns. In order to understand the logic of this unorthodox thinking, which does not characterize the Soviet takeover as a complete watershed in East German economic practice, we must take a closer look at the communication flow between the two German states. As Rainer Gries has pointed out, East German automobility discourse addressed its domestic citizens as much as the West German audience. He even goes so far as to portray the East German automobile world as divided into two independent communication spheres, represented by one or the other of the two automobiles on the East German market: the Wartburg and the Trabant. The Trabant was the symbol of mass mobility at home, while the semiotics of the Wartburg were intended to penetrate the Iron Curtain. In this respect, the name

Wartburg was supposed to transmit an all-German message closely linked to historical figures (Martin Luther) and events (the student protests of 1830). It thus claimed to be the true heir of the German past. The Wartburg's mission was to convey proof of the viability and superiority of the Socialist system across the border.[38]

The leaflet, issued in 1966, is an extended version of this communication strategy at the European level. The Wartburg represents the perfect choice in all possible contexts and settings, both in the GDR and other Socialist countries, as well as on capitalist soil. Although the photos it contains were taken before the Volga advertisement analyzed above, its technique is more refined and its concept is elaborate in every detail, yet with a simple and efficient layout. Besides the introductory lines, the descriptive text is reduced to a minimum. The starting point is the Sans Souci castle in Potsdam, where the car is simply introduced with the sentence: "Now here it is. From here on the Wartburg tours through all of Europe." In a quick reading exercise, we can note the following series of laudatory adjectives: unbeatable, elegant, economical, appealing, stylish, peppy, hill-climbing, indispensable, sturdy, and spacious.[39] These telegraphic messages are easy to remember. While leafing through the brochure, a wide range of places is revealed one by one before the viewer's eyes. This rapid change of scenery encourages daydreaming and anticipates the pleasure of driving in all these far and near places. Again, glamorous requisites function as a pretext for introducing the new automobile model.

Looking carefully at one photo after the other, one can hardly overlook the fact that the snapshots were not taken on location, but that car and people were added to the pictures afterwards. Although the color hues were carefully matched and the proportions skillfully adjusted, it is quite obvious that the scene is a collage. If we follow the paradoxical logic of efficient advertising that Paul Frosch has marvelously put into words, namely that a certain setting is staged to look real while at the same time it is really staged, our example turns into a hilarious pose.[40] In this respect the leaflet is a double forgery. On the one hand, it should not be understood as an advertisement for travel by potential East German tourists, for whom most of the Western settings were taboo—only the Wartburg was allowed to cross the strictly demarcated border of the Cold War map. On the other hand, it stands for the Socialist wishful thinking of conquering the international automobile market. Socialist cars could rarely be encountered on Western roads, as the advertisements tried to portray them. Although some appreciated the qualities of the Wartburg, it could not survive the harsh competition on the Western automobile market. Since future models did not benefit from technical improvements (they still had an old-fashioned two-gear motor), the Wartburg was soon to be forgotten by its initial Western admirers.[41] This clearly reveals the limitations of this sort of campaign, and brings us back to the Potemkin villages mentioned at the beginning of the chapter.

In sum, Socialist automobility tells the story of a shared history beyond the demarcations of the Cold War. From the Socialist perspective, a wide range of contacts, exchanges, learning processes, and emulation patterns accompanied the evolution of the Socialist automobile industry. The analysis also revealed that the borders between East and West were not only geographical, but also inside people's heads. The crossing of these borders did not dispel the bipolar division of the world. I attempted to illustrate this ambivalence by focusing on two different moments in the lives of Socialist cars—the production process and the selling of these cars on Western markets. All actions in the realm of automobiles were perceived through the lens of systemic competition. The use of Western licenses to improve domestic automobile production was inscribed into the Khrushchevian logic of "overtaking the Cold War enemy without catching up." Even when asking the West for help, the superiority of the Socialist production system had to be emphasized. The same discursive patterns are to be observed in the soft domain of envisioning a Socialist lifestyle. Socialist states not only sold cars to the West, but also a specific Socialist way of life. The Socialist superiority complex was inscribed into very modest leaflets, even if the images chosen openly emulated Western lifestyles. Thus, the "ironies of détente"[42]—cooperation with the West on the one hand and rejection of the West on the other—become apparent on both levels.

Notes

I would like to thank the organizers and participants of the conference "European Cold War Cultures?" in Potsdam from 26 to 28 April 2007 for the lively discussion. Klaus Gestwa read an early draft of this paper. I want to thank him for his time and useful comments.
 1. "Stoi! Der Milizionär in der Gorkistrasse winkt mit einer roten Flagge. Anhalten und stehen bleiben! erklärt er freundlich. Wir werden Zeugen einer Begebenheit seltsamer Art.... Zunächst passiert nichts. Nur der Milizionär wedelt aufgeregt mit der Flagge herum. Vor uns drängen sich die schon gestoppten Autos. Links und rechts füllen sich die Lücken. Nach 5 Minuten ist auch hinter uns alles proppenvoll mit Wagen. Entweder kommt jetzt Chruschtschow oder da vorn fehlt ein Stück Strasse.... Ein Flaggenwinken ohnegleichen setzt sich ein. Auch ohne die Flaggen kapieren wir, worum es geht: dawai, dawai, los, los. Der gestaute Autopulk wird in Marsch gesetzt.... Innerhalb einer halben Minute fängt der gesamte Stauwagen an zu rollen.

Auf dem Balkon wird eine Kamera sichtbar, die mit Weitwinkel- und Teleobjektiven in das Gewühl der Gorkistrasse hineinsieht. Wir sind völlig perplex. Erst nach einigen Metern geht uns ein Licht auf. Da filmt irgendeine Wochenschau oder das Fernsehen den 'Riesenverkehr' auf der Gorkistrasse. Die kompakte, unheimliche Walze sich schiebender Autokolonnen. ... Und die Genossen in Komi oder Kasachstan werden nach Luft schnappen, wenn sie diese Bilder sehen. Sie werden mit ehrlicher Überzeugung dem Fremden aus dem Ausland auf die Schulter klopfen und sagen: 'Ich habe ja neulich einen Filmstreifen aus Moskau gesehen, na – den hätten sie sich mal ansehen sollen! Dann hätten sie einen Eindruck davon bekommen, wie unser Verkehr schon heute im Begriff ist, den Westen zu überrunden.' Ja ja Genossen ... Schon mal von Potemkin gehört?" in Helmut Müller, *So sah ich Rußland* (Hamburg, 1962), 93.
2. Vladimir Tismaneanu, *Stalinism for all Seasons* (Berkeley, 2003); Manfred Hildermeier, *Geschichte der Sowjetunion, 1917–1991* (Munich, 1998).
3. Susan E. Reid, "Cold War in the Kitchen," *Slavic Review* 61 (2002), no. 2: 212–252.
4. Dietrich Beyrau, "Die befreiende Tat des Wortes," in *Samizdat*, ed. Wolfgang Eichwede (Bremen, 2000), 26–37.
5. Judd Stitziel, *Fashioning Socialism* (London, 2005), 1ff.
6. Lewis Siegelbaum, "Cars, Cars and More Cars," *Les Actes du GERPISA* 39 (2005): 171–182, 173.
7. ANIC (Archivele Naționale Istorice Centrale), Fond C.C. al P.C.R., Cancelarie, File no. 105/1966, Hotărîrea Consiluilui de Miniștri 2000/1965 anexa XII/6 poz. 26, Autoturismul.
8. Lewis Siegelbaum, *Cars for Comrades* (Ithaca, 2008), 84–87.
9. Ibid., 235–238.
10. Bruce Parrott, ed., *Trade, Technology, and Soviet-American Relations* (Bloomington, 1985).
11. Valerio Castronovo, *Fiat 1899–1999* (Milan, 1999), 1056; Jean-Louis Loubert, *Renault* (Boulogne, 2000), 217ff.
12. Castronovo, *Fiat*, 1057.
13. Michael David-Fox, "Multiple Modernities vs. Neo-Traditionalism," *Jahrbücher für Geschichte Osteuropas* 54 (2006), no. 4: 535–555, 554.
14. ANIC, Fond C.C. al P.C.R., Cancelarie, file no. 52/1970, Stenograma ședinței Comitelului Executiv al C.C. al P.C.R., 28 April 1970, 12.
15. Dan Cătănuș, "Divergențele româno-sovietice din C.A.E.R. și consecințele lor asupra politicii externe a României, 1961–1962," *Archivele Totalitarismului* 48/49, no. 3–4 (2005): 68–80, 77.
16. ANIC, Fond C.C. al P.C.R., Cancelarie, file no. 105/1966, Stenograma ședinței Comitelului Executiv al C.C. al P.C.R., 16 August1966.
17. Tamara Keating, *Constructing the Gaullist Consensus* (Baden-Baden, 2004); Alina Pavelescu, "Charles de Gaulle și marile ambiții ale comuniștilor români, mai 1968," *Archivele Totalitarismului* 48/49 (2005), no. 3–4: 191–98, 191.
18. Pavelescu, "Charles de Gaulle," 192.
19. "Bun venit președintelui Franței," *Scânteia* 27, no. 7702, 14 May 1968, 1.
20. A. Kosygin, "Povyshchenie nauchnoi obosnovannosti planov—vazheishaia zadacha planovykh organov," *Planovoe Khoziaistvo* 42 (1965), no. 4: 3–10.
21. Parrott, *Trade*, 84ff.
22. Siegelbaum, "Cars," 176.
23. Central Intelligence Agency, *USSR: Role of Foreign Technology in the Development of the Motor Vehicle Industry* (Washington, October 1979).

24. "Die Arbeitsbedingungen in Turin und Togliatti unterscheiden sich beträchtlich. An dem von italienischen Fachleuten ausgearbeiteten Projekt wurden wesentliche Änderungen mit dem Ziel vorgenommen, die Arbeitsbedingungen maximal zu verbessern. Ein Vertreter des ZK der zuständigen sowjetischen Gewerkschaft hielt sich eigens in Turin auf, um sicherzustellen, daß bei der Projektierung des Werkes die Vorschriften der sowjetischen Arbeitsgesetzgebung berücksichtigt wurden.... Die Werkhallen sind höher und geräumiger als die Hallen in Turin, die hellen Farben der Wände und Träger üben selbst bei trübem Wetter einen wohltuenden Einfluß aus. Die Leistung der Belüftungs- und Klimaanlagen wurde auf das Drei- bis Fünffache erhöht." Evgeni Dvornikov, "Das Werk an der Wolga," *Sowjetunion heute*, no. 18 (1973): 4–7, 5.
25. "Der Schiguli Modell WAS 2101 entspricht aber keineswegs dem Fiat 124. Die sowjetischen und italienischen Konstrukteure gaben sich sehr viel Mühe, um den sowjetischen Wagen den rauhen Naturverhältnissen der Sowjetunion anzupassen. So kam man zu guter Letzt zu einem neuen Modell, das seinen Vorgängern nicht mehr ähnelt als der russische Winter dem italienischen." Nikolai Golubzov, "Togliatti," *Sowjetunion heute*, no. 1 (1971): 10–13, 12.
26. Raymond L. Garthoff, *Détente and Confrontation* (Washington, 1984), 410.
27. Thomas Lindenberger, "Einleitung," in *Massenmedien im Kalten Krieg*, ed. Thomas Lindenberger (Cologne, 2006), 9–21, 13f.
28. Reid, "Cold War," 223ff.
29. Stitziel, *Fashioning Socialism*, 4.
30. Adrian Cioroian, *Pe umerii lui Marx* (Bucharest, 2005), 397.
31. "Der Moskwitsch 407—das Jedermann-Auto. Er ist ein 'Echter Viersitzer' mit bequemen Sitzen für 4 Erwachsene und hat einen großen Kofferraum für viel Gepäck, 4 Türen ermöglichen ein leichtes Ein und Aussteigen. ... Auf langen Reisen ist das Fahren angenehm und nicht ermüdend. Der M 407 ist gegen Wind und Kälte unempfindlich, sein Innenraum bleibt auch bei Schnee und klirrender Kälte behaglich. Er schafft jeden Weg und kommt durch jedes Gelände. Anhänger und Wohnwagen zieht er willig. Für all diese Dienste verlangt der Moskwitsch jedoch keine besondere Wartung, er bleibt genügsam und wirtschaftlich sein ganzes Leben lang. Seine Konstrukteure hielten nichts von technischen Spielereien und Modeauswüchsen. Sie bauten den M 407 für die Autofahrer, die mit Überlegung kaufen wollen." "Jedermann-Auto: Moskwitsch 407," 1959/1960, in Guido Esling collection, Berlin.
32. http://www.forum-auto.com/marques/dacia/sujet15.htm, last visited on 25 May 2010.
33. Peter Hamilton, "The Lada," in *Autopia: Cars and Culture*, ed. Peter Wollen and Joe Kerr (London, 2002), 191–198, 194.
34. Paul Frosch, *The Image Factory* (London, 2003), 107.
35. "Die schönen, weichgepolsterten Sitze mit zweckmäßig geformten Rücklehnen sind für die Fahrgäste sehr bequem. Jeder Vordersitz läßt sich leicht vorstellen.... Die Sitze lassen sich für Schlafangelegenheiten umlegen. Der Wagen hat ein Transistor-Radio mit Lang-, Mittel und Ultrakurzwellenbereich, mit Entstörmittel und automatische ausschiebbarer Antenne." "Mercedes des Ostens, Wolga Gaz-24," 1970, in Guido Esling collection, Berlin.
36. Wolfgang Schröder, *AWO, MZ, Trabant und Wartburg* (Bremen, 1995).
37. http://www.die-besten.de/wartburg/homepage800x600prospektewartburg353htm, last visited on 25 May 2010.
38. Rainer Gries, "Perfekte Panne, perfide Performance," in *"Ins Gehirn der Masse kriechen!" Werbung und Mentalitätsgeschichte*, ed. Rainer Gries (Darmstadt, 1995), 172–192, 183ff.

39. http://www.die-besten.de/wartburg/homepage800x600.htm.
40. Frosch, *Image Factory*, 107.
41. Gries, "Perfekte Panne," 186.
42. Jussi Hanhimäki, "Ironies and Turning Points," in *Reviewing the Cold War*, ed. Odd Arne Westad (London, 2000), 326–342.

Bibliography

Agerpress. "Bun venit președintelui Franței." *Scânteia* 27, no. 7702, 14 May 1968.
ANIC (Archivele Naționale Istorice Centrale). Fond C.C. al P.C.R., Cancelarie. file no. 105/1966, Hotărîrea Consiliul de Miniștri 2000/1965, anexa XII/6 poz. 26, Autoturismul.
——. File no. 105/1966, Stenograma ședinței Comitelului Executiv al C.C. al P.C.R. [Transcript of the meeting of the executive committee of the C.C. of the P.C.R., Supplement, XII/6. 26, the Passenger Car], 16 August 1966.
——. File no. 52/1970, Stenograma ședinței Comitelului Executiv al C.C. al P.C.R., 28 April 1970.
Beyrau, Dietrich. "Die befreiende Tat des Wortes." in *Samizdat: Alternative Kulturen in Zentral- und Osteuropa; die 60er bis 80er Jahre*, ed. Wolfgang Eichwede (Bremen, 2000), 26–37.
Castronovo, Valerio. *Fiat 1899–1999: un secolo di storia italiana*. Milan, 1999.
Cătănuș, Dan. "Divergențele româno-sovietice din C.A.E.R. și consecințele lor asupra politicii externe a României, 1961–1962," *Archivele Totalitarismului* 48/49 (2005), no. 3–4: 68–80.
Central Intelligence Agency. *USSR: Role of Foreign Technology in the Development of the Motor Vehicle Industry*. Washington, October 1979.
Cioroian, Adrian. *Pe umerii lui Marx: o introducere în comunismul românesc*. Bucharest, 2005.
David-Fox, Michael. "Multiple Modernities vs. Neo-Traditionalism: On Recent Debates in Russian and Soviet History." *Jahrbücher für Geschichte Osteuropas* 54 (2006), no. 4: 535–555.
Dvornikov, Evgeni. "Das Werk an der Wolga." *Sowjetunion heute*, no. 18 (1973): 4–7.
Frosch, Paul. *The Image Factory: Consumer Culture, Photography and the Visual Content Industry*. London, 2003.
Garthoff, Raymond L. *Détente and Confrontation: American-Soviet Relations from Nixon to Reagan*. Washington, 1984.
Golubzov, Nikolai. "Togliatti: Autostadt an der Wolga." *Sowjetunion heute*, no. 1 (1971): 10–13.
Gries, Rainer. "Perfekte Panne, perfide Performance. Opel baut in Eisenach: Bemerkungen zu einer Einheits-Anzeige." In *"Ins Gehirn der Masse kriechen!" Werbung und Mentalitätsgeschichte*, ed. Rainer Gries (Darmstadt, 1995), 172–192.
Hamilton, Peter. "The Lada: A Cultural Icon." In *Autopia: Cars and Culture*, ed. Peter Wollen and Joe Kerr (London, 2002), 191–198.
Hanhimäki, Jussi. "Ironies and Turning Points: Détente in Perspective." in *Reviewing the Cold War*, ed. Odd Arne Westad (London, 2000), 326–342.
Hildermeier, Manfred. *Geschichte der Sowjetunion, 1917–1991*. Munich, 1998.

Keating, Tamara. *Constructing the Gaullist Consensus: A Cultural Perspective on French Policy toward the United States in NATO, 1958–2000.* Baden-Baden, 2004.
Kosygin, A.N. "Povyshennie nauchnoi obosnovannosti planov—vazheishaya zadacha planovykh organov." *Planovoe Khoziaistvo* 42 (1965), no. 4.
Lindenberger, Thomas. "Einleitung." In *Massenmedien im Kalten Krieg: Akteure, Bilder, Resonanzen,* ed. Thomas Lindenberger (Cologne, 2006), 9–21.
Loubert, Jean-Louis. *Renault: histoire d'une entreprise.* Boulogne, 2000.
Müller, Helmut. *So sah ich Rußland.* Hamburg, 1962.
Parrott, Bruce, ed. *Trade, Technology, and Soviet-American Relations.* Bloomington, Ind., 1985.
Pavelescu, Alina. "Charles de Gaulle și marile ambiții ale comuniștilor români, mai 1968." *Archivele totalitarismului* 48/49 (2005), no. 3–4: 191–198.
Reid, Susan E. "Cold War in the Kitchen: Gender and the De-Stalinisation of Consumer Taste in the Soviet Union under Khrushchev." *Slavic Review* 61 (2002), no. 2: 212–252.
Schröder, Wolfgang. *AWO, MZ, Trabant und Wartburg: Die Motorrad und Pkw-Produktion in der DDR.* Bremen, 1995.
Siegelbaum, Lewis. "Cars, Cars and More Cars: The Faustian Bargain of the Brezhnev Era." *Les Actes du GERPISA* 39 (2005), 171–182.
———. *Cars for Comrades: The Life of the Soviet Automobile.* Ithaca, N.Y., 2008.
Stitziel, Judd. *Fashioning Socialism: Clothing Socialism, Politics and Consumer Culture in East Germany.* London, 2005.
Tismaneanu, Vladimir. *Stalinism for all Seasons: A Political History of Romanian Communism.* Berkeley and Los Angeles, 2003.

Internet resources

http://www.forum-auto.com/marques/dacia/sujet15.htm
http://www.die-besten.de/wartburg/homepage800x600.htm

Further documents

"Jedermann-Auto: Moskwitsch 407," 1959/1960, in Guido Esling collection, Berlin.
"Mercedes des Ostens, Wolga Gaz-24," 1970, in Guido Esling collection, Berlin.

Chapter 8

Advertising, Emotions, and "Hidden Persuaders"
The Making of Cold-War Consumer Culture in Britain from the 1940s to the 1960s

Stefan Schwarzkopf

Introduction

Anxieties surrounding the introduction of new forms of consumer marketing are an integral part of the study of Cold War Culture.[1] Like many other fields of popular culture, advertising attracted the keen interest of the Cold War political elite, intellectuals, and critical journalists. On the one hand, America's and Europe's "Cold Warriors" saw private consumption as a key area for the self-assertion of their respective ideologies, which generated conflicting views in East and West of what constitutes a consumers' paradise.[2] On the other hand, Western intellectuals in particular began to warn that the new consumer affluence opened the door for intrusive, harmful, unethical, and potentially undemocratic forms of product communication. The list of anxieties compiled by the concerned liberal intelligentsia was topped by the new medium of television, which seduced consumers in their living rooms. This was followed by revelations about psychoanalytical consumer research techniques developed by Ernest Dichter, which allowed the "hidden persuaders" to turn consumers into marionettes of invented desires.³ Social commentators in the West noted with unease the increased use of sexual stereotypes in advertising. On top of that, the advent of American products and American advertising agencies on the European markets fueled traditional middle-class fears of "Americanization."⁴

In order to counter widespread criticism, the Western European advertising industries began to use Cold War rhetoric to defend themselves against charges of being "brainwashers," "hidden persuaders," or manipulators of consumer emotions. Advertising was presented as a weapon of paramount importance in the arsenal of "Freedom," and those who demanded tighter regulation of advertising were drawn into a battle about the "freedom of choice" and consumer sovereignty. Thus advertising, new advertising media (TV), new forms of consumer research (Dichter's motivation research), and new forms of advertising creation (sexualized brand images) were at the heart of an emerging Cold War Culture that still today influences the way Western societies make sense of consumer culture. In this chapter I will look at the debates over advertising and consumer culture in Britain between the late 1940s and the 1960s, in order to ascertain whether there was something specifically "European" in the way the British discussed and "ordered" the place of advertising and marketing in their society. The Cold War, it turns out, not only strongly promoted the politicization of advertising and consumption.⁵ The global struggle of empires acted as a ferment that provided for the emergence of a transatlantic consensus on how marketing and consumer culture were either politically defended or critically challenged by various constituencies.

Putting Advertising and Consumer Culture Back into Cold War History

Historians are now becoming more and more aware of the fact that during the Cold War, cultural proxy wars were fought on nations' home fronts and battled out between political parties, ideologues, civil-society organizations, and the emerging think tanks.⁶ The Cold War was a global and a "total" war in that all aspects of life, not just diplomatic and macroeconomic issues but also the arts and sciences, economic and social research, businesses and industries, and education and popular culture, were forced to position themselves in the global system struggle.⁷ In this respect, the role of consumer politics in the making of a distinct Cold War Culture has received attention for the cases of divided Germany and the United States.⁸ Britain, in comparison, proves to be a much more complicated case. The unclear future of the Empire, the ongoing debates about nation-alized industries, rationing, retail price maintenance, and the performance of sensitive export industries ensured that the domestic economic policy agenda in Britain was considerably different from those of other European countries and the United States.[9] While political visions of consumption and the issue of consumer protection feature prominently in accounts of postwar British consumer culture, the role of advertising remains largely untouched.[10] Moreover, only a few authors use the Cold War as an explanatory paradigm for their reconstruction of the British political debates over consumption. According to these accounts, the emergence of an affluent society and the contested notion of materialistic, individualized consumerism took place in a postwar but not necessarily a Cold War Britain.

Advertising had already been fiercely debated in the Victorian, Edwardian, and interwar eras by Fabian, Socialist, and liberal intellectuals who tried to expose its long-term economic ill effects.[11] At the same time, the advertising industry had attracted similar criticism from conservatives, senior economists, and upper-middle-class professionals until the mid 1940s.[12] With the accession of the Labour Party to power in 1945, however, the issue of advertising, which had clearly been a *political* issue since the 1890s, became an *ideological* issue debated along the lines of party-political fronts.

The rise of "affluent Britain" was marked by intensifying hostility towards advertising.[13] From the 1940s until well into the 1970s, the Labour Party stood in the vanguard of left-wing political attacks on the advertising industry. As soon as Labour came into power in 1945, Chancellor Hugh Dalton floated a scheme under which only half a company's advertising budget could be written off against tax.[14] Although this measure was avoided by a voluntary agreement to cut down advertising across all sections of the consumer goods industry, throughout the following two decades the advertising industry continued to fear the introduction of punitive taxation by a Labour government.[15] Numerous voices on the Left, ranging from libertarian Labour Party revisionists such as Anthony Crosland to the Communist Party, called for a tax on advertising or for other forms of regulation to quell the influence of advertising messages on society.[16]

Probably the most prolific critic of advertising within the ranks of the Labour Party was the MP for Swindon, Francis Noel-Baker. Noel-Baker campaigned relentlessly for the setting up of state-funded advertising watchdogs in order to liberate society from "high-pressure salesmanship and the need to 'create demand.'"[17] In 1958, Noel-Baker tried unsuccessfully to get the House of Commons's support for the establishment of a Royal Commission on advertising. Only a few months later, however, in March 1959, Noel-Baker did manage to form a cross-party group, the Advertising Inquiry Council, which demanded stronger independent regulation of the advertising industry and measures to protect consumers from misleading advertising.[18] In 1966, Labour published the *Report of a Commission of Enquiry into Advertising* (the Reith Report), which proposed a levy on advertising in order to finance a National Consumer Board, charged with testing the claims advertisers made about their clients' products. Labour's 1972 *Green Paper on Advertising* made a similar recommendation.

"And Brain-Washing As Well"

The impact of the Cold War on British advertising culture became palpable in the discourse about market research and advertising psychology. Here, the idiom of the Cold War entered advertising debates mainly in the form of scares about subversion, covert intelligence methods, subconscious infiltration, and brainwashing. If the angst-ridden middle classes of 1950s America were convinced the "Commies" had invented flying saucers as the latest weapon to attack the "free world," the Left believed that capitalism had invented unknown techniques to tap and influence people's minds. Many, it seems, feared that the application of psychological brainwashing techniques—made famous in films such as *The Manchurian Candidate* (1962) and *The Ipcress File* (1965)—were already a reality in the world of advertising and salesmanship.

Popular culture in the 1950s and early 1960s was obsessed with the power of suggestion techniques, psychoanalysis, and hypnosis, all of which threatened to undermine traditional ideas of the self-determined, rational, and fully responsible individual. Similarly, analyses of advertising in the 1950s and 1960s described the industry openly as "hidden persuaders" and as a "persuasion industry."[19] The journalist Vance Packard, for example, argued that advertisers used manipulative techniques to exploit subconscious desires and anxieties. The fear that "free will" was being compromised not only informed criticism of the industry in the 1950s and 1960s but gave it much of its urgency and political intensity.[20] The export of certain American advertising research cultures to Britain was seen by some as vindicating the industry's critics. In the early 1950s, advertising psychologists and market researchers such as Ernest Dichter of the Institute for Motivational Research and Louis Cheskin of the Color Research Institute demonstrated that there was a large gap between consumers' stated, rational intentions and their actual behavior.[21] Dichter and Cheskin, the two leading representatives of motivational research, successfully convinced American and later European business clients that chocolate, cars, cigarettes, and fashion had to appeal to people's unconscious or "hidden" desires and fears.[22]

In late summer of 1957, the press reported how a new advertising technique was being employed in a cinema in New Jersey, namely the flashing onto screens of slogans or words for a few milliseconds. The resulting furor surrounding James Vicary's idea of "subliminal advertising" became the fulcrum of Cold War fantasies concerning the advertising industry.[23] British commentators as well as their U.S. counterparts pointed not only at the ethical complications of trying to compel consumers against their will to buy certain products. More importantly, the political dangers of this new advertising technique—the idea that the political fringe could subvert the law-abiding minds of middle England—rendered it necessary for the advertising industry to clamp down on subliminal messages in order to pacify fears "among the British that their subconsciousness was attacked by subliminal advertising."[24] The Institute of Practitioners in Advertising, the professional body of the U.K. advertising industry, set up a committee to study the ethical aspects of subliminal advertising, while the three American media networks NBC, CBS, and ABC, as well as the State of New York, directly banned subliminal advertising.[25] Francis Noel-Baker again summarized left-wing criticism when he demanded an enquiry into modern advertising techniques: "There was talk of hypnosis, psycho-analysis, motivation, conditioned reflex, psycho-persuasion, mental perception, and ... brain-washing as well."[26]

The use of psychological fear factors, subconscious pressures, and allusions to sexual success or social failure in consumer advertising in the 1950s added considerably to the negative image of the advertising industry. The Institute of Practitioners in Advertising soon became aware that scare stories about people being persuaded against their will to rush out and buy unwanted products were a serious threat to the reputation of the advertising profession.[27] As a means to avoid further alienation of public confidence in advertising, the IPA issued a pamphlet in 1957 which explained the basics of motivational research in simple terms to a wider audience.[28] In 1958, the IPA eventually banned its member agencies from using and experimenting with subliminal advertising, on the grounds of growing concern over the ethical and professional standing of the advertising industry.[29]

How Advertising "Sold" the Cold War

Faced with a growing and diverse range of critics consisting of politicians, intellectuals, and consumer movements, the advertising industry began to develop strategies to improve its public image. In contrast to the interwar years, when economists saw advertising largely as a wasteful and inefficient means of distribution, the advertising industry was now able to draw on political and economic theory as a major source of support.[30] Economists such as Schumpeter and Hayek advanced theories in which the freedom of consumer choice and of entrepreneurial activities featured as pillars of democratic society. From this perspective, the state had the task of safeguarding the individual's freedom to choose and consume, rather than restricting that right in favor of the "common good."[31]

As the intellectual contest between the systems of collective economic planning and of private ownership unfolded, the British advertising industry actively began to use the language of the Cold War. Advertising clubs in London invited right-wing politicians to deliver speeches about the need to "defend the consumer's freedom of choice."[32] Through such meetings and public speeches, the industry introduced into the public discourse the argument that advertising was not a threat to consumer sovereignty, but one of its essential assets. In an editorial in July 1951, the *Times* celebrated this new positive role of advertising in a society of growing affluence: "The danger, today, lies not in too much competition, taking expensive forms, but in too little, not in too much duplication of efforts to satisfy consumers' wants but in too many limitations."[33]

A network of right-wing economists, journalists, and politicians emerged in those years who advanced a public-interest argument for advertising, and who could be called upon by the industry to defend it. Think tanks such as the Bow Group, the Institute of Directors, or the Institute of Economic Affairs provided the advertising profession with much-needed theoretical ammunition. In a whole series of publications, members of these organizations argued that advertising was not a form of organized consumer deception, but an essential tool for modern consumers to exercise their freedom of choice in an affluent society abounding with ever more media, products, and services.[34] With such allies, the industry was able to argue that advertising contributed to the institutional culture of commercial competition, without which essential "Western" freedoms (namely individualism and democracy) were in danger. Critics and opponents of advertising were portrayed as trying to curtail the freedoms of capitalist competition in the way the Communists did. The political punch line of this argument lay in the concept of the "citizen consumer," which was seized upon by pro-advertising lobbyists. Ralph Harris and Arthur Seldon of the Institute of Economic Affairs, for example, stressed that being able to choose from among all the messages sent out by commercial competitors was a right every citizen in a democracy should be entitled to. The only alternative to this system of entertaining a "variety of persuaders" was the introduction of the state as "single persuader." This system however, according to Harris and Seldon, would inevitably degenerate into "veiled coercion" by the state.[35]

Throughout the 1950s, the Institute of Directors conducted campaigns telling people that free enterprise gave "everyone a chance—and a choice."[36] The advertising industry profited from the propaganda battles between "free enterprise" campaigners and successive Labour governments by working for both sides in their attempts to devise creative and convincing campaigns. Advertising—with a capital A—also joined the battle. An important move in this propaganda war was to connect values of freedom, citizenship, and choice with the business of advertising. While the Left in Britain always contended that advertising was essentially a device to dishonestly influence the free and informed choice of consumers, the advertising industry successfully managed to associate itself with the cause of defending freedom and democracy.

The public battles over advertising in Britain increased in intensity during the early 1950s, when the Labour Party was ousted from government and a newly elected Conservative government began to remove restrictions imposed on industries. Most importantly, the rationing of consumer products like butter and detergents was terminated, which meant that commercial suppliers of these products began competitive advertising for the first time since the beginning of World War II. The *Times* duly referred to the newly started competition among the several brands as "freedom's battlefield."[37] Similarly, the new advertising medium of commercial television, introduced in September 1955, was promoted to the British public by the Conservative Party's Central Office as "a moment of triumph in the history of the free mind."[38]

A few years later, the market researcher Harry Henry summarized this view in a speech under the title "Market research and the new consumer democracy."[39] Here, Henry argued that higher income levels, increased product choice, stronger emphasis on market research, and the framework of a free, competitive market economy had turned British consumers into a more democratic, sovereign people. While before the age of market research manufacturers tended to "talk down" to consumers, the new environment forced them to listen to those people whose prerogative it was to "vote" in favor of or against a product. In this new environment the market researcher and motivational psychologist had an important role to play, not only by giving manufacturers control over their market, but by giving "the housewife and the ordinary people of the country control of the manufacturer, too."[40]

One of the most important events in the Cold War propaganda battle over the meanings of "freedom" and "consumer choice" was staged by the

U.K. advertising industry in London in the summer of 1951. After several years of careful preparation, the Advertising Association, the overarching trade organization of all advertising-related industries, hosted the International Advertising Convention, devoted to "The Task of Advertising in a Free World." London experienced an invasion of almost 3,000 advertising men and women from 37 countries, who gathered in Westminster's Central Hall in July 1951. The cardinal theme of the conference, which linked advertising to the discourse of freedom and society, ran through all the major addresses and the specialized sessions, which were given titles such as "How direct advertising contributes to the task of selling in a free world," "The Contribution of Market Research in a Free world," and "The Task and Responsibilities of Local Newspapers in a Free World" (International Advertising Conference 1951).

This invention of a close connection between commercial advertising and the freedom of Western societies pervaded the conference from the very first opening remarks made by the conference's patron, the Duke of Gloucester, who said he believed "that the most important task for all of us is to keep that free world free." Lord Halifax of Mackintosh, the conference president, reminded the several thousand delegates that "advertising in all its forms can be a very powerful force in maintaining freedom. It is closely linked with freedom of speech, freedom of the press, freedom of choice, and I believe that if any one of these goes, freedom itself will soon depart."[41]

Some of the discussion panels at the conference saw Labour leaders and representatives of the British consumer movement expressing their ideas about and voicing their criticisms of advertising. In these sessions, the long-standing tensions between the Left and the world of "free enterprise" and commercialism eventually erupted in sharp and pointed remarks from both sides. William Beveridge, for example, strongly questioned the role of advertising in a modern society. Not only did he question the title of the conference, he also reminded the advertising profession of its social responsibilities to the community, to keep the landscape free from billboards and to abstain from cheating consumers into buying things they did not need: "The service of advertising to the community is to enable citizens to get the most and the best out of their vital freedom, the consumer's freedom in spending his income. The condition on which alone this service can be rendered is that those who conduct advertising shall recognize responsibilities both for what they say and for how they say it."[42] Similarly, the Scottish president of the National Council of Women, Lady Tweedsmuir, attacked advertisers for letting the consumer down. In her speech on "What the Consumer Expects of Advertising," Tweedsmuir accused the industry of not listening to consumers' needs and of failing to give them sufficient guidance and information.[43] Thus, the Left contested the commercial and cultural dominance of advertising with a competing vision of a "free" citizen consumer.

But despite these attacks, the U.K. advertising industry saw the conference as a clear public-relations victory for itself. The industry had used the conference to boast that "advertisers can keep the world free."[44] Fairfax Cone, chairman of the U.S. Advertising Council, was happy to accept the challenge proposed by the representatives of the Left on behalf of his British colleagues. Using their experience of successfully selling consumer products, Cone proposed, advertising agencies could successfully "knock out" Communist propaganda. George Patterson, Governing Director of a large Australian advertising agency, called upon his international colleagues to combat the "impudent activities of the fifth column among the free peoples, which seeks to destroy man's faith in himself."[45]

While the Labour government presented the achievements of a Socialist Britain and the idea of equality at the South Bank Exhibition of the Festival of Britain, the U.K. advertising industry simultaneously staged its own little festival of choice and free enterprise on the opposite side of the river.[46] Reviewing the conference, the advertisers were pleased with the public response to the speeches and discussions. In its 1951 Annual Report, the Advertising Association announced that the conference had created sufficient momentum that it had decided to launch a "permanent programme of publicity activity on behalf of advertising."[47] Consequently, the Advertising Association began to use the considerable amount of money left in the organization fund in order to devise a long-term public relations campaign to promote a better image of the industry.[48] Among other measures, the Advertising Association employed two press officers, organized a panel of public speakers, created a Public Affairs Committee which lobbied MPs, trade union leaders, and other public figures, and filmed several short documentaries that explained the business of advertising to the public.[49] In order to support the panel of public speakers, the public relations officers of the Advertising Association compiled dossiers about the attitudes of Labour leaders toward advertising, which were distributed to speakers talking in the run-up to the 1959 election.[50] Between 1956 and 1958 alone, over 800 meetings were addressed by the association's speakers, who taught schoolchildren, women's cooperative guilds, Rotary clubs, and worker's educational associations up and down the country about the service advertising rendered to the freedom and welfare of British consumers.[51]

The public-relations activities of the Advertising Association offer an insight into a whole network of communicators in the 1950s, which revolved around the aim of winning over British public opinion to the ideas of "freedom of choice" and the politics of free enterprise. The essential feature that gave this network its Cold War character was the degree to which its members looked to the United States for guidance on questions of ideological principle. The Cold War propaganda services that U.S. advertising professionals in the Advertising Council and the Psychological Strategy Board rendered to policy-makers in the White House became important role models for pro-advertising campaigners in the U.K. working in organizations such as Aims of Industry, the Advertising Association, and the Institute of Directors.[52] By serving and connecting Conservative Party politicians and industrialists, the advertising industry played a major role as interlocutor within this industrial-political complex, which had embarked on a campaign to fight and win the Cold War in British society.

Conclusion: The Cold War as "Americanization's" Gateway?

By bringing party politics and advertising together in a way unknown before World War II, the Cold War deepened a political split within British society that had already started to emerge over consumer politics before 1939, and turned it into a non-negotiable ideological rift. In an age of ideology, advertising and consumer culture became part of a belief system that saw brands, shopping malls, and commercials as necessary parts of a "free" society. Criticizing advertising, either morally, economically, or politically, became associated with opposition to certain innate human freedoms, in a manner akin to communism. Since the late nineteenth century, advertising agents in Britain had been struggling to improve the public image of their profession in the face of widespread hostility. With the onset of the Cold War, however, the political coordinates that framed the image of advertising changed. By employing the language of "freedom" and "choice," the advertising industry sought to capitalize on the current freedom-versus-totalitarianism discourse. The newly developed image of the industry as an advocate of "freedom of choice" fitted neatly into a Cold War Culture that governed American and British foreign politics. Influenced by the climate of the political Cold War, the advertising industry linked the rebuttal of its cultural and social critics to the task of defending "freedom"—a value beyond criticism. Thus, those who advanced the alternative conception of the consumer as critical, informed, and educated were presented as opponents not simply of the industry but of democracy. The long-term consequences of the ideological Cold War battles over the role of advertising in modern society cannot be overestimated. When, in the 1980s, the rhetoric of "free enterprise" reemerged in the form of Reaganomics and Thatcherism, the ever-increasing power of multinational corporations and the influence of their advertising on people's lives were once again sold as an increase in "freedom" that consumers were allegedly allowed to exercise.[53]

As mentioned earlier, the political struggles within British society over the demise of the Empire and the sensitive issue of economic policies (British export industries; the balance of payments and the need to earn dollars; nationalization of coal, steel, and transport industries, etc.) meant that the British historical experience of how the Cold War permeated and finally hijacked the agenda of consumer politics was different from that of the United States and other European countries. And yet, the Cold War as a global political and cultural phenomenon steered the British debate over the right place of advertising in society in essentially the same direction as was experienced in North America and Western Europe. In all of these societies, the advertising industry tended to be treated with suspicion and hostility by trade unions, left-wing civil society groups, intellectuals and muckraking journalists, academic economists, policy-makers with an eye on consumer prices and industrial monopolies, women's groups, consumer advocates, and many more. During the 1940s and 1950s, however, advertising businesses across the Western hemisphere reemerged from the rubble of World War II as self-appointed knights in shining armor to the rescue of democracy.[54]

Moreover, the attempts launched in Britain at connecting advertising to the political battles of the Cold War resulted in a kind of love affair between the British and the American advertising industries, which before the 1940s would perhaps have been much more difficult to entertain because of the fierce economic competition and the strong cultural differences between the two industries.[55] In a sense, therefore, the Cold War brought American and British advertising both politically and culturally much closer together, and provided the gateway through which American marketing expertise and ownership structures of agencies entered the British market during the mid and late 1950s. In this way, the British experience was perhaps unique compared to the French and the German markets, where the tendency towards "Americanization" was resisted for much longer within home-grown advertising circles. This opening up of the British advertising world to the American-inspired Cold War rhetoric seems to have been characteristic especially of the 1950s. A brief look into the British advertising trade journals and other marketing-related publications of the 1960s and 1970s supports the view that a European Cold War Culture of the fierce "American type" seems to have been limited to the 1950s. During the 1960s, which saw Harold Wilson's refusal to join the Americans in Vietnam, the beginning of the policy of détente in Germany (*Ostpolitik*), and the emergence of a European common market, British marketers had to position their profession vis-à-vis new and far more relevant challenges, such as the unfavorable Sterling exchange rate on the world markets, the protracted and painful death of Britain's manufacturing industries, and the rise of a distinctly liberal and permissive teenage market segment. Thus, the paradoxical concomitance in the 1960s of a "cultural explosion" (Arthur Marwick) and a rationalization and bureaucratization of political and market relationships under the European Economic Community's common-market regime rendered the Cold War an obsolete epistemological model for understanding the world for Europeans well before the breakdown of communism in 1989.

Notes

1. See Lizabeth Cohen, *A Consumer's Republic* (New York, 2003); David Crewe, "Consuming Germany in the Cold War," in *Consuming Germany in the Cold War*, ed. David Crewe (Oxford, 2003), 1–19; Stefan Schwarzkopf, "They Do it with Mirrors," *Contemporary British History* 19, no. 2 (June 2005): 133–150; Mark Tadajewski, "The Ordering of Marketing Theory," *Marketing Theory* 6 (2006), no. 2: 163–199.
2. See Rainer Gries, *Produkte und Politik* (Vienna, 2006); Katherine Pence, "Shopping for an 'Economic Miracle,'" in *The Expert Consumer*, ed. Alain Chatriot, Marie-Emanuelle Chessel and Matthew Hilton (Aldershot, 2006), 105–120.
3. See Vance Packard, *The Hidden Persuaders* (New York, 1957).
4. See Heide Fehrenbach and Uta Poiger, eds., *Transactions, Transgressions, Transformations* (New York, 1999); Rob Kroes, "American Empire and Cultural Imperialism," *Diplomatic History* 23 (1999), no. 3: 463–477.
5. See Frank Mort, "The Commercial Domain," in *Commercial Cultures*, ed. Peter Jackson et al. (Oxford, 2000), 35–53.
6. See Walter Hixson, *Parting the Curtain* (Basingstoke, 1997); Kenneth Osgood, *Total Cold War* (Lawrence, Kans., 2006); Yale Richmond, *Cultural Exchange and the Cold War* (University Park, Penna., 2003); Stephen Whitfield, *The Culture of the Cold War* (Baltimore, 1996).
7. See Volker Berghahn, *America and the Intellectual Cold Wars in Europe* (Princeton, 2001); Nils Gilman, *Mandarins of the Future* (Baltimore, 2007); Joel Isaac, "The Human Sciences in Cold War America," *The Historical Journal* 50 (2007), no. 3: 725–746; Rebecca Lowen, *Creating the Cold War University* (Berkeley, 1997); Julia Mickenberg, *Learning from the Left* (Oxford, 2006); Susan Reid, "The Khrushchev Kitchen," *Journal of Contemporary History* 40 (2005), no. 2: 289–316; Axel Schildt and Detlef Siegfried, eds., *Between Marx and Coca-Cola* (New York, 2006); Christopher Simpson, *Science of Coercion* (New York, 1994); Bert Spector, "The Harvard Business Review Goes to War," *Management & Organizational History* 1 (2006), no. 3: 273–295; Peter Vodosek and Wolfgang Schmitz, eds., *Bibliotheken, Bücher und andere Medien in der Zeit des Kalten Krieges* (Wiesbaden, 2005).
8. See Elaine Tyler May, *Homeward Bound* (New York, 1988); Gary Cross, *An All-consuming Century* (New York, 2000); Cohen, *A Consumer's Republic*; Crewe, "Con-

suming Germany"; Erica Carter, *How German Is She?* (Ann Arbor, 1997); Greg Castillo, "Domesticating the Cold War," *Journal of Contemporary History* 40 (2005), no. 2: 261–288; Helen Laville, "'Our country endangered by Underwear,'" *Diplomatic History* 30 (2006), no. 4: 623–644.

9. See Lawrence Black, *The Political Culture of the Left in Affluent Britain, 1951–64* (Houndmills: Palgrave, 2003); Lawrence Black and Hugh Pemberton, eds., *An Affluent Society?* (Aldershot, 2004); Richard Findley, "The Conservative Party and Defeat," *Twentieth-century British History* 12 (2001), no. 3: 327–353; Matthew Hilton, "Consumer Politics in Post-war Britain," in *The Politics of Consumption*, ed. Martin Daunton and Matthew Hilton (Oxford, 2001), 241–259; Matthew Hilton, *Consumerism in Twentieth-century Britain* (Cambridge, 2003); Michael Hopkins, Michael Kandiah, and Gillian Staerck, eds., *Cold War Britain, 1945–1964* (New York, 2003); Anne Massey, *The Independent Group* (Manchester, 1995); James Obelkevich, "Consumption," in *Understanding Post-war British Society*, ed. James Obelkevich and Peter Catterall (London, 1994), 141–154; Catherine Schenk, "Austerity and Boom, 1945–1955," in *Twentieth-century Britain*, ed. Paul Johnson (London, 1994), 300–319; Ina Zweiniger-Bargielowska, *Austerity in Britain* (Oxford, 2000).

10. Excellent exceptions are Sean Nixon, "In Pursuit of the Professional Ideal," in Jackson et al., *Commercial Cultures*, 55–74, and Frank Mort, "The Commercial Domain: Advertising and the Cultural Management of Demand," ibid. 35–53.

11. G.W. Goodall, *Advertising* (London, 1914); G.D.H. Cole, et al., eds., *Is Advertising Today a Burden—or a Boon?* (London, 1930); F.R. Leavis, *Mass Civilisation and Minority Culture* (Cambridge, 1930); F.R. Leavis and Denys Thompson, *Culture and Environment* (London, 1933); Denys Thompson, *The Voice of Civilisation* (London, 1943); Albert Baster, *Advertising Reconsidered* (London, 1935).

12. Richardson Evans, *The Age of Disfigurement* (London, 1893); Richardson Evans, *An Account of the SCAPA Society* (London, 1926); Frank Patrick Bishop, *The Economics of Advertising* (London, 1944), 132–144; idem, *The Ethics of Advertising* (London, 1949); Dorothea Braithwaite and S. Patrick Dobbs, *The Distribution of Consumable Goods* (London, 1932), 104.

13. Jeremy Tunstall, *The Advertising Man in London Advertising Agencies* (London, 1964).

14. See Terrence Nevett, *Advertising in Britain* (London, 1982).

15. "Advertising tax," *Times*, 19 November 1947, 2; "Limitation of advertising: Chancellor accepts F.B.I. scheme," *Times*, 19 February 1948, 2. See similar arguments in Labour Party, *Signposts for the Sixties* (London, 1960), 9, and C. Taylor, "What's Wrong with Capitalism?" *New Left Review* 2 (1960): 8.

16. See Elaine Frances Burton, *The Battle of the Consumer* (London: 1955); Anthony Crosland, *The Conservative Enemy* (London, 1962); Max Corden, *A Tax on Advertising?* (London, 1961); Communist Party of Great Britain, "Memorandum of Evidence to the Royal Commission on the Press," *Royal Commission on the Press: Documentary Evidence* (London, 1962), vol. 3 (Cmd. 1812-4–9); Francis Williams, *The American Invasion* (London, 1962), 21ff.; Colin Harbury, *Efficiency and the Consumer* (London, 1958); Labour Party, *Fair Deal for the Shopper* (London, 1961).

17. See Francis Noel-Baker, "We Need More Light on Advertising," *Labour Woman*, July 1959, 99.

18. The Advertising Inquiry Council was led by the journalist Elizabeth Gundrey, who also edited the BSI Consumer Advisory Council's Shopper's Guide, while Noel-Baker sat on the Executive Committee together with Richard Hoggart, the author of *The Uses of Literacy* (1957). The AIC published the critical newsletter *Scrutiny*, which exposed false advertising claims. See Francis Noel-Baker, "Enquiry into Advertis-

ing," *Socialist Commentary* (March 1959): 8ff.; idem, "The Role of the Consumer Organizations," in *Advertising and the Community*, ed. Alexander Wilson (Manchester, 1968), 147–156.
19. See Vance Packard, *The Hidden Persuaders*; idem, *The Status Seekers* (Harmondsworth, 1959); Graham Turner and John Pearson, *The Persuasion Industry* (London, 1966).
20. See J.A.C. Brown, *Techniques of Persuasion* (Harmondsworth, 1963), 165–193.
21. See Ernest Dichter, *Strategy of Desire* (New York, 1960); George H. Smith, *Motivation Research in Advertising and Marketing* (New York, 1954); Louis Cheskin, *Why People Buy* (London, 1960); Harry Henry, *Motivation Research* (London, 1958); Max Adler, *Modern Market Research* (London, 1956).
22. See Ernest Dichter, *Getting Motivated by Ernest Dichter* (New York, 1979); Daniel Horowitz, "The Emigré as Celebrant of American Consumer Culture," in *Getting and Spending: European and American Consumer Societies in the Twentieth Century*, ed. Susan Strasser et al. (Cambridge, 1998), 149–166; Stefan Schwarzkopf, "'Culture' and the Limits of Innovation in Marketing Research," *Management & Organizational History* 2 (2007), no. 3: 219–236.
23. "Split Second Advertising: Aiming at the Subconscious," *Times*, 16 September 1957, 7; J. Brooks, "The Little Ad That Isn't There," *Consumer Reports* 23 (1958): 7–10; T.E. Moore, "Subliminal Advertising," *Journal of Marketing* 46 (1982): 38–47.
24. "Case for press advertising: meeting the subliminal 'threat,'" *Times*, 28 September 1957, 3. Commentators in the press again stressed the possible political implications of subliminal advertising when it was realized that the Soviet Union had started its own research program on this new persuasion technique. See *Times*, 5 July 1958, 5.
25. "Subconscious Advertising Criticized: Study Planned of New Technique," *Times*, 7 October 1957, 5; "Ban on Subliminal Advertising: Decisions by Three U.S. Networks," *Times*, 5 December 1957, 10; "Ban on Subliminal Advertising," *Times*, 14 March 1958, 10; "Subliminal Advertising," *Times*, 19 March 1958, 4; "Motive Research," *Times*, 17 April 1959, 15. See also Frank Whitehead, "Advertising and Our Lives," *The Listener*, 16 March 1961, 471–473.
26. "Demand for Inquiry into Advertising Refused: Reliance on Voluntary Code of Conduct," *Times*, 22 November 1958, 10.
27. "Subconscious Advertising Criticized: Study Planned of New Technique," *Times*, 7 October 1957, 5.
28. Harry Henry, *Motivation Research*, 234.
29. IPA, *Subliminal Communication* (London, 1958); Brown, *Techniques of Persuasion*, 184.
30. See Kent Lancaster and Duke Yaguchi, "How economists have treated advertising: 1890–1940," *The Journal of Advertising History* 7 (October 1983): 14–29.
31. See S.M. Amadae, *Rationalizing Capitalist Democracy* (Chicago, 2003); Friedrich von Hayek, *Road to Serfdom* (London, 1944).
32. "Role of Advertising: Mr. Stanley's Defence of Consumer's Choice," *Times*, 16 December 1947, 2.
33. "Advertisers Take Stock," *Times*, 9 July 1951, 7.
34. See B. Baynes, *Advertising on Trial* (London, 1956); and Ralph Harris and Arthur Seldon, *Advertising in a Free Society* (London, 1959); idem, *Advertising and the Public* (London, 1962); idem, *Advertising in Action* (London, 1962).
35. Harris and Seldon, *Advertising in a Free Society*, 81f.
36. See *Times*, 10 July 1951, 2; 11 May 1959, 4; 4 June 1959, 8; "'Free Enterprise' Ad. Campaign Launched: £200,000 Outlay in the First Year," *Advertiser's Weekly*, 5 July 1951, 7.

37. "Cautious buying of 'freed' butter," *Times*, 11 May 1954, 5; "Soap Powder War on TV," *Times*, 28 August 1968, 24.
38. "Government Determined on TV 'a Triumph'—Conservative Central Office," *Advertisers' Weekly*, 23 July 1953, 147, 187.
39. Harry Henry, *Perspectives in Management, Marketing and Research* (London, 1971), 138–144.
40. Ibid., 143.
41. The International Advertising Conference, 1 and 5; "Flags Are Out for 40 Nations: Royal Welcome for 2600 Conference Delegates," *Advertisers' Weekly*, 5 July 1951, 3; and the conference report in *Advertisers' Weekly*, 10 July 1951, 2.
42. The International Advertising Conference, 7, and "The Beveridge Challenge to Advertising," *Advertisers' Weekly*, 10 July 1951, 3.
43. "What the Consumer Expects," *Advertisers' Weekly*, 10 July 1951, 5; "Fair Play for Consumers: Lady Tweedsmuir and Advertising Ethics," *Times*, 11 July 1951, 3.
44. See the speech by Sam Gale, past chairman of the U.S. Advertising Council, *Advertisers' Weekly*, 12 July 1951, 84, and *Daily Mail*, 10 July 1951, 3.
45. *International Advertising Conference (Great Britain) 1951* (London, 1951), 9ff.
46. Becky Conekin, "*The Autobiography of a Nation*" (Manchester, 2003).
47. Annual Report of the Advertising Association (1950–51), 17 (History of Advertising Trust Archive, AA 15/5); "Conference Has a Good Press," *Advertisers' Weekly*, 10 July 1951, 11; "Aims of Advertising Will Ring Round the Free World," *Advertisers' Weekly*, 19 July 1951, 127.
48. "P.R. Plan Needed Now," *Advertisers' Weekly*, 16 August 1951, 290.
49. "A.A. will appoint P.R.O. to tell public about benefits of advertising," *Advertisers' Weekly*, 29 November 1951; "How advertising is helping the housewife," *Advertisers' Weekly*, 31 January 1958, 4.
50. Advertising Association 1958.
51. See the memorandum "Public Relations for Advertising" (Advertising Association, 1958) at History of Advertising Trust (HAT), AA 8/1/2; "How advertising protects the public," *Advertisers' Weekly*, 25 October 1957, 8.
52. See William Crofts, *Coercion or Persuasion?* (London, 1989); Richard Kisch, *The Private Life of Public Relations* (London, 1964), 32ff.
53. Milton Friedman and Rose Friedman, *Free to Choose* (New York, 1979); Burt Neubourne, *Free Speech, Free Markets, Free Choice* (New York, 1987).
54. See William Bird, *Better Living* (Evanston, 1999); Inger Stole, *Advertising on Trial* (Urbana, 2006).
55. See Stefan Schwarzkopf, "Who Said 'Americanization'?" in *Decentering America*, ed. Jessica Gienow-Hecht, Explorations in Culture and International History (New York, 2007), 33–100; idem, "Transatlantic Invasions or Common Culture?" in *Anglo-American Media Interactions, 1850–2000*, ed. Mark Hampton and Joel Wiener (London, 2007), 254–274.

Bibliography

Adler, Max. *Modern Market Research: A Guide for Business Executives*. London: Crosby Lockwood, 1956.

Advertising Association. *The Labour Party and Advertising*. London: Advertising Association, 1958.
Amadae, S.M. *Rationalizing Capitalist Democracy: The Cold War Origins of Rational Choice Liberalism*. Chicago: University of Chicago Press, 2003.
Baster, Albert. *Advertising Reconsidered: A Confession of Misgiving*. London: P.S. King, 1935.
Baynes, B. *Advertising on Trial: The Case for the Consumer*. London: Bow Group, 1956.
Berghahn, Volker. *America and the Intellectual Cold Wars in Europe*. Princeton: Princeton University Press, 2001.
Bird, William. *Better Living: Advertising, Media and the New Vocabulary of Business Leadership, 1935–1955*. Evanston: Northwestern University Press, 1999.
Bishop, Frank Patrick. *The Economics of Advertising*. London: Robert Hale, 1944.
———. *The Ethics of Advertising*. London: Robert Hale, 1949.
Black, Lawrence. *The Political Culture of the Left in Affluent Britain, 1951–64*. Houndmills: Palgrave, 2003.
Black, Lawrence, and Hugh Pemberton, eds. *An Affluent Society? Britain's Post-war Golden Age Revisited*. Aldershot: Ashgate, 2004.
Braithwaite, Dorothea, and S. Patrick Dobbs. *The Distribution of Consumable Goods*. London: Routledge, 1932.
Brooks, J. "The Little Ad That Isn't There." *Consumer Reports* 23 (1958): 7–10.
Brown, J.A.C. *Techniques of Persuasion: From Propaganda to Brainwashing*. Harmondsworth: Penguin, 1963.
Burton, Elaine Frances. *The Battle of the Consumer*. London: Labour Party, 1955.
Carter, Erica. *How German Is She? Post-War West German Reconstruction and the Consuming Woman*. Ann Arbor: University of Michigan Press, 1997.
Castillo, Greg. "Domesticating the Cold War: Household Consumption as Propaganda in Marshall Plan Germany." *Journal of Contemporary History* 40 (2005), no. 2: 261–288.
Cheskin, Louis. *Why People Buy: Motivation Research and Its Successful Application*. London: B.T. Batsford, 1960.
Cohen, Lizabeth. *A Consumer's Republic: The Politics of Mass Consumption in Post-war America*. New York: Alfred A. Knopf, 2003.
Cole, G.D.H., ed. *Is Advertising Today a Burden—or a Boon?* London: New Advertisers Press, 1930.
Communist Party of Great Britain. "Memorandum of Evidence to the Royal Commission on the Press." In *Royal Commission on the Press: Documentary Evidence* (London: HMSO, 1962), vol. 3 (Cmd. 1812-4-9).
Conekin, Becky. *'The Autobiography of a Nation': The 1951 Festival of Britain*. Manchester: Manchester University Press, 2003.
Corden, Max. *A Tax on Advertising?* London: Fabian Research Series 222, 1961.
Crewe, David. "Consuming Germany in the Cold War: Consumption and National Identity in East and West Germany, 1949–1989." In *Consuming Germany in the Cold War*, ed. David Crewe (Oxford: Berg, 2003), 1–19.
Crofts, William. *Coercion or Persuasion? Propaganda in Britain after 1945*. London: Routledge, 1989.
Crosland, Anthony. *The Conservative Enemy*. London: Jonathan Cape, 1962.
Cross, Gary. *An All-consuming Century: Why Commercialism Won in Modern America*. New York: Columbia University Press, 2000.
Dichter, Ernest. *Strategy of Desire*. New York: Boardman, 1960.
———. *Getting Motivated by Ernest Dichter: The Secret behind Individual Motivations by the Man Who Was Not Afraid to Ask "Why."* New York: Pergamon, 1979.

Evans, Richardson. *The Age of Disfigurement*. London: Remington, 1893.
———. *An Account of the SCAPA Society*. London: Constable, 1926.
Fehrenbach, Heide, and Uta Poiger, eds. *Transactions, Transgressions, Transformations: American Culture in Western Europe and Japan*. New York: Berghahn, 1999.
Findley, Richard. "The Conservative Party and Defeat: The Significance of Resale Price Maintenance for the General Election of 1964." *Twentieth-century British History* 12 (2001), no. 3: 327–353.
Friedman, Milton, and Rose Friedman. *Free to Choose: A Personal Statement*. New York: Harcourt Brace, 1979.
Gilman, Nils. *Mandarins of the Future: Modernization Theory in Cold War America*. Baltimore: Johns Hopkins University Press, 2007.
Goodall, G.W. *Advertising: A Study of Modern Business Power*. London: Constable, 1914.
Gries, Rainer. *Produkte und Politik: zur Kultur- und Politikgeschichte der Produktkommunikation*. Vienna: Facultas, 2006.
Harbury, Colin. *Efficiency and the Consumer*. London: Fabian Research Series 199, 1958.
Harris, Ralph, and Arthur Seldon. *Advertising in a Free Society*. London: Institute of Economic Affairs, 1959.
———. *Advertising and the Public*. London: Andre Deutsch, 1962.
———. *Advertising in Action*. London: Hutchinson, 1962.
Hayek, Friedrich von. *Road to Serfdom*. London: Routledge, 1944.
Henry, Harry. *Motivation Research: Its Practice and Uses for Advertising, Marketing and Other Businesses*. London: Crosby Lockwood, 1958.
———. *Perspectives in Management, Marketing and Research*. London: Crosby Lockwood, 1971.
Hilton, Matthew. "Consumer Politics in Post-war Britain." In *The Politics of Consumption: Material Culture and Citizenship in Europe and America*, ed. Martin Daunton and Matthew Hilton (Oxford: Berg, 2001), 241–259.
———. *Consumerism in Twentieth-century Britain: The Search for a Historical Movement*. Cambridge: Cambridge University Press, 2003.
Hixson, Walter. *Parting the Curtain: Propaganda, Culture and the Cold War, 1945–1961*. Basingstoke: Macmillan, 1997.
Hopkins, Michael, Michael Kandiah, and Gillian Staerck, eds. *Cold War Britain, 1945–1964*. New York: Routledge, 2003.
Horowitz, Daniel. "The Emigré as Celebrant of American Consumer Culture: George Katona and Ernest Dichter." In *Getting and Spending: European and American Consumer Societies in the Twentieth Century*, ed. Susan Strasser, Charles McGovern, and Matthias Judt (Cambridge: Cambridge University Press, 1998), 149–166.
International Advertising Conference (Great Britain) 1951. London: The Times Publishing Co., 1951.
IPA (Institute of Practitioners in Advertising). *Subliminal Communication*. London: IPA, 1958.
Isaac, Joel. "The Human Sciences in Cold War America." *The Historical Journal* 50 (2007), no. 3: 725–746.
Jackson, Peter, Michelle Lowe, Daniel Miller, and Frank Mort, eds. *Commercial Cultures: Economies, Practices, Spaces*. Oxford: Berg, 2000.
Kisch, Richard. *The Private Life of Public Relations*. London: MacGibbon & Kee, 1964.
Kroes, Rob. "American Empire and Cultural Imperialism: A View from the Receiving End." *Diplomatic History* 23 (1999), no. 3: 463–477.
Labour Party. *Signposts for the Sixties*. London: Labour Party, 1960.
———. *Fair Deal for the Shopper*. London: Labour Party, 1961.

———. *Report of a Commission of Enquiry into Advertising* (the Reith Commission Report). London: Labour Party, 1966.
Lancaster, Kent, and Duke Yaguchi. "How economists have treated advertising: 1890–1940." *Journal of Advertising History* 7 (October 1983), 14–29.
Laville, Helen. "'Our country endangered by Underwear': Fashion, Femininity and the Seduction Narrative in *Ninotchka* and *Silk Stockings*." *Diplomatic History* 30 (2006), no. 4: 623–644.
Leavis, F.R. *Mass Civilisation and Minority Culture*. Cambridge: Minority Press, 1930.
Leavis, F.R., and Denys Thompson. *Culture and Environment: The Training of Critical Awareness*. London: Chatto & Windus, 1933.
Lowen, Rebecca. *Creating the Cold War University: The Transformation of Stanford*. Berkeley and Los Angeles: University of California Press, 1997.
Massey, Anne. *The Independent Group: Modernism and Mass Culture in Britain, 1945–59*. Manchester: Manchester University Press, 1995.
May, Elaine Tyler. *Homeward Bound: American Families in the Cold War Era*. New York: Basic Books, 1988.
Mickenberg, Julia. *Learning from the Left: Children's Literature, the Cold War, and Radical Politics in the United States*. Oxford: Oxford University Press, 2006.
Moore, T.E. "Subliminal Advertising: What You See Is What You Get." *Journal of Marketing* 46 (1982): 38–47.
Mort, Frank. "The Commercial Domain: Advertising and the Cultural Management of Demand." In Jackson et al., *Commercial Cultures*, 35–53.
Neubourne, Burt. *Free Speech, Free Markets, Free Choice: An Essay on Commercial Speech*. New York: Association of National Advertisers, 1987.
Nevett, Terrence. *Advertising in Britain: A History*. London: Heinemann, 1982.
Nixon, Sean. "In Pursuit of the Professional Ideal: UK Advertising and the Construction of Commercial Expertise, 1953–64." In Jackson et al., *Commercial Cultures*, 55–74.
Noel-Baker, Francis. "We Need More Light on Advertising." *Labour Woman*, July 1959, 99.
———. "The Role of the Consumer Organizations." In *Advertising and the Community*, ed. Alexander Wilson (Manchester: Manchester University Press, 1968), 147–156.
Obelkevich, James. "Consumption." In *Understanding Post-war British Society*, ed. James Obelkevich and Peter Catterall (London: Routledge, 1994), 141–154.
Osgood, Kenneth. *Total Cold War: Eisenhower's Secret Propaganda Battle at Home and Abroad*. Lawrence: University of Kansas Press, 2006.
Packard, Vance. *The Hidden Persuaders*. New York: Doubleday, 1957.
———. *The Status Seekers*. Harmondsworth: Penguin, 1959.
Pence, Katherine. "Shopping for an 'Economic Miracle': Gendered Politics of Consumer Citizenship in Divided Germany." In *The Expert Consumer: Associations and Professionals in Consumer Society*, ed. Alain Chatriot, Marie-Emanuelle Chessel and Matthew Hilton (Aldershot: Ashgate, 2006), 105–120.
Reid, Susan. "The Khrushchev Kitchen: Domesticating the Scientific-Technological Revolution." *Journal of Contemporary History* 40 (2005), no. 2: 289–316.
Richmond, Yale. *Cultural Exchange and the Cold War: Raising the Iron Curtain*. University Park: Pennsylvania State University Press, 2003.
Schenk, Catherine. "Austerity and Boom, 1945–1955." in *Twentieth-century Britain: Economic, Social and Cultural Change*, ed. Paul Johnson (London: Longman, 1994), 300–319.
Schildt, Axel, and Detlef Siegfried, eds. *Between Marx and Coca-Cola: Youth Cultures in Changing European Societies, 1960–1980*. New York: Berghahn, 2006.

Schwarzkopf, Stefan. "They Do it with Mirrors: Advertising and British Cold War Consumer Politics." *Contemporary British History* 19, no. 2 (June 2005), 133–150.

———. "'Culture' and the Limits of Innovation in Marketing Research: Ernest Dichter, Motivation Studies and Psychoanalytic Consumer Research in Great Britain, 1950–1970." *Management & Organizational History* 2 (2007), no. 3: 219–236.

———. "Who said 'Americanization'? The Case of Twentieth-Century Advertising and Mass Marketing from a British Perspective," in *Decentering America: New Directions in Culture and International History*, ed. Jessica Gienow-Hecht. Explorations in Culture and International History (New York: Berghahn Books, 2007), 33–100.

———. "Transatlantic Invasions or Common Culture? Modes of Cultural and Economic Exchange Between the American and the British Advertising Industries, 1951–1989." In *Anglo-American Media Interactions, 1850–2000*, ed. Mark Hampton and Joel Wiener (London: Palgrave, 2007), 254–274.

Simpson, Christopher. *Science of Coercion: Communication Research and Psychological Warfare, 1945–1960*. New York: Oxford University Press, 1994.

Smith, George H. *Motivation Research in Advertising and Marketing*. New York: McGraw-Hill, 1954.

Spector, Bert. "The Harvard Business Review goes to war." *Management & Organizational History* 1 (2006), no. 3: 273–295.

Stole, Inger. *Advertising on Trial: Consumer Activism and Corporate Public Relations in the 1930s*. Urbana: University of Illinois Press, 2006.

Tadajewski, Mark. "The Ordering of Marketing Theory: The Influence of McCarthyism and the Cold War." *Marketing Theory* 6 (2006), no. 2: 163–199.

Taylor, C. "What's Wrong with Capitalism?" *New Left Review* 2 (1960): 8.

Thompson, Denys. *The Voice of Civilisation: An Enquiry into Advertising*. London: Frederick Muller, 1943.

Tunstall, Jeremy. *The Advertising Man in London Advertising Agencies*. London: Chapman & Hall, 1964.

Turner, Graham, and John Pearson. *The Persuasion Industry*. London: Readers Union 1966.

Vodosek, Peter, and Wolfgang Schmitz, eds. *Bibliotheken, Bücher und andere Medien in der Zeit des Kalten Krieges*. Wiesbaden: Harrassowitz, 2005.

Whitehead, Frank. "Advertising and Our Lives: The Dangers of Mass Suggestion," *The Listener*, 16 March 16, 471–473.

Whitfield, Stephen. *The Culture of the Cold War*. Baltimore: Johns Hopkins University Press, 1996.

Williams, Francis. *The American Invasion*. London: Anthony Blond, 1962.

Zweiniger-Bargielowska, Ina. *Austerity in Britain: Rationing, Controls and Consumption, 1939–1955*. Oxford: Oxford University Press, 2000.

Chapter 9

SURVIVAL IN THE WELFARE COCOON
The Culture of Civil Defense in Cold War Sweden

Marie Cronqvist

> Which war are you Swedes planning to participate in since you are building all these massive shelters for humans, machines, and war ships?[1]

In his memoirs, the Swedish prime minister Tage Erlander recalls a 1954 luncheon at Winston Churchill's country home Chequers, when the British Minister of Supply Duncan Sandys challenged him on the matter of civil defense. In the 1950s and 1960s, Sweden was sometimes—and occasionally with a hint of mockery as in the words of Sandys—simply referred to as "the nation that strives underground."[2] Extensive emergency evacuation plans, mandatory civil defense duty, frequent atomic air-raid drills, necklace identification tag campaigns, and the construction of massive public shelters marked the Swedish Cold War experience. In the spirit of total defense, "if war comes" was the catch phrase constantly repeated in the daily lives of Swedish citizens as well as at military and political conferences, generating a militarization of everyday life that surpassed that of many other countries. Still in the 1980s, Sweden's civil defense budget per capita rose well above those of greater powers such as the Soviet Union, Great Britain, France, and the United States.[3]

Why would a small, neutral country on the northern periphery of Europe put so much time and effort into digging itself into solid granite, preparing not only for war but for the end of days? In this chapter, I will discuss this question central to any understanding of Cold War Sweden, though my main interest is not civil defense policy alone, but also the cultural process by which policy-makers and citizens alike domesticated war and made military preparedness a home and family affair.

First, I am interested in how the national security program connected with collective identity at the grass-roots level of experience. How was the rhetoric of everyday vigilance constructed under the Swedish maxim "if war comes?" What were its historical frames of reference? Second, I shall discuss to what extent and in what ways narratives of the good society interacted with the Cold War narrative in the context of civil defense. The Swedish welfare model, a middle way between state Socialism and capitalism, embodied in the concept of the *folkhem*—literally "people's home"—and enforced by the hegemonic Social Democratic Party (SAP) from the 1930s on throughout the Cold War era, seems to have supplied citizens with a deep sense of security and stability during the age of uncertainty and fear of nuclear annihilation.

In order to investigate how warfare meets welfare and how images of neutrality and *folkhem* intersect in the early Cold War period, I will refer to one very significant civil defense instruction manual, *If War Comes: Instructions for Sweden's Citizens* (*Om kriget kommer: vägledning för Sveriges medborgare*). This brochure was reissued in a number of updated versions throughout the Cold War period and distributed to all households in Sweden, although in this context I will focus on the three editions from 1943, 1952, and 1961. In *If War Comes*, warm welfare and cold war are two sides of the same coin. The topics dealt with include not only preparedness for war, but also moral values, family ideals, work ethos, welfare, and cleanliness. At the end of this journey through early postwar Swedish history, I will argue that the case of civil defense culture in Sweden allows for a new interpretation of the shift from World War to Cold War, which also questions some of the basic assumptions of international historiography on Cold War culture.

The Atomic Age and Cultures of Civil Defense

In his groundbreaking book *By the Bomb's Early Light*, Paul Boyer argues that within hours after the attack on Hiroshima, the bomb became "one of those categories of Being, like Space and Time," that by now are well rooted in our conceptual universe and "built into the very structure of our minds, giving shape and meaning to all our perception."[4] For Americans, not only did the glorious triumph in World War II suddenly threaten to transform into a Pyrrhic victory, it also became clear that living with the bomb raised things such as fear, despair, fatalism, helplessness, psychic numbing, moral erosion, and mental apocalypse.[5] The threat of atomic holocaust evoked a metamorphosis of the world known to man and unleashed a host of doomsday fantasies. At once, nuclear culture seemed to advance the crumbling of distinctions between physics and philosophy, politics and poetry, reality and science fiction. In the field of fiction, imagining World War III or a postatomic future became a powerful leitmotif, from novelist Neville Shute's sinister dystopia *On the Beach* (1957) to film director Stanley Kubrick's dark satire *Dr. Strangelove* (1964).

Whereas Kubrick seemingly found the topic of nuclearism far too bizarre for any realistic interpretation, practical instructions and blunt realism were indeed central concerns in the grave world of civil defense. In the vast research on American Cold War Culture, scholars such as Laura McEnaney, Guy Oakes, and Kenneth D. Rose have established the culture of civil defense as a branch of its own.[6] The key perspective in these studies of the nuclear age mindset is a particular interest not primarily in the organizational or propagandistic aspects of civil defense, but more importantly in the cultural construction of meaning. Inquiries into how civil defense messages were designed, received, appropriated, and adjusted paint a much broader picture of American everyday life in the Cold War era.

Elaine Tyler May set out early to explore such cultural aspects of civil defense rhetoric in a section of her book *Homeward Bound*, published in 1988 and by now a frequently cited classic in the field of Cold War Culture research. Through her main focus on the lives and experiences of American families, May suggests that the information management of civil defense establishes a link between private and public, intimate life and politics, the safety of the family environment and the unfathomable threat of total war. She strikingly illustrates the 1950s connection between homemaking and shelter culture, as well as the link between unleashed female sexuality and nuclear warfare. In the cultural milieu of 1950s America, societal rupture and devastating chaos could arrive in the shape of either nuclear devices or sex bombs.[7]

Civil defense instructions, however, were intended as much to encourage hopes of security as to draw attention to the profound threat of nuclear war. Problems of psychology related to life in the shadow of the bomb proved to be a gripping task for civil defense authorities in the 1950s and 1960s. Following May's *Homeward Bound*, several scholars have investigated this aspect of civil defense rhetoric—to conceive the inconceivable and to manage nuclear terror. Margot A. Henriksen, who investigates existential anxiety in 1950s America, shows for example that nuclear anxiety was considered an illness, diagnosed as "nuclearosis." Appropriate treatment included a fallout shelter to make the patient feel safe and to clear the mushroom clouds from his or her sight.[8]

The same rationale to confront hopelessness and despair could be found in the classic civil defense cartoon *Duck and Cover*, released in 1950 and featuring Bert the Turtle, who advises school children to duck and cover under their desks in the face of nuclear attack, as well as in the 1950 booklet *Survival Under Atomic Attack*, issued by the Federal Civil Defense Administration (FCDA). Guy Oakes discusses such messages in terms of a civil defense system of emotion management, "a strategy for the mobilization, administration, and control of emotional life," involving cognitive standards defining possible feelings, practical norms defining which emotions are to be expected, and a technology of controls and strategies defining what to do under specific circumstances and how people could convert their negative emotions into constructive advantages while awaiting the apocalypse.[9]

In addition to the psychological handling of nuclear anxiety, Laura McEnaney characterizes civil defense discourse as a far-reaching militarization of everyday life. Civil defense was a paramilitary program, McEnaney argues, with one foot in the defense establishment and the other in the cultural domain of the postwar home front—a quaint fusion of military priorities and idealized domestic life.[10] Sometimes married life itself symbolized a protection against the horrors of war, which May illustrates in *Homeward Bound* by referring to *Life* magazine's 1959 article on the honeymoon couple cuddling up in their bomb shelter for two weeks of "unbroken togetherness."[11]

McEnaney's use of the concept of everyday militarization is interesting because while earlier research on the culture of civil defense—as with Cold War Culture in general—has almost exclusively focused on the United States, everyday militarization was in certain ways a much more far-reaching phenomenon in other countries. In European historiography, considering the number of human lives profoundly affected by the grim everyday realities of aerial bombardment through two world wars and the constant outcries for efforts to protect civilians, literature on the cultural history of civil defense is remarkably scarce. In Germany, a few recent studies have addressed the issue of civil protection,[12] and in Sweden the strictly political and organizational aspects of civil defense propaganda have also been discussed,[13] but the cultural dimensions of the civil defense mindset have thus far not been sufficiently addressed.

Following May, McEnaney, Oakes, Rose, and others, I regard civil defense instructions not only as a question of policy, but in the broader context of social life and everyday culture. Instead of speaking about one singular culture of civil defense, I suggest identifying various local cultures of civil defense. Not only could an inquiry into the variety of local responses to the threat of total war tell us much about the structures and cultural values of the societies that produce these responses, it could also contribute to a more complex and multiperspective discussion of Cold War Culture. Taking into consideration that scholarly discourse thus far has primarily targeted the experiences of key actors or regimes during the Cold War, neutral countries present interesting cases for comparison. Countries such as Sweden and Switzerland were situated at the periphery and yet, at the same time, at the very center of the Cold War. Interestingly, both countries were deeply committed to civil defense. According to Lawrence J. Vale, enforcing everyday militarization and upholding the cultural identity of neutrality in these countries seem to have been two sides of the same coin. Neutrality has rendered possible the undisturbed development of large-scale and ambitious civil defense programs.[14]

Accordingly, a case study of Swedish civil defense culture can make important contributions, not only to the history of Sweden in the Cold War and Swedish Cold War Culture, but also to the history of different European Cold War Cultures. The Swedish example may also serve as an interesting illustration of how a Social Democratic welfare state handled issues of military defense, national security, and domesticity in an age of total war. Here, civil defense could be seen as a manifestation of national identity, and a reflection of the values of Swedish modernity and sense of exceptionalism during the Cold War era. What was unique about the situation in Sweden? How were Swedish citizens to tackle the impending World War III?

One People, One Home, and One Defense

As in many other European countries, the postwar civil defense program in Sweden has its roots in the unruly 1930s, when the threat of air war loomed on all sides. Apocalyptic visions of a coming total war abounded, a war that would expose civilians to an unprecedented level of violence through aerial bombardment. Measures for civilian defense were taken in a number of European countries, and in Sweden the first air-raid protection association was founded in 1937, with the task of training civilians in methods of defense and relief with instructive titles such as *How to Act When the Bombs Are Falling*.[15] A series of investigations and commissions followed, and during the war years—which in Sweden to this day are called "the preparedness years" since the country declared itself neutral early on and remained materially unaffected by the conflict—the scattered and at times improvised local air-protection activities were gradually institutionalized. In 1944, the earlier state air-raid protection program and the evacuation commission established at the beginning of the war merged into a new central authority, the Swedish Civil Defense Administration. Civil defense duty was mandatory for every citizen.[16]

Two aspects are crucial to this spirit of preparedness and the growing militarization in Sweden during World War II. One is that the Swedish Social Democrats had completely abandoned their critical stance toward the military and adopted a much more sympathetic one. Already at the beginning of World War II, they had successfully overcome the ideological gulf between military defense and Socialism that followed in the wake of World War I and was at that time manifest in the critical expression "the fortified poorhouse" (*det befästa fattighuset*). Now, in the words of one contemporary commentator, it was rather a question of "the fortified *folkhem*"—total defense in an age of total war.[17] Following a 1939 conference on the relationship between people and defense, an initiative by the Social Democratic Youth Movement, the new umbrella organization for civil and voluntary defense organizations in Sweden, was founded in 1940 under the name of *Folk och försvar*, literally "people and defense."[18] During, and especially after World War II, securing the home front implied total commitment to militarization, and the belief in an all-encompassing *folkförsvar* ("people's defense") continued to be a characteristic trait of Sweden throughout the Cold War.

A second aspect central to the first few years of planning Swedish postwar civil defense in general, and the organization *Folk och försvar* in particular, was the larger cultural context provided by the late nineteenth-century popular movements in Sweden (*folkrörelserna*): the temperance movement, the workers' movement, and the revivalist movement. Bo Stråth and Øystein Sørensen identify a late nineteenth-century merging of images of individual freedom with those of collectivism and state authority under the concept of *folk* (people). Accordingly, there is a great degree of continuity between the pragmatism of the nineteenth-century Scandinavian popular movements and the Swedish Social Democrats when they redefined themselves as a *folk* party rather than a class party in the 1930s.[19] This remains an important consideration when analyzing the frequent concept of *folk* in the context of postwar Swedish culture of civil defense and its insistence on the individual's adaptation to the collective. The term *folk* should not be understood lightly as "people in general," but rather as one specific organism: the Swedish people.[20]

Besides *folk* and *folkhem*, other concepts are important for understanding the cultural embeddedness of civil defense in Sweden, including the tone in which citizens were addressed. In the Nordic popular movement tradition, education (*bildning*) was considered a key instrument and temperance and conscientiousness (*skötsamhet*) were honored virtues. The popular movements expressed very specific educational ideals in which the responsibility of the individual was essential, ideals and traits that were imperative in the cultural and ideological foundation of the workers' movement as well as the Swedish Social Democratic Party. The Swedish citizen was imagined as an individual not only with a profound thirst for knowledge, but also with a deeply rooted sense of collectiveness and undivided loyalty to the common good.

Lars Trägårdh has argued that the popular movements were crucial in the construction of a pragmatic, individual-oriented Protestant ethic of responsibility, in contrast to the holistic collectivism that signified continental Romanticism. Contrary to the common perception of the collectivist nature of the Nordic welfare state, he argues that what in fact characterizes these states in general, and Sweden in particular, is the unmediated *alliance* between the state and the individual—a "statist individualism." It is a relationship in which benefits provided by the state are directly received by the individual, thus bypassing other potential mediating institutions in civil society such as the job or the family. Thus, as Trägårdh puts it, using the terminology of Ferdinand Tönnies, "behind the *Gemeinschaft* of the so-called 'home of the people' one finds a *Gesellschaft* of atomized, autonomous individuals."[21] This individualistic collectivism, the construction of a folk community out of autonomous individuals unbound by any obligations or direct responsibilities for other family members, but bound by their devotion to, and dependence on the state, of course presents an interesting and sharp contrast between Sweden and not only the American model of civil defense culture, but also those of most other countries.

Neutrality as Self-awareness

The popular movements and their way of constructing the conscientious individual with a profound loyalty to the collective is thus one important cultural framework for any understanding of how Swedish Cold War civil defense successfully fused the Swedish people and the nation's defense in the concept of *folkförsvar*—implying the people *as* the defense. Another important context is unquestionably what some Swedish historians have interchangeably called the myth of neutrality, neutrality as self-awareness, or neutrality as a state of mind.

Politically, the fragile geostrategic position of Sweden in World War II and during the first decades of the Cold War contributed to the development of a security policy based on the idea of nonalignment in peacetime, and aiming at neutrality in wartime. This credo of neutrality, a blueprint of the early Cold War era and fundamentally contested for the first time as late as the 1990s,[22] was founded on the solid base of a strong and total defense, with civil resistance as a particularly important feature in the event of war. After World War II, neutrality increasingly became not only the chosen security policy, under the maxim of "small-state realism," but also a state of mind that invested the Swedish national identity with rationality, peacefulness, and modernity, in contrast to the war-ravaged continent heavily burdened with callous ideologies and past traumas.[23]

The process of making modernity and neutrality the quintessence of the Swedish way entailed a flight from tradition and history. There were hardly any lessons to be learned from past experiences, and turning away from history implied a turning away from Europe. Swedish historians have referred to the complex relationship between Sweden and Europe in terms of a *Berührungsangst*, a need for demarcation and an anxiety about contact with the Dark Continent of Europe. Whereas the continent evoked fearful images of brutality and war, tradition and history, Sweden and Swedishness implied peace, modernity, and the brightest of futures.[24]

The social and political ethos, which emphasized perpetual peace before all other values, thus nurtured a cultural narrative of Swedish exceptionalism, which was marked by a distinct continuity between World War II and Cold War Sweden—a continuity also addressed by civil defense planners and instructors. This narrative was sustained not only by a detachment from the disarray of postwar Europe and a sense of immunity to world crises at large, but also by a spirit of rational collaboration and consensus among social groups and between labor and capital, as well as universal and centrally steered solutions with elements of social engineering. In the first decade of the Cold War, neutrality and *folkhem* had become not merely hegemonic, but sanctified concepts. Social Democracy had melded with Swedishness to the extent that non-Socialists risked damaging their own causes when contending with their opponents. Alf W. Johansson speaks about a social liberal culture of consensus that permeated Sweden after World War II, an egalitarian culture in which the focus was not on the splendor of the strong in society, but on the needs of the weak. Safety and security were the fundamental guiding values: "Sweden sought its glory by being most successful in security: from the cradle to the grave the Swede would rest in a sheltering net of societal safety. The condition for this was societal homogeneity and a dominating Puritan ethos: diligence, conscientiousness, moderation, thriftiness."[25]

The goal of establishing a fully dependable and safe haven permeated postwar civil defense. More than anything, the military preparedness slogan "if war comes" expressed the outlines of the cultural milieu of Cold War Sweden—an obsession with social and national security evolving around the neutral *folkhem*. Here, the threat of war did not result in a romantic sense of a community seeking its foundation in history, but instead in a national identity fabricated out of order, cleanliness, modernity, and an optimistic outlook on the future. Internal security was coupled with security from an outside world. In the following sections, empirical examples will illustrate the argument outlined so far.

Between Warfare and Welfare

Odd as it may seem, the first version of the civil defense instruction manual *If War Comes* was written in the winter of 1943, when World War II had taken a different turn and the direct threat of war had in fact decreased, largely due to grave German misfortunes on the eastern front. Swedish concessions to Germany in the first few years of the war, among them the rail transit of soldiers to Norway and Finland, were now withdrawn. A stricter policy of neutrality was proclaimed, although Sweden at the same time began to adjust itself politically, economically, and culturally to the Western powers whose victory now seemed inevitable. Military rearmament as well as the neutrality policy, however, continued to enjoy popular support among the Swedes, and in the later years of World War II, the Swedish postwar total defense organization was built.

A preliminary draft entitled *Wartime ABC for Swedish Citizens* (*ABC för svenska medborgare i krig*) was presented and discussed at the Swedish Defense Ministry in the winter of 1943, but in the version that was eventually printed, the title was adjusted to *If War Comes* (*Om kriget kommer*).[26] The edition was almost 2.3 million, and the royal character assigned to the brochure was quite important, not only because it was signed by King Gustav V and had the stately royal seal on the front page, but also due to the fact that Crown Prince Gustav Adolf allegedly was involved in the first draft of the manuscript.[27] The overall message in this 16-page manual was that total war calls for total defense and that resistance is paramount at all times.

In comparison with later Cold War versions, *If War Comes* from 1943 has a formal and authoritarian tone, addressing not primarily citizens but rather the king's loyal subjects. However different in the form of address, it nevertheless establishes the later recurrent image of a small fortress, a peaceful neutral island, a realm of security in an unsafe world. This cocooning narrative is perhaps even more clearly enforced in another civil defense publication dated two years earlier, which had been distributed by *Folkberedskapen*, the main branch of the wartime State Information Agency devoted to issues of civil defense and preparedness. It was a correspondence course in six parts for local study groups, entitled *The Swedish Way of Life (Den svenska livsformen)*.[28] The series of letters contained information about Swedish democracy, citizenship, and the political system, but also Swedish cultural values and mentality.

Already the title conceives Swedish society as an organism, a nonconforming but idyllic and peaceful way of life fundamentally different from that in the conflict-ridden continent of Europe. In the fourth letter, entitled *Social Security with Individual Responsibility*, which exemplifies what Trägårdh has defined as the Scandinavian model of "statist individualism," one illustration in particular captures the idea of an island of hope in a sea of despair.[29] A handful of people, perhaps not necessarily a family but individuals symbolizing the different stages of life, are sheltered by a protective wall distancing them from the irrational, fearful, and dark storm outside. The bricks of the wall constitute a bulwark against harmful influences from the outside world by means of industrial welfare or workers' protection, national basic pension, medical care, owner-occupied housing programs, maternity care, and general holidays. In this illustration, Swedish welfare meets European warfare; rationality and order meet rupture and chaos.

In *The Swedish Way of Life*, as in the first version of *If War Comes*, messages of civil defense and popular resistance are constantly reasserted. These two examples of civil defense rhetoric from the preparedness era evoke the image of a national community based on every individual's sense of duty, honesty, and obedience to the law and the state. Moreover, they evoke the image of a small but righteous country simultaneously on the periphery and at the very center of a war between greater powers. This sense of watching the world from a distance would linger into a new era of equally Cold War.

Civil Defense Housekeeping in the 1950s and 1960s

In sharp contrast to most other countries in Europe, Sweden was in an advantageous position after World War II. The forestry and steel industries were intact, opening up the opportunity of manufacturing goods and products for an insatiable European market. On account of the flourishing economy, the first two decades of the Cold War saw not only the coming of affluence, but also the realization of the welfare state outlined in the 1930s and marked by the ethos of social engineering. A number of social and political reforms were carried out, such as the universal child allowance in 1947, obligatory health insurance in 1955, and a national supplementary pension plan in 1959. A comprehensive agreement on the labor market between the confederation of trade unions and the employers' confederation was also achieved in this era of harmony and consent. However, harmony and stability were evidently threatened by evil forces inside the four walls of the people's Swedish home. At the beginning of the 1950s, fears of treacherous fifth columnists received extensive public attention and became a vital incentive to civil defense activities. This occurred against the backdrop not only of the exposure of international spy networks, but also of two widely discussed cases of Communist espionage in Sweden in 1951 and 1952. In the context of civil defense, the old World War II messages about total resistance at all times, such as the *Silence Campaign* (including posters entitled "A Swede Keeps Quiet" and "The Spy is Doing a Jigsaw Puzzle"), were recycled. Between 1950 and 1954, *Folk och försvar* launched a large-scale propaganda campaign on the topic of psychological defense and the spirit of resistance, focusing on the present danger of the fifth column.[30]

The fear of spies and traitors also left a distinct mark on the 1952 version of *If War Comes*, which by this time had grown from sixteen to thirty-five informative pages, each one illustrated. The strict and authoritative tone of the 1943 version was now replaced by an informal and complaisant tone, addressing the individual citizen as an equal. On the first page, the introductory address was signed by both King Gustav VI Adolf and Prime Minister Tage Erlander, again establishing the monarchy's natural place in the home of the people.[31]

A deceitful spider's web, the classic metaphor of espionage, covers a spread in *If War Comes* in 1952. In the contemporary print media, the clear and present danger of espionage was frequently described in terms of smelly filth that had somehow infiltrated the otherwise perfectly sanitary *folkhem*. One example is a witty drawing in *Stockholms-Tidningen* in February 1952, when a second spy scandal had hit the front pages. Here, the Swedish housewife—or the symbolic "Mother Svea"—encounters a rotten communist egg in her kitchen cabinet. The need for a thorough spring cleaning seems to be quite urgent.

If War Comes from 1952 introduced the issue of how to maintain high-quality civil defense housekeeping. As other researchers have shown, domesticity and sound atomic housewifery according to traditional gender roles were essential in American civil defense culture of the 1950s.[32] This was equally important in Cold War Sweden. On the pages of *If War Comes* from 1952 and 1961, the *folkhem* housewife takes pride in her duty to prepare the home for both attack and recovery, all in a calm and assured manner. The paramilitary housewife was responsible for containing fear and avoiding panic, which involved everything from comforting frightened children to preparing first-aid kits, stocking food and water, and packing the family automobile with enough supplies for an extended trip in case of emergency.

Naturally, the housewife would also engage in her usual endless dusting, brushing, cleaning, and washing—although these everyday hygiene and sanitation practices were now carried out in the service of national security. As Mary Douglas once pointed out, dust and dirt emerge as a question of "matter out of place" and a disruption of order. Thus, cleaning is concomitant with the creation (or recreation) of order and stability.[33] In the context of civil defense housekeeping, the homemaker was expected to wash away any lingering airborne radioactive particles on pots and pans, thus creating solid harmony out of potential chaos. Keeping every domestic item in its right place, according to *If War Comes*, is a prerequisite for national security.[34]

Thus there are some striking similarities between the American and the Swedish cults of domesticity in the 1950s, but there are also noteworthy differences. Compared to U.S. civil defense culture as described by May, McEnaney, Oakes, and others, the Swedish home was something much larger than the individual household. Equally important as the domestic microcosm of the nuclear family was the sense of the community as a whole, encapsulated in the powerful *folkhem* metaphor and supported by the paramilitary spirit of preparedness firmly anchored in the World War II mindset. Indeed, the patriarchal *folkhem* model, the trust in nurturing state institutions, laid considerably more stress on "home" than on "family." The cherished connection between the two faces of domestic life, the individual household and the larger collective home, had to be clear and obvious to every citizen. The former was but a miniature version of the latter.

Nevertheless, emphasizing the home also meant the possibility of having to leave it behind. From its beginnings in the late 1930s on, the Swedish civil defense model had centered on two issues: the planning of evacuation and the construction of shelters. In the late 1950s, evacuation and relocation planning became the primary topic of concern in Sweden, which radically differed from the civil defense models in other Western European countries such as France or Great Britain, where the order was to stay at home until further instructions were issued by the authorities—the so-called stay-put policy.[35] If the issues of spies and psychological defense were at the heart of *If War Comes* in 1952, the concern with evacuation took center stage in the next version, published in 1961. Against the backdrop of the discussion on the hydrogen bomb in civil defense planning during the late 1950s, the front page portrays ominous dark clouds in an otherwise bright sky.[36]

Around 1960, extensive evacuation drills were held in a number of Swedish cities, such as the one that took place in the capital, Stockholm, in April 1961. This public sociodrama, "Operation Stockholm," was said to be the world's largest emergency evacuation rehearsal of its time, with around 30,000 participating civilians, who found themselves woken up by the telephone alarm at around six o'clock in the morning and fully evacuated from the city center to the countryside just in time for lunch. Celebrities, politicians, and royalty alike participated, and again we notice the symbolic place of the monarchy in the civil defense culture of Sweden, when enthusiastic news dailies showed press photos of King Gustav VI Adolf evacuating the royal castle, riding the underground railway with his fellow evacuees, and later being served the mandatory bowl of meat soup at the rural assembly point. However frightening a scenario, the press framed the event in a peaceful and idyllic setting far from the horrific scenery of nuclear war. It was, according to the papers and television newscasts, a beautiful morning, perfect for a nice outing in the countryside, with city dwellers enjoying a picnic in the sun awaiting further orders, in good spirits and seemingly untroubled by the nuclear holocaust that had purportedly struck their nation's capital.[37]

The question of evacuation was also central to the version of *If War Comes* published the same year, 1961. One of its pages features a family standing by for evacuation. The group consists of a mother with two children and a grandfather, wearing what seems to be an old woolen overcoat from the preparedness years' Home Guard. The father is absent, already at his assigned post in the military defense. "Keep the family together during evacuation," the instructions say, and the evacuees are requested to bring money and valuables, protective clothing, gas masks, identification tags, and ration cards. Symptomatically, they are also requested to bring along their health insurance papers and their trade-union books—allowing for the survival of the evacuated and relocated Swedish welfare state.[38] Here, the trade-union book is not only an indicator of the weight given to the possibilities for employment at the relocation site; it also symbolizes the *folkhem*'s faith in the Swedish model of consensus and cooperation on the labor market.

Thus far, I have focused on the period from World War II to the beginning of the 1960s. However, a quick look at the following decades is revealing. At the end of the 1960s and during the 1970s, Swedish defense policy gradually turned towards the conception of an advance-warning period of several months or even years. The 1959 civil defense film *Let's*

Go Underground (*Vi går under jorden*) is an example of a mindset that came to prevail in the decades to come. In the mid 1960s, the civil defense pendulum had swung back from evacuation/relocation to a focus on the construction of public shelters, which at this time numbered 43,000, with room for 3 million people, almost half the population of Sweden.[39] Already in 1965, the vast emergency evacuation plans for Sweden were in part obsolete, even if evacuation continued to be a vital feature of civil defense instructions in the 1970s and 1980s. "If war comes" was still an important motto, and updated versions of *If War Comes* were published annually in the telephone directories, including everything from practical instructions to extensive maps of evacuation routes for those citizens who in the case of an emergency evacuation would be traveling in their own vehicles.[40] The durable wartime preparedness slogan was eventually replaced by another motto: "Total defense is everyone's concern." However, this was not until after the end of the Cold War.[41]

Welfare Cocooning and the Persistence of Preparedness

In his introduction to *Recasting America* in 1989, Lary May singled out the end of World War II as a crucial moment, after which Americans experienced a paradigm shift of major proportions in terms of beliefs and values.[42] In the 1990s, other historians joined in the chorus and agreed that 1945 signified a departure from a familiar world into unknown territory. As far as nuclear culture is concerned, many scholars have taken their lead from Paul Boyer, who highlights the significance of the bomb in terms of a Kantian category of Being that fundamentally reshapes our understanding of the world.[43]

Undoubtedly, such arguments could be made, but it is also interesting to turn the question around by highlighting other regions or experiences. I have argued that the case of Sweden presents a correction to the narrative of the fundamental conceptual break of 1945, in which the World War mindset gave way to Cold War Culture. In many ways, at its core the Swedish civil defense propaganda of the 1950s was World War II translated to Cold War. The presence and importance of World War II in the Swedish cultural narratives of the 1950s cannot be overemphasized, and the intimate connection between people and defense established at the beginning of World War II ("the preparedness years") is constantly reasserted. In this sense, one may very well argue that to bystanders such as the Swedes, the war continued throughout the 1950s, as they maintained a culture of readiness and a siege mentality to which historians so far have paid insufficient attention.[44]

In Sweden, everyday life in the first two decades of the Cold War did not differ much from that in World War II—a high degree of everyday militarization, popular narratives of an invisible yet tangible threat of war, and breathless anticipation of the coming apocalypse. However, there was also room for the fundamentally optimistic narrative of Swedish life or the Swedish way, and a sanguine belief in the future. A parallel can be drawn to 1950s America, and to Tom Engelhardt's observation that the U.S. at this time exhibited a simultaneous mobilization and demobilization. On the one hand, America was preparing for nuclear apocalypse, while on the other hand it was awaiting a life of endless promise and abundance.[45] This was equally true of Sweden in the first two decades of the Cold War.

The combination of modernism, social engineering, and the economic model known as the "Swedish model," whose primary goals were full employment and social equality, all helped to create a collective identity intimately and strongly connected with peace, cooperation, and neutrality. Here, history and remembering were essential, but if the art of forgetting was exercised in the political arena, in everyday culture the myth of the war experience was kept alive. Strains of sentimental militarism endured throughout the 1950s, evoking a humble and romantic nostalgia for the preparedness years. These stories were not about bombs or combat, but about the endless clipping of ration coupons, the taste of surrogate coffee, the blackout curtains, and last but not least the feeling of nostalgia that plagued popular culture in the war years and was captured in the radio hit *Somewhere in Sweden* (*Någonstans i Sverige*). In this song, a woman sings about her fiancé who is away, not at the European front and not in bloody battle, but indeed "somewhere in Sweden"—a national fireguard in the preparedness army of the peaceful and orderly, neutral *folkhem*.

In *Civil Defense Begins at Home*, Laura McEnaney makes the argument that in the U.S., domestication was not only a psychological but a political affair, since it served to legitimize the privatization of civil defense.[46] In Swedish civil-defense culture, this element of privatization did not take place, nor was there ever a debate on public versus private responsibilities regarding national security. People were allowed, but not requested, to construct their own shelters. The credo was always: every citizen's individual responsibilities and the state's responsibilities, seldom the family or any other social affiliation. Keeping the family intact was an instrument rather than a goal in securing the Swedish way.

In conclusion, the home is constantly reasserted in Swedish civil-defense culture, though not primarily the individual home, but the collective people's home. The domesticism of civil defense in Sweden did not result, as in the U.S., in an enforcement of the nuclear family as the key unit in society, but rather in a grand vision of survival in the welfare cocoon. Within the walls of the people's homes, myths of sheltering, paternal care, and egalitarian solidarity flourished, while *Folk och försvar* merged the people with the nation's defense under the fatherly wings of the king and the Social Democratic Prime Minister. In the face of nuclear disaster, the precautions taken by the Social Democratic government would ensure the subterranean survival of the Swedish *folkhem*, a home in which all Swedes would be cared for as members of a family and where values such as equality, cooperation, order, and security would prevail. Thus the narrative of the *folkhem* community and the Cold War narrative of successful civil defense in a nuclear world strongly amplified one another, and maintained the comprehensive militarization of everyday life that had characterized Sweden in the preparedness years—a cocoon of extreme readiness, and an overindulging in narratives of homesickness in endless anticipation of war.

Notes

1. Tage Erlander, *Tage Erlander: 1940–1949* (Stockholm: Tiden, 1973), 23, my translation.
2. See for example I.I. Österström, "Det nya civilförsvaret," *Statstjänstemannen* (1961): 12; *Vi går under jorden: en film om våra skyddsrum*, Civilförsvarsstyrelsen (1959).
3. Lawrence J. Vale, *The Limits of Civil Defence in the USA, Switzerland, Britain, and the Soviet Union* (Hampshire, 1987), 9.
4. Paul Boyer, *By the Bomb's Early Light* (New York, 1994), xviii.
5. ibid., xix, 3–26.
6. Guy Oakes, *The Imaginary War* (Oxford, 1994); Margot A. Henriksen, *Dr. Strangelove's America* (Berkeley, 1997); Laura McEnaney, *Civil Defense Begins at Home* (Princeton, 2000); Kenneth D. Rose, *One Nation Underground* (New York, 2001); Andrew D. Grossman, *Neither Dead nor Red* (New York, 2001); Alice L. George, *Awaiting Armageddon* (Chapel Hill, 2003); Dee Garrison, *Bracing for Armageddon* (New York, 2006).
7. Elaine Tyler May, *Homeward Bound* (New York, 1999), 80–99.
8. Henriksen, *Dr. Strangelove's America*, 107.
9. Oakes, *The Imaginary War*, 46–71. Quote on p. 46.
10. McEnaney, *Civil Defense Begins at Home*, 5.
11. May, *Homeward Bound*, ix–xi, 94.
12. See for example Bernd Lemke, *Luftschutz in Großbritannien und Deutschland 1923 bis 1939* (Munich, 2005); Clemens Heitmann, *Schützen und helfen?* (Berlin, 2006); Dietmar Süss, ed., *Deutschland im Luftkrieg* (Munich, 2007).
13. Magnus Hjort, "Nationens livsfråga" (Stockholm, 2004).
14. Vale, however, makes this comment only about Switzerland. Vale, *The Limits of Civil Defence*, 94–122.

15. Karl-Gunnar Bäck, *50 års frivillighet* (Stockholm, 1987), 9.
16. Bäck, *50 års frivillighet;* Wilhelm Agrell, *Ett samhällsskydd för alla väder?* (Stockholm, 1988).
17. Ole Jödal, "Det befästa folkhemmet," in *Frihet* 24 (1940), no. 3: 2.
18. Rune Eriksson, *Folk och försvar 50 år: 1940–1990* (Stockholm, 1990).
19. Øystein Sørensen and Bo Stråth, "Introduction: The Cultural Construction of Norden," in *The Cultural Construction of Norden*, ed. Øystein Sørensen and Bo Stråth (Oslo, 1997), 1–24; Bo Stråth, "The Swedish Image of Europe as the Other," in *Europe and the Other and Europe as the Other*, ed. Bo Stråth (Brussels, 2000), 359–383, 365.
20. However, compared to the German *Volk*, the Swedish *folk* connoted much more pragmatism than holism. Sørensen and Stråth, "Introduction." A comparison between the German *Volksgemeinschaft* and the Swedish *folkhem* is made in Norbert Götz, *Ungleiche Geschwister* (Baden-Baden, 2001).
21. Lars Trägårdh, "Statist Individualism: On the Culturality of the Nordic Welfare State," in Sørensen and Stråth, *The Cultural Construction of Norden*, 253–285, quote on p. 253.
22. Following an intense public debate on the question of Swedish neutrality, the Neutrality Commission's report *Had there been a war...* (Stockholm, 1994) showed that the Swedish preparations for accepting military aid from the western NATO countries were extensive during the first two decades of the Cold War.
23. Alf W. Johansson, "Neutrality and Modernity," in *War Experience, Self Image and National Identity*, ed. Stig Ekman and Nils Edling (Stockholm, 1997), 163–85, 170; Bo Stråth, "Neutrality as Self-Awareness," in *The Swedish Success Story?*, ed. Kurt Almqvist and Kay Glans (Stockholm, 2004), 147–60.
24. Johansson, "Neutrality and Modernity," 178; Stråth, "The Swedish Image of Europe as the Other," 369. The term *Berührungsangst*, when referring to Sweden's uneasy relation to Europe, was first used by Swedish historian Klaus Misgeld.
25. Alf W. Johansson, "Inledning: Svensk nationalism och identitet efter andra världskriget," in *Vad är Sverige?*, ed. Alf W. Johansson (Stockholm, 2001), 7–17, 11, my translation.
26. Marie Cronqvist, "Det befästa folkhemmet: Kallt krig och varm välfärd i svensk civilförsvarskultur," in *Fred i realpolitikens skugga*, ed. Magnus Jerneck (Lund: Studentlitteratur, 2009).
27. Cronqvist, "Det befästa folkhemmet."
28. Marie Cronqvist, *Mannen i mitten* (Stockholm, 2004), 66–69.
29. *Den svenska livsformen*, letter 4: "Social Security with Individual Responsibility" (Stockholm, 1941–42), 1.
30. Cronqvist, *Mannen i mitten*, 88–136; Hjort, "Nationens livsfråga," 175–224.
31. *Om kriget kommer: Vägledning för Sveriges medborgare* (Stockholm, 1952).
32. May, *Homeward Bound*; Oakes, *The Imaginary War*; McEnaney, *Civil Defense Begins at Home*.
33. Mary Douglas, *Purity and Danger* (London, 1966), 36.
34. *Om kriget kommer* (1952), 11–13; *Om kriget kommer: Vägledning för Sveriges medborgare* (Stockholm, 1961), 31–42.
35. Vale, *The Limits of Civil Defence*, 124.
36. *Om kriget kommer* (1961).
37. Marie Cronqvist, "Utrymning i folkhemmet," *Historisk tidskrift* 3 (2008): 451–476.
38. *Om kriget kommer* (1961), 19.
39. Agrell, *Ett samhällsskydd för alla väder?*, 12–17.

40. Cronqvist, "Det befästa folkhemmet."
41. Eino Tubin, *Förfäras ej* (Stockholm, 2003), 218.
42. Lary May, "Introduction," in *Recasting America*, ed. Lary May (Chicago, 1989), 1–16.
43. Boyer, *By the Bomb's Early Light*, xx.
44. Cronqvist, *Mannen i mitten*, 82–87, 316.
45. Tom Engelhardt, *The End of Victory Culture* (Amherst, 1998), 74–81.
46. McEnaney, *Civil Defense Begins at Home*, 74.

Bibliography

Agrell, Wilhelm. *Ett samhällsskydd för alla väder? Om det civila försvarets problem*. Stockholm: Sveriges civilförsvarsförbund, 1988.

Bäck, Karl-Gunnar. *50 års frivillighet: En bildkavalkad genom SCF:s historia*. Stockholm: Sveriges civilförsvarsförbund, 1987.

Boyer, Paul. *By the Bomb's Early Light: American Thought and Culture at the Dawn of the Atomic Age*. New York: Pantheon Books, 1994.

Cronqvist, Marie. *Mannen i mitten: Ett spiondrama i svensk kallakrigskultur*. Stockholm: Carlssons bokförlag, 2004.

———. "Utrymning i folkhemmet: Kalla kriget, välfärdsidyllen och den svenska civilförsvarskulturen 1961." *Historisk tidskrift* 3 (2008), 451-476.

———. "Det befästa folkhemmet: Kallt krig och varm välfärd i svensk civilförsvarskultur." In *Fred i realpolitikens skugga*, ed. Magnus Jerneck (Lund: Studentlitteratur, 2009).

Douglas, Mary. *Purity and Danger: An Analysis of the Concepts of Pollution and Taboo*. London: Routledge, 1966.

Engelhardt, Tom. *The End of Victory Culture: Cold War America and the Disillusioning of a Generation*. Amherst: University of Massachusetts Press, 1998.

Eriksson, Rune. *Folk och försvar 50 år: 1940–1990*. Stockholm: Centralförbundet Folk och försvar, 1990.

Erlander, Tage. *Tage Erlander: 1940–1949*. Stockholm: Tiden, 1973.

Garrison, Dee. *Bracing for Armageddon: Why Civil Defense Never Worked*. New York: Oxford University Press, 2006.

George, Alice L. *Awaiting Armageddon: How Americans Faced the Cuban Missile Crisis*. Chapel Hill: University of North Carolina Press, 2003.

Götz, Norbert. *Ungleiche Geschwister: Die Konstruktion von nationalsozialistischer Volksgemeinschaft und schwedischem Volksheim*. (Baden-Baden: Nomos, 2001).

Grossman, Andrew D. *Neither Dead nor Red: Civilian Defense and American Political Development During the Early Cold War*. New York: Routledge, 2001.

Heitmann, Clemens. *Schützen und helfen? Luftschutz und Zivilverteidigung in der DDR 1955 bis 1989/90*. Berlin: Christoph Links Verlag, 2006.

Henriksen, Margot A. *Dr. Strangelove's America: Society and Culture in the Atomic Age*. Berkeley and Los Angeles: University of California Press, 1997.

Hjort, Magnus. *"Nationens livsfråga": Propaganda och upplysning i försvarets tjänst 1944–1963*. Stockholm: Santérus förlag, 2004.

Jödal, Ole. "Det befästa folkhemmet." *Frihet* 24 (1940), no. 3: 2.

Johansson, Alf W. "Neutrality and Modernity: The Second World War and Sweden's National Identity." In *War Experience, Self Image and National Identity: The Second World War as Myth and History*, ed. Stig Ekman and Nils Edling (Stockholm: Gidlunds förlag, 1997), 163–185.

———. "Inledning: Svensk nationalism och identitet efter andra världskriget." In *Vad är Sverige? Röster om svensk nationell identitet*, ed. Alf W. Johansson (Stockholm: Prisma, 2001), 7–17.

Lemke, Bernd. *Luftschutz in Großbritannien und Deutschland 1923 bis 1939: Zivile Kriegsvorbereitungen als Ausdruck der staats- und gesellschaftlichen Grundlagen von Demokratie und Diktatur*. Munich: Oldenburg Wissenschaftsverlag, 2005.

McEnaney, Laura. *Civil Defense Begins at Home: Militarization Meets Everyday Life in the Fifties*. Princeton: Princeton University Press, 2000.

May, Elaine Tyler. *Homeward Bound: American Families in the Cold War Era*. New York: Basic Books, 1999.

May, Lary, ed. *Recasting America: Culture and Politics in the Age of the Cold War*. Chicago: University of Chicago Press, 1989.

Oakes, Guy. *The Imaginary War: Civil Defense and American Cold War Culture*. Oxford: Oxford University Press, 1994.

Österström, I.I. "Det nya civilförsvaret." *Statstjänstemannen* 12 (1961).

Rose, Kenneth D. *One Nation Underground: The Fallout Shelter in American Culture*. New York: New York University Press, 2001.

Sørensen, Øystein, and Bo Stråth, eds. *The Cultural Construction of Norden*. Oslo: Scandinavian University Press, 1997.

Stråth, Bo. "The Swedish Image of Europe as the Other." In *Europe and the Other and Europe as the Other*, ed. Bo Stråth (Brussels: PIE Lang, 2000), 359–383.

———. "Neutrality as Self-Awareness." In *The Swedish Success Story?*, ed. Kurt Almqvist and Kay Glans (Stockholm: Axel and Margaret Ax:son Johnson Foundation, 2004), 147–160.

Süss, Dietmar, ed. *Deutschland im Luftkrieg: Geschichte und Erinnerung*. Munich: Oldenburg Wissenschaftsverlag, 2007.

Trägårdh, Lars, "Statist Individualism: On the Culturality of the Nordic Welfare State," in *The Cultural Construction of Norden*, ed. Øystein Sørensen and Bo Stråth (Oslo: Scandinavian University Press, 1997).

Tubin, Eino. *Förfäras ej: 50 år med det psykologiska försvaret—en biografi över en svensk myndighet*. Stockholm: Styrelsen för psykologiskt försvar, 2003.

Vale, Lawrence J. *The Limits of Civil Defence in the USA, Switzerland, Britain, and the Soviet Union: The Evolution of Policies Since 1945*. Hampshire: Macmillan, 1987.

Further documents

Den svenska livsformen, letter 4: "Social security with individual responsibility." Stockholm: Statens informationsstyrelse, Folkberedskapen, 1941–42.

Neutrality Commission. *Had there Been a War… Preparations for the Reception of Military Assistance 1949–1969*. Stockholm: Fritze, 1994.

Om kriget kommer: Vägledning för rikets medborgare i händelse av krig. Stockholm: Statens informationsstyrelse, 1943.

Om kriget kommer: Vägledning för Sveriges medborgare. Stockholm: Kungl. Civilförsvarsstyrelsen, 1952.

Om kriget kommer: Vägledning för Sveriges medborgare. Stockholm: Kungl. Civilförsvarsstyrelsen, 1961.

Vi går under jorden: En film om våra skyddsrum, Kungl. Civilförsvarsstyrelsen/Suecia Film (1959).

Part III

CROSSING THE BORDER
Interactions with the "Other"

Chapter 10

THE PEACE AND THE WAR CAMPS
The Dichotomous Cold War Culture in Czechoslovakia: 1948–1960

Roman Krakovsky

During the Cold War, both the East and the West developed representations of themselves as well as "the Other." For each, the initial image of itself was, arguably, created in isolation, without reference to the Other. For instance, the East defined itself in terms of the fight for peace, and the West in terms of the fight for democracy. These images were then expanded upon, attaining new meanings from the wider context of the East-West relationship. Thus, the representation of Self was always completed by the representation of the Other. For the East, the West came to represent an imperialist war camp. For the West, the East became the anti-democratic, even totalitarian camp.

My purpose is to analyze Socialist representations of Self and Other, particularly their dynamics in Czechoslovakia during the founding period of the 1950s. A number of collective social events could provide a reasonable basis for analyzing East-West representations: such examples include Liberation Day[1] or mass sporting contests such as the "Peace Race" for cyclists.[2] However, the best occasion to analyze is probably the May Day celebration. Every year, the East-West relationship was made explicit through contrasts on May Day—the most important celebration in the

Socialist camp. The main goal of the day was to strengthen camaraderie within the Socialist community.[3] Above all, however, May Day was a proud display of the power of proletarian internationalism. Consequently, representing both the "Socialist" and the "imperialist" camps was one of the key aims of the ritual.[4]

An examination of May Day celebrations also provides the opportunity to examine sources that have thus far not been sufficiently exploited by historians of Communist regimes. Important aspects of such an examination are iconography and dramatic performances. I will use materials collected in the Czech Historical Archives and in the archives of the Czech Press Agency (ČTK), the successor to the Czechoslovak Press Agency. In order to interpret these visual performances in the broader context of the time, I will rely on the principal daily newspaper of the Czechoslovak Communist Party, *Rudé právo* (Red Law), and the newspaper of the Czechoslovak Youth Union, *Mladá fronta* (Young Front).

After investigating the origins of the peace movement and its protagonists, I will analyze how the "peace" and the "war" camps were represented, and how the representation of the Other (in this case, the West) also revealed the self-images and intentions, both idealized and actual, of those groups that constructed the representation—particularly the Communist regime in Czechoslovakia (see Illustration 10.1).

The Genesis of the Dual Representation of the World

In order to reveal the origins of the peace and the war camps' representations, it is necessary to return to two speeches made at the beginning of 1946, which inaugurated a new phase of international politics. After a period of collaboration in the anti-Fascist coalition (1942–1946), divisive issues came to dominate the Soviet-American relationship.[5] It became apparent that the superpowers' policies were no longer connected by the common interests that had held the wartime alliance together. On 9 February 1946, Stalin made his "two camps speech" before the assembly of electors of Moscow. For the first time since the entry of the USSR into World War II, he reaffirmed the Leninist conception of international relations. He declared that crises and conflicts between nations were unavoidable during the stage of "monopolistic capitalism," and that the two world wars were proof of the contradictions of capitalism. He stated that communism and capitalism belonged to two different camps, fundamentally incompatible and irreconcilable, and defended the idea that peace was impossible until capitalism could be vanquished and replaced by communism.[6] This speech provided the first element necessary for the

Illustration 10.1. The poster for the 6th Peace Race (Poland, Czechoslovakia, RDG, 1953).
(Personal archives of the author.)

creation of the peace camp image: peace is incompatible with capitalism, which implies that it is compatible only with communism. Accordingly, it would be vain to entertain the hope of real international cooperation. One month later, in March 1946, Winston Churchill recognized this reality in his Iron Curtain speech, given at Westminster College in Fulton.[7] The division between the two camps had been firmly established.

The division between the peace camp and the war camp (to follow the Socialist labels), while seemingly a radically new concept, did not come to Communist leaders out of the blue. Its evolution between 1946 and 1949 depended upon two separate but synergistic elements: the creation of a peace discourse, and the techniques used to establish organizations.

In 1946, Soviet leaders made a number of speeches emphasizing the new peace issue. In March 1946, during the Iran crisis, Stalin explained the causes of the prevailing fear of war by attributing the responsibility to "the actions of certain political groups engaged in the propaganda of a new war."[8] In his interview in *Pravda* in October 1948, Stalin called upon "the social forces in favor of peace" to unseat the leaders of Great Britain and the U.S.A., who were pursuing "a policy of unleashing a new war."[9] Stalin's view was reinforced by Molotov in his speech on the anniversary of the October Revolution a week later, and this perspective became the basis for the Communist peace movement.

At the same time, the Soviet Union developed the foundation for an international anti-war coalition. On 5 October 1947, in reaction to Truman's doctrine of containment (12 March 1947) and the Marshall Plan (rejected by Eastern European states in July 1947),[10] Cominform, an organization of East European countries, was founded.[11] Its principal task was to consolidate Soviet control over East European countries and to coordinate their own foreign policy within the allied sphere. In his address to the founding meeting of Cominform, Zhdanov outlined the doctrinal competition between communism and capitalism. According to his appraisal, the world was divided into two opposing blocs. "The cardinal purpose of the imperialist camp is to strengthen imperialism, to hatch a new imperialist war, to combat Socialism and democracy." Conversely, the purpose of the anti-imperialist camp was to "resist the threat of new wars and imperialist expansion, to strengthen democracy and to extirpate the vestiges of Fascism."[12] Cominform's official newspaper, *For a Lasting Peace, For a People's Democracy*, stressed the same peace issue. The integration of public opinion and the mobilization of local authorities came with the Peace Congresses, at which keen interest was shown for Western scientists troubled by the consequences of their work in the development of nuclear weapons, writers and artists disturbed by the excess of congressional investigations of Communists in the U.S.A., and (particularly in

France) anyone who saw the growing American influence in Europe as a threat to European culture.[13]

Following the signing of the North Atlantic Treaty on 4 April 1949, the peace movement entered a new phase. The universalist character of the movement was definitively abandoned and the fight for peace was allocated to the working class and to the countries composing the peace camp. This new situation was reflected two weeks later in the World Peace Congress, which took place on 20 April 1949. Two sessions were held simultaneously in two different European cities. The first was opened in Paris.[14] The second session was held in Prague, and brought together those delegates to whom the French authorities had refused visas: those from the countries of the new Eastern bloc.[15]

One fundamental difference separated the outcomes of the two sessions. In Paris, the struggle for peace remained the key issue of international interest. The delegates adopted a manifesto that made peace a global issue: "The defense of peace is the concern of all nations."[16] In Prague, on the other hand, the articulation of the peace struggle was re-

Illustration 10.2. Poster of World Congress of Defenders of Peace (France, 1949).
(Personal archives of the author.)

Illustration 10.3. First Polish Peace Congress (Poland, 1950).
(Personal archives of the author.)

Illustration 10.4. Members of the Youth Union carrying the banner "Peace is for the People—War for Capitalists!" (May Day, Prague, 1949).
(Czech National Archives, fond Centralni katalog FFKD [86965/77].)

stricted to a well-defined group of countries: "For peace and against the imperialist instigators of the new war."[17]

From 1949 onwards, the peace movement charted a political rather than a territorial frontier, dividing the world into two opposing camps. The peace movement gave the population in the Eastern bloc a comprehensible and meaningful explanation of the political globe. The political space of a "Socialist man" was built around this objective, which increasingly became a symbolic system, a sort of curtain through which one looked without even noticing it.

The organization of the world around a binary concept of East and West, Communist and capitalist, was thus based on the opposition between friend and foe. According to Carl Schmitt, this distinction is not only political, but also cultural, because it divides the world not into rival states but into rival societies.[18] Affiliation with the Eastern bloc was founded on common values, on a sense of membership in the Socialist society defending peace.[19] May Day celebrations exemplified this cultural identification, and during the 1950s one part of the May Day parade was specifically devoted to allegories of the Socialist camp in contrast to the imperialist camp (see Illustration 10.5).

The media stressed the spontaneous and authentic character of these allegories, which was supposed to reflect the profound feelings of the population. The 1957 capitalist allegory depicted a limousine surrounded and protected by American police officers in uniform. The limousine was driven by "resuscitated German imperialism," with the face of General Speidel, then commander-in-chief of the NATO forces in Europe.[20] When his limousine approached the official parade gallery, he raised his

Illustration 10.5. Allegory of peace camp (May Day, Prague, 1949).
(Czech National Archives, fond Centralni katalog FFKD [859228/57].)

hand in a Nazi salute. At that moment, according to the media, "the pioneers joined the play and forced him to accept a dove. Speidel rejected it, but he was suddenly surrounded by a gaggle of doves."[21] Of course, the scene was staged, and each pioneer who "spontaneously" joined the play executed a carefully rehearsed part. However, the important thing here is not (real or staged) spontaneity, but rather the intention of the parade's organizers to represent an allegory—a performance that seemed to originate naturally from the people, from popular imagery.[22]

The principal creators and performers of the allegories were students, especially those from the Academy of Arts, Architecture, and Design of Prague (UMPRUM, Vysoká škola uměleckoprůmyslová). This role is to be attributed chiefly to their talent in the art of modeling and sculpture. However, the representations also had input from more senior persons associated with the Academy. During the 1950s, a senior official of the Communist Party occupied an important place in the management of the Academy and supervised the design of the May Day allegories.[23] Although the political symbolism of their allegories was carefully scrutinized by the Communist Party, their designers also had extensive personal experience with representing social "reality" for a general audience. Therefore, these allegories ultimately reflected the perspectives of those who conceptu-

Illustration 10.6. The Hydra of the Reaction (May Day, Prague, 1951).
(Czech National Archives, fond Centralni katalog FFKD [47223/52].)

alized and designed them as much as they did any underlying political conditions.

The symbolic attributes of the Other were rarely the original creations of the Communist regime: traditional codes and embodiments were "recycled," although fresh associations were frequently linked with these older symbols. In 1950, the hydra of capitalism was represented as a hybrid being, half man, half animal. It had the face of Uncle Sam (the image made popular by Thomas Nast during World War I), and the symbol of the dollar and the American and British flags (on the hat) evoked associations with Wall Street bankers. Joining this composite figure of superpowers recently designated as "imperialist," a hook-nosed figure with a beard recalls the image of a Jewish financier. Paradoxically, this anti-Semitic symbol was juxtaposed with a swastika that topped the crest of the hydra, suggesting that the potential new world war was being enabled by Jewish capital. The inscription on the hydra's body, "Capitalism: the biggest danger for the world" ended with the exhortation "People, stay vigilant!"[24] This expression was the emblematic call of Julius Fučík, the hero of the Czech anti-Fascist resistance, who was executed by the Nazis. Thus, for the Czechoslovak audience of 1950, well-known symbols of America, anti-Semitism, and its own anti-Fascist resistance movement were reconfigured to depict a new political reality, facilitating its integration into Czechoslovak culture. Thus, the Other was normalized and neutralized: "difference" was brought under control by defining it in already-familiar terms and icons.[25]

Working the Dualist Representation of East and West

The East-West representation systematically followed a number of fundamental operating principles. The first was the creation of a clear dichotomy. A representation of oneself was always preceded by a representation of the Other. Consequently, the Eastern spectator was first confronted with the representation of the Western war camp and only then was shown that of the Eastern peace camp. The distinction between, and defi-

Illustration 10.7. Allegory of war camp (May Day, Ostrava, 1951). On the banner: "United with the Communist Party, the Trade Union and the Youth Union, we will vanquish it" and "Producing more coal will demolish the plans of the reaction."
(*Source:* ČTK [FO01226557].)

Illustration 10. 8. Allegory of peace camp (May Day, Ostrava, 1951). On the banner: "Socialism = Peace / War = Ruins, Misery, Death / Peace = Life and Happiness of our children."
(*Source:* ČTK [FO01226558].)

nition of, the Self versus the Other thus becomes clear by comparing the two, and the invention of the Other arises from this comparison.

On May Day 1951, two allegorical parade floats followed one another through Ostrava, the capital city of the mining region of northern Moravia. The first float, named the "Hydra of Reaction," represented a seven-headed monster with the faces of the leaders of "imperialist states": Truman, De Gaulle, British Prime Minister Attlee, German chancellor Adenauer, and Churchill. A mineworker—emblematic figure of the region and new hero of the regime—was shooting it down.[26] The inscription on the float described the scene: "United with the Communist Party, the trade union and the youth union, we will vanquish it," and "Producing more coal will demolish the plans of the reaction." The float representing the "Hydra of Reaction" was followed immediately by the "Float of Socialism." The portraits of the heads of state or Communist party leaders of the Eastern bloc (Dimitrov, Zápotocký, Stalin, and Gottwald) were joined together under the image of the same dove symbol that had been introduced by Picasso at the Paris Peace Conference in 1949. This peace symbolism was underlined by the inscriptions beneath the portraits: "Socialism=Peace," "War=Ruins, Misery, Death," and "Peace=Life and the Happiness of our

Children."[27] The contrasting depictions of the Other reveal that the difference between the Eastern Self and the Western Other was not only profound, but that it arose out of a single fundamental and even challenging issue: peace.

By clearly placing the peace camp in the moral center and by talking about it in terms of contrast with the war camp, the construction of the Other was just another way to talk about and invite a much more complex definition of oneself. In this process, respect for reality was not necessarily an issue: neither Adenauer, De Gaulle, or Churchill truly threatened peace any longer. After his electoral defeat in 1945, Churchill no longer played a role in British policy. He came back only in October 1951. De Gaulle resigned his presidency in the provisional government in January 1946. Until 1959, he stood in opposition to the official establishment.[28] These men, however, represented Great Britain and France, respectively, in the allegory of the imperialist camp on May Day 1951. Consequently, the allegory of the Other did not reflect contemporary reality, but exposed its creators' perceptions of the postwar climate. The allegorical floats, in terms that were not only iconically familiar to Czechoslovaks but remained frozen during the immediate postwar period, translated the strategy of the Other. The alternative—to show that the political system in the West was developing, to show that people and governments could change—did not correspond to the Soviet geopolitical discourse that was elaborated immediately during the postwar period. The Other was to be displayed as a perpetually unalterable entity.

In order to make the Other a more authentic, immediate threat, it was necessary to establish a concrete and potentially physical relation with it.[29] This relationship was necessarily negative, and it was built on feelings of revulsion and disdain (and their corollaries—laughter and mockery). The allegories often represented fantastic and intentionally horrible monsters (dragons, hydras, mythical animals) or the subjects that elicited the greatest fear during the Cold War: the atomic bomb, the revival of Fascism, or the extreme outcome of such enmity—a new world war. However, these creatures and concepts were not primarily intended to frighten the Czechoslovak audience: reports describing May Day's allegorical floats often mention them as eliciting laughter and mockery. In 1950, the allegory of the Hydra of Capitalism, some thirty meters long, provoked not terror but mockery in the spectators. The youth newspaper *Mladá fronta* described the audience's reaction: "We laugh at you, as the workers carrying the banners with the sign of the dollar and the message: brigades and tractors will destroy these monsters!"[30] The same year, in Ostrava, the float of the war camp elicited "widespread mockery."[31] In 1951, "the culture of kitsch from Hollywood" was a target of fun.[32]

However, in the midst of the Cold War during the 1950s, laughing at the potential danger of a looming war was not enough. The police, the army, and the People's Militia (the Communist Party's paramilitary force), immediately followed the allegorical representations during the May Day parades, announcing that it was necessary to "be vigilant."[33] Laughter was permitted because it was the only way to fight against the repressed content of the collective imagination of the regime and its own fears,[34] but it was imperative that people be prepared to face those fears and fight to "defend peace"—with arms, if necessary.

Laughter and its antithesis, fear, are intimately connected. To tame the Other and to dominate it by laughter and mockery allows admitting the existence of one's own fears. The disturbing strangeness of the Other was, above all, a shock to Czechoslovaks, who like any audience felt astonishment when confronted with the unusual, the weird, and the horrible. A startling revelation occurs when the borders between imagination and reality disappear, when the symbolic is no longer just a symbol, when the fantastic is no longer just fantasy, because the symbolic and fantastic have suddenly become real.[35] This impression was particularly easy to promulgate in the Eastern bloc, given the fact that the true nature of the Other was barely known by the population during these years. The transmission of images, information, and people was still very limited, leaving the collective imagination of the Czechoslovak population free to visualize Westerners as monsters. Despite this false perception, the anxiety created by such an antagonistic relationship was, at times, a positive phenomenon. The shock of an encounter with the Other helped to identify those who might violate the very fragile and uncertain limits of the regime's own identity. This shock can provoke disorder that can endure and evolve into a collective psychosis. Or it can progress as part of any traditional relationship.

The allegory of the Other was a sort of interaction between the representations of both East and West, which tangibly instrumentalized the boundary between them. This tension remained intact throughout the Cold War, and paradoxically was enriching for both sides. The conflict affected the way in which both sides developed, since the need to have an enemy is at the heart of political psychology.[36] Imperialism could not be disconnected from communism. The one without the other simply could not exist, particularly in the sense we are discussing here: that the perception of the Other is created by, perpetuated by, and ultimately defines the Self to a significant degree. In the political sphere, the distinction between friend and foe is at the heart of the sovereign entity's political existence, allowing the formation, maintenance, and updating of power. Having an enemy thus ensures the stability of the group identity.[37]

Evolving Representations of the Other (1948–1960)

During the 1950s, belligerence remained the key characteristic attributed to the Other. In the first half of the 1950s, during the period of Eastern reconstruction, this theme was exemplified by the dichotomy between the West's "plans" to wage war and the East's establishment of socialism. On May Day in 1950, one allegorical float of imperialism displayed a Wall Street skyscraper covered in inscriptions from top to bottom: "Coca Cola" and "Texas Bar" indicated Western consumption. "Terror," "third war today," and "atomic puma" were suggestive of the war supposedly being plotted by the West. The financial exploitation of mankind was represented by sacks of American currency and the inscriptions "Wall Street" and "We want the benefits." The banker mounted at the top of the skyscraper held the reins of soldiers of different capitalist countries,

Illustration 10.9. Allegory of war camp (May Day, Prague, 1950), with Wall Street skyscraper covered with inscriptions: "Coca-Cola, Texas Bar, Third War-to-day, Atomic Puma, War, Wall Street, We want benefits, Tito, Dollarium Trumans, Mormon Mess, Terror." The capitalist banker is sitting on the building and holding a carrot, driving the soldiers of Western armies. The Wall Street Capital, protected by members of the KKK, is followed by the monster of war. In the background, the beginning of the Allegory of the peace camp, with the banner: "Peace is stronger than war. With USSR, we are 900 million!"
(*Source:* National Czech Archives, fond Centralni katalog FFKD [84572/56].)

who pulled the whole building in a comic effort to obtain the bait dangling from a fishing rod, also held by the banker. A representation of the Ku Klux Klan, marching along, kept a protective and vigilant eye on the proceedings. The foolishness of capitalism's proclivity to ensure continued growth by financing new wars was summarized by the inscription on top of the banker's head: "Dollarium Trumans," a word play relating "delirium tremens" to the name of the U.S. president.

In contrast to this Other, the peace camp was represented by symbols of the peaceful reconstruction of the country and additional achievements: new factories and housing for workers, cooperative farmers on tractors, and the potential economic success of Socialist competition were depicted for all to see.[38]

By the mid 1950s, this peace-vs.-war theme was completed by the addition of a new factor: the atomic bomb. A sense of ultimate opposition and contrast between the East and the West arose from the simultaneous development of nuclear weapons by the Soviet Union and the U.S.A. The American nuclear monopoly had already been broken in 1949, when the first Soviet nuclear bomb was successfully tested.[39] The most drastic Eastern improvements came in the middle of the 1950s. The USSR developed a "boosted fission" bomb in August 1953 and tested a "true" multistage hydrogen bomb in November 1955.[40]

When the Other found the means for absolute protection via a weapon with absolute power, the dualism between East and West also became absolute.[41] Those who aim these weapons at others, however, are first obliged to "annihilate" their victims figuratively. They must find a way to perceive the Other as entirely criminal and inhuman, as totally worthless. Otherwise, they are themselves criminal and inhuman. Thus, the first allegorical "burial" of the Western atomic bomb appeared in 1950, in reaction to the first Soviet nuclear bomb test that occurred in August 1949.[42] The deepest criminalization and devaluation of the war camp ensued in representations of its funeral, which appeared more and more frequently during the second half of the 1950s. Unsurprisingly, the atomic bomb was generally present in these scenes.

The launching of the first Soviet Sputnik satellite (August 1957) showed the world that the USSR had accurate and deadly missiles that could hit targets located anywhere on the planet. Consequently, that year, the allegorical float of the Other represented the funeral of NATO.[43] The funeral opened with the "Ghost of Hitler," followed by monstrous-looking creatures called *atomčíci*—men with atomic bombs for heads. On the tops of their heads they carried fighter planes, and on their foreheads was the symbol of NATO. The military's use of atomic technology (the rocket was labeled "Made in NATO") predicted the future death of the

Illustration 10.10. The first allegorical "burial" of the Western atomic bomb (May Day, Prague, 1950). On the coffin: "Atomic Puma—Rest in Peace."
(*Source*: National Czech Archives, fond Centralni katalog FFKD [2/6297].)

Atlantic pact. The scene was followed by the coffin of NATO, which was surrounded by the "specters of war": members of the Ku Klux Klan as completely dehumanized figures identified only by their symbol of the cross.[44]

From 1957 onwards, rockets and satellites would also systematically appear in the floats representing the peace camp. Strange as it may seem, they would constantly be presented as symbolic of the possible peaceful uses of atomic power, such as the exploration of space. Indeed, the Socialist countries, always peaceable and good, were shown using atomic technology only for peaceful and never for evil purposes.[45] The message was altogether clear: for the war camp, the discovery of the atom was synonymous with the atomic bomb. For the peace camp, conversely, the atom was equated with forms of atomic power that could be employed for the well-being of the population.

In 1960, the allegories of the peace camp and the war camp disappeared from the May Day parades. However, the thematic notion of the defense of peace in the world persisted on streamers and banners. It simply changed its target: the peace camp/war camp dichotomy was replaced by calls for international solidarity between the Eastern working

Illustration 10.11. The burial of the war camp (May Day, Prague, 1957). The procession opens with the "Ghost of Hitler" followed by men with atomic bombs for heads and the coffin of NATO.
(*Source:* ČTK FO01087359.)

Illustration 10.12. The burial of the war camp (May Day, Prague, 1957).
(*Source:* ČTK FO01087357.)

class and the oppressed peoples of Vietnam, Chile, and in colonies. Were the signs of decreasing anti-Western propaganda an indicator that the peace movement was beginning to decline? If the East were to eliminate the Other, what would remain of its self-conceptualization? The elimination of the Other was, possibly, an aspiration that could never be wholly achieved, for if the Other were destroyed, the Self, in turn, would likely be destroyed as well. Otherwise, an alternate self-definition should arise from the construction of another, new perspective on the Other. Does the disappearance of the allegorical representations of the war camp from May Day parades indicate that, beginning in 1960, the peace camp no longer defined itself in relation to its traditional enemy?

There might be several explanations for this change. The first is geopolitical, and was exemplified by the profoundly altered perspective from which the Soviet military viewed the Other in its policies towards the end of the 1950s. In November 1958, the U.S.A. and the USSR began an informal moratorium on nuclear testing that lasted three years (1958–1960). In September 1959, Khrushchev made his first visit to the United States, and in 1961 he met President Kennedy in Vienna. The twenty-second Congress (1961) modified the military doctrine on the basis of growing soberness about the effects of modern weapons. The new position was: war can be eliminated even before the final liquidation of capitalism. Soon after the Cuban Missile Crisis (October 1962), talks about a test ban treaty and nuclear arms control ensued. In 1963, Khrushchev described the new situation with the term "peaceful coexistence," suggesting that the frontier between "us" and "them" would remain intact, yet did not entail inevitable hostilities. However, the meanings of "us" and "them" were profoundly transformed, becoming more indicative of an economic and political competition between the Soviet Union and the United States rather than a thermonuclear competition leading to war.

The second reason for the transformation of the East/West dichotomy is related to the development of societies in East European countries. The fading of the antagonistic us-vs.-them representation testifies to the weakening of the dualistic thought pattern typical of the 1950s. In the majority of East European countries, society became more liberal. The peace camp opened up to the Other. In Czechoslovakia and East Germany, economists negotiated fiscal reforms. The victims of the show trials of the 1950s (like Gustáv Husák or Laco Novomeský) were gradually rehabilitated. Culture was discussed more widely in the media, and television and cinema contributed to making the image of the West more familiar as well as more nuanced. The radical dual structure of thinking about the West no longer fit the niche it had previously inhabited in society at the beginning of the 1960s.[46]

The final reason is ideological, and relates even more closely to Czechoslovak society. After the Soviet Union, Czechoslovakia was the first country in the Eastern bloc to achieve socialism (in 1960), at which time a new Socialist constitution was also approved. At this new stage, the Other no longer existed within the country. The realization of the ultimate goal of socialism confirmed that the enemy had been eliminated from society. There was no place for it any more at the May Day parade. The peace camp no longer defined *itself* in contrast to the war camp. The process was reversed, as the war camp was increasingly defined by the engagement of the peace camp abroad. The Other was portrayed, in contrast, by the East's actions in support of decolonization in the first half of the 1960s, and by the material help given to the people of Vietnam in fighting against American imperialism during the second half of the 1960s and at the beginning of the 1970s.

Representations of the peace and the war camps at May Day parades testify to the dual character of thought and aesthetics within the Communist societies during their founding period. In the 1950s, the people's democracies adopted the bipolar aesthetic of good and evil, hero and villain, as developed in the Soviet Union during the interwar period.[47] This approach contributed to the establishment, between 1946 and 1949, of a new Soviet vision of the border, which was less material or strategic and more geopolitical, and therefore more malleable. Its limits were defined politically via the peace/war dichotomy. The Western countries, especially the U.S.A., were affected by this new concept and developed their own reaction, based on the geopolitics of the blocs that dominated Cold War policy. In the 1960s, the view of the world became much more complex, and this radical, bipolar conception became obsolete as shades of gray entered the previously black-and-white conception of the Other and the Self. However, as particular segments of East European societies continued to maintain and further developed the roots of this bipolar conception of the world over the next forty years, the East European self-definition as the peace camp requires further analysis.

Notes

1. For an analysis of Liberation Day as political ritual, see Christel Lane, *The Rites of Rulers* (Cambridge, 1981). See also idem, "Legitimacy and Power in The Soviet Union Through Socialist Ritual," *British Journal of Political Science* 14 (1984): 207–217.
2. On the Peace Race, see Jiří Černý, Ladislav Sošenka, and Jaroslav Staněk, *Závod míru* (Prague, 1987) and Horst Schubert and Horst Werner, *Friedensfahrt* (Berlin, 1962).

3. For an extended analysis of the May Day ritual, see Roman Krakovsky, *Rituel du 1ᵉʳ mai en Tchécoslovaquie 1948–1989* (Paris: L'Harmattan, 2004).
4. On Socialist ritual, see Karen Petrone, *Life Has Become More Joyous, Comrades* (Bloomington, 2000) and Christopher A.P. Binns, "The Changing Face of Power, Part 1," *MAN (n.s.)* 4 (1979): 585–606 and "Part 2," *MAN (n.s.)* 1 (1980): 170–187. On the aesthetics of Communist ritual, see Rosalinde Sartorti, "Stalinism and Carnival," in *The Culture of the Stalin Period*, ed. Hans Günther (London, 1990), 41–77. For more extensive bibliography of the history of symbolic politics in Communist regimes, see Roman Krakovsky, *Rituel du 1ᵉʳ mai*.
5. These included the German question and the Iran dispute, over the continued Soviet occupation of the Azerbaijan region of northern Iran, among others.
6. Benjamin Frankel, ed., *The Cold War 1945–1991: Vol. 3* (Detroit, 1992), 56f.
7. Walter La Feber, *America, Russia, and the Cold War 1945–1975* (New York, 1976), 39. On the origins of the Cold War in the U.S.A., see Fraser J. Harbutt, *The Iron Curtain* (New York, 1986). For Stalin's response to Churchill's speech, see his interview with a *Pravda* correspondent (14 March 1946): "Stalin's Reply to Churchill", 14 March 1946 (interview with *Pravda*), *The New York Times*, p. 4.
8. *Pravda*, 23 March 1946. Quoted in Marshall D. Shulman, *Stalin's Foreign Policy Reappraised* (Cambridge, Mass., 1963), 83.
9. *Pravda*, 29 October 1948.
10. Martin A. Schain, ed., *The Marshall Plan* (New York, 2001), 132.
11. Cominform, created in place of Comintern, was dissolved in 1956.
12. For Zhdanov's speech at the founding meeting of Cominform, see http://www.cnn.com/SPECIALS/cold.war/episodes/04/documents/cominform.html.
13. The first among them, the World Congress of Intellectuals for Peace, was organized by Polish communists in Wroclaw in August 1948. The congress was successful in attracting a number of prominent non-Communists, including British biologist Julian Huxley, an American prosecutor of the Nazi sedition trials, O. John Rogge, and the "red priest" Abbé Boulier from France. Alexander Fadeyev, head of the Soviet Writers' Union, provided the climax to the congress with a violently anti-American speech. Several International Peace Congresses followed, organized on the same basis, among others in Paris and New York (1949), in Wroclaw and Berlin (1950), and in Vienna (1952). For the international and Euro-American context of the peace movement, see Phillip Deery, "The Dove Flies East," *Australian Journal of Politics and History* 48 (2002): 449–468. For the French context in particular, see Yves Santamaria, *Le Parti de l'ennemi?* (Paris, 2006).
14. The poster for the conference was designed by Pablo Picasso. He used his lithograph with the dove, which was already one of the most recognized symbols of peace.
15. The Soviet Union, China, Czechoslovakia, Yugoslavia, Hungary, Romania, East Germany, "free Greece," "democratic Spain," Mongolia, Korea, Indonesia, and the World Student Union.
16. "Le Congrès Mondial des Partisans de la Paix proclamme hautement que la défense de la Paix est désormais l'affaire de tous les peuples." See "Manifesto," *L'Humanité*, 27 April 1949.
17. "Z Paříže a Prahy zní mohutný hlas národů světa za mír," *Rudé právo*, 21 April 1949.
18. Carl Schmitt, *La Notion de politique / La Théorie du partisan* (Paris, 1992), 64f.
19. In reaction to the Nobel Peace Prize, on 21 December 1949 the Soviet Union created the International Stalin Peace Prize. It was awarded to notable individuals who had "strengthened peace among peoples." Following Nikita Khrushchev's denuncia-

tion of Stalin at the Twentieth Congress held in 1956, the prize was renamed the International Lenin Peace Prize.
20. General Hans Speidel (1897–1987) was head of Rommel's general staff during World War II. He took part in the attempted assassination of Hitler in 1943. From April 1957 to September 1963, he was commander-in-chief of NATO forces in Europe.
21. "Jdou jednotné šíky, jdou," *Rudé právo*, 2 May 1957.
22. In Eastern Europe, spreading or propagating war was condemned and prosecuted under the law. For Czechoslovakia, see *Zákon na ochradu míru 165/1950*.
23. Archives of Prague, collection Vysoká škola uměleckoprůmyslová, box no. 31, Politická výchova 1949–1951.
24. "Kapitalismus—tot' věčné nebezpečí. Lidé bděte!" Czech National Archives, Centrální Katalog FFKD, 1950, picture without reference.
25. On the construction of the image of the Other through the already-familiar cultural codes, see Mondher Kilani, "Découverte et invention de l'autre dans le discours anthropologique," in *L'Invention de l'autre*, ed. Mondher Kilani (Lausanne, 1994).
26. "KSČ-ROH-ČSM—Společně ji ubijem" and "Reakce plány maříme když víc uhli těžíme." Archives of the Press Agency ČTK, picture FO01226557 (František Nesvadba).
27. "Socialismus = Mír; Válka = trosky—bída—smrt"; "Mír = život—štěstí našich dětí." Archives of the Press Agency ČTK, picture FO01226558 (František Nesvadba).
28. [29.] From 1953 to 1959, De Gaulle led a quiet life in Colombey-les-deux-Eglises and did not play any role in French politics.
29. Howard F. Stein, "Psychological Complementarity in Soviet-American Relations," *Political Psychology* 2 (1985): 249–261, 257.
30. "Smějeme se vám, směje se vám náš dělník, který spolu s vaším dolarem nese nápis: 'Úderky a traktory zničí tyhle potvory!'" The slogan "Brigades and tractors will destroy these monsters" also uses the refrain of the phrase ("Úderky a traktory zničí tyhle potvory!"). See "Se sovětským svazem za mír, za vlast, za socialismus," *Mladá fronta*, 3 May 1950.
31. "Slavný 1. máj v Ostravě," *Mladá fronta*, 3 May 1950.
32. "Smějí se ukázkám kýčové kultury, vyplodům Hollywoodu." See "Míru patří naše srdce—násilníkům pěst," *Mladá Fronta*, 2 May 1951.
33. "Posměch však nestačí, je nutno zvýšit revoluční bdělost a stát na stráži!" See "Slavný 1. máj v Ostravě," *Mladá fronta*, 3 May 1950.
34. Julia Kristeva, *Etrangers à nous-même* (Paris, 1991).
35. Sigmund Freud, *L'Inquiétante étrangeté et autres essais* (Paris, 1998), 251.
36. Vamik D. Volkan, "The Need to Have Enemies and Allies," *Political Psychology* 2 (1985): 219–247.
37. Ofer Zur, "The Love of Hating," *History of European Ideas* 4 (1991): 345–369.
38. Czech National Archives, Centrální katalog FFKD, 1952, picture 40391/52.
39. The first Soviet atomic test took place on 29 August 1949. It was a replica of the American "fat man" bomb, the design of which the Soviets knew from espionage.
40. The first Soviet test of a hydrogen bomb took place on 12 August 1953. However, it was more a "boosted" fission bomb than a staged thermonuclear device.
41. Vilho Harle, "European Roots of Dualism and its Alternatives in International Relations," in *European Values in International Relations*, ed. Vilho Harle (London and New York, 1990), 10.
42. Czech National Archives, Centrální katalog FFKD, 1951, picture 38224/52.
43. Archives of the Czech Press Agency ČTK, 1957, pictures FO01087357, FO01087359, and FO01226564. The funeral of NATO is not a coincidence. NATO was originally

founded to defend peace. After the creation of the Warsaw Pact in 1955, it was not possible to admit that the Other shared the same objective. It would have meant that the two camps were, fundamentally, the same.

44. "Divíte se, kde se vzal uprostřed májové nálady pohřební průvod? Ano, byl tam! V jeho čele byl Hitlerův duch, doprovod tvořili raketové zbraně, esesáci a atomická strašidla. Koho že to pochovávali? Na rakvi napsáno— NATO." See "Pohřeb v průvodu," *Rudé právo*, 2 May 1957. See also Archives of the Press Agency ČTK, picture FO0107357.
45. See for example "Strhující proud radosti a odhodlání," *Rudé právo*, 2 May 1958.
46. On the thaw in Czechoslovakia, see Karel Kaplan, *Kořeny československé reformy 1968*, 2 vols. (Brno, 2000–2002).
47. The bipolar conception of the world in the Russian interwar culture was analyzed by Katherine Clark in *The Soviet Novel* (Bloomington, 1981) and Victoria E. Bonnel, *Iconography of Power* (Berkeley, 1999).

Bibliography

Binns, Christopher A.P. "The Changing Face of Power: Revolution and Accomodation in the Development of the Soviet Ceremonial System, Part 1," *MAN (n.s.)* 4 (1979), 585–606 and "Part 2," *MAN (n.s.)* 1 (1980), 170–187.
Bonnel, Victoria E. *Iconography of Power: Soviet Political Posters under Lenin and Stalin.* Berkeley and Los Angeles: University of California Press, 1999.
Clark, Katherine. *The Soviet Novel: History as Ritual.* Bloomington: Indiana University Press, 1981.
Černý, Jiří, Ladislav Sošenka, and Jaroslav Staněk, *Závod míru* (Prague: Olympia/Sport, 1987).
Deery, Phillip. "The Dove Flies East: Whitehall, Warsaw and the 1950 World Peace Congress," *Australian Journal of Politics and History* 48 (2002): 449–468.
Frankel, Benjamin, ed. *The Cold War 1945–1991: Vol. 3: Resources: History, Concepts, Events, Organizations, Bibliography, Archives.* Detroit, Washington, and London: Gare Research Inc., 1992.
Freud, Sigmund. *L'Inquiétante étrangeté et autres essais.* Paris: Gallimard, 1998. In English
Freud, Sigmund. "The 'Uncanny'." In *On Creativity and Unconscious. Papers on the Psychology of Art, Literature, Love, Religion* (New York: Harper & Row, 1958), 122–161.
Harbutt, Fraser J. *The Iron Curtain: Churchill, America, and the Origins of the Cold War.* New York and Oxford: Oxford University Press, 1986.
Harle, Vilho. "European Roots of Dualism and its Alternatives in International Relations." In *European Values in International Relations*, ed. Vilho Harle (London and New York: Pinter Publishers, 1990).
Kaplan, Karel. *Kořeny československé reformy 1968.* 2 vols., Brno: Doplněk, 2000–2002.
Kilani, Mondher. "Découverte et invention de l'autre dans le discours anthropologique: de Christophe Colomb à Claude Lévi-Strauss." In *L'Invention de l'autre: essais sur le discours anthropologique*, ed. Mondher Kilani (Lausanne: Payot, 1994).
Krakovsky, Roman. *Rituel du 1er mai en Tchécoslovaquie 1948–1989.* Paris: L'Harmattan, 2004.
Kristeva, Julia. *Etrangers à nous-même.* Paris: Gallimard, 1991. In English Kristeva, Julia. *Strangers to Ourselves.* New York: Harvester Wheatsheaf, 1991.

La Feber, Walter. *America, Russia, and the Cold War 1945–1975*. New York: Wiley, 1976.

Lane, Christel. *The Rites of Rulers: Ritual in Industrial Society: The Soviet Case*. Cambridge: Cambridge University Press, 1981.

———. "Legitimacy and Power in The Soviet Union Through Socialist Ritual." *British Journal of Political Science* 14 (1984): 207–217.

Petrone, Karen. *Life Has Become More Joyous, Comrades: Celebrations in the Time of Stalin*. Bloomington: Indiana University Press, 2000.

Santamaria, Yves. *Le Parti de l'ennemi? Le PCF dans la lutte pour la paix (1947–1958)*. Paris: Armand Colin, 2006.

Sartorti, Rosalinde. "Stalinism and Carnival: Organisation and Aesthetics of Political Holidays." In *The Culture of the Stalin Period*, ed. Hans Günther (London: McMillan, 1990), 41–77.

Schain, Martin A., ed. *The Marshall Plan: Fifty Years After*. New York: Palgrave, 2001.

Schmitt, Carl. *La Notion de politique/La Théorie du partisan*. Paris: Flammarion, 1992 (1st edition 1932).

Schubert, Horst, and Horst Werner. *Friedensfahrt*. Berlin: Sportverlag, 1962.

Shulman, Marshall D. *Stalin's Foreign Policy Reappraised*. Cambridge, Mass.: Harvard University Press, 1963.

Stein, Howard F. "Psychological Complementarity in Soviet-American Relations." *Political Psychology* 2 (1985): 249–261.

Volkan, Vamik D. "The Need to Have Enemies and Allies: A Developmental Approach." *Political Psychology* 2 (1985): 219–247.

Zákon na ochradu míru 165/1950

Zur, Ofer. "The Love of Hating: The Psychology of Enemy." *History of European Ideas* 4 (1991): 345–369.

Further documents

Archives of the Press Agency ČTK
Archives of Prague
Czech National Archives
http://www.cnn.com/SPECIALS/cold.war/episodes/02/1st.draft/pravda.html
http://www.cnn.com/SPECIALS/cold.war/episodes/04/documents/cominform.html
L'Humanité, "Manifesto," 27 April 1949

Various articles from the newspapers:
Mladá fronta
Pravda
Rudé právo

Chapter 11

ARTISTIC STYLE, CANONIZATION, AND IDENTITY POLITICS IN COLD WAR GERMANY, 1947–1960

Joes Segal

Introduction

The early years of the twenty-first century witnessed a strong scholarly interest in the cultural aspects of the Cold War. It was recognized that literature, the visual arts, music, theatre, cinema, and other cultural expressions not only reflected existing political tensions, but were also debated and sometimes celebrated as carriers of collective identities and ideologies. Culture became an important factor in the mental mapping of the Cold War and in the process of ideological inclusion and exclusion in East and West, not just for the cultural elite but also for the public at large.

The visual arts make an interesting case in point, illustrating the cultural politics of the Cold War in its full complexity, partly due to the wide range of possible interpretations of artworks and images. In fact, the visual arts sometimes functioned as a mirror, or projection screen, of diverging political outlooks. Artistic styles and conceptions were interpreted as reflections of shared (or inimical) values and identities, not only in art theory and art criticism, but in cultural politics as well. However, the association of the visual arts with political identities was always contested, and often paradoxical.

This chapter will analyze the process of politicization and canonization of the visual arts in postwar Germany, against the background of the unfolding "artistic Cold War." In divided Germany, the ideological struggle between liberal democracy and communism had to take the burden of the recent national past into account. The negative heritage of National Socialism played a central role in defining an anti-capitalist identity in East and an anti-totalitarian one in West Germany, with regard to the visual arts as well. What resulted was a complex and sometimes paradoxical set of associations between the visual arts on the one hand and both national and ideological identities on the other. I will argue that with regard to German Cold War art politics there were striking structural similarities in East and West, but some important differences as well. Finally, the question will be raised as to how much the German art debates provide insight into the specific character of European Cold War Cultures.

The Canonization of Socialist Realism: The Soviet Occupation Zone and the GDR

During the first years after World War II, most German artists and intellectuals agreed on the necessity of coming to terms with the recent past and constructing a new political and cultural foundation for life in Germany. Therefore there was a widespread (though by no means universal or unconditional) readiness among them to join forces with the cultural initiatives of the Allied Forces. Following the Potsdam Agreement of August 1945, the Allies officially cooperated in the administration of occupied Germany. And although they had their own program and style of political and cultural reeducation, they all actively promoted anti-Fascism, humanism, and democracy.[1]

This ideological and cultural correspondence between the Allied Forces in the first years following the war also had its repercussions on the world of art. There was as yet no emphasis on Socialist Realism in the Soviet zone, or on modern art in the Western zones. Throughout Germany, exhibitions represented artists who had been marked "degenerate" by the Nazis and who had been forced into actual or "inner emigration," irrespective of their political conviction or painting style. The Soviet Military Administration (SMAD) was especially active in organizing cultural events. Cultural officers of the *Informationsverwaltung der sowjetischen Militäradministration in Deutschland* persuaded German artists and intellectuals to contribute to the cultural and spiritual revival of Germany.[2]

Already in June 1945, the KPD (*Kommunistische Partei Deutschlands*) called for the foundation of a popular front of anti-Fascist and democratic forces on the basis of humanist tolerance.³ It was in this spirit that in July 1945, the *Kulturbund zur demokratischen Erneuerung Deutschlands* was founded, a cultural organization of German artists and intellectuals aimed at humanist values and a democratic spirit in the tradition of the German "classical" heritage. The *Kulturbund*, headed by the poet Johannes R. Becher, who had spent the years from 1934 to 1945 in exile in the Soviet Union, claimed to be apolitical and strove to reconcile *Geist* and *Macht*, culture and politics. Nonetheless, the organization was strictly hierarchical, with Communist party members at the top.⁴ The *Kulturbund* also established itself in the Western zones (under the name *Kulturliga* in Munich, as *Freie deutsche Kulturgesellschaft* in Frankfurt, and under its own name in the British zone), but it was mistrusted by the Western Allies and finally banned in 1947.⁵ Because of the liberal and pragmatic organization of cultural life and the activities of the *Kulturbund*, the Soviet zone attracted quite a number of artists and intellectuals.

The first official art exhibitions in this zone had an open character. This also holds true for the first major exhibition: the *Allgemeine deutsche Kunstausstellung* in Dresden in 1946, the main organizer of which was art historian Will Grohmann. Together with the painter Hans Grundig, he traveled through Germany to select works from, among others, the abstract painters Willi Baumeister and Max Ackermann.⁶ Also on display were many modern painters who were known to the general public, if at all, only through the notorious National Socialist exhibition *Degenerate Art* in Munich in 1937. During the festive opening on 25 August 1946, Major Alexander Dymshitz, leader of the Cultural Office of the Soviet Military Administration, who would later play a prominent role in the enforcement of the doctrine of Socialist Realism, proclaimed the end of "denkfauler Nazinaturalismus" ("intellectually lazy National Socialist naturalism") in art. He also contributed an introduction to the exhibition catalogue.⁷ Although the first reviews in the press were favorable, negative public reactions soon began to be heard. The *Sächsische Zeitung* approvingly published quotations from visitors, varying from "gehe in die Ausstellung und lache dich tot" ("visit the exhibition and laugh your head off") to "Nichts als entartete Kunst" ("nothing but degenerate art"). During the opening of the exhibition, Herbert Gute, director of the East German Public Education Administration's Art and Literature section, had remarked that after twelve years of Nazi dictatorship, finally a free art without regulations from above could develop, but less than two months later he wrote in the *Sächsische Zeitung* that art had never been "for its own sake" and that the slogan *l'art pour l'art*, which he identified with the modern works on display in Dresden, was nothing but a poisonous shot from the bourgeoisie.[8] This would mark the beginning of a cultural chill to the east of the Elbe.

In October 1946, one week after the publication of Gute's sneering article, at a congress of the *Sächsische Landesverwaltung* on the arts, Lieutenant Colonel Tulpanov cited the "democratic" art of Soviet Russia as an inspiring example to East German painters. He stressed that art should always appeal to the people, and he defended Soviet art policy under Stalin against criticism from the West. The timing of his speech seems no coincidence. In the Soviet Union, after a short period of relative liberalism in the art world following World War II, Andrei Zhdanov, the Leningrad Party leader, advisor to Stalin and future organizer of the Cominform (founded in September 1947), issued three decrees in August 1946, condemning formalist tendencies, a lack of ideology, and bourgeois decadence in Russian literature, theatre, and film. (A fourth decree, attacking "false originality" in Russian opera, would follow in February 1948.[9]) These decrees immediately affected the visual arts as well, and the official art policy in the Soviet zone followed suit, especially after the intensification of the international East-West divide as a consequence of the failure of the 1947 Moscow Conference of the Allied Secretaries of State on the future of Germany, and the proclamation of the Truman Doctrine in the United States.[10]

In order to enforce the introduction of a Soviet-inspired cultural life in East Germany, the Soviets opened their *Haus der Kultur der Sowjetunion* and founded the *Gesellschaft zum Studium der Kultur der Sowjetunion* in 1947. To be sure, the official art magazine *bildende kunst* (1947–49) published some articles by modern art critics and art historians (Adolf Behne, Werner Haftmann), but it also criticized modern tendencies (especially abstract art) and discussed Socialist Realism from the Soviet Union and other Eastern European countries in spite of protests from one of its editors, the painter Karl Hofer (see below).[11] An important element in the cultural struggle between East and West in Germany was the meaning of "National Socialism" in evaluating art and culture. Whereas in the Western zones Socialist Realism was criticized as a variation on National Socialist realism (both were propagandistic art forms in a totalitarian context), Soviet and East German politicians connected modern art and culture with the origins of National Socialism. Otto Grotewohl, for example, the future prime minister of the GDR, in his speech to the first cultural conference of the SED (*Sozialistische Einheitspartei Deutschlands*) in May 1948, discussed Nietzsche and Spengler as the spiritual fathers of National Socialism, and stressed that the contemporary bourgeois philosophy of existentialism, which was popular among modern Western artists and intellectuals, amounted to a return to Nietzsche.[12] Alexander Dymshitz, the Russian major who had opened the first *Allgemeine deutsche Kunstausstellung* in 1946, two years later spoke out against formalism, modernism, and decadence in the arts and condemned Pablo Picasso, a member of the French communist party, for his "decadent" desire to be "original" at all costs and for his lack of any idealist content.[13]

It is interesting to note in this context that Picasso caused ideological problems in both East and West, since he combined a Communist outlook with a modern painting style. In Soviet art criticism after 1946, Picasso was the preeminent symbol of Western bourgeois decadence,[14] whereas he was hailed at various international conferences organized by the Cominform and even received an international peace prize from the Soviet Union.[15] This artistic and ideological schizophrenia was omnipresent in the Soviet Union under Stalin; Dmitri Shostakovich, who was a prominent target of Zhdanov's 1948 decree on "false originality" in Russian opera, was forced to join the Soviet delegation to the Cultural and Scientific Conference for World Peace held at the Waldorf Astoria in New York in March 1949, organized by the Cominform, to represent official Soviet culture for an international audience.[16]

Because of the strongly centralized cultural politics in the Soviet zone and the lack of private galleries, artists were more or less forced to comply with the directives as formulated by the military administration, which in the end boiled down to the rejection of all art forms save Soviet-modeled Socialist Realism. In the years following the war (1945–47), many artists and intellectuals had been attracted to the Soviet zone with its blooming cultural life. During the years 1948–49, many of them at least considered moving to the West.[17] This illustrates one of the paradoxes of the Socialist bloc's cultural politics in the early years of the Cold War: in order to enforce "art for the people" and a recognizable Socialist artistic identity, the politicians alienated themselves not only from the artists, who were more or less reduced to illustrators of a political idea, but also from the public, which did not warm to the artistic results. The political leadership of the GDR would explain this discrepancy in terms of a lack of artistic quality and political conviction among the artists.

Following the foundation of the German Democratic Republic in October 1949, the political control of art and culture intensified through a series of institutional reorganizations. In 1950, the *Verband Bildender Künstler Deutschlands* (Union of Visual Artists in Germany) was partly modeled after its counterpart in the Soviet Union. Membership was compulsory for visual artists who wanted to exhibit and to qualify for commissions by the state—which in the GDR was of particular importance since there were no private galleries where artworks could be sold. The specific aim of the organization was the fight against the "Kulturbarbarei des amerikanischen Imperialismus in allen seinen Formen" ("the cultural barbarism of American imperialism in all its manifestations") and the production of Socialist Realist art in accordance with Soviet painting. Modern, "formalist" influences in art were by now generally ascribed to the Americans. In his essay "Die Hauptaufgaben auf dem Gebiete der Kunst" ("The major tasks in the field of the arts") from 1950, Walter Ulbricht, Secretary General of the SED, wrote that the symptoms of decadence in art, to a large extent imported from the United States, had to be defeated,[18] while one year later N. Orlov fulminated in the *Tägliche Rundschau* that formalism in art was not only undemocratic (because not related to the people), but also anti-aesthetic, pathological, and degenerate—using the very vocabulary of National Socialism.[19]

The radicalization of art politics was not just a matter of rhetoric. Socialist artists who were well prepared to devote themselves to the construction of socialism were heavily criticized when their work showed even the slightest influence of modern painting styles. Socialist content in art was deemed worthless unless it was packed in an immaculate "Socialist" style. At the Dresden art academy, references to modern art history were carefully removed; the library even banned books on such "classical" modern artists as Pierre-Auguste Renoir and Vincent van Gogh.[20]

It was only between 1953 and 1956 that the political leadership of the GDR was practically forced to reconsider its harsh cultural politics. The effects of Stalin's death in March 1953 were not immediately felt, but after the workers' revolt three months later, which was crushed with the support of Soviet tanks, East German intellectuals seized the opportunity to complain about the gap that had arisen between the Party and the people, and demanded a revision of Stalinist cultural politics as well as a return to artistic pluralism. In June 1953, the *Deutsche Akademie der Künste* published a whole catalogue of demands, aiming to end all political interference with the arts. The Party leadership was afraid to lose the support of artists and intellectuals completely, and made some concessions, also, in the words of Ulbricht, in acknowledgment of their loyalty in the days of "Fascist provocation" (that is to say, the workers' revolt of 17 June). In 1955–56, the newly founded art magazine *Bildende Kunst* (now written with capitals) started a discussion about Picasso. The Spanish painter was praised for his political engagement for communism and world peace, but there remained a difference of opinion with regard to his painting style. Some of the debaters still accused him of formalism, while others maintained that he had found an appropriate contemporary pictorial language for his ideas.[21] Around the same time, as an indirect result of Khrushchev's de-Stalinization politics, there was some discussion about

Picasso in the Soviet Union as well, and in 1956 a small exhibition of his work even opened in Moscow.[22]

But whereas the relative "thaw" in cultural matters largely remained in effect in the Soviet Union until 1962,[23] the "liberal" phase in the GDR did not last long. Following the Hungarian uprising of October 1956, the SED launched a campaign against "revisionists" and "counterrevolutionaries." In January 1957, Ulbricht proclaimed the end of all artistic discussions in the GDR; painters had to stop talking and start painting again, unconditionally supporting the cause of socialism. According to Alexander Abusch, State Secretary of Culture, the artists had failed to understand the true meaning of socialism and therefore had been susceptible to the organized incitements from its enemies.[24] When a regional exhibition in Halle and Magdeburg provoked angry reactions by party officials because of alleged "formalist" tendencies, a delegation of 6,000 workers was sent there to "spontaneously" condemn the works on display "in the name of the people."[25] All in all, it is clear that the interpretation of art as a weapon in the Cold War was unconditionally adopted from the Soviet Union. The only difference seems to have been that the GDR under Ulbricht was more stubborn in its political control and ideological interpretation of art than the Soviet Union under Khrushchev. De-Stalinization never really reached East Germany in the 1950s.

The Canonization of Modern Art: The Western Occupation Zones and the FRG

Gradually, modern art became the cultural symbol of freedom and democracy in the Western occupation zones. Would this association ever have occurred if Hitler had been an admirer of modern art? This rhetorical question is not as absurd as it may sound. On the one hand, several officials of the NSDAP (Joseph Goebbels, among others) were interested in modern art, and tended to accept at least German expressionism as an appropriate artistic expression of the German people until the Führer placed a ban on it. On the other hand, quite a few modern artists in Germany had readily accepted the National Socialist assumption of power in 1933, and sometimes directly subscribed to the National Socialist ideology. A famous case in point is the expressionist painter Emil Nolde, who in letters to Goebbels and Minister of Education Bernhard Rust vehemently protested the inclusion of his work in the exhibition *Degenerate Art* in 1937, in view of his "German" painting style and his unabated loyalty to the National Socialist cause.[26] Willi Baumeister, an abstract painter in the entourage of the Bauhaus who after 1945 would become one of the most eloquent and popular spokesmen of abstract art, had been convinced that the rejection of his work by the Nazis was based on a fundamental misunderstanding, and before retreating into "inner emigration" he considered moving to Italy, where the Fascist regime, so he thought, welcomed avant-garde art.[27] Interestingly, such former political convictions played no role in postwar Germany. Nolde and Baumeister figured prominently in the West German art world as free creative spirits who were victimized by the Nazi regime.

In the three Western occupation zones, cultural politics was much more decentralized than in the Soviet zone, and largely left to the federal states and local authorities. Nonetheless, the Allied Powers (with the Americans leading the way) tried to influence public opinion directly as well as indirectly. Not only did they operate their own cultural institutions in Germany; they were also actively involved in German cultural initiatives. Former victims of National Socialist art policy, especially modern artists, were appointed as professors at art academies and jurors at important exhibitions. After 1947, this tendency to give preference to modern artists became stronger as the East-West divide deepened.

That is not to say that the canonization of modern art in the Western zones was uncontested. However, the main reason for condemning modern art was not that it was formalist, bourgeois, or decadent, but that it was inaccessible and obscure or that it lacked human feeling and a spiritual essence. After 1945, several religious intellectuals tried to explain the rise of National Socialism in Germany as the final consequence of the process of secularization since the Renaissance, and especially the Enlightenment.[28] This line of reasoning was extrapolated to the world of art by the Austrian art historian Hans Sedlmayer, who in his bestselling book *Verlust der Mitte* (1948) maintained that modern art was the true symptom of a culture which had lost its spiritual essence.[29] Without mentioning the word "degeneration," Sedlmayr, who had been a party member of the NSDAP, echoed National Socialist (and Socialist, for that matter) rhetoric by characterizing modern art as a symbol of cultural decadence, albeit this time from a religious standpoint. But opposition to modern art in the Western zones did not come exclusively from conservatives or former National Socialists like Sedlmayr. In 1949, the Social Democrat Wilhelm Hausenstein, appointed German Consul in Paris, published his book *Was bedeutet die moderne Kunst?*, in which he argued that the modern experiment in art had since long become obsolete and that abstract art was a consequence of the human defection from God and an artistic reflexion of the nihilist *Zeitgeist*.[30]

Nevertheless, abstract art quietly gained ground in the Western zones at the expense of realist tendencies, whether modern or conservative. An interesting case in point is the postwar career of the realist but modern painter Karl Hofer. Already in June 1945, the Soviet Military Administration had appointed Hofer as president of the *Hochschule für bildende Künste* in Berlin-Charlottenburg. During the Nazi rule, Hofer, who in his work combined influences from his teacher Hans Thoma (paradoxically one of Hitler's favorite artists) with modern elements from, among others, Hans van Marées and Paul Cézanne, had been declared "degenerate" and was prohibited from exhibiting his work. Although Charlottenburg was in the American sector in Berlin, the Soviets had made this appointment before the entry of the Americans.[31] At first, Hofer remained in close contact with the Soviet zone. Together with the Communist painter Oskar Nerlinger, he became editor of the official Soviet-zone art magazine *bildende kunst*. Nevertheless, he spoke out against its publication of the article "Dreißig Jahre sowjetischer Malerei" ("Thirty years of Soviet painting"), which came down to a defense of Soviet-type Socialist Realism. One year later, Hofer defended the priority of art over politics in *bildende kunst* (whereas his coeditor did exactly the opposite in the same issue). Thereupon Major Dymshitz launched a biting attack against the painter in his article "Über die formalistische Richtung in der deutschen Malerei" ("On formalism in German painting") in the *Tägliche Rundschau*, accusing him of "decadence."[32] Thus, Hofer finally decided for the West. In 1950, he became president of the West German *Deutscher Künstlerbund*, and in the catalogue of its 1951 exhibition he warned that "the Hydra of Hitlerean non-art," referring to Soviet Socialist Realism and its counterpart in the GDR, had brutally lifted its head again.[33] But Hofer's own artistic realism found little appreciation in the FRG,[34] and when he commented on the "unfruitfulness" of abstract art in 1954, a storm of protest ensued within the West German art world. Several influential abstract painters, such as Baumeister, consequently resigned their membership in the DKB.[35] Fundamental criticism of abstract art had become something of a taboo in the meantime.[36]

Many West German artists and critics described abstract art as a revelation of some metaphysical order. Art historian Will Grohmann (who, as mentioned above, had changed camps in 1947) wrote that pure art develops a positive relationship towards "fundamental reality" and is capable of answering questions "about the meaning of life in time and space," whereas his colleague Werner Hofmann stated that the modern artist relates the fate of art to philosophical, religious, and existential questions.[37] Be that as it may, an important reason for the overwhelming success of modern (abstract) art in the Western zones and subsequently in the early years of the FRG, at least within the art world and among cultural politicians, seems to have been its radical rejection by both Hitler and Stalin. It was clear that modern art was conceived as some sort of threat or *Fremdkörper* ("foreign body") within both totalitarian systems.[38] How could it otherwise be explained that the highest ranks of the political leadership in the Third Reich and in Stalin's Soviet Union spared no pains in attacking modern art and persecuting its producers? As a victim of totalitarian regimes, modern art could easily be associated with individual freedom, and consequently with liberal democracy. This corresponded seamlessly with the anti-Communist Cold War propaganda according to which the Soviet system was yet another variation of totalitarianism. According to Jutta Held, it was around 1949 that several art critics began to reject *all* realist art as an instrument of totalitarianism and as contrary to the "natural" development of free art.[39] This line of thought was to be continued into the first decade of the FRG. In 1950, the *Deutscher Künstlerbund* proclaimed that it would protect art against any attempt at corruption by external demands and prevent it from deteriorating into "Tendenzkunst"[40]—an exact reversal of the foundation statement of the VBKD in the GDR in the same year, which stated that the organization would protect art against cultural barbarism from the West (see above). In 1957, in their *Einführung in die Kunstsoziologie* ("Introduction to the Sociology of Art"), Martha Mierendorff and Heinrich Tost argued that realist art is always susceptible to ideological abuse, whereas abstract art is undogmatic, does not carry any national symbols, and recognizes no borders. Therefore, the authors conclude, modern art is always distrusted by dictatorial regimes. Two years later, art historian Werner Haftmann, in the introduction to the catalogue of the second *documenta* exhibition in Kassel (1959), called modern art an exquisite example of universal human culture because it had developed a transnational communication that transcended language barriers, local norms, racist ideas, and folklore.[41]

To mention the *documenta* is to mention a feature of central importance to the art world of the FRG. The first exhibition under this name, aimed at presenting the main currents in international modern art since the beginning of the twentieth century and reintroducing modern German artists into the international art scene, was organized in Kassel in 1955, one year after the FRG to a large extent officially regained its political autonomy following the successful political and economic *Westbindung* by Chancellor Konrad Adenauer. The positive reception at home and abroad incited the organizers to turn it into a recurrent manifestation of international contemporary art. One could argue that this was the West German "answer" to the East German *Deutsche Kunstausstellungen* ("German art exhibitions") in Dresden, which presented the state of the art in German Socialist Realism roughly every four years. There is no doubt that the *documenta*, as the single most important art event in the

FRG, contributed significantly to the canonization of modern art in West Germany.

Was the institutionalization and canonization of modern art in West Germany directly influenced by political incitements from the United States, comparable to the impact of Soviet art policy on the GDR? This appears to be a complex and highly contested matter. Since the 1970s, several art historians have commented upon the alleged connection between the international success of American Abstract Expressionism and attempts by the American government and government-related institutions to influence public opinion abroad by means of cultural propaganda, especially in the form of traveling exhibitions.[42] For instance, it is argued that the CIA wanted to counter the cultural offensive of the Cominform and, through cooperation with the New York Museum of Modern Art and private institutions, used modern American painting, especially Abstract Expressionism, as a symbol of cultural freedom in the United States.[43]

First of all, it has to be observed that modern art in America was not exactly uncontroversial after World War II. Frances Stonor Saunders quotes President Harry Truman, who in 1948, after visiting a room in the National Gallery of Washington containing works by Holbein and Rembrandt, wrote in his diary: "It's a pleasure to look at perfection and then think of the lazy, nutty moderns. It is like comparing Christ with Lenin."[44] It seems more than a coincidence that Truman chose Lenin, the father of the Russian Revolution, as the political counterpart of modern art. One year later, George Dondero, a Senator from Michigan, complained in an interview: "Modern art is communist because it is distorted and ugly, because it does not glorify our beautiful country. Art which does not glorify our beautiful country in plain, simple terms that everyone can understand breeds dissatisfaction. It is therefore opposed to our government, and those who create and promote it are our enemies."[45] Thus at least American politicians' enthusiasm for modern art as a representation of American culture has to be qualified. The fact that the FBI kept files on several Abstract Expressionists as possible "fellow travelers" underpins the point.[46]

Another problem arises when studying the public statements of the Abstract Expressionists themselves. Many of them had gone through a Socialist phase in the 1930s, but were eventually scared off by rumors about the Soviet gulags, the Moscow show trials, Stalinist art politics, and the notorious Molotov-Ribbentrop (or Hitler-Stalin) pact of August 1939.[47] But that is not to say that they were willing to engage in a Cold War propaganda struggle on the side of the United States. On the contrary: in the context of Joseph McCarthy's anti-Communist imputations, they distanced themselves not only from political totalitarianism (as in the Soviet Union) but also from what some of them called "economic totalitarianism" (as in the United States). Many followed Jean-Paul Sartre and other left-wing European intellectuals in their plea for a "third way" between communism and capitalism. Barnett Newman, for instance, stated in an interview with Dorothy Gees Seckler that those who could "read" his work properly would recognize in it the end of all state capitalism and totalitarianism.[48]

Thus one has to assume that American artistic Cold War propaganda, insofar as it actually existed as such, took place without the consent of important parts of the political elite as well as the artists themselves. That is not impossible. In fact, leading personalities of the Museum of Modern Art publicly related modern art to democracy. René d'Harnoncourt, vice-president of the museum, called modern art a "foremost symbol" of a democratic society. Director Alfred Barr, Jr. formulated it the other way round: "The modern artist's nonconformity and love of freedom cannot be tolerated within a monolithic tyranny and modern art is useless for the dictator's propaganda,"[49] a statement that comes remarkably close to that of Mierendorff and Tost in their *Einführung in die Kunstsoziologie*, quoted above. However, this of course does not necessarily imply that Barr and d'Harnoncourt were actively engaged in cultural propaganda.

The question whether American cultural propaganda activities really influenced the Western European art world has mostly been discussed in connection with American traveling exhibitions during the 1950s in Europe. However, as recent studies by Sigrid Ruby and Nancy Jachec have convincingly argued, these travel exhibitions contained a wide variety of painting styles (also including folk art, academic realism, and Social Realism), and it was not until the very end of the decade that the United States Information Agency (USIA)—which was founded in 1953 as a subdivision of the National Security Council in order to promote American culture abroad—directly cooperated with the International Council of the Museum of Modern Art in presenting Abstract Expressionist art in Europe.[50] By that time, the association between modern art and Western political values was already well established throughout Europe. That is not to say, of course, that American influences did not deeply affect cultural life in the Western zones and the FRG already at an early stage. Especially in movies, popular music, youth culture, and "lifestyle," this influence can hardly be overestimated.[51] But in the case of the visual arts, the assessment looks different.

An endlessly repeated central element in the defense of modern art was its "freedom." Since abstract art did not represent reality, it could not be used by any political system as a means of propaganda. However, there is a paradox involved in the practical consequences of this view. The freedom of artistic production, explicitly laid down in the constitution of the FRG, boiled down not to an individually motivated artistic pluralism, but to the absolute predominance of one specific kind of painting that came to be associated with "artistic freedom." In the context of the Cold War, this noninstrumental art was ideologically contrasted with the totalitarian perversion of art under (National) Socialism. The West German authorities were actively involved in this process by acquiring modern artworks for museums, granting modern artists official assignments, appointing them at art academies, and presenting their works at the *documenta*. There was no need for a large-scale American cultural offensive in order to develop this kind of artistic identity politics in Germany.

Conclusion

The cultural Cold War in East and West provides a striking example of what in social psychology is called "ingroup- and outgroup-homogenization": the urge to enhance one's own group identity by minimizing internal and exaggerating external differences. The Soviets and the Americans, the East Germans as well as the West Germans, constructed an ordered universe with razor-sharp borders between East and West, good and evil, freedom and totalitarianism, socialism and decadence. Since it is evident that such clear-cut identities do not exist in this world, it was deemed necessary to locate elements within one's own culture that supposedly corresponded to the enemy: modern art in the Soviet realm, realism in the West (but then again modern art in conservative America). This "splitting" symbolically identified the antagonistic camps of the Cold War. What was at stake, in the words of philosopher Susan Buck-Morss, was the "outlawing (of) the enemy's interpretation of the world."[52]

Of course, there were fundamental differences between the two camps, and much of what we call "Cold War rhetoric" has a firm base in historical reality. Nevertheless, it is interesting to note some striking similarities with regard to cultural politics, and more specifically the role of the visual arts in East and West Germany. First of all, it is clear that both camps from 1946 onwards gradually identified themselves exclusively with a specific type of painting: Socialist Realism in the East, modernism (especially abstract art) in the West. From a traditional "Western" art-historical standpoint, this may seem to be a strange observation, since modern art has generally been described after World War II as the "logical" outcome of an autonomous historical process, whereas (National) Socialist Realism was seen as a fatal deviation from the right path. However, this art-historical rhetoric has to be historicized itself as integral to the cultural context of the Cold War period. The strict identification of political ideology and artistic style was partly based on a process of exclusion: whereas the *Verband Bildender Künstler Deutschlands* in 1950 saw it as one of its main tasks to fight "American" influences in East German art, its West German counterpart, the *Deutscher Künstlerbund*, claimed that very same year to protect "free" art against any totalitarian (read: Communist) influences. In the Western context, the free (nonpolitical) character of modern art turned into something of a political message, especially as it actually resulted not in artistic pluralism but in the predominance of one specific type of painting that could be associated with "freedom."

Furthermore, it is remarkable that one finds more or less the same splits in Soviet and American artistic propaganda. In both countries, modern art was condemned at home as art from the enemy, a kind of fifth column. Senator Dondero and other followers of Joseph McCarthy thundered against "Communist art," whereas Soviet art critics following Zhdanov's decrees attacked the same art as "capitalist bourgeois decadence." Paradoxically, for international audiences both countries promoted modern art (Picasso, Léger, Guttuso, and other Communist modern artists in the case of the Soviet Union; Abstract Expressionists and other modern American painters in the case of the United States) to present themselves as culturally open and progressive states. Actually, both realist *and* modern art formed an integral part of Soviet, American, and German art history, underscoring the fact that reality in the context of the Cold War had largely become a matter of rhetoric.

All the same, the parallels between East and West seem to end where the actual influence of the United States and the Soviet Union in Germany is concerned. Compared to Soviet cultural policy, American cultural propaganda could not be as purposeful and straightforward, in light of the fundamental controversies over questions of cultural identity and the possible role of the arts. The first unequivocal attempts to present American modern art as the very symbol of Western spiritual freedom and liberal democracy came at a time when this very association had long since taken root in West Germany.

It remains to be asked what the postwar German art debates can teach us about European Cold War Cultures. In the case of Germany, it will be clear that there was no room for deviation between "internal" and "external" art policy, as there was in the Soviet Union and the United States. In this sense, the divided country was more object than subject of Cold War propaganda, even more than in the rest of Europe. Germany makes an interesting case, not only because the cultural and ideological divide split the nation in two parts, but also because the country, leaving the catastrophic heritage of Nazism behind, had to start all over again (the term *Stunde Null,* "zero hour," was regularly used after 1945), and was therefore especially susceptible to new political projections. Cold War rhetoric in the German case often boiled down to an association of the enemy with the blackest pages from national history: the FRG and the GDR as "logical" continuations of the Third Reich. The harshness of this rhetoric might be explained by the closeness and common history of East and West Germans. The Cold War offered them an opportunity to come to terms with (or forget) the past and to redefine their own identity.

Notes

1. Manfred Görtemaker, *Geschichte der Bundesrepublik Deutschland* (Munich, 1999), 208–212.
2. Hermann Glaser, *Deutsche Kultur* (Bonn, 1997), 103.
3. Jutta Held, *Kunst und Kunstpolitik 1945–1949* (Berlin, 1981), 12.
4. Martin Damus, *Malerei der DDR* (Reinbek, 1991), 48f.
5. Not quite without reason, as it turned out: Walter Ulbricht and Josef Stalin had discussed the *Kulturbund* as a useful "Trojan horse" to attract West German artists and intellectuals. Glaser, *Deutsche Kultur*, 105.
6. Glaser, *Deutsche Kultur*, 172. In 1947, Grohmann was appointed director of the *Hochschule für Werkkunst* in Dresden, where he introduced ideas from the Bauhaus. However, later that year, restricted by the increasingly narrow art politics in the Soviet zone, he moved to the West, where he would play an important role in the art world of the FRG.
7. Damus, *Malerei der DDR*, 43; Bernd Lindner, *Verstellter, offener Blick* (Cologne, 1998), 71.
8. Lindner, *Verstellter, offener Blick*, 72–75.
9. Matthew Cullerne Bown, *Socialist Realist Painting* (London, 1998), 222–227.
10. Görtemaker, *Geschichte*, 250.
11. Held, *Kunst und Kunstpolitik*, 384.
12. Glaser, *Deutsche Kultur*, 106.
13. Cited in Karin Thomas, *Zweimal deutsche Kunst nach 1945* (Cologne, 1985), 33.
14. Bown, *Socialist Realist Painting*, 246.
15. Gertje R. Utley, *Picasso* (New Haven, 2000), 101–134. See also David Caute, *The Dancer Defects* (Oxford, 2003), 568–588.
16. Frances Stonor Saunders, *Who Paid the Piper?* (London, 1999), 50f. On the extensive discussion about Shostakovich in the context of the Cold War, see Caute, *The Dancer Defects*, 415–440.
17. Glaser, *Deutsche Kultur*, 172.
18. Lindner, *Verstellter, offener Blick*, 93.
19. N. Orlow, "Wege und Irrwege der modernen Kunst," *Tägliche Rundschau* (20 January 1951), cited in Damus, *Malerei der DDR*, 78. Damus does not mention the fact that "N. Orlow" was the pseudonym of Vladimir Semjonovich Semjonov, who in 1953 became the first Soviet ambassador to the GDR. He was not the first Russian to use a medical vocabulary with regard to modern art. In 1947, art critic Kemenov

had already described modern artworks as the products of pathological minds. See Caute, *The Dancer Defects*, 516. On Orlow, see also Barbara McCloskey, "Dialectic at a Standstill: East German Socialist Realism in the Stalin Era," in *Art of Two Germanys*, ed. Stephanie Barron and Sabine Eckmann (New York and Los Angeles 2009), 109.
20. Lindner, *Verstellter, offener Blick*, 112f.
21. Damus, *Malerei der DDR*, 139ff.; Lindner, *Verstellter, offener Blick*, 117.
22. Bown, *Socialist Realist Painting*, 246; Michael Scammel, "Art as Politics and Politics in Art," in *Nonconformist Art*, ed. Alla Rosenfeld and Norton T. Dodge (Rutgers, 1995), 49–63, here 50.
23. Not without reservations, however. In August 1957, for instance, Khrushchev published his essay "For the Close Link of Literature and Art with the People," where he stated that although he wanted to do away with the excesses of Stalin's art policy, the basic assumptions of his politics and of Zhdanov's decrees remained in effect. Bown, *Socialist Realist Painting*, 386–387.
24. Damus, *Malerei der DDR*, 152.
25. Lindner, *Verstellter, offener Blick*, 120f.
26. Stephanie Barron, ed., *"Degenerate Art"* (Los Angeles, 1991), 319; Rose-Carol Washton Long, ed., *German Expressionism* (London, 1993), 307.
27. Held, *Kunst und Kunstpolitik*, 18.
28. Görtemaker, *Geschichte*, 204f.
29. Hans Sedlmayr, *Verlust der Mitte* (Salzburg, 1948), passim.
30. Thomas, *Zweimal deutsche Kunst*, 19. Remarkably, just before and during the First World War, Hausenstein had been an early proponent of German expressionism and had defended Wassily Kandinsky against reactionary criticism in Herwarth Walden's avant-garde art magazine *Der Sturm*. Joes Segal, *Krieg als Erlösung* (Munich, 1997), 51, 134.
31. Damus, *Malerei der DDR*, 52.
32. Martin Damus, *Kunst in der BRD 1945–1990* (Reinbek, 1995), 116; idem, *Malerei der DDR*, 62.
33. Damus, *Kunst in der BRD*, 116.
34. Held, *Kunst und Kunstpolitik*, 30.
35. Damus, *Kunst in der BRD*, 178. Nevertheless, there was also some public support for Hofer, among others from Günter Grass in the cultural magazine *Der Monat*. On Hofer and abstract art, see also Ursula Peters and Roland Prügel, "The Legacy of Critical Realism in East and West," in Barron and Eckmann, *Art of Two Germanys*, 66.
36. In 1955, Hans Sedlmayer published a second book against modern art: *Die Revolution der modernen Kunst* (Hamburg 1955), which found its supporters, but hardly within the West German art world.
37. Will Grohmann, ed., *Neue Kunst nach 1945* (Cologne, 1958), 192; Werner Hofmann, *Zeichen und Gestalt* (Frankfurt, 1957), 10, 38.
38. The term is used by Franz Roh, *Geschichte der deutschen Kunst von 1900 bis zur Gegenwart* (Munich, 1958), 151, with regard to National Socialist art. He also comments on the striking parallelism between National Socialism and Bolshevism in this respect.
39. Held, *Kunst und Kunstpolitik*, 388.
40. Gerhard Grohs, "Zur Soziologie der bildenden Künste in der Bundesrepublik," in *Die Gesellschaft in der Bundesrepublik*, ed. Hans Steffen (Göttingen, 1971), 45.
41. Cited in Damus, *Kunst in der BRD*, 183–185.

42. Max Kozloff, "American Painting During the Cold War," *Artforum* 11 (1973), no. 9: 43–54; Eva Cockcroft, "Abstract Expression: Weapon of the Cold War," *Artforum* 12 (1974), no. 10: 39–41; David Shapiro and Cecile Shapiro, "Abstract Expressionism," *Prospect* 3 (1976): 175–214; Serge Guilbaut, *How New York Stole the Idea of Modern Art* (Chicago and London, 1983).
43. Saunders, *Who Paid the Piper?*, 257–263.
44. Ibid., 252.
45. From an interview with art critic Emily Genauer in *Harper's Magazine*, cited in David Craven, *Abstract Expressionism as Cultural Critique* (Cambridge, 1999), 98. Excerpts from Dondero's Congressional speeches on modern art and communism are reproduced in Charles Harrison and Paul Wood, eds., *Art in Theory, 1900–1990* (Oxford and Cambridge, Mass., 1992), 654–658.
46. Craven, *Abstract Expressionism as Cultural Critique*, 79–104.
47. Jonathan Harris, "Modernism and Culture in the USA, 1930–1960," in *Modernism in Dispute*, by Jonathan Harris et al. (New Haven and London, 1993), 3–76, here 13–14, 38.
48. Ibid., 65. Compare to Guilbaut, *How New York Stole the Idea of Modern Art*, 196–198, and Nancy Jachec, *The Philosophy and Politics of Abstract Expressionism, 1940–1960* (Cambridge, 2000), 2–9.
49. D'Harnoncourt in Harris, "Modernism and Culture," 57; Barr in his article "Is Modern Art Communistic?" *New York Times Magazine* (14 December 1952), cited from Caute, *The Dancer Defects*, 549.
50. Sigrid Ruby, *Have we an American Art?* (Bonn, 1999); Jachec, *The Philosophy and Politics of Abstract Expressionism*, passim; Michael Krenn, *Fall-Out Shelters for the Human Spirit* (Chapel Hill, 2005).
51. See for instance Ralph Willett, *The Americanization of Germany, 1945–1949* (London, 1989); Kaspar Maase, *Bravo Amerika* (Hamburg, 1992); Anselm Doering-Manteuffel, *Wie westlich sind die Deutschen?* (Göttingen, 1999); Uta G. Poiger, *Jazz, Rock, and Rebels* (Berkeley, 2000).
52. Susan Buck-Morss, *Dreamworld and Catastrophe* (Cambridge, Mass., 2000), 5.

Bibliography

Barron, Stephanie, ed. *"Degenerate Art:" The Fate of the Avant Garde in Nazi Germany* Los Angeles: Los Angeles County Museum of Art, 1991.

Barron, Stephanie, and Sabine Eckmann, eds. *Art of Two Germanys: Cold War Cultures*. New York and Los Angeles: Abrams, 2009.

Bown, Matthew Cullerne. *Socialist Realist Painting*. New Haven: Yale University Press, 1998.

Buck-Morss, Susan. *Dreamworld and Catastrophe: The Passing of Mass Utopia in East and West*. Cambridge, Mass.: MIT Press, 2000.

Caute, David. *The Dancer Defects: The Struggle for Cultural Supremacy during the Cold War*. Oxford: Oxford University Press, 2003.

Cockcroft, Eva. "Abstract Expressionism: Weapon of the Cold War." *Artforum* 12 (1974), no. 10: 39–41.

Craven, David. *Abstract Expressionism as Cultural Critique: Dissent During the McCarthy Period*. Cambridge: Cambridge University Press, 1999.

Damus, Martin. *Malerei der DDR: Funktionen der Kunst im Realen Sozialismus*. Reinbek bei Hamburg: Rowohlt, 1991.

———. *Kunst in der BRD 1945–1990: Funktionen der Kunst in einer demokratisch verfaßten Gesellschaft*. Reinbek bei Hamburg: Rowohlt, 1995.

Doering-Manteufel, Anselm. *Wie westlich sind die Deutschen? Amerikanisierung und Westernisierung im 20. Jahrhundert*. Göttingen: Vandenhoeck & Ruprecht, 1999.

Glaser, Hermann. *Deutsche Kultur: Ein historischer Überblick von 1945 bis zur Gegenwart*. Bonn: Bundeszentrale für Politische Bildung, 1997.

Görtemaker, Manfred. *Geschichte der Bundesrepublik Deutschland: Von der Gründung bis zur Gegenwart*. Munich: Beck, 1999.

Grohmann, Will, ed. *Neue Kunst nach 1945: Malerei*. Cologne: Dumont Schauberg, 1958.

Grohs, Gerhard. "Zur Soziologie der bildenden Künste in der Bundesrepublik." In *Die Gesellschaft in der Bundesrepublik: Analysen II*, ed. Hans Steffen (Göttingen: Vandenhoeck & Ruprecht, 1971), 43–63.

Guilbaut, Serge. *How New York Stole the Idea of Modern Art: Abstract Expressionism, Freedom, and the Cold War*. Chicago and London: University of Chicago Press, 1983.

Harris, Jonathan. "Modernism and Culture in the USA, 1930–1960," in *Modernism in Dispute: Art since the Forties*, by Jonathan Harris, Francis Frascina, Dr. Charles Harrison, and Paul Wood (New Haven and London: Yale University Press, 1993), 3–76.

Harrison, Charles, and Paul Wood, eds. *Art in Theory, 1900–1990: An Anthology of Changing Ideas*. Oxford and Cambridge, Mass.: Blackwell, 1992.

Held, Jutta. *Kunst und Kunstpolitik 1945–1949: Kulturaufbau in Deutschland nach dem Zweiten Weltkrieg*. Berlin: Elefanten Press, 1981.

Hofmann, Werner. *Zeichen und Gestalt: Die Malerei des 20. Jahrhunderts*. Frankfurt am Main: Fischer, 1957.

Jachec, Nancy. *The Philosophy and Politics of Abstract Expressionism, 1940–1960*. Cambridge: Cambridge University Press, 2000.

Kozloff, Max. "American Painting during the Cold War." *Artforum* 11 (1973), no. 9: 43–54.

Krenn, Michael. *Fall-Out Shelters for the Human Spirit: American Art and the Cold War*. Chapel Hill: University of North Carolina Press, 2005.

Lindner, Bernd. *Verstellter, offener Blick: Eine Rezeptionsgeschichte bildender Kunst im Osten Deutschlands, 1945–1995*. Cologne: Böhlau, 1998.

Maase, Kaspar. *Bravo Amerika: Erkundungen zur Jugendkultur der Bundesrepublik in den fünfziger Jahren*. Hamburg: Junius, 1992.

Mierendorff, Marta, and Heinrich Tost. *Einführung in die Kunstsoziologie*. Köln: Westdeutscher Verlag, 1957.

Poiger, Uta G. *Jazz, Rock, and Rebels: Cold War Politics and American Culture in a Divided Germany*. Berkeley and Los Angeles: University of California Press, 2000.

Roh, Franz. *Geschichte der deutschen Kunst von 1900 bis zur Gegenwart*. Munich: F. Bruckmann, 1958.

Ruby, Sigrid. *Have We an American Art? Präsentation und Rezeption amerikanischer Malerei in Westdeutschland und Westeuropa der Nachkriegszeit*. Weimar: VDG, 1999.

Scammel, Michael. "Art as Politics and Politics in Art." In *Nonconformist Art: The Soviet Experience 1956–1986*, ed. Alla Rosenfeld and Norton T. Dodge (New York: Thames and Hudson, 1995).

Sedlmayr, Hans. *Verlust der Mitte: Die bildende Kunst des 19. und 20. Jahrhunderts als Symptom und Symbol der Zeit*. Salzburg: O. Müller, 1948.

———. *Die Revolution der modernen Kunst*. Hamburg: Rowohlt, 1955.

Segal, Joes. *Krieg als Erlösung: Die deutschen Kunstdebatten 1910–1918.* Munich: scaneg, 1997.

Shapiro, David, and Cecile Shapiro, "Abstract Expressionism: The Politics of Apolitical Painting." *Prospect* 3 (1976): 175–214.

Stonor Saunders, Frances. *Who Paid the Piper? The CIA and the Cultural Cold War.* London: Granta Books, 1999.

Thomas, Karin. *Zweimal deutsche Kunst nach 1945: 40 Jahre Nähe und Ferne.* Cologne: DuMont, 1985.

Utley, Gertje R. *Picasso: The Communist Years.* New Haven: Yale University Press, 2000.

Washton Long, Rose-Carol, ed. *German Expressionism: Documents from the End of the Wilhelmine Empire to the Rise of National Socialism.* Berkeley, Calif. and London: University of California Press, 1993.

Willett, Ralph. *The Americanization of Germany, 1945–1949.* London: Routledge, 1989.

Chapter 12

WHAT DOES DEMOCRACY LOOK LIKE? (AND WHY WOULD ANYONE WANT TO BUY IT?)
Third World Demands and West German Responses at 1960s World Youth Festivals

Quinn Slobodian

In the plans of their Communist organizers, the World Youth Festivals of the 1960s were supposed to win the sympathies of young leaders from Asia, Africa, and Latin America, and serve as catalysts for a global Soviet-friendly youth movement. In reality, the festivals became occasions for heated, and even violent, debates between delegates from the three worlds about which model of democracy—liberal capitalist, state-Socialist, or a more radical alternative—was viable in a postcolonial world. This chapter follows the West German intervention in the three festivals of the decade, and shows how Third World demands challenged West Germans involved with cultural diplomacy and student activists to ask themselves how they could represent their version of democracy.[1] In the early years of the decade, West German cultural Cold Warriors seeking to infiltrate and subvert the Communist festivals found that their attack on Soviet-bloc imperialism, in the name of "freedom," had little effect on Third World delegates emerging, in most cases, from a recent history of Western colonialism and more drawn to the Soviet language of "equality." By the end of the decade, the West German New Left was looking to the Third World for political alternatives beyond a U.S.-bloc liberalism that sanctioned the Vietnam War. The "Maoism" of West German students at the 1968 Sofia festival appropriated and reworked a political idiom originating in the Third World to reveal the deficiencies of both Soviet and Western-bloc democracy.

Vienna 1959: Universal Problems

The seventh World Youth Festival in Vienna in 1959 was the first to be aimed primarily at the decolonizing world. Like those before it, the festival was a participatory pageant of sport, performance, and mass demonstration, allowing 18,000 young people from 112 countries to enact a ritual of Socialist togetherness under the motto of "Peace and Friendship."[2] The opening ceremony set the aesthetic tone: it began with a crowd of small children running into the stadium with bouquets, followed by seven gong clangs and one hundred flag-waving motorcyclists circling the track while the participants paraded in to the sounds of Wagner's "Tannhäuser."[3] In West Germany, the festival was an object of concern for the large and shifting network of academic experts, politicians, church leaders, and student activists engaged in the project of defending the West German image and containing Soviet, and especially East German, influence at home and abroad. Decolonization meant new challenges for cultural diplomats worried about "losing" postcolonial nations to the Communist bloc.[4] To anti-Communist cultural Cold Warriors, particularly officials from the Ministry of Family and Youth (*Bundesministerium für Familie und Jugend*), the Ministry for German Issues (*Bundesministerium für Gesamtdeutsche Fragen*) and experts on the Soviet bloc, the apparent success of the Vienna Festival in building global good will was alarming.[5]

West German cultural Cold Warriors were undecided on whether Soviet influence could be confronted on the "home territory" of the Communist-organized festivals. Albert Feller, associated with the *Bonner Büro Berichte*, a federal agency in charge of publishing information on the Soviet bloc, argued in a commercial metaphor that "one would not expect, for example, the owner of a department store to clear a floor so that the competition could display their offerings."[6] Hans-Wilhelm Tölke pointed out in response that the Soviet offer of a positive political vision to youth from developing nations left them no choice but to invade the "Soviet department store." At Vienna, the Soviets had "sold their 'progressive democracy' against our old 'backward democracy' [to delegates from developing nations]. This situation will naturally get immediately and inevitably worse for us if we … do not commit to our own attempt to sell. We could not and cannot afford to say, this market is too dirty (*dreckig*) for us!"⁷

Leadership in countering the World Youth Festivals came from the Ministry of Family and Youth (BMFa) as well as academics connected to the "political education" (*politische Bildung*) institutes that had been established with federal money after the war, to strengthen West German civic culture from backsliding into fascism, and more pointedly against the threat of communism from the East. Heinz Asendorf, the leader of one of these institutes—the *Gesamteuropäische Studienwerk e.V.* (GESW), founded in 1954—and author of books on Soviet education and public-opinion methods, worried that youth from "Afro-Asian developing countries" had left the festival with a "global feeling" (*Weltgefühl*) of being "people in a world of peace and friendship."⁸ Sociologist Walter Hildebrandt, another board member of the GESW and author of books on Soviet communism, agreed that the Soviets seemed to be monopolizing the universal notion of "the world." This "one world," he said, "is certainly no communist invention, but we cannot ignore the fact that the Soviets are profiting from it."⁹

The attempt by 120 West German anti-Communist students within the umbrella student organization *Verband deutscher Studentenschaften* (VDS) to subvert the festival's intentions by staging an "anti-festival" in collaboration with Austrian students and the BMFa in Vienna had been deemed a failure. The anti-festival, funded with over 100,000 DM by the West German state, and consisting of information booths, film screenings, and the distribution of literature, had articulated no positive visions of Western democracy.¹⁰ To extend Feller's metaphor, they tried to sell West German democracy by defaming the competition. Festival participants passing anti-festival booths were confronted with questions that slandered Soviet communism through comparisons to fascism:

> Why does the party control all areas of life? Does it mistrust its adherents? Or is the character of its members and followers so inferior that they require constant surveillance as in fascism? … Why is there so much forced labor in the USSR? Why not still concentration camps? (sic) … Why does communism demand that one has to *hate* the "capitalists"? … Why are mothers from the so-called GDR not allowed to visit their children in the Federal Republic when they are sick?¹¹

Ranging from mockery to specious historical analogy to pathos, the questions of the West Germans sparked little interest in festival participants.

Attempts by West German students to denounce Soviet "imperialism" were equally unsuccessful, and easily turned around as critiques of Western imperialism. As one member of the VDS anti-festival asked in retrospect about African and Asian delegates: "Did anyone seriously believe in light of their historical experience that the tragic fate of Tibet and Hungary could touch them as deeply as it does us? ... Their forefathers, and to a large extent they too, have had their experience with Western, not Soviet imperialism."[12] Fritz Cramer, an anti-festival organizer, reported hearing from individuals from developing countries that Western prosperity "came from colonialism" and the "robbery" (*Raub*) of raw materials that could have been used for domestic development.[13] Although Germany had lost its colonies after the First World War, delegates from developing countries insisted that West Germany was still "colonialist" because of its indirect financial support for continued imperial regimes through the European Economic Community.[14] Cramer pointed out that showcasing Western prosperity—as in the idea of labeling goods in Viennese shop windows with information on the relative buying power of workers' wages in Eastern and Western Europe—was counterproductive, because "the higher living standard of the West is not felt as an attraction, rather as 'inequality,' i.e., something negative ... arrived at through imperialism."[15] "Equality" and not "freedom," he observed, was the guiding "formula" of the festival.[16]

A telegram from the West German ambassador in Morocco confirmed official concerns about the festival's effects, reporting that Moroccan youth leaders returning from Vienna were giving presentations on their "admiration ... for the progress of the Soviet Union not only in terms of their prosperity but also their humanitarian spirit (*Geist der Humanität*)."[17] The 1959 festival and its aftermath suggested that the Soviet bloc was winning supporters worldwide by evoking a more equitable and humane form of democracy than that of Western capitalism.[18] The vocabulary of anti-communism used at home through the 1950s, which portrayed the "threat from the East" as non-Western, bellicose, and expansionist, would need revising to fit the demands of a postcolonial world that linked the West first with its own lived and national history of imperial exploitation. Implicitly conceding that their own imaginative capacity could not match the great "charismatic effect" (*Ausstrahlungskraft*)[19] of Soviet rhetoric, West Germans focused on the demand for financial aid, concluding, as Cramer had, that "industrialization through Western capital" was the "only way" to defend developing countries against communism.[20] In the years of the early 1960s, as West Germans were simultaneously pushed by American pressure and pulled by Third World demands into large-scale foreign aid financing, appeals to abstract freedom receded in favor of the rhetoric of economic modernization.[21]

Helsinki 1962: West Germany Itself as a Symbol of Capitalist Democracy

Development lending did not end official attempts to represent West German democracy symbolically. Cultural Cold Warriors judged the invitation of Third World delegates back to West Germany as one of the few bright spots of the Vienna anti-festival, a tactic that allowed capitalist democracy, in effect, to act as a symbol of itself.[22] The cities, factories, and people of West Germany were to be themselves convincing evidence of the superiority of the Western worldview. One hundred festival participants accepted invitations in Vienna, primarily delegates from Tunisia, Morocco, and Algeria.[23] West German "anti-festival" measures at the 1962 Helsinki festival (see Illustration 12.1) concentrated solely on convincing over four hundred young people, mostly from North Africa, West Africa, and South Asia, to spend between one and three weeks in West Germany.[24]

Illustration 12.1. Helsinki World Youth Festival of 1962, promotional brochure. International Preparatory Committee of the VIIIth World Festival of Youth and Students for Peace and Friendship, Helmut Rödl.

(International Union of Socialist Youth [IUSY] section of the APO Archive, Freie Universität Berlin. Every effort has been made to trace the copyright holder and to obtain permission for this image.)

A typical tour for Third World youth leaders began by meeting members of the youth wing of one of the political parties (tailored to the politics of the delegation), followed by a factory visit to an automobile manufacturer, a presentation on the economic structure of West Germany, a meeting with the board of the transport union, and concluding with another factory visit.[25] The itinerary wove together party, industry, and union in a way that illustrated the form of democracy around which Social Democrats, Christian Democrats, and Free Democrats had united, one in which the relationship between state, union, and capital was harmonious and voluntary.[26] The freely chosen cooperative relationship between labor and industry was presented as a countermodel to the fusion of Party and union in the Soviet Communist system. West German social democratic and trade union delegations overseas carried a similar message, urging the dissolution of bonds between specific political parties and unions and arguing for the independence of labor as a central element of the West German state form.[27]

At times, attempts to woo festival participants literally looked like seductions. One proposal for a "counter-festival" by a West German student group suggested a small industrial exhibition showing off West German products with "no talk of politics."[28] "Good-looking and charming hostesses" would provide "consultation" (their quotation marks) and hand out free airplane tickets to West Germany.[29] Though the deployment of attractive women "would not convert any hard-boiled communists," the proposal went on with a wink, "it has happened before."[30] The literature and publicity material of Communist festival organizers used prominent displays of femininity in their own cause as well. "Miss Festival" beauty pageants were highlighted events, and festival publications consistently featured large images of women, usually from Asia, in traditional costume.[31] The only image on the pamphlet advertising the 1965 Algiers Festival (canceled after the overthrow of Ben Bella) was a large close-up of a made-up young Arab woman in fashionable headscarf (more Hepburn than *hijab*), pearl necklace, and a flower in her hair (see Illustration 12.2).[32] This image could be read alternately as a sign of confident, emancipated modernity or as the most recent use of the exoticized non-Western body to stimulate in the Western viewer the prospect of a rarified form of sexual encounter, this time at an international Socialist youth gathering.

In the first half of the 1960s, festival seductions were running into everyday realities. Nigerian student Theophilus Okonkwo, one of the first students at the Patrice Lumumba University in Moscow, withdrew from the Helsinki festival, complaining of the inconsistency between the Soviet lionization of Africans as symbols and their daily mistreatment.[33]

Illustration 12.2. Algiers World Youth Festival (planned for 1965, not realized), promotional brochure. Arbeitskreis Festival 65, F. Werkmeister.
(International Union of Socialist Youth [IUSY] section of the APO Archive, Freie Universität Berlin. Every effort has been made to trace the copyright holder and to obtain permission for this image.)

Okonkwo mentioned a photograph of him sparring in a Moscow gym that had been transformed, without his consent, into a photomontage for a Soviet political poster, depicting him as a slave breaking out of chains to attack a white slave-master.[34] A large non-Communist delegation from Ceylon also left the festival early in protest of their marginalization.[35] West German officials noted that Third World delegates were "significantly more self-confident" in Helsinki, and were often making their dissatisfaction heard about the "one-sidedness of the festival and the manipulation of many discussions."[36] In 1962, embassies in Moscow reported that the number of students from Lumumba University applying for scholarships in the Western bloc was continually growing, with foreign students complaining about racially motivated attacks, the prohibition of relationships with Russian women, and the "disgusting conditions of life in the USSR."[37]

The New Left Turns to the Third World

The disenchantment was not only with the Soviets. To critical observers, the events of the early 1960s provided ample grounds for skepticism about the benevolent intentions of Western-bloc foreign policy. Armed interventions in the Congo, Algeria, and the Dominican Republic, and the continued support of repressive regimes through foreign aid fed growing criticism in left-leaning circles worldwide. By the middle of the decade, public discussion of Africa, Asia, and Latin America in West Germany had spread from specialized circles of state and civil society and the pages of newsweeklies into the fora of the emerging student movement.

In their discussions and activism, the New Left adopted the term "Third World." As West German–based Iranian intellectual Bahman Nirumand pointed out, "Third World" had the advantage of being expressly political, rather than the imperial terms still common in West Germany at the time, which described nations in terms of their economic utility to the metropole ("coffee countries," "cotton countries") or in terms of their backwardness relative to the West ("developing countries").[38] Between Helsinki in 1962 and the next World Youth Festival in Sofia in 1968, the political Third World would become a reservoir of alternatives for many West Germans, driven by the Vietnam War and domestic repression to search beyond Western-bloc liberalism and Soviet "bureaucratic socialism."

Of the institutions mediating the relationship between West Germany and the Third World, the first to be attacked was foreign aid. Criticism of Western development policy was heard first and loudest from African,

Asian, and Latin American students, who by 1962 had arrived at universities all over West Germany and West Berlin in large enough numbers for one observer to call it an "invasion."[39] The number of students from the Third World had tripled between 1957 and 1960, rising from 3,053 to 9,282, and peaking at 11,460 students in 1962.[40] The leftist critique heard from many foreign students was that development aid was unable to fill its original promises and was being used strategically to enrich a comprador class of Third World elites. In 1965, Johannes Glathe, rector of Justus Liebig University in Gießen, appealed directly to the Ministry of the Interior about a Nigerian student's presentation, complaining that the Third World students' political opinions on foreign aid contradicted the official West German position.[41]

The Third World critique of development aid expanded within emerging New Left circles in the mid 1960s. Exposing development aid as an "instrument of imperialism and neocolonialism" was one of the four focal points of the work of the leading student organization SDS (*Sozialistischer Deutscher Studentenbund*) in West Berlin in the summer semester of 1964.[42] In 1967, Nirumand published a book under the ironic title *Persia, a Model Developing Country*, which would enter its fifth printing within months of its release and ultimately sell over 100,000 copies.[43] In his book, Nirumand described the situation in a "modernizing" Iran: "Every Cadillac sits next to a broken-down donkey cart, every villa next to dozens of mud huts, and in Hilton hotels and nightclubs, people enjoy themselves on carpets woven by children working fourteen-hour days."[44] Nirumand condemned Western development aid and investment for having only helped exaggerate and give new form to local class differences, without addressing basic structural inequalities and injustices.

Local critiques from Third World students and intellectuals in West Germany aligned with the "Chinese standpoint" that entered New Left conversations in the mid 1960s. The Chinese Communist Party's official analysis posited a shift in the global order, so that the most significant division was no longer East-West but North-South, between the industrialized and the nonindustrialized countries. Nirumand himself wrote that the Third World as a bloc only took on substance with the Sino-Soviet split in 1962–63, "the reaction to which was the rich nations of all ideologies and shades forming a common front against the poor."[45] Rudi Dutschke, SDS leader and influential opinion-maker within the New Left, was already publishing articles on the Chinese position in 1964, having heard about it through the writings of the American economist Paul A. Sweezy, likely in the pages of the *Monthly Review*.[46] Author Hans Magnus Enzensberger also took the Chinese position and argued it in the pages of the widely read journal *Kursbuch*.[47]

New Left thought incorporated Third World critiques of development into a larger, overarching critical philosophy that saw consumerism, technocracy, and imperialism as a bundled whole, simultaneously sating and sedating complacent Western populations while driving Third World populations into ever more abject positions of violent oppression.[48] To the New Left, the most telling evidence of this dynamic was the Vietnam War. By 1968, many saw the war not as a distortion of the capitalist world system but as the truth of it. To a speaker at the 1968 Vietnam Congress in West Berlin, the war had displaced liberal capitalist democracy as a viable reference point for politics:

> If it's true that the United States of North America are in the process of exterminating a people, if it's true that American pilots are daily, hourly roasting children, dismembering the sick, women, and old men, if it's true that the Americans are gassing Vietnamese farmers and poisoning them with chemicals, and if it's true that they are pushing prisoners from flying helicopters and if it's furthermore true that the Federal Republic of Germany and their Senate and the delegates in Bonn and West Berlin are supporting this gigantic slaughter, then it has to finally be said: we are not governed by idiots, we are governed by criminals.[49]

The war, in the words of one former activist, "consigned the 'free West's' entire arsenal of ideological legitimation to the dustbin of history."[50] A former SDS member and sociologist remembers the war as "inverting the preexisting 'coordinate system' of political understanding."[51] The gap between liberal norm and the reality represented by the war led many, including former reformists, to search for radical alternatives. Critiques of parliamentary democracy, circulating for years, began to take on more urgency and the search for options beyond mainstream Western-bloc democracy became more pressing.

The turn of West German students to the Third World is routinely dismissed by historians as "naïve" and as "romanticized sympathy" for liberation movements, and is rarely seen as productive.[52] Yet the rejection of liberal democracy and attraction to the Third World was not an entirely destructive move. Widespread revulsion for a form of democracy that could sanction mass murder in Vietnam also threw the question of *democracy* open to redefinition. As sociologist Oskar Negt, Jürgen Habermas's assistant at Frankfurt University in the 1960s, argues, what was "new" in the New Left was the reclaiming of the concept of democracy from political party-style representation and refilling it with the historical tradition of direct democracy.[53] Rejecting a West German present in which former National Socialists still held leading positions in state and industry, students looked to the pre-Nazi German past and the Third World present, giving attention to strains of heterodox Weimar radicalism, in particular the communist councils (*Räte*) that emerged after the First World War, along with the Chinese Cultural Revolution, which they saw as a contemporary site of radical democracy in action.[54]

From 1967 on, enthusiasm for Mao was evident everywhere in West Germany. Images of the Chinese leader were ubiquitous at protest events, where students bought Chinese-published newspapers and viewed Chinese-produced films.[55] In 1967, students from the Stuttgart art school marched through the streets with a ten-foot-high portrait of Mao, reciting passages from Mao's book, and handed out flyers announcing the necessity of a cultural revolution in Baden-Württemberg.[56] In 1969, a group of former SDS activists in Munich self-consciously referred to Mao's lesson of "encircling the city from the countryside," mapping out youth detention centers, discotheques, and other gathering places in the Bavarian countryside as likely sites for recruiting cadres.[57] Members of a West Berlin commune decorated their Christmas tree in 1969 with forty "Mao Bibles" to "document the particularity of our position, also to Christmas."[58]

Though the omnipresence of Mao on the West German New Left is often remarked on, usually by former activists ruing their naiveté, no one has yet ventured an explanation of *how* Mao was being used in West Germany.[59] Kristin Ross argues that in France, Maoism was used as a means of rediscovering the "French utopian tradition" of socialism and mass organization.[60] Philosopher Alain Badiou, himself a Maoist for many years, sees the ethics of French Maoism as having been informed by a perceived fidelity to the Cultural Revolution. The fact that their version of the event never actually existed does not, in his analysis, diminish its productivity for their own ethics and politics.[61] I would argue that a comparable phenomenon took place on the West German New Left. Fidelity to an imaginary Chinese Cultural Revolution led to a rediscovery not of utopian socialism, but of forms of radical democratic practice that undermined what the New Left saw as the ossified consensus-obsessed form of politics practiced in the postwar state. "West German Maoism," which would be a central feature of the West German presence at Sofia in 1968, dictated a form of anti-authoritarian practice that privileged constant discussion and the inclusion of minority views, and proscribed arbitrary closure, hierarchy, and "bureaucratic" procedure.

Sofia 1968: West German Maoism in Practice

The Sofia World Youth Festival in 1968 was perhaps the only chance that the West German Maoists of the New Left had to put their ideas into practice in an international context, with extensive contact with members of the Third World. By late 1968, West Germans active on the New Left had begun to gravitate around one of two poles: "traditionalism," with its orientation toward the Soviet Union, and "anti-authoritarianism," which combined a reception of revolutionary ideas from the Third World with diverse strains of European radical thought, including Reichian psychoanalysis, anarchism, and Situationism.[62] The anti-authoritarian faction included most of the SDS and the liberal and social democratic youth groups as well as the umbrella student group.[63] The anti-authoritarian Maoists' express aim at the Sofia festival was to "break open" the "front" created between Party and youth leaders from the Soviet bloc and to "make the general line the object of discussion."[64] As they saw it, "a festival like this must contain critique and self-critique, information and argumentation, as well as make possible discussion on strategy and tactics against imperialism at a national as well as international level."[65]

The anti-authoritarian majority did not include everyone in the West German delegation. The diversity of the five hundred–person group became visible and audible in the opening ceremonies, as the anti-authoritarians greeted the Soviet delegation by shouting "Mao!" and carried portraits of the Chinese leader they had secured from the Chinese embassy the day before, the Soviet party-line "traditionalists" shouted "Lenin!" and the moderates, including Christian Democrats, were the only ones to applaud the Czechoslovak delegation as they came in carrying pictures of Alexander Dubček, the reformist leader of Prague Spring whom Soviet tanks would remove from power later that month.[66] There was no official counterstrategy on the part of the West German state at the festival. As a confidential report to the Ministry of Family and Youth suggests, this may have been because "the world Communist movement has changed in an extremely dramatic fashion in the last six years."[67] The apparently united front that the Soviets were building at the beginning of the decade, with China and Cuba as their primary partners, had all but dissolved, with neither country in attendance at the festival; the former increasingly estranged from the Soviets since 1963 and the latter having withdrawn when the organizers refused to add "revolutionary action" to the official slogan of "For Solidarity, Peace, and Friendship."[68] The anti-authoritarians saw themselves, in effect, as both stand-ins and ambassadors for the excluded Third World elements, visiting both the Chinese and Cuban embassies and demonstratively chanting "Castro-Mao-Guevara!" at the closing ceremonies.[69]

Beyond vocal provocation at the mass events, the anti-authoritarians worked to support minority delegations at the festival who were critical of the Soviet "general line." Students observed that "revolutionary

Third World organizations" at the festival had been replaced by "revisionist CP-loyal" organizations or delegations put together from students at the Lumumba University.[70] Anti-authoritarians sought to create connections and give voice to delegations that deviated from the Soviet Communist Party line. They convinced the group from Okinawa to leave the orthodox line of the Japanese delegation and take part in an unregistered demonstration.[71] The Yugoslav and Czechoslovak delegates, also alienated from the Soviets for their intolerance toward reform, agreed to form a coalition with the anti-authoritarians.[72] The Czechoslovaks expressed their alliance at one of the festival's mass events with a chant of "Rudi Dutschke!"[73] Festival organizers had also attempted to replace the Confederation of Iranian Students (CISNU), a large exile group critical of both the U.S. and the Soviet Union and the "oldest sister organization" of the West German SDS, with a small group of pro-Soviet students.[74] When CISNU students marched with the West German SDS, they had the Iranian flag and their placard seized from them by Bulgarian secret police.[75] The West German delegation sat down on the street in protest, delaying the opening ceremonies for an hour with no result, and the Iranian students left the festival early.[76] West German students criticized the official exclusion of the exile student organization CISNU on leaflets and in teach-ins in the following days.[77]

Supporting marginalized delegations, West German anti-authoritarians sought to act on their intention "to lead a discussion of revolutionary strategies and tactics represented in Sofia by minority groups."[78] In the eyes of festival participants who followed the Soviet Party line, this strategy only served to dissolve the potential strength of a consistent bloc and "furnish the imperialists with gloating commentary on the festival."[79] The anti-authoritarians insisted in response that they *were* "interested in creating unity, but not an unreflected-on (*unreflektierte*) united front. This," they believed, "can be created first only on the basis of discussion."[80] Anti-authoritarian obsession with discussion was made concrete in a series of teach-ins in their section of the festival, which were "hardly attended by Soviet youth."[81] Some members of the West German group chanted the word itself "Discussion, discussion!" during long speeches in the seminars, and staged a "spontaneity test" in which several of them stood and vigorously applauded a "demonstrably unimportant" section of the speech.[82] "The room," they noted smugly, "rose to their feet" in imitation "and clapped frenetically."[83]

Asked by a Soviet student at Sofia what program his organization had, a West German anti-authoritarian replied that they had no program.[84] Their program, in their version of West German Maoism, was provocation; its strategy: "unmask bureaucracy and annihilate depoliticization."[85]

The West German Maoists' most visible provocation was an unregistered demonstration against the Vietnam War, in front of the American embassy. They announced the event on a smuggled-in banner at the opening ceremonies, and spent much effort in recruiting student groups to join them in an action that orthodox delegations saw as impugning their Bulgarian hosts and the Soviet Union.[86] At the demonstration, West German anti-authoritarians, led by Karl-Dietrich Wolff, physically clashed with orthodox party-line members of their own delegation who were working alongside Bulgarian secret police.[87] At what would be the last SDS delegates' conference in September 1968 in Frankfurt, five "traditionalists" were expelled from the organization for cooperating with Bulgarian secret police to repress the demonstration in Sofia.[88] Other students left the SDS with those expelled, founding the *Marxistischer Studentenbund Spartakus*, the first of many splinter groups that would contribute to the ultimate dissolution of the SDS, the central organization of the West German New Left, by spring of 1970.[89]

Conclusion

At the heart of the Cold War as a cultural conflict was an argument about what democracy was, and what it might look like. Both sides of the Cold War in Europe claimed to be the rightful heirs of the humanist democratic tradition, and both based their legitimacy on divergent interpretations of democracy. At the 1960s World Youth Festivals, actors from both sides were compelled to perform their version of democracy for an international audience and, in particular, for delegates from the Third World. The features that they emphasized were telling. In Vienna in 1959, West German cultural Cold Warriors compared the festival to a department store, and considered using consumer goods in shop windows to advertise their social model. They linked democracy to market freedom, against the principle of economic equality promoted by the Soviet bloc. West German attacks on Soviet imperialism backfired as Asian and African delegates reminded them of the ongoing history of Western European empire, and gravitated more toward the Soviets' unifying idea of "one world."

At Helsinki in 1962, West German cultural Cold Warriors retreated from moral language, focusing instead on inviting delegates to visit the Federal Republic. There they presented the factory, and the voluntary collaboration between trade union, political party, and industry, as the central fixtures of the West German social model. This was a vision of democracy as consensus, and in its emphasis on social peace and economic production, it resembled its East German counterpart more than organizers realized. West German cultural Cold Warriors downplayed the role of dissent and debate in democracy in the early 1960s, in favor of an emphasis on what Charles Maier has called the "politics of productivity."[90] Like the domestically produced consumer durables that entered the world market in this period, West German democracy was supposed to be the best because it was the most efficient.

In the course of the 1960s, the economistic definition of democracy came under attack from the West German New Left. New Leftists were outspoken critics of the European Cold War Culture that had emerged since the war. They felt that the bloc mentality had narrowed the space of political expression domestically, as expressed by the 1956 ban on the West German Communist Party. It had also carried friend-enemy distinctions over from wartime, sanctioning a continuation of National Socialist anti-communism and rejecting calls for the leveling of class distinctions. With the thaw of bloc tensions in the 1960s, they saw popular animus turning toward them, and claimed that student protesters had become a new, shared antagonist for West Germans, to "divert attention from internal problems and integrate the population."[91]

The most damning New Left charge against Cold War culture was its ability to justify the military actions of the U.S. in the Third World. Putting European Cold War culture in a global perspective, New Leftists saw the smoothly functioning West German factory as part of a complex that also produced suffering in Vietnam. For them, consensus was not a goal but a means of avoiding confrontation with the human consequences of what was called "defending the free world." By 1968, most New Leftists believed that direct action was the most defensible way to dismantle the Cold War culture of rigidity and conformism they saw on both sides of the continent's Iron Curtain. At Sofia, West German New Leftists all but abandoned economic questions and staged their version of democracy as a process of endless discussion, disobedience, and disruption.

The global perspective of the New Left, though frequently schematic and even distorted, illuminates gaps in the historiography of German Cold War Culture. Cultural histories of divided Germany have largely accepted the capitalist-Communist binary as given. They have also focused overwhelmingly on the encounter with the United States. Debates over how, when, and whether West Germany was "Americanized" dominated scholarship in the 1990s and early 2000s. This chapter adds to the work of a small group of scholars in contending that the emerging postcolonial and developing world was an important but often overlooked third term in the coalescence of a West German political culture, particularly in the 1960s.[92] The festivals were vulnerable moments of encounter for West

Germans. When they sought to represent their own political culture to individuals from the Third World, they found rebuke as often as they found admiration. Yet such encounters challenged insularities, both national and continental, and suggest that histories of European Cold War Cultures must not forget to look south.

Notes

1. Johannes Paulmann has emphasized the development of "self-understanding" that often accompanied projects of postwar German cultural diplomacy. See Johannes Paulmann, *Auswärtige Repräsentationen* (Cologne, 2005), 2.
2. Erwin Breßlein, *Druschba! Freundschaft?* (Frankfurt am Main, 1973), 109.
3. Klaus Holzmann, "Bericht über die VII. Weltfestspiele der Jugend und Studenten" an das BMFa, Bundesarchiv Koblenz (hereafter BA) B153/1928, 4.
4. For the more formal West German diplomatic efforts of the 1960s, see William Glenn Gray, *Germany's Cold War* (Chapel Hill, 2003). See also Young-Sun Hong, "Kalter Krieg in der Ferne," in *Umworbener Klassenfeind*, ed. Uta Balbier and Christiane Rösch (Berlin, 2006), 77–94, 77f.
5. Though the concern was not party-specific, the Social Democratic Party was worried enough that the entire leadership (*Vorstand*) met specially to discuss means of countering the festival's influence. Flor BMFa, Vermerk, Betr.: Weltjugendfestspiele, 2. Dez. 1959. BA/B153/1928.
6. "Es sei z.B. nicht zu erwarten, dass ein Kaufhausbesitzer der Konkurrenz eine Etage einräume, damit sie ihr Angebot in seinem Hause zeige." Albert Feiler, Büro Bonner Berichte, Rednerdienst, Betr.: Gespräch im Gesamteuropäischen Studienwerk e.V. in Vlotho am 30. Sept. 1959. 8 October 1959, BA/B153/1928, 8.
7. "[Sie] verkauften ihre 'fortschrittliche Demokratie' gegenüber unseren alten 'rückschrittlichen Demokratie.' ... Diese Situation verschlechterte sich natürlich sofort unabsehbar für uns, wenn ... wir kein Verkaufsengagement eingeht. Wir konnten und können es uns eben nicht leisten zu sagen: uns ist dieser Markt zu dreckig!" Tölke, in "Protokoll des Auswertungsgespräche über das Festival 1959 in Wien," BA/B153/1928, 7.
8. Asendorf in ibid., 2.
9. The English term "one world" was used in the original. Dr. Hildebrandt in ibid., 17.
10. Arbeitskreis '59, Formblatt an den BMFa and BMI. "Anlage zum Antrag vom 23. Mai 1959," 23 May 1959, BA/B153/1928; "Bericht über die Teilnahme einer Reisegruppe des VDS am Gästeprogramm der österreichischen Hochschülerschaft in der Zeit vom 26.7 bis 4.8.1959 in Wien," BA/B166/1304, 1, 6; "Bericht über die Tätigkeit und Erfahrungen während der 7. Weltjugendfestspiele in Wien. Gruppe 5," BA/B166/1304, 4.
11. "Warum kontrolliert die Partei alle Lebensgebiete? Mißtraut sie ihre Anhängern? Oder sind ihre Mitglieder und Anhänger charakterlich so minderwertig, daß sie ständig überwacht werden müssen wie im Faschismus? ... Warum gibt es in der UdSSR soviel Zwangsarbeit? Warum noch immer Konzentrationslager? ... Warum verlangt der Kommunismus, daß man die 'Kapitalisten' *hassen* muß? ... Warum dürfen Mütter

aus der sogenannten DDR ihre Kinder in der Bundesrepublik nicht besuchen, wenn sie krank sind?" Arbeitsgemeinschaft für gesellschaftspolitische Studien, Bonn, "Erster Bericht der internationalen Studiengruppe über die VII. Weltfestjugendspiele," 31 August 1959. Enclosure. BA/B153/1928, 2–3.

12. "Glaubte wirklich jemand im Ernst, daß angesichts ihrer eigenen historischen Erfahrungen sie das tragische Schicksal Tibets und Ungarns so tief berühren konnte, wie uns? Mit dem westlichen Imperialismus hatten ihre Vorfahren, haben zum großen Teil auch sie noch ihre Erfahrungen gemacht, nicht mit den sowjetischen." "Bericht über die Teilnahme einer Reisegruppe des VDS," 17.
13. Fritz Cramer comité international d'information et d'action sociale (CIAS)/Volksbund für Frieden und Freiheit an das BMFa, Betr.: Weltjugendfestspiele in Wien. 3 November 1959, BA/B153/1928, 1ff.
14. "Bericht über die Teilnahme einer Reisegruppe des VDS," 27.
15. Cramer, Betr.: Weltjugendfestspiele in Wien.
16. Ibid.
17. Bundesminister für Gesamtdeutsche Fragen an den BMFa Wuermeling, Betr.: VII. Weltjugendfestspiele, 30 October 1959, attached telegram from embassy in Rabat, 2.
18. Internationalist rhetoric was also backed up by over 12,000 positions at Soviet universities for students from developing countries by 1959, particularly in trade schools. Werner Richter DAAD an das Bundesministerium für Arbeit, Betr.: Vermittlung von Vorpraktikantenstellen für ausländische Studienanwärter, 27 January 1959. BA/B149/6307.
19. "Bericht über die Teilnahme einer Reisegruppe des VDS," 17.
20. Cramer, Betr.: Weltjugendfestspiele in Wien.
21. For U.S. pressure on West Germany to share its overseas financial commitments, see Heide-Irene Schmidt, "Pushed to the Front: The Foreign Assistance Policy of the Federal Republic of Germany, 1958–1971," *Contemporary European History* 12 (2003), no. 4: 473–507.
22. Referat J4 BMFa, Vermerk Draft, Betr.: Jugendfestspiele, 5 Jan 1962, BA/B153/1929, 1.
23. Flor J6, Vermerk, Betr.: Weltjugendfestspiele 1959 in Wien, 20 Aug 1959, BA/B153/1928, 18.
24. Günter Scheer, "Bericht über die VIII. Weltfestspiele der Jugend und Studenten für Frieden und Freundschaft Helsinki/Finnland 28. Juli bis 6. Aug. 1962," 31 August 1962. BA/B153/1930, 21.
25. Eva H.J. Walk Arbeitskreis 59 an Flor BMFa, 7 Juli 1959, Anlage, BA/B153/1928, 5.
26. On the crystallization of the front around "consensus capitalism," see Julia Angster, *Konsenskapitalismus und Sozialdemokratie* (Munich, 2003).
27. This was the primary message, for example, of the DGB delegation on their two-month trip through Southeast Asia in 1958. See "Trade Unionism and Politics Should Not Mix Says Visiting German Trade Union Leader," *Sunday Gazette* (Malaysia), 19 October 1958, Politisches Archiv des Auswärtigen Amts (hereafter PA-AA) B85/410.
28. "Jugendfestival in Algier." *Civis* 12 (December 1964): 4.
29. "Frieden und Freundschaft." *Civis* 11 (November 1964): 17.
30. Ibid., 17.
31. A journalist noted that the "beautiful" Chinese and Korean women in traditional costume were the only ones met with "spontaneous applause" on entering the stadium in Helsinki. Walter Günzel, "Spießrutenlaufen in Helsinki," *Die Welt*, 1 August 1962, 3.

32. Festival Algier brochure, Archiv "APO und soziale Bewegungen" (APO-Archiv) Freie Universität Berlin, Otto-Suhr-Institut für Politikwissenschaft (hereafter APO), "Festival Algier (1965)" folder.
33. Rolf Ekmanis, "Disenchantment in Helsinki," *Bulletin*, n.d, BA/B153/1930, 25.
34. Ibid.
35. Scheer, "Bericht," 17.
36. Walter Günzel, "Die ungebetenen Gäste wurden kühl empfangen," *Die Welt*, 30 Juli 1962, 3; Flor, Anlage 3 zum Protokoll der Sitzung des Aktionsausschusses für Jugendfragen vom 1. März 963, "Weltjugendfestspiele in Helsinki: Bericht und Folgerungen," BA/B153/1930, 8.
37. Jaguttis-Emden Botschaft der BRD Moskau an das AA, 1 Feb 1962, BA/B212/26881; A.R. Amar aus Uganda für den Exekutivausschuss der afrikanischen Studentenvereinigung in der UdSSR, "Offener Brief an alle afrikanischen Regierungen," 20 September 1960, BA/B212/26881, 4; Ali Mohamed El Wagie to the Cultural Attaché, German Embassy, Moscow, 26 November 62, BA/B212/26881; Mustafa Abdel Mageed to the Cultural Attaché, Embassy of Federal Republic, 1962, BA/B212/26881.
38. Bahman Nirumand, *Persien, Modell eines Entwicklungslandes oder Die Diktatur der freien Welt* (Reinbek, 1967), 9.
39. Karl Fritz Heise, "Politische Aktivitäten ausländischer Studenten innerhalb und außerhalb der Hochschule (1962)," in *30 Jahre Reintegrationsdiskussion an den deutschen Hochschulen*, ed. Afrikanisch-Asiatische Studentenförderung e.V. (Göttingen, 1998), 146–150, 146. On foreign students as catalysts for West German student protest see Quinn Slobodian, "Dissident Guests," in *Migration and Activism in Europe since 1945*, ed. Wendy Pojmann (New York, 2008), 33–56.
40. Dieter Bielenstein, VDS Pressereferat an den Abgeordneten des Deutschen Bundestages Herrn Dr. Fritz. Anlage. 26 April 1961, BA/B166/1172; "Das Ausländerstudium in der Bundesrepublik," Dokumentation III/63, *ew—Entwicklungsländer Informationen*, 24 May 1963, BA/B106/47386, 4f.
41. Glathe, Rektor der Justus Liebig Uni Gießen an das BMI, 4. Mai. 1965, PA-AA/B82/803, 1.
42. SDS Landesverband Berlin, "Arbeitskreis Programm Sommersemester 1964," APO/Urs Mueller-Plantenberg Privatarchiv/"SDS II Jan 1964—Dec 1964," Folder 1.
43. Bahman Nirumand, *Persien*. See also Bahman Nirumand, Hansi Scharbach, and Peter Schneider, "Ringvorlesung vom 15. Juni 1988," *Kalaschnikow* 8 (February 1997): 58–63, 58.
44. "Jedem Cadillac steht ein klapperiger Eselskarren gegenüber, jeder Villa Dutzende von Lehmhutten, und in den Hilton-Hotels und Amüsierlokalen erfreut man sich an Teppichen, die Kinder in vierzehnstündiger Arbeit pro Tag geknüpft haben." Nirumand, *Persien*, 11.
45. Ibid.
46. Rudi Dutschke, *Jeder hat sein Leben ganz zu leben* (Cologne, 2003), 20; Ingo Juchler, *Die Studentenbewegungen in den Vereinigten Staaten und der Bundesrepublik Deutschland der sechziger Jahre* (Berlin, 1996), 81f. Sweezy, cofounder and frequent contributor to the *Monthly Review*, wrote frequently on the Chinese position in the 1960s. Max Elbaum, *Revolution in the Air* (London, 2002), 60.
47. Rüdiger Sareika, *Die Dritte Welt in der westdeutschen Literatur der sechziger Jahre* (Frankfurt am Main, 1980), 29, 66.
48. On the connections made between consumerism and imperialism in the late 1960s, see Uta G. Poiger, "Imperialism and Consumption," in *Between Marx and Coca-Cola*, ed. Axel Schildt and Detlef Siegfried (New York, 2006), 582–623.

49. Raute at the Berlin Vietnam Congress, 1968, quoted in "Internationale Solidarität und intellektuelle Wünschlandschaft," in *Linksintellektueller Aufbruch zwischen "Kulturrevolution" und "kultureller Zerstörung,"* ed. Siegward Lönnendonker (Opladen, 1998), 235–251, 236.
50. Eckhard Siepmann, "Vietnam—der große Katalysator," in *CheSchahShit*, ed. E. Siepmann (Hamburg, 1984), 195–201, 195.
51. Ulf Kadritzke, "Produktive und unproduktive Illusionen in der Studentenbewegung," in *Radikalisierte Aufklärung*, ed. Heinz Bude and Martin Kohli (Weinheim, 1989), 239–282, 248.
52. Konrad Jarausch, *After Hitler* (New York, 2006), 65, 165.
53. Oskar Negt, *Achtundsechzig* (Göttingen, 1995), 141.
54. Ibid., 143f. For the complicated relationship between the New Left and former Weimar radicals see Claus-Dieter Krohn, "Die westdeutsche Studentenbewegung und das 'andere Deutschland,'" in *Dynamische Zeiten*, ed. Axel Schildt, Detlef Siegfried, and Karl Christian Lammers (Hamburg, 2000), 695–718.
55. The newspapers sold were received free from the Chinese embassy in East Berlin and smuggled out. A former salesman and member of Kommune I smirked that the tabloids "in this sense were a little bit right when they claimed that we were financed from Beijing." Dieter Kunzelmann, *Leisten Sie keinen Widerstand!* (Berlin, 1998), 55.
56. Detlef Michel, "Maos Sonne über Mönchengladbach," in *CheSchahShit*, ed. E. Siepmann, 251–260, 260.
57. Eckart Spoo, "'Die Städte von den Dörfern her einkreisen,'" *Frankfurter Rundschau*, 5 June 1969.
58. Karl Heinz Heinemann, "Lutz von Werder," in *Ein langer Marsch*, ed. Karl-Heinz Heinemann and Thomas Jaitner (Cologne, 1993), 11–28, 17.
59. Typical is Peter Schneider's self-description as one of the first "pedagogical victims" (*Lektüreopfer*) of Mao's Little Red Book and his subsequent painful realizations about the Cultural Revolution on visiting China. Nirumand, Scharbach, and Schneider, "Ringvorlesung," 60.
60. Kristin Ross, *May '68 and its Afterlives* (Chicago, 2002), 97.
61. Alain Badiou, *Ethics* (London, 2001), 42.
62. See Ingrid Gilcher-Holtey, "Kritische Theorie und Neue Linke," in *1968—Vom Ereignis zum Gegenstand der Geschichtswissenschaft*, ed. Ingrid Gilcher-Holtey (Göttingen, 1998), 168–187.
63. These groups were the Liberaler Studentenbund Deutschlands, the Sozialistischer Hochschulbund, and the VDS, respectively. Marianne Henkel, Vorsitz. des internationalen Ausschusses VDS, "Bericht über die Reise der VDS Delegation zu den 9. Weltjugendfestspiele in Sofia vom 27. Juli bis zum 8. Aug. 1968," BA/B166/1303, 1 (hereafter cited as "Henkel").
64. Reinhard Selka, Hochschulausschuss VDS, "Bericht über die Reise der VDS Delegation zu den 9. Weltjugendfestspiele in Sofia vom 27. Juli bis zum 8. Aug. 1968," 25 Sept 1968, BA/B166/1303, 2 (hereafter "Selka").
65. Günther Dengel, Vorsitzender des internationalen Ausschusses VDS, "Bericht über die Reise der VDS Delegation zu den 9. Weltjugendfestspielen in Sofia vom 27. Juli bis zum 8. Aug. 1968," BA/B166/1303, 13 (hereafter "Dengel").
66. Several students had been arrested for the visit to the Chinese embassy. Antiauthoritarians also visited the Cuban embassy during the festival. Dengel, 1, 3; Selka, 4.
67. "Der deutsche Bundesjugendring in Sofia/Vorläufiger Bericht," BA/B145/4003, 3.
68. Ibid., 4.
69. Dengel, 8.

70. Selka, 1.
71. Henkel, 5.
72. Ibid., 5.
73. Breßlein, *Drushba! Freundschaft?*, 148.
74. CISNU was critical of the Soviet Union for its economic support of the Shah. See Afshin Matin-Asgari, *Iranian Student Opposition to the Shah* (Costa Mesa, 2001), 99; Joscha Schmierer, "Der Zauber des großen Augenblicks," in *Die Früchte der Revolte*, ed. Lothar Baier et al. (Berlin, 1988), 107–126, 123; Dengel, 3.
75. Dengel, 3.
76. "Der deutsche Bundesjugendring in Sofia," 20; Breßlein, *Drushba! Freundschaft?*, 138.
77. Dengel, 8.
78. Henkel, 8.
79. Dengel, 9.
80. Henkel, 7.
81. "Der deutsche Bundesjugendring in Sofia," 30; Henkel, 13.
82. Dengel, 7.
83. Selka, 5.
84. Dengel, 12.
85. Johann-Wolfgang Landsberg an den VDS, "Bericht über die Reise der VDS Delegation zu den 9. Weltjugendfestspielen in Sofia vom 27. Juli bis zum 8. Aug. 1968," BA/B166/1303, 3.
86. Henkel, 7.
87. Breßlein, *Drushba! Freundschaft?*, 140; Dengel, 4.
88. Tilman Fichter and Siegward Lönnendonker, *Kleine Geschichte des SDS* (Berlin, 1977), 157.
89. Michael Schmidtke, *Der Aufbruch der jungen Intelligenz* (Frankfurt am Main, 2003), 276.
90. Charles S Maier, "The Politics of Productivity," in *The Cold War in Europe*, ed. Charles S. Maier (Princeton, 1991), 190–194.
91. Knut Nevermann, *Der 2. Juni 1967* (Cologne, 1967), 9.
92. For similar efforts see Hong, "Kalter Krieg in der Ferne." See also Jennifer Ruth Hosek, "'Subaltern Nationalism' and the West Berlin Anti-Authoritarians," *German Politics and Society* 26, no. 1 (Spring 2008): 57–81; Niels Seibert, *Vergessene Proteste* (Münster, 2008).

Bibliography

Angster, Julia. *Konsenskapitalismus und Sozialdemokratie: Die Westernisierung von SPD und DGB*. Munich: R. Oldenbourg Verlag, 2003.
Badiou, Alain. *Ethics: An Essay on the Understanding of Evil*. London: Verso, 2001.
Breßlein, Erwin. *Drushba! Freundschaft? Von der Kommunistischen Jugendinternationale zu den Weltjugendfestspielen*. Frankfurt am Main: Fischer, 1973.
Dutschke, Rudi. *Jeder hat sein Leben ganz zu leben: Die Tagebücher 1963–1979*. Cologne: Kiepenheuer & Witsch, 2003.
Elbaum, Max. *Revolution in the Air: Sixties Radicals Turn to Lenin, Mao and Che*. London: Verso, 2002.

Fichter, Tilman, and Siegward Lönnendonker. *Kleine Geschichte des SDS: Der Sozialistische Deutsche Studentenbund von 1946 bis zur Selbstauflösung.* Berlin: Rotbuch, 1977.
Gilcher-Holtey, Ingrid. "Kritische Theorie und Neue Linke." In *1968—Vom Ereignis zum Gegenstand der Geschichtswissenschaft,* ed. Ingrid Gilcher-Holtey (Göttingen: Vandenhoeck & Ruprecht, 1998), 168–187.
Gray, William Glenn. *Germany's Cold War: The Global Campaign to Isolate East Germany, 1949–1969.* Chapel Hill: University of North Carolina Press, 2003.
Günzel, Walter. "Die ungebetenen Gäste wurden kühl empfangen." *Die Welt,* 30 July 1962, 3.
———. "Spießrutenlaufen in Helsinki." *Die Welt,* 1 August 1962, 3.
Heinemann, Karl Heinz. "Lutz von Werder: Die Auseinandersetzung mit der Realität hat einem die Scheuklappen beseitigt." In *Ein langer Marsch: '68 und die Folgen,* ed. Karl-Heinz Heinemann and Thomas Jaitner (Cologne: PapyRossa, 1993), 11–28.
Heise, Karl Fritz. "Politische Aktivitäten ausländischer Studenten innerhalb und außerhalb der Hochschule (1962)." In *30 Jahre Reintegrationsdiskussion an den deutschen Hochschulen,* ed. Afrikanisch-Asiatische Studentenförderung e.V. (Göttingen: IKO-Verlag, 1998), 146–150.
Hong, Young-Sun. "Kalter Krieg in der Ferne: Dekolonisierung, Hygienediskurse und der Kampf der DDR und der USA um die Dritte Welt." In *Umworbener Klassenfeind: Das Verhältnis der DDR zu den USA,* ed. Uta Balbier and Christiane Rösch (Berlin: Links Verlag, 2006), 77–94.
Hosek, Jennifer Ruth. "'Subaltern Nationalism' and the West Berlin Anti-Authoritarians." *German Politics and Society* 26, no. 1 (Spring 2008): 57–81.
Jarausch, Konrad. *After Hitler: Recivilizing Germans, 1945–1995.* New York: Oxford University Press, 2006.
Juchler, Ingo. *Die Studentenbewegungen in den Vereinigten Staaten und der Bundesrepublik Deutschland der sechziger Jahre: Eine Untersuchung hinsichtlich ihrer Beeinflussung durch Befreiungsbewegungen und -theorien aus der Dritten Welt* (Berlin: Duncker & Humblot, 1996)
Kadritzke, Ulf. "Produktive und unproduktive Illusionen in der Studentenbewegung." In *Radikalisierte Aufklärung: Studentenbewegung und Soziologie in Berlin 1965 bis 1970,* ed. Heinz Bude and Martin Kohli (Weinheim: Juventa Verlag, 1989), 239–282.
Krohn, Claus-Dieter. "Die westdeutsche Studentenbewegung und das 'andere Deutschland.'" In *Dynamische Zeiten: Die 60er Jahre in den beiden deutschen Gesellschaften,* ed. Axel Schildt, Detlef Siegfried, and Karl Christian Lammers (Hamburg: Christians, 2000), 695–718.
Kunzelmann, Dieter. *Leisten Sie keinen Widerstand! Bilder aus meinem Leben.* Berlin: Transit, 1998.
Lönnendonker, Siegward, ed. *Linksintellektueller Aufbruch zwischen "Kulturrevolution" und "kultureller Zerstörung": Der Sozialistische Deutsche Studentenbund (SDS) in der Nachkriegsgeschichte (1946–1969).* Opladen: Westdeutscher Verlag, 1998.
Maier, Charles S. "The Politics of Productivity: Foundations of American International Economic Policy after World War II." In *The Cold War in Europe: Era of a Divided Continent,* ed. Charles S. Maier (Princeton, N.J.: Markus Wiener, 1991), 169–194.
Matin-Asgari, Afshin. *Iranian Student Opposition to the Shah.* Costa Mesa, Calif.: Mazda, 2001.
Michel, Detlef. "Maos Sonne über Mönchengladbach: Die Sehnsucht der Intellektuellen nach dem Einfachen." In *CheSchahShit: Die sechziger Jahre zwischen Cocktail und Molotow,* ed. Eckhard Siepmann et al. (Hamburg: Rowohlt, 1984), 251–260.

Negt, Oskar. *Achtundsechzig: Politische Intellektuelle und die Macht.* Göttingen: Steidl Verlag, 1995.
Nevermann, Knut. *Der 2. Juni 1967: Studenten zwischen Notstand und Demokratie: Dokumente zu den Ereignissen anläßlich des Schah-Besuchs.* Cologne: Pahl-Rugenstein, 1967.
Nirumand, Bahman. *Persien, Modell eines Entwicklungslandes oder Die Diktatur der freien Welt.* Reinbek: Rowohlt, 1967.
Nirumand, Bahman, Hansi Scharbach, and Peter Schneider. "Ringvorlesung vom 15. Juni 1988: Internationalismus als Realitätsflucht." *Kalaschnikow* 8 (1997): 58–63.
Paulmann, Johannes. *Auswärtige Repräsentationen: Deutsche Kulturdiplomatie nach 1945.* Cologne: Böhlau, 2005.
Poiger, Uta G. "Imperialism and Consumption: Two Tropes in West German Radicalism." In *Between Marx and Coca-Cola: Youth Cultures in Changing European Societies, 1960–1980,* ed. Axel Schildt and Detlef Siegfried (New York: Berghahn, 2006), 582–623.
Ross, Kristin. *May '68 and its Afterlives.* Chicago: University of Chicago Press, 2002.
Sareika, Rüdiger. *Die Dritte Welt in der westdeutschen Literatur der sechziger Jahre.* Frankfurt am Main: R.G. Fischer Verlag, 1980.
Schmidt, Heide-Irene. "Pushed to the Front: The Foreign Assistance Policy of the Federal Republic of Germany, 1958–1971." *Contemporary European History* 12 (2003), no. 4: 473–507.
Schmidtke, Michael. *Der Aufbruch der jungen Intelligenz: Die 68er Jahre in der Bundesrepublik und den USA.* Frankfurt am Main: Campus, 2003.
Schmierer, Joscha. "Der Zauber des großen Augenblicks: Der internationale Traum von '68." In *Die Früchte der Revolte: Über die Veränderung der politischen Kultur durch die Studentenbewegung,* ed. Lothar Baier et al. (Berlin: Verlag Klaus Wagenbach, 1988), 107–126.
Seibert, Niels. *Vergessene Proteste: Internationalismus und Antirassismus 1964–1983.* Münster: Unrast Verlag, 2008.
Siepmann, Eckhard, ed. *CheSchahShit: Die sechziger Jahre zwischen Cocktail und Molotow.* Hamburg: Rowohlt, 1984.
Slobodian, Quinn. "Dissident Guests: Afro-Asian Students and Transnational Activism in the West German Protest Movement." In *Migration and Activism in Europe Since 1945,* ed. Wendy Pojmann (New York: Palgrave, 2008), 33–56.

Chapter 13

DRAWING THE EAST-WEST BORDER
Narratives of Modernity and Identity
in the Northeastern Adriatic (1947–1954)

Sabina Mihelj

The northeastern Adriatic[1] has long functioned as an integral part of the symbolic fracture cutting through the European continent, dividing it, in the eyes of Western Europeans, into its civilized Western and underdeveloped Eastern or Balkan parts. The main contours and early history of the fracture, first formed in the period of the Enlightenment, have by now received considerable attention. Often inspired by Edward Said's influential study of the Western perceptions of the Orient,[2] historians, anthropologists, and political scientists have produced a number of detailed studies exploring the historical formation and varied uses of Western imagery of the Balkans and Eastern Europe in the late nineteenth and early twentieth centuries, pointing to its links with racism and nationalism as well as its affinities with established power relations.[3] More recently, these studies are being complemented by examinations of symbolic mappings of Europe in regions stigmatized as Eastern or Balkan, whose inhabitants often react to the stigma by pushing the symbolic boundary of the West further East, or by producing equally distorting images of the West.[4]

We know relatively little, however, about exactly what happened with these mutual misperceptions during the Cold War period. On the surface, the answer seems straightforward: in the eyes of its inhabitants, the European continent continued to be divided into its Western and Eastern parts, but the differences between the two were no longer seen as a matter of race, nation, culture, or civilization. Instead, the roots of the division were thought to lie in ideology, politics, and economy: the democratic, liberal West was now facing the Communist, totalitarian East. Yet as this chapter aims to demonstrate, this answer is at best partial, if not misleading: it neglects the persistence of older mental mappings, and tells us nothing about the competing images of Europe formed on different sides of the Iron Curtain.

The lack of literature addressing the symbolic mappings of Europe after World War II is no coincidence. This blind spot is part and parcel of two closely related tendencies that long dominated the study of the Cold War: the tendency to avoid the discussion of culture, and the associated assumption that during the Cold War ethnicity, nationality, and race were trumped by ideology, international politics, or class. Over the past two decades, both tendencies have been challenged and in part overturned, though predominantly in studies looking at the U.S. The rapid increase in the volume of books and articles dealing with various aspects of Cold War Culture has prompted one author to talk of a "cultural turn" in Cold War studies.[5] The number of works exploring the intricate relationships between Cold War, ethnic conflict, nationalism, and racism is increasing as well,[6] and so is the range of books exploring the possibilities of applying the concept of Orientalism to various aspects of American Cold War Culture.[7] This chapter aims to add to this body of work by looking at Cold War identity constructions in the northeastern Adriatic. Having functioned as one of the epicenters of East-West confrontations in the early post–World War II years, the region provides an ideal case study for exploring the mutations of nationalist, racist, and Orientalist discourses during the Cold War. Unlike existing examinations of Cold War Orientalism, this chapter adopts a comparative approach, and examines not only the pro-Western visions of the East, but also their counterparts produced in the pro-Yugoslav camp. In doing so, the chapter echoes the ideas of those who have argued for a comparative approach to the history of the region,[8] as well as those urging an analysis that explores the construction of symbolic boundaries between the East and the West from both Western and Eastern points of departure.[9]

The examination is limited to the years between 1947 and 1954, which coincides with the period of existence of the Free Territory of Trieste (FTT). FTT was an unusual political formation, established on a patch of bitterly disputed territory that was claimed by Italy on the one hand and the Yugoslav federation on the other hand. The border dispute has a long and turbulent history, which is closely tied to the rise of nation-states and the accompanying attempts to make culture and ethnicity coincide with state borders. Given the region's complex ethnic and cultural patchwork, establishing a border based on national principles was bound to trigger processes of national assimilation and ethnic unmixing, as well as to provoke violence. The rise of fascism in Italy gave way to increasingly ruthless forms of Italianization of Slovenians and Croatians in the region,[10] which in turn prompted a hardening of anti-Italian sentiments among growing numbers of the affected populations, and gave rise to several clandestine anti-Fascist organizations that regularly resorted to violent means.[11] Though intermittently broken by forms of Italo-Slav anti-Fascist collaboration, this spiral of violence and suspicion continued throughout World War II and into the postwar period.

In the years following World War II, the border dispute acquired a wider strategic significance. Poised on the southern end of what came to be known as the Iron Curtain, its fate appeared too important to be left to Italy and Yugoslavia alone. After prolonged negotiations, most of the northeastern Adriatic was carved up between the two neighboring states, while the remaining patch of territory, comprising the port city of Trieste and its immediate surroundings, was declared a Free Territory. The FTT was divided into two zones, controlled respectively by the Allied Military Government (Zone A) and the Yugoslav army (Zone B). In line with the early Cold War politics of containment, Zone A came to function as the last bulwark against Soviet expansionism,[12] which was seen as operating not only through the Yugoslav government, but also through the mass appeal of Italy's own Communist Party. At the same time, Zone B was becoming ever more incorporated into the Yugoslav economic, political, and ideological system.[13] After the electoral defeat of the Communist Party in Italy in 1948 and Yugoslavia's expulsion from Cominform later in the same year, the double-headed threat of Soviet expansion into Italian territory suddenly receded. With Trieste no longer functioning as a site of East-West confrontation, the solution to the "Trieste question" again became a largely bilateral problem, to be resolved between Italy and Yugoslavia themselves. In 1954, FTT was finally dismembered and the two zones annexed to the two neighboring states.

Throughout the existence of FTT, the local mass media were heavily involved in the border dispute, projecting different ideas about the "true" identity of the region and its people, as well as dissimilar convictions about where the borders should lie. Divided along both national and ideological lines, the newspapers in particular provide an excellent insight into the multiple cleavages cutting through the public representations of identity, space, and place in the region. The analysis presented in this chapter covers newspapers published in all three major languages of the region—Italian, Slovenian, and Croatian—and includes pro-Western and pro-Yugoslav as well as pro-Soviet outlets. Among newspapers published in the Yugoslav part of the northeastern Adriatic, the sample includes the Croatian daily *Riječki list* (1947–1954), later renamed to *Novi list* (1954–), the Slovenian biweekly *Nova Gorica* (1947–1953), later renamed to *Primorske novice* (1953–), and the Italian daily *La Voce del Popolo* (1945–). Together with the Slovenian biweekly *Slovenski Jadran* (1952–1963), published in Zone B, and the Slovenian minority daily *Primorski Dnevnik* (1945–), published in Zone A, most of these newspapers had their roots in clandestine anti-Fascist, pro-Communist periodicals established during World War II.[14] Under the Federal People's Republic of Yugoslavia, all publications were legally free, but were in fact rather tightly regulated by the Communist authorities, which resorted to a variety of direct and indirect means, including the banning of distribution, denial of paper supplies, etc.[15] As a result, all the pro-Yugoslav newspapers included in the sample represented the identities and boundaries of the northeastern Adriatic similarly, more or less in line with the positions of the Communist Party of Yugoslavia.[16]

The remaining materials examined in the chapter, all published in Zone A, are much more varied in terms of both their political affiliations and their approach to identities and borders. The official outlet of the regional branch of the Italian Communist Party, *Il Lavoratore* (1945–1964), and its Slovenian counterpart *Delo* (1949), offer an insight into the specificities of pro-Soviet Cold War discourse in the region after Tito's break with Stalin in 1948. The two pro-Italian dailies, *La Voce Libera* (1945–1949) and *Giornale di Trieste* (1947–1954), although affiliated with political groups at different ends of the political spectrum, both unequivocally supported the annexation of Trieste to Italy,[17] and represented the voices of those Triestines who "recognized themselves in . . . the Western, Atlantic, and European camp."[18] The weekly *Trieste* (1954–1978) followed broadly similar lines of argument. Finally, the Slovenian weekly *Demokracija* (1947–1963), tied to the Catholic and liberal factions within the Slovenian minority in Zone A, provides an insight into Slovenian appropriations of pro-Western discourses.[19]

The Northeastern Adriatic As a Civilizational Fault Line

A cursory glance at the pro-Western newspapers published in the northeastern Adriatic in the post–World War II years reveals that the perceptions of Europe prevalent at the time cannot be assessed fully without taking into account their continuities with prewar mental mappings. Far from being swept away by Cold War divisions, beliefs in the fundamental influence of racial, cultural, and civilizational differences continued to hold sway throughout the existence of the FTT. The Cold War mapping of Europe, based on the division of the world into two economically and politically radically opposed blocks, was simply grafted onto preexisting layers of nineteenth- and early twentieth-century distinctions. The long-standing notion of Italy as a cultural nation, for instance, now regularly appeared in conjunction with that of a liberal, democratic Western civilization,[20] while the Yugoslav nations were repeatedly depicted as belonging to the illiberal, Communist Eastern civilization. Moreover, the core ideas that coalesced into the Cold War mapping were themselves of an older date. The notion of Europe's being divided into a civilized West and an underdeveloped East can be traced back to the period of the Enlightenment.[21] Similarly, ideologically motivated cleavages between liberals, Socialists, and clerics, both within and across the various national groups coexisting in the northeastern Adriatic, have a much longer history and were largely established in the late nineteenth century. However, in the post–World War period, Churchill's metaphorical "Iron Curtain" gave these divisions an unprecedented fixity, largely resolving the old ambiguities, including those related to the exact position of Germany and the Slavic nations in Central Europe.[22]

The symbolic geographies drawn by the pro-Italian, anti-Communist Triestine newspapers often coincided with, and sometimes even explicitly mentioned, the notion of an Iron Curtain, emphasizing that it marked a border not only between nations, but also between radically different civilizations and races. In an article published in *Trieste*, the northeastern Adriatic is deemed to be "a sensitive meeting point between three worlds: the Latin world, the German world, and the Slavic world—a point that, depending on the historical moment and temperature, can be either a point of strife or a point of agreement."[23] For the author of the article, there is no doubt about how the East-West divide fits into the picture: according to him, it is "the march of Slavism that threatens to submerge Western civilizations" and only Italianness could reinstate the equilibrium in the region—the very same Italianness that "prevented the Germans from grabbing the Mediterranean."[24] This juxtaposition of the Slavic and German threats, and the concomitant neglect of the Italian totalitarian past, finds its parallels in other pro-Italian publications from the period. According to an editorial published in *Giornale di Trieste*, for example, Pan-Slavism "is, at least as far as its mental forms are concerned, a direct heir" of Pan-Germanism.[25]

Arguably, representations such as these were an echo of the broader Western discourse at the time, within which both Nazism and communism were thought of as essentially alien to Western civilization,[26] and were lumped together under the label "totalitarian" or "authoritarian" and contrasted to the "democratic West."[27] The dichotomy of the democratic West and the illiberal, totalitarian East frequently appeared in the pro-Italian Triestine press as well. The crucial addendum, however—and in fact the focus of attention in such representations—was the position of Italy. When drawing a parallel between Nazism and communism, Italian nationalists in the region were in fact appropriating Cold War bipolarities to buttress their own nationalist claims. Typically, the pro-Italian press would endorse the notion of Trieste as the bulwark protecting the Italian nation from the Slavic threat, and tie it to Western Allied aims to protect the Western block. The conclusion of the above-mentioned article published in *Trieste* provides a fitting example of how this strategy worked in practice:

> It is clear today that Trieste, along with the part of the Julian Venetia indispensable to it, can fulfill its important and delicate function of an equilibrator between the East and the West of Europe only if it is included in its natural nest, that is into the Italian state, into an Italy that is reconstituting itself ... as a bulwark of democracy and of Western civilization. Without Trieste and its territory, however, Italy itself is weakened and much less able to resist the pressure of the East.[28]

An integral part of this convergence of nationalist claims and Cold War mappings was the marrying of national and racial categories to political and economic orientation. In line with this, some nations—or even whole races—were assumed to be inherently predisposed to developing a democratic political system and adopting a market economy, while others were believed to be condemned to a totalitarian outlook and centrally planned economy. The pro-Italian Triestine press regularly drew on these distinctions and equations when discussing the allegedly unique fate of the city and the broader region. "For the Italians of Trieste and Istria ... the idea of homeland is indissolubly tied to the idea of freedom," read an editorial published in *Trieste*. Yet these freedom-loving Italians, continued the article, "live close to an environment where the civil, political, and social liberties and the respect for the autonomy of the peoples are considered to be simple propagandistic formulas, to be exploited often but never applied."[29] Very similar distinctions were drawn in an editorial published in *La Voce Libera*, which concluded that true democratic liberties could be secured only with the return of the FTT to Italy—a country that, according to another article published in the same daily, also "gave the world Roman law" and should therefore certainly be involved in the administration of justice in the Free Territory.[30]

A characteristic element of the discourse that tied national and racial categories to political and economic orientations was the term *slavo-communista* (Slavo-communist), a derogatory label that at least partly fed on the assumption that communism had its roots in the innately totalitarian character of the Slavs.[31] The articles published in *Giornale di Trieste* offer numerous examples. One such article describes the cruel behavior of Yugoslav Communists towards the local Italian population and refers to the perpetrators as "human beasts."[32] Even more telling are the derisive caricatures in which *slavo-communisti* are regularly pictured with a grim, stern expression on their faces, wearing a uniform, with no distinguishing individual features, and often even barefoot.[33] Suggesting a propensity to militarism, collectivism, and violence, as well as primitivism, such caricatures provided a fitting visual backdrop to newspaper stories warning of the imminent threat of a "Slavo-communist invasion" in Trieste. In one such article, the author claims that the Slavs are using "complex mechanisms of infiltration," drawing closer and closer to the heart of the city, casting a dense net of institutions that is centrally controlled in a machine-like manner and can easily be used to stir up the obedient masses in the city.[34]

Another frequently invoked characteristic that functioned to demonstrate Italy's privileged link to Western civilization—and, by default, Yugoslavia's detachment from the West—was religion. Historically, the Italian national origin myth relied heavily on Catholicism. Particularly in the turbulent period after World War II, Catholicism provided one of the foundational myths that helped rebuild Italian national unity, as defined in opposition to two main Others: the Fascist past and the Communist threat.[35] In this period, Catholics' repugnance toward communism took precedence over their traditional antipathy toward liberalism, and facilitated their reconciliation with the values of modern Western society.[36] If the Cold War setting provided external pressure, Catholicism was thus the glue that was used to restore Italian postwar nationhood and sense of belonging to the West from within. This was in tune with the wider function of religion in the construction of the West during the Cold War, namely the fact that the Christian West was contrasted to the atheist East.[37]

The convergence of Italian religious nationalism and Cold War rhetoric came very clearly to the fore in *Giornale di Trieste*'s reporting on the violent incidents in the autumn of 1953. The incidents were sparked by an announcement, issued jointly by the United States and Great Britain on 8 October, in which the two Allies informed the involved parties that they intended to withdraw their troops from Zone A of the Free Territory and hand over the administration to Italy. Yugoslavia responded with public denunciations, mass protests, and finally a mobilization of armed forces along the Italian border.[38] The pro-Italian part of the population in Trieste, cheer-led by *Giornale di Trieste*, greeted the prospect of the arrival of Italian troops with excitement, organizing mass displays of national loyalty. The demonstrations that escalated in early November provoked repressive measures on the side of the Allied administration and resulted in bloodshed.[39] One of the major clashes with the police took place in front of one of Trieste's Catholic churches, Sant'Antonio Nuovo. *Giornale di Trieste* found this fact particularly repugnant, claiming that the events were an affront to the religious feelings of the people,[40] and "offended the most sacred values, using violence against the flag and against the crucifix."[41] However, while denouncing the measures adopted by the Allied forces, *Giornale di Trieste* nevertheless resorted to Cold War metaphors. As usual, the Cold War rhetoric was used to promote claims to an Italian Trieste, this time combined with explicit references to the Christian—and thereby supposedly inescapably Western—character of the city. What was at stake in the conflicts, argued one of the editorials, was "the honor of a western city that prides itself on being Christian, the honor of our Allies … , the salvation of a democratic Europe," all threatened by an atheist, uncivilized nation and its totalitarian regime.[42]

Yet another set of oppositions that often surfaced in pro-Italian constructions of the border, and overlapped with the contrast between civilized Italians and barbaric Slavs, was one that pitched civilized coastal cities against the untamed rural hinterland. This opposition has its origins in the Venetian Enlightenment, when Venetians often criticized the Dalmatian "Morlacchi"—a now nonexistent category referring to the people living in the rural hinterland of Dalmatia—as lazy, irrational, and prone to violence.[43] Over the course of the nineteenth century, the rural/urban divide gradually acquired racist and nationalist overtones, thereby linking the urban settings to Italian civilization and the rural hinterland to Slavic tribes. It is in this radicalized form that the distinction became an integral element of Fascist ideology. Fascists often spoke of Dalmatia as a land in need of being civilized by the Italians, or singled out particular cities in Dalmatia as superior to other towns that were permeated by barbarism, low levels of hygiene, and, more generally, balkanism.[44] The aristocracy of the "new" Fascist civilization was believed to be morally responsible for saving humanity, including the inhabitants of the Balkans, from the combined threats of democracy, communism, and Jewish conspiracy, and thereby also to secure "vital space" for the expansion of the Fascist New Order.[45] In the postwar period, the specifically Fascist inflections of the rural/urban contrast largely receded, but the fundamental polarity, intertwined with the Italian/Slav split, continued to function as one of the core instruments of boundary maintenance, this time combined with typical Cold War elements. One article commenting on the festivities and protests organized on Labor Day in 1947 provides a case in point. According to the author, a substantial part of the "tired people who tramped ... the streets of the city center" on Labor Day was "undoubtedly foreign" and "did not belong to the city," but was instead brought over from the villages in Zone B.[46] Not only were the protesters alien because they were Communist and supposedly came from the Yugoslav part of the Free Territory, but also because their rural origins made them appear an alien body in the urban environment of Trieste.

While the above-discussed polarities—East/West, totalitarianism/democracy, atheism/Christianity, etc.—were particularly characteristic of identity constructions appearing in the pro-Italian press, one should note that the same rhetorical devices were also used by the anti-Communist factions of the Slovenian minority in Zone A. Like their Italian counterparts, Slovenian anti-Communists relied on Cold War rhetoric to buttress their own nationalist demands and claim a privileged Western character for Slovenians. These rhetorical devices are clearly evident in the opening issue of the weekly *Demokracija*, a publication affiliated with the major anti-Communist Slovenian party at the time, the Slovenian Democratic Union. One of the main aims of the new weekly, claims the editorial, is to reveal to the world the true face of the Slovenian nation, and help rebuild the image of Slovenians as a "truly democratic, cultured, and Christian nation (*narod*)." Communist rule, argued the editorial, was imposed on the nation from the outside and is essentially alien to its historical roots. With time, the Slovenian nation should "return to the family of free nations belonging to the democratic and Christian culture and civilization."[47] As did the pro-Italian press, *Demokracija* thus presented the northeastern Adriatic as a major civilizational fault line, yet one that should be shifted further East to incorporate Slovenians into the West. Unsurprisingly, the same line of argumentation was adopted also in Slovenian-language publications of the Allied Military Government aimed at promoting pro-Western sentiments among local Slovenians. In one such publication, the Slovenians of the Free Territory were described as "one of the rare branches of the Slovenian national family that has the opportunity to freely and actively participate in the cultural, political, and economic life of European nations" and that was able "to maintain its historical ties with the West."[48]

The Northeastern Adriatic As an Ideological Battleground

If the pro-Western press clearly perpetuated older identity constructions, couching them in Cold War rhetoric, the pro-Communist press followed a very different vision, one that was, at least initially, firmly intent on breaking away from racist and nationalist discourses of the past, and instead divided the world according to ideological, political, and economic criteria. The ideological premises of these criteria were of course in direct opposition to those at work in dominant Western Cold War discourses. In line with the historical-materialist interpretation of history, the pro-Communist vision rejected the assumption that modernization went hand in hand with the advancement of the market economy and liberal democracy. Instead, it invested its hopes in an egalitarian, worker-led society in which the distribution of profits is subject to social control. Especially in the immediate postwar period, it also rejected the idea that sovereign political units should coincide with culturally and nationally homogeneous units—a fact that is habitually overlooked in existing analyses of identity construction in the region.[49] As a consequence, the Italo-Yugoslav border in pro-Communist identity constructions assumed a radically different function: it did not serve primarily as a national boundary, but instead functioned as the marker of an ideological divide.[50] To be sure, references to national identities and interests were far from absent, yet their fulfillment seemed coextensive with the Communist cause.[51]

Despite this fundamental difference, pro-Communist constructions of identity and difference continued to be based on the fundamental premise of modern identity construction also shared by the anti-Communist press, namely the opposition between the modern, civilized Self and the underdeveloped, backward, and primitive Other.[52] However, in contrast to the Western-oriented identity constructions explored earlier, representations of the Self and the Other that prevailed in the pro-Communist press associated progressiveness, civilization, and modernity with political and economic doctrines and practices adopted in "the East": internationalism, a centrally planned economy, and working-class rule. This alternative narrative of progress and modernity drew on the broader narrative that saw the Soviet politico-economic model as more advanced than that of capitalist Europe,[53] and often amounted to an exact reversal of the civilizational hierarchy found in the anti-Communist newspapers. Instead of the contrast between civilized Italians and underdeveloped, barbaric Slavs, pro-Communist papers were regularly drawing on the distinction between the progressive working peoples of Yugoslavia and the uncivilized Italian bourgeoisie. It is important to note that this distinction did not coincide with national, racial, and more broadly geocultural divisions: the "progressive working peoples of Yugoslavia" often expressly included the local Italian working class. Instead of being divided into two blocs, the world as seen through the lens of pro-Communist newspapers in the region was divided into two fronts: "the front of the imperialist instigators of war" on the one hand, and "the huge front of peoples of all countries who want peace" on the other. The latter was believed to include "the invincible Soviet Union, the new Yugoslavia, Poland, Czechoslovakia, Romania, Bulgaria, Albania, the democratic forces of Greece and Hungary, and the great majority of the people of America, England, France, Italy, and all other countries not only in Europe, but across the whole world."[54]

Apart from Fascist Italy, which featured as the major enemy of the "working people" in the region before 1945, pro-Communist newspapers repeatedly also attacked "contemporary imperialists," above all those in the U.S.A. The democracy, civilization, and culture of contemporary imperialists, claimed one article, is only a veil covering their "spiritual poverty," while "the true democracy" can only be found among the "progressive powers rallying around Soviet culture."[55] Another article presented an even more damning picture of "the Western world, and particularly America," referring to their use of "uncivilized instruments" such as "the atomic bomb" and "the barbaric dollar-democracy," which are "unworthy of civilized people."[56] A further indicator of the assumed backwardness of the imperial forces, including the Italian bourgeoisie, was their alleged propensity for patriarchal family relations. According to one article, the revolution "swept away the shameful stains of the inequality of women and the outdated beliefs about the worthlessness of women, their subordination to men, and their inability to contribute to social, political, and economic life."[57] In contrast, however, the women on the other side of the Italian-Yugoslav border, "are continuing to carry the burden of foreign domination."[58] The women living in the coastal cities in Zone B were seen to be no better off: the inhabitants of these cities, allegedly consisting mostly of the "Italian bourgeoisie," were purportedly "extremely backward" and "patriarchal."[59]

Another criterion of civilization and progress habitually invoked in the pro-Yugoslav press was the presence (or absence) of fascism, chauvinism, and nationalism. These phenomena, one article claimed, "were thoroughly extinguished in Yugoslavia," but continued to be "tolerated, allowed, and even supported" in the Free Territory, where "democratic principles and human rights exist only on paper."[60] One could easily be tempted to conclude that the charge of fascism was indiscriminately directed at all Italians, thereby creating a fitting ideological counterpart to the stereotype of the "Slavo-Communist" in the pro-Italian nationalist press. Intermittently, pro-Yugoslav newspapers leveled the charge of fascism not only at the pre-1943 Italian regime, but at postwar Italy as well,[61] thus indeed reinforcing the stereotypical connection between Italians and fascism. However, pro-Communist, including pro-Yugoslav newspapers, normally avoided the equation between Italians and Fascists, and instead emphasized that the common struggle against Fascist Italy unified the local populations regardless of national allegiance. Predictably, the distinction between anti-Fascist and pro-Fascist Italians was most often drawn in *Il Lavoratore*, the official outlet of the regional branch of the Italian Communist Party. Its articles regularly criticized the Italians of Trieste who "continue to be victims of nationalism,"[62] and condemned the persistence of "Fascist terrorism" in the city,[63] yet without losing sight of anti-Fascist activities and convictions among Italians in the region. Similar arguments could also be found in the Croatian and Slovenian pro-Communist press. According to an article, "one could expect that the struggle against Italian fascism, which was the most visible expression of Italy in this region, would lead to a fight against all Italians." However, continued the article, the national liberation struggle helped turn the developments in a different direction: "The great idea of brotherhood and unity of nations in the struggle against the common oppressor, for the common freedom and well-being, united both Italians and Croatians of Istria into a common front."[64]

The various imperialist, fascism-prone Others, and particularly so Fascist Italy, were also the ones to be blamed for the poor economic and social condition of the working class in the northeastern Adriatic. According to one article, Fascist Italy "was preventing any education of Slovenians and Croatians and the Italian working classes."[65] "Our working people," claimed another article, "were consciously and calculatingly diverted from theater ... and deliberately entertained by farce and comedy to turn them away from political and social problems."[66] Even the irresponsible exploitation of natural resources such as forests, for example, was seen as a consequence of similarly irresponsible behavior of "foreign imperialists" and "capitalists."[67] The low level of transport infrastructure in the country was equally blamed on the "internal exploiters and foreign imperialists, people who for twenty years have been exporting what was best out of our country."[68] Upon the dismantling of the Free Territory, when Zone B was annexed to Yugoslavia, the president of the local Socialist alliance was reported as saying that he hoped for a "new era, one that would do away with the dark past and the damaging consequences of the hundred-years long enslavement."[69] "We are left with a sad heritage," lamented another article published in the same period. "Our highland villages do not have good drinkable water, and we will have to tear down all the hovels in which the working people used to live in the times of the 'high civilization.'"[70] Given that the "imperial forces of the West" were seen as generally hostile to progress and true democracy, the guiding light and measure of progress was to be sought at the other end of the symbolic map of the world: in "the East." Where geographic and natural obstacles hindered the strengthening of ties with the East, argued one article, railways and tunnels should therefore be built to overcome these obstacles and turn the alienated regions in the right direction.[71]

However, only a few years after the establishment of the Free Territory, the lines of division drawn by the pro-Communist press were reshuffled, and among pro-Yugoslav newspapers "the East" suddenly lost its previous appeal. Tito's split with Stalin in 1948 was followed by a clear bifurcation within the pro-Communist press in the region. For *Il Lavoratore* and the newly established, pro-Soviet Slovenian newspaper *Delo*, Yugoslavia now joined the ranks of imperial enemies: its supporters deserved to be labeled "Fascist," "nationalist," and "chauvinist,"[72] and were accused of paving the way for the establishment of capitalism in Yugoslavia.[73] Upon the announcement of the partition of the Free Territory in 1954, both newspapers decried the decision, arguing that it went against the will of the population and presented a threat to peace in the region.[74] The pro-Yugoslav newspapers, on the other hand, believed the true traitor was the Soviet Union itself. The reports on developments in the Soviet Union were now far from the glittering portrayals of the immediate postwar years. Instead, articles warned against "Soviet expansionism"[75] and portrayed the Soviet elite as the new imperialists who were enjoying a luxurious lifestyle while the living conditions of Soviet workers deteriorated.[76] Following the same interpretive framework, Triestine supporters of the Soviet Union were accused of misleading the proletarian masses in Trieste and supporting nationalist, imperialist, and capitalist aims.[77] The former ally now joined the list of Yugoslavia's main Others: together with capitalist regimes and colonies, it was now regarded as a country whose workers were "oppressed, deprived of all rights, denied freedom."[78]

The break with the Soviet Union also marked the beginning of a slight shift in the relative weight of nationalist aspirations and class struggle in favor of the former. Geocultural demarcations now regularly appeared side by side with socioeconomic ones. Particularly in the realm of foreign policy, Yugoslavia was beginning to adopt a new geopolitical identity, positioning itself as outside of the two "imperialist" blocs, belonging neither to the East nor to the West. "We are following our own path to socialism," argued Tito in a speech in 1954, "and we will not let anyone, neither those in the East nor those in the West, lead us astray from this path."[79] This liminal position allowed Yugoslav leaders to draw selectively on cultural, political, and ideological elements associating them with both poles of the symbolic map, acting simultaneously as a bridge between and a bulwark against both East and West, while at the same time refusing to join either of them.[80] This symbolic positioning became particularly prominent from the late 1950s onwards, when it found its political expression in the Nonaligned Movement.

Within Yugoslavia itself, geocultural principles of identification, in particular nationalist ones, took hold as well: Slovenian representatives were disappointed by the increasingly real prospect of "losing" Trieste, which among other things meant that the borders of Yugoslavia would not coincide with the ethnic distribution of the Slovenian population. In the public realm, these stirrings became visible in occasional disagreements between newspaper commentaries written by Slovenian Communist leaders and the official positions defended by Tito,[81] as well as in the continuing insistence on the London Memorandum as an ultimately unjust, provisional solution. In a speech delivered by France Bevk, reproduced in *Primorske novice*, the Slovenian writer commended the Memorandum as the best possible solution under the circumstances, and emphasized its role in maintaining peaceful relations with Italy. However, he also clearly signaled that the new arrangement of borders was not there to stay, since it did not coincide with ethnic distribution: "If we look into the more distant future, we should not forget that unnatural borders, which unjustly cut into the body of a nation, cannot endure."[82] Although ultimately accepting the border settlement, voices such as this made it clear that the Communist vision of the northeastern Adriatic continued to draw on national and cultural lines of division—though to a much lesser extent than pro-Western discourses produced in the region at the time.

Conclusion

As we have shown, symbolic mappings of Europe produced in the northeastern Adriatic after World War II continued in many ways to perpetuate much older lines of identification and exclusion. Especially ideas fostered in pro-Western newspapers, which centered on the perception of the northeastern Adriatic as a civilizational fault line, remained deeply embedded in nationalist discourses, and resorted to Cold War rhetoric primarily as a means of furthering nationalist claims and territorial demands. However, pro-Soviet and pro-Yugoslav outlets provided a significantly different vision, one that perceived the region primarily as an ideological battleground. Although both mappings and the corresponding sets of identifications were tied to the same basic narrative of progress, and operated with distinctions such as progressive vs. backward and civilized vs. barbaric, they were premised on radically different understandings of what it meant to be "modern": one was consistent with the dominant Western narrative, culminating in industrialization and the development of a market economy; the other was based on Socialist ideas and resulted in an egalitarian, worker-led society in which the distribution of profits is subject to social control.

Notes

1. Among Italians, the region is known as the Julian Venetia (*Venezia Giulia*), while Slovenians and Croats refer to it as the Julian March (*Julijska krajina*). In order to avoid the nationalist, emotional connotations of these terms, this article will use the neutral label "northeastern Adriatic." For a discussion of the symbolic struggles involved in naming the area, see Bogdan C. Novak, *Trieste, 1941–1954* (Chicago, 1970), 3–6.
2. Edward Said, *Orientalism* (London, 1978).
3. E.g. Georges Corn, *Orient-Occident, la fracture imaginaire* (Paris, 2003); Larry Wolff, *Inventing Eastern Europe* (Stanford, 1994); idem, *Venice and the Slavs* (Stanford, 2001); Maria Todorova, *Imagining the Balkans* (Oxford, 1997); Vesna Goldsworthy, *Inventing Ruritania* (London and New Haven, 1998); David A. Norris, *In the Wake of the Balkan Myth* (Basingstoke and London, 1999); Iver B. Naumann, *Uses of the Other* (Manchester, 1999); Božidar Jezernik, *Wild Europe* (London, 2004).
4. E.g., Milica Bakić-Hayden and Robert M. Hayden, "Orientalist Variations on the Theme 'Balkans,'" Slavic Review 51 (1992), no. 1: 1–15; Merje Kuus, "Europe's Eastern Expansion and the Reinscription of Otherness in East-Central Europe," Progress in Human Geography 28 (2004), no. 4: 472–489; Wendy Bracewell, "Orijentalizam, okcidentalizam i kozmopolitanizam: balkanski putopisi o Evropi," Sarajevo Notebook 6–7 (2004): 179–193.
5. Robert Griffith, "The Cultural Turn in Cold War Studies," *Reviews in American History* 29 (2001), no. 1: 150–157.
6. See, for example, Robert Knight, "Ethnicity and Identity in the Cold War," *The International History Review* 22 (2000), no. 2: 253–504; Mary L. Dudziak, *Cold War Civil Rights* (Princeton, 2000); Thomas Borstelmann, *The Cold War and the Color Line* (Cambridge, Mass., 2003).
7. Melani McAlister, *Epic Encounters* (Berkeley, 2001); Christina Klein, *Cold War Orientalism* (Berkeley, 2003).
8. E.g. Marina Cattaruzza, "Introduzione," in *Nazionalismi di frontiera*, ed. Marina Cattaruzza (Soveria Mannelli, 2003), 9–21, 12.
9. See Bo Stråth, "A European Identity," *European Journal of Social Theory* 5 (2002), no. 4: 387–401; Patrick Major and Rana Mitter, "East is East and West is West?," *Cold War History* 4 (2003), no. 1: 1–22.
10. Cf. Marina Cattaruzza, *L'Italia e il confine orientale* (Bologna, 2007), 168–181.
11. Cf. Rolf Wörsdörfer, *Krisenherd Adria 1915–1955* (Paderborn, 2004), 263–273.
12. Raoul Pupo, *Guerra e dopoguerra al confine orientale d'Italia (1938–1954)* (Udine, 1999), 161.
13. See Nevenka Troha, "Ukrepi jugoslovanskih oblasti v conah B Julijske krajine in Svobodnega tržaškega ozemlja v Italijani na Koprskem," *Annales—Series historia et sociologia* 10 (2000), no. 1: 203–216.

14. See Bojan Pavletič, ed., *Primorski dnevnik 1945–1995* (Trst, 1995); Branko Marušič, "Povojni slovenski tisk," in *Zbornik Primorske—50 let* (Koper, 1997); Božidar Novak, *Hrvatsko novinarstvo u 20. stoljeću* (Zagreb—, 1995), 344–347.
15. Carol S. Lilly, *Power and Persuasion* (Boulder, 2001), 43f.
16. That being said, I should add that the Yugoslav press at the time did not always accurately reproduce the official line of the Communist Party of Yugoslavia (CPY). In the early post–World War II years, this was largely due to the lack of educated and skilled editors and journalists, which forced the CPY to rely on inexperienced and non-Communist personnel. From the early 1950s onwards, other factors came into play, most prominently the press reform, which required all newspapers to follow consumer demand and rely on sales rather than state support. See Lilly, *Power and Persuasion*, 68 and 207f.
17. See Luciano Becker, Roberto de Rosa, and Silvano Benvenuti, "La Voce Libera," and Cesare Vetter, "Il Giornale di Trieste," both in *Nazionalismo e neofascismo nella lotta politica al confine orientale 1945–75* (Trieste, 1977), 27–61 and 112–42, respectively.
18. Guido Botteri, ed., *Un secolo un giornale: Il Piccolo, 1881–1981* (Trieste, 1981), 43.
19. Due to limitations of space, this chapter avoids the discussion of identity- and border constructions in the pro-independence daily *Il Corriere di Trieste* (1945–1958). Suffice it to say that this newspaper bears witness to the continued existence of supranational, cosmopolitan forms of identification in the region. Many of its founders and contributors were known for their disdain for nationalism and support for supranational, yet not exclusively Socialist, forms of identification and political legitimation.
20. Elio Apih, *Trieste* (Rome, 1988), 170.
21. Wolff, *Inventing Eastern Europe*.
22. Martin K. Lewis and Kären A. Wigen, *Myth of Continents* (Berkeley, 1997), 60.
23. "Questa regione ... è un punto sensibile d'incontro, che può essere scontro o accordo, a seconda del momento e della temperatura storica, fra tre mondi: il mondo latino, il mondo tedesco, e il mondo slavo." From Giani Stuparich, "La funzione di Trieste," in *Trieste* 1 (1954), no. 1: 3.
24. "E come nel passato soltanto l'italianità della regione potè ristabilire l'equilibrio e impedire ai tedeschi di allungare le mani sul Mediterraneo, così nel presente soltanto l'italianità della Venezia Giulia può arrestare nel Sud d'Europa la marcia dello slavismo che minaccia di sommergere le civiltà occidentali." Ibid.
25. "Il 'panslavismo' non è un'invenzione polemica degli italiani, ma una realtà, come lo fu al suo tempo il 'pangermanismo', di cui—almeno per le forme mentali—è l'erede diretto." From D.M., "I comunisti, Trieste e l'URSS," in *Giornale di Trieste*, 10 September 1947, 1.
26. Lewis and Wigen, *Myth of Continents*, 59f.
27. Naumann, *Uses of the Other*, 103. To fit the dichotomizing pattern, the fact that the supposedly "democratic" West included countries governed by military dictatorships—Portugal, Spain, Turkey, and Greece—was conveniently forgotten. See Gerard Delanty, *Inventing Europe* (New York, 1995), 125.
28. "Oggi è chiaro che Trieste con quella parte della Venezia Giulia che le è indispensabile può risolvere la sua importante e delicata funzione equilibratrice fra Oriente e Occidente europeo, soltanto se è inclusa nel suo nesso naturale, cioè nello Stato italiano, in un'Italia che si ricostituisce solidamente nella coscienza e nella volontà d'essere un baluardo della democrazia e della civiltà occidentale. Ma senza Trieste e il suo territorio, l'Italia stessa è indebolita e molto meno capace di resistere alla pressione dell'Oriente." In Stuparich, "La funzione di Trieste," 3.

29. "Per gli italiani di Trieste e dell'Istria ... il concetto di Patria è indissolubilmente connesso a quello di libertà.... Gli italiani di questa regione vivono vicini ad un ambiente dove le libertà civili, politiche e sociali ed il rispetto dell'autonomia dei popoli sono considerate ancora semplici formule propagandistiche, da sfruttarsi spesso ma da applicarsi mai." From "Posizioni ferme," in *Trieste* 1 (1954), no. 1: 1.
30. "L'Italia che ha dato al mondo il diritto romano ... non potrà certamente essere assente dall'Amministrazione della giustizia nel T.L.," in Bruno Attilio Latini, "Ordinamento giuridico e 'Territorio libero,'" *La Voce Libera*, 1 March 1947, 1.
31. Pamela Ballinger, *History in Exile* (Princeton, 2003), 66.
32. Piero Almerigogna, "Il 'pestaggio' prima della foiba," *Giornale di Trieste*, 2 October 1953, 4.
33. E.g. "Chiamate 00," *Giornale di Trieste*, 2 November 1953, supplement *Cittadella*, 2.
34. "La grande mistificazione," *Giornale di Trieste*, 21 March 1948, 2.
35. Enzo Pace, *La Nation italienne en crise*, trans. Patrick Michel (Paris, 1998).
36. Mikael af Malmborg, "The Dual Appeal of 'Europe' in Italy," in *The Meaning of Europe*, ed. Mikael af Malmborg and Bo Stråth (Oxford, 2002), 68.
37. Delanty, *Inventing Europe*, 123.
38. Roberto G. Rabel, *Between East and West* (Durham, 1988), 150ff.
39. Novak, *Trieste*, 418–448.
40. "Stile e silenzio," *Giornale di Trieste*, 6 November 1953, 2.
41. "I nuovi lutti denunciano," *Giornale di Trieste*, 7 November 1953, 1.
42. "Cosa si vuole?" *Giornale di Trieste*, 6 November 1953, 1.
43. Wolff, *Venice and the Slavs*, 132–138.
44. Ibid., 355.
45. Davide Rodogno, "Italian Soldiers in the Balkans," *Journal of Southern Europe and the Balkans* 6 (2004), no. 2: 125–144.
46. "Gli incidenti del Primo Maggio nelle ripercussioni al Consiglio di Zona," *Giornale di Trieste*, 3 May 1947, 2.
47. "Nasproti zunanjemu svetu bo 'Demokracija' stremela tolmačiti pravo politično mišljenje in hotenje našega naroda ... da si bo tujina spet ustvarila o nas predstavo resnično demokratičnega, kulturnega in krščanskega naroda.... da bo prej ali slej ... se tako vrnil v družino svobodnih narodov demokratične in krščanske kulture in civilizacije." In "Uvodna beseda," *Demokracija*, 25 April 1947, 1.
48. "... ena izmed redkih vej slovenske narodne družine, ki ima možnost za svobodno in aktivno udejstvovanje v kulturnem, poličnem in gospodarskem življenju evropskih narodov. Zaradi tega so lahko ohranili zgodovinske vezi z Zahodom ..." in European Recovery Program, *Tržaški Slovenci sodelujejo pri evropskem obnovitvenem načrtu* (Trieste: La Editoriale Libreria, 1949), 1.
49. For a compatible argument see Glenda Sluga, *The Problem of Trieste and the Italo-Yugoslav Border* (New York, 2001).
50. Raoul Pupo, "Med zgodovino in geografijo," trans. Devana Jovan, *Prispevki za novejšo zgodovino* 15 (2000), no. 1: 285–299.
51. The rise of communism, both in Yugoslavia and elsewhere, owes a great deal to the manipulation of nationalist aspirations condoned by both Marx and Lenin as an acceptable means of furthering the Communist cause in prerevolutionary societies. Yet contrary to the expectations of Leninist national policy, Communist revolutions proved unable to diffuse national sentiments. See Walker Connor, *The National Question in Marxist-Leninist Theory and Strategy* (Princeton, 1984).
52. Cf. Michael Pickering, *Stereotyping* (Basingstoke, 2001), 51ff.
53. Naumann, *Uses of the Other*, 104.

54. "Oggi nel mondo esistono due fronti ... fronte degli alzatori di guerra imperialisti e l'enorme fronte dei popoli di tutti i paesi che vogliono la pace. Di questo fronte fa parte l'invincibile Unione Sovietica, a questo fronte appartengono la nuova Jugoslavia, la Polonia, la Cecoslovacchia, la Romania, la Bulgaria, l'Albania, le forze democratiche della Grecia e della Ungheria e appartiene l'enorme maggioranza del popolo dell'America, dell'Ingilterra, della Francia, dell'Italia e di tutti gli altri paesi non solo d'Europa, ma anche di tutto il mondo." From "Esposizione del maresciallo Tito sulla politica estera della R.F.P.J.," in *La Voce del Popolo*, 1 April 1947, 1.
55. "Svjetski značaj sovjetske kulture," *Riječki list*, 5 September 1947, 3.
56. "Izmedju FNR Jugoslavije i Republike Madžarske potpisana je konvencija o kulturnoj saradnji," *Riječki list*, 17 October 1947, 1.
57. "Ljudska revolucija je pometla sramotne madeže neenakopravnosti žene in preživele nauke o manjvrednosti žene, o njeni podrejenosti možu, o njeni nesposobnosti sodelovanja v družbenem političnem in gospodarskem življenju." From Mir, "Žena ni več manjvredno bitje," in *Primorske novice*, 3 June 1954, 10.
59. Photo credit accompanying the article "Eighth of March—Women's Day," *Slovenski Jadran*, 5 March 1954, 1.
59. Jurij Beltram, "Dosedanji rezultati dela ljudske oblasti v Koprščini in Bujščini," *Primorski dnevnik*, 3 September 1947, 1.
60. "Dočim je v Jugoslaviji fašizem v vseh svojih odrazih in odtenkih dokončno uničen in se ljudstvo vzgaja v pravem, bratskem in demokratičnem duhu, se pri nas dopušča in omogoča ali celo podpira porajanje šovinizma, nacionalne mržnje in neofašizma. Demokratična načela in ljudske pravice so pri nas le na papirju ali pa lepo izražene fraze." From "29 XI 1953–29 XI 1947," in *Primorski dnevnik*, 29 November 1947, 1.
61. E.g. "Naš praznik," *Primorske novice*, 3 September 1954, 1.
62. "A vantaggio di chi?" *Il Lavoratore*, 1 March 1947, 1.
63. "Primo Maggio 1947: vittoria di popolo," *Il lavoratore*, 2 May 1947, 1.
64. "... moglo se očekivati da će se borba protiv talijanskog fašizma, koji je tu bio najvidljiviji izraz Italije, dovesti do borbe protiv svih Talijana ... No s pojavom narodno-oslobodilačke borbe stvari su i kod nas poprimile drugi izgled.... Velika ideja bratsva i jedinstva naroda u borbi protiv zajedničkog tlačitelja, za zajedničku slobodu i blagostanje, ujedinila je u čvrst front Talijane i Hrvate Istre." From Andrea Casassa, "Naša štampa sluši učvršćenju bratsva i jedinstva Hrvata i Talijana naše pokrajine" [Our press serves the strengthening of the brotherhood and unity of Croatians and Italians of our region], in *Riječki list*, 2 March 1947, 2. The official proclamations of Italo-Yugoslav brotherhood of course provide little insight into the struggles taking place on the ground, which often contradicted ideas of brotherhood and continued to be fuelled by mutual suspicion and nationalist prejudices as well as violence, and prompted a mass exodus from Istria. For a synthetic overview and critical assessment of various interpretive approaches to the issue of interethnic relations and migrations in the northeastern Adriatic during and after World War II, see Raoul Pupo, *Il lungo esodo—Istra* (Milan, 2005), 187–204.
65. Beltram, "Dosedanji rezultati," 3.
66. "Naši radni ljudi, koje je stara vlast svjesno i proračunato odvajala od kazališta, kao što jih je svjesno zabavljala lakrdijaštvom i cirkusanstvom, kako bi jih time odvratila od političkih i socialnih problema...." From J.K., "Plan rada Narodnog kazališta u novoj sezoni," in *Rječki list*, 5 September 1947, 3.
67. M.D., "Uloga šumskog gospodarstva u privredi i kulturnom razvitku našeg naroda," *Riječki list*, 17 September 1947, 2.

68. "Jugoslavija se ne straši groženj in tuje propagande," *Primorski dnevnik*, 3 September 1947, 1.
69. "... novi časi, ki bodo odpravili z mračno preteklostjo in škodljivimi posledicami stoletnega zasužnjevanja," from "Veliko slavje v Kopru," in *Primorske novice*, 26 November 1954, 1.
70. "Mi smo podedovali žalostno dediščino. ... Naše višinske vasi nimajo dobre pitne vode, porušiti bo treba brloge, v katerih so živeli delovni ljudje za časa 'visoke civilizacije.'" "Končna priključitev k socialistični domovini," *Slovenski Jadran*, 7 October 1954, 1–2.
71. Tone Peruško, "Veze Istre s Hrvatskom," *Riječki list*, 29 November 1947, 4.
72. "Ob izidu," *Delo*, 8 January 1949, 1.
73. "Protisovjetizem Titove klike," *Delo*, 8 January 1949, 1.
74. See, e.g., articles on the cover page of *Il Lavoratore*, 4 October 1954.
75. "Sibillina nota da Mosca per minare la sicurezza dell'Occidente," *La Voce del Popolo*, 2 April 1954, 1.
76. Z.B., "A Mosca, città delle file, una rarità le prugne e le mele," *La Voce del Popolo*, 15 June 1954, 3.
76. "Kominform in tržaško vprašanje," *Primorske novice*, 3 September 1954, 2.
78. Vittorio Drog, "Per un avvenire radioso e felice," *La Voce del Popolo*, 1 May 1954, 1.
79. "... mi imamo svojo lastno pot, po kateri gremo v socializem, in nikomur, ne tistim na Vzhodu, ne tistim na Zahodu ne bomo dovolili, da bi nas odvrnil od te poti." "Mi bomo nadaljevali lastno pot v socializem," *Primorske novice*, 2 April 1954, 1.
80. This kind of symbolic positioning is part and parcel of a more widespread phenomenon that can be conceptualized as "frontier Orientalism," a variety of Orientalism characteristic of European empires without overseas colonies, as well as the modern states established in their stead. Cf. Andre Gingrich, "Frontier Myths of Orientalism," in MESS—*Mediterranean Ethnological Summer School, Vol. II*, ed. Bojan Baskar and Borut Brumen (Ljubljana, 1996), 99–127.
81. See Jože Pirjevec, "Londonski memorandum 1954," in *Vojna in mir na Primorskem*, ed. Jože Pirjevec, Gorazd Bajc, and Borut Klabjan (Koper, 2005), 23f.
82. "Če pa pogledamo v daljšo bodočnost, ne pozabimo, da nenaravne meje, ki se krivično zarežejo v telo kakega naroda, ne morejo biti trajne." Mir, "Nenaravne meje ne morejo ostati trajne," *Primorske novice*, 15 October 1954, 1.

Bibliography

Apih, Elio. *Trieste: La storia politica e sociale*. Rome: Editori Laterza, 1988.

Almerigogna, Piero. "Il 'pestaggio' prima della foiba." *Giornale di Trieste*, 2 October 1953, 4.

Bakić-Hayden, Milica, and Robert M. Hayden. "Orientalist Variations on the Theme 'Balkans': Symbolic Geography in Recent Yugoslav Cultural Politics." *Slavic Review* 51 (1992), no. 1: 1–15.

Ballinger, Pamela. *History in Exile: Memory and Identity at the Borders of the Balkans*. Princeton: Princeton University Press, 2003.

Becker, Luciano, Roberto de Rosa, and Silvano Benvenuti, "La voce libera," in *Naziona-*

lismo e neofascismo nella lotta politica al confine orientale 1945–75 (Trieste: La Editoriale Libreria, 1977), 27–61.

Borstelmann, Thomas. *The Cold War and the Color Line: American Race Relations in the Global Arena*. Cambridge, Mass.: Harvard University Press, 2003.

Botteri, Guido, ed. *Un secolo un giornale: Il Piccolo, 1881–1981*. Trieste: Società Editrice Triestina, 1981.

Bracewell, Wendy. "Orijentalizam, okcidentalizam i kozmopolitanizam: balkanski putopisi o Evropi." *Sarajevo Notebook* 6–7 (2004): 179–193.

Cattaruzza, Marina. "Introduzione." In *Nazionalismi di frontiera: Identità contrapposte sull'Adriatico nord-orientale 1850–1950*, ed. Marina Cattaruzza. (Soveria Mannelli: Rubbettino, 2003), 9–21.

———. *L'Italia e il confine orientale*. Bologna: Il Mulino, 2007.

Connor, Walker. *The National Question in Marxist-Leninist Theory and Strategy*. Princeton: Princeton University Press, 1984.

Corn, Georges. *Orient-Occident, la fracture imaginaire*. Paris: Le Découverte, 2003.

Delanty, Gerard. *Inventing Europe: Idea, Identity, Reality*. New York: St. Martin's Press, 1995.

Dudziak, Mary L. *Cold War Civil Rights: Race and the Image of American Democracy*. Princeton, N.J.: Princeton University Press, 2000.

European Recovery Program. *Tržaški slovenci sodelujejo pri evropskem obnovitvenem načrtu*. Trieste: La Editoriale Libreria, 1949.

Gingrich, Andre. "Frontier Myths of Orientalism: The Muslim World in Public and Popular Culture of Central Europe." In *MESS—Mediterranean Ethnological Summer School*, Vol. II, ed. Bojan Baskar and Borut Brumen (Ljubljana: Institut za multikulturne raziskave, 1996), 99–127.

Goldsworthy, Vesna. *Inventing Ruritania: The Imperialism of the Imagination*. London and New Haven: Yale University Press, 1998.

Griffith, Robert. "The Cultural Turn in Cold War Studies." *Reviews in American History* 29 (2001), no. 1: 150–157.

Jezernik, Božidar. *Wild Europe: The Balkans in the Gaze of Western Travellers*. London: SAQI, in association with the Bosnian Institute, 2004.

Klein, Christina. *Cold War Orientalism: Asia and the Middlebrow Imagination, 1945–1961*. Berkeley and Los Angeles: University of California Press, 2003.

Knight, Robert. "Ethnicity and Identity in the Cold War: Carinthian Border Dispute, 1945–1949." *The International History Review* 22 (2000), no. 2: 253–504.

Kuus, Merje. "Europe's Eastern Expansion and the Reinscription of Otherness in East-Central Europe." *Progress in Human Geography* 28 (2004), no. 4: 472–489.

Latini, Bruno Attilio. "Ordinamento giuridico e 'Territorio libero.'" *La Voce Libera*, 1 March 1947, 1.

Lewis, Martin K., and Kären A. Wigen. *The Myth of Continents: A Critique of Metageography*. Berkeley and Los Angeles: University of California Press, 1997.

Lilly, Carol S. *Power and Persuasion: Ideology and Rhetoric in Communist Yugoslavia*. Boulder, Colo.: Westview Press, 2001.

McAlister, Melani. *Epic Encounters: Culture, Media, and U.S. Interests in the Middle East, 1945–2000*. Berkeley and Los Angeles: University of California Press, 2001.

Major, Patrick, and Rana Mitter. "East is East and West is West? Towards a Comparative Socio-Cultural History of the Cold War." *Cold War History* 4 (2003), no. 1: 1–22.

Malmborg, Mikael af. "The Dual Appeal of 'Europe' in Italy." In *The Meaning of Europe*, ed. Mikael af Malmborg and Bo Stråth (Oxford: Berg, 2002), 51–76.

Marušič, Branko. "Povojni slovenski tisk." In *Zbornik Primorske—50 let*, ed. Slobodan Valentinčič (Koper: Primorske novice, 1997), 256–261.
Naumann, Iver B. *Uses of the Other: "The East" in European Identity Formation*. Manchester: Manchester University Press, 1999.
Norris, David A. *In the Wake of the Balkan Myth: Questions of Identity and Modernity* (Basingstoke and London: Macmillan; New York: St. Martin's Press, 1999).
Novak, Bogdan C. *Trieste, 1941–1954: The Ethnic, Political, and Ideological Struggle*. Chicago: University of Chicago Press, 1970.
Novak, Božidar. *Hrvatsko novinarstvo u 20. stoljeću*. Zagreb: Golden marketing—Tehnička knjiga, 2005.
Pace, Enzo. *La Nation italienne en crise: Perspectives européennes*. Trans. Patrick Michel. Paris: Bayard, 1998.
Pavletič, Bojan, ed. *Primorski dnevnik 1945–1995*. Trst, Gorica, and Čedad: Družba za založniške pobude d.d., 1995.
Pickering, Michael. *Stereotyping*. Basingstoke: Palgrave Macmillan, 2001.
Pirjevec, Jože. "Londonski memorandum 1954." In *Vojna in mir na Primorskem*, ed. Jože Pirjevec, Gorazd Bajc, and Borut Klabjan (Koper: Založba Annales, 2005), 11–46.
Pupo, Raoul. *Guerra e dopoguerra al confine orientale d'Italia (1938–1954)*. Udine: Del Bianco Editore, 1999.
———. "Med zgodovino in geografijo: Razmišljanja o italijanski vzhodni meji." Trans. Devana Jovan. *Prispevki za novejšo zgodovino* 15 (2000), no. 1: 285–299.
———. *Il lungo esodo—Istra: le persecuzioni, le foibe, l'esilio*. Milan: Rizzoli, 2005.
Rabel, Roberto G. *Between East and West: Trieste, the United States, and the Cold War, 1941–1954*. Durham: Duke University Press, 1988.
Rodogno, Davide. "Italian Soldiers in the Balkans: The Experience of the Occupation (1941–1943)." *Journal of Southern Europe and the Balkans* 6 (2004), no. 2: 125–144.
Said, Edward. *Orientalism*. London: Penguin Books, 1995.
Sluga, Glenda. *The Problem of Trieste and the Italo-Yugoslav Border: Difference, Identity, and Sovereignty in Twentieth-Century Europe*. New York: SUNY Press, 2001.
Stråth, Bo. "A European Identity: To the Historical Limits of a Concept." *European Journal of Social Theory* 5 (2002), no. 4: 387–401.
Stuparich, Giani. "La funzione di Trieste." *Trieste* 1 (1954), no. 1: 3.
Todorova, Maria. *Imagining the Balkans*. Oxford: Oxford University Press, 1997.
Troha, Nevenka. "Ukrepi jugoslovanskih oblasti v conah B Julijske krajine in Svobodnega tržaškega ozemlja in Italijani na Koprskem." *Annales—Series historia et sociologia* 10 (2000), no. 1: 203–216.
Vetter, Cesare. "Il Giornale di Trieste." In *Nazionalismo e neofascismo nella lotta politica al confine orientale 1945–75* (Trieste: La Editoriale Libreria, 1977), 112–142.
Wolff, Larry. *Inventing Eastern Europe: The Map of Civilization on the Mind of the Enlightenment*. Stanford: Stanford University Press, 1994.
———. *Venice and the Slavs: The Discovery of Dalmatia in the Age of Enlightenment*. Stanford: Stanford University Press, 2001.
Wörsdörfer, Rolf. *Krisenherd Adria 1915–1955: Konstruktion und Artikulation des Nationalen im italienisch-jugoslawischen Grenzraum*. Paderborn: Ferdinand Schöningh, 2004.

Part IV

THE LEGACIES OF THE COLD WAR
Remembrance and Historiography

Chapter 14

A 1950s Revival
Cold War Culture in Reunified Germany

Andrew H. Beattie

> ... at issue here is the continuation of the systemic struggle
> between democracy and dictatorship
> after the end of the real socialist systems of rule.
> —Hartmut Koschyk (CSU)

Extensive research has demonstrated that the Cold War had a decisive impact on a central element of postwar German culture and political culture: public memory.[1] Some commentators have suggested that the Cold War's conclusion marked the end, if not of "history," then at least of the "memory regimes" that had emerged in East and West Germany.[2] The implication is that public memory in unified Germany was now free to develop along decidedly post–Cold War lines.[3] Yet such a view overlooks numerous continuities across the apparent caesura of 1989–90.[4] It also ignores that the history and legacies of the Cold War became a major subject of public as well as scholarly debate. From conservative *Rote Socken* scare campaigns (an updated equivalent of "Reds under the bed") to negotiations between Social Democrats and the post-Communist Party of Democratic Socialism (PDS) over how to characterize the foundation of the Socialist Unity Party of Germany (SED) in 1946, the Cold War past was vigorously contested and instrumentalized.⁵ Clearly, the Cold War's impact on German political culture did not end in 1989–90.

Far from simply offloading its Cold War baggage, German memory politics remained deeply indebted to the political and ideological legacy of the conflict. Indeed, in contrast to those commentators who posit the almost immediate demise of Cold War–era conflicts and mentalities, other commentators have perceived their persistence, or even their strengthening after 1989–90. Stefan Berger, for instance, notes the "predominance of anti-Communist Cold War rhetoric" in official discourse on the history of the German Democratic Republic (GDR), while Mary Fulbrook criticizes the wider ascendancy of a "Checkpoint Charlie view of history."⁶ Prompted not least by the revival of the totalitarian paradigm and the propagation of a renewed "anti-totalitarian consensus," other commentators similarly perceive correspondences between the anti-Communist discourses of 1950s West Germany and unified Germany.⁷ However, the purported similarities and continuities require more sustained consideration than they have received.

The literature has overlooked the fact that such parallels were themselves the subject of public debate after 1990. Like some scholarly observers, post-Communist commentators and politicians construed and unsurprisingly opposed a perceived return to the climate of the height of the Cold War, which for them was synonymous with dogmatic 1950s-style anti-communism. Numerous Social Democrats and liberals assumed similar positions. Meanwhile, the anti-Communists they criticized did not openly advocate such a return, but did expend considerable energy mourning the loss of what they regarded as the noble anti-totalitarianism of the early postwar decades; this, they believed, had been undermined in West Germany by Social Democratic rule, détente, generational change, and "1968," the negative effects of which they now hoped to reverse. Although divided over its assessment, both sides thus appeared to believe in the existence of a historical West German Cold War Culture that had been dominated by the binary division of the world and by anti-Communists' pervasive fear of and strident opposition to Communists and their fellow travelers, whose efforts at subversion and infiltration, and indeed whose mere existence, were deemed an existential threat to Western values.

This chapter examines the contours of this shared but contested belief in Cold War Culture and the question of its revival after unification. Empirically, it draws primarily on discussions before the Bundestag's Commissions of Inquiry "Working through the History and Consequences of the SED Dictatorship in Germany" and "Overcoming the Consequences of the SED Dictatorship in the Process of German Unity." Operating between 1992 and 1998, these parliamentary inquiries constituted a locus for the investigation and discussion of the Cold War's history and legacy in Germany. Having brought together politicians, scholars, intellectuals, and eyewitnesses, the inquiries provide a focused snapshot of postunification discourse on the Cold War.[8] That discourse touched more or less explicitly on many of the questions that are central to the present volume's investigation of Cold War Culture, including the origins and periodization of the Cold War; its impact on political cultures, mentalities, and identities; the divisions within the hostile blocs; and the connections across them.

Above all, the discourse offers insights into the debate between post–Cold War triumphalism and its critics. The Bundestag inquiries constituted a forum in which the "victors" of the Cold War sought symbolic and enduring affirmation of its historical and ideological outcome, while the "losers" sought to rescue what they could. This division is often misrepresented as running between West and East. Yet Cold War and post–Cold War divisions cut across the East-West divide. On numerous matters, in fact, a Western *and* Eastern anti-Communist majority sought to discredit a largely Eastern post-Communist minority. On many other questions, meanwhile, Western conservatives (with support from Eastern dissidents) sought to attack their traditional Western left-liberal opponents for being fellow travelers or for their alleged softness on communism, indeed for their complicity in undermining West German Cold War Culture. In lamenting the decline and rebuffing criticism of Cold War Culture, academics, intellectuals, and politicians on the Right sought its rehabilitation and to a considerable extent also its revival, while their counterparts on the Left highlighted its democratic and liberal deficits.[9]

Western Cold War Culture was thus a crucial element of a debate that is frequently misunderstood as having revolved primarily or exclusively around East German history. By examining the debate about the 1950s, I hope to show, first, that Western history was also vigorously contested; secondly, that Cold War era conflicts continued well into the 1990s; thirdly, that the perceived similarities between the 1950s and 1990s were the result not of unconscious reflexes but of deliberate attempts to censure and reverse ideological and intellectual trends of the preceding decades; but that, fourthly, those actors and commentators who perceive a straightforward revival of 1950s Cold War Culture in unified Germany fail to acknowledge the significant change that 1989–90 had brought about: the Cold War's transition from global conflict to the subject of historical debate.

Cold War Culture in Retrospect

While Eastern-bloc communism and Communists are undoubtedly the primary targets of post–Cold War triumphalism, their supporters, sympathizers, and observers in the West have not escaped attention. East Germany was certainly the primary focus of Germany's post–Cold War transitional justice and the process of "working through" the postwar past. In contrast, the Federal Republic of Germany (FRG) featured largely as an implicit point of comparison and an unquestioned norm.[10] Yet various aspects of Western history were also vigorously contested. So far, West German policy towards the GDR (*Deutschlandpolitik*) is the only one whose postunification reexamination has been thoroughly considered in the literature.[11] However, the speedy collapse of the East German regime and Soviet-bloc communism as a whole provoked a broader reevaluation of how communism had been viewed in the West. Such a reappraisal seemed particularly necessary in the early 1990s, given both the West German government's evident lack of a plan for unification in 1989 and the stability with which so many experts had credited East Germany. Revelations about the extent of Stasi repression and the rediscovery of the massive death toll at internment camps in the Soviet Occupation Zone (SBZ) added to the perceived need for a critical review of Western opinion. Many Easterners and Westerners asked why the Communist regime's fragility had not been recognized, and how and why its shady sides were so underrepresented in public and scholarly discourse.

The ensuing, wide-ranging debate provided Western conservatives and Eastern dissidents with a welcome opportunity to scold the Western Left for its insufficiently critical stance. Two examples from the Bundestag debate on the establishment of the first commission of inquiry in March 1992 can stand for many. According to minister for women and youth (and future chancellor) Angela Merkel of the Christian Democratic Union (CDU): "We were often amazed in the East about the illusions one had about the GDR in the West. I think we also need to discuss that. How was it possible that so-called progressive groupings in the West granted the dictatorships in the East a bonus of which right-wing dictators in other states could only dream?"[12] And according to the parliamentary leader of the CDU and the Christian Social Union (CSU) (and later Merkel's interior and then finance minister), Wolfgang Schäuble (CDU): "It appears at the moment as though the extent of misery and repression is becoming visible for the first time.... But are all these terrible discoveries really so new? Didn't we hear and were we not able to know at least vaguely about most of this even in the early years—if we wanted to know and believe it? Is it perhaps not the case that many truths were increasingly repressed in recent years and decades, equally in both parts of Germany?"[13] Such criticism set the tone for the commissions' work, not least because the governing coalition of the CDU/CSU and the Free Democratic Party (FDP) had a majority on the inquiry.

Space does not allow a full account of the public debate about the alleged intellectual "failings," "moral bankruptcy," "collaboration," or "betrayal of liberty" of which scholars, the media, public intellectuals, and left-wing political parties were accused, or of the competition between Left and Right over whose understanding of the GDR had been more realistic.[14] Clearly, questions about the (in)accuracy of assessments, representations, and prognoses about the GDR were linked with moral and ideological considerations, and a moralized discourse emerged in the early 1990s about who enjoyed, or had somehow sacrificed, the right to write East German history.[15] The answers to these questions reflected convictions about how the GDR should be viewed in the present, and these in turn were connected with wider political and identitarian projects for unified Germany.[16] For the current discussion, however, it is more important to consider that—as exemplified by Schäuble's references to the "repression" of what had been known earlier—the debate about recent failings exposed understandings of how East Germany had been seen before then. Indeed, it revealed a belief in a West German Cold War Culture whose defining characteristic was strident anti-communism.

The contours of Cold War Culture as perceived by the center-Right became evident in their critique of the post–Cold War Culture that supposedly had developed in West Germany during the era of détente. In the context of the commissions of inquiry, such criticism was expressed both in dedicated research papers and more incidentally during discussions of other topics. The first major set of complaints about what one might call the culture of détente that had allegedly become dominant since the late 1960s was that it had downplayed the dictatorial nature of the regime and paid insufficient attention to its repressive apparatus and practices, to its victims, and to the opposition. Conservative historian and expert witness to the commission Manfred Kittel argued that "the mental climate of a tendency to trivialize GDR injustice" had "become increasingly influential in the Federal Republic since the seventies."[17] Historian, prominent *Kommunistenfresser* ("devourer of Communists"), and expert witness Hubertus Knabe posited the need for self-critical reflection on Westerners' nonreceptiveness to critiques of Communism such as that of Alexander Solzhenitsyn.[18] Historian, sociologist, and expert commissioner for the CDU Manfred Wilke displayed an equally harsh view of the Western Left, wondering why viewing anti-Communist resistance as a fight for freedom had given way to seeing it as an activity of "Cold Warriors" that endangered détente.[19] His colleague Alexander Fischer suggested in similar terms that the publicist and victim of Stalinism Gerhard Finn, who was appearing before the commission, would have been decried as a "Cold Warrior" five years before.[20] And witness and former West German minister for expellees and for intra-German relations Heinrich Windelen (CDU) lamented widespread Western disinclination to campaign against GDR human-rights abuses, and the concomitant tendency to view doing so as a "relic of the Cold War."[21]

Such statements constituted not only a rejection of the anti-anti-communism of the culture of détente, but an implicit endorsement of prior readiness to register, highlight, and protest Communist crimes during the height of the Cold War in the 1950s. Long-standing anti-Communists sought to rehabilitate the Cold War Culture that anti-anti-Communists had assailed, and the repeated criticism of the pejorative use of terms such as "Cold Warrior" implied the rehabilitation of Cold Warriorhood.[22] This was evident again in an account given by theologian and historian Peter Maser, a member of the secretariat of the first inquiry and CDU commissioner of the second, of the commission's preferred terminology: "To refer to the GDR as the SED dictatorship had become unusual in wide circles in West Germany. Whoever used such a term was inevitably reviled by notorious do-gooders as a 'Cold Warrior,' opponent of détente, and 'anti-Communist.' ... On this the commission of inquiry provided again for an unambiguous form of expression that helped to blow away the fog from minds programmed toward accommodation."[23] As Maser's use of "again" suggests, at issue was not just the appropriate characterization of the GDR in the present, or even the errors of the culture of détente, but also the previous, putatively superior Cold War Culture.[24] Maser's distinction between wayward apologists and clear-sighted, anti-Communist democrats was characteristic of much postunification discourse, and indicated considerable continuity with Cold War era *Lagerdenken* ("thinking within ideological trenches").[25]

Conservatives' second major criticism of West German approaches to the GDR specifically targeted academic scholarship for its abandonment of the totalitarian paradigm, which they identified as a key ingredient of Cold War Culture.[26] Calls from the center-Right for the notion's reinstatement were invariably accompanied by condemnatory statements about its "marginalization" since the 1970s.[27] Its advocates focused more on rebuking those who allegedly had placed a "taboo" on the concept—or lauding the steadfastness of those who had continued to employ it—than on justifying it or addressing specific criticisms raised against it.[28] Yet it is possible to elucidate its perceived merits from the disparagement of its "system-immanent" rival. The main virtues with which totalitarianism was credited were of evaluative and political rather than analytical or explanatory nature. The "system-immanent" school was taken to task primarily for its normative abstentionism and its depoliticization of images of the GDR.[29] According to a paper by political scientist Eckhard Jesse on scholarship on the GDR, the paramount, justified criticism of the system-immanent mainstream of West German scholarship on the GDR in the 1970s and 80s was its "relinquishing of the application of Western-normative positions in evaluating the GDR.... A spade was not always called a spade where the nonexistent legitimacy of the second German state was concerned."[30] In contrast, totalitarianist approaches were lauded for their explicitly normative stance and for their ability to demonstrate similarities between communism and Nazism.[31] Thus despite all protestations that totalitarianism was no Cold War *Kampfbegriff* ("battle slogan"), its perceived virtues were precisely those that made it suitable as such, and its advocates seemed to want to return to the highly normative, indeed deeply politicized approach to the GDR of the 1950s and 60s.[32]

At issue was not just the relative emphasis given to dictatorial rule, repression, or resistance, but the total assessment of the East German regime. The center-Right insisted—here we have their third major complaint—that the insight that these phenomena were intrinsic to communism had been lost after the 1960s. According to the second inquiry's report, "this clear evaluation of the realities that are *innate* in Communist dictatorships increasingly disappeared from view after the hot phase of the Cold War subsided, not least due to seemingly necessary political considerations."[33] Only the total condemnation of totalitarian regimes that had characterized Cold War Culture was regarded as legitimate.

Intimately related to the issue of the absoluteness of the critique of the *regime* was the question of the illegitimacy of the East German *state*, and the importance of that illegitimacy for the Federal Republic.[34] The fourth major complaint about Western approaches to the GDR since the late 1960s—and here government policy and the media were implicated more than academic scholarship—was the apparent slide from absolute nonrecognition to granting the GDR legitimacy through recognition. Conservative parliamentarian Günther Müller (CSU) complained about liberal journalists' insistence on not questioning the GDR's "right to exist," and economist and inquiry witness Hannsjörg Buck bemoaned the system-immanent approach's failure to question the GDR "existentially."[35] Experts Bleek and Bovermann reflected at greater length on the fact that "the self-understanding of the Bonn Republic in its first two decades [rested] on its self-definition as the German democratic core state, which implied political nonrecognition of the GDR on the one hand and the ideological front position against the real Socialist dictatorship in Germany on the other."³⁶ Cold War Culture had thus entailed not only the absolute rejection of the East German state, but the centrality of this stance to West German identity. Such a position was grounded not least in seeing the GDR exclusively as an artificial creation of the Cold War, an insight, as Eckhard Jesse remarked, that was later repressed in favor of the notion that postwar division was the Germans' punishment for Auschwitz. The latter view, it was suggested, had emerged only in tandem with the decline of Cold War Culture, which had upheld a more clear-headed understanding of the second German state's origins, unencumbered by a wayward, moralistic sense of causality or responsibility.³⁷ Such arguments suggested that the Cold War had been (rightly) the defining feature of West German politics, culture, and identity in the 1950s and into the 1960s.

Closely connected with questions of recognition and legitimacy, a fifth component of the critique by conservatives and others concerned the unresolved national question and attempts to maintain or redefine German national identity during the period of division. Christian Democrats, Free Democrats, some Social Democrats, and numerous Eastern dissidents in various parties excoriated widespread Western indifference to East Germany and the national question in the decades before 1989, as well as the common tendency to regard the Federal Republic as "Germany." Manfred Wilke, for example, blamed détente not only for increasingly unrealistic assessments of communism, but also for declining belief in the nation; and Eckhard Jesse criticized mainstream GDR research for its conspicuous "lack of interest in Germany unity."³⁸ At the same time, conservatives criticized Social Democrats and liberals for their various efforts at elaborating on the identitarian consequences of continuing division, including the notion that the Germans constituted "two states, one nation," which was regarded as signaling acceptance of the status quo. According to the second commission's final report, "the previous view of the GDR was axiomatically determined by the latter's democratic and national illegitimacy," but developments from the late 1960s onwards saw the depoliticization not only of views of the GDR but also of the concept of "nation."³⁹ The apparent nadir in the mid to late 1980s was the tendency within the SPD and the Greens to regard the GDR just like any other foreign country (*normales Ausland*), and their readiness to consider recognizing separate East German citizenship.⁴⁰

In contrast to these seemingly postnational developments, Cold War Culture had entailed spirited national orientation. According to Bleek and Bovermann, "SBZ scholarship in the fifties was largely a scholarship for reunification."⁴¹ Similarly, Federal Chancellor Helmut Kohl (CDU) reported to the commission with considerable pride that in the 1970s he had appeared to many even in his own party to be a "diehard" (*Ewiggestriger*), because "I advanced views that we had earlier actually advanced together in the fifties and sixties," such as that the German people's will for national unity required the "recreation of the identity of nation and state." Kohl insisted with some justification that "that sounds today just like a self-evident statement, but at that time it had long ceased to be self-evident."[42]

Far from being content with highlighting the waywardness of détente-era approaches to the GDR and the nation, the Cold War's triumphant anti-Communist victors hoped to discredit their left-wing opponents from East and West Germany morally. The commissions paid considerable attention to the SED's role in fostering the various developments described above. The GDR's *Westarbeit* ("ideological work in the West") could not be shown conclusively to have been a decisive factor in undermining the view of the GDR as a dictatorial or totalitarian regime, or as a crime against the nation. Nevertheless, anti-Communists sought to discredit the Western Left by highlighting its apparent susceptibility to Communist manipulation, which was held to have both reflected and reinforced the decline of Cold War Culture.[43] Such arguments implied that the pervasive fear of Communist infiltration and subversion that had dominated West German Cold War Culture had not been unfounded.

If the features of Cold War Culture discussed thus far were more or less implicit in center-Right criticism of its demise, they were confirmed by occasional explicitly positive statements. According to conservative historian and expert witness Horst Möller, in West Germany:

> There was—and one shouldn't disregard this—a double anti-totalitarian basic consensus among the Germans. It was anti-National Socialist and anti-Communist. This—together with the positive value orientation toward the West—formed the constituent ingredient of the democratic parties and indeed of all the democratic parties after the Second World War and in the early Federal Republic. For me as a historian it is one of the regrettable developments that this anti-totalitarian basic consensus with its positive value orientation is apparently disappearing from memory.[44]

Similarly, political scientist and expert witness Gerd Langguth argued that "in the fifties and sixties the rejection of real existing communism was one of the supporting pillars, I almost want to say of the philosophy of state in West Germany—I think rightly, by the way."[45] However imprecisely, such statements expressed the same basic understanding and endorsement of Cold War Culture that emerged from the more frequent excoriation of its subsequent abandonment and the rise of the culture of détente. They also indicate again that Möller and others saw the Cold

War as being the defining feature of West German political culture in the first postwar decades.

The origins and merits of Cold War Culture were by no means unanimously agreed upon. The view of committed anti-Communists such as those quoted thus far was unambiguous: its crucial ingredient, anti-communism, was a response, indeed the only appropriate reaction to communism in general and to developments in eastern Germany after 1945 in particular. According to commissioner and former West German minister for intra-German relations Dorothee Wilms (CDU):

> The anti-Communist stance of the population in Germany, in West Germany—but I think also in the SBZ/GDR—was no hysteria and no ideology, but was fed by the experience that people had at the end of the war. The whole Stalinist policy after war's end, Korea, Berlin blockade, CSSR 1948, that was all freshly remembered, and we as West Germans—I am to that extent an eyewitness—experienced how hundreds of thousands came over from the then GDR. They came full of horror, full of antipathy. It was no illusion—everyone who came over wasn't crazy—they just wanted to get out of the system of bondage. So to that extent I reject the notion that the whole period of the fifties was hysteria, that it was an invention of Adenauer that people became anti-Communist. No, it was the experiences of a whole generation.[46]

On this reading, the origins of (West) German anti-communism (and of the Cold War itself) were to be found only in the years after 1945. Other accounts, meanwhile, did not go so far as to dispute its merits, but did acknowledge longer, less salubrious continuities and suggested, too, that the Cold War's origins also reached further back. Political scientist and FDP commissioner Hans-Adolf Jacobsen insisted: "Anticommunism was not fed alone by the developments of 1945, but one could also seamlessly connect to what [Nazi] demons had already proclaimed about Bolshevism and annihilation. But it has to be seen very differently, as the Americans also have to be considered, as well as the expellees, prisoners, etc."[47] Such differentiation and openness to continuities from the Third Reich into the Federal Republic was rather rare among those who sought to defend Cold War Culture.

Post-Communists agreed with the center-Right on the central features of Cold War Culture, although they differed markedly over its assessment and its origins. For them, it amounted to the stigmatization, political persecution, and criminalization of Communists, epitomized by the banning of the Western Communist Party of Germany (KPD) in 1956.[48] They objected fiercely to the perceived "heightening of the anti-Communist climate" in reunified Germany, which was "reminiscent of the earliest periods of the Cold War."[49] Extending Jacobsen's historical trajectory of anti-communism even further back, former East German expert on Western conservative thought and PDS commissioner Ludwig Elm emphasized even older traditions that were "anti-liberal and inimical to progress," dating back to the "counterrevolution of 1848/49," on which West German anti-communism had allegedly drawn. The "barbaric anti-bolshevism of the Nazi movement" had radicalized these traditions, but was itself discredited by 1945. Nevertheless, "the older and deeper layers—lying below the Nazi element—of bourgeois-conservative and nationalist enmity towards Marxism and the labor movement" continued into the postwar era.[50] In this view, "problems and conflicts" associated with developments in the SBZ and the GDR were merely "utilized" to promote extant anti-communism, "modified in accordance with the age."[51] Such a view limited the distinctiveness of Cold War Culture, but not Elm's opposition to it.

Social Democrats and liberals resisted and sought to diffuse conservative critiques of the 1970s and 80s, but addressed the earlier decades less forthrightly.[52] They appeared to share the same basic understanding of Cold War Culture, but their assessments were rather ambivalent. On occasion, Social Democrats evinced a desire not to be outdone retrospectively in their anti-communism or their nationalism, stressing especially postwar SPD leader Kurt Schumacher's rigor on both counts.[53] At other times, however, Social Democrats and liberals highlighted the negative aspects of Cold War Culture, offering moderate renditions of the more hysterical positions of post-Communists such as Elm. Publicist and invited expert Ilse Spittmann-Rühle, for example, claimed that the "climate of the Cold War" had inhibited accurate reporting on the GDR.[54] Publicist and inquiry witness Peter Bender similarly reminded the commission of the widespread fear of Communist infiltration in West Germany.[55] The SPD even spoke of criminalizing the KPD as a sign of the "deformation" of the Federal Republic, and Social Democrats argued that anti-communism had been used to tar the entire Left with the Communist brush.[56] Liberal philosopher and inquiry witness Jürgen Habermas also highlighted anti-communism's function in the internal politics of the Federal Republic, saying it had been used to create domestic political enmities (*innerpolitische Feinderklärungen*) "that do not belong in a democratic state ruled by law."[57] In addition to these significant concerns, the center-Left criticized the primacy that had been accorded to the confrontation with present communism over that with past Nazism.[58] It thus maintained much of the New Left's traditional critique of Federal Republican anti-communism and pointed to the illiberal tendencies of West German Cold War Culture, which on this reading had much in common with McCarthyism in the U.S.A.

The center-Right majority on the commissions of inquiry was clearly perturbed by the most vocal criticism directed against the Federal Republic's foundational Cold War Culture, and sought to deny any parallels between the GDR's persecution of political opponents and the persecution of Communists in 1950s West Germany. The second inquiry commissioned an expert report on the latter issue, and its final report offered a rather defensive account of the West's "legislation for the protection of the state." The inquiry's report conceded certain less-than-desirable outcomes, but gave no ground on the fundamental questions of the liberal and democratic acceptability of banning the KPD and otherwise discriminating against Communists.[59] A dissenting statement by the left-wing Alliance 90/The Greens commented perceptively that a critical reappraisal of Western practice would have been more worthwhile than the majority report's trite rejection of the comparison of the FRG and the GDR in this respect.[60] Such a reassessment, however, did not suit the reendorsement of Cold War Culture by the Right, which remained unapologetic about the illiberal aspects of a militant anti-communism that cast political opponents as traitors and enemies and was obsessed with real and imagined Communist infiltration. Any regrettable features were apparently marginal compared to the clear-sighted and morally rigorous condemnation of communism and its supporters and sympathizers. Such refusal to broach any serious criticism of West German anti-communism was consistent with conservatives' rejection of the culture of détente and their rehabilitation of Cold War Culture.

The Revival of Cold War Culture?

As mentioned at the outset, the totalitarian paradigm's return to prominence and the commission of inquiry's propagation of an anti-totalitarian consensus for reunified Germany prompted numerous commentators to remark on similarities with West German discourse of the 1950s. But to what extent is it meaningful to speak of a revival, rather than merely the rehabilitation of Cold War Culture? For all the attempts to restore the honor of once-decried Cold Warriors, had conservative positions remained unchanged since the 1950s, and were they now hegemonic?

Many on the Right certainly hoped to replace the left-leaning, postnational *Zeitgeist* of the 1970s and 80s with a more strident anti-communism and renewed national identification. Christian Democrats and Free Democrats—supported on many points also by Social Democrats, liberals, and members of Alliance 90/The Greens—painted an overtly normative picture of the GDR that largely resembled its 1950s predecessor: it was dominated by Communist crimes and abuses, and paid considerable attention to opposition to the regime, as well as the latter's victims; it saw repression as intrinsic to the regime, foregrounded the GDR's fundamental democratic and national illegitimacy, and sought thereby to attach further legitimacy to the Federal Republic.[61] With less enthusiastic support—and indeed against some opposition—from the moderate Left, Christian Democrats and Free Democrats also condemned the regime as totalitarian, and rejected suggestions of any positive side or democratic potential to East German Socialism. Moreover, conservatives sought to delegitimize not just official Marxist-Leninist ideology but Socialism generally, and thus to discredit the ideological heritage of the SPD, and of many Greens and Eastern dissidents (who naturally resisted this familiar political strategy).[62] In these respects, it is possible to speak of a conservative attempt to resurrect key features of Cold War Culture, which thus did not simply disappear or become irrelevant with the end of the Cold War itself.

Some post-Communists certainly perceived (and rejected) the revival of Cold War Culture. Hard-line PDS representatives repeatedly inveighed against the dangerous similarities between contemporary discourse and that of the 1950s, dramatizing in particular alleged parallels between past and present "criminalization" of communism and its adherents. During the debate on establishing the first inquiry, Uwe Jens Heuer (PDS) argued that "the current atmosphere can in many respects be compared only with the atmosphere of the fifties, the atmosphere at the time of the banning of the KPD."[63] Post-Communists also protested against the renewed use of the term "totalitarianism" and the anti-totalitarian consensus. According to Heuer: "Today the enlarged Federal Republic has returned to a considerable degree to the terminology of the Cold War. The much-criticized scholarship on the GDR again reaches for the term totalitarianism. Honecker is well on the way to becoming the Stalin of today."[64] Indeed, for the PDS the revival of "totalitarianism" merely served to justify the renewed discrimination against Communists. Ludwig Elm argued as follows:

> Members of the commission and some experts and eyewitnesses contributed to the fact that today the tendentious drawing of parallels between the GDR and the National Socialist criminal state occurs almost daily and without being contradicted in politics, media, and in areas of education and scholarship. It poisons the political climate by reviving images of the enemy from the coldest years of the Cold War and additionally—whether intentionally or through neglect—tends to play down the Nazi policy of conquest and eradication. Some statements and resolutions of the commission promote political discrimination and special laws in eastern Germany.[65]

For the PDS, Cold War Culture past and present was synonymous with anti-Communist persecution and exculpation of Nazism, legitimized by anti-totalitarianism.

Yet for all the concerns of the PDS and others, the 1990s did not witness a straightforward 1950s revival. Indeed, the most significant differences between the 1950s and the 1990s emerged, ironically, in the two areas that prompted the most concern about an ostensible restoration: the supposed persecution of (post-)Communists and the alleged anti-communist primacy or equationism that characterized the renewed "anti-totalitarian consensus." On the latter point, members of the Right insisted more or less sincerely that they did not want to equate the Nazi and Communist regimes or their crimes; they seemed to accept the continuing centrality and singularity of the Holocaust as the outcome of history debates in the 1980s and early 90s, perspectives on which both the moderate and the radical Left had insisted.[66] Perhaps even more important, however, was the change brought by 1989–90. Now that the GDR was consigned to history like the Third Reich, the need—already perceived in the 1950s—to focus on the present Communist threat rather than past Nazism—and thus to limit the reckoning with the latter largely to rhetorical distancing rather than genuine engagement with Germans' responsibility and complicity—had evaporated.[67] One should not regard the 1990s as witnessing the straightforward emergence of a liberal-democratic "Holocaust identity" that placed responsibility for Nazi crimes at the center of German memory.[68] Yet one can hardly say of Germany in the 1990s, as one can of West Germany in the 1950s, that it was more concerned with communism than with Nazism.

The GDR's demise and the end of the Cold War also account for the other main difference between the 1990s and the 1950s. PDS claims of the criminalization of (post-)Communists and communism were exaggerated. There is no doubt that the German state and its political establishment went to considerable lengths after 1990 to delegitimize the GDR, its representatives, and its ideology.[69] Yet they cannot be said to have criminalized (post-)Communists in general. While some on the Right lamented the fact that the party had not been outlawed, the mere presence of PDS representatives in the Bundestag and on the commissions of inquiry falsified its own arguments about a return to the hysteria and persecution of the height of the Cold War (just as Elm's claim that equationist parallels between the GDR and the Third Reich were passing uncontradicted was itself contradicted by his very speech).[70] Unification removed any threat that communism had ever posed to the legitimacy or stability of the Federal Republic, such that the criminalization of (post-)Communists was superfluous. Instead of criminalization, anti-Communists could be content with the politicization of Cold War history and the delegitimization of the GDR and its defenders. The Right's attempted rehabilitation of Cold Warriorhood and of historical Cold War Culture should therefore not be confused with the latter's resurrection in the present.

Yet certain continuities remained. Whereas political persecution had once been the harbinger of the illiberal aspects of Cold War Culture, now a certain illiberal intolerance was revealed in debates about the past: those who did not subscribe to the dominant interpretation of the past were politically suspect. According to conservative parliamentarian Hartmut Koschyk (CSU): "It can have quite negative consequences for the liberal, rule-of-law democracy in Germany if the SED dictatorship is seen as a legitimate alternative to the constitutional state of the Federal Republic of Germany, as intended by the historical interpretations of the PDS."[71] Such statements suggested that some anti-Communists had not reached the level of tolerance and relaxation that Jürgen Habermas deemed necessary for a genuinely liberal and democratic society, for they revealed the "general suspicion against internal enemies" that had once characterized Cold War Culture.[72] Now, however, those enemies were identified by their views on Cold War history. The relative importance of a Koschyk or a Habermas should not be neglected in assessing the significance of such intolerance in unified Germany. Nevertheless, Koschyk's statement highlighted not just the transition from criminalized politics to politicized history. It also demonstrated the stakes of the debate about Cold War history, a debate in which the delegitimization of the culture of détente and the relegitimization of Cold War Culture played a central role.

Notes

1. See for example Jürgen Danyel, ed., *Die geteilte Vergangenheit* (Berlin, 1995); Jeffrey Herf, *Divided Memory* (Cambridge, Mass., 1997); Norbert Frei, *Vergangenheitspolitik* (Munich, 1999).
2. Eric Langenbacher, "Changing Memory Regimes in Contemporary Germany?" *German Politics and Society* 21 (2003), no. 2: 46–68.
3. Bill Niven, *Facing the Nazi Past* (London, 2002), 6; Mary Nolan, "The Politics of Memory in the Berlin Republic," *Radical History Review* 81 (2001): 113–32, 114; Robert G. Moeller, "What Has 'Coming to Terms with the Past' Meant in Post–World War II Germany?" *Central European History* 35 (2002), no. 2: 223–256, 230.
4. For a discussion of some such continuities, see Andrew H. Beattie, "The Victims of Totalitarianism and the Centrality of Nazi Genocide," in *Germans as Victims*, ed. Bill Niven (Basingstoke, 2006), 147–163.

5. Andrew H. Beattie, "The Past in the Politics of Divided and Unified Germany," in *Partisan Histories*, ed. Max Paul Friedman and Padraic Kenney (New York, 2005), 17–38.
6. Stefan Berger, *The Search for Normality* (Providence, 1997), 254–255; Mary Fulbrook, "Heroes, Victims and Villains in the History of the GDR," in *Rewriting the German Past*, ed. Reinhard Alter and Peter Monteath (Atlantic Highlands, 1997), 175–196.
7. For a recent example, see Petra Haustein, *Geschichte im Dissens* (Leipzig, 2006), 184, 374f.; cf. Beattie, "Victims of Totalitarianism," 148, 155, 158f.
8. See Andrew H. Beattie, *Playing Politics with History* (New York, 2008).
9. Cf. Jerry Z. Muller, "German Neoconservatism and the History of the Bonn Republic, 1968–1985," *German Politics and Society* 18 (2000), no. 1: 1–32.
10. Cf. Jörn Leonhard and Lothar Funk, eds., *Ten Years of German Unification* (Birmingham, 2002); Beattie, *Playing Politics with History*, esp. chapter 3 and conclusion.
11. On the debate about *Deutschlandpolitik* before the commission of inquiry, see A. James McAdams, *Judging the Past in Unified Germany* (Cambridge, 2001), 92–116.
12. "Verwundert waren wir im Osten oft darüber, welche Illusionen man sich im Westen über die DDR machte. Auch darüber müssen wir, so meine ich, diskutieren. Wie war es denn möglich, daß im Westen die sogenannten fortschrittlichen Gruppierungen den Diktaturen im Osten einen Bonus einräumten, den sich rechte Diktaturen in anderen Staaten nur erträumen konnten?" Deutscher Bundestag, ed., *Materialien der Enquete-Kommission "Aufarbeitung von Geschichte und Folgen der SED-Diktatur in Deutschland" (12. Wahlperiode des Deutschen Bundestages)*, 9 vols. (Frankfurt am Main: Suhrkamp, 1995), 1:110.
13. "Es scheint ja, als würde derzeit das Ausmaß von Elend und Unterdrückung erst richtig sichtbar....
    Aber sind alle diese schrecklichen Erkenntnisse wirklich so neu? Hatten wir das meiste nicht wenigstens in Umrissen auch schon in früheren Jahren gehört und wissen können, wenn wir es denn wissen und glauben wollten? Ist es vielleicht also so, daß manches an Wahrheiten in den letzten Jahren und Jahrzehnten zunehmend verdrängt wurde, und zwar in beiden Teilen Deutschlands gleichermaßen?" Ibid., 1:59.
14. Jens Hacker, *Deutsche Irrtümer* (Berlin, 1992); Henryk M. Broder, "Ein moralischer Bankrott," *Der Spiegel* 51 (1991): 205–208; Cora Stephan, ed., *Wir Kollaborateure* (Reinbek, 1992); Konrad Löw, ... *bis zum Verrat der Freiheit* (Munich, 1993).
15. The Western debate in fact merged with an Eastern debate about the renewal of the historical sciences. See Mitchell G. Ash, "Geschichtswissenschaft, Geschichtskultur und der ostdeutsche Historikerstreit," *Geschichte und Gesellschaft* 24 (1998), no. 2: 283–304.
16. Konrad H. Jarausch, "The German Democratic Republic as History in United Germany," *German Politics and Society* 15 (1997), no. 2: 33–48, 35.
17. Deutscher Bundestag, *Materialien ... Aufarbeitung*, 9:647.
18. Ibid., 7:125–26; Heike Haarhoff, "Ein Mann auf der Lauer," *Die Tageszeitung*, 29 November 2006, 4-5, http://www.taz.de/1/archiv/archiv/?dig=2006/11/29/a0146.
19. Deutscher Bundestag, *Materialien ... Aufarbeitung*, 7:53.
20. Ibid., 66.
21. Ibid., 5:811.
22. In some respects, this constituted self-rehabilitation. Space does not allow a detailed discussion of personal biographies, but individuals such as Karl Wilhelm Fricke and Gerhard Finn represented personal continuities with Cold War Culture of the 1950s and 60s.
23. "Von der DDR als SED-Diktatur zu reden, war auch in Westdeutschland in breiten Kreisen unüblich geworden. Wer solch ein Wort in den Mund nahm, mußte sich von

den notorisch Gutmeinenden als 'Kalter Krieger,' Entspannungsgegner und 'Antikommunist' beschimpfen lassen.... Die Enquete-Kommission hat hier wieder für eine eindeutige Ausdrucksweise gesorgt, die dazu beigetragen hat, die Nebel aus den auf Anpassung programmierten Hirnen wegzublasen." Peter Maser, "Auf dem Weg zur deutschen Einheit," in *Unrecht überwinden: SED-Diktatur und Widerstand*, ed. Gerhard Finn et al. (Sankt Augustin, 1996), 69–77, 71.

24. The accuracy of the depictions of Cold War Culture was of secondary importance. In fact, before the "fog" of détente had set in, the GDR was generally called the "Zone," "Ostzone," "Sowjetzone," or "SBZ," terms that highlighted the Soviet occupier's role. Highlighting the SED's responsibility after 1990 was in fact a departure from the erasure of German Communism's historical roots from West German memory in the 1950s. See Eric Weitz, "The Ever-Present Other," in *The Miracle Years*, ed. Hanna Schissler (Princeton, 2001), 219–232. Cf. Corey Ross, *The East German Dictatorship* (London, 2002), 8.

25. Antonia Grunenberg, "Antitotalitarianism versus Antifascism," *German Politics and Society* 15 (1997), no. 2: 76–90.

26. Eckhard Jesse, "Doppelte Vergangenheitsbewältigung in Deutschland," in *Vergangenheitsbewältigung*, ed. E. Jesse and Konrad Löw (Berlin, 1997), 11–26, 17f.

27. Such depictions underestimated the plurality of approaches in Western scholarship. Cf. Ross, *The East German Dictatorship*, 14.

28. For example, Bernhard Marquardt, "Totalitarismustheorie und die Aufarbeitung der SED-Diktatur," in *Materialien ... Aufarbeitung*, ed. Deutscher Bundestag, 3:1530–1549, 1545. See Beattie, *Playing Politics with History*, chapter 6. For an exceptional acknowledgement that anti-communism had hindered the understanding of the GDR in the 1950s and 60s, see Jesse "Doppelte Vergangenheitsbewältigung," 17f.

29. See the report of the second commission of inquiry, Deutscher Bundestag, ed., *Materialien der Enquete-Kommission "Überwindung der Folgen der SED-Diktatur im Prozess der deutschen Einheit" (13. Wahlperiode des Deutschen Bundestages)*, 8 vols. (Frankfurt am Main: Suhrkamp, 1999), 1:697; and Eckhard Jesse, "Die politikwissenschaftliche DDR-Forschung in der Bundesrepublik Deutschland," in *Dem Zeitgeist geopfert*, ed. Peter Eisenmann and Gerhard Hirscher (Munich, 1992), 13–58. Cf. Ross, *The East German Dictatorship*, 17.

30. "den Verzicht auf das Geltendmachen westlich-normativer Positionen bei der Beurteilung der DDR.... Die fehlende Legitimität des zweiten deutschen Staates wurde nicht immer beim Namen genannt." Eckhard Jesse, "Die DDR-Forschung vor und nach der 'Wende' 1989/90," in *Materialien ... Überwindung*, ed. Deutscher Bundestag, 4:1191–1221, 1198f.

31. Deutscher Bundestag, *Materialien ... Aufarbeitung* 2:157f.

32. Horst Möller and Bernhard Marquardt both insisted that totalitarianism was no Cold War *Kampfbegriff* because it predated the Cold War, but they failed to demonstrate that it had not become—or was not still—a *Kampfbegriff*. Ibid., 9:577; Marquardt, "Totalitarismustheorie," 1531. Cf. Abbott Gleason, *Totalitarianism* (New York, 1995); Ross, *The East German Dictatorship*, 17, 21f.

33. "Diese klare Bewertung der den kommunistischen Diktaturen systemimmanenten Gegebenheiten geriet nach dem Abklingen der heißen Phase des Kalten Krieges auch aus notwendig erscheinenden politischen Rücksichtnahmen immer mehr aus dem Blickfeld." Deutscher Bundestag, *Materialien ... Überwindung*, 1:455, emphasis added.

34. On the differing degrees to which distinctions were made between socialism, the SED regime, and the GDR state, see Beattie, *Playing Politics with History*, especially chapters 3 and 4.

35. Deutscher Bundestag, *Materialien ... Aufarbeitung*, 1:121; idem, *Materialien ... Überwindung*, 3:236.
36. "[So] basierte das Selbstverständnis der Bonner Republik in ihren ersten zwei Jahrzehnten auf der Selbstdefinition als deutscher demokratischer Kernstaat, womit die politische Nichtanerkennung der DDR einerseits und die ideologische Frontstellung gegen die realsozialistische Diktatur in Deutschland andererseits impliziert war." Wilhelm Bleek and Rainer Bovermann, "Die Deutschlandpolitik der SPD/FDP-Koalition 1969–1982," in Deutscher Bundestag, *Materialien ... Aufarbeitung*, 5:1141–1187, 1157.
37. Jesse, "DDR-Forschung," 1199. See also Hans-Jürgen Fischbeck, Ludwig Mehlhorn, and Stephan Bickhardt, "Das Mauersyndrom: Die Rückwirkung des Grenzregimes auf die Bevölkerung der DDR," in Deutscher Bundestag, *Materialien ... Aufarbeitung*, 5:1188–1211, 1200.
38. Deutscher Bundestag, *Materialien ... Aufarbeitung*, 7:372; Jesse, "DDR-Forschung," 1199f. More moderately, Bleek and Bovermann, "Deutschlandpolitik," 1179.
39. Deutscher Bundestag, *Materialien... Überwindung*, 1:696f.
40. Ibid., 709; Deutscher Bundestag, *Materialien ... Aufarbeitung*, 1:110.
41. Bleek and Bovermann, "Deutschlandpolitik," 1178.
42. "Ich bin da [in the Catholic Academy, Munich] total durchgefallen als ein Ewiggestriger, weil ich Meinungen vertrat, wie wir sie eigentlich vorher gemeinsam in den 50er und 60er Jahren vertreten hatten. Ich will mich selbst zitieren: 'Die Menschen, die in beiden Teilstaaten leben, gehören unstreitig zum deutschen Volk. Auch wenn sie als Deutsche in verschiedenen Gesellschaftsordnungen leben. Sie sind nach wie vor deutscher Nationalität, auch wenn die Gemeinsamkeiten, die ein Volk als Einheit verbinden, durch die Trennung geschwächt werden.' Und dann fügte ich hinzu, 'daß der Wille zur Einheit der Nation ständig aktualisiert' werden müsse. Dazu gehört nach unserem Verständnis, nach dem Verständnis des Grundgesetzes die staatliche Einheit, die Wiederherstellung der Identität von Nation und Staat. Das hört sich heute eigentlich als eine bare Selbstverständlichkeit an, war aber zu jenem Zeitpunkt schon längst keine Selbstverständlichkeit mehr." Deutscher Bundestag, *Materialien ... Aufarbeitung*, 5:917.
43. Ibid., 1:489f.; Jochen Staadt, "Versuche der Einflußnahme der SED auf die politischen Parteien der Bundesrepublik nach dem Mauerbau," and Peter Schütt, "Die Kulturpropaganda der DKP als Teil der SED-Deutschlandpolitik," in ibid., 5:2406–2600 and 2331–2358 respectively, esp. 2415f. and 2356f.
44. "Es gab eben, und man sollte dieses nicht geringschätzen, einen doppelten antitotalitären Grundkonsens der Deutschen. Der war antinationalsozialistisch und antikommunistisch. Diese, verbunden mit der positiven Wertorientierung nach Westen, bildete die Konstituentien der demokratischen Parteien, und zwar aller demokratischen Parteien nach dem 2. Weltkrieg und in der frühen Bundesrepublik. Es gehört für mich als Historiker zu den bedauerlichen Entwicklungen, daß dieser antitotalitäre Grundkonsens mit seiner positiven Wertorientierung offensichtlich aus dem Gedächtnis verschwindet." Ibid., 5:299.
45. "[Aber] es war in den fünfziger, sechziger Jahren die Ablehnung des real existierenden Kommunismus eine der tragenden Säulen, jetzt möchte ich fast sagen, der Staatsphilosophie in Westdeutschland, wie ich meine, übrigens zu Recht." Ibid., 611.
46. "Die antikommunistische Haltung der Bevölkerung in Deutschland, in Westdeutschland, aber ich denke auch in der SBZ/DDR, war keine Hysterie und keine Ideologie, sondern sie war gespeist aus den Erfahrungen, die die Menschen am Ende des Krieges

erlebt hatten. Die ganze Stalinsche Politik nach Kriegsende, Korea, Berliner Blockade, CSSR 1948, das alles war ja in bester Erinnerung, und wir als Westdeutsche—ich bin insoweit Zeitzeugin—haben ja erlebt, wie Hunderttausende aus der damaligen DDR kamen. Sie kamen voller Entsetzen, voller Abscheu. Das war keine Illusion, das waren doch nicht alles Spinner, die herübergekommen sind, sondern sie wollten raus aus dem System der Unfreiheit. Insoweit verwahre ich mich dagegen, daß die ganze Zeit in den 50er Jahren eine Hysterie gewesen sei und daß es eine Erfindung von Adenauer gewesen sei, daß die Menschen antikommunistisch wurden. Nein, das waren die Erfahrungen einer ganzen Generation." Ibid., 284.

47. "Natürlich war der Antikommunismus nicht alleine gespeist von der Entwicklung von 1945, sondern man konnte ja fast nahtlos anknüpfen an das, was Ungeister schon vorher einmal im Hinblick auf Bolschewismus und Vernichtung proklamiert hatten. Aber das ist sehr differenziert zu sehen, zumal dabei auch die Amerikaner zu berücksichtigen sind, zudem die Vertriebenen, die Gefangenen usw." Ibid., 287.
48. Ibid., 1:694–695; Deutscher Bundestag, Materialien ... Überwindung, 1:806; Ludwig Elm, Das verordnete Feindbild (Cologne, 2001), 54. Cf. Patrick Major, The Death of the KPD (Oxford, 1997).
49. Elm, Das verordnete Feindbild, 52.
50. Ibid., 55, 59.
51. Ibid., 60.
52. Deutscher Bundestag, Materialien ... Überwindung, 1:457–459.
53. Deutscher Bundestag, Materialien ... Aufarbeitung, 5:257–260. For a recent account that similarly stresses Social Democrats' prominence in anti-Communist campaigns and commemoration during the 1950s, see Friedhelm Boll, Sprechen als Last und Befreiung (Bonn, 2003), 274–334.
54. Deutscher Bundestag, Materialien ... Überwindung, 8:52.
55. Deutscher Bundestag, Materialien ... Aufarbeitung, 5:508f.
56. Deutscher Bundestag, Materialien ... Überwindung, 1:765–769; Bernd Faulenbach, "Geteilte Vergangenheit—eine Geschichte?" in Deutsche Vergangenheiten—eine gemeinsame Herausforderung, ed. Christoph Kleßmann, Hans Misselwitz, and Günter Wichert (Berlin, 1999), 15–34, 31.
57. Deutscher Bundestag, Materialien ... Aufarbeitung, 9:738f.
58. Ibid., 3:167. Numerous scholars argue similarly that confronting the Nazi past for its own sake, or that of justice, took second place to unspecified exhortations to stand up to the threat of Communist totalitarianism "this time around." Sigrid Meuschel, "Legitimationsstrategien in der DDR und in der Bundesrepublik," in Kleßmann, et al., Deutsche Vergangenheiten, 115–127, 117; Bernhard Giesen, Intellectuals and the Nation (Cambridge, 1998), 148; Helmut Dubiel, "The Acceptance of Democracy," in Coping with the Past, ed. Kathy Harms, Lutz R. Reuter, and Volker Dürr (Madison, 1990), 130–139, 135; Robert G. Moeller, War Stories (Berkeley, 2001). On considerable conservative defensiveness after 1990 about alleged inadequacies in the FRG's confrontation with Nazism, see Beattie, Playing Politics with History, chapter 5.
59. Deutscher Bundestag, Materialien ... Überwindung, 1:711ff., 782.
60. Ibid., 714.
61. See Beattie, Playing Politics with History, esp. chapter 3.
62. On totalitarianism, see ibid., chapter 6, and on democratic potential and the delegitimation of the moderate Left, chapter 4. Cf. Anne Sa'adah, Germany's Second Chance (Cambridge, Mass., 1998), 252.
63. Deutscher Bundestag, Materialien ... Aufarbeitung, 1:80. Communist-dominated organizations of the victims of Nazism, such as the Auschwitz Committee in the Fed-

eral Republic of Germany, were similarly reminded of the "language and politics of the Cold War," ibid., 9:562. Cf. Haustein, *Geschichte im Dissens*, 220f., 252f.
64. "Heute ist die größere Bundesrepublik in großem Umfang zur Terminologie des Kalten Krieges zurückgekehrt. Die vielkritisierte DDR-Forschung greift wieder zur Vokabel des Totalitarismus. Honecker ist auf dem besten Wege, zum Stalin von heute zu werden." Deutscher Bundestag, *Materialien ... Aufarbeitung*, 1:80.
65. "Mitglieder der Kommission und manche Experten und Zeitzeugen trugen dazu bei, daß die tendenzielle Parallelisierung von DDR und nationalsozialistischem Verbrecherstaat heute in Politik, Medien, in Teilen von Bildung und Wissenschaft nahezu alltäglich und unwidersprochen stattfindet. Sie vergiftet das politische Klima, indem Feindbilder aus den kältesten Jahren des kalten Krieges wiederbelebt und übrigens—ob beabsichtigt oder fahrlässig—tendenziell die nazistische Eroberungs- und Ausrottungspolitik verharmlost werden. Manche Aussagen und Beschlüsse der Kommission förderten politische Diskriminierung und Sonderrechte in Ostdeutschland." Deutscher Bundestag, *Materialien ... Überwindung*, 1:827. Cf. Elm, *Das verordnete Feindbild*, 54.
66. Beattie, "Victims of Totalitarianism," 157–163.
67. Cf. Boll, *Sprechen als Last*, 218, 220, 293; Frei, *Vergangenheitspolitik*.
68. Jan-Werner Müller, "East Germany," in *The Politics of Memory and Democratization*, ed. Alexandra Barahona De Brito, Carmen Gonzalez Enriquez, and Paloma Aguilar (Oxford, 2001), 248–274. On Holocaust identity, see Giesen, *Intellectuals and the Nation*, chapter 7. Cf. A. Dirk Moses, "The Non-German German and the German German," *New German Critique* 34 (2007), no. 2: 45–94, 45–50.
69. McAdams, *Judging the Past*; Beattie, *Playing Politics with History*.
70. Rudolf Wassermann, "Vergangenheitsbewältigung nach 1945 und nach 1989," *Jahrbuch Extremismus und Demokratie* 5 (1993): 29–50, 38.
71. "Es kann durchaus negative Folgen für die rechtsstaatliche und freiheitliche Demokratie in Deutschland haben, wenn die SED-Diktatur als legitime Alternative zum Rechtsstaat Bundesrepublik Deutschland betrachtet wird, wie es die historischen Deutungsbemühungen der PDS beabsichtigen." Deutscher Bundestag, *Materialien ... Überwindung*, 1:121f.
72. Ibid., 690.

Bibliography

Ash, Mitchell G. "Geschichtswissenschaft, Geschichtskultur und der ostdeutsche Historikerstreit." *Geschichte und Gesellschaft* 24 (1998), no. 2: 283–304.

Beattie, Andrew H. "The Past in the Politics of Divided and Unified Germany." In *Partisan Histories: The Past in Contemporary Global Politics*, ed. Max Paul Friedman and Padraic Kenney (New York: Palgrave MacMillan, 2005), 17–38.

———. "The Victims of Totalitarianism and the Centrality of Nazi Genocide: Continuity and Change in German Commemorative Politics." In *Germans as Victims: Contemporary Germany and the Third Reich*, ed. Bill Niven (Basingstoke: Palgrave, 2006), 147–163.

———. *Playing Politics with History: The Bundestag Inquiries into East Germany*. New York: Berghahn, 2008.

Berger, Stefan. *The Search for Normality: National Identity and Historical Consciousness in Germany since 1800.* Providence, R.I.: Berghahn, 1997.

Boll, Friedhelm. *Sprechen als Last und Befreiung: Holocaust-Überlebende und politisch Verfolgte zweier Diktaturen. Ein Beitrag zur deutsch-deutschen Erinnerungskultur.* Bonn: Dietz, 2003.

Broder, Henryk M. "Ein moralischer Bankrott." *Der Spiegel* 51 (1991): 205–208.

Danyel, Jürgen, ed. *Die geteilte Vergangenheit: Zum Umgang mit Nationalsozialismus und Widerstand in beiden deutschen Staaten.* Berlin: Akademie Verlag, 1995.

Deutscher Bundestag, ed. *Materialien der Enquete-Kommission "Aufarbeitung von Geschichte und Folgen der SED-Diktatur in Deutschland"* [Working through the history and consequences of the SED dictatorship in Germany] *(12. Wahlperiode des Deutschen Bundestages).* 9 vols., Frankfurt am Main: Suhrkamp, 1995.

———. *Materialien der Enquete-Kommission "Überwindung der Folgen der SED-Diktatur im Prozess der deutschen Einheit"* [Overcoming the consequences of the SED dictatorship in the process of German unity] *(13. Wahlperiode des Deutschen Bundestages).* 8 vols., Frankfurt am Main: Suhrkamp, 1999.

Dubiel, Helmut. "The Acceptance of Democracy: Intellectual and Political Culture in West Germany." In *Coping with the Past: Germany and Austria after 1945,* ed. Kathy Harms, Lutz R. Reuter, and Volker Dürr (Madison: University of Wisconsin Press, 1990), 130–139.

Elm, Ludwig. *Das verordnete Feindbild: Neue deutsche Geschichtsideologie und "antitotalitärer Konsens."* Cologne: PapyRossa, 2001.

Faulenbach, Bernd. "Geteilte Vergangenheit—eine Geschichte? Eine Bestandsaufnahme." In *Deutsche Vergangenheiten—eine gemeinsame Herausforderung: Der schwierige Umgang mit der doppelten Nachkriegsgeschichte,* ed. Christoph Kleßmann, Hans Misselwitz, and Günter Wichert (Berlin: Christopher Links, 1999), 15–34.

Frei, Norbert. *Vergangenheitspolitik: Die Anfänge der Bundesrepublik und die NS-Vergangenheit.* Munich: Deutscher Taschenbuch, 1999.

Fulbrook, Mary. "Heroes, Victims and Villains in the History of the GDR." In *Rewriting the German Past: History and Identity in the New Germany,* ed. Reinhard Alter and Peter Monteath (Atlantic Highlands, N.J.: Humanities Press, 1997), 175–196.

Giesen, Bernhard. *Intellectuals and the Nation: Collective Identity in a German Axial Age.* Cambridge: Cambridge University Press, 1998.

Gleason, Abbott. *Totalitarianism: The Inner History of the Cold War.* New York: Oxford University Press, 1995.

Grunenberg, Antonia. "Antitotalitarianism versus Antifascism: Two Legacies of the Past in Germany." *German Politics and Society* 15 (1997), no. 2: 76–90.

Haarhoff, Heike. "Ein Mann auf der Lauer." *Die Tageszeitung,* 29 November 2006, 4–5.

Hacker, Jens. *Deutsche Irrtümer: Schönfärber und Helfershelfer der SED-Diktatur im Westen.* Berlin: Ullstein, 1992.

Haustein, Petra. *Geschichte im Dissens: Die Auseinandersetzungen um die Gedenkstätte Sachsenhausen nach dem Ende der DDR.* Leipzig: Leipziger Universitätsverlag, 2006.

Herf, Jeffrey. *Divided Memory: The Nazi Past in the Two Germanys.* Cambridge, Mass.: Harvard University Press, 1997.

Jarausch, Konrad H. "The German Democratic Republic as History in United Germany." *German Politics and Society* 15 (1997), no. 2: 33–48.

Jesse, Eckhard. "Die politikwissenschaftliche DDR-Forschung in der Bundesrepublik Deutschland." In *Dem Zeitgeist geopfert: Die DDR in Wissenschaft, Publizistik und politischer Bildung,* ed. Peter Eisenmann and Gerhard Hirscher (Munich: v. Hase & Koehler Verlag, 1992), 13–58.

———. "Doppelte Vergangenheitsbewältigung in Deutschland: Ein Problem der Vergangenheit, Gegenwart und Zukunft," in *Vergangenheitsbewältigung*, ed. Eckhard Jesse and Konrad Löw (Berlin: Duncker & Humblot, 1997), 11–26.

Langenbacher, Eric. "Changing Memory Regimes in Contemporary Germany?" *German Politics and Society* 21 (2003), no. 2: 46–68.

Leonhard, Jörn, and Lothar Funk, eds. *Ten Years of German Unification: Transfer, Transformation, Incorporation?* Birmingham: Birmingham University Press, 2002.

Löw, Konrad. *... bis zum Verrat der Freiheit: Die Gesellschaft der Bundesrepublik und die "DDR."* Munich: Langen Müller, 1993.

McAdams, A. James. *Judging the Past in Unified Germany*. Cambridge: Cambridge University Press, 2001.

Major, Patrick. *The Death of the KPD: Communism and Anti-Communism in West Germany, 1945–1956*. Oxford: Clarendon Press, 1997.

Maser, Peter. "Auf dem Weg zur deutschen Einheit: Anmerkungen zur neuen Enquete-Kommission des Deutschen Bundestages." In *Unrecht überwinden: SED-Diktatur und Widerstand*, ed. Gerhard Finn, Frank Hagemann, Peter Maser, Helmut Müller-Enbergs, Günther Wagenlehner, Hermann Wentker (Sankt Augustin: Konrad Adenauer Stiftung, 1996), 69–77.

Meuschel, Sigrid. "Legitimationsstrategien in der DDR und in der Bundesrepublik." In *Deutsche Vergangenheiten—eine gemeinsame Herausforderung: Der schwierige Umgang mit der doppelten Nachkriegsgeschichte*, ed. Christoph Kleßmann, Hans Misselwitz, and Günter Wichert (Berlin: Christopher Links, 1999), 115–127.

Moeller, Robert G. *War Stories: The Search for a Usable Past in the Federal Republic of Germany*. Berkeley and Los Angeles: University of California Press, 2001.

———. "What Has 'Coming to Terms with the Past' Meant in Post-World War II Germany?" *Central European History* 35 (2002), no. 2: 223–256.

Moses, A. Dirk. "The Non-German German and the German German: Dilemmas of Identity after the Holocaust." *New German Critique* 34 (2007), no. 2: 45–94.

Müller, Jan-Werner. "East Germany: Incorporation, Tainted Truth, and the Double Division." In *The Politics of Memory and Democratization: Transitional Justice in Democratizing Societies*, ed. Alexandra Barahona De Brito, Carmen Gonzalez Enriquez, and Paloma Aguilar (Oxford: Oxford University Press, 2001), 248–274.

Muller, Jerry Z. "German Neoconservatism and the History of the Bonn Republic, 1968–1985." *German Politics and Society* 18 (2000), no. 1: 1–32.

Niven, Bill. *Facing the Nazi Past: United Germany and the Legacy of the Third Reich*. London: Routledge, 2002.

Nolan, Mary. "The Politics of Memory in the Berlin Republic." *Radical History Review* 81 (2001): 113–132.

Ross, Corey. *The East German Dictatorship: Problems and Perspectives in the Interpretation of the GDR*. London: Arnold, 2002.

Sa'adah, Anne. *Germany's Second Chance: Trust, Justice and Democratization*. Cambridge, Mass.: Harvard University Press, 1998.

Stephan, Cora, ed. *Wir Kollaborateure: Der Westen und die deutschen Vergangenheiten*. Reinbek bei Hamburg: Rowohlt, 1992.

Wassermann, Rudolf. "Vergangenheitsbewältigung nach 1945 und nach 1989." *Jahrbuch Extremismus und Demokratie* 5 (1993): 29–50.

Weitz, Eric. "The Ever-Present Other: Communism in the Making of West Germany." In *The Miracle Years: A Cultural History of West Germany, 1949–1968*, ed. Hanna Schissler (Princeton: Princeton University Press, 2001), 219–232.

Chapter 15

THE MIKSON CASE
War Crimes Memory, Estonian Identity Reconstructions, and the Transnational Politics of Justice

Valur Ingimundarson

Introduction

The end of the Cold War not only discredited communism but also destabilized other ideological truisms. In the early 1990s, the Soviet successor states and the countries of Eastern Europe began to grapple with the legacy of communism, usually opting for lustration or purges rather than prosecution, trials, or truth commissions. The initial anti-Communist focus fitted well with attempts by the political elite in the Baltic states to portray resistance against the Soviets in heroic terms and to use victimization narratives (e.g., the Soviet annexation during World War II) as a tool to reconstruct new Western-oriented national identities with the strategic goal of joining the European Union and NATO. As with all such reconfigurations, however, the narrative sanitized important aspects of their national pasts. Not only was the anti-democratic character of the interwar right-wing regimes downplayed, but the collaboration with Nazi Germany in World War II, including participation in war crimes, was rationalized by the struggle against Soviet repression.

It was logical to point to the travesty of Soviet justice, as symbolized by show trials over alleged Baltic war criminals during the Cold War. But since the Holocaust had already in the 1970s become the dominant narrative of World War II, it was impossible to avoid political scrutiny of the wartime past in the final phases of the Cold War and beyond. Indeed, Western governments, including the United States and France, were heavily involved in projects promoting the lessons of the Holocaust.[1] This development was highlighted by media spectacles in the 1980s and 1990s surrounding the extradition of the accused war criminal John Demjanjuk (a U.S. citizen of Ukrainian descent whose death sentence was later repealed by the Israeli Supreme Court on the grounds of mistaken identity) and the war-crimes trials of French Nazi collaborators Paul Touvier and Maurice Papon.

In this chapter, I discuss how various discourses on war crimes, especially Estonian, Icelandic, and Jewish, but also Russian and American ones, were used to influence, revise, and question national identities, individual and collective guilt, and governmental behavior during and after the Cold War. The purpose is not only to explore—from a transnational perspective—the ideological tension between anti-communism, a defining feature of the cultural Cold War, and memories of the Holocaust. These metanarratives are also juxtaposed against microhistorical, individual, and biographical representations of wartime collaboration. As a case study, I have chosen the so-called Mikson case.[2] It centered on charges—first put forward by Sweden in 1945, then by the Soviet Union in the 1960s, and finally by the Israel-based Simon Wiesenthal Center in the 1990s—against an Estonian policeman, Evald Mikson, who later became a citizen of Iceland, for killing Communists and Jews during the late phase of the Russian occupation of Estonia in 1940–41 and the German occupation from 1941 to 1944.[3]

As Alon Confino has argued, historians have been more successful in conceiving memory through historical sites, buildings, monuments, films, or novels—that is, through cultural and political representation in the public sphere—than in explaining human experiences such as mass atrocities.[4] I seek to address this problem here by focusing on the intersection between individual representations based on experiences, on the one hand, and reconfigurations of structural power relations and collective memories on the other. First, I explain how Cold War interpretations, in Estonia and Iceland, of Mikson's heroic struggle against Soviet communism were pitted against accusations of war crimes against Communists and Jews. Second, I show that geopolitical and ideological paradigm shifts—from World War II to the Cold War and beyond—led to radically different political and judicial responses to the case. Thus, from a broader perspective, the narrative deals with the production and reproduction of conflicting "truths" about national pasts, and with the destabilization of fixed political and cultural identities.

Mikson's Background: Serving the Old Guard in Estonia in the 1930s and 1940s

Evald Mikson's career was closely linked to political developments in Estonia. After serving in the army, he joined the police in the early 1930s. When Estonia's parliamentary system was abolished in the mid 1930s to pave the way for a conservative authoritarian regime, Mikson took part in the coup, and remained a government servant until the Soviets occupied the country in the summer of 1940.[5] The occupation resulted in the dismissal of most members of the security police, including Mikson, who went into hiding. It has been estimated that during the Soviet occupation over 7,000 people were arrested, the vast majority of whom were executed or died in prison. What caused the most serious trauma was the deportation to the Soviet Union of more than 10,000 Estonians—including 5,000 women and 2,500 children—associated with the former regime. The Estonian anti-Soviet resistance was largely sparked by these deportations, and by the German invasion of the Soviet Union in June 1941.

Mikson was among the organizers of the so-called Forest Brothers and its successor movement, the *Omakaitse*, whose goal was to resist the Soviets and to punish collaborators.[6] It has been estimated that over 7,800 Estonian citizens were killed during the German occupation.[7] Most of these killings, which took place in the first months following the German invasion, were committed by members of the *Omakaitse* who were later incorporated into the Estonian police. Despite its anti-Communist agenda, the Germans felt that the *Omakaitse* had acted illegally and arbitrarily when dealing with suspected collaborators. The accusations against Mikson stem partly from his activities as an *Omakaitse* leader in July and August 1941, that is, before the Germans had established full control in Estonia.

Of course, the Germans did not only target Communists and Soviet sympathizers in Estonia. Roundups and killings of Jews were committed by the extermination squad *Einsatzkommando (Sonderkommando)* 1A under Martin Sandberger, which was part of *Einsatzgruppe A*. However, 75 percent of Estonia's Jewish community, which numbered about 4,500, managed to escape to the Soviet Union; virtually all remaining people (between 950 and 1000 men, women, and children) were killed before the end of 1941.[8] Estonians, among them Mikson, collaborated closely with the Germans in arresting Jews, and according to German sources they also took part in the killings.[9]

The Soviet annexation of Estonia explains why most Estonians saw the Germans as "friendly occupiers." The Germans never planned to restore Estonia's republican status or to grant it sovereignty.[10] But given the high racial status of Estonians in German eyes, they were given a large degree of self-administration.[11] In September 1941, Mikson was appointed deputy to the head of the Information Department of the Political Police of the Tallinn-Harju prefecture. During his tenure, he not only interrogated many suspected Communists and Jews, but signed the arrest warrants of almost thirty individuals: Estonians, Jews, and Russians. Most of them were later executed. At the end of November 1941, however, Sandberger ordered Mikson's arrest. The reason is not fully clear. In postwar testimonies, most of those with knowledge of the case cited two different reasons: that he stole valuables from prisoners or that he was engaged in unauthorized killings.[12]

Mikson always denied these allegations. In his autobiography, he claimed that the Germans were furious over his failure to divulge important details of his interrogation of Karl Säre, the head of the Estonian Communist Party.[13] No evidence has been produced to link Mikson's arrest with Säre, and contrary to Mikson's postwar assertions, other people were also involved in the interrogation.[14] Mikson, who received a three-year sentence, was released in 1943.[15] It was alleged that he had become a German informant during his prison sentence[16]—a charge made more plausible by his subsequent work for the *Abwehr*, the German military intelligence organization. Mikson fails to address the question in his autobiography, but makes much of Sandberger's supposed ill will toward him.[17] In any case, Mikson was not released until after Sandberger left his Tallinn position in 1943. Little is known about Mikson's work for the *Abwehr* before he fled to Sweden in September 1944—on the same day the Soviets reoccupied Tallinn. But given his police career and his role in the Estonian resistance movement, he had no chance of surviving in Soviet Estonia.

War-Crimes Allegations: Mikson in Sweden, 1944–1946

In Sweden, the first war-crimes accusations against Mikson were put forward by Estonian refugees. They testified that he had spied for the Germans, killed Communists and Jews, raped Jewish women, beaten prisoners and stolen from them, and pronounced death sentences.[18] As a result, he was incarcerated in a Swedish detention camp for many months from 1944 to 1945. Having concluded that Mikson was guilty of war crimes, the Swedish authorities decided to deport him to Estonia in late 1945. The implementation of the decree, however, was delayed until October 1946. In the meantime, Mikson—with the assistance of a sympathetic anti-Communist Swedish lawyer, Yngve Schartau—managed to receive a special hearing at Stockholm's Magistrate Court, which allowed countertestimonies in his favor by other Estonian refugees. The hearing had no bearing on the order. But at the last moment a Swedish official came to Mikson's rescue and brought him safely to the Norwegian border, where he boarded a ship heading for South America.[19] By pure chance, however, Mikson settled in Iceland after the ship was stranded near the island.

Mikson's intention had always been to emigrate to the United States. With the emerging Cold War, Mikson's lawyer used his anti-Soviet credentials to back his application. It was turned down in 1947, however, no doubt because of his collaboration with the Germans. The Icelandic authorities, in contrast, did not pay much attention to his past. In the intense climate of the Cold War, Mikson's anti-communism was a sign of strength. Moreover, the Soviet annexation of the Baltic states generated sympathy for the plight of Estonians, Latvians, and Lithuanians in Iceland. Mikson married an Icelandic woman, gained Icelandic citizenship in 1955, and acquired a new Icelandic name, Eðvald Hinriksson. With his experience as a goalkeeper on the Estonian national football team in the 1930s, he worked in Iceland mainly as a sports coach and masseur. In the early 1960s, he opened up his own sauna and massage parlor, which was soon frequented by the Icelandic political elite.

The Second Round: Soviet War Crimes Accusations in 1961

Mikson's past came back to haunt him in 1961, when the organ of the Icelandic Socialist Party, Þjóðviljinn, charged him with the mass murder of Communists and Jews during World War II, based on evidence introduced at a trial in Estonia of three collaborators, Ain-Ervin Mere, Ralf Gerrets, and Jaan Viik.[20] Despite the seriousness of the charges, Morgunblaðið, the most influential newspaper in Iceland and the mouthpiece of the largest party (the center-Right Independence Party) gave him its full backing. It was affiliated with Minister of Justice Bjarni Benediktsson, a staunch anti-Communist who had approved Mikson's citizenship application.[21] Mikson's strategy was to depict himself as an opponent of both Nazism and communism. He had been imprisoned by the Nazis for his "services to the Estonian Republic" and because he had refused to join the German secret services. Even if Mikson was an anti-Soviet Estonian nationalist, he had, as noted, worked for the Germans in 1941 and after his release from prison in 1943. Postwar condemnation of Nazism made it necessary to equate the activities of the Germans with those of the Soviets,[22] but his anti-communism was far stronger.

The allegations became part of a heated Cold War debate. Morgunblaðið harped on Mikson's patriotism when faced with Communist evil, suggesting that the Soviets had fabricated the charges to stage a show trial.[23] Moreover, it sought to establish a common link between Iceland's independence struggle and that of the Baltic states.[24] This Cold War narrative proved to be effective and long-lived. It was based on the notion that the accusations against Mikson were part of a Communist smear campaign. The moral lesson was that if the Icelanders failed to respond forcefully to communism, they could face the same fate as the Baltic states.

When *Þjóðviljinn* published copies of new Estonian documents in the spring of 1961, showing that Mikson had signed arrest warrants for Communists and Jews in 1941,[25] the Ministry of Justice refused to reconsider its decision not to open an investigation. These documents were more reliable than the KGB testimonies, which had been based on leading questions twenty-five years after the alleged events. However, in the politically charged atmosphere they were not deemed to warrant further examination.

One puzzle is why Mikson—unlike Mere, Gerrets, and Viik—was not indicted in absentia for war crimes. The notion that Icelandic newspaper accounts had anything to do with the case lacked credibility. *Þjóðviljinn* had only reported about the charges against Mikson, not initiated them. As part of the Estonian investigation, material on Mikson's activities in Estonia was collected and witnesses were interrogated about his role in opposing the Soviets. Yet in September 1961, the Estonian KGB decided to halt the investigation, on the pretext that Mikson's whereabouts were unknown. This was absurd, because *Þjóðviljinn* had already published his address. When the case was reexamined in 1971 and 1983, this proved to be a recurring stumbling block. Since the KGB possessed this information, it does not explain why the investigation was closed.[26] The Estonian authorities investigated the matter based on the *Þjóðviljinn* articles and requests by several Estonians. What may have played a role was that Icelandic Socialist leaders had advised against it, believing that the political timing was not ripe.

Given Mikson's anti-Communist record, it is unlikely that the KGB tried to recruit him. Even if the motive was to blackmail him, he could always rely on Icelandic support. Before the show trials in Estonia, the KGB approached Mere, but when he turned down the offer,[27] he was charged and sentenced in absentia. In February 1993, the chief of the Estonian Supreme Court, Rait Maruste, suggested that the KGB had been interested in having Mikson extradited because of his information on Karl Säre, the head of the Estonian Communist Party.[28] Although the Soviets did not close the case in 1961, they never requested Mikson's extradition. Perhaps they calculated—plausibly—that the Icelandic government would never grant it; perhaps they believed that not enough political capital was to be extracted from war-crimes trials so long after the war;[29] or perhaps they felt that the evidence against Mikson was too weak to warrant a major political effort. Whatever the reason, the Soviets did not pursue the matter following the 1961 trial.

The Simon Wiesenthal Center Revives the Mikson Case in 1992

The Mikson case remained dormant until the end of the Cold War.[30] Mikson witnessed the demise of the Soviet Union and the reestablishment of Estonia's former status as an independent state in 1991. Iceland played a part by being the first country to grant the Baltic states diplomatic recognition. Symbolically, this act also brought an Icelandic Cold War narrative—the notion of close cultural-political bonds between Iceland and the Baltic states—to a successful conclusion. That they had, in fact, never had much in common, except their small size, was immaterial. What the new Baltic political elites shared with the Icelandic one was their satisfaction with the fall of the Soviet empire. Hence, it was seen as only natural to portray the anti-Communist struggle as the founding myth of the restored Baltic states.

At first, this selective narrative was not questioned. But in 1992, the Mikson case was suddenly and dramatically reopened. Ironically, it was Mikson himself who was responsible for this, by giving an interview to an Estonian newspaper, *Eesti Express*, where he recounted his version of Estonia's wartime history, especially his interrogation of Säre.[31] An Estonian Jew who read the interview and lived in Israel remembered Mikson for a different reason, namely in connection with the persecution of Jews. After he notified the Simon Wiesenthal Center, its director, Efraim Zuroff, made this a priority case. To ensure maximum publicity, he chose the visit to Israel in early 1992 of the Icelandic Prime Minister Davíð Oddsson, head of the center-Right Independence Party, to publicize the accusations against Mikson.[32]

The reaction in Iceland, where the case received a lot of media attention, was characterized by rejection and moral indignation. First, several politicians and editors made much of the point that the Israeli government had made a mockery of Oddsson's visit by such a blatant breach of protocol. This opinion was seconded by Foreign Minister Jón Baldvin Hannibalsson, the head of the Social Democratic Party, the Independence Party's coalition partner. Hannibalsson, who was far more critical of Israel than Oddsson, argued that the Israeli government had entrapped the latter. What may also have influenced Hannibalsson was that he had pushed for the recognition of the Baltic states and was deeply respected in Estonia.³³ Second, the Israeli-Palestinian conflict was evoked as an argument against both Mikson's extradition to Israel (which was never a realistic possibility) and Israel's moral authority to demand it. A parallel was drawn between the Holocaust and crimes against Palestinians.

Thirdly, when it became known that the allegations were based on the same KGB documents that were used in the 1961 trials, Hannibalsson questioned their authenticity.³⁴ Oddsson was more careful, stressing Mikson's rights and warning against jumping to conclusions about events that had taken place half a century ago. Acknowledging that the Simon Wiesenthal Center was respected internationally and had often been proven right, he pointed out—with obvious reference to the Demjanjuk case³⁵—that it had also been proven wrong. As in 1961, it was clear from the start that the Icelandic government was not going to take legal action against Mikson.

Mikson rejected all the allegations. His son, Atli Eðvaldsson, formerly an internationally known football player and at the time coach of the national football team, became his chief spokesman. As in 1961, Mikson was most concerned about possible extradition requests. Claiming that Bjarni Benediktsson, the Minister of Justice in 1961, had informed him during the height of the Cold War that Russian courts would never reach Icelanders, he now pinned his hopes on Oddsson.³⁶ While Mikson could still rely on considerable public support, the demise of communism robbed him of his strongest political weapon. While *Morgunblaðið* had acted as his mouthpiece in 1961, it was not willing to defend his wartime record any more. Nonetheless, it remained deeply skeptical of the use of KGB evidence and, consistent with its establishment credentials, was respectful of Mikson's social standing in Iceland.³⁷

There was far more overt support for Mikson in Estonia, where he was seen by many as a heroic anti-Communist resistance fighter. The Estonian Foreign Ministry declared that Mikson was not guilty of any crimes, least of all against Jews.³⁸ The Ministry of Justice subsequently offered Mikson the chance of letting an Estonian court decide whether he was guilty or not—a proposition that lacked credibility given the government's categorical stand on the issue.³⁹ Legally, he could be tried for collaborating with the Germans and for signing arrest warrants for Jews. However, this could hardly be achieved, as this was only one such case among many.⁴⁰ While the Cold War spell on the Mikson case had showed some signs of weakening in Iceland, the opposite was the case in Estonia. There was no interest in undermining the dominant memory of anti-Communist resistance by drawing attention to Nazi collaboration.

The defensive reaction in Iceland and Estonia only made Efraim Zuroff more determined to pursue the case.⁴¹ His options, however, were limited.

Mikson had committed no crimes in Iceland. The Icelandic government would not extradite him to Estonia, Russia, or Israel because of apprehensions concerning the judicial systems in these countries. Moreover, no war-crimes legislation existed in Iceland. Because of the statute of limitations, the only charge that could be brought against him was that of murder. Finally, in contrast to U.S. law, foreign immigrants in Iceland could not be deprived of their citizenship and deported if they had lied about their past when applying for a residence permit. Nothing suggests that Mikson's wartime role played any part in the decision to grant him Icelandic citizenship. As noted, his anti-Communist credentials had been an asset during the Cold War.

The Simon Wiesenthal Center, however, continued to put pressure on the Icelandic government. It produced copies of documents about Mikson from the Estonian archives. Those included arrest warrants and interrogation reports from his time in the Estonian Security Police. Moreover, Zuroff referred to a damaging report, hitherto unknown in the context of the Mikson case, by a Finnish security policeman, Olavi Viherluoto, who had met Mikson in 1941 when he was working for the Estonian security police.[42] Viherluoto, who had visited Tallinn to interrogate Säre,[43] claimed that Mikson had spoken of his involvement in killing Jews. Mikson mentions Viherluoto's visit in his autobiography, but claims he was a drunk and a Communist spy.[44] Viherluoto's report is open to interpretation. After the Finnish military defeat against the Soviet Union, the Soviets infiltrated the Finnish security police. Yet since they never used this information against Mikson, the purported motive for planting it makes little sense.[45]

In October 1992, two Icelandic legal experts commissioned by the government published their opinion that there was no need to open an investigation into Mikson's past "as things now stand."[46] Yet this conclusion did not silence government critics. Atli Eðvaldsson interpreted it as "proof" of Mikson's innocence.[47] However, Efraim Zuroff claimed that it was a whitewash and a "joke."[48] He pointed out that the lawyers had not asked for—or examined—the relevant documents or interviewed potential witnesses.[49] Indeed, their reasoning would have ruled out any war-crimes trials, such as those of Papon and Touvier. Similar investigations were already being conducted in the United States, Germany, Canada, Australia, and New Zealand.[50] The Icelandic government's inaction was also criticized at home, especially by the sensationalist weekly *Pressan*, which became Zuroff's main vehicle for publishing his side of the story.[51] *Pressan* was the only Icelandic newspaper that published the allegations in detail and gathered new material on the story by contacting Estonian witnesses. Yet Zuroff's belligerent tactics also alienated many Icelanders, who resented what they saw as a witch-hunt—a view reflected in some media accounts of the case.[52]

It was not only the Simon Wiesenthal Center that found the legal opinion flawed. Despite their interest in the Mikson case during the Cold War, the Russians had stayed out of it when it flared up again. But in late 1992, the Russian Ambassador to Iceland Yuri Reshetov, who had also served in Reykjavik during the Cold War, broke his silence. In his capacity as an "expert in international law," in an article in *Morgunblaðið* he criticized not only the two lawyers, but also the government for failing to initiate an investigation.[53] Foreign Minister Hannibalsson interpreted this act as bordering on interference in Icelandic domestic affairs and officially cautioned Reshetov.[54]

In early February 1993, Zuroff came to Iceland armed with KGB documents from the 1961 investigation, notably the testimony of 43 witnesses.[55] He stated that Mikson was guilty of murdering 30 people and ordering the killing of 150 others. Thus, he accepted without reservation the testimony of not only the 7 people who claimed to have seen Mikson commit murders, but also of the 36 people who had second-hand knowledge of his activities. What is clear is that the witnesses linked Mikson to at least 9 murders, mostly of Communists but also of two Jewish women.[56] This was surely damaging evidence, involving the unregulated activities of the *Omakaitse* during the summer of 1941. However, the testimony had been gathered by the KGB, whose heavy-handed questioning tactics undermined it as evidence. It is known that the *Omakaitse* formed field courts and sentenced people to death. No documentary proof to that effect has been found for Mikson's unit, and no death warrants signed by Mikson have been unearthed.[57] Nonetheless, it is possible, of course, that Mikson participated in sentencing and executing people, as the 1961 testimony and the Viherluoto report claim.

Zuroff's visit to Iceland[58] was also meant to confront Icelandic purist self-conceptions by exhorting the government to join those states that favored bringing war criminals to justice instead of sheltering them. The Icelandic Minister of Justice, Þorsteinn Pálsson, however, refused to open an investigation, stating that it was up to the Director of Public Prosecutions to pursue the matter if warranted.[59] Zuroff's claim that he was not representing the Israeli government was correct, even if he enjoyed its diplomatic support.[60] However, another important fact is that the Israeli state prosecutor concluded in 1993 that the evidence was not sufficient to bring Mikson to trial in Israel or to request his extradition.[61] On a specific Israeli government request, the Estonian Prime Minister Mart Laar promised his government's assistance in the search for further documentary evidence. Subsequently, Laar entrusted two Estonian historians with the task of collecting material on war crimes committed during the German as well as the Russian occupations. The Estonian government had never wanted to separate these two issues. It had subscribed to the dominant view that the Soviet Union was to blame for Estonia's hardships.[62] Hence the decision to examine Estonian collaboration with the Germans by focusing on the Mikson case was a major policy change. Rait Maruste, the president of the Estonian Supreme Court, acknowledged that the previous government had lacked the political will to investigate the charges against Mikson. In a rare display of Estonian self-criticism, he argued—at a time when Estonia was actively seeking Western integration—that Estonian respect for the rule of law would be questioned if the allegations were not investigated.[63]

A War-Crimes Investigation in Iceland

In August 1993, the Icelandic Director of Prosecutions finally opened a formal legal investigation into the charges against Mikson[64]—forty-two years after they first surfaced in Iceland. A law professor at the University of Iceland, Jónatan Þórmundsson, who headed the criminal investigation[65] together with his assistant, Þórir Oddsson, gathered material on Mikson's activities from Estonia, Finland, Sweden, and the United States. When they went to Estonia, they experienced first-hand how politicized this case had become. The requested documentary material was first submitted to the Estonian President and then to the Prime Minister before it was released to them. Although Þórmundsson was aided by the chief of the Estonian Interpol as well as archivists, he also encountered much obstruction. On the grounds that no treaty on criminal cooperation had been concluded between Iceland and Estonia, the Estonian authorities made it clear that any requests for testimony of potential witnesses—and even interviews—had to go through diplomatic channels. For this reason, no Estonians were interviewed. This was not at all consistent with official Estonian statements calling for full disclosure.

The investigators had planned to finish the inquiry at the end of 1993. Judging by a preliminary report written in December, however, they still had a considerable way to go.[66] They had not even interviewed Mikson himself. And even if they had wanted to arrange for the translation of documents based on the "plausibility of criminal charges," as they put it, they did not indicate that a firm decision to recommend prosecution had been reached.[67] They did not need to do that. Before preparing a final report to the Icelandic Director of Prosecution and the State Criminal Investigation Police,[68] Mikson died in a hospital at the end of December

1993. In accordance with Icelandic law, the Director of Prosecution immediately closed the case.[69]

The Political Fallout from the Mikson Case

Efraim Zuroff was disappointed by what he clearly saw as an anticlimactic outcome. As he later put it: "The guy" (Mikson), whom he described as a "big murderer, a rapist," had "croaked on us."[70] The day after Mikson's death, he wrote letters to Oddsson and Minister of Justice Pálsson, pressing for the continuation of the investigation. Ironically, Atli Eðvaldsson agreed with his nemesis, although for an altogether different reason. He wanted to seek closure to clear his father's name of what he termed "the disgusting allegations made by the Simon Wiesenthal Center."[71] Yet in the absence of legal precedents, the Ministry of Justice[72] upheld the decision to terminate the inquiry.

However, the skirmishes between Atli Eðvaldsson and Efraim Zuroff continued. In 1999, Eðvaldsson attempted to restore his father's reputation in an interview in *Morgunblaðið*, under the headline "The Devil Never Sleeps." Revealing that his family had received death threats from individuals, including Jews, he claimed that Lennart Meri, the President of Estonia, had promised to assist him in clearing Mikson's name. Zuroff responded immediately by writing a very personal attack against Mikson, arguing that he was no victim of Communist persecution but a Nazi collaborator, and repeating all the charges against him in gory detail.[73]

Given the strong language of this *ad hominem* attack, *Morgunblaðið* decided to balance it with the 1992 statement by the Estonian foreign ministry absolving Mikson of all crimes. While *Morgunblaðið* had played an instrumental role in this story as a vehicle for Mikson's defense during the Cold War, it had sought to distance itself from overtly supporting him in the changed political climate of the 1990s. But this intervention—which made no sense because the Estonian government had distanced itself from its 1992 statement—undermined its effort. The criminal investigation itself showed that the Estonian version[74] was not backed by the Director of Public Prosecutions.[75]

Ironically, it was an international commission appointed by Lennart Meri to investigate war crimes in Estonia during the Soviet and German occupations that weakened Eðvaldsson's efforts. In its 2001 report, it specifically mentioned the war-crimes "roles of the following: Ain-Ervin Mere, Julius Ennok, Ervin Viks, and Evald Mikson, who signed numerous death warrants."[76] Actually, no documents had been found to show that Mikson had signed such warrants. But judging on the basis of the cumulative weight of the evidence, the commission associated him with the executions.[77]

While the international commission used only Estonian and Soviet documents, five types of incriminating evidence against Mikson have surfaced: first, testimony by Estonian refugees in Sweden after World War II; second, Estonian testimony collected by the KGB in connection with the 1961 trial; third, Estonian police records from 1941; fourth, the Finnish policeman's report from 1941; and fifth, the testimony of Estonians in West German trials of war criminals in the 1960s. Most of the Swedish testimony against Mikson was based on hearsay, even if there were eyewitness accounts of beatings and thefts. Some of the more serious allegations, such as indiscriminate killings during the summer of 1941, resurfaced in the 1961 testimony.[78] The KGB documents are flawed because the testimony was based on leading questions and possibly coercion many years later. They should not, however, be entirely dismissed. KGB material on war criminals has been accepted by Western courts in other cases.[79] However, they probably would not have sufficed to ensure a conviction in the Mikson case.

The report of the Finnish policeman, Viherluoto, is extremely damaging to Mikson because it ties him directly to the killing of Jews. Only a copy of the original has been preserved, and it is not backed up by additional documentary evidence. In West German trials of war criminals in the 1960s, two former Estonian policemen incriminated Mikson.[80] The international commission concluded that the material in the Estonian and KGB files was enough to associate Mikson with war crimes and death sentences. Taken together, the allegations have weight, not least because they are based on different sources. Whether the incriminatory evidence would have sufficed to convict Mikson of war crimes, however, will never be known.

While the findings of the international commission's investigation were reported factually in the Icelandic press in 2001,[81] the reaction was muted. No attempts were made to reopen public debate on the issue. Predictably, it was Zuroff who had the last word. In an article in *Morgunblaðið*, he wanted to alert "the Icelandic nation" about the futility of hiding Mikson's reputation behind the cloak of Estonian nationalism; neither could his children continue to dismiss the allegations as Communist fabrications. For all this, he said, the Estonian government should be thanked—a government that originally had defended Mikson when the allegations were first put forward. He also had a moral lesson for Icelanders: this story showed how important it was not to sideline the crimes of the Holocaust or to let fleeting popularity hide participation in persecution and murder. What was at stake was the integrity of Icelandic society as a whole.[82]

Zuroff's praise for the Estonian Government did not last long. He had, of course, been highly critical of it in the 1990s for failing to confront Estonia's past. As he put it, "not a single Baltic Nazi war criminal has been prosecuted, in the wake of Lithuanian, Latvian, and Estonian independence."[83] While the international commission had focused as much on the Soviet occupation period as on the German one, he hoped that the Estonians had abandoned their protective position vis-à-vis Estonian war criminals. But after it became clear that the Estonian authorities were unwilling to open war-crimes investigations, the Simon Wiesenthal Center began criticizing them again. Zuroff even received public support from the United States. The U.S. Ambassador to Estonia, Joseph M. DeThomas, urged the Estonian government to address the issue of Nazi war criminals more vigorously and to increase public awareness of the Holocaust.[84] The initial reaction in Estonia was characterized by hostility, not only because of the ambassador's intervention but also because his message weakened the dominant narrative of Soviet/Communist crimes. Nonetheless, the Estonian government decided to make 27 January (the liberation day of Auschwitz in 1945) Holocaust Commemoration Day. This move was obviously meant to address the discrepancy of bringing Estonian Communist criminals to justice while doing nothing about Estonians who had committed crimes against Jews.

Zuroff went much further, however. He launched a project dubbed "Operation: Last Chance" in 2002, offering a substantial monetary reward for information leading to the prosecution of war criminals during the German occupation. Again, this was met with a storm of indignation in the Baltic states. Among the many critics was former Estonian president Lennart Meri, who had sought to reconcile the two metanarratives of World War II by establishing the international commission.[85] Yet Zuroff refused to back down.[86] Jewish organizations also hoped that Estonia's application for NATO membership would be tied to its handling of war-crimes cases.[87] Pressure was brought to bear on the Estonian government by Western politicians, including U.S. senators. The Estonians took these threats seriously and tried to fend off the criticism, even if this issue never became a major stumbling block in the Baltic states' quest to join NATO—a goal they accomplished in 2004.

In 2006, the Estonian State Prosecutor cleared Harry Männil, a former policeman who had served under Mikson in Tallinn, of wrongdoing.[88] Zuroff's angry reaction to the decision met with little understanding in Estonia.[89] He was vilified in the media and by officials. The evidence he presented in war-crimes cases by no means always met the legal criteria for criminal prosecutions. However, the fact that the Estonian government has not convicted any Estonian of war crimes related to the German occupation period raises questions about its willingness, especially in the 1990s, to pursue such cases.[90] Again, the predominant focus on Communist crimes not only reflects the far longer Soviet domination of Estonia, it is also consistent with the predominant anti-Communist national discourse.

Conclusion

War-crimes cases are usually characterized by an acute tension between individual experiences and collective representations. Mikson's own biographical narrative relies not only on a self-serving interpretation of his actions during World War II, but also on a certain set of broader political and ideological paradigms. As an Estonian nationalist, he equated his own life trajectory with that of the Estonian nation, portraying these merged experiences in terms of victimization as a result of Soviet, and to a lesser extent German repression.[91] Mikson's ability to evade capture and rebuild his life after World War II was due not least to favorable political circumstances. The public backlash in Sweden against the decision to hand over to the Soviet Union Estonian refugees suspected of collaboration with Nazi Germany helps explain why Mikson was allowed to leave the country, even if he had not been cleared of any charges and faced a deportation order. After he settled in Iceland, there was no chance—at the height of the cultural Cold War—that he would be extradited to the Soviet Union. That the Icelandic political elite, including the most influential newspaper, Morgunblaðið, felt the need to defend Mikson without reservation in 1961 showed that it did not want the allegations to undermine the dominant anti-Communist discourse in Iceland. His case was also actively used to buttress this metanarrative by establishing—artificially, it may be argued—a fraternal link between the Icelandic people, who had "escaped the fate" of communism, and the Baltic victims of Soviet imperialism. It was easy to discredit the Icelandic Socialist Party because of its support for the Soviet Union. And even if the non-Communist opposition wanted to investigate the charges against Mikson, it did not push forcefully for an inquiry.

Indeed, anti-communism became Mikson's most effective defense during the Cold War. He invariably used it to defend himself against those who had accused him of murder and theft, including Viherluoto and Sandberger; he branded his accusers as Communist spies or faulted them for punishing him for not revealing information from his interrogations of Communists. Anti-communism also became the key element in the foundation myth of a restored Estonian state. Hence Mikson's quasi-heroic status in Estonia in the early 1990s, where he enjoyed the support and respect of the political elite. It fitted well with the Estonian preoccupation with crimes committed under the Soviet occupation after the Baltic states regained their independence. As Andres Kasekamp has argued, this was to some extent understandable, since for more than forty years Estonians were constantly reminded by the Soviets of Nazi crimes. There had been total silence on Soviet crimes in 1940–41 and again from 1945 to 1990. During the Cold War, moreover, the Soviets punished Estonians for collaboration with the Germans, culminating in the most famous war-crimes trials in the early 1960s.[92] As noted, these convictions were based on anti-Soviet charges, not anti-Jewish ones. The Soviet investigation of Mikson's wartime activities and the publication of his alleged atrocities showed their interest in his case. However, their handling of the case leaves open the question of why they did not try him in absentia or pursue him more aggressively by requesting his extradition. The attitude of Icelandic Socialist leaders may provide the explanation.

After the end of the Cold War, the Mikson case turned into something far more than individual wartime experiences against Soviet communism. It became a question of Estonia's complicity in the Holocaust. It was impossible to rationalize the extermination of the Jews by referring to the Soviet terror campaign in Estonia. Also, it was far more difficult to defend Mikson against the charges pushed by the Simon Wiesenthal Center in the post–Cold War period than against the Soviets during the Cold War.

Indeed, when the case flared up again in 1992, the anti-Communist consensus had lost much of its political force, because it had become part of a different metanarrative. In Iceland, this was reflected in the far more cautious reaction to the charges by the Icelandic political elite than in 1961. In contrast to its hard-line defense of Mikson in 1961, *Morgunblaðið* was now careful not to dismiss the charges against him. The Icelandic government, to be sure, did not want to reopen the case; by commissioning a legal opinion, which predictably did not recommend a prosecution, and by turning the case over to the Director of Prosecution, it demonstrated its unwillingness to engage the issue. In the 1990s, however, it also refrained from defending Mikson.

Zuroff's interpretations of these national pasts were often marked by exaggerations. Many Icelanders sympathized with Mikson, not because they condoned murder but because of Zuroff's tactics. They also pitied a senile old man who was obviously not fit to deal with the media frenzy. There was a similar reaction in France during the Papon and Touvier trials in the 1990s. The idea that the Israelis were in no position to take the high ground on war crimes because of their treatment of the Palestinians was a defensive mechanism and a diversionary tactic, even if many Icelanders genuinely sympathized with the Palestinians. But Zuroff made too much of Icelandic support for Mikson on the grounds of his family's high social standing. It was by no means the main reason for the Icelanders' reluctance to pursue the case. The Icelandic government also wanted to grant a citizen legal protection in the face of serious charges.

One irony of the Mikson case is that the ideological attempt to establish a fraternal relationship with Baltic people during the Cold War became far more credible after the breakup of the Soviet Union. After all, Iceland had granted them formal recognition before all other countries. The Estonian government did not want to harm Mikson personally or let the allegations of the Simon Wiesenthal Center spoil its ties with Iceland. Conversely, the Icelandic government sought to prevent the Mikson case from having an adverse impact on its relationship with Estonia. The initial hostile reaction of Foreign Minister Hannibalsson, who of course was personally instrumental in recognizing the Baltic states, to the Simon Wiesenthal Center's charges is a case in point. This informal bilateral collusion between Iceland and Estonia served Mikson's interests because it favored inaction. But Oddsson's pro-Israeli stance and his friction with Hannibalsson complicated Iceland's position. Oddsson straddled a middle ground between the Israeli and Estonian positions: he was careful not to absolve Mikson of any wrongdoing publicly, to the satisfaction of the Israelis, while not doing anything to bring him to justice—a stance favored by the Estonians. The Estonian government also did not want to damage its relations with Israel, as the decision to give Zuroff access to documents on the Mikson case shows. Yet it had no intention of sacrificing the founding myth of a newly independent Estonia on the grounds of complicity in the Holocaust.

The Simon Wiesenthal Center was pivotal in reopening the Mikson case and in pressuring the Icelandic Director of Prosecution to investigate it. Zuroff's controversial methods can be criticized for their excessiveness. At the outset, although he had little evidence, he had no qualms about calling Mikson a murderer and rapist. He always stated as fact the highest number of Mikson's alleged victims cited in Estonian testimonies, although it was only based on hearsay. Even the Israeli government did not think that there was enough evidence against Mikson to warrant an extradition request. Furthermore, his exclusive focus on Jewish victims almost made it look like they were the only ones killed by Estonians after the retreat of the Soviets in 1941, whereas Communist sympathizers had been by far more numerous.

However, Zuroff was right to point out that the extermination of the Jews did not hinge on their affiliation with communism. He played an important role in forcing a change in the handling of the Mikson case by the Estonian and Icelandic authorities. Of course, he received diplomatic assistance from the Israeli government in his cause. Irrespective of this fact, however, his intervention helped spark a debate over the national pasts in Estonia and, to a lesser degree, in Iceland. This contributed to the decision of the Estonian government to pay more attention to the German occupation period and to crimes committed by Estonians, including participation in the Holocaust. In Iceland, critical questions were raised about complicity in sheltering potential war criminals.

The Germans were the driving force behind the Holocaust, even if they relied on Estonian collaborators. The highest-ranking German official in Estonia from 1941 to 1943, Martin Sandberger,[93] who imprisoned Mikson, lived as a free man in Stuttgart until his death in 2010. Considering the American intervention in the case of Estonian war criminals, it is ironic that the U.S. government was directly responsible for not only sparing his life but also assuring his early release from prison.[94] He was sentenced to death by a U.S. military court in Nuremberg in 1948 for crimes against humanity and mass murder. However, the U.S. High Commissioner John McCloy commuted his sentence to life in prison in 1951, after much pressure from influential German government officials and politicians, and even from a U.S. senator.[95] At that time, Cold War interests, especially the integration of West Germany into the Western alliance, had outweighed the importance of punishing Nazi criminals. War-crimes cases only complicated that effort because of West German insistence that the sentences of those convicted be shortened, or that they be released or pardoned. In 1958, Sandberger was pardoned.[96] Just as political necessity had influenced the U.S. government's position on war crimes in the postwar period and that of the Icelandic government during the Cold War, the demand for a new founding myth in post–Cold War Estonia created amnesia about a more troubled past—a past that conflicted with the political needs of the present.

Notes

1. The activities of the U.S. Office of Special Investigations (OSI), the Holocaust Memorial Museum in Washington, D.C., and U.S. government investigations on Nazi gold in Switzerland testify to U.S. efforts to promote Holocaust awareness. The same applies to the French government's push to expose the crimes of the Vichy regime in the 1980s and 1990s through war-crimes trials.
2. The Mikson case poses some historical-methodological problems, including the evaluation of witness testimonies given long after the alleged crimes took place. As Henry Rousso has pointed out, it is not the task of historians to assume the role

of judges on the question of individual guilt or innocence. Still, since the evidence underpinning the allegations against Mikson became a most contentious issue, I will address the problem of culpability here.
3. The Estonian security police forces cooperated with the Germans during the occupation. See Ruth Bettina Birn, *Die Sicherheitspolizei in Estland 1941–1944* (Paderborn, 2006); see also idem, "Collaboration with Nazi Germany in Eastern Europe," *Contemporary European History* 10 (2001), no. 2: 181–198; Seppo Myllyniemi, *Die Neuordnung der baltischen Länder 1941–1944* (Helsinki, 1973). As Birn shows, Estonia, which was allowed to maintain forms of self-government during World War II, had a specific place in German ideological plans in Eastern Europe. Estonians were seen as most "racially desirable" and with the greatest potential for "Germanization." See Birn, "Collaboration with Nazi Germany," 182–183.
4. See Alon Confino, "Telling about Germany," *Journal of Modern History* 76, no. 2 (June 2004): 401–402. As for individual experiences, see Christopher Browning's *Ordinary Men* (New York, 1992), which addresses the psychological motives of perpetrators of mass killings in World War II. Daniel Jonah Goldhagen's *Hitler's Willing Executioners* (New York, 1996) also analyzes the same police battalion, although he comes to a radically different conclusion. Despite its serious methodological flaws and reductionism, it is valuable for its desanitization of brutal war experiences. These works do not, however, place these microhistorical experiences into broader national, social, or political contexts (except for Goldhagen's misguided attempt to essentialize—historically—collective German killing instincts).
5. The coup followed a fierce struggle between the conservative Right, representing the army and government institutions, and the radical Right—the so-called VASP-populist movement. See Margus Kastehein and Lauri Lindström, "The Activities of E. Mikson in the Southern Part of Tartu District and in Tallinn in 1941" (Tallinn, 1992), 8–9. This unpublished report was commissioned by the Estonian Prime Minister Mart Laar and written by two Estonian historians. It deals with Mikson's activities in 1941 on the basis of historical documents of the Estonian security police and testimonies of witnesses conducted by the KGB in 1961. This was part of an investigation into alleged war crimes committed by Mikson.
6. The Forest Brothers movement was revived after the second Soviet occupation in 1944. Former Prime Minister Mart Laar, a historian who became Estonian Prime Minister, wrote a book on this topic, based on oral histories, in which he glorifies the movement's memory in the struggle against the Soviets. See Laar, *War in the Woods*, trans. Tiina Ets (Washington, 1992). Mikson's *Omakaitse* managed to take power in two Estonian districts in July 1941 without the assistance of the German army.
7. See "Conclusions: Report of the Estonian International Commission for the Investigation of Crimes against Humanity. Part III—The German Occupation of Estonia, 1941–1944," http://www.historycommission.ee/temp/conclusions.htm.
8. It has been surmised that fewer than a dozen Jews survived. See "Conclusions: Report of the Estonian International Commission for the Investigation of Crimes against Humanity. Phase II—The German Occupation of Estonia, 1941–1944," http://www.historycommission.ee/temp/conclusions.htm, xviii.
9. See Birn, "Collaboration with Nazi Germany," 188.
10. Ibid., 182.
11. Ibid., 185.
12. See the testimony by Ewald Piirisild, 3 October 1968, and Karl Toom, 12 November 1968, Bestand EL 317 III Bü. 782, Staatsarchiv Ludwigsburg; see also the testimonies of Uno Richard Andrussen, 27 October 1944, and Eik Varep, 2 March 1945 in

Sweden, Swedish immigration records, Archives of the Icelandic Director of Public Prosecutions, mál Eðvalds Hinrikssonar [The Mikson case], 30.30.3/5; ibid., 40.30.2; see finally various testimonies based on KGB interrogations—obtained by the Simon Wiesenthal Center—from the 1961 trials in Estonia, Archives of the Icelandic Director of Public Prosecutions, mál Eðvalds Hinrikssonar, 10.50.2, 3.

13. See Einar Sanden, Úr eldinum til Íslands, trans. Þorsteinn Sigurlaugsson (Reykjavik, 1988), 140–141. Mikson claimed that the Germans wanted to punish him for not letting them know that Säre spoke German and for failing to report Säre's dealings with an English agent, Richard Sorge, in the Far East. These were false allegations, according to Mikson, since Säre had not told him anything about Sorge's activities. After the end of the Cold War, English writer Chapman Pincher suggested that Sorge was Sir Richard Hollis, the head of MI5, the British counterintelligence agency, who had been suspected by his own colleagues of being a Soviet spy. Prime Minister Margaret Thatcher claimed that the evidence could not be substantiated, and after an internal inquiry he was given the benefit of the doubt.

14. E-mail correspondence: Ruth Bettina Birn to Valur Ingimundarson, 31 May 2006. During Mikson's imprisonment, his activities with the *Omakaitse* were investigated, but the German files on him have not been found.

15. Estonian Foundation for the Investigation of Crimes against Humanity (Meelis Maripuu) to Valur Ingimundarson, 24 September 2004; see also Kastehein and Lindström, "Activities of E. Mikson," 19.

16. Estonian Foundation for the Investigation of Crimes against Humanity (Meelis Maripuu) to Valur Ingimundarson, 24 September 2004; the *Abwehr* was the intelligence branch of the German Army that financed the *Omakaitse* at that time. See Birn, "Collaboration with Nazi Germany," 184.

17. Mikson thanked patriotic Estonians close to the puppet regime headed by Hjalmar Mäe for his release. In addition, he believed that the *Abwehr* had saved him from the clutches of Sandberger. See Sanden, *Úr eldinum*, 143–144, 156.

18. See, for example, the testimonies of Erik Jaarma, 22 December 1944, and August Rei, 22 December 1944, Swedish immigration records, Archives of the Icelandic Director of Public Prosecutions, mál Eðvalds Hinrikssonar, 30.30.3/5; cf. also Karl Eduard Lindma, 26 October 1941; Uno Richard Andrussen, 27 October 1944; Heldo Tönisson, 21 February 1945; Eik Varep, 2 March 1945; ibid., 40.30.2.

19. See Sanden, *Úr eldinum*, 189–192.

20. See *Þjóðviljinn*, 14 March 1961. The evidence, which *Þjóðviljinn* reproduced, had been published in a booklet by an Estonian Communist, Ants Saar. Ain-Ervin Mere had been made the head of the Estonian section of the political police after Mikson was imprisoned. Garrets and Viik were executed in Estonia. The allegations were based on eyewitness testimony collected by the Estonian KGB in connection with the trial. Mere had managed to escape to Britain and was convicted to death in absentia. Interestingly enough, the Soviet KGB tried to recruit Mere in England, but when he refused and did not appear at his trial, he received the death penalty. See letter: Estonian Foundation for the Investigation of Crimes against Humanity (Meelis Maripuu) to Valur Ingimundarson, 24 September 2004.

21. See *Morgunblaðið*, 15 March 1961.

22. Ibid.

23. See the editorial in *Morgunblaðið*, 16 March 1961. In order to circumvent calls for an investigation, *Morgunblaðið* accused *Þjóðviljinn* of wanting to hand Mikson over to the Russians, who would torture and execute him. Such "Red Magic" had never been practiced in Iceland. See *Morgunblaðið*, 17 March 1961.

24. Ibid.
25. See *Þjóðviljinn*, 18 April 1961; see also Hjörtur Torfason (Mikson's lawyer in Iceland) to Yngve Schartau, 27 April 1961, and Yngve Schartau to Hjörtur Torfason, 4 May 1961, Archives of the Icelandic Director of Public Prosecutions, mál Eðvalds Hinrikssonar, 60.30.2.
26. No conclusive documentary evidence has been found to clarify the matter.
27. Estonian Foundation for the Investigation of Crimes against Humanity (Meelis Maripuu) to Valur Ingimundarson, 24 September 2004.
28. Maruste's theory was in line with Mikson's own explanation in the early 1990s about his interrogations of Säre, even if its importance was probably exaggerated. See *Morgunblaðið*, 13 February 1993.
29. It should be noted, however, that the Soviets supplied Western prosecutors with documentary material on war crimes in other cases until the breakup of the Soviet Union.
30. When Mikson's autobiography, which was written by the Estonian writer Einar Sanden, was published in 1988, it had little impact and aroused no interest in the case. In this rambling account, Mikson focuses as much on Estonia's history as on his own life, even if he addresses in some detail his activities in Estonia and, to a lesser degree, in Iceland. The main thesis is familiar: that Mikson was a faithful supporter of the Estonian Republic against Nazi Germany and the Soviet Union. All war-crimes charges are firmly denied as Communist propaganda. See Sanden, *Úr eldinum*, passim.
31. See *Eesti Express*, 1 November 1991.
32. In a letter delivered to Oddsson with the assistance of Israeli foreign ministry officials, he accused Mikson not only of signing arrest warrants but also of murdering eight Jews. Efraim Zuroff to Davíð Oddsson, 18 February 1992, Archives of the Icelandic Director of Public Prosecutions, mál Eðvalds Hinrikssonar, 10.10. 4; see also *Morgunblaðið*, 19 February 1992.
33. *Morgunblaðið*, 19 February 1992.
34. Hannibalsson vehemently argued that information from the KGB could not be taken at face value by the Icelandic government. Ibid.
35. Demjanjuk was accused of being "Ivan the Terrible," the notorious Treblinka guard. But the Israeli Supreme Court came to the conclusion that this was a case of a mistaken identity. Thus, he escaped a death sentence and was released. He was, however, later identified as another guard at the Sobibor camp. He has been stripped of his U.S. citizenship and was later convicted for war crimes in Germany; *Morgunblaðið*'s reporting of the Mikson case was factual, but it did not, in contrast to some other Icelandic media, publish any details of atrocities allegedly committed by Mikson based on the 1961 testimonies. See, for example, *Morgunblaðið*, 26 February 1992.
36. In his defense, he made the point that this was the third episode of a continuing conspiratorial attack against him. First, he had been accused of war crimes in Sweden in 1945–46; then, he had been persecuted by the communist newspaper *Þjóðviljinn* in 1961; and now in the early 1990s, the Jews were after him. But given his advanced age—he was 81 years old—he was unprepared for the media attention and got caught up in contradictions about his career. See *Morgunblaðið*, 19 February 1992.
37. See, for example, *Morgunblaðið*, 19, 20, 22, and 26 February; 4 and 27 March, 1992.
38. It parroted exactly the same arguments that Mikson had used in his defense: that the KGB had feared that he would divulge information that could compromise its intelligence activities in Russia and the Nordic countries. Thus, the Soviets had whipped up the charges against him and insisted on his extradition from Sweden and Iceland.

39. *Morgunblaðið*, 20 February 1992.
40. *Morgunblaðið*, 4 March 1992.
41. Efraim Zuroff to Þorsteinn Pálsson, Minister of Justice, 23 February 1992, Archives of the Icelandic Director of Public Prosecutions, mál Eðvalds Hinrikssonar, 10.10.4.
42. Portions of this report were reproduced in Hannu Rautkallio's *Finland and the Holocaust*, trans. Paul Sjöblom (New York, 1987). Zuroff referred to this book, but copies of the report were also found in the Finnish National Archives. Finnish National Archives, Supreme Court File, KKO 982 VD 1948. The original, however, has not been found. And the copy was an abbreviation and an excerpt. After the war, Viherluoto confirmed the veracity of the report. It was introduced as evidence in the trial of the head of the Finnish Security Police, Arno Anthoni, in 1948, with the intention of proving that he knew of the killings of the Jews far earlier than he had claimed.
43. See Sanden, *Úr eldinum*, 136–137; Estonian Foundation for the Investigation of Crimes against Humanity (Meelis Maripuu) to Valur Ingimundarson, 24 September 2004; "Travel Report" (Olavi Viherluoto), 21 October 1941. English translation of the original report. See Archives of the Director of Prosecutions, mál Eðvalds Hinrikssonar, 40.40.3.
44. Sanden, *Úr eldinum*, 136–137. In 1992, Mikson did not address the charges made by Viherluoto. But in response his son, Atli Eðvaldsson, referred to passages of his autobiography. See *Pressan*, 12 March 1992.
45. Despite this incriminating piece of evidence against Mikson, the anti-Semitic policies adopted in Estonia were initiated by the German occupation forces. Estonians took part in the killings, but it was a German-led and -driven project. See Birn, *Sicherheitspolizei*, 259–260.
46. To the legal experts, it was not only that a long time had passed since the alleged crimes took place. The documents that could prove or disprove the allegations were "probably lost." Moreover, the experts assumed that most of the potential witnesses were dead. The report was published in its entirety in *Morgunblaðið*, 3 October 1992.
47. See *DV*, 5 October 1992; *Morgunblaðið*, 6 October 1992.
48. *Morgunblaðið*, 4 October 1992; see also *Pressan*, 8 October 1992.
49. Their task was only to offer a legal opinion, not to investigate the merits of the case. See *Morgunblaðið*, 16 October 1992.
50. *Morgunblaðið*, 14 October 1992.
51. See *Pressan*, 8 October 1992.
52. See, for example, *DV*, 5 October 1992.
53. *Morgunblaðið*, 20 October 1992.
54. Reshetov escaped a reprimand, however. See *Morgunblaðið*, 21 October 1992.
55. Zuroff had managed to get a meeting with Estonian Prime Minster Mart Laar and access to Estonian archives.
56. Kastehein and Lindström, "Activities of E. Mikson," 16.
57. Estonian Foundation for the Investigation of Crimes against Humanity (Meelis Maripuu) to Valur Ingimundarson, 24 September 2004.
58. *Morgunblaðið*, 3 February 1993; *Alþýðublaðið*, 2 February 1993; *Tíminn*, 2 February 1993; transcripts of a newscast, TV Channel 2, 2 February 1992.
59. *Morgunblaðið*, 2 February 1993; *Alþýðublaðið*, 3 February 1992; *DV*, 3 February 1993.
60. *Morgunblaðið*, 4 February 1993; see also *Pressan*, 4 February 1992.
61. Copy of a memorandum from the Israeli Foreign Ministry to the Icelandic Foreign Ministry, Archives of the Director of Public Prosecutions, mál Eðvalds Hinrikssonar, 60. 97.1.

62. *Morgunblaðið*, 4 February 1993.
63. *Morgunblaðið*, 13 February 1993.
64. Memorandum, Director of Public Prosecutions, 10 August 1993, Icelandic State Criminal Investigation Police, Archives of the Director of Public Prosecutions, mál Eðvalds Hinrikssonar, 10.20.4B; Zuroff gleefully suggested that the decision had something to do with a letter from eighty-five parliamentarians, representing all the Jewish parties in the Israeli Knesset. The only party that was not involved in writing the letter was the Democratic Arab Party; it did not have the right to be associated with such actions. In the letter, the Icelandic authorities were asked to respond to the accusation that they were harboring a war criminal and to file charges against Mikson. Among those who signed it were former Prime Minister Yitzhak Shamir and former Foreign Minister David Levy. Similarly, Zuroff's intimation that the Icelandic government was behind the investigation was false. But having achieved his main goal, of course he applauded the decision (See *Morgunblaðið*, 14 August 1993). Israeli foreign minister Shimon Peres also discussed the Mikson case with Oddsson during his visit to Iceland a week later. The Israeli government did not want to be perceived as being behind Zuroff's campaign. Thus Peres freely admitted that at this point the evidence was not sufficient to ensure a conviction, even if he had high hopes that more documents would be found in the Estonian archives. He also went out of his way not to criticize the Icelandic government for its handling of the matter, claiming to have full confidence in Icelandic democracy and its judicial system. See *Morgunblaðið*, 13 and 24 August 1993.
65. *Morgunblaðið*, 14 August 1993.
66. They had not received responses to requests for documentary evidence from countries such as Germany, Russia, and Canada.
67. *Morgunblaðið*, 10 December 1993.
68. Jónatan Þórmundsson, "Mál Eðvalds Hinrikssonar: Áfangaskýrsla um stöðu rannsóknar og yfirlit yfir næstu aðgerðir" [The Eðvald Hinriksson case: a preliminary report about the state of the investigation and a summary of planned actions], 2 December 1993, Archives of the Director of Public Prosecutions, mál Eðvalds Hinrikssonar, 10.20.6.
69. *Morgunblaðið*, 28 December 1993.
70. Jana Wendt, interview with Efraim Zuroff, *The Bulletin*, 4 April 2006, to be found on the Web site "Operation: Last Chance," http://www.operationlastchance.org/ARTICLES_145-65.htm.
71. Atli Eðvaldsson to Þorsteinn Pálsson, 24 March 1994, Archives of the Director of Public Prosecutions, mál Eðvalds Hinrikssonar, 10.20.13.
72. Ministry of Justice and Ecclesiastic Affairs to Atli Eðvaldsson, 13 June 1994, Archives of the Director of Public Prosecutions, mál Eðvalds Hinrikssonar, 10.20.15.
73. Dr. Efraim Zuroff, "Letter to Morgunblaðið," *Morgunblaðið*, 5 November 1999.
74. Efraim Zuroff, "Enn um mál Eðvalds Hinrikssonar" [More about the case of Eðvald Hinriksson], *Morgunblaðið*, 17 November 1999.
75. *Morgunblaðið* defended itself by referring to its anti Communist roots. If allegations of murder and rape were found in KGB files, it said, they should not be taken at face value, especially since they came from the "vultures of the Gulag." As Zuroff pointed out, *Morgunblaðið* could have mentioned the Estonian, Finnish, and Swedish documents instead of only singling out the KGB files. The paper was more convincing in arguing that when people's reputations are at stake, it is appropriate to proceed with caution—to rely on confessions or proper judicial proceedings, *Morgunblaðið*, 17 November 1999.

76. See "Conclusions: Report of the Estonian International Commission for the Investigation of Crimes against Humanity. Phase II—The German Occupation of Estonia, 1941–1944," http://www.history commission.ee/temp/conclusions.htm.
77. Estonian Foundation for the Investigation of Crimes against Humanity (Meelis Maripuu) to Valur Ingimundarson, 24 September 2004.
78. Identical descriptions, for example, were given by two different witnesses about Mikson's executing every third prisoner in a lineup. See the testimony by Johannes Sooru from 8 June 1961; KGB documents obtained by the Simon Wiesenthal Center stemming from the 1961 trials in Estonia, Archives of the Icelandic Director of Public Prosecutions, mál Eðvalds Hinrikssonar, 10.50.2, 3. See also the testimony by Eik Varep, 2 February 1945; Swedish immigration documents, Archives of the Icelandic Director of Public Prosecutions, mál Eðvalds Hinrikssonar, 40.30.3.
79. See an interview with Alfred Streim, a German prosecutor, in *Morgunblaðið*, 6 February 1992, on the question of the authenticity of KGB documents.
80. One claimed to have seen the German file on Mikson's arrest in 1941, which revealed that he was imprisoned because of unlawful killings of Estonians. The other stated that he had heard that Mikson had stolen valuables from prisoners. See the testimony by Ewald Piirisild, 3 October 1968, and Karl Toom, 12 November 1968, Bestand EL 317III Bue 782, Staatsarchiv Ludwigsburg.
81. See, for example, *Morgunblaðið*, 20 June 2001.
82. Efraim Zuroff, "Sannleikurinn lítur loksins dagsins ljós" [The truth finally comes to light], *Morgunblaðið*, 29 June 2001.
83. Efraim Zuroff, "The Failure to Prosecute Nazi War Criminals in Lithuania, Latvia and Estonia, 1991–1998," *Antisemitism Research* 11, 1 (Summer 1998), http://www.cidi.n1/dossiers/an/art1-02-nl.html.
84. Joseph M. DeThomas wrote an article in an Estonian newspaper to press the issue. See *Eesti Päevaleht*, 28 May 2001. See also Andres Kasekamp, "What Really Happened—Estonia and the Holocaust," Estonian Foreign Ministry, 26 February 2003, http://www.vm.ee/eng/kat_411/3525.html.
85. See the official website of "Operation: Last Chance," News, Estonia, http://www.operationlastchance.org/ESTONIA_65-5.htm.
86. Zuroff accused the Estonian government of protecting Nazi war criminals, and went so far as to call for the resignation of the Chief of the Estonian Security Police for not producing documentary evidence to build a case against alleged Estonian war criminals. See Kasekamp, "What really happened."
87. See, for example, Adam B. Ellick, "Attitude toward Holocaust activities could sink Estonia's bid to join NATO," Global News Service of the Jewish People, 29 July 2002, http://www.jta.org/page_view_story.asp.
88. See *European Jewish Press*, 1 January 2006.
89. The Simon Wiesenthal Center had been instrumental in getting the Estonian state prosecutor to launch an investigation into Männil's wartime activities in 2001. Like Mikson after World War II Männil managed to escape from Sweden to Venezuela, where he amassed a fortune as a businessman. When the accusations against Mikson resurfaced in 1992, he accused Männil of being a Communist collaborator and stated—wrongly—that he was behind the Simon Wiesenthal Center's campaign. Since no firm evidence was produced to link Männil to killings, the investigation was formally closed at the end of 2005. See, for example, *Jerusalem Post*, 5 January 2006.
90. It is unlikely, however, that this will happen, since most potential suspects are dead.

91. See a very interesting report on Estonian nationalism by Martin Sandberger, entitled "Grundsätzliche Fragen des Einsatzes der Baltendeutschen in Estland," [1943], R90, 209, Bundesarchiv (Berlin).
92. See also Kasekamp, "What really happened."
93. On Sandberger's career, see "Nachlass Martin Sandberger," Bestand EL 317 III Bü 785; see also SA (ehem. BDC), Film Nr. 163 B, Bundesarchiv (Berlin).
94. See Michael Wildt, *Generation des Unbedingten* (Hamburg, 2002), 785–790.
95. About the case, see National Archives (NA) (Maryland), Record Group 338, "Records Relating to Post-Trial Activities," box 11.
96. See Norbert Frei, *Vergangenheitspolitik* (Munich, 1996), 195–228.

Bibliography

Books and articles

Birn, Ruth Bettina. "Collaboration with Nazi Germany in Eastern Europe: The Case of the Estonian Security Police." *Contemporary European History* 10 (2001), no. 2: 181–198.

———. *Die Sicherheitspolizei in Estland 1941–1944: Eine Studie zur Kollaboration im Osten.* Paderborn: Schöningh, 2006.

Browning, Christopher. *Ordinary Men: Reserve Police Battalion 101 and the Final Solution in Poland.* New York: Aaron Asher Books, 1992.

Confino, Alon. "Telling about Germany: Narratives of Memory and Culture." *Journal of Modern History* 76, no. 2 (June 2004): 389–416.

Frei, Norbert. *Vergangenheitspolitik: Die Anfänge der Bundesrepublik und die NS-Vergangenheit.* Munich: Beck Verlag, 1996.

Goldhagen, Daniel Jonah. *Hitler's Willing Executioners: Ordinary Germans and the Holocaust.* New York: Knopf, 1996.

Laar, Mart. *War in the Woods: Estonia's Struggle for Survival, 1944–1956.* Trans. Tiina Ets. Washington, D.C.: The Compass Press, 1992.

Myllyniemi, Seppo. *Die Neuordnung der baltischen Länder 1941–1944: Zum nationalsozialistischen Inhalt der deutschen Besatzungspolitik.* Helsinki: Historiallisia Tuckimuksia, 1973.

Rautkallio, Hannu. *Finland and the Holocaust: The Rescue of Finland's Jews.* Trans. Paul Sjöblom. New York: Holocaust Library, 1987.

Sanden, Einar. *Úr eldinum til Íslands: Ævisaga Eðvalds Hinrikssonar.* Trans. Þorsteinn Sigurlaugsson. Reykjavik: Almenna bókafélagið, 1988.

Wildt, Michael. *Generation des Unbedingten. Das Führungskorps des Reichssicherheitshauptamtes.* Hamburg: Hamburger Edition, 2002.

Media

Alþýðublaðið, 1992–1993
DV, 1992–1993
Eesti Express, 1991

Eesti Päevaleht, 2001
European Jewish Press, 2006
Morgunblaðið, 1961, 1992, 1992,1993, 2001
Pressan, 1992
Tíminn, 1993
Þjóðviljinn, 1961
Transcripts of a newscast, Iceland TV Channel 2, 2 February 1992

Letters and e-mail correspondence

Ruth Bettina Birn to Valur Ingimundarson, 31 May 2006
Estonian Foundation for the Investigation of Crimes against Humanity (Meelis Maripuu) to Valur Ingimundarson, 24 September 2004

Web resources

"Conclusions: Report of the Estonian International Commission for the Investigation of Crimes against Humanity. Part III—The German Occupation of Estonia, 1941-1944." http://www.historycommission.ee/temp/conclusions.htm
Ellick, Adam B., "Attitude toward Holocaust activities could sink Estonia's bid to join NATO," Global News Service of the Jewish People, 29 July 2002. http://www.jta.org/page_view_story.asp.
Kasekamp, Andres. "What Really Happened—Estonia and the Holocaust." Estonian Foreign Ministry, 26 February 2003. http://www.vm.ee/eng/kat_411/3525.html.
"Operation: Last Chance." News, Estonia. http://www.operationlastchance.org/ESTONIA_65-5.htm.
Wendt, Jana. Interview with Efraim Zuroff, *The Bulletin*, 4 April 2006. http://www.operationlastchance.org/ARTICLES_145-65.htm. *Jerusalem Post*, 5 January 2006.
Zuroff, Efraim. "The Failure to Prosecute Nazi War Criminals in Lithuania, Latvia and Estonia, 1991–1998." *Antisemitism Research* 11, 1 (Summer 1998). http://www.cidi.nl/dossiers/an/art1-02-nl.html.

Unpublished Sources

Archives of the Icelandic Director of Public Prosecutions, Reykjavik. "Mál Eðvalds Hinrikssonar [The Mikson case]" (Archival Material from Estonia and Iceland), 10.10.4; 10.20.6; 10.20.13; 10.20.15; 10.50.2, 3; 30.30.3/5; 40.30.2; 40.30.3; 60.30.2
Kastehein, Margus, and Lauri Lindström. "The Activities of E. Mikson in the Southern Part of Tartu District and in Tallinn in 1941." Tallinn, 1992.
Staatsarchiv Ludwigsburg. "Nachlass Martin Sandberger." Bestand EL 317 III Bü. 782, 785.
National Archives, Maryland. Record Group 338, "Records Relating to Post-Trial Activities," box 11.
Bundesarchiv, Berlin. R90, 209 SA (formerly BDC), Film Nr. 163 B.

Chapter 16

THE FIRST COLD WAR MEMORIAL IN BERLIN
A Short Inquiry into Europe, the Cold War, and Memory Cultures

Petra Henzler

Unquestionably, the Cold War was the metastructure for the postwar era, influencing nearly every important development after World War II. In a certain sense, we can understand the Cold War as an extension of nineteenth-century nationalism. However, it was a successor that did not erase the effects of nationalism. Rather it had a transforming affect: it fostered and partly reactivated transnationality, especially for the European states. Hence the concept of Cold War Culture, which links changing lifestyles, mass consumption, and mass culture as well as educational systems with the overarching systemic conflict between the United States and the Soviet Union, is ultimately very convincing. But can we also apply this concept to European Cold War Cultures?[1] This will be the central question of this contribution on the historicization of the Berlin Blockade and its first Cold War memorial, the "Luftbrückendenkmal" ("Airlift Memorial"), at Tempelhof airport in Berlin.

Historicization and memory are of course part of a cultural system. Following Maurice Halbwachs, who disclaimed purely personal memory, the *mémoire collective* is the formative base for any kind of collective.[2] Thus, rethinking Cold War memory in a European context requires some thoughts about Europe. In the first part of this inquiry, I will investigate whether it makes sense in scholarly terms to use the term "European," and will point out the advantages of the concept of Cold War Cultures. In the second part, I will outline the emotional impacts of memory, and in the third part illustrate the historicization and narratives of the Berlin Blockade.

Europe

"By and large, 'Europe' was of no major concern; instead, it showed a presence that was beyond doubt and therefore did not require any further questioning and theorizing."[3] Ute Frevert's words about Europe during the early twentieth century could also be a comment on contemporary Europe, although today Europe exists and is of serious concern not only for scholarly discourse, but also for the broader public. What has changed is the level of theorizing about Europe, as well as its political appeal and form. Since 1945, Europe's form, borders, and shape have been (and still are) subject to intense discussion. Despite that fact that Europe undoubtedly exists, it is still difficult to define where its borders lie, and more importantly, who and what is "European."

At this point it is necessary to outline briefly the epistemological debate concerning space, which can be summarized under the headline "spatial turn." During the prewar era, space was understood mainly in terms of geopolitics, which purportedly existed independently of human beings. Space was understood as a universal truth, like time, and an object of concrete political and economic interventions. Today, space is regarded as a product of human perspectives and interventions.[4] There appears to be academic consensus on the perception that the borders, forms, and meanings of space are a product of mental constructions. Space is neither homogeneous, nor does it have an essential meaning; borders and spatial mappings are the result of a cultural-political system.[5] Accepting this deconstructive concept (that space is a product of human orders and based on social practices[6]), we can better understand why Europe has no clear borders and such a fluid discursive structure. *Europe* is a concept that has a history as well as various political connotations.[7]

In fact, *Europe* was and still is subject to continuous change. It appears in different shapes and with different cultural connotations. Two prominent examples are the concepts of Central Europe (*Mitteleuropa*) and the Christian Occident. *Central Europe* was chiefly a political term, with changing targets. In the mid nineteenth century, it was used as a concept for federalism in order to strengthen Germany's position vis-à-vis Russia and the United States. In the late nineteenth century, it was used as an alternative concept to the "Greater German Solution" (*Großdeutsche Lösung*) in the Habsburg Monarchy. Then, the term evolved from a political to an economic concept that was instrumentalized for the Central European Tariff Union. After World War II, the concept disappeared, due to the fact that Europe was now structured along the East-West divide. Since the end of the Cold War, the term has experienced a revival: Central Europe has acquired a certain appeal for constructing a new cultural and political identity for former Eastern-bloc states. Moreover, based upon a new interpretation of "Central Europe" as a concept for a decidedly transnational cultural history, a new type of historical narrative has been established—especially in the Austrian academic field.[8]

The concept of *Christian Occident* has an even longer history. Closely tied to religion, it suggests that Europe has homogenous cultural roots. Christianity promises to transcend the complex experiences in Europe. However, this promise cannot be fulfilled. Despite that fact that the term *Christian Occident* still attracts distinguished historians like Hagen Schulze[9] or Hans Ulrich Wehler,[10] European regions display a variety of versions of Christianity, and—more importantly—Islam and Judaism as well. These religions are undeniably important aspects of cultural processes in Europe, although we must also concede that in the process of modernization, the cultural frame of religion lost its prominent structuring power.

In the postwar era, the identification of what Europe is and who is European became notions used for inclusion and exclusion. As economic concepts, neither capitalism nor communism were assessed merely on the basis of their economic benefits, but rather functioned as distinct societal orders. Moreover, specific moral attributes were ascribed to these competing societal orders. Europe was (and still is) narrated as a success story of transnational processes against "old" nationalism. The U.S.A. and the Soviet Union regarded their respective societal systems, as well as the blocs established in their wake, as a promise for securing the peace in Western or Eastern Europe, respectively.[11] This way, the "old" nationalisms were to be overcome via transnational relations, and the former national conflicts gave way to a transnational conflict based on system competition.

However, it is doubtful whether the narrative of "Europe"—without any clear definition of the spatial concept—is a fitting interpretive model for the postwar era in Europe. Although it is a widely employed narrative in public as well as academic discussions, using "European" as the main interpretive model always entails the danger of entanglement in politics instead of scholarly analysis. In the context of the eastern expansion of the EU, discussions surrounding where Europe begins and where it ends were very intense. During the public debate over whether Austria should become a member of the European Union, the discussion came under the umbrella of being European or not, which meant being part of the Western world or being part of the "Balkans," a synonym for the alleged cultural as well as economic and social underdevelopment of the former Eastern bloc.[12] Now that the borders are being drawn anew, the European Union embraces some former Eastern-bloc states and shares a border with Turkey.

This example shows that the term *Europe* has a tendency to raise discussions surrounding cultural identity which are not tied to geography. As part of our research, we are rather confronted with political facts, motivations, and social negotiations. Moreover, using Europe as an interpretive model for Cold War Cultures raises more questions than it clarifies. In contrast, the approach of pluralizing the term *Cold War Culture* opens up new perspectives. It is an exciting challenge to integrate cultural plurality into the design, as this entails a complex theoretical question surrounding the internal relationship between culture (in a broad sense), politics, and economy, which can be discussed on the basis of empirical data. This way, we can discuss defined markets, consumption behavior, lifestyles, etc., and introduce a transnational perspective into the research question. However, European Cold War *Cultures* implies plurality, which is an important characteristic of the continent. It raises once more the question surrounding what constitutes Europe and what is European. This is an important concern for political interests as well as for European self-conceptualization. Indeed, it is tempting to create a new metanarrative. Konrad Jarausch has pointed out that it is always part of a convincing (historical) narrative to interpret all aspects in light of their significance for the present. Depending on how this present is perceived, history is defined as a tragedy, a comedy, or a heroic history. In any case, the result is perceptible in advance: the present. Certainly this is theoretically problematic, as there is never only "one" history, just as there is never only "one" present. Thus, this tendency to homogenize, which is psychologically understandable, is not scientifically viable. This makes it very difficult to avoid the homogenizations of older metanarratives, for example "the nation," even in the academic field.[13] Of course we are used to teleological narrations and this is a lesson we still have to learn concerning our expectations. We have to accept that the cultural and social identities built upon social clusters, with relations based on social practices, education, or consumption behaviors, are extremely strong, and that an awareness of this circumstance might explain more than the teleological concept. We must take the consequences of the criticism of metanarratives and of "old-fashioned" national history seriously. Of course, this means that we have to deal with more heterogeneity, fragmentation, and ruptures in our academic work. But education, academic behavior, and communication styles are a strong cultural bond that will help us better understand the complex past "reality." Finally, we may find that fragmentation and particular developments are and were in fact not problematic, as these two aspects are central features of modernity and are often integrated by individuals in surprisingly uncomplicated ways. The advantage is that we can identify all this empirically and that this identification does not require any spatial concept.

With his notion of "imagined communities"[14] Benedict Anderson contributes one of many important points: the mental construction of nations was only possible by establishing imagined communities. Moreover, collective imagination was a product of mass media, education systems, and the loss of other collective narratives.

Europe cannot be defined merely as the Christian Occident: we should not forget that the concept of Europe has a long and complex history, and Europe is also defined by its past as colonizer, its war experiences, its complex network of global relations, and much more. "Europe" is not a universal term. It has even been questioned whether Europe is actually a continent at all.[15]

The Cold War was a strong political structure, with complex impacts on the economy and on culture. It established certain emotional conditions, such as *angst*, and was a vehicle for social change. We can identify factors such as mass media, economic incentives, and political reorientations that help to analyze local manifestations of global events in this context. Bringing up "Europe" raises a number of important questions that unfortunately do not, however, help us understand the cultural influence of the Cold War in Europe. Transnationality is not a linear exchange between close neighbors. The awareness of transnationality leads to an increasing awareness of complex global networks of academics, artists, interest groups, and others. The network can encompass many different regions all over the world, and is not necessarily tied to geographical spaces, but more often to social, intellectual, or even consumption spaces.

The remembrance and historicization of the Berlin Blockade focused solely on the "Westernization" of the Federal Republic of Germany and West Berlin. It established a transatlantic link, not a European one. The event is part of the symbolic "Western" shift of the Federal Republic of Germany. We will see that there is no historicization of the Airlift in the German Democratic Republic, because the occasional reference to the event and sporadic historical and political analyses does not amount to historicization. Historicization refers to the process of forming memory in a broader sense—anchoring an event in the cultural memory of a society.

Hence, I propose to treat the Airlift as a *place of remembrance* only for the United States and the FRG, including their transatlantic relationship.

In order to understand the power of this historicization and remembrance, the sporadic oblivion of events, and their reactivation, we must take a closer look at the emotional quality of memory.

Memory and Fear

Memory is part of a cultural system. All forms of memory, such as commemoration, published memoirs, movies, or school textbooks—even the orally narrated memories of grandfathers, for example—are tied to social experiences of not only the "producers" but also the recipients. "Historical" truth (or better: the convincing truth of remembrance) is measured by evidence, but evidence does not necessarily mean proven facts. Evidence refers to a subjective and social narrative that is adaptable to subjective and social experiences and backgrounds. This type of truth is completely different from historical, judicial, or academic truth.[16] Social experiences, based upon the individual horizon defined by family structure, education, economic background, or other social boundaries, are the basis for the evaluation of narrations and their plausibility. Memory (remembrance, commemoration, recollection) is always embedded in narrative structures. Narrations are generally reflexive: the mediation of the past focuses on the audience. Hence, the narrative structure almost automatically includes the recipient.

Autobiographical memory is linked to emotions, enabling temporal perspectives and with them practical orientations. The positive/negative axis constitutes an *emotional index* of autobiographical memory. Life experiences are interpreted within a set of possible human emotions and thus made accessible. This emotional index has importance neither for semantic memory, which saves knowledge, nor for the episodic memory of events. Only this specifically human ability to experience space and time reflexively and self-consciously, as a retrospective narration from the past to the present, creates the possibility of concepts and values oriented towards the future.[17] This narration is more instrumental and not so much tied to facts. In this respect, we see that oblivion is a functional process of memory. Concerning the total sum of past events, forgetting is an absolutely necessary condition for constituting reasonable and convincing pasts—depending on the needs and requirements of the present.[18]

These considerations on the development of the human memory, which stem from the field of anthropology, underline the relevance of

Maurice Halbwachs's findings. Thus the construction of social relations by memory and remembrance (Halbwachs) structurally anchors emotional assessments. In contrast to the not-yet-narrated fragments and bits of the past that do not serve a function and are therefore like "free spirits," active narrations of the past follow their own inherent dramaturgy. Simply the fact that they are active means that they have emotional indexes for a significant group in a given society that considers them to be important for the present. (However, this does not mean that this narration's emotional index is the same for everyone.)

Based on these anthropological findings concerning the functions of memory, we can better understand the oscillation between communicative and cultural memory. The concept of memory as a formative aspect of social relations reinforces the necessity of memory for the practical use of this category. Elemental are questions concerning how and when any kind of memory appears, and which perceptions structure identity offers, steer policy, and explain situations.[19] This is not a treatment of memory as part of a simple political representation in a "forced" or politically steered commemoration culture. It calls for an academic treatment of memory that takes into consideration the field of representation in mass media, within a family, or in education systems, public spaces, and the like. In conclusion, we can state that memory is essential for orientation, but to a greater degree also for inclusion and exclusion into a group. Thus, it is about relations that may be established by political orders, but also by shared experiences based on mass media, the arts, entertainment, consumption, education, and the like.

Collective memory is a hybrid concept.[20] A society is not a single group, but consists of various constellations that are engaged in a constant process of exchange and subject to social dynamics. It is a complex field. Thus it is important to be aware of the necessity of translating between the level of autobiographical (individual) experience and the broader societal level. In order to understand the dynamics of memory and the oscillation between communicative and cultural memory, we must keep this in mind. Memory theory or the history of memory is concerned with identity or identity offers within a society. Finally, it is a framework within which to reflect on "cultural identity" without the need for a new master narrative. It offers the possibility of linking fragmented but entangled experiences on the basis of their differences and exchanges. As such, it is a promising approach for a discipline to avoid the regression into old structures of teleological narratives, and one that fosters the understanding of transnational boundaries and clarifies the heterogeneous interactions in Europe. One important layer in this context is the "Westernization" of Europe in terms of the Cold War dichotomy. Moreover, the historicization and memory of the Airlift is intimately connected with this rapid Westernization of the FRG and West Berlin.

Angst: The Berlin Blockade and the Steadfastness of the Berliners

Seized and damaged by the Red Army in 1945, Berlin's Tempelhof airport was taken over by the Americans, who completed the architect Ernst Sagebiel's design in 1950. In 1948–49, Tempelhof airport was the focal point of the Berlin Airlift, when Douglas C-47 and C-54 airplanes shipped food and other supplies into the western part of Berlin besieged by the Soviets. Its Nazi origins were thus redeemed.[21]

The process of commemoration was not based only on a political decision. The memory of the Airlift was clearly alive in the postwar society, in light of its presence in the mass media, movies, memoirs, and the like. We must thus take a closer look at the emotional index of the Airlift. Closely connected with this is the question concerning fields of representation and what kinds of relations were established with this memory.

First of all, the Airlift was a collective experience for Berliners that was mostly frightening. However, the local fear in Berlin turned into the global fear of a third world war and the horror of the atomic bomb. The conflict had global significance and was therefore globally observed. Visibility was the key for the "battle" in Berlin, which was narrated in terms of "the steadfastness of the Berliners (West)," the state of siege, and the defense of Western democracy. Visibility became an essential tool for the Cold War.[22]

Fields of Representation for the Airlift: Mass Media

The assessment of the Airlift as a historical event appeared simultaneously with the events themselves. It somehow geminated from the Airlift. Individual survival in a precarious situation was synchronically part of a narration that placed the events into a sort of Cold War dichotomy. One was in the middle of a key historical event. Individual survival and individual worries concerning one's very existence were perceived as a collective concern. It was a successfully narrated historicization of the present as resistance to the good values and, in the background, as resistance to worldwide peace. It was a bond that linked Berliners with the refugees from East Germany and with the Western world, as epitomized by the United States.

This strange and powerful concept of prospective historicization—the inflated evaluation of the present as a key historical moment—was mainly narrated by the cinema; by newsreels; on the radio, not only in the news but also in the entertainment section ("Stimme Berlins," RIAS); and in newspapers. Concerning Berlin, it is interesting that the mediated daily life was renarrated from an Eastern as well as a Western perspective.

Already before the Berlin Blockade, the mass media were used as an important tool to influence postwar Germany. All Allies agreed fully with the assumption that German society had completely internalized National Socialist propaganda, and that this "contamination" could be reversed only by the extensive employment of quality counterpropaganda.[23]

This resulted in a general production and distribution prohibition for all German media directly after the war. In turn, the Allies tried to transform the meaning of the term *propaganda* into a less negatively connoted tool for manipulation. However, in the growing conflict with the Soviet Union, the climate of mutual suspicion, denunciation, and weakening made cooperation difficult: a memorandum sent to the Soviet Military Administration in Germany in 1946 by Sergei Tulpanov (the director of the Propaganda Administration), highlighted the anti-Soviet tone in Western propaganda. Meanwhile, General Lucius D. Clay (military governor for the U.S. Zone in Germany from 1947 to 1949) commented on the Soviet propaganda as follows:

> We do propose to attack communism and the police state before the German people, whereas in the past we have confined our efforts to presenting the advantages of democracy.... Under these conditions we cannot wait for Washington's approval when our adversaries speak to the German public. If I get the Department of Army in trouble, I will apologize; on the other hand, I shall not let Soviet attacks go unanswered and have both our press and the German people believe that we are afraid to answer. There could be nothing more harmful to our success.[24]

The run-up to the Cold War was already a battle of narrations and ideologies. The agitation and propaganda started in 1946, and was a preview of sorts of the Berlin Blockade/Berlin Airlift two years later. The propaganda was mainly carried out through a bipolar narration structure that became a topological standard for any kind of media narration. Because of the Blockade, Berlin was defined as the arena for the East-West conflict. Visible performances of affiliation and symbolic actions were an essential part of this political as well as ideological conflict. In this context, "visible" implies distributed through the media and oriented towards mass perception.

In the struggle for the position of West Berlin, the Allies constantly worried about the steadfastness of the population. It is important to consider the terminology "morale of the Berliners," which became a crucial incantation during the conflict. This terminology had a strong impact, and still feeds some urban myths concerning Berlin. Ernst Reuter, the mayor of West Berlin from 1948 to 1953, played a prominent role in mobilizing the resistance of the Berliners, and indeed had a strong sense of the connection between political decision-making and public relations. This strong sense was used to mobilize the Berliners, but also to vigorously mobilize the Allies, especially the U.S.A. Here, Reuter speaks on the occasion of the Social Democratic Party's manifestation in the City Hall of Schöneberg on 11 July 1948:

> The world cannot abandon us! If we have achieved something, then we have achieved through our attitude that the Allies stay, that they have to stay, because they could never justify before the public opinion of their own countries delivering this people to a one-sided dictatorship.[25]

And again on the occasion of a trip to the United States, Ernst Reuter spoke to the City Council on 7 April 1949:

> The actual mission of my trip, by virtue of this invitation of American mayors, was to take this opportunity to inform the American public about what is happening here in our city of Berlin, and alongside the many occasions that resulted from official visits, I have also used every possible occasion in order to address the American public. Hence I have not missed the opportunity to speak four times via broadcasts, namely on television, and on one occasion half an hour on the popular broadcast "Meet the Press," in which one is examined and interrogated and put to the acid test by no less than four hard-boiled journalists.[26]

Reuter's talent for influencing public opinion and especially "the morale of the Berliners" resulted in an accompanying popular myth. Supposedly there was an informal agreement between General Clay and Reuter to divide the task between them: General Clay was to take care of all technical and organizational aspects of the Airlift, and Reuter was to be responsible for the morale of the Berliners. However, the Allies did not leave the perseverance of the Berliners only to the concern of the then mayor of Berlin. Besides the gigantic technical endeavor of breaking the Blockade through the air, the Allied media policy was quite active. In 1945, before the Berlin Blockade, the Allies started to rebuild the media for the "new Germany." However, the joint project failed and resulted in separate media projects such as newsreels like *Welt im Film* ("The World on Film"), as a coproduction of the United States and Great Britain, *Blick in die Welt* ("View of the World"), as a French production, and *Der Augenzeuge* ("Eyewitness") as a so-called German newsreel, which was actually under Soviet control.²⁷ Broadcast and print media were also newly structured and organized. Several local and regional broadcasts were established. In the American sector, RIAS became the most popular.²⁸ Central broadcasts were also launched in the French and British zones.

Already on 13 May, the first broadcast was transmitted from the old broadcast building on Masurenallee in Berlin. This program was under Soviet control and later became the state broadcast of the GDR. In contrast to the Western zones, in the Soviet zone Germans were responsible for it. Despite strict Soviet control, this circumstance itself became part of the Communists' anti-Western propaganda. The Eastern program became the "true" voice of the Germans.²⁹

The Airlift was an effective media demonstration, advertising the efficiency of the Western system. A large number of newsreels and documentaries were produced during the Blockade (by the Allies) and shown all over Germany—not only in Berlin. Equally important and intensively used were the radio and print media. William F. Heimlich, a member of the U.S. Military Intelligence in Germany and head of RIAS from 1948 to 1949, remarked on the occasion of the opening of the new RIAS building on 7 July 1948: "We will continue to serve the population of Berlin and it is my wish that people in Berlin and in the Eastern zone regard RIAS as a weapon in their struggle for freedom and democracy."³⁰

Crucial for further developments was the fact that this information policy, which mainly targeted Berlin and Germany, reverberated through all the Allied countries, most of all in the United States. The information was in part explicitly aimed at the United States, not only in newspapers or newsreels but also in entertainment productions. One example is the movie *The Big Lift* from 1950, directed by George Seaton. It is a semi-documentary film about the Berlin Airlift, featuring the stories of two fictitious U.S. Air Force members: Sgt. Hank Kowalski (Paul Douglas), whose hatred of the Germans proves resistant to change, and Sgt. Danny McCullough (Montgomery Clift), whose pursuit of an attractive German war widow gives him a crash course in the seamy side of occupied Berlin. This widow represents the "bad" Germans. She was married to and still is in contact with a former Nazi who lives in St. Louis without any legal problems. She tries to use Sgt. McCullough's naiveté to get a ticket to the United States. Sgt. Hank Kowalski is in some ways the evil twin of Sgt. Danny McCullough. He also has a German "Schatzi." However, his "Schatzi" was successfully reeducated from the Nazi brainwashing to become a true democratic believer. This reeducation also leads to a reeducated American, who better understands the problems of the Germans and comes to the conclusion that Germans are basically also good and freedom-loving people. With the exception of Paul Douglas, Montgomery Clift, Cornell Borchers, and Bruni Löbel, the military and civilian staff play themselves. It is an interesting plot in the context of the establishment of the transatlantic relationship. Two models of German women can be identified: the German *Fräulein* as unconvincible, selfish, and dangerous, and the German *Fräulein* as good, innocent, and willing to learn and to build the foundation for a new Germany. Annette Brauerhoch interprets *The Big Lift* with regard to the narrative "*deutsches Fräulein*." Based on a media analysis, she convincingly highlights the feminization of postwar Germany and women's roles in the reeducation and reconstruction of West Germany.[31] *The Big Lift* was also very successful in the United States, as reflected in the Golden Globe nomination for "best film promoting international understanding" in 1950. However, the role of Cornell Borchers as the abysmal widow was feared to be too negative for Germany. The movie was reedited for the German market and released in 1953.

The resistance of the Berliners and the image of West Berlin as a "front city" was emanated all over Germany. The American historian Brian Ladd wrote:

> The suffering of these victims redeemed all Germans. Since the Airlift of 1948–49, Berliners, more than other Germans, had been able to claim the hearts of their former enemies in the West. In a famous speech during the Airlift, West Berlin's mayor, Ernst Reuter, demanded, "Peoples of the world, look upon this city!" At least in the West, they looked, and they saw freedom-loving heroes where only a few years before they had seen Hitler's minions.... West Berlin celebrated its new identity with its first major post war monument, the Airlift Memorial dedicated by Reuter at Tempelhof airport in 1951.[32]

The famous speech by Ernst Reuter in front of the Reichstag was heard and seen all over the world.[33] Its claim on the global perspective and the visibility of events became crucial for all actions and strategies employed in the Cold War. West Berlin's demonstrated membership in the Western world was a fundamental aspect in the further development of the new Germany. It was used to link this new Germany unshakably to the Western Allies.[34] The Blockade ended on 12 May 1949. Its termination had already been announced in the newspapers on 5 May. The headlines of the newspapers in the Western sector on 12 May read: "In Memoriam," with a swift claim for commemoration of the victims of the Airlift (*Tagesspiegel*), "Die Blockade ist gesprengt" ("The blockade is broken"), and "Berlin verdient die Achtung der Welt" ("Berlin deserves the world's attention") (*Telegraf*), as well as a detailed chronicle and historical evaluation of the Airlift in all the newspapers of West Berlin. The reports in Western newsreels were similar.

In contrast, the GDR made few comments on the end of the "Western blockade." The Soviets denied that there was a blockade at all, and only in response to the "counterblockade" from the Western sectors was it officially possible to speak about the Berlin Blockade in the GDR at all. Typical of narrations in the GDR, the first announcement of the Blockade's termination on page 1 of the *Berliner Zeitung* was accompanied by a report about the inauguration of the Soviet Honor Memorial in Treptow on 8 May.

Ironically, in 1994 the departure of all Allies from Berlin had similarities to that event: On 8 September, France's President François Mitterrand, British Prime Minister John Major, and U.S. Secretary of State Warren Christopher commemorated the victims of the Airlift at Airlift Square (*Platz der Luftbrücke*). The official farewell of the Soviets had already taken place on 31 August at the Soviet Honor Memorial in Treptow. Here, President Boris Yeltsin commemorated the victims of the capture of Berlin.

Fields of Representation for the Airlift, Part II: Urban Space

Already on 1 June 1949, Kronprinzenallee, in Berlin's Steglitz-Zehlendorf district, was renamed Clayallee, and on 25 June the area to the northwest of the Tempelhof airport was ceremoniously inaugurated as Airlift Square (*Platz der Luftbrücke*). The quick museumization of the Airlift by codifying urban space can be seen as the result of the parallel character of event and narration, or the geminating of the perception, which helped to cement the now positive relationships between former enemies, and especially West Germany's transatlantic relation to the United States.

Two years later, on 10 July 1951, the Airlift Memorial was inaugurated. This memorial was dedicated to commemorate the victims of the Airlift. The Minister for All-German Affairs, Jakob Kaiser, called the memorial a "symbol of a world-moving solidarity between the people of Berlin and yesterday's victors.... [The] Airlift Memorial is a memorial of the fact that Berlin has incontestably acquired the right to be the capital of our fatherland."[35] The efforts to retain West Berlin were mainly the result of the intensive commitment of the Americans and the British. Although the French were politely mentioned, the commemoration was linked to them. To be more precise, the commemoration was an act of fraternization especially with the United States. Great Britain was regarded more as a "good friend" of the United States.

In the 1950s and 60s, the intensive commemoration of the Berlin Airlift of 1948–49 was still a vivid expression of the event's significance for all

Berliners as well as for West Germans. President John F. Kennedy's Berlin visit in 1963—apart from the legendary words *"Ich bin ein Berliner"*—reactivated and simultaneously utilized this memory with statements like: "I am proud to come to this city as the guest of your distinguished mayor (Willy Brandt), who has symbolized throughout the world the fighting spirit of West Berlin."[36] The reactivation was achieved not only through words, but also through the ritualized visits to sensitive sights in the city such as the Airlift Memorial and the freshly constructed Wall, and all this in the company of General Lucius D. Clay, the famous Airlift hero. Each stage of the visit and the President's departure were broadcast, and thus swiftly adapted to the central Cold War paradigm of visibility.

All presidents of the United States had to lay a wreath at the Airlift Memorial; it was part of the ritual. However, the reactions of the Berliners to this ritual, at first wholly positive and later more ambivalent, could always be taken as an indicator of the current state of transatlantic relations.

Détente and the End of the Airlift

Although Kennedy's Berlin visit called to mind the significance of the Airlift as well as the strong bond between Berlin and the U.S.A. (the people of Berlin greeted him euphorically), we have to concede that two principles of the Cold War faded slowly. The insuperable strength of the United States to guarantee Western freedom lost its power of persuasion with the Berlin Wall and the disasters of Vietnam. In addition, the policy of détente, which John F. Kennedy and West Germany's chancellor Willy Brandt pursued, diffused the atmosphere of direct and constant threat. With this change, the positive relations between the United States and the Berliners slowly eroded. It is important also to mention the context of the "Generation of '68," or the protest generation. Based on their criticism of Richard Nixon's government, a fraction of this movement took on a radical anti-American stance. The Airlift narration became one of American imperialism and an argument against the parent generation. The GDR counternarrative of the Airlift as part of the "imperialist strategy" of the United States and its Western allies was widely received in the protest movement, and remains one of the most important narratives of certain left-wing groups until today.[37]

The Airlift as well as Tempelhof airport became a stage again, but this time for a vanished Berlin that had been an ally and a ward of the Americans. The Airlift commemoration lost its unambiguous meaning in the course of the generational conflict. This conflict was certainly not limited to Berlin, but rather was a transnational trend. It was a phenomenon that transformed the rigid Cold War society. The generational conflict transformed the previously close relationship between Berlin and the United States into a critical interrogation of both the past and the value of commemorating not only the Airlift, but history in general.

Concerning the Berlin Airlift, Andreas Anderhub wrote: "In 1984, the events dated back only thirty-five years, not much more than the lifespan of a generation. Then nobody would have presumed that such an important event, witnessed by millions of people, could here and today in Berlin apparently vanish from public consciousness."[38] Obviously, such a claim for commemoration is much more a sign of oblivion than of any kind of lively and active remembrance in Berlin. Still, it had its importance for the Allies residing in the city. The museumization of the Airlift[39] was frequently repeated but did not elicit the broad public enthusiasm it once had. However, Tempelhof airport and Airlift Square did not lose their connotation with the Airlift, and were still associated with the U.S.A. in the mental map of Berlin. The emotional *angst* index, the fear of the loss of position in the Western world, did not make sense in the perspective of the 1980s. The position of West Berlin was secure—partly thanks to the Wall. It was secure enough so that it was possible to distance oneself from U.S. interests. This oblivion opened up new possibilities for criticism. For example, there are some myths surrounding the Berlin Blockade that should be critically discussed, such as the blockade's purported "totality."[40]

The Allies Have Left the City: Is the Story Over?

> Especially in a mature Europe that is growing together, programs committed to the German language and the cultural heritage of the German-speaking realm are particularly justified.... Because a society defines itself through shared culture. If factors that enhance identification vanish, this weakens the cohesion and finally the efficiency of a community.... What sorts of "identity benefactors" do I have in mind? Even if it might be dangerous to pick out only two examples, I would like to mention "the Airlift" and "Dresden" as illustrations.[41]

The Bavarian Prime Minister Edmund Stoiber is here referring to the German TV production *Nur der Himmel war frei*, a two-part television movie that retold the story of the Airlift and was broadcast in November 2005. The end of the Cold War, the fall of the Berlin Wall, and German reunification lie between the comments of Andreas Anderhub and Edmund Stoiber. They imply a radical change of frame for the Airlift narration. Preliminarily, we can conclude that both comments express a positive view of the events. With regard to what I have argued about the emotional index, the most astonishing difference between these comments is the transformation from the fear of oblivion to a vivid memory of a crucial event for German identity.

How should we interpret this reactivation of the Airlift, concerning all that was said about the emotional index? The index of the Airlift was obviously *angst*, a fear that was in the background of the event's historicization especially in the first twenty years of the Cold War. However, it no longer has a contemporary basis, as the original conflict has been resolved. Concerning the Airlift's commemoration, we can conclude that due to the loss of the underlying context—the Cold War—the recurring and ritualized community-building via the Airlift Memorial also vanished. This loss affected all Western allies, but most strongly the United States. As already mentioned, this shared memory and its value for the involved "participants" must be regarded as an unsteady flow, transformed and renarrated according to contemporary needs. Thus, we cannot understand the reactivation of the Airlift memory if we do not consider some other factors and emotions connected with it.

The end of the Cold War opened up a new space that allowed for a nostalgic view of the lost transatlantic community. This loss is more or less at the center of publications on the memory of the Berlin Airlift, such as books, radio and print features, or movies. The Cold War was a strong frame for the meaning of Berlin, and before the political turnover in 1989, the Airlift narration was mostly centered on the scandal of the siege. The resistance of the Berliners and the friendship with the Western Allies was important, but more a by-product of being a freedom-loving member of the freedom-loving West. The stamp "freedom-loving Germans" was—a point which we also have to take into account—the ticket for the Germans to be integrated into the process of a forming the (West) European Community. In addition, it was the initial situation that shifted the image of Germany away from that of aggressive Prussia to the democratic FRG.

The time after 1989 was accompanied by the shift of Berlin's identity from front city to "Berlin Republic." This period also changed the Airlift narration. Most prominent is the increase in nostalgically colored narrations surrounding the Berlin Blockade, which focus more on friendship and warm solidarity than on the scandal of the Blockade itself. Again, the special relationship between the U.S.A. and Berlin still dominates. This is most likely due to the fact that most written and filmed memoirs are produced by Germans and Americans, such as Gail S. Halvorsen's *The Berlin Candy Bomber* (1990, 2002, 2004) and *Kaugummi und Schoko-*

lade ("chewing gum and chocolate"); the German TV production *Nur der Himmel war frei* ("only the sky was clear") (2005); *Tempelhof: Das fliegende Herz Berlins* ("the flying heart of Berlin") (2005), a book by Mareike Knoke; *The Berlin Airlift: First Battle of the Cold War* (1998), a TV documentary on the American History Channel; and many more.

Indeed, Gail S. Halvorsen is an important and very popular figure in the context of Tempelhof nostalgia. He was a pilot during the Blockade and started "little vittles," the airdrop of small chocolate parcels. This action was already very popular during the Airlift, and was accompanied by intense public collections in the United States (a point we can consider a further step in the fraternization of Germans and Americans). Last but not least, this was the reason for the famous renaming of the war planes as "candy bombers" (*Rosinenbomber*).

Another phenomenon can also be observed: the concentration in published pictures of the airport on the interwar years. On the level of images, there is a strong connection, shaped by heroism and technical high performance, between the airport and the 1920s and the airport of 1948–49. Likewise remarkable is the fact that the two airport periods "Airlift" and "interwar years" are hardly connected with the National Socialist airport. Tempelhof as a monument of Nazi architecture is generally treated separately and not incorporated into nostalgic views.

In fact, debates about the final closure of Tempelhof Airport were partly dominated by historical arguments. The first referendum, entitled "Tempelhof bleibt Verkehrsflughafen" ("Tempelhof remains a passenger airport"), was initiated by "Interessengemeinschaft City-Airport Tempelhof" ("Tempelhof City Airport Syndicate," ICAT) in 2006. The syndicate and its 1250 members were supported by various groups, including "Aktionsbündnis be-4-tempelhof." On 6 May 2008, 60.1 percent of voters were in favor of maintaining Tempelhof as a City Airport. However, because of relatively low participation, these 60.1 percent represented only 21.7 percent of Berlin's population, and the federal state of Berlin refused to accept the referendum.[42]

While the initiators of this first referendum argued that the closure would harm Berlin economically,[43] a second and more successful referendum was initiated by "Aktionsbündnis be-4-tempelhof," a former supporter of ICAT. This time it was argued that Tempelhof should be kept open for historical reasons. On 7 June 2009, 37.1 per cent of the total population of Berlin supported the referendum, which was consequently accepted by the Senate of Berlin.[44] The success of this referendum was obviously linked to a campaign that targeted the meaning of Tempelhof during the Cold War rather than its economic significance. For example, an open letter from the initiators to the political leaders of Berlin recalled both the famous Ernst Reuter "Schaut auf diese Stadt" speech[45] and candy-bomber pilot Gail S. Halvorsen's dictum: "In America, we've got a symbol of freedom, it is called 'Statue of Liberty.' I believe that Tempelhof Airport is the German equivalent of the Statue of Liberty."[46] In fact, the second referendum was more successful because it addressed Tempelhof's symbolic meaning and the emotional index of its memory.

As we have said, the element of *angst* was overwritten by nostalgia. Remarkably, the aim of the second referendum was to claim the airport and airfield as the Airlift's stage, and thus as a world heritage. This notion of Tempelhof as a Cold War memorial confirms that there is a deep divide between the Nazi and the postwar memory of Tempelhof as a showcase for freedom-loving Berlin. In fact, the second referendum's initiators never said a word about the Nazi origins of the building. Today, Berlin is in search of a new name for the "Tempelhofer Feld" ("Tempelhof field"), which is now open to the public and widely accepted as a local recreation area. Not surprisingly, one of the favored names is "Park der Luftbrücke" ("Airlift Park").[47]

Finally, a place of remembrance has emerged around the actual commemoration, which I would like to call the Tempelhof airport "archive"—a place for recalling contradicting memories and a location for potential identification for various groups. The place represented and still represents transnational experiences, and could be a pivotal point for analyzing differing affiliations and expectations. Moreover, it is a symbol of shared interests and values during the long Cold War period, and it is a place where the interdependence of politics and culture becomes obvious. Hence it is a place of remembrance that embraces three important narrations of modernity: the history of aviation, the Nazi past, and the Cold War. All narrations have their memorials directly on location: the building itself; a memorial for the forced laborers under the Nazi regime; in one of the airport's courts a memorial to the first aviators, donated by the British government in the 1970s; two memorials to the Airlift; and last but not least a memorial to the U.S. victory over the Nazis: the Eagle at the Eagle Square.

Austrian research on places of remembrance has demonstrated that the history of memory is not necessarily connected to national history.[48] Henry Rousso criticizes projects currently being carried out in France, Italy, and Germany.[49] The concept of collective memory, as well as that of places of remembrance as metaphorical "locations" for cumulative memories, foster our understanding of the interdependence and transnationality of cultures. At this point, the history of memory can take its place in the research on Cold War Cultures in Europe.

Notes

1. Thomas Lindenberger, "European Cold War Cultures?," *Potsdamer Bulletin für Zeithistorische Studien*, no. 38/39 (2006): 21–23.
2. Maurice Halbwachs, *Das kollektive Gedächtnis* (Stuttgart, 1967).
3. Ute Frevert, "Europeanizing Germany's Twentieth Century," *Histories and Memories of Twentieth-Century Germany, History & Memory* 17 (2005): 87–116, 90.
4. Frithjof B. Schenk, *Der spatial turn und die Osteuropäische Geschichte*, in: H-Soz-u-Kult, 6 January 2006, http://hsozkult.geschichte.hu-berlin.de/forum/2006-06-001; Jörg Dünne and Stephan Günzel, eds., *Raumtheorie* (Frankfurt am Main, 2006).
5. Stefan Troebst, *Region und Epoche statt Raum und Zeit*, http://www.europa.clio-online.de/2006/Article=161.
6. Georg Simmel, *Soziologie*, Gesamtausgabe Band II (Frankfurt am Main, 1995), 687–697.
7. Heike Karge, James Kaye, and Bo Stråth, "Europe," in *Briefingbook des Ludwig Boltzmann Instituts für Europäische Geschichte*, 15 May 2007, 166–169, http://ehp.lbg.ac.at/docs/briefing_book_lf_homepage.pdf.
8. Jürgen Elvert, "Mitteleuropa," *Historische Mitteilungen*, Beiheft no. 35 (Stuttgart, 1999); H. Mitterbauer and A.F. Balogh, eds., *Zentraleuropa* (Vienna, 2006); M. Csáky, A. Kury, and U. Tragatschnig, eds., *Kultur, Identität, Differenz* (Innsbruck, 2004); Jacques Le Rider, Moritz Csáky, and Monika Sommer, eds., *Transnationale Gedächtnisorte in Zentraleuropa* (Innsbruck, 2002).
9. Hagen Schulze, *Staat und Nation in der europäischen Geschichte* (Munich, 1999). The concept of a Christian Occident is not explicit, but rather remains implicit, for example with the supposed beginning of European history around 1000 A.D. and the emphasis on the importance of the split between the eastern and western churches. Cf. ibid., 13–17.
10. Hans Ulrich Wehler, "Das Türkenproblem," *Die Zeit*, no. 38 (2002), http://www.zeit.de/2002/38/200238_tuerkei.contra.xml?page=1.
11. Frevert, "Europeanizing Germany's Twentieth Century," 102–109.
12. Ruth Wodak, Rudolf de Cillia, and Martin Reisigl, *Zur diskursiven Konstruktion nationaler Identität* (Frankfurt am Main, 1998).
13. Konrad Jarausch, "Die Krise der deutschen Meistererzählung," in *Die historische Meistererzählung*, ed. Konrad Jarausch and Martin Sabrow (Göttingen, 2002), 140–162.
14. Benedict Anderson, *Imagined Communities* (London, 1983).
15. Karge, James, and Stråth, "Europe," 166f.
16. Harald Welzer, "Warum Menschen sich erinnern können und warum sie Geschichte haben," in *Erinnerung* (Berlin, 2007), 42–65.
17. Ibid., 44–47.
18. Ibid., 53.
19. Alon Confino and Peter Fritzsche, "Introduction: The Noise of the Past," in *The Work of Memory*, ed. Alon Confino and Peter Fritzsche (Urbana, 2002), 1–24.
20. Elisabeth Bronfen, Benjamin Marius, and Therese Steffen, eds., *Hybride Kulturen* (Tübingen, 1997).
21. Jordan Glancy, "Board Now, Gate Closing," *The Guardian*, 26 July 2004, http://arts.guardian.co.uk/critic/feature/0,1270210,00.html.
22. Andres W. Daum, *Kennedy in Berlin* (Paderborn, 2003), 8–17, 146–150.
23. Deutsches Technik Museum, *Auftrag Luftbrücke*, exhibition catalogue (Berlin: 1998), 8; Jutta Gröschl, *Die Deutschlandpolitik der vier Großmächte in der Berichterstattung der deutschen Wochenschauen 1945–1949* (Berlin, 1997).

24. Gröschl, *Deutschlandpolitik*, 106f.
25. "Die Welt kann uns gar nicht im Stich lassen. Wenn wir eines erreicht haben, dann haben wir durch unsere Haltung erreicht, dass die Alliierten hier bleiben, dass sie hier bleiben müssen, weil sie es vor der öffentlichen Meinung ihrer eigenen Völker niemals würden verantworten können, dieses Volk einer einseitigen Diktatur auszuliefern." H. Reichhardt, ed., *Ernst Reuter* (Berlin, 1974), vol. 3, p. 418.
26. "Es war die eigentliche Aufgabe meiner Reise, auf Grund dieser Einladung der amerikanischen Bürgermeister, die Gelegenheit zu benutzen, die amerikanische Öffentlichkeit über das was hier bei uns in Berlin vor sich geht, zu unterrichten, und ich habe neben den zahlreichen Gelegenheiten, die sich aus offiziellen Besuchen ergeben haben, auch jede andere Gelegenheit ausgenutzt, um die amerikanische Öffentlichkeit anzusprechen. Ich habe infolgedessen die Gelegenheit nicht versäumt, viermal über den Rundfunk, und zwar über die Television, zu sprechen, einmal in der Länge von einer halben Stunde in einer in Amerika gern gehörten und weit verbreiteten Sendung 'Meet the Press,' in der man von nicht weniger als vier sehr hart gesottenen Reportern ausgefragt und auf Herz und Nieren geprüft wird." Reichhardt, *Ernst Reuter*, 683.
27. Gröschl, *Deutschlandpolitik*, 141–202.
28. Herbert Kundler, *RIAS Berlin* (Berlin, 2002).
29. Gröschl, *Deutschlandpolitik*, 130–140.
30. "Wir werden der Berliner Bevölkerung weiter dienen und es ist mein Wunsch, daß Berlin und die Ostzone den RIAS als Waffe in ihrem Kampf für Freiheit und Demokratie ansehen." William F. Heimlich, "Eine Waffe im Kampf um die Freiheit," *Tagesspiegel*, 7 July 1948, Berlin section.
31. Annette Brauerhoch, *Fräuleins und GIs* (Frankfurt am Main, 2006).
32. Brian Ladd, *The Ghosts of Berlin* (Chicago, 1997), 29.
33. Reichhardt, *Ernst Reuter*, 477ff.
34. Daum, *Kennedy in Berlin*, 14–17; Gröschl, *Deutschlandpolitik*, 85–89, 141–202.
35. "Symbol einer weltbewegenden Solidarität zwischen den Berlinern und den Siegern von Gestern.... [Das] Luftbrückendenkmal ist ein Mahnmal dafür, dass Berlin sich unbestreitbar das Recht erworben hat, die Hauptstadt unseres Vaterlandes zu sein." "Feierlichkeiten am Platz der Luftbrücke," *Tagesspiegel*, 11 July 1951, 1f.
36. Quoted in Daum, *Kennedy in Berlin*, 201.
37. Gerhard Keiderling, *Zur Berlinkrise 1948* (Berlin, 1982); MSZ online, "Westberlin: Eine Sumpfblüte des Imperialismus," *Marxistische Streit- und Zeitschrift* 1982, 6, http://www.gegenstandpunkt.com/msz/html/82/82_6/berlin.htm, and more currently: Weltrevolution 90, "Berliner Luftbrücke 1948," http://de.internationalism.org/welt90/1998_berlinerluftbr.
38. "Die Ereignisse liegen 1984 dreieinhalb Jahrzehnt zurück, nicht viel länger als die Zeitspanne einer Generation. Wer hätte damals vermutet, dass ein derartig bedeutendes Ereignis, von Millionen elementar miterlebt, hier und heute in Berlin offensichtlich weitgehend dem öffentlichen Bewusstsein entglitten ist?" Andreas Anderhub, *Blockade, Luftbrücke und Luftbrückendank* (Berliner Forum 2/84), 5.
39. Cf. Daum, *Kennedy in Berlin*.
40. Heinz-Gerd Reese, ed., *Blockade und Luftbrücke: Legende oder Lehrstück? Die Berlin-Krise von 1948/49 und ihre Folgen*, touring exhibition: "Blockade u. Luftbrücke—Legende oder Lehrstück?" (Stiftung Luftbrückendank).
41. "Gerade in einem mündigen und zusammenwachsenden Europa haben Programme ihre besondere Berechtigung, die sich in besonderer Weise der deutschen Sprache und dem kulturellem Erbe unseres Sprachraums verpflichtet wissen.... Denn eine

Gesellschaft definiert sich über kulturelle Gemeinsamkeiten. Fallen Identitätsstiftende Faktoren weg, schwächt das den Zusammenhalt und letztlich die Leistungsfähigkeit einer Gemeinschaft.… An welche 'Identitätsstifter' denke ich?… Auch wenn es gefährlich ist, jetzt nur zwei Beispiele herauszugreifen, so möchte ich doch 'Die Luftbrücke' und 'Dresden' zur Erläuterung nennen." Edmund Stoiber, 1. *Berliner Medienrede des Bayrischen Ministerpräsidenten*, 22 November 2006, http://www.ekd.de/medien/vortraege_predigten/061122_stoiber_berlin_medienrede.html.

42. For a brief overview of statistics, press, etc. see http://www.wahlen-berlin.de/wahlen/framesets/ve-2008.htm.
43. "Wir meinen, dass eine Schließung die schlechteste, weil unwirtschaftlichste und für die Stadt nachteiligste Lösung ist." Initial Statement by ICAT, 22 December 2007, http://www.openpr.de/news/179193/ICAT-Volksbegehren-Keine-Pause-im-Kampf-fuer-Flughafen-Berlin-Tempelhof.html.
44. Cf. http://www.berlin.de/ba-tempelhof-schoeneberg/organisationseinheit/buerger/wahl/ergebnis_be_tempelhof.html.
45. Press release, Berlin, 6 September 2008, http://www.be-4-tempelhof.de/news/presseerklaerungenderinitatoren/offenenerbriefschautaufdiesestadt/index.htm.
46. Quoted in: http://flughafentempelhof.blogspot.com/2008_12_01_archive.html; see also http://www.be-4-tempelhof.de/hintergrund/freiheitsstatuefuerdeutschland/index.html.
47. "Namen für Tempelhofer Feld gesucht." *Berliner Morgenpost*, 6 July 2010.
48. Moritz Csáky and Peter Stachel, eds., *Die Verortung von Gedächtnis* (Vienna, 2001); Moritz Csáky and Peter Stachel, *Mehrdeutigkeit* (Vienna, 2000). For more information, see http://www.oeaw.ac.at/kkt/projekte/odg/odg.html.
49. Henry Rousso, "History of Memory," in *Conflicted Memories*, ed. Konrad Jarausch and Thomas Lindenberger (New York, 2007), 23–36.

Bibliography

Anderson, Benedict. Benedict Anderson, *Imagined Communities: Reflections on the Origin and Spread of Nationalism*. London: Verso, 1983.

Brauerhoch, Annette. *Fräuleins und GIs: Geschichte und Filmgeschichte*. Frankfurt am Main: Stroemfeld, 2006.

Bronfen, Elisabeth, Benjamin Marius, and Therese Steffen, eds. *Hybride Kulturen: Beiträge zur anglo-amerikanischen Multikulturalismusdebatte*. Tübingen: Stauffenburg, 1997.

Confino, Alon, and Peter Fritzsche. "Introduction: The Noise of the Past." In *The Work of Memory: New Directions in the Study of German Society and Culture*, ed. Alon Confino and Peter Fritzsche (Urbana: University of Illinois Press, 2002), 1–24.

Csáky, M., A. Kury, and U. Tragatschnig, eds. *Kultur, Identität, Differenz: Wien und Zentraleuropa in der Moderne. Gedächtnis—Erinnerung—Identität 4*. Innsbruck: Passagen, 2004.

Csáky, Moritz, and Peter Stachel. *Mehrdeutigkeit: Die Ambivalenz von Gedächtnis und Erinnerung*. Vienna: Passagen, 2000.

Csáky, Moritz, and Peter Stachel, eds. *Die Verortung von Gedächtnis*. Vienna: Passagen, 2001.

Daum, Andres W. *Kennedy in Berlin*. Paderborn: Schöningh, 2003.

Dünne, Jörg, and Stephan Günzel, eds. *Raumtheorie: Grundlagentexte aus Philosophie und Kulturwissenschaft*. Frankfurt am Main: Suhrkamp, 2006.

Elvert, Jürgen. "Mitteleuropa: Deutsche Pläne zur europäischen Neuordnung 1918–1945." *Historische Mitteilungen*, Beiheft no. 35. Stuttgart: Steiner, 1999.

Frevert, Ute. "Europeanizing Germany's Twentieth Century." *Histories and Memories of Twentieth-Century Germany, History & Memory* 17 (2005): 87–116.

Glancy, Jordan. "Board Now, Gate Closing." *The Guardian*, 26 July 2004. http://arts.guardian.co.uk/critic/feature/0,1270210,00.html.

Gröschl, Jutta. *Die Deutschlandpolitik der vier Großmächte in der Berichterstattung der deutschen Wochenschauen 1945–1949: Ein Beitrag zur Debatte um den Film als historische Quelle*. Berlin: Walter de Gruyter, 1997.

Halbwachs, Maurice. *Das kollektive Gedächtnis*. Stuttgart: Enke, 1967.

Heimlich, William F. "Eine Waffe im Kampf um die Freiheit." *Tagesspiegel*, 7 July 1948, Berlin section.

Jarausch, Konrad. "Die Krise der deutschen Meistererzählung." In *Die historische Meistererzählung: Deutungslinien der deutschen Nachkriegsgeschichte nach 1945*, ed. Konrad Jarausch and Martin Sabrow (Göttingen: Vandenhoek & Ruprecht, 2002), 140–162.

Karge, Heike, James Kaye, and Bo Stråth. "Europe." In *Briefingbook des Ludwig Boltzmann Instituts für Europäische Geschichte*, 15 May 2007, 166–169, http://ehp.lbg.ac.at/docs/briefing_book_lf_homepage.pdf.

Keiderling, Gerhard. *Zur Berlinkrise 1948*. Schriften des Zentralinstituts für Geschichte, Akademie der Wissenschaften der DDR, 69. Berlin: Akademie Verlag, 1982.

Kundler, Herbert. *RIAS Berlin: Eine Radiostation in einer geteilten Stadt. Programme und Menschen: Texte-Bilder-Dokumente*. Berlin: Reimer, 2002.

Ladd, Brian. *The Ghosts of Berlin: Confronting German History in the Urban Landscape*. Chicago: University of Chicago Press, 1997.

Le Rider, Jacques, Moritz Csáky, and Monika Sommer, eds. *Transnationale Gedächtnisorte in Zentraleuropa. Gedächtnis—Erinnerung—Identität 1*. Innsbruck: Passagen, 2002.

Lindenberger, Thomas. "European Cold War Cultures? Massenmedien im Kalten Krieg in transnationaler Perspektive." *Potsdamer Bulletin für Zeithistorische Studien*, no. 38/39 (2006): 21–23.

Mitterbauer, H., and A.F. Balogh, eds. *Zentraleuropa: Ein hybrider Kommunikationsraum*. Vienna: Praesens-Verlag, 2006.

Reese, Heinz-Gerd, ed. *Blockade und Luftbrücke: Legende oder Lehrstück? Die Berlin-Krise von 1948/49 und ihre Folgen*, touring exhibition: "Blockade u. Luftbrücke—Legende oder Lehrstück?" (Stiftung Luftbrückendank).

Reichhardt, H., ed. *Ernst Reuter: Artikel, Briefe, Reden: 1946–1949*. 3 vols., Berlin: Propyläen, 1974.

Rousso, Henry. "History of Memory: Policies of the Past: What for?" In *Conflicted Memories: Europeanizing Contemporary Histories*, ed. Konrad Jarausch and Thomas Lindenberger (New York: Berghahn Books, 2007).

Schenk, Frithjof B. *Der spatial turn und die Osteuropäische Geschichte*. In H-Soz-u-Kult, 6 January 2006, http://hsozkult.geschichte.hu-berlin.de/forum/2006-06-001.

Schulze, Hagen. *Staat und Nation in der europäischen Geschichte*. Munich: C.H. Beck, 1999.

Simmel, Georg. *Soziologie: Untersuchung über die Formen der Vergesellschaftung*. Gesamtausgabe Band II. Frankfurt am Main: Suhrkamp, 1995.

Stoiber, Edmund. *1. Berliner Medienrede des Bayrischen Ministerpräsidenten*. 22 November 2006. http://www.ekd.de/medien/vortraege_predigten/061122_stoiber_berlin_medienrede.html.

Troebst, Stefan. *Region und Epoche statt Raum und Zeit: "Ostmitteleuropa" als prototypische Geschichtsregionale Konzeption*. http://www.europa.clio-online.de/2006/Article=161.

Wehler, Hans Ulrich. "Das Türkenproblem." *Die Zeit*, no. 38 (2002). http://www.zeit.de/2002/38/200238_tuerkei.contra.xml?page=1.

Welzer, Harald. "Warum Menschen sich erinnern können und warum sie Geschichte haben." In *Erinnerung*, ed. Biosphärenreservat Mittelelbe, Kulturstiftung Dessau Wörlitz, et al. UNESCO—Stätten im Raum Dessau-Wittenberg (Berlin, 2007), 42–65.

Wodak, Ruth, Rudolf de Cillia, and Martin Reisigl. *Zur diskursiven Konstruktion nationaler Identität*. Frankfurt am Main: Suhrkamp, 1998.

Further Documents

Deutsches Technik Museum. *Auftrag Luftbrücke*. Exhibition catalogue. Berlin, 1998.

Weltrevolution 90. *Berliner Luftbrücke 1948: Ein Versuch, die Verbrechen der Alliierten zu vertuschen*. http://de.internationalism.org/welt90/1998_berlinerluftbr.

MSZ online. *Westberlin: Eine Sumpfblüte des Imperialismus. Marxistische Streit- und Zeitschrift* 1982, 6. http://www.gegenstandpunkt.com/msz/html/82/82_6/berlin.htm.

Notes on Contributors

Andrew H. Beattie received his doctorate in European history from the University of Sydney in 2005. He currently teaches German and European studies at the University of New South Wales in Sydney. His research addresses the politics of memory in contemporary Germany, especially remembrance of East Germany and how it relates to remembrance of the Nazi past.

Marie Cronqvist received her doctorate in history from Lund University, Sweden, in 2004 and is currently an associate professor in Journalism and Media History at the Department of Communication and Media at Lund University. Her research interests include Cold War narratives, the history of journalism, and science and the media.

Luminita Gatejel studied modern history and German literature at the University of Tübingen (Germany). She wrote her Ph.D. dissertation at the Berlin School for Comparative European History on cars and consumerism in the Soviet Union, the GDR, and Romania. Currently she is a Max Weber Fellow at the European University Institute in Florence (Italy).

Petra Henzler studied history, sociology, and philosophy at the universities of Graz, Bologna, and Amsterdam. Since 1998 she has been a researcher at Forschungsgesellschaft Mobilität FGM/Austrian Mobility Research, Akademie der Künste (Berlin), and Brandenburgische Technische Universität (Cottbus). For her doctoral thesis about the memory of Tempelhof Airport in Berlin, she was affiliated with the Center for Metropolitan Studies at the Technical University, Berlin. Today, she is a freelance author in Berlin.

Valur Ingimundarson received his Ph.D. from Columbia University in New York. He is a professor of contemporary history and chair of the Historical Institute and of EDDA—Center of Excellence in Critical Contemporary Research at the University of Iceland. He has published extensively on the Cold War, U.S.-European relations, Icelandic foreign and security policy, and postconflict politics in the Balkans.

Roman Krakovsky is preparing his doctorate at the Sorbonne University, Paris. He is an assistant and lecturer in contemporary European history at the Institut d'études politiques in Paris. In 2004, he published *Rituel du 1er mai en Tchécoslovaquie*.

Edward Larkey received his doctorate in cultural theory from the Humboldt-Universität, Berlin, in 1986 and is Professor of German Studies and Intercultural Communication at the University of Maryland, Baltimore County. His most recently published book is entitled *Rotes Rockradio: Populäre Musik und die Kommerzialisierung des DDR-Rundfunks*, published by LIT-Verlag (2007). His current research engages in transcultural analyses of fictional television narratives in Germany and the U.S.

Thomas Lindenberger received his doctorate from the Technical University, Berlin, and his habilitation from Potsdam University. He was a research director at the Potsdam Centre for Contemporary History Research and is currently the director of the Ludwig Boltzmann Institute for European History and Public Spheres in Vienna. He held guest professorships at EHESS Paris, Thomas Masaryk University (Brno), and CEU Budapest.

Sabina Mihelj received her doctorate from the Ljubljana Graduate School of the Humanities. She is currently Senior Lecturer in Media, Communication, and Culture at Loughborough University, U.K. Her research focuses on issues of collective identity and mass communication, comparative media research, and the cultural and social history of Cold War Culture. She has published several articles and book chapters and is the author of *Media Nations: Communicating Belonging and Exclusion in the Modern World* (Palgrave, 2011).

Marcus M. Payk received his doctorate in modern history from the University of Bochum in 2005. He is a specialist in German and transatlantic history in the twentieth century and is currently a research fellow at the Department of History, Humboldt-Universität, Berlin.

Monique Scheer received her doctorate in European ethnology (*empirische Kulturwissenschaft*) from the University of Tübingen, where she is currently Assistant Professor at the Ludwig Uhland Institute. Her research interests include popular Catholic piety, German evangelicalism, and the historical and cultural anthropology of emotions.

Stefan Schwarzkopf received his doctorate in history from Birkbeck College, University of London. He is an associate professor at the Department of Management, Politics and Philosophy at Copenhagen Business School. His field of interest is the history of marketing and the cross-links between Cold War Cultures and the European advertising industries.

Joes Segal received his doctorate in art history from the University of Amsterdam. He is currently Assistant Professor of History at Utrecht University, The Netherlands, specializing in East European cultural history and in art and politics in times of crisis. In 2009/2010 he was Fulbright Guest Curator at the Wende Museum, Los Angeles, and a guest professor at UCLA.

Marsha Siefert received her doctorate from the University of Pennsylvania and is Associate Professor of History at the Central European University in Budapest. Her research focuses on cultural and communications history with particular attention to music and film. In the field of Cold War Culture she has published articles on radio diplomacy, sound recording in Hungary and Russia, music biopics, and Americanization in the Soviet Union.

Quinn Slobodian received his doctorate in modern European history at New York University. He is Assistant Professor of History at Wellesley College and is the author of *Foreign Front: Third World Politics in Sixties West Germany* (Duke University Press). He has published articles on labor internationalism, the activism of foreign students, and the politics of gore in West Germany in the 1960s.

Olga Voronina received her doctorate from Harvard University. Together with Dmitri Nabokov and Brian Boyd, she is currently translating Vladimir Nabokov's letters to his wife for publication by Knopf. As Assistant

Professor of Russian at Bard College, New York, she specializes in Russian literature and Cold War studies.

Annette Vowinckel received her doctorate from Universität Essen, Department of History, in 1999 and her habiliation from Humboldt-Universität, Berlin, Department of Cultural Studies, in 2006. She is a specialist in cultural history of the Renaissance and the twentieth century. As a researcher at the Zentrum für Zeithistorische Forschung, Potsdam, she has recently published a book on the cultural history of skyjacking.

Index

1968, 168n17, 168n19, 184–85n18, 186n37, 233n46, 300
    Berlin Vietnam Congress, 263, 272n49
    Czechoslovakia 1968, 29. *See also* Prague Spring
    Film releases and TV-series during the Sixties, 36–8, 47n67, 47n72, 82n82, 96
    Mexico Games 1968, 116. *See also* Olympics/Olympic Games
    New Left and 1968, 261, 265, 268, 271n62–64. *See also* New Left
    World Youth Festival, Sofia 1968, 13, 255, 261, 264–65

A

ABC, 176, 123n16
A Burnt-Out Case (novel), 104
Abstract Expressionism, 245, 251n42, 251nn45–46, 251n48, 251n50
Abusch, Alexander, 241
Ackermann, Max 237
Activism, 261, 271n39. *See also* New Left and "Third World"
Adenauer, Konrad, 16, 130, 144n7, 222–3, 244, 306, 316–17n46
Advertisements. *See also* Automobile
    Advertising Association (AA), 179–81, 186n47, 186n50, 186n51
    Advertising Inquiry Council, 175, 184n18
    Institute of Practitioners in Advertising (IPA), 176
    Subliminal Advertising, 176, 185n23–25
Afghanistan, 114
Africa, 5, 14
    Film Festivals, 37
    Public discussions/criticism of Western development, 261, 267. *See also* New Left, "Third World"
    World Youth Festivals, 254, 257–58, 260. *See also* Patrice Lumumba University
Airlift memorial, Tempelhof, 16, 347, 352–64
Air-raid protection, 195–96
Akhmatova, Anna, 9, 55–67, 70, 71–73nn4–75
Algeria, 258, 261
Allgemeine Deutsche Kunstausstellung (Dresden), 237, 239, 244
Alliance 90/The Greens, 310. *See also* The Greens
Amateur sports, 113, 120. *See also* Olympics/Olympic games, Sports
"Americanization", 6, 18n24, 27, 45n22, 45n24, 46n48, 107m5, 173, 181–82, 186n55, 251n51
Anarchism, 265
Anti-authoritarianism, 265
Anti-communism, 7, 11, 15, 16, 257, 322
    1950's style anti-communism, 300
    anti-anti-communism of the culture of détente, 304
    Mikson, anti-communism, 325, 335. *See also* Mikson Case
    National Socialist anti-communism, 268
    Religion and anti-communism, Billy Graham, 131, 145n8
    West-Germany (Cold War Culture) and anti-communism, 303, 308–10, 315n28
Anti-Semitism, 220
Anti-totalitarian consensus/anti-totalitarianism, 300, 310–12
Apocalypse/apocalyptic, 12
    Apocalypse in people, America, 193–94
    Apocalyptic Cold-War narratives, 143
    Awaiting apocalypse, apocalyptic

visions, Sweden, 195, 205. *See also* everyday militarization
Graham's apocalyptic message, 131
Nuclear apocalypse, 106, 205
"woman of the apocalypse", 143, 146n31
Armenia, 34
Asia
    Central Asia, 34
    Film Festival, 37
    Public discussions/ criticism of Western development, 261–62, 267. *See also* New Left, "Third World"
    World Youth Festival, 254, 256–59, 270n27, 270n39
Atomic bomb, 95, 223, 226–27, 286, 354. *See also* nuclear bomb
Attlee, Clement, 222
Auschwitz, 306, 317n63, 334
Austria, 16
    Austrian academic field and research, 349, 364
    Austrian art historian Hans Sedlmayer, 242
    Austrian EU-membership, 350
    Austrian students, anti-Communists, anti-festival, 256
Automobile, 152, 164, 165–66, 202
    Automobile production and industry, 11, 154–58, 165, 167
    Dacia, 157, 161–62
    Fiat Zhiguli, 157–58
    Ford, 156
    Moskvich, 159–61, 164
    Socialist/ Western automobile, 153–55, 159, 160, 161, 166, 167, 259
    Volga, 156, 159, 162–66
    Wartburg, 160, 165–67
Azerbaijan, 34, 231n5

B

Bahr, Egon, 102
Bain, Barbara, 97
Balbier, Uta, 114–5, 108–9n27, 122n2, 123n7, 269n4
Baltic states, 24, 321, 325–27, 334–37
    Baltic war criminals, 321, 334
    images of villains of Baltic origin in TV-Series, 103
Banionis, Donatas, 40–41
Barcelona, 121. *See also* Olympics/Olympic Games
Barr, Alfred Jr., 246

Bauhaus, 241, 249n6
Baumeister, Willi, 237, 241–43
Becher, Johannes R., 237
Behne, Adolf, 238
Ben Bella, Ahmed, 259
Bender, Peter, 309
Benin, 121
Berlin Blockade, 308, 347–48, 351, 354–56, 359, 361–62
Berlin, Isaiah, 9, 55–56
Berlin, West, 10, 78, 88, 262–4, 273n92, 352, 354–6, 358–61
Beveridge, William, 179
Bild-Zeitung, 118
biopics, 38, 41
Bond, James, 96, 100, 103–06, 108n11, 108n20, 108n23, 108–9n27
Bourdieu, Pierre, 114
Bovermann and Bleek, 305–06, 316n36, 316n38, 316n41
Bow Group, 177
Brainwashing, 12, 173, 175
    Nazi Brainwashing, 357
Brandt, Willy, 41, 360
Brezhnev, Leonid, 153–4
Buck, Hansjörg, 305
Buck-Morss, Susan, 2, 8, 16–17, 247
Budapest, 23, 37, 42–43, 47n67, 47n72, 48n92, 49n101–2, 100
Bulgaria, 24, 34, 37, 38, 41, 45n32, 293n54, 266–7, 286
Bunce, Valerie, 29, 46n37

C

Capitalism, 2, 14, 17, 155, 160, 175, 184n15
    communism and Capitalism, 116, 214, 216, 226, 229, 246, 257, 349
    Consensus capitalism, 270n26
    Global capitalism, 43, 66
    "Hydra of capitalism", 220, 223
    Industrial capitalism, 77
    "monopolistic capitalism", 214
    Swedish welfare model. *See also* folkhem, 192
Car production. *See* Automobile
Carter, Jimmy, 114
Castro, Fidel, 104, 265
Catholicism/Catholics, 11, 130–34, 137, 139, 143–44, 145n14, 146n18, 147n37, 282
    Catholic Church, 121, 130, 145–46n17, 283
CBS, 97, 176
Ceaușescu, Nicolae, 153–6, 159
Central Asia, 34. *See also* Asia

Central Intelligence Agency (CIA), 25, 157, 245
Cézanne, Paul, 243
Cheskin, Louis, 175, 185n21
Chile, 40, 229
China, 68, 231n15, 265, 272n59
Chinese Communist Party, 262
Christian Democratic Union (CDU), 146n23, 259, 265, 302–3, 306, 308, 310–11
Christian Social Union (CSU), 302–3, 305, 313
Christianity, 28, 284, 349
    Christian, 63, 130–31, 135, 138, 143, 145n14, 146n26, 146n28, 147nn36–37, 148n48, 148n58, 282–84
    Concept of Christian Occident, 348–49, 351, 365n9
Church, 121, 130–35, 137–40, 142–44, 145–46n17, 255, 283, 365n9
Churchill, Randolph, 57–58, 62–63, 72n33
Churchill, Winston, 62–63, 66, 70, 71n4, 72n42, 191, 216, 222–3, 231n7, 280
Civil defense, culture of, 191, 193–196
Civilization
    Christian civilization, 63, 284
    Dichotomy - Eastern and Western civilization, 158, 277, 279, 280–83, 285–87, 289
Class, 95, 114, 196, 262, 268, 277, 288
    Middle-class, 173–76
    Upper class, 113
    Working class, 90n8, 217, 227–29, 285, 287
Clay, Lucius D., General, 355
Coca Cola, 183n7, 225, 271n48
Cold Warrior, 11, 108n9, 122, 172, 303–4, 310
    Cold Warriorhood, 304, 313
    Cultural Cold Warriors, 254–5, 258, 267–8
Colonialism, 254, 257, 262
Color Research Institute, 175
COMECON, 30
Cominform, 30, 216, 231, 234, 238, 245
    Kominform, 294n76
Comintern, 30, 231n11
Communist Party, 3, 9, 101, 174, 299
    Chinese Communist Party, 262
    Communist Party of Great Britain, 184n16
    Communist Party of Yugoslavia, 279, 291n16
    Communists' anti-Westernism, 56, 229, 357
    Czechoslovak Communist Party, 214, 219, 222, 224
    Estonian Communist Party, 324, 326. *See also* Mikson Case
    French Communist Party, 145–46n17, 156, 239
    German Communist Party, 122, 237, 268, 308. *See also* German Communist Party
    Italy's Communist Party, 278–79, 287. *See also* Il lavoratore
    Soviet Communist Party, 29, 55, 60, 266
Cone, Fairfax, 180
Congo, 104, 261
Congress of Cultural Freedom, 25, 27, 30
Conservative Party, 178, 181, 184n9
Consumerism, 8, 11–12, 173–74, 178n9, 263, 271n48
    Consumer Research, 172, 173
    Consumer Sovereignty, 173, 177
Co-produced films, 38
Coubertin, Pierre de, 113–4
Cox, Michael, 28, 45n27
Crosland, Anthony, 174, 184n16
Croatia/Croatians, 14, 278–79, 287, 293n64
Crowley, David, 8, 18n32, 32, 47n57
Cuba, 29, 37–38, 104, 265, 272n66
Cuban Missile Crisis, 106, 146n31, 229
Cultural diplomacy, 24, 27, 29–30, 46n42, 254, 269n1
Cultural enlightenment, 26
Cultural exchange, 24–25, 29, 183n6
Czech Republic, 24
Czechoslovakia, 6, 8, 13, 31–2, 213–15, 231n15, 232n22, 233n46, 286
    Film industry and film festivals, 34–5, 37–8
    Prague Spring, 28, 32
    Reasons for the transformations of East/West dichotomy, 229–230
    Socialist representations of self and other, 213–215. *See also* Peace Race

D

Dacia. *See* Automobile
Dalton, Hugh, 174
DEFA 38, 40–41, 48n93, 48n94, 106
Delo (newspaper), 279, 288, 294n72, 294n73
Democracy, 3, 17, 63, 89, 114, 213, 181–82, 198, 200, 213, 216, 246, 254–57, 259, 263–64, 299, 343n64

Capitalist democracy, 185n31, 258, 262
Demokracija (newspaper), 279, 284, 292n47
Ideology, 116, 177–78, 236, 241, 255, 267–68, 281, 283–84, 286–87, 354–55, 357
Liberal democracy, 7, 8, 13–14, 120, 236, 244, 248, 263, 285, 313
Détente 98,102–3, 106,152, 154, 167, 300, 306, 310, 360
Détente, culture of, 303, 304, 307, 313
Détente, policy of, 182
Deutsche Akademie der Künste, 240
Deutscher Künstlerbund, 243–4, 248
Developing countries, 256, 257, 26, 270n18. See also "Third World", Asia, Africa, Latin America
Development aid, 262
Dichter, Ernest, 172–73, 175, 185n21–22
Die fünfte Kolonne (TV-Series), 96
Digital media, 122
Dimitrov, Georgi Mikhailov, 222
Dissidents, 8, 33
Eastern dissidents, 301–2, 306, 311
DKP. See German Communist Party
Dobrenko, Evgeny, 35, 47n68, 47n69
Dokumenta (Kassel), 244, 247
Dominican Republic, 261
Dondero, George, 245, 248, 251n45
Dr. No (movie), 96
Dr. Strangelove; or, How I Learned Stop Worrying and Love the Bomb (movie), 102, 108m18, 193, 206n6, 206n8
Dubček, Alexander, 265
Dutschke, Rudi, 262, 266, 271n46
Dymshitz, Alexander, 237, 239, 243

E

Eisenhower, Dwight D., 130
East Germany. See also German Democratic Republic/GDR
Eastern Europe, 1–2, 4, 8, 10, 13–14, 16, 23–44, 45n29, 45n32, 45n36, 46n39, 45n46, 46n50, 46n53, 47n56, 47n65, 47n72, 49n108, 55, 77, 103, 122, 147n37, 216, 232n22, 238, 276, 290n3, 291n21, 321, 339n3, 249
Elm, Ludwig, 309, 311–12, 317n48, 317n49, 318n65
England, 59, 71n4, 120, 176, 286, 340n20
Entertainment, 115, 120
Espionage, 37, 232n39

Communist espionage in Sweden, 201
Espionage narratives in U.S. and West German TV-series and literature, 94–97, 98–100, 104–7
Estonia, 15–16
Estonian national identities, war crimes, 321–345. See also Mikson Case
Film studios and festivals, 34, 40
European Economic Community, 183, 257
Eurovision, 30
Everyday militarization, 194–95, 205

F

Fabian Society, 174
Factories, 226, 258
Fair play, 3, 113–4. See also Olympics/Olympic Games
Fascism, 106, 216, 223, 236, 256, 278, 286–87, 191n17, 315n25
Fatima/Portugal, cult of Fatima, 11, 135–39, 142–44, 144–45n7, 146n29, 146n30, 146n31, 146–47n32, 147n35, 147n40, 147n41, 147n42
Blue army of Fatima, 138
Federal Bureau of Investigation (FBI), 245
Federal Republic of Germany/West Germany, 7, 9, 10, 13–14, 153, 159, 161–62
Art in West Germany, 245, 247–48
Berlin Blockade, remembrance of, 351
Media, Olympic Games and Sports, 112, 115–16, 118, 120–21
Media in/from West Germany, 38, 81, 95, 100, 105–07
Political and memory culture in FRG, 255–59, 261–64, 268, 270n21, 299–300, 302–4, 307–10, 312–13, 338, 359–60
Religion in West Germany, 130–31, 137, 143, 148n47
Women's roles in reeducation and reconstruction, 158
Festival of Britain, 180
Feuchtwanger, Leon, 40
Film festivals, 36–37, 40, 42
Film industries, 33–42
Finn, Gerhard, 304, 314n22, 315n23
First World War/World War I, 95, 135, 196, 220, 250n30, 257, 264
Fischer, Alexander, 304
Fleig, Anne, 116, 123n9
Folk (Swedish context), 196–97, 201, 206, 207n18, 207n20

Folkförsvar (people's defense), 196–97
Folkhem/Folkhemmet (people's home), 12, 192, 196, 198–99, 201–03, 205–06, 207n17, 207n20, 207n26, 207n27, 207n37, 208n40
For eyes only – Streng geheim (movie), 106
Ford Foundation 25, 30
Forman, Miloš, 38
France, 11–12, 38, 48n86, 68–69, 87, 103, 120, 130, 192, 217, 223, 231n13, 286, 322, 336, 359, 364
    Automobile production, 156
    Civil defense model, 202
    Lourdes, Marian apparition, 134
    Maoism in France, 264. *See also* Maoism
    Worker-priest movement, 132, 145–46n17
Frankenheimer, John, 38
Free Democratic Party (FDP), 303, 308, 316n36
Free Territory of Trieste, 14, 278. *See also* Trieste
Freedom, 3, 10, 12, 25, 29, 32–32, 35, 46n38, 88, 131, 173, 196, 241, 254, 257, 267, 281, 287–88, 303, 357–58, 360, 362, 364
    artistic freedom, 244–48
    Budapest's Freedom Square, 23, 42–43
    Freedom and mobility, 154–55
    freedom of choice, 177–82
Freie Deutsche Kulturgesellschaft, 237
Friedman, Milton, 186n53
Friedrichsen, Uwe, 100
From Russia with love (movie), 96
Funeral in Berlin (movie), 96

G

Gaulle, Charles de, 156, 168n17, 168n18, 222–3, 232n28
GDR media culture, 77
Genauer, Emily, 251n45
Get Smart (TV-Series), 104–05
Georgia, 34
German Communist Party/DKP (*Kommunistische Partei Deutschlands KPD*). *See also* Communist Party, 122, 237, 265, 268, 308–11, 316n43, 317n48
German Confederation of Trade Unions (DGB), 270n27
German Cultural Industries, 76–79, 87–89, 89n6

German Democratic Republic/East Germany/GDR, 34, 37, 38, 40–41, 76–84, 88–89, 90n9, 90n14, 91n25, 102–3, 106, 115–18, 121–22, 152–53, 159, 165–66, 229, 231n15, 236, 238–41, 243–45, 249, 249n19, 256, 300, 302–13, 314n16, 315n24, 315n28, 315n34, 318n68, 351, 354, 357, 359–60
Giornale di Trieste (newspaper), 279–80, 282–83, 291n17, 291n25, 292n32–34, 292n40–42, 292n46
Globalization, 121
Goebbels, Joseph, 241
Gogh, Vincent van, 240
Goldfinger (movie), 96
Goskino (USSR State Committee for Cinematography), 34, 36, 39, 48n79
Gottwald, Klement, 222
Goya, 40
    Goya (movie), 41–2
Graham, Billy, 131, 145n11
Grass, Günther, 250
Graves, Peter, 97
Great Britain, 6, 12, 30, 63, 66–70, 87, 103, 184n16, 186n45, 191, 216, 223, 282, 356, 359
    Civil defense model, 202
    TV-series and shows, 103, 105
Greeks, 113
Green, Graham, 104
Greens, The 306, 310–1
Grohmann, Will, 237, 243, 249n6, 250n37
Grotewohl, Otto, 238
Grundig, Hans, 237
Guevara, Che, 266
Gumbrecht, Hans-Ulrich, 113, 122n3
Gundrey, Elizabeth, 184n18
Gute, Herbert, 237–8
Guttuso, Renato, 248

H

Habermas, Jürgen, 263, 309, 313
Haftmann, Werner, 238, 244
Halvorsen, Gail S., 362–63
Harnoncourt, René d', 246, 251n49
Harris, Ralph, 177–78, 185n34–35
Hausenstein, Wilhelm, 242, 250n30
Hayek, Friedrich August, 177, 185n31
Heimlich, William F., 357
Held, Jutta, 244
Hellmann, Angelika, 118
Helsinki, 1962, World Youth Festival, 13, 258–59, 261, 267, 270n24, 270n31, 271n33, 271n36
Henry, Harry, 178, 185n21, 185n28, 186n39

Heroldsbach-Thurn/West-Germany, 139, 148n53
Heuer, Uwe Jens, 311
Hill, Steven, 48n80, 97
Hitler, Adolf 114, 241, 243, 245, 272n52, 339n4, 358
    Anti-Hitler Coalition, 55, 232n20
    "Ghost of Hitler", 226, 228, 233n44
Hofer, Karl, 238, 243, 250n35
Hofmann, Werner, 243, 250n37
Hoggart, Richard, 184n18
Holbein, Hans, 245
Hollywood, 25–7, 34, 36, 38, 40, 44n9, 47n60, 96, 108n18, 109n28 223, 232n32
Holocaust, 193, 203, 312, 318n68, 321–22, 328, 333–34, 336–38, 338n1, 342n42, 344n84, 344n87
Hungary, 6, 8, 16, 24, 28, 34, 35, 37, 38, 41, 43, 48n82, 101, 103, 108n17, 231n15, 257, 286
Husák, Gustáv, 229

I

I Led Three Lives (TV-Series), 96
Icelandic Politics, 15, 325–33, 335–38, 339–40n12, 340n18, 341n25, 342n32, 341n34, 342n61, 343n64, 344n78. See also Mikson Case
Ideology, 32, 130, 142, 154, 181, 238, 277, 283, 308, 312
    Cold War ideology in TV series, 94–5, 103
    Ideological paradigm shifts, 322
    Ideology and Olympic Games, 112–14, 116, 118–20, 122. See also Sports, Olympic Games, Korbut Olga
    Political ideology, 11, 86, 90n8, 248
    Socialist ideology, 32, 241, 311
Il Lavoratore (Italian Communist Party), 279, 287–8, 293n62, 294n74
Imagined Community, 351, 365n14
Imperialism, 216, 224–25
    Critique of imperialism, 262–63, 265. See also Development aid
    Cultural imperialism, 45n20, 183n4
    Soviet imperialism, 6, 254, 256–57, 267, 335
    Western imperialism, 14, 218, 230, 240, 257, 270n12, 360
Indianerfilme, 38. See also DEFA
Industry
    Advertising industry, 12, 174–182
    American cultural industry, 105–6
    Automobile industry, 156–58, 165, 168n23
    Cultural industry in the GDR, 78, 87–88
    Entertainment industry, 89, 95–96
    Film industry, 24, 27, 34, 36, 39, 47n64, 95
    West German social model, 258, 263, 267
Infotainment, 120
Institute of Directors, 177–78, 181
Institute of Economic Affairs (IEA), 177
Intervision, 30
Invention of tradition, 113, 123n4
Iordanova, Dina, 34–7, 45n32, 47n66, 47n71–72, 47n76
Iran
    Confederation of Iranian Students (CISNU), 266, 273n74. See also World Youth Festival
    Iran Crisis, 216, 231n5. See also Stalin
    Iranian intellectual Bahman Nirumand, 261–262. See also "Third World"
"Iron Curtain", 11–12, 17, 28, 44, 101–2, 115, 134, 153–54, 158–59, 165, 216, 231n7, 268, 277–78, 280
Iskusstvo Kino (magazine) 40, 41, 48n90
Istria, 281, 287, 292n29, 293n64
Italy, 7, 14, 18n25, 37, 68, 72n29, 87, 103, 130, 242, 277–82, 286–7, 289, 292n36, 364

J

Jachec, Nancy, 246, 251n48, 251n50
Jacobsen, Hans-Adolf, 308–9
Janz, Karin, 10, 113, 117, 119
Jesse, Eckhard, 305–6, 315n26, 315n28–30, 316n37–38
John Klings Abenteuer (TV-Series), 10, 95, 100, 102–5

K

Kaldor, Mary, 28–29, 45n33
Kamper, Dietmar, 117, 123n
Kandinsky, Wassily, 250n30
Kennedy, John Fitzgerald, 146n31
    Visit in Berlin, 360, 356n22, 366n34, 366n36, 366n39
    Visit in Vienna, 229
Keleti, Márton, 41
Kittel, Manfred, 303
Knabe, Hubertus, 303
Kohl, Helmut, 306–7

Kommunistische Partei Deutschlands
  (KPD), 237, 308–11, 317n48
Korbut, Olga, 10, 112–3, 117–20, 123n14,
  123n17, 123n18, 125. See also Olympic
  Games/Olympics
Koschyk, Hartmut, 299, 313
Khrushchev, Nikita, 3, 13, 146n31, 152–54,
  156, 159, 167, 229, 231n19, 240–1,
  250n23
Ku Klux Klan, 226–7
Kulturbund zur Demokratischen Erneuerung
  Deutschlands, 237, 249n5
Kulturliga, 237

L

La Voce del Popolo (newspaper), 279,
  293n54, 294n75–76, 294n78
La Voce Libera (newspaper), 279, 281,
  291n17, 292n30
Labor, 8, 34, 198, 259
    Forced labor, 64, 68, 256, 364
    Labor Day, 284
    Labor market, 201, 203
    Labor Movement, 309
    Soviet labor legislation, 158
Labour Party, 174, 178, 184n15, 184n16
Lada/Zhiguli. See Automobile
Landau, Martin, 97
Lange, Helmut, 100
Langguth, Gerd, 307
Lasch, Christopher, 25, 44n6
Latin America, 37. See also "Third World"
    Cinema, 37
    Criticism of Western development
      policy, 261. See also development
      aid
    Public discussions of Latin America,
      261
    World Youth Festival, 254
Latvia
    Film Studios/Film Festival, 34, 40
    Plight of Latvians to Iceland after
      the Soviet annexation, 325
    Prosecution of Nazi War Criminals,
      334, 344n83
Leavis, F.R., 184n11
Léger, Fernand, 248
Lenfilm, 41
Lenin, Vladimir Ilyich, 245, 265
    International Lenin Peace Price,
      231–2n19
    Leninist, 214, 292n51
    Marxist-Leninist Ideology, 292n51,
      311
Liehm, Anton J., 41, 48n88, 48n95

Liehm, Mira, 41, 48n88, 48n95
Lithuania, 34, 39–41, 48n92, 325, 334,
  344n83
Lublin/Poland, 134, 146n27
Lucas, Scott, 29, 46n38

M

Mackintosh, Harold Vincent (Lord Halifax
  of Mackintosh), 179
Mandelstam, Osip, 58, 61, 64
Marées, Hans von, 243
Marshall Plan, 216, 231n10
Mao Zedong, 264–5, 272n56, 272n59
Maoism
    French Maoism, 264
    West German Maoism, 255, 264–67
Market research, 175, 178–79, 185n21–22
Marwick, Arthur, 108n24, 183
Maser, Peter, 304, 314–5n23
Mata Hari, 95–96
May Day, 213–4, 218–25, 227–31
May, Lary, 2, 17n4, 26, 44n12, 204, 208n42
McCarthy, Joseph, 13, 245, 248
    McCarthyism, 4, 309
Melbourne, 115, 121
Menschen im Netz (TV-Series), 96
Merkel, Angela, 302
Mexico City, 116. See also The Olympic
  Games
Mierendorff, Martha, 244, 246
Mikson Case, 15–16, 321–22, 327–333,
  336–37, 338n2, 339–40n12, 341n35,
  343n64
Ministry of Family and Youth, 255–6, 265
Mission: Impossible (TV-Series), 10, 95, 97,
  100, 102–5
Mladá Fronta (newspaper), 214, 223,
  232n30, 232n32–33
Modernity, 6, 8,14, 17, 44n13, 116, 159,
  259, 351
    European modernity, 43, 49n106, 77
    Modernization, 90n15, 139, 257,
      285, 349
    Narratives of modernity, 276, 285,
      364
    Socialist modernity, 155
    Swedish modernity, 195, 198–99,
      207n23, 207n24
Moldavia, Soviet republic of, 34, 40
Möller, Horst, 307, 315n32
Molotov, Viatcheslav, 62, 216, 245
Monat, Der, 25, 250n35
Morocco, 257–8
Morris, Greg, 97
Moscow, 114, 122

Moscow Does Not Believe in Tears (movie), 41–2, 48n99
Moskvich. *See also* automobile
Motivation Research, 173, 175–76, 185n21, 185n28
    Institute for Motivational Research, 175
Müller, Günther, 305
Munich, 112–4, 117–9, 122–4
Museum of Modern Art (New York), 245–6

N
Nast, Thomas, 220
Nationalism, 8
American Nationalism, 3
    Block identity and nationalism, 29
    Estonian nationalism, 333, 345n91
    Nationalism and Northeastern Adriatic, 277, 286–87, 291n19
    Nineteenth century nationalism, 276, 347, 349. *See also* Orientalism, Imagined Communities
    Religious nationalism, 282
    Social democrats and nationalism, 309
    Subaltern Nationalism, 273n92
    Swedish Nationalism, 207n25
National Consumer Board, 175
National security, 98–99, 104–05, 192, 195, 199, 202, 205
    National Security Council (NSC), 246
National Socialism, 114, 236, 238, 240, 242, 247, 250n38. *See also* "Third Reich"
Nationalsozialistische Deutsche Arbeiterpartei (NSDAP), 241–42
Nazism, 133, 248, 280–81, 305, 309, 312, 317n58, 317n63, 325
NBC, 176
Negt, Oskar, 263, 272n53
Nerlinger, Oskar 243
Neutrality (Swedish context), 192, 195, 197–99, 205, 207n22–24
New Left, 184n15
    German New Left, 14, 255, 261–65, 267–68, 272n54, 309. *See also* "Thirld World", Maoism, Vietnam
Newman, Barnett, 246
Nicolescu, Sergiu, 38
Nietzsche, Friedrich, 238–9
Nigeria, 259, 262. *See also* "Third World"
Nirumand, Bahman, 261–2, 271n38, 271n43–44, 272n59

Nobody Wants to Die (movie), 39–40, 42
Noel-Baker, Francis, 174, 176, 184n17–18
Nolde, Emil, 241–42
North Atlantic Treaty, 217–8, 226–7
Northeastern Adriatic, 276, 290n1
    Cold War identity constructions in the northeastern Adriatic, 277–80, 284, 287, 289, 293n64
Nova Gorica, 279
Novi list (newspaper), 279
Novomeský, Laco, 229
Nuclear bomb, 67, 68, 133, 226. *See also* atomic bomb
Nuclear war, 193, 203
Nur der Himmel war frei (movie), 361

O
Olympics/Olympic Games, 10, 31, 112–17, 120–22, 123n16. *See also* Sports, Olga Korbut, fair play
Orientalism, concept of, 277
    Cold War Orientalism, 277, 290n7
    Frontier Orientalism, 294n80
    Said, Edward, 290n2
Orlov, N. (Vladimir Semjonovich Semjonov), 240, 249–50n19
Ostpolitik, 41, 102, 183
Ostrava, 221–23
Our Man in Havana (novel), 104

P
Packard, Vance, 175, 183n3, 185n19
Palestinian terrorism, 114. *See also* Munich and Olympic Games
Pan-Slavism, 280
Party of Democratic Socialism (PDS)/post-Communists, 15, 299, 308–9, 311–13, 318n71
Pasternak, Boris, 25, 42, 56, 64
Patrice Lumumba University, 259. *See also* World Youth Festivals
Peace movement, 214, 216–18, 229, 231
Peace Race, 213–15, 230
Peru, 121
Petelska, Ewa, 41
Petelski, Czeslaw, 41
Picasso, Pablo, 222, 231n14, 239–241, 248, 249n15
Poland, 6, 8, 24, 28, 34–5, 37, 39, 41, 46n39, 68, 134, 215, 217, 286
Political education (*politische Bildung*), 256. *See also* World Youth Festivals
Politics of memory, 313n3, 318n68. *See also* Airlift Memorial
    Cold War Memorial, 347, 364

Cold War Memory Politics, 4
Different approaches on memory, 347–54, 364
German memory politics, 300, 307, 312, 315n24
Instrumentalization of memory, 360–64
Public memory, 15, 299
War crimes memory, 321–322, 328, 339n6
Politics of productivity, 268, 273n90
Pope John Paul II, 11, 144
Pope Pius XII, 133, 135–7, 145n14
Popular culture, 5, 8, 26, 28, 108n20, 120, 172–3, 175, 205
Popular music policies, 78
Postwar Soviet propaganda, 355
"Prague Spring", 32, 265
Pravda, 216, 231n7–9
Leningradskaia Pravda, 60
Preparedness, 12, 192, 195–96, 198, 200, 202–6
Preuves, 25
Primorske novice (newspaper), 279, 289, 293n57, 293n61, 294n69, 294n76, 294n79, 294n82
Primorski dnevnik (newspaper), 279, 291n14, 293n59–60, 294n68
Protestantism/Evangelicals/Lutherans/Pietism, 131, 145n12, 145n14–15
Psychoanalysis
Reichian psychoanalysis, 265
Suggestion techniques, Hypnosis and Psychoanalysis, 175. See also Popular Culture
Psychological Strategy Board, 181

R

Racism, 276–77
Radio Free Europe, 30, 46n41, 48n82
Radio Liberty, 30, 46n41, 48n82
Reagan, Ronald, 12, 42–43, 49n101, 144
Reaganomics, 182
Reid, Susan, 8, 18n32, 32, 47n56–57, 168n3, 169n28, 183n7
Reith Report, 175
Religion, 11
Concept of Christian Occident, 349. See also Christianity
Function of religion in the construction of the West, 282
Religion and the Cold War, 129–31, 142, 145n8–9, 145n16, 145–46n17, 146n19, 148n58
Rembrandt, 245

Renoir, Pierre-Auguste, 240
Reuter, Ernst, 356
Rigby, Cathy, 119, 123n16
Riječki list (newspaper), 279, 293n55–56, 293n64, 293n67, 294n71
Rijn, Rembrandt van. See Rembrandt
Roh, Franz, 250n38
Romania, 24, 31, 37
Rome, 139, 146n32
Rome Olympics, 115. See also Olympic Games
Contract with Fiat, 157. See also Automobile
Rosary, 137–38. See also Fatima
"Rosary Crusades", 138
Ruby, Sigrid, 246, 251n50
Rudé právo (newspaper), 214, 231n17, 232n21, 233nn44–45
Rust, Bernhard, 241

S

Said, Edward, 276, 290n2. See also Orientalism
Salazar, António de Oliveira, 135, 146n29
SALT I and II, 106
Sartre, Jean-Paul, 246
Saunders, Frances Stonor, 44n7, 72n41, 245, 249n16, 251n43
Schäuble, Wolfgang, 302–3
Schmitt, Carl, 218, 231n18
Schumacher, Kurt, 309
Schumpeter, Joseph Alois, 177
Seckler, Dorothy Gees, 246
Secret police
Bulgarian secret police, 266–67
Hungarian secret police, 101. See also John Klings Abenteuer
Rakhlin's secret police, 72n33
Volga and secret police, 164
Sedlmayer, Hans, 242, 250n36
Seldon, Arthur, 177–78, 185n34–35
Semjonov, Vladimir Semjonovich. See also N. Orlov
Sexual/sexuality, 4, 99, 101, 104, 173, 176, 193, 259
Shostakovich, Dmitri, 239, 249n16
Situationism, 265
Slavo-communists (*slavo-communista*), 14, 282, 286
Slovakia, 24
Slovenia/Slovenians, 14, 278–79, 284, 287–89, 289n1
Slovenski Jadran (magazine), 279, 293n59, 294n70
Snyder, Timothy, 43, 49n108

Soccer, 112–3, 115–6, 118, 120, 122
Social Democracy, 148
Social Democratic Party of Germany (SPD), 306, 309, 311, 316n36, 356
Socialist Unity Party of Germany (Sozialistische Einheitspartei Deutschlands) (SED), 15, 77, 79, 238, 240–42, 299
SED Dictatorship in Germany, 300–01, 304, 313, 314n12, 314–15n23, 315n28–29, 315n34, 315n43, 318n71
Socialism, 13–14, 17, 29, 31–33, 43, 77, 152, 153, 159, 168n5, 192, 196, 216, 222, 225, 230, 232n27, 232n30, 240–42, 247, 261, 264, 288, 299, 311, 315n34
    National Socialism. *See* National Socialism
    Socialism and Sports, 120–22
    Socialist Realism, 35, 77
    Socialist Style, 32
Sofia
    Film Studio, 41
    World Youth Festival 1968, 13–14, 255, 261, 264–68, 272n63–65, 272n67, 273n76, 273n81, 273n85
Solovieva, Ina, 40, 48n90
Solzhenitsyn, Alexander, 42, 303
Soviet Union, 1, 2, 7–13, 16, 157, 191, 206n3, 216, 226, 229–31, 234, 286–88
    Automobile Culture in Soviet Union, 152–159, 185n24
    Becher in exile, 237
    Berlin/Akhmatova, Churchil/Stalin, 57, 61–62, 65, 67
    Film and arts, 24–44, 103–4
    Financial aid, British loan, 68–70
    Mikson Case, 322–23, 327, 329, 331, 335, 337, 341nn29–30
    New Left's orientation, 265, 266–67, 273n74
    Olympic Games, sports, 114, 117–21
    Religion and Soviet Union, 133, 135, 137–40, 142, 144
    Soviet anti-British propaganda, 1946, 66
    Soviet Film, 36, 37, 39, 40, 47n64, 47n77, 48n79, 48n83, 48n89, 48n96
    Soviet Filmmakers Union, 31, 41–42
    Soviet friendship societies, 30, 46n39
    Soviet Military Administration (SMAD), 236–37, 243, 355
    Soviet occupation zone (SBZ), 236, 302, 308–9, 315n24, 316n46
    Soviet patriotism, 56
    U.S. vs. Soviet Union, 347, 349, 355
Sovinfilm, 36
Sozialistischer Deutscher Studentenbund (SDS), 262–67, 271n42, 273n88
Sozialistische Einheitspartei Deutschlands (SED). *See* Socialist Unity Party of Germany
Sparwasser, Jürgen, 112
Spengler, Oswald, 238
Speidel, Hans, 218–19, 232n20
Spittmann-Rühle, Ilse, 309
Sport, 10–11, 30, 87, 92n33, 112–16, 118–22, 122n1, 123nn5–6, 325
Sputnik, 226
Stalin, Joseph, 214, 216, 222, 231–34, 238–40, 244, 249–50
Stalinism, 29, 35, 71n16, 72n41, 168n2, 231n4, 304
Students, 13, 29
    Students' activism, 219, 255, 262–64, 256, 259, 261, 265–67, 270n18, 271n39, 272n66. *See also* May Day, Patrice Lumumba University, World Youth Festival
Sweden, 6, 12, 15–16, 191–192, 194–206, 207n24. *See also* civil defense, preparedness, folk
    Mikson case in Sweden, 322, 324, 331, 333, 335, 339–40n12, 241n36, 341n38, 344n89
Szabó, István, 38, 49n102

T

Talankin, Igor, 41
Tchaikovsky Competition, 31
Technocracy, 263
Television, 4, 9, 11, 21, 25. *See also* Cold War Culture
    Airlift, 361
    Archbishop Futton Sheen's TV show, 138
    Censorship board (Lektorat) for television in the GDR, 79
    Commercial television, 172, 178
    Ernst Reuter's speech on television, 356, 366n26
    Images of the West, 229
    Media coverage of sports in East and West Germany, Olympic Games, 112, 115–17, 120–22, 123n16, 124n23
    Russian television, 40

384 • Index

Spy television and TV series during the 50's and 60's, 10, 94–97, 100, 102–6, 107n4, 108n9, 108n12, 108n21, 108n25, 109n29
Television newscasts on the evacuation of King Gustav VI Adolf, 203
West German Constitutional Court's decision to permit private television, 81
Thatcherism, 182
The Big Life (movie), 357
The British Loan, 67, 69–70, 73n66
The Comedians (novel), 104
The Hidden Persuaders (book), 183n3, 185n19
The Ipcress File (movie), 175
The Man from U.N.C.L.E. (TV-Series), 104–5, 108n25
The Manchurian Candidate (movie), 175
The Spy Who Came in From the Cold (movie), 96
"Third Reich", 244, 249, 308, 312. See also National Socialism, Totalitarianism
"Third Reich" in TV series, 100, 104
"Third World", 13–14, 27, 37, 100, 104, 120, 158, 354
public discussions on colonialism, 254–55, 257–69. See also Students, World Youth Festival, New Left
Thoma, Hans, 243
Thompson, J. Lee, 38
Thunderball (movie), 106
Tokyo, 115
Tost, Heinrich, 244, 246
Totalitarianism, 6, 7, 181, 244
Anti-totalitarianism, 300, 311–12, 315n25
Totalitarianism as an ideological frame, variations of, 244–47, 284, 304–05, 311, 313n4, 314n7, 315n32, 317n58, 317n62, 317n66
Trade Unions, 182, 201
Trieste/Free Territory of Trieste, 14, 277–84, 287–89, 290n1, 291n17–20, 291n23, 291n25, 291n25, 292n29, 292n39, 292n49
Truman, Harry 69, 222, 225–26, 245
Truman's doctrine, 55, 216, 238
Tulpanov, Sergei, 238, 355
TV-Union Berlin (company), 100

U
Ulbricht, Walter, 240–1, 249n5

Uncle Sam, 220
United States of America, 2–5, 7, 9–10, 12–13, 16, 23–27, 30, 191, 216, 226, 229–31, 268, 322
Advertising Association, 181
Art policy in the U.S., 238, 240, 245–48
Consumer politics in the U.S., 173–74, 182
Everyday militarization, 194
Ideological confrontation between Soviet Union and the U.S.A., 55, 67, 229, 238, 347, 349
Information policy on Germany, 356–58
Khrushev's Visit in the U.S., 229
Mikson, 325, 329, 331, 334, 341n35
Religious Culture of the Cold War, 129–30, 137, 145n9
Representation and memory of Airlift, 325, 354, 359, 360–63
Sports, Olympic Games, 114, 120–21
U.S. advertising council, 189, 186n44
U.S. images in TV and film, 34, 37, 95, 97–98, 104–5
U.S. involvement in the Northeast Adria, 282
United States Information Agency (USIA), 246
US Congress, anti-Soviet message in, 69–70
Vietnam War, 263. See also The New Left, World Youth Festivals

V
Vatican, 130, 132, 137, 144, 145n17, 147n33–34, 147n37
Verband Bildender Künstler Deutschlands (VBKD), 239, 244, 248
Verband Deutscher Studentenschaften (VDS), 256–57, 269n10, 170n12, 270n14, 270n19, 271n40, 272n63–65, 273n85
Vicary, James, 176
Vienna, 138, 229, 231n13
World Youth Festival 1959, 13, 255–58, 267
Vietnam, 29, 182, 229–30, 272n49–50
Vietnam War, 3, 14, 26, 44n14, 255, 261, 263, 267–68, 360
Virgin Mary, 129, 132, 145n9, 146n27. See also Catholicism
Apparition of, 11, 138, 140

Volga. *See* Automobile
Völkerfreundschaft, 118
VOKS, 30, 46n41

W

Walden, Herwarth, 250n30
Wall Street, 220, 225
Watergate affair, 107
War Crimes, 16, 321–22, 324–26, 329, 331–36, 338, 338n1, 339n5, 341n29, 341n30, 341n36. *See also* Mikson Case
Wartburg. *See* Automobile
Welfare state, 6
    Nordic welfare state, 195, 197, 200, 203, 207n21
West Germany/Federal Republic of Germany (FDR). *See Federal* Republic of Germany
"Westernization", 16, 27, 351, 354–54
Whitfield, Stephen, 2–4, 17n6, 25–26, 32, 44n11, 107n3, 145n8, 145n11, 183n6
Wilke, Manfred, 303, 306
Wilms, Dorothee, 308
Wilson, Harold, 182
Windelen, Heinrich, 304
Wolf, Karl-Dietrich, 267
Wolf, Konrad, 40–41
Women, 39, 261
    Feminization of post war Germany, 358
    Images of women in movies and TV series, 99, 357–58
    National Council of Women, 179
    Socialist image of women, 164, 286
    Women and religious revival, 140
    Women's gymnastics, 117. *See also* Olga Korbut, Olympic Games/Olympics
World Peace Congress (1949), 217, 233
World War II, 1, 5–8, 10, 12, 15, 17, 43, 165, 214, 232n20, 349
    Arts after the WWII, 236, 238, 245, 247
    Consumption after the WWII, 153, 178, 181, 193, 195–96
    Films about the WWII, 38, 96
    Marian apparition during and after the WWII, 134–35, 137. *See also* Fatima
    Memories of the WWII, 313n3, 347
    Narratives of the WWII, 43, 67, 321–22
    Olympic Games after the WWII, 121
    Sweden and the WWII, 195–200
    Symbolic mappings of Europe in the northeastern Adriatic after WWII, 277–79, 282, 289, 291n16, 293n64
    War Criminals, 325, 333–335. *See also* War Criminals, Mikson Case
World Youth Festivals, 13, 254–56, 258, 260–61, 264, 267

Y

Youth, 10, 46n49, 60, 106, 142, 246
    Czechoslovak Youth Union, newspaper of, 210, 222–23. *See also* Mláda Fronta
    Minister for Women and Youth, Angela Merkel, 302
    Social democratic youth movement, 196
    World Youth Festivals, 13–14, 31, 254–61, 264–67
    Youth broadcasting networks, culture, music in the GDR, 68–81, 84–88, 90n8, 92n33
    Youth Union, 214, 218, 221–22
Yugoslavia, 8, 29
    Border dispute with Italy, 278–79, 282, 285–89, 291n16, 292n51. *See also* Trieste/Free Territory of Trieste
    Film 24, 37–38, 41
Yurchak, Alexei, 35, 47n70

Z

Zápotocký, Antonín, 222
Žalakevičius, Vytautas, 39–40
Zhdanov, Andrei, 60, 64–65, 71n2, 71n22, 71n25, 73n53, 73n76, 216, 231n12, 238–39, 248, 250n23
Zonenrandgebiet, 122
Zubkova, Elena, 32, 47n58
Zuchold, Erika 117
Zvezda and *Leningrad*, the Party resolution on, 59–60, 63–66

www.ingramcontent.com/pod-product-compliance
Lightning Source LLC
Chambersburg PA
CBHW072141100526
44589CB00015B/2039